T5-DHH-346

Guinness
Book of
Essential
Facts

THIS BOOK IS THE PROPERTY OF
THE FOOD NEWS DEPARTMENT OF
THE NEW YORK TIMES

Guinness
Book of
Essential
Facts

Compiled by
NORRIS McWHIRTER

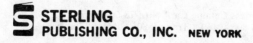
STERLING
PUBLISHING CO., INC.   NEW YORK

The compilers wish to thank Edward W. Egan for the
sections on Literature, Philosophy, Art, Music (in part),
Drama, Radio and Television, and Black Americans.

Copyright © 1979 by Sterling Publishing Co., Inc.
Two Park Avenue, New York, N.Y. 10016
Based on "The Guinness Book of Answers" copyright © 1978
by Guinness Superlatives Ltd. and Norris McWhirter
and on "The Dunlop Illustrated Encyclopedia of Facts"
copyright © 1970, 1969, 1966, 1964 by Dreghorn Publications Ltd.
and Guinness Superlatives Ltd.
Manufactured in the United States of America
All rights reserved
Library of Congress Catalog Card No.: 78-66315
Sterling ISBN 0-8069-0160-8 Trade 0-8069-0161-6 Library

Table of Contents

Introduction

The *Guinness Book of Essential Facts* is intended to be a useful supplement to existing reference books. The condensation of facts into clear, readable lists will provide easier access to comparative information than most other reference texts can provide. Whereas searching in an encyclopedia to find, for example, the relative lengths of tunnels or bridges might require looking up two or more references (often in separate volumes), this new book places the information at your fingertips.

The Guinness Book of Essential Facts covers a wide range of subjects that is unique to itself. No other reference work offers an equivalent variety of data that is as concise. Herein can be found such diverse items as the proper layout of a lacrosse field, the most popular television programs, a chronological history of the development of music, complete metric conversion tables, the tallest buildings, and the odds in contract bridge. Collecting such information might normally require access to six or seven books.

Perhaps the most important feature of this book, though, is that the information it contains is every bit as entertaining as it is useful. Although crammed with facts, the list format makes this book easy to read and understand. This is a reference book that can be read and enjoyed from cover to cover.

Days of the Week

ENGLISH	LATIN	SAXON
Sunday	Dies Solis	Sun's Day
Monday	Dies Lunae	Moon's Day
Tuesday	Dies Martis	Tiu's Day
Wednesday	Dies Mercurii	Woden's Day
Thursday	Dies Jovis	Thor's Day
Friday	Dies Veneris	Frigg's Day
Saturday	Dies Saturni	Saternes' Day

Tiu was the Anglo-Saxon counterpart of the Nordic Tyr, son of Odin, god of war, who came closest to Mars (Greek, Ares) son of the Roman god of war Jupiter (Greek Zeus). Woden was the Anglo-Saxon counterpart of Odin, Nordic dispenser of victory, who came closest to Mercury (Greek, Hermes), the Roman messenger of victory.

Thor was the Nordic god of thunder, eldest son of Odin and nearest to the Roman Jupiter (Greek, Zeus), who was armed with thunder and lightning. Frigg (or Freyja), wife of Odin, was the Nordic goddess of love, and equivalent to Venus (Greek Aphrodite), goddess of love in Roman mythology. Thus four of the middle days of the week are named after a mythological husband and wife and their two sons.

Months

January (31 days)
Latin, *Januarius*, or *Ianuarius*, named after Janus, the two-faced Roman god of doorways (*ianuae*) and archways (*iani*), as presiding over the "entrance," or beginning of the year.

February (29 days)
Latin, *Februarius* (*februare*, to purify), from *februa*, a festival of purification held on February 15.

March (31 days)
Latin, *Martius*, the month of Mars, the Roman god of war and the protector of vegetation.

April (30 days)
Latin, *Aprilis*, from *aperire* (to open), the season when trees and flowers begin to "open."

May (31 days)
Latin, *Maius*, either from Maia, an obscure goddess, or from *maiores* (elders), on the grounds that the month honored old people, as June honored the young.

June (30 days)
Latin, *Junius*, either from the goddess Juno, or from *iuniores* (young people), as the month dedicated to youth.

July (31 days)
Latin, *Julius*, after Gaius Julius Caesar (born July 12, probably in 102 B.C., died March 15, 44 B.C.), the Roman soldier and statesman. (Formerly known by the Romans as *Quintilis*, the fifth month.)

Months (continued)

August (31 days)
Latin, *Augustus*, after Augustus Caesar (born Gaius Octavius), the first Roman emperor. (Originally called *Sextilis*, the sixth month.)

September (30 days)
Latin, from *septem* (seven), as it was originally the seventh month.

October (31 days)
Latin, from *octo* (eight), originally the eighth month.

November (30 days)
Latin, from *novem* (nine), originally the ninth month.

December (31 days)
Latin, from *decem* (ten), originally the tenth month.

Calendars

OLD STYLE (JULIAN) AND NEW STYLE (GREGORIAN) DATES

The Julian Calendar, introduced by Julius Caesar in 45 B.C., on the advice of the Egyptian astronomer Sosigenes, was in use throughout Europe until 1582 when Pope Gregory XIII ordained that Oct. 5 should be called Oct. 15. The discrepancy occurred because of the Augustinian ruling of A.D. 4 that every fourth year shall be of 366 days and hence include a Leap Day.

Countries switched from the Old Style (Julian) to the New Style (Gregorian) system as follows:

1582	Italy, France, Portugal, Spain
1583	Flanders, Holland, Prussia, Switzerland, and the Roman Catholic states in Germany
1586	Poland
1587	Hungary
1600	Scotland
1700	Denmark and the Protestant states in Germany
1700–40	Sweden (by gradual process)
1752	England and Wales, Ireland and the Colonies, including North America
1872	Japan (12 day lag)
1912	China (13-day lag)
1915	Bulgaria (13-day lag)
1917	Turkey and the U.S.S.R. (13-day lag)
1919	Romania and Yugoslavia (13-day lag)
1923	Greece (13-day lag).

LEAP YEAR

Leap years occur in every year the number of which is divisible by four, e.g. 1964, except centennial years, e.g. 1700, 1800, or 1900, which are treated as common or non-leap years *unless* the number of the *century* is divisible by four, e.g. 1600 was (NS) a leap year and 2000 will be a leap year.

The whole process is one of compensation for over-retrenchment of the discrepancy between the calendar year of 365 days and the mean solar year of 365.24219878 days. The date when it will be necessary to suppress a further leap year, sometimes assumed to be A.D. 4000, A.D. 8000, etc., is not in fact yet clearly specifiable, owing to minute variations in the earth-sun relationship.

EASTER DAY

Easter Day

Easter, the Sunday on which the resurrection of Christ is celebrated in the Christian world is, unlike Christmas which is fixed, a "moveable feast."

The celebration of Easter is believed to have begun in about A.D. 68. The English word Easter probably derives from *Eostre*, a Saxon goddess whose festival was celebrated about the time of the vernal equinox.

Easter Days and Leap Years 1978–2000

(Years in bold type are leap years.)

1978	March 26	1986	March 30	1994	April 3
1979	April 15	1987	April 19	1995	April 16
1980	April 6	**1988**	April 3	**1996**	April 7
1981	April 19	1989	March 26	1997	March 30
1982	April 11	1990	April 15	1998	April 12
1983	April 3	1991	March 31	1999	April 4
1984	April 22	**1992**	April 19	**2000**	April 23
1985	April 7	1993	April 11		

The date of Easter has been a matter of constant dispute between the eastern and western Christian churches. Almost the entire calendar of the Christian religion revolves around the date upon which, in any given year, Easter falls. The repercussions extend in Christian countries into civil life.

According to English Statute Law by Act of 1751 (24 Geo. II, c. 23) Easter Day is the *first* Sunday after the full moon which occurs on, or next after, Mar. 21, but if this full moon occurs on a Sunday, Easter Day is on the Sunday after. The moon, for the purposes of this Act, is not the real moon but the paschal moon which is a hypothetical moon, the full details of which can be found in the *Book of Common Prayer*. Thus Easter may fall on any one of the thirty-five days from Mar. 22 (as last in 1818) to Apr. 25 (as last in 1943) inclusive.

The United Nations in 1949 considered the establishment of a perpetual world calendar, which would automatically and incidentally have fixed Easter, but the proposals were shelved indefinitely in 1956.

The Vatican Council in Rome in October 1963 approved the resolution to fix the date of Easter, subject to the agreement of other Christian churches, by 2058 votes to nine against.

The boldest scheme for calendar reform, which is winning increasing support, is that the year should be divided into four quarters of thirteen weeks, with each day of the year being assigned a fixed day of the week. By this scheme it is thought likely that Easter would always fall on Sunday, Apr. 8. For this calendar to conform with the mean solar year a "blank day" would be required each year.

THE HEBREW CALENDAR

This calendar is based on solar years and lunar months. The 11 days by which the solar year exceeds 12 lunar months are accommodated by having a 13th month (*Veadar* of 30 days) in the 3rd, 6th, 8th, 11th, 14th and 17th year of a 19-year-cycle.

The months are:

Tishri	(30 days)	*Veadar*	(or II Adar)
Heshvan	(29 or 30 days)	*Nisan*	(30 days)
Kislev	(29 or 30 days)	*Iyar*	(29 days)
Tebet	(29 days)	*Sivan*	(30 days)
Shebat	(30 days)	*Tammuz*	(29 days)
Adar	(30 days in a leap year)	*Ab*	(30 days)
		Elul	(29 days)

The Hebrew Calendar (continued)

Note: *Yom Kippur* (the Day of Atonement) falls on the 10th day of *Tishri* and *Pesach* (Passover) spans the 15th to 22nd days of *Nisan*.

The calendar day starts at 6 P.M. and is subdivided into hours, then into 1,080 parts of an hour called *Halaquim* with each *Heleq* lasting about 3½ seconds. A *Heleq* can be divided into 76 *rega'im*.

A Hebrew year is 355 days (i.e., a *shelema*—meaning a complete year), if *Heshvan* and *Kislev* are of the full length of 30 days; or 354 days if only *Heshvan* has only 29 days, *i.e.* is a "defective" month, which is called a *sedur* or normal year; or 353 days if both these months are defective when a so-called *hasera* year occurs. In leap years the number of days are 383, 384 and 385 respectively.

Current Hebrew years (*Anno Mundi*) can be converted to the Gregorian date by ignoring the thousands and adding 239, provided this is between the Jewish New Year (*Rosh Hashanah* usually in September) and before December 31. For the rest of the year from January 1 to the eve of the Jewish New Year celebrations it is necessary to add 240 to ascertain the Gregorian year.

THE ISLAMIC CALENDAR

The Mohammedan era started in 622 A.D., when Mohammed fled from Mecca to Medina. The years are designated A.H., meaning *anno Hegirae*. To convert to our calendar multiply A.H. by .97 and add 622.

The calendar consists of 12 months of alternately 30 and 29 days. With the exception that *Dulheggia* sometimes has 30 days, there is no provision to keep in gear with the solar year, so Moslem months slide back through the seasons in a 32½-year cycle. The months are:

Muharram	30 days		*Rajab*	30 days
Saphar	29		*Shaaban*	29
Rabia I	30		**Ramadan*	30
Rabia II	29		*Shawwal*	29
Jomada I	30		*Dulkaada*	30
Jomada II	29	* The month of fasting.	*Dulheggia*	29 (or 30)

THE CHINESE CALENDAR

The traditional Chinese calendar assigns an animal to each year in repeating 12-year zodiacal cycles, thus:

1969	Year of the Rooster	1976	Dragon
1970	Dog	1977	Snake
1971	Pig	1978	Horse
1972	Rat	1979	Ram
1973	Ox	1980	Monkey
1974	Tiger	1981	again Rooster
1975	Hare		

The origin of this practice is often fancifully dated to 2637 B.C. but any date prior to 1766 B.C. in Sinic civilization is now regarded as lacking historicity.

Roman Numerals

Roman numerals, although their use is waning, are still far from extinct. They are used consistently to differentiate Popes, Monarchs and even artificial satellites as succession numbers, *viz.* Pope John XXIII, King Henry VIII and Gemini XI. They are also used on coinage, statutes, formal documents and buildings to denote dates or the years of origin.

The seven basic symbols used are I = 1, V = 5, X = 10, L = 50, C = 100, D = 500, M = 1,000.

In Roman numerology there are four rules:

(1) A letter repeated indicates a doubled value. Thus XX = 20.

(2) A letter following one of greater value adds to it. Thus VIII = 8.

(3) A letter preceding one of greater value subtracts from it. Thus IX = 9.

(4) A dash over a letter multiplies it by 1,000. Thus $\overline{M}$ = 1,000,000.

I	1	XI	11	XXX	30	CD	400
II	2	XII	12	XL	40	D	500
III	3	XIII	13	L	50	DC	600
IV or IIII	4	XIV	14	LX	60	DCC	700
V	5	XV	15	LXX	70	DCCC	800
VI	6	XVI	16	LXXX	80	CM	900
VII	7	XVII	17	XC	90	M	1,000
VIII	8	XVIII	18	C	100	$\overline{V}$	5,000
IX	9	XIX	19	CC	200	$\overline{X}$	10,000
X	10	XX	20	CCC	300	$\overline{M}$	1,000,000

The year 1968 is thus written MCMLXVIII.

The Seasons

The four seasons in the northern hemisphere are astronomically speaking:

Spring from the vernal equinox (about Mar. 21) to the summer solstice (about June 21).

Summer from the summer solstice (about June 21) to the autumnal equinox (about Sept. 21).

Autumn from the autumnal equinox (about Sept. 21) to the winter solstice (about Dec. 21).

Winter from the winter solstice (about Dec. 21) to the vernal equinox (about Mar. 21).

In the southern hemisphere, of course, autumn corresponds to spring, winter to summer, spring to autumn and summer to winter.

The solstices (from Latin *sol*, sun; *stitium*, standing) are the two times in the year when the sun is farthest from the equator and appears to be still. The equinoxes (from Latin *aequus*, equal; *nox*, night) are the two times in the year when day and night are of equal length when the sun crosses the equator.

The Zodiac

The zodiac (from the Greek *zodiakos kyklos*, circle of animals) is an unscientific and astrological system devised in Mesopotamia *c.* 3000 B.C.

The zodiac is an imaginary belt of pictorial constellations which lie as a backdrop quite arbitrarily 8 degrees on either side of the annual path or ecliptic of the sun. It is divided into twelve sections each of 30 degrees. Each has been allocated a name from the constellation which at one time coincided with that sector. The present lack of coincidence of the zodiacal sectors with the constellations from which they are named has been caused mainly by the lack of proper allowance for leap days. The old order is nonetheless adhered to.

The traditional "signs" are:
Aries, the Ram March 21–April 19.
Taurus, the Bull April 20–May 20.
Gemini, the Twins May 21–June 21.
Cancer, the Crab June 22–July 22.
Leo, the Lion July 23–Aug. 22.
Virgo, the Virgin August 23–September 22.
Libra, the Balance September 23–October 23.
Scorpio, the Scorpion October 24–November 21.
Sagittarius, the Archer November 22–December 21.
Capricornus, the Goat December 22–January 19.
Aquarius, the Water Carrier January 20–February 18.
Pisces, the Fish February 19–March 20.

Watches at Sea

A watch at sea is four hours except the period between 4 P.M. and 8 P.M., which is divided into two short watches termed the first dog watch and the second dog watch. The word dog is here a corruption of "dodge." The object of dog watches is to prevent the same men always being on duty during the same hours each day.

Midnight–4 A.M.	Middle watch
4 A.M.–8 A.M.	Morning watch
8 A.M.–noon	Forenoon watch
noon–4 P.M.	Afternoon watch
4 P.M.–6 P.M.	First dog watch
6 P.M.–8 P.M.	Second dog watch
8 P.M.–Midnight	First watch

BELLS

Each four-hour watch is divided for time-keeping purposes into half-hours, which are marked by an increasing number of strokes on the ship's bell.

For example, "Three bells in the first watch" means 9:30 P.M. (or 21.30 hours), i.e., three half-hour periods after the start (8:00 P.M. or 20.00 hours) of the first watch.

Thus a full four-hour watch ends with 8 bells, while a dog watch ends with only 4 bells. The traditional exception is that at midnight on December 31st, 16 bells are rung to mark the New Year.

In practice a ship's bell is not (for time-keeping purposes) rung at sea, but only in harbor before "taps." Time is, however, still traditionally referred to by the number of bells of the given watch.

Wedding Anniversaries

The choice of object or material attached to specific anniversaries is in no sense "official." The list below is a combination of commercial and traditional usage.

First—Cotton
Second—Paper
Third—Leather
Fourth—Fruit, flowers
Fifth—Wooden
Sixth—Sugar
Seventh—Wool, copper
Eighth—Bronze, pottery
Ninth—Pottery, willow
Tenth—Tin
Eleventh—Steel
Twelfth—Silk, linen

Thirteenth—Lace
Fourteenth—Ivory
Fifteenth—Crystal
Twentieth—China
Twenty-fifth—Silver
Thirtieth—Pearl
Thirty-fifth—Coral
Fortieth—Ruby
Forty-fifth—Sapphire
Fiftieth—Golden
Fifty-fifth—Emerald
Sixtieth—Diamond
Seventieth—Platinum

Birthdays

Below are given dates of birth and death, where accurately known, of people generally accepted as being famous or infamous. Included are also the dates of highly memorable occasions.

JANUARY (31 days)

DERIVATION
Latin, *Januarius,* or *Ianuarius,* named after Janus, the two-faced Roman god of doorways *(ianaue)* and archways *(iani),* as presiding over the "entrance," or beginning of the year.

1 J. D. Salinger b. 1919
2 Isaac Asimov b. 1920
3 Marcus Tullius Cicero b. 106 B.C.
4 Augustus John b. 1878
5 German National Socialist Party founded 1919; Alvin Ailey b. 1931
6 Joan of Arc b. *c.* 1412; Sun Myung Moon b. 1920; Jet propulsion invented 1944
7 Butterfly McQueen b. 1911
8 Elvis Presley b. 1935
9 George Balanchine b. 1904; Simone de Beauvoir b. 1908; Richard Nixon b. 1913; Joan Baez b. 1941
10 League of Nations founded 1920
11 Rod Taylor b. 1930
12 Edmund Burke b. 1729
13 Gwen Verdon b. 1925
14 Albert Schweitzer b. 1875; Cecil Beaton b. 1904; Casablanca Conference 1943
15 Martin Luther King, Jr. b. 1929
16 Ivan the Terrible crowned 1547; Ethel Merman b. 1909; Federal prohibition of alcohol introduced, 1920
17 Benjamin Franklin b. 1706; David Lloyd George b. 1863; Konstantin Stanislavski b. 1863
18 A. A. Milne b. 1882; Scott reached South Pole 1912; Muhammad Ali b. 1942
19 James Watt b. 1736; Edgar Allan Poe b. 1809; Paul Cézanne b. 1839
20 Federico Fellini b. 1920
21 Paul Scofield b. 1922; Jack Nicklaus b. 1940
22 Francis Bacon b. 1561; George (later Lord) Byron b. 1788
23 Edouard Manet b. 1832
24 Frederick the Great b. 1712; Gold discovered in California 1848

25 Robert Burns b. 1759
26 Eartha Kitt b. 1928
27 Wolfgang Amadeus Mozart b. 1756; Samuel Gompers b. 1850; Mikhail Baryshnikov b. 1948
28 Susan Sontag b. 1933
29 Thomas Paine b. 1737; Anton Chekhov b. 1860; W. C. Fields b. 1880; Paul Newman b. 1925; Germaine Greer b. 1939
30 Charles I executed 1649; Franklin Delano Roosevelt b. 1882; Harold Prince b. 1928; Vanessa Redgrave b. 1937; Mohandas Gandhi assassinated 1948
31 Franz Schubert b. 1797; Anna Pavlova b. 1881; Jersey Joe Walcott b. 1914

FEBRUARY (29 days)

DERIVATION
Latin, *Februarius* (*februare,* to purify), from *februa*, a festival of purification held on Feb. 15.

1 Victor Herbert b. 1859
2 Nell Gwyn b. 1650; Fritz Kreisler b. 1875; James Joyce b. 1882; Jascha Heifetz b. 1901; German capitulation at Stalingrad 1943
3 Felix Mendelssohn-Bartholdy b. 1809; Norman Rockwell b. 1894; Yalta conference began 1945
4 Submarine warfare by Germany 1915
5 Hank Aaron b. 1934
6 Babe Ruth b. 1895; Queen Elizabeth II succeeded to throne 1952
7 Sir Thomas More b. 1478; Charles Dickens b. 1812
8 Mary, Queen of Scots, executed 1587; Russo-Japanese War began 1904
9 Mia Farrow b. 1945
10 Académie Française founded 1635; Charles Lamb b. 1775; Harold Macmillan b. 1894
11 Thomas Alva Edison b. 1847; Vatican City independence 1929
12 Abraham Lincoln b. 1809; Charles Darwin b. 1809; Alice Longworth Roosevelt b. 1884
13 Georges Simenon b. 1903
14 Copernicus b. 1473; Malthus b. 1766; John Barrymore b. 1882; Jimmy Hoffa b. 1913
15 Galileo Galilei b. 1564
16 Edgar Bergen b. 1903; George F. Kennan b. 1904
17 Edward German b. 1862; Marian Anderson b. 1902; Chaim Potok b. 1929; Jim Brown b. 1936
18 *Pilgrim's Progress* published 1678
19 David Garrick b. 1717; Eddie Arcaro b. 1916
20 Ansel Adams b. 1902
21 Cardinal John Henry Newman b. 1801; Andrés Segovia b. 1893; Hubert de Givenchy b. 1927
22 George Washington b. 1732; Luis Buñuel b. 1900
23 Samuel Pepys b. 1633; George Frederick Handel b. 1685
24 Andrew Johnson impeached 1868
25 Enrico Caruso b. 1873
26 Victor Hugo b. 1802; Johnny Cash b. 1932
27 Henry Wadsworth Longfellow b. 1807; Elizabeth Taylor b. 1932
28 Linus Pauling b. 1901
29 Gioacchino Antonio Rossini b. 1792

19

BIRTHDAYS (continued)

MARCH (31 days)

DERIVATION
Latin, *Martius*, the month of Mars, the Roman god of war and the protector of vegetation.

1 Frédéric Chopin b. 1810
2 Dr. Seuss b. 1904; Tom Wolfe b. 1931
3 Alexander Graham Bell b. 1847
4 US Constitution in force 1789
5 Rex Harrison b. 1908; Churchill's Iron Curtain speech 1946
6 Michelangelo b. 1475; Elizabeth Barrett Browning b. 1806
7 Bell's telephone patented 1876
8 Cyd Charisse b. 1923; Lynn Redgrave b. 1943
9 Amerigo Vespucci b. 1451; André Courrèges b. 1923; Bobby Fischer b. 1943
10 Russian Troops mutiny in Petrograd 1917
11 Sir Harold Wilson b. 1916; Ralph Abernathy b. 1926; German troops enter Austria 1938
12 Russian revolution, 1917; Edward Albee b. 1928; Liza Minelli b. 1946
13 Uranus discovered 1781
14 Albert Einstein b. 1879; First trans-Atlantic broadcast 1925
15 Julius Caesar assassinated 44 B.C.
16 Czechoslovakia annexed by Germany 1939
17 Rudolf Nureyev b. 1938
18 Ingmar Stenmark b. 1956
19 David Livingstone b. 1813
20 Napoleon's "Hundred Days" began 1815; B. F. Skinner b. 1904
21 Johann Sebastian Bach b. 1685; Modest Mussorgsky b. 1839
22 Marcel Marceau b. 1923
23 Werner von Braun b. 1912
24 Union of English and Scottish Crowns 1603
25 Rome Treaty signed by Six 1957; Simone Signoret b. 1921; Gloria Steinem b. 1934
26 Tennessee Williams b. 1911
27 U.S. Navy created 1794
28 Britain and France entered Crimean War, 1854; Spanish Civil War ended 1939
29 Pearl Bailey b. 1918
30 Francisco de Goya b. 1746; Vincent van Gogh b. 1853
31 Josef Haydn b. 1732; Cesar Chavez b. 1927; Jack Johnson b. 1878

APRIL (30 days)

DERIVATION
Latin, *Aprilis*, from *aperire* (to open), the season when trees and flowers begin to open.

1 Prince Otto von Bismarck b. 1815
2 Charlemagne b. 742; Hans Christian Andersen b. 1805; Emile Zola b. 1840
3 Pony Express established in U.S. 1860; Henry R. Luce b. 1898; Marlon Brando b. 1924
4 North Atlantic Treaty signed 1949

5   Joseph (later Lord) Lister b. 1827; Algernon Charles Swinburne b. 1837; Spencer Tracy b. 1900; Bette Davis b. 1908
6   U.S. Declaration of War 1917
7   William Wordsworth b. 1770; Francis Ford Coppola b. 1939
8   Mary Pickford b. 1893; Entente Cordiale signed 1904; Betty Ford b. 1918; Jacques Brel b. 1929
9   U.S. Civil War ended 1865
10 Joseph Pulitzer b. 1847; Max Von Sydow b. 1929
11 Joel Grey b. 1932
12 U.S. Civil War began 1861; Yuri Gagarin orbits earth 1961
13 John Dryden became first Poet Laureate 1668; Thomas Jefferson b. 1743; Eudora Welty b. 1909
14 Lillian Gish b. 1896; John Gielgud b. 1904
15 Leonardo da Vinci b. 1452; Abraham Lincoln d. 1865 (wounded by assassin); "Titanic" sank, 1912
16 Sir Charles Chaplin b. 1889; Lily Pons b. 1904; Peter Ustinov b. 1921; Kareem Abdul-Jabbar b. 1947
17 John Pierpont Morgan b. 1837; Nikita Khrushchev b. 1894
18 San Francisco earthquake 1906; Republic of Ireland established 1949
19 Battle of Lexington and Concord 1775
20 Adolf Hitler b. 1889; Joan Miro b. 1893
21 Foundation of Rome 753 B.C.; Charlotte Brontë b. 1816; John Muir b. 1838; Anthony Quinn b. 1916; Queen Elizabeth II b. 1926
22 Lenin b. 1870; Yehudi Menuhin b. 1916
23 Confederate Memorial Day
24 Anthony Trollope b. 1815; Robert Penn Warren b. 1905; Shirley MacLaine b. 1934; Barbra Streisand b. 1942
25 Oliver Cromwell b. 1599; Ella Fitzgerald b. 1918
26 Emma, Lady Hamilton, b. 1765; John James Audubon b. 1785; Anita Loos b. 1893; Bernard Malamud b. 1914
27 Ulysses S. Grant b. 1822
28 Mutiny on the *Bounty* 1789; Benito Mussolini killed 1945; Japan regained independence 1952
29 William Randolph Hearst b. 1863; Emperor Hirohito of Japan b. 1901; Zubin Mehta b. 1936
30 George Washington became first U.S. President 1789; Adolf Hitler committed suicide 1945

MAY (31 days)

DERIVATION
Latin, *Maius*, either from Maia, an obscure goddess, or from *maiores* (elders), on the grounds that the month honored old people, as June honored the young.

1   Duke of Wellington b. 1769; Judy Collins b. 1939
2   Catherine the Great b. 1729; Benjamin Spock b. 1903; Bing Crosby b. 1904; Hussein I (King) b. 1935
3   Niccolò Machiavelli b. 1469; Golda Meir b. 1898; Pete Seeger b. 1919
4   Haymarket Square riot (Chicago) 1886
5   Sören Kierkegaard b. 1813; Karl Marx b. 1818
6   Pushkin b. 1799; Sigmund Freud b. 1856; Theodore White b. 1915; Orson Welles b. 1915; Willie Mays b. 1931; First 4 min. mile by Roger Bannister at Oxford 1954
7   Johannes Brahms b. 1833; Pyotr Tchaikovsky b. 1840; *Lusitania* sunk 1915
8   VE-Day 1945

BIRTHDAYS (continued)

9 Sir James Barrie b. 1860; Pancho Gonzalez b. 1928
10 Fred Astaire b. 1899; Winston Churchill became Prime Minister 1940
11 Irving Berlin b. 1888; Martha Graham b. 1894
12 Florence Nightingale b. 1820; Yogi Berra b. 1925
13 Sir Arthur Sullivan b. 1842; Joe Louis b. 1914
14 State of Israel proclaimed 1948
15 Pierre Curie b. 1859
16 First film "Oscars" awarded 1929
17 Dennis Hopper b. 1936
18 Walter Gropius b. 1883; Frank Capra b. 1897; Margot Fonteyn b. 1919
19 Anne Boleyn executed 1536
20 John Stuart Mill b. 1806; James Stewart b. 1908; Moshe Dayan b. 1915
21 Alexander Pope b. 1688; Fats Waller b. 1904; Lindbergh landed in Paris 1927
22 Richard Wagner b. 1813; Sir Arthur Conan Doyle b. 1859; Sir Laurence Olivier b. 1907
23 Rosemary Clooney b. 1928; Joan Collins b. 1933
24 Queen Victoria b. 1819; Mikhail Sholokhov b. 1905; Bob Dylan b. 1941
25 Ralph Waldo Emerson b. 1803; Josip Broz Tito b. 1892; Bennett Cerf b. 1898; Miles Davis b. 1926; Beverly Sills b. 1929
26 Al Jolson b. 1886; John Wayne b. 1907
27 Vincent Price b. 1911; Sam Snead b. 1912; Henry Kissinger b. 1923; Dunkirk evacuation began, 1940
28 William Pitt (the younger) b. 1759; Jim Thorpe b. 1888
29 Bob Hope b. 1903; John F. Kennedy b. 1917; Mount Everest climbed 1953
30 Joan of Arc executed 1431
31 Pepys' Diary ends 1669; Battle of Jutland 1916; Joe Namath b. 1943

JUNE (30 days)

DERIVATION
Latin, *Junius*, either the goddess Juno, or from *iuniores* (young people), as the month dedicated to youth.

1 Brigham Young b. 1801; John Masefield b. 1878; Marilyn Monroe b. 1926
2 Thomas Hardy b. 1840; Coronation of Queen Elizabeth II 1953
3 Allen Ginsberg b. 1926
4 Robert Merrill b. 1919
5 John Maynard Keynes b. 1883; Marshall Plan 1947
6 D-Day 1944
7 George ("Beau") Brummell b. 1778
8 Frank Lloyd Wright b. 1869
9 Peter the Great b. 1672; Cole Porter b. 1893
10 Duke of Edinburgh b. 1921; F. Lee Bailey b. 1933
11 Ben Jonson b. 1573; John Constable b. 1776; Richard Strauss b. 1864
12 Vic Damone b. 1928
13 William Butler Yeats b. 1865; Boxer Rising in China 1900; Red Grange b. 1903
14 Burl Ives b. 1909
15 Magna Carta sealed 1215; Edward, the Black Prince, b. 1330
16 Katharine Graham b. 1917; Joyce Carol Oates b. 1938
17 Battle of Bunker Hill 1775; Igor Stravinsky b. 1882

18 U.S. declared war on Britain 1812; Battle of Waterloo 1815; Sylvia Porter b. 1913
19 Lester Flatt b. 1914; Lou Gehrig b. 1903
20 Black Hole of Calcutta 1756; Jacques Offenbach b. 1819; Lillian Hellman b. 1907
21 Jean-Paul Sartre b. 1905; Françoise Sagan b. 1935
22 Anne Morrow Lindbergh b. 1906
23 Duke of Windsor b. 1894; Alfred Kinsey b. 1894; Bob Fosse b. 1927
24 Jack Dempsey b. 1895; Phil Harris b. 1906
25 Custer's Last Stand 1876; Robert Venturi b. 1925; Korean War began 1950
26 UN Charter signed 1945
27 Charles Stewart Parnell b. 1846
28 Peter Paul Rubens b. 1577; Archduke Franz Ferdinand assassinated 1914
29 Robert Evans b. 1930
30 Lena Horne b. 1917

JULY (31 days)

DERIVATION
Latin, *Julius*, after Gaius Julius Caesar (b. July 12, probably in 102 B.C., d. March 15, 44 B.C.), the Roman soldier and statesman. (Formerly known by the Romans as *Quintilis*, the fifth month.)

1 Amandine Aurore Dupin (alias George Sand) b. 1804
2 Thurgood Marshall b. 1908
3 Quebec founded 1608
4 Declaration of Independence approved 1776; Ann Landers b. 1918; Neil Simon b. 1927
5 Cecil Rhodes b. 1853
6 Della Reese b. 1932
7 Gustav Mahler b. 1860; Satchel Paige b. 1906
8 John D. Rockefeller b. 1839; Nelson A. Rockefeller b. 1908
9 Edward Heath b. 1916; O. J. Simpson b. 1947
10 John Calvin b. 1509; Saul Bellow b. 1915; Arlo Guthrie b. 1947
11 E. B. White b. 1899; Yul Brynner b. 1920
12 Julius Caesar b. 100 B.C.; Oscar Hammerstein II b. 1895; Van Cliburn b. 1934
13 Sidney Webb b. 1859
14 Storming of the Bastille began 1789; Isaac Bashevis Singer b. 1904; Gerald Ford b. 1913; Ingmar Bergman b. 1918
15 Inigo Jones b. 1573; Rembrandt van Rijn b. 1606;
16 Sir Joshua Reynolds b. 1723; First atomic bomb exploded 1945
17 Spanish Civil War began 1936; Newport Jazz Festival began 1954
18 William Makepeace Thackeray b. 1811; Yevgeny Yevtushenko b. 1933.
19 Edgar Degas b. 1834
20 First moon landing by man 1969
21 Ernest Hemingway b. 1899; Marshall McLuhan b. 1911
22 Alexander Calder b. 1898
23 Haile Selassie b. 1892
24 Simon Bolivar b. 1783
25 Louis Blériot flew Channel 1909
26 George Bernard Shaw b. 1856; Carl Jung b. 1875; Aldous Huxley b. 1894
27 Korean Armistice signed 1953; Leo Durocher b. 1906
28 Jacqueline Kennedy Onassis b. 1929
29 Spanish Armada defeated 1588; Benito Mussolini b. 1883
30 Henry Ford b. 1863
31 Don Murray b. 1929

BIRTHDAYS (continued)

AUGUST (31 days)

DERIVATION
Latin, *Augustus*, after Augustus Caesar (born Gaius Octavius), the first
Roman emperor. (Originally called *Sextilis*, the sixth month.)

1 Battle of the Nile 1798
2 James Baldwin b. 1924
3 Rupert Brooke b. 1887
4 Percy Bysshe Shelley b. 1792; Britain declared war on Germany
   1914
5 Guy de Maupassant b. 1850; John Huston b. 1906; Neil Armstrong
   b. 1930
6 Alfred, Lord Tennyson, b. 1809; Alexander Fleming b. 1881;
   Atomic bomb dropped on Hiroshima 1945
7 British Summer Time Act 1924
9 John Dryden b. 1631; Atomic bomb dropped on Nagasaki 1945;
   Zino Francescatti b. 1905; Bob Cousy b. 1928
10 Herbert Hoover b. 1874
11 Cardinal John Henry Newman d. 1890
12 Norris and Ross McWhirter b. 1925
13 Alfred Hitchcock b. 1899
14 Buddy Greco b. 1926; David Crosby b. 1941
15 Napoleon Bonaparte b. 1769; Julia Child b. 1912; Panama Canal
   opened 1914; VJ-Day 1945
16 Cyprus became independent 1960
17 Davy Crockett b. 1786; Mae West b. 1892
18 Berlin Wall completed 1961; Robert Redford b. 1937; Rafer
   Johnson b. 1935
19 World record Buffalo Bigmouth caught Lock Lorna, Mo. 1976;
   Willie Shoemaker b. 1931
20 Isaac Hayes b. 1942
21 Princess Margaret b. 1930; Wilt Chamberlain b. 1936
22 English Civil War began 1642; Claude Debussy b. 1862; Henri
   Cartier-Bresson b. 1908; Ray Bradbury b. 1920
23 Gene Kelly b. 1912
24 Aubrey Beardsley b. 1872
25 Ivan IV "The Terrible" b. 1530; Paris liberated 1944; Leonard
   Bernstein b. 1918
26 Prince Albert b. 1819
27 Confucius b. 551 B.C.; Krakatoa erupted 1883
28 Wolfgang von Goethe b. 1749
29 Oliver Wendell Holmes, Sr. b. 1809; Ingrid Bergman b. 1915
30 Fred MacMurray b. 1908; Elizabeth Ashley b. 1939; Jean-Claude
   Killy b. 1943
31 Queen Wilhelmina of the Netherlands b. 1880; Alan Jay Lerner
   b. 1918; Ted Williams b. 1918

SEPTEMBER (30 days)

DERIVATION
Latin, from *septem* (seven), as it was originally the seventh month.

1 Germany invaded Poland 1939
2 Great Fire of London began 1666; Jimmy Connors b. 1952
3 Britain declared war on Germany 1939
4 Henry Ford II b. 1917
5 Louis XIV of France b. 1638
6 *Mayflower* sailed from Plymouth 1620

7   Queen Elizabeth I b. 1533; London Blitz began 1940
8   Richard Coeur de Lion b. 1157; Antonín Dvořák b. 1841; First V2 landed in England 1944
9   Tolstoy b. 1828
10 Jose Feliciano b. 1945; Arnold Palmer b. 1929
11 O. Henry b. 1862
12 Herbert Henry Asquith b. 1852; Jesse Owens b. 1913
13 Jacqueline Bisset b. 1946
14 Gregorian Calendar in Britain 1752
15 James Fenimore Cooper b. 1789
16 Lauren Bacall b. 1924
17 U.S. Constitution signed 1787; Ken Kesey b. 1935
18 Samuel Johnson b. 1709; Claudette Colbert b. 1905; Greta Garbo b. 1905
19 Joseph Pasternak b. 1901
20 Sophia Loren b. 1934
21 H. G. Wells b. 1866
22 Michael Faraday b. 1791
23 Augustus, Emperor of Rome, b. 63 B.C.; Ray Charles b. 1931
24 Horace Walpole b. 1717
25 Barbara Walters b. 1931
26 T. S. Eliot b. 1888; Pope Paul VI b. 1897; *Queen Mary* launched 1934
27 *Queen Elizabeth* launched 1938
28 Georges Clemenceau b. 1841; Marcello Mastroianni b. 1924
29 Battle of Marathon 490 B.C.
30 Truman Capote b. 1924; Elie Wiesel b. 1928

OCTOBER (31 days)

DERIVATION
Latin, from *octo* (eight), originally the eighth month.

1   Louis Untermeyer b. 1885; Vladimir Horowitz b. 1904; Jimmy Carter b. 1924
2   Mohandas Gandhi b. 1869
3   Gore Vidal b. 1925
4   Damon Runyon b. 1884; Charlton Heston b. 1924; Sputnik I launched 1957
5   Philip Berrigan b. 1923
6   Thor Heyerdahl b. 1914
7   June Allyson b. 1923
8   Rev. Jesse Jackson b. 1941
9   Jacques Tati b. 1908
10 Henry Cavendish b. 1731
11 Eleanor Roosevelt b. 1884
12 Nurse Edith Cavell executed 1915; Dick Gregory b. 1932; Luciano Pavarotti b. 1935
13 Margaret Thatcher b. 1925
14 Battle of Hastings 1066; William Penn b. 1644; Dwight D. Eisenhower b. 1890
15 Publius Vergilius Maro (Virgil) b. 70 B.C.; Friedrich Wilhelm Nietzsche b. 1844; John Kenneth Galbraith b. 1908; Mario Puzo b. 1920
16 Marie Antoinette executed 1793; Oscar Wilde b. 1854; Eugene O'Neill b. 1888
17 Delaware & Chesapeake Canal op. 1829
18 Pierre Trudeau b. 1919
19 Retreat from Moscow by French 1812
20 Sir Christopher Wren b. 1632; Art Buchwald b. 1925; Mickey Mantle b. 1931

BIRTHDAYS (continued)

21 Samuel Taylor Coleridge b. 1772; Battle of Trafalgar 1805
22 Franz Liszt b. 1811; Doris Lessing b. 1919; Robert Rauschenberg b. 1925
23 Battle of El Alamein began 1942; Pelé b. 1940
24 U.N. Organization established 1945
25 Battle of Agincourt 1415; Charge of the Light Brigade at Balaklava 1854; Pablo Picasso b. 1881
26 Jaclyn Smith b. 1948
27 Erasmus b. 1466; Theodore Roosevelt b. 1858
28 Evelyn Waugh b. 1903; Jonas Salk b. 1914
29 Sir Walter Raleigh executed 1618; James Boswell b. 1740; New York stock market crash 1929; Johnny Carson b. 1925
30 Ezra Pound b. 1885
31 Vermeer bapt. 1632; John Keats b. 1795; Chiang Kai-shek b. 1887

NOVEMBER (30 days)

DERIVATION
Latin, from *novem* (nine), originally the ninth month.

1 Benvenuto Cellini b. 1500; First hydrogen bomb exploded 1952
2 Marie Antoinette b. 1755
3 William Cullen Bryant b. 1794; Karl Baedeker b. 1801
4 Will Rogers b. 1879
5 Gunpowder Plot 1605
6 John Philip Sousa b. 1854
7 Marja Sklodowska (later Marie Curie) b. 1867; Isamu Noguchi b. 1904; Billy Graham b. 1918; Al Hirt b. 1922
8 Katharine Hepburn b. 1909; Munich Putsch 1923
9 German Republic proclaimed 1918
10 Martin Luther b. 1483; H. M. Stanley met David Livingstone at Ujiji 1871; Richard Burton b. 1925
11 Fyodor Dostoyevsky b. 1821; Armistice Day 1918; Alger Hiss b. 1904; Kurt Vonnegut, Jr. b. 1922
12 Auguste Rodin b. 1840
13 Robert Louis Stevenson b. 1850
14 Jawaharlal Nehru b. 1889; Charles, Prince of Wales b. 1948
15 William Pitt (the Elder) b. 1708; Erwin Rommel b. 1891; Georgia O'Keeffe b. 1887; Averell Harriman b. 1891
16 Tiberius b. 42 B.C.; Suez Canal opened 1869
17 Bernard (later Viscount) Montgomery b. 1887; Tom Seaver b. 1944
18 W. S. (later Sir William) Gilbert b. 1836; Amelita Galli-Curci b. 1889; Eugene Ormandy b. 1899
19 Charles I b. 1600; Indira Gandhi b. 1917
20 Alistair Cooke b. 1908; Robert Kennedy b. 1925; Wedding of Queen Elizabeth II 1947
21 Voltaire b. 1694; Stan Musial b. 1920
22 André Gide b. 1869; Charles de Gaulle b. 1890; Geraldine Page b. 1924; Billie Jean King b. 1943; John F. Kennedy assassinated 1963
23 Manuel de Falla b. 1876; Vera Miles b. 1930
24 Charles Darwin's *Origin of Species* published 1859
25 Andrew Carnegie b. 1835; Joe DiMaggio b. 1914
26 Eugene Ionesco b. 1912
27 Alexander Dubcek b. 1921; David Merrick b. 1912
28 William Blake b. 1757
29 Louisa May Alcott b. 1832
30 Jonathan Swift b. 1667; Samuel Clemens (alias Mark Twain) b. 1835; Sir Winston Churchill b. 1874

DECEMBER (31 days)

DERIVATION
Latin, from *decem* (ten), originally the tenth month.

1   Queen Alexandra b. 1844; Mary Martin b. 1913; Woody Allen b. 1935
2   Battle of Austerlitz 1805; Maria Callas b. 1923; Julie Harris b. 1925; First nuclear chain reaction 1942
3   Joseph Conrad b. 1857
4   Samuel Butler b. 1835; Francisco Franco b. 1892
5   Walt Disney b. 1901
6   Warren Hastings b. 1732; Otto Graham b. 1921
7   Mary, Queen of Scots, b. 1542; Pearl Harbor attacked 1941
8   Jean Sibelius b. 1865; Sammy Davis, Jr. b. 1925
9   John Milton b. 1608
10 César Franck b. 1822; Arthur Fiedler b. 1894
11 Hector Berlioz b. 1803; Edward VIII abdicated 1936; Aleksandr Solzhenitsyn b. 1918
12 First trans-Atlantic radio signal 1901; Frank Sinatra b. 1915
13 Heinrich Heine b. 1797; Archie Moore b. 1916
14 Amundsen reached South Pole 1911
15 Sitting Bull killed 1890
16 Ludwig van Beethoven b. 1770; Boston Tea Party 1773; Jane Austen b. 1775; Margaret Mead b. 1901
17 First airplane flight 1903; Erskine Caldwell b. 1903
18 Slavery abolished in U.S.A. 1865; Robert Moses b. 1888; Ty Cobb b. 1886
19 Sir Ralph Richardson b. 1902; Leonid Brezhnev b. 1906
20 Sir Robert Menzies b. 1894
21 Pilgrim Fathers landed 1620; Benjamin Disraeli b. 1804; Josif Stalin b. 1879; Kurt Waldheim b. 1918; Chris Evert b. 1954
22 Jean Racine b. 1639; James Wolfe b. 1726; Giacomo Puccini b. 1858
23 Sir Richard Arkwright b. 1732
24 Matthew Arnold b. 1822
25 Sir Isaac Newton b. 1642; Humphrey Bogart b. 1899; Anwar el-Sadat b. 1918
26 Henry Miller b. 1891; Mao Tse-tung b. 1893; Radium discovered 1898
27 Louis Pasteur b. 1822
28 Woodrow Wilson b. 1856
29 St. Thomas à Becket killed 1170; William Ewart Gladstone b. 1809; Pablo Casals b. 1876; Mary Tyler Moore b. 1937
30 Rudyard Kipling b. 1865; Stephen Leacock b. 1869; Grigory Rasputin assassinated 1916
31 Henri Matisse b. 1869; Odetta b. 1930

Prominent Black Americans

Note: NAACP = National Association for the Advancement of Colored People

ALDRIDGE, Ira (1807–67). Actor acclaimed for his performances throughout Europe. Played Othello with the famous British actor Edmund Kean as Iago.

ALLEN, Richard (?1760–1831). Slave who bought his freedom and became a Philadelphia clergyman, civic leader and opponent of racism. Established the African Methodist Episcopal Church in 1794.

ANDERSON, Marian (1902–). Opera and Negro spiritual singer who gained recognition in the United States after acclaimed performances in Europe. In 1939, the Daughters of the American Revolution denied her permission to sing at Constitution Hall in Washington, D.C.

ARMSTRONG, Louis (1900–71). Trumpet player, singer, band leader and showman. Important contributor to the development of jazz.

ATTUCKS, Crispus (?1723–70). Former slave who led an angry crowd in a confrontation with British troops in colonial Boston, resulting in the Boston Massacre, in which he was killed.

BALDWIN, James (1924–). Novelist, playwright and essayist. Author of *Another Country, The Fire Next Time* and other books.

BANNEKER, Benjamin (1731–1806). Mathematician, astronomer, surveyor, almanac publisher and civic-minded citizen. Served on the commission that designed Washington, D.C.

BETHUNE, Mary McLeod (1875–1955). Educator and advisor on ethnic minorities to President Franklin D. Roosevelt.

BRADLEY, Thomas (1917–). Former lawyer, police lieutenant and city councilman. Elected Democratic mayor of Los Angeles in 1973.

BROOKE, Edward W. (1919–). Lawyer and Republican politician. Attorney General of Massachusetts, 1962–1966. United States Senator from Massachusetts, 1966–1978. First black elected to United States Senate since Reconstruction era.

BUNCHE, Ralph (1904–71). Educator, United States government official and United Nations diplomat. Won the Nobel Peace Prize in 1950 for his efforts as United Nations mediator of the Palestine dispute.

IRA ALDRIDGE (left) actor, and RICHARD ALLEN (right) clergyman who bought his freedom from slavery, were prominent in the early 19th century.

BENJAMIN BANNEKER (left) was one of the learned men of his time, and helped design Washington, D.C. CRISPUS ATTUCKS (right) was killed in the Boston Massacre in 1770.

CARVER, George Washington (?1864–1943). Scientist who headed the agricultural research program at Tuskegee Institute in Alabama. Developed methods of soil improvement and crop diversification, and discovered hundreds of uses for the peanut, sweet potato and soybean.

CULLEN, Countee (1903–46). Poet. Author of *Copper Sun, On These I Stand* and other books of poetry.

DOUGLASS, Frederick (?1817–95). Self-educated slave who escaped to the North and became an eloquent opponent of slavery, editor (of *North Star*, an abolitionist newspaper), lecturer (with the Massachusetts Anti-Slavery Society) and writer.

THOMAS BRADLEY (left) who was elected mayor of Los Angeles in 1973, followed in the political tradition of FREDERICK DOUGLASS (right) who led the fight in the mid-19th century for freedom for blacks.

EDWARD KENNEDY "DUKE" ELLINGTON (1899-1974), American jazz musician and composer, formed a jazz band which became world famous for its playing of the blues.

DU BOIS, William E. B. (1868–1963). Scholar, educator and life-long opponent of racism and colonialism. A founder (in 1910) of the NAACP and editor of its magazine, *Crisis.* Author of *The Souls of Black Folk* and other books.

DUNBAR, Paul Laurence (1872–1906). Poet and novelist. Author of *Lyrics of Lowly Life* and other works.

ELLINGTON, Duke (1899–1974). Innovative jazz musician, composer and band leader.

ELLISON, Ralph (1914–). Novelist. Author of *Invisible Man* and other books.

FARMER, James (1920–). Civil rights leader. Founder (in 1942) and leader of the Congress of Racial Equality (CORE). Assistant Secretary of Health, Education and Welfare (1969–1970) in the administration of President Nixon.

GARVEY, Marcus (1887–1940). Jamaica-born advocate of black nationalism. Founded the Universal Negro Improvement Association in 1914, moved to New York City in 1916 and led a "Back to Africa" movement until imprisoned for mail fraud (1925–1927) and then deported.

HENSON, Matthew A. (1866–1955). Seaman and explorer. Assistant to Robert E. Peary on several Arctic explorations, including Peary's 1908–1909 expedition to the North Pole. Placed United States flag at the Pole.

HUGHES, Langston (1902–67). Poet, playwright and novelist. Author of *Shakespeare in Harlem, I Wonder as a I Wander* and other books.

JOHNSON, Jack (1878–1946). Boxer who in 1908 became the first black to win the world heavyweight boxing championship.

JOHNSON, James Weldon (1871–1938). Poet, novelist, editor, translator, song writer, teacher and United States diplomat in Venezuela and Nicaragua. Official of the NAACP, 1916–1930. Author of *The Autobiography of an Ex-Colored Man* and other books.

JOPLIN, Scott (1868–1917). Innovative pianist and composer of ragtime music.

JORDAN, Barbara (1936–). Lawyer and Democratic politician. Texas state senator, 1966–1972. Elected to House of Representatives, 1972.

KING, Martin Luther, Jr. (1929–68). Baptist minister and foremost leader of the non-violent civil rights movement that brought desegregation

JOE LOUIS held the world heavyweight crown longer than anyone else —almost 12 years.

of public facilities in the South and other civil rights gains. Founder (in 1957) and president of the Southern Christian Leadership Conference (SCLC). Assassinated in Memphis, Tennessee.

LOUIS, Joe (1914–   ). World heavyweight boxing champion, 1937–1949, longest reign.

MALCOLM X (1925–65). Former prison inmate who became an eloquent spokesman for the Nation of Islam (Black Muslims). Later became disillusioned with Black Muslim policies and was assassinated after leaving that organization to pursue an independent course.

MARSHALL, Thurgood (1908–   ). Civil rights lawyer who successfully argued the case against racial segregation in the public schools before the Supreme Court in 1954. Solicitor General of the United States, 1965–1967. First black Supreme Court Justice, 1967–present.

MUHAMMAD, Elijah (1897–1975). Leader (1934–1975) of the black nationalist Nation of Islam (Black Muslims).

OWENS, Jesse (1913–   ). Track athlete who won four gold medals at the 1936 Olympic Games in Berlin.

PAIGE, Leroy "Satchel" (1906–   ). Baseball player (pitcher) in the Negro League, 1924–1948. Allowed into major leagues at age 42. Elected to National Baseball Hall of Fame in 1971.

RANDOLPH, A. Philip (1889–   ). Leader of the struggle for Negro representation in the labor movement. Founder and president of the Brotherhood of Sleeping Car Porters, and vice president of the AFL-CIO.

ROBESON, Paul (1898–1976). Athlete, actor and concert singer who was blacklisted for his militant advocacy of racial equality and his admiration for the Soviet Union.

ROBINSON, Jackie (1919–72). Baseball player for the Brooklyn Dodgers. The first black to play in the major leagues. Elected to the National Baseball Hall of Fame in 1962.

TRUTH, Sojourner (?1797–1883). Former slave who advocated abolition of slavery, women's rights and better working conditions.

TUBMAN, Harriet (?1823–1913). Maryland slave who escaped and became a "conductor" on the Underground Railroad, secretly venturing into the South many times to guide slaves to freedom in the North. Served as nurse, spy and scout for the Union Army during the Civil War.

TURNER, Nat (1800–31). Slave who led a revolt in Southampton, Virginia, in 1831. The rebellion was crushed, and Turner and his followers were hanged.

NAT TURNER led a slave revolt in Virginia in 1831 which was crushed. He was captured and hanged, but became a martyr.

VESEY, Denmark (?1767–1822). Former slave who planned a slave rebellion in South Carolina, was betrayed by informers and hanged along with his followers.

WASHINGTON, Booker T. (1856–1915). Educator who advocated the attainment of social and economic equality for Negroes through vocational training rather than by political struggle. Founder (in 1881) of the Tuskegee Institute in Alabama and the author of *Up From Slavery*.

WATTS, André (1946–   ). Concert pianist. Made debut with New York Philharmonic in 1963.

WHEATLEY, Phillis (?1753–84). Poet. The first notable Negro writer in the United States. Originally the slave of a Boston merchant.

WHITE, Walter F. (1893–1955). Writer and civil rights leader who investigated and fought against the lynching of blacks. Executive secretary of the NAACP, 1931–1955. Author of *Fire in the Flint* and other books.

PHILLIS WHEATLEY (left), first black poet, and HARRIET TUBMAN (right), who helped slaves escape via the "Underground Railroad."

BLACK AMERICANS (continued)

WILKINS, Roy (1901–). Civil rights leader and executive director of the NAACP, 1955–1977.

WILLIAMS, Daniel Hale (1858–1931). Surgeon and hospital administrator. Established the first Negro hospital in the United States—Provident Hospital in Chicago—and founded the first training school for black nurses. Performed one of the first heart operations in 1893.

WRIGHT, Richard (1908–60). Novelist. Author of *Native Son* and other books.

YOUNG, Andrew (1932–). Clergyman, civil rights leader and politician. Official of the Southern Christian Leadership Conference (SCLC), 1964–1971. Democratic congressman from Georgia, 1972–1977. United States Ambassador to the United Nations, 1977– .

YOUNG, Whitney, Jr. (1921–71). Executive director of the National Urban League (1961–1971), writer, lecturer.

BLACK AMERICAN ENTERTAINERS

Amos, John	actor	—
Armstrong, Louis	musician	1900–71
Baker, Josephine	dancer	1906–75
Basie, Count (William)	orchestra leader	1904–
Beavers, Louise	actress	1904–62
Calloway, Cab	orchestra leader	1907–
Cambridge, Godfrey	actor	1933–76
Carroll, Diahann	actress	1935–
Checker, Chubby	singer	1941–
Cole, Nat "King"	singer	1919–65
Cosby, Bill	actor, comedian	1937–
Dandridge, Dorothy	actress	1924–65
Davis, Ossie	actor	1917–
Davis, Sammy, Jr.	actor, entertainer	1925–
Dee, Ruby	actress	1924–
Dixon, Ivan	actor	1931–
Domino, Fats	singer	1928–
Dunham, Katherine	dancer	1910–
Ellington, Duke	Composer	1899–1974
Fitzgerald, Ella	singer	1918–
Flack, Roberta	singer, composer	1939–
Foxx, Redd	actor	1922–
Gillespie, Dizzy	musician, composer	1917–
Gunn, Moses	actor	1929–
Hampton, Lionel	orchestra leader	1914–
Handy, W. C.	composer	1873–1958
Hendrix, Jimi	singer	1943–70
Hines, Earl (Fatha)	pianist, songwriter	1905–
Holder, Geoffrey	choreographer	1930–
Holiday, Billie	singer	1915–59
Hooks, Robert	actor	1937–
Horne, Lena	singer, actress	1917–
Hyman, Earle	actor	1926–
Ingram, Rex	actor	1895–1969
Jackson, Mahalia	singer	1911–72
Jones, James Earl	actor	1931–
King Oliver	musician, band leader	1885–1938
Kitt, Eartha	actress	1928–
Ledbetter, Huddie (Leadbelly)	singer	1888–1949
Lee, Canada	actor	1907–52
Little, Cleavon	actor	1939–
Mathis, Johnny	singer	1935–
McDaniel, Hattie	actress	1895–1952
McQueen, Butterfly	actress	1911–
Moore, Melba	actress, singer	1945–

JOHNNY MATHIS made a record album in 1958 that stayed on the best seller chart for more than 9 years.

Morris, Greg	actor	1934–
Morton, Ferdinand (Jelly Roll)	composer	1885–1941
Odetta	singer	1930–
Peters, Brock	actor	1927–
Poitier, Sidney	actor	1927–
Price, Leontyne	opera singer	1927–
Pryor, Richard	actor	—
Reese, Della	singer	1932–
Rhodes, Hari	actor	1932–
Robeson, Paul	(see other list)	
Robinson, Bill (Bojangles)	dancer	1878–1949
Rolle, Esther	actress	—
Ross, Diana	actress, singer	1944–
Roundtree, Richard	actor	1942–
Russell, Nipsey	comedian	1924–
Sands, Diana	actress	1934–73
Scott, Hazel	pianist	1920–
Short, Bobby	singer, pianist	1936–
Smith, Bessie	singer	1894–1937
Strode, Woody	actor	1948–
Turner, Ike	singer	1934–
Turner, Tina	singer	1941–
Uggams, Leslie	actress	1943–
Vaughan, Sarah	singer	1924–
Vereen, Ben	actor	1946–
Verrett, Shirley	opera singer	1933–
Waller, Thomas (Fats)	singer, composer	1904–43
Warwicke, Dionne	singer	1941–
Waters, Ethel	actress	1900–77
Williams, Mary Lou	pianist, composer	1910–
Williamson, Fred	actor	1937–
Wilson, Flip	comedian	1933–
Wonder, Stevie	singer	1950–

BLACK AMERICAN SPORTS FIGURES

Aaron, Henry	baseball	1934–
Abdul-Jabbar, Kareem	basketball	1947–
Ali, Muhammad	boxing	1942–
Ashe, Arthur	tennis	1943–
Blue, Vida	baseball	1949–
Boozer, Emerson	football	1943–
Brock, Lou	baseball	1939–
Brown, Jimmy	football	1936–
Campanella, Roy	baseball	1921–
Chamberlain, Wilt	basketball	1936–

WILT CHAMBERLAIN is generally acknowledged to be the best basketball player of all time. He holds more records than any other player.

HENRY AARON set the major league record with 755 home runs in 23 seasons.

KAREEM ABDUL-JABBAR in 8 years of pro basketball sank more than half of the baskets he attempted.

WYOMIA TYUS set a record as the world's fastest sprinter in 1965.

BLACK AMERICAN SPORTS FIGURES (continued)

Erving, Julius	basketball	1950–
Foreman, George	boxing	1949–
Frazier, Joe	boxing	1944–
Frazier, Walt	basketball	1945–
Howard, Elston	baseball	1930–
Jackson, Reggie	baseball	1946–
Johnson, Jack	boxing	1878–1946
Johnson, Rafer	decathlon	1935–
Louis, Joe	boxing	1914–
Mays, Willie	baseball	1931–
McCovey, Willie	baseball	1938–
Mitchell, James	football	1948–
Moore, Archie	boxing	1916–
Owens, Jesse	track	1918–
Paige, Leroy (Satchel)	baseball	1906–
Patterson, Floyd	boxing	1935–
Reed, Willis	basketball	1942–
Robinson, Frank	baseball	1935–
Robinson, Jackie	(see other list)	
Robinson, Sugar Ray	boxing	1920–
Rudolph, Wilma	track	1940–
Simpson, O. J.	football	1947–
Tyus, Wyomia	track	1945–
Walcott, Joe	boxing	1914–
Wills, Maury	baseball	1932–

JESSE OWENS broke 6 world records in one day in 1935—in running, hurdling and long jumping.

Sports

BASEBALL

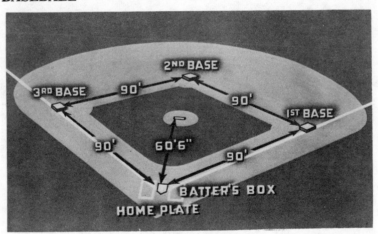

How the infield looks.

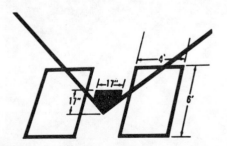

The batter's box.

BADMINTON

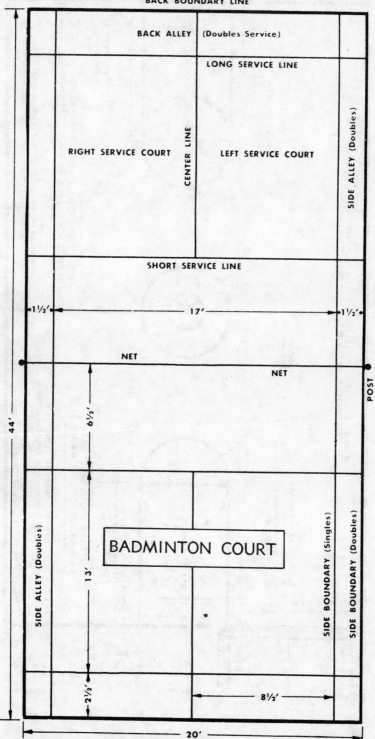

THE BASKETBALL COURT

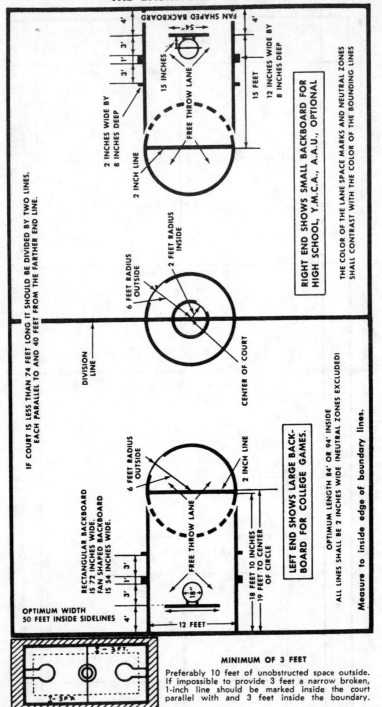

FAN SHAPED BACKBOARD

54"

15 INCHES

15 FEET

FREE THROW LANE

12 INCHES WIDE BY
8 INCHES DEEP

2 INCHES WIDE BY
8 INCHES DEEP

2 INCH LINE

4'   3'   1'   3'

RIGHT END SHOWS SMALL BACKBOARD FOR
HIGH SCHOOL, Y.M.C.A., A.A.U., OPTIONAL

THE COLOR OF THE LANE SPACE MARKS AND NEUTRAL ZONES
SHALL CONTRAST WITH THE COLOR OF THE BOUNDING LINES.

IF COURT IS LESS THAN 74 FEET LONG IT SHOULD BE DIVIDED BY TWO LINES,
EACH PARALLEL TO AND 40 FEET FROM THE FARTHER END LINE.

DIVISION
LINE

6 FEET RADIUS
OUTSIDE

2 FEET RADIUS
INSIDE

CENTER OF COURT

RECTANGULAR BACKBOARD
IS 72 INCHES WIDE.
FAN SHAPED BACKBOARD
IS 54 INCHES WIDE.

6 FEET RADIUS
OUTSIDE

FREE THROW LANE

2 INCH LINE

18"

18 FEET 10 INCHES
19 FEET TO CENTER
OF CIRCLE

OPTIMUM WIDTH
50 FEET INSIDE SIDELINES

4'   3'   1'   3'

12 FEET

LEFT END SHOWS LARGE BACK-
BOARD FOR COLLEGE GAMES.

OPTIMUM LENGTH 84' OR 94' INSIDE
ALL LINES SHALL BE 2 INCHES WIDE (NEUTRAL ZONES EXCLUDED)

Measure to inside edge of boundary lines.

3 FT.

3 FT.

MINIMUM OF 3 FEET

Preferably 10 feet of unobstructed space outside.
If impossible to provide 3 feet a narrow broken,
1-inch line should be marked inside the court
parallel with and 3 feet inside the boundary.

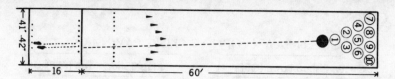

BOWLING : The lane with a ball aimed at the head pin.

1	2	3	4	5	6	7	8	9	10
☒	7⧄	8Ⓞ	7⧄	9⁄	☒	8⁄	☒	9⁄	☒8⁄
20	38	46	65	74	94	114	133	142	162

HOW BOWLING IS SCORED: The first ball you roll is a strike, and is marked with an X in the first small box of the first frame. The first ball you roll in the second frame knocks down 7 pins, and that is recorded in the first small box of the second frame. Before you finish this frame, you down the other 3 pins, giving you a spare, which is scored with a slanted line in the other small box of frame 2. Also, at this time you record the final score for the first frame—a strike (10) plus the next 2 balls (10) gives you 20. In frame 3, you roll an 8 and leave a split (2 pins far apart) which is represented by a circle. Since you fail to "convert" this, it remains a zero. You now enter the score for frame 2—a spare (10) plus the next ball (8), a total of 18, added to the 20 equals 38. If you had converted the split it would have been a circle with the spare slash through it. At the end of frame 10, you get 2 balls after your strike, and the extra is scored in the 3rd small box.

BRIDGE (Contract)   Point-Count Bidding

OPENING BIDS

Points	Bid
12 or 13, with good suit	1 of suit
14, with any suit	1 of suit
16 to 18, with stoppers	1 NT
22 to 24, with stoppers	2 NT
25 to 27, with stoppers	3 NT
25 or more, with good suit	2 of suit

RESPONSES TO 1 OF A SUIT

6 to 16	1 of new suit
9 to 16	2 of lower suit
17 or more	Jump in new suit
6 to 10, with trump support	Raise to 2
13 to 16	Raise to 3
8 or less, with trumps and void or singleton	Raise to 4
6 to 9	1 NT
13 to 15, with stoppers	2 NT
16 or 17, with stoppers	3 NT

RESPONSES TO 2 OF A SUIT

5 or less	2 NT
6 or more	Positive response

RESPONSES TO 2 NT

0 to 3	Pass
4 to 10	Bid game
11 or more	Aim for slam

REBIDS BY OPENER

13 to 16	Minimum or pass
17 to 19	Invite a game
20 or more	Force to game

REBIDS BY RESPONDER

6 to 9	Minimum or pass
10 to 12	Invite a game
13 or more	Force to game

CHESS

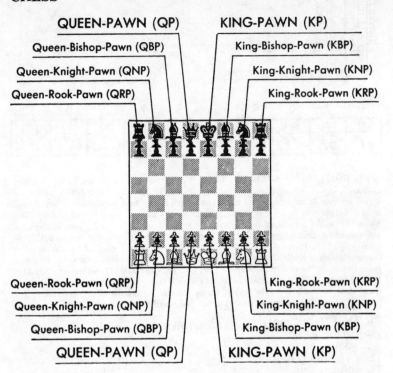

QUEEN-PAWN (QP)   KING-PAWN (KP)

Queen-Bishop-Pawn (QBP)   King-Bishop-Pawn (KBP)

Queen-Knight-Pawn (QNP)   King-Knight-Pawn (KNP)

Queen-Rook-Pawn (QRP)   King-Rook-Pawn (KRP)

Queen-Rook-Pawn (QRP)   King-Rook-Pawn (KRP)

Queen-Knight-Pawn (QNP)   King-Knight-Pawn (KNP)

Queen-Bishop-Pawn (QBP)   King-Bishop-Pawn (KBP)

QUEEN-PAWN (QP)   KING-PAWN (KP)

The opening position

CROQUET   # CRICKET

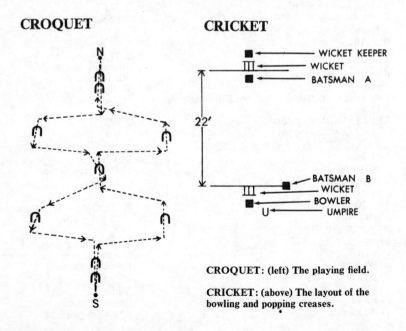

CROQUET: (left) The playing field.

CRICKET: (above) The layout of the bowling and popping creases.

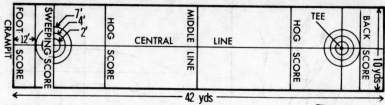

CURLING: (Above) How the rink is laid out. (Right) A stone.

FENCING

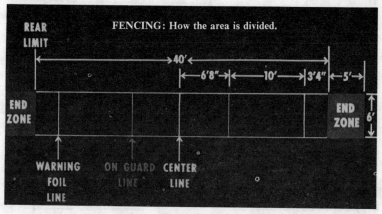

FENCING: How the area is divided.

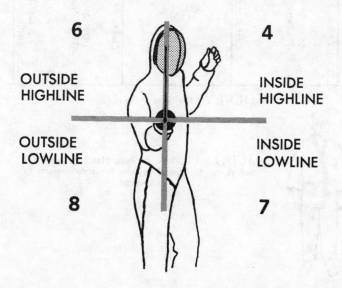

6   4

OUTSIDE HIGHLINE   INSIDE HIGHLINE

OUTSIDE LOWLINE   INSIDE LOWLINE

8   7

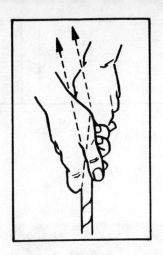

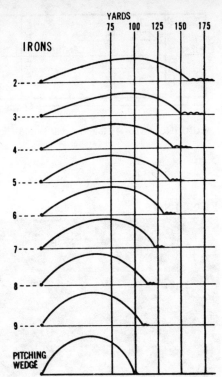

YARDS
75 100 125 150 175

IRONS

2
3
4
5
6
7
8
9
PITCHING WEDGE

GOLF : (Above) The overlapping grip. (Right) Average length of shot with each iron.

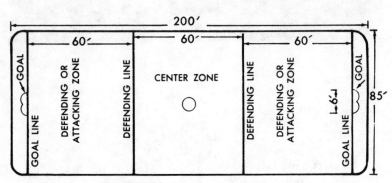

200'

60'   60'   60'

GOAL

DEFENDING OR ATTACKING ZONE

DEFENDING LINE

CENTER ZONE

DEFENDING LINE

DEFENDING OR ATTACKING ZONE

GOAL

GOAL LINE

GOAL LINE

85'

HOCKEY : Divisions of the rink.

JUDO : A Judoka or Judo player dressed in a Judogi, the traditional costume for Judo contests or exhibitions.

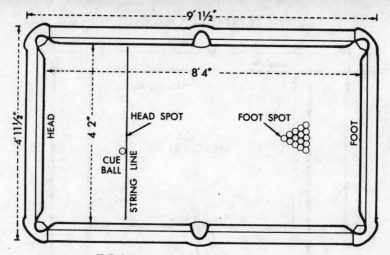

POOL: The table set up for the break.

POLO: The mallet

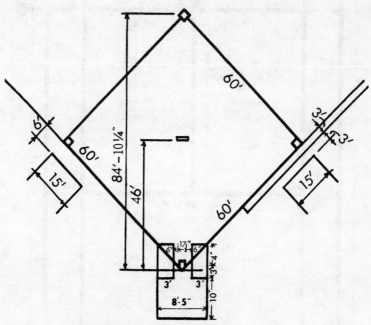

SOFTBALL: Infield and batter's box.

TENNIS COURT

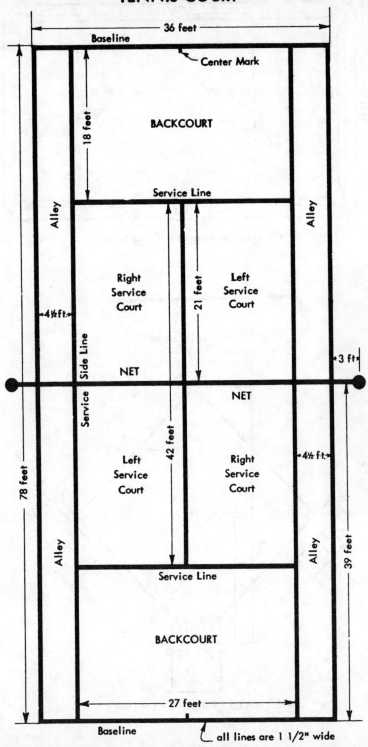

Baseline

36 feet

Center Mark

BACKCOURT

18 feet

Alley

Service Line

Right
Service
Court

Left
Service
Court

21 feet

4½ ft.

Service Side Line

NET

NET

3 ft.

Left
Service
Court

42 feet

Right
Service
Court

4½ ft.

78 feet

Alley

Alley

39 feet

Service Line

BACKCOURT

27 feet

Baseline

all lines are 1 1/2" wide

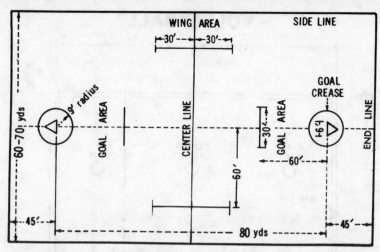

LACROSSE : The playing field.

LOW HURDLE

30"

HIGH HURDLE

39"

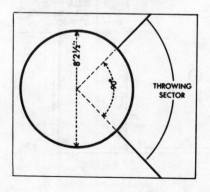

TRACK & FIELD

DISCUS THROW: The circle and its rim with the 90-degree sector.

VOLLEYBALL

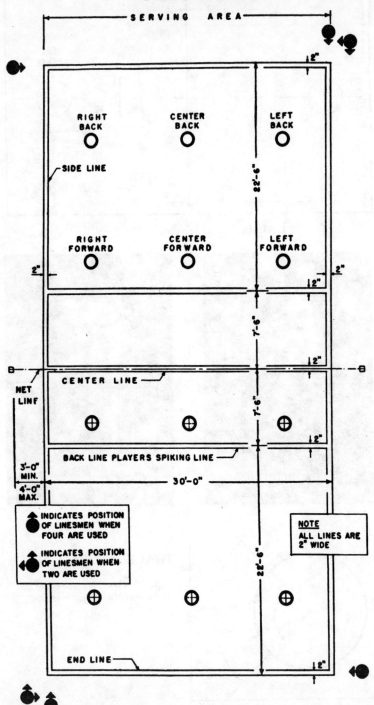

SERVING AREA

2"

RIGHT BACK

CENTER BACK

LEFT BACK

SIDE LINE

22'-6"

RIGHT FORWARD

CENTER FORWARD

LEFT FORWARD

2"

2"

2"

7'-6"

2"

NET LINE

CENTER LINE

7'-6"

2"

BACK LINE PLAYERS SPIKING LINE

3'-0" MIN.

30'-0"

4'-0" MAX.

INDICATES POSITION OF LINESMEN WHEN FOUR ARE USED

INDICATES POSITION OF LINESMEN WHEN TWO ARE USED

NOTE
ALL LINES ARE 2" WIDE

22'-6"

END LINE

2"

Summary Olympic Games

I	1896	Athens, Greece	April 6–15
II	1900	Paris, France	May 20–Oct. 28
III	1904	St. Louis, Missouri	July 1–Nov. 23
*	1906	Athens, Greece	April 22–May 2
IV	1908	London, England	April 27–Oct. 31
V	1912	Stockholm, Sweden	May 5–July 22
VI	1916	Berlin, Germany	not celebrated owing to war
VII	1920	Antwerp, Belgium	April 20–Sept. 12
VIII	1924	Paris, France	May 4–July 27
IX	1928	Amsterdam, Netherlands	May 17–Aug. 12
X	1932	Los Angeles, Calif.	July 30–Aug. 14
XI	1936	Berlin, Germany	Aug. 1–16
XII	1940	Tokyo, then Helsinki	not celebrated owing to war
XIII	1944	London, England	not celebrated owing to war
XIV	1948	London, England	July 29–Aug. 14
XV	1952	Helsinki, Finland	July 19–Aug. 3
XVI	1956	Melbourne, Australia [1]	Nov. 22–Dec. 8
XVII	1960	Rome, Italy	Aug. 25–Sept. 11
XVIII	1964	Tokyo, Japan	Oct. 10–24
XIX	1968	Mexico City, Mexico	Oct. 12–27
XX	1972	Munich, West Germany	Aug. 26–Sept. 10
XXI	1976	Montreal, Canada	July 17–Aug. 1
XXII	1980	Moscow, U.S.S.R.	July 19–Aug. 3
XXIII	1984	Los Angeles, Calif.	—

* *This celebration (to mark the 10th anniversary of the modern Games) was officially intercalated but is not numbered.*

[1] *The equestrian events were held in Stockholm June 10–17, 1956.*

Winter Olympic Games

I	1924	Chamonix, France	Jan. 25–Feb. 4
II	1928	St. Moritz, Switzerland	Feb. 11–19
III	1932	Lake Placid, N.Y.	Feb. 4–12
IV	1936	Garmisch-Partenkirchen, Germany	Feb. 6–16
V	1948	St. Moritz, Switzerland	Jan. 30–Feb. 8
VI	1952	Oslo, Norway	Feb. 14–25
VII	1956	Cortina d'Ampezzo, Italy	Jan. 26–Feb. 5
VIII	1960	Squaw Valley, Calif.	Feb. 18–28
IX	1964	Innsbruck, Austria	Jan. 29–Feb. 9
X	1968	Grenoble, France	Feb. 6–18
XI	1972	Sapporo, Japan	Feb. 3–13
XII	1976	Innsbruck, Austria [2]	Feb. 4–15
XIII	1980	Lake Placid, N.Y.	—
XIV	1984	Sarajevo, Yugoslavia	

[2] *Originally awarded to Denver, Colo.*

Speed in Sport

m.p.h.	Record	Name	Place	Date
2,193.167	Official air speed record (paramilitary)	Capt. Eldon Joersz & Maj. George Morgan	over Beale Air Base, California	July 28, 1976
631.637	Highest land speed (four-wheeled rocket powered)	Gary Gabelich (U.S.) in *The Blue Flame*	Bonneville Salt Flats, Utah	Oct. 23, 1970
614	Parachuting free-fall in mesosphere (military research)	Capt. J. W. Kittinger (U.S.)	Tularosa, N.M.	Aug. 16, 1960
429.311	Highest land speed (wheel-driven)	Donald Campbell (G.B.) in *Bluebird* (gas-turbined)	Lake Eyre, S. Australia	July 17, 1964
418.504	Highest land speed (four wheel direct drive)	Robert Summers (U.S.) in *Goldenrod*	Bonneville Salt Flats, Utah	Nov. 12, 1965
345.42	Highest water-borne speed	Ken Warby (Australia) in *The Spirit of Australia*	Blowering Dam, N.S.W., Australia	Nov. 20, 1977
319.627	Official water speed record	Ken Warby (Australia) in *The Spirit of Australia*	Blowering Dam, N.S.W., Australia	Oct. 8, 1978
307.692	Highest speed motorcycle	Don Vesco (U.S.)	Bonneville Salt Flats, Utah	Sept. 28, 1975
221.160	Auto racing—closed circuit	Mark Donohue Jr. (U.S.)	Talladega, Alabama	Aug. 9, 1975
213.70	Model aircraft (jet model)	V. Goukoune (U.S.S.R.)	Klementyeva, U.S.S.R.	Sept. 21, 1971
202.42	Hydroplane record (propeller-driven)	Larry Hill (U.S.)	Long Beach, Calif.	Aug. 1973
200.624	Lap record 500 miles auto racing	Johnny Rutherford (U.S.)	Indianapolis	May 13, 1977
180	Pelota (Jai-alai)	Jose Areitio	Palm Beach, Florida	Feb. 2, 1978
170	Golf ball	(Electrically timed)	U.S.A.	1960
155.627	Lap record (practice) 24 hr. endurance auto racing	Jackie Oliver	Le Mans, France	Apr. 18, 1971
140.5	Cycling, motor-paced	Dr. Allan V. Abbott (U.S.)	Bonneville Salt Flats, Utah	Aug. 25, 1973
134.33	Water skiing	Grant Torrens (Australia)	Australia	Feb. 1978
117–185	Sky diving—lower atmosphere	Terminal velocity (varies with altitude)		post 1950
124.41	Downhill schuss (Alpine skiing)	Steve McKinney (U.S.)	Portillo, Chile	Oct. 1, 1978

SPEED IN SPORT (continued)

118	Ice hockey—puck	Bobby Hull (Canada)	Chicago	1965
102.74	Gliding (*100 km* triangular course)	K. Briegleb (U.S.) in a *Kestrel I*	over the U.S.A.	July 18, 1974
90	Tobogganing—Cresta Run	Poldi Berchtold (Switz.)	St. Moritz, Switzerland	Jan. 1975
76.342	Cycling behind pacemaker—1 hr.	Leon Vanderstuyft (Belgium)	Montlhery Motor Circuit, France	Sept. 30, 1928
63.894	Downhill Alpine skiing (Olympic course) (average)	Franz Klammer (Austria)	Innsbruck, Austria	Feb. 5, 1976
52.46	Speedway (4 laps of 430 yd.)	Dave Morton (G.B.)	Crewe, England	Aug. 12, 1974
43.26	Horse racing (440 yd. in 20.8 s.)	Big Racket	Mexico City	Feb. 5, 1945
42.16	Track cycling (*200 m* unpaced in 10.61 s.)	Omari Phakadze (U.S.S.R.)	Mexico City	Oct. 22, 1967
41.72	Greyhound racing (410 yd. straight 26.13 s.)	The Shoe (Australia)	Richmond, N.S.W., Australia	Apr. 25, 1968
38.46	Sailing—60 ft. proa *Crossbow II* (33.4 knots)	T. J. Coleman (U.K.) *et al.*	Portland, Dorset, England	Oct. 4, 1977
35.06	Horse racing—The Derby (1 mile 885 yd.)	Mahmoud	Epsom, Surrey, England	June 1936
35	Boxing—speed of punch	Sugar Ray Robinson (U.S.)	U.S.A.	Jan. 1957
30.715	Cycling—1 hr., unpaced	Eddie Merckx (Belgium)	Mexico City, Mexico	Oct. 25, 1972
29.80	Steeplechasing—The Grand National (4 miles 856 yd. in 9 min. 1.9 s.)	Red Rum ridden by Brian Fletcher	Aintree, Liverpool, England	Mar. 31, 1973
29.43	Ice speed skating (500 m. in 37.00 s. on 400 m rink)	Yevgeniy Kulikov (U.S.S.R.)	Medeo, U.S.S.R.	Mar. 29, 1975
27.89	Sprinting (during 100 yd.)	Robert Hayes (U.S.)	St. Louis	June 21, 1963
21.49	Cycling—average maintained over 24 hr.	Teuvo Louhivuori (Finland)	Tampere-Kolari, Finland	Sept. 10, 1974
13.46	Rowing (2,000 m)	East German Eight	Montreal, Canada	July 16, 1976
12.24	Marathon run (26 miles 385 yd.)	Derek Clayton (Australia)	Antwerp, Belgium	May 30, 1969
8.96	Walking—1 hr.	Daniel Bautista (Mexico)	Madrid, Spain	May 29, 1978
4.52	Swimming (100 m)—Long Course in 49.44 s.	Jonty Skinner (S.A.F.)	Philadelphia	Aug. 14, 1976
2.4	Channel swimming (effective speed)	Nasser el Sahzli (Egypt)	England to France	Aug. 21, 1977
0.00084	Tug o' war (2 hr. 41 min. pull—12 ft.)	2nd Derbyshire Regt. (U.K.)	Jubbulpore, India	Aug. 12, 1889

Origins of Sports

Date	Sport	Location and Notes
B.C.		
c. 3000	Coursing	Egypt. Saluki dogs. Greyhounds used in England A.D. 1067.
c. 2350	Wrestling	Tomb of Ptahhotap, Egypt; ancient Olympic games *c.* 708 B.C., Greco-Roman style, France *c.* A.D. 1860, Internationalized 1912.
c. 2050	Hockey	Beni Hasan tomb, Egypt. Lincolnshire, England A.D. 1277. Modern forms *c.* 1875. Some claims to be of Persian origin in 2nd millennium B.C.
c. 1600	Falconry	China-Shang dynasty. Earliest manuscript evidence points to Persian origin.
c. 1520	Boxing	Thera fresco, Greece. First ring rules 1743 England. Queensberry Rules 1867.
c. 1360	Fencing	Egyptians used masks and blunted swords. Established as a sport in Germany *c.* A.D. 1450. Hand guard invented in Spain *c.* 1510. Foil 17th century, épée mid-19th century, and sabre in Italy, late 19th century.
c. 1300	Athletics (track & field)	Ancient Olympic Games. Modern revival *c.* A.D. 1810, Sandhurst, England.
c. 800	Ice skating	Bone skates superseded by metal blades *c.* A.D. 1600.
c. 776	Gymnastics	Ancient Olympic Games. Modern sport developed *c.* A.D. 1780.
c. 648	Horse racing	Thirty-third ancient Olympic Games. Roman diversion *c.* A.D. 210 Netherby, Yorkshire, England. Chester course 1540.
c. 600	Equestrianism	Riding of horses dates from *c.* 1400 B.C. Anatolia, Turkey. Show jumping Paris A.D. 1886.
c. 525	Polo	As *Pulu*, Persia. Possibly of Tibetan origin.
c. 10	Fly fishing	Earliest reference by the Roman Martial.
ante 1	Jiu-Jitsu	Pre-Christian Chinese origin, developed as a martial art by Japan.
A.D.		
c. 300	Archery	Known as a neolithic skill (as opposed to a sport). Natal, South Africa *ante* 46,000 B.C. Practiced by the Genoese, Italy. Internationalized 1931.
c. 1050	Tennis (royal)	Earliest surviving court, Paris, 1496. First "world" champion *c.* 1740.
1278	Fox hunting	Earliest reference in England. Popularized at end 18th century. Previously deer, boar or hare hunted.
ante 1300	Bowls	On grass in Britain, descended from the Roman game of boccie.
1429	Billiards	First treatise by Marot (France) *c.* 1550. Rubber cushions 1835, slate beds 1836.

Date	Sport	Location and Notes
c. 1450	Golf	Earliest reference: parliamentary prohibition in March 1457, Scotland. Rubber core balls 1902, steel shafts 1929.
1474	Shooting	Target shooting recorded in Geneva, Switzerland.
ante 1492	Lacrosse	Originally American Indian *baggataway*. First non-Indian club, Montreal, 1856.
c. 1530	Football (association)	26-a-side, Florence, Italy. Rules codified, Cambridge University, England 1846. Eleven-a-side standardized 1870. Chinese ball-kicking game *Tsuchin* known c. 350 B.C.
c. 1550	Cricket	Earliest recorded match, Guildford, Surrey, England. Earliest depictment c. 1250. Eleven-a-side Sussex, England 1697. Earliest recorded women's match, Surrey, England 1745.
c. 1560	Curling	Netherlands. Scotland 1716.
1600	Ice yachting	Earliest patent in Low Countries. Sand yacht reported Belgian beach 1595.
1603	Swimming	Inter-school contests in Japan by Imperial edict. Sea-bathing at Scarborough, England by 1660. Earliest bath, Liverpool, England in 1828.
c. 1660	Ice hockey	Netherlands. Kingston, Ontario, Canada, 1855. Rules devised in Montreal 1879.
1661	Yachting	First contest Thames (Sept. 1). Earliest club in Cork, Ireland, 1720.
c. 1676	Caving	Pioneer explorer, John Beaumont, Somerset, England.
1698	Mountaineering	Rock climbing in St. Kilda, Australia. First major ascent (Mont Blanc, France) 1786. Continuous history since only 1854.
c. 1700	Bull fighting	Francisco Romero of Ronda, Andalusia, Spain. Referred to by Romans c. 300 B.C.
1716	Rowing	Earliest contest, sculling race on Thames (Aug. 1). First English regatta, 1775, Henley Regatta 1839.
1744	Baseball	Princeton, N.J. Rules codified 1845 by Cartwright, Hoboken, N.J.
c. 1750	Trotting	Harness racing sulky introduced 1829.
1760	Roller skating	Developed by Joseph Merlin (Belgium). Modern type devised by J. L. Plimpton (U.S.) in 1866.
1771	Surfing	Canoe surfing first recorded by Capt. James Cook in the Hawaiian Islands. Board surfing reported by Lt. James King, 1779. Sport revived by 1900 at Waikiki, Honolulu.
1793	Lawn tennis	Field tennis, as opposed to court tennis, first recorded in England (Sept. 29). Leamington Club, England, founded 1872. Patent as *sphairistike* by Major W. C. Wingfield Feb. 1874.
1798	Rackets	Earliest covered court, recorded, Exeter, England.

Date	Sport	Location and Notes
1823	Rugby	Traditional inventor Rev. William Webb Ellis (c. 1807–72) at Rugby School, England (Nov.). Game formulated at Cambridge, 1839. The Rugby Union founded in 1871.
c. 1835	Croquet	Ireland as "Crokey." Country house lawn game in England, c. 1856. First rules 1857. The word dated back to 1478.
1843	Skiing (Alpine)	Tromsö, Norway. Kiandra Club, New South Wales, Australia 1855. California 1860. Alps 1883.
1845	Bowling (ten-pin)	Connecticut, to evade ban on nine-pin bowling. Kegel—a German cloister sport known since 12th century.
1847	Rodeo	Sante Fe, New Mexico. Steer wrestling, 1900.
c. 1850	Squash rackets	Evolved at Harrow School, England. First U.S. championship 1906.
1853	Gliding	Earliest flight by John Appleby, coachman to Sir George Cayley, Brompton Hall, Yorkshire, England. World championships 1948.
c. 1863	Badminton	Made famous at Badminton Hall, Avon, England.
1865	Canoeing	Pioneered by John Macgregor (Scotland).
1868	Cycling	First International Race May 31, Parc de St. Cloud, Paris.
1869	Water polo	Developed in England from "water soccer." An Olympic event since 1900.
1873	Football (American)	Harvard College, Mass. Intercollegiate Football Association, Oct. 1873. First game Harvard vs. McGill Univ. (Canada) May, 1874, Cambridge, Mass.
1875	Snooker (pool)	Devised by Col. Sir Neville Chamberlain, Ootacamund Club, India, as a variant of "black pool."
1876	Greyhound racing	Railed "hare" and windlass, Hendon, North London (Sept.). Race with mechanical hare, Emeryville, Calif., 1919. First race in U.K., Manchester July 24, 1926.
1879	Ski jumping	Huseby, near Oslo, Norway.
1882	Judo	Devised (February) by Dr. Jigora Kano (Japan) from Jiu-Jitsu (see above).
1884	Bobsledding	First toboggan contests, St. Moritz, Switzerland. Skeleton (one-man), 1892.
1886	Equestrianism (show jumping)	Paris. Pignatelli's academy, Naples c. 1580.
1889	Table tennis	Devised by James Gibb as "Gossima" from a game known in 1881. Ping Pong Association formed in London, 1902. Sport resuscitated, 1921.
1891	Weightlifting	First international contest, Cafe Monico, London (Mar. 28).

ORIGINS OF SPORTS (continued)

Date	Sport	Location and Notes
1891	Netball	Invented in U.S. Introduced to England 1895.
1891	Basketball	Invented by Dr. James A. Naismith. First played Jan 20, 1892, Springfield, Mass. Mayan Indian game *Pok-ta-Pok* dated *c.* 1000 B.C.
1895	Auto racing	Earliest competitive race Paris-Bordeaux, France (June 11–13). 20 kilometer race, Longchamps, Paris, 1891.
1895	Rugby league	Professional breakaway, 1895 (Aug. 29). Team reduced from 15 to 13 in 1906 (June 12).
1895	Volleyball	Invented by William G. Morgan at Holyoke, Mass. as *Minnonette*. Internationalized 1947.
1896	Marathon running	Marathon to Athens, 1896 Olympics. Standardized at 26 miles 385 yds., in 1924. Named after the run from the Marathon battlefield, Greece, by Phidippides in 490 B.C.
1897	Motorcycle racing	Earliest race over a mile, Sheen House, Richmond, Surrey, England (Nov. 29).
c. 1900	Water skiing	Aquaplaning, U.S. Pacific coast; plank-riding behind motor boat, Scarborough, England 1914; shaped skis by Ralph Samuelson, Lake Pepin, Minnesota, 1922; devised ramp jump at Miami, Florida, 1928.
1901	Small-bore shooting	.22 calibre introduced as a Civilian Army training device.
1912	Modern Pentathlon	First formal contest, Stockholm Olympic Games.
1918	Orienteering	Invented by Major Ernst Killander, Sweden.
1922	Skiing (slalom)	Devised by Sir Arnold Lunn, Mürren, Switzerland (Jan. 21).
1923	Speedway	West Maitland, N.S.W., Australia (Nov.); first World Championships Sept. 1936.
1936	Trampoline	Developed by George Nissen (U.S.) First championships 1948. Used in show business since 1910.
1951	Sky diving (parachuting)	First world championships in Yugoslavia.
1958	Hang gliding	Modern revival by Prof. Rogallo; origins attributable to Otto Lilienthal (Germany) 1893.
1960	Aerobatics	First world championships instituted. First aerobatic maneuver 1913.
1966	Skateboarding	First championship in U.S.; upsurge from 1975; motorized boards from 1977.

Literature

(See also Dramatists)

William Shakespeare's signature.

British and Irish Writers

14th century
LANGLAND, William (*c.* 1332–*c.* 1400). *Vision of Piers Plowman.*
CHAUCER, Geoffrey (?1340–1400). *Canterbury Tales.*

15th century
MALORY, Sir Thomas (d. 1471?). *Morte D'Arthur.*
MORE, Sir Thomas (1478–1535). *Utopia.*

16th century
SPENSER, Edmund (?1552–99). *The Faerie Queene.*
LYLY, John (*c.* 1553–1606). *Euphues.*
SIDNEY, Sir Philip (1554–86). *The Countesse of Pembrokes Arcadia;
Astrophel and Stella; The Defence of Poesie.*
BACON, Francis (1561–1626). *Essayes.*
MARLOWE, Christopher (1564–1593). *Tamburlaine The Great; Dr.
Faustus.*
DONNE, John (?1571–1631). *Poems; Songs and sonnets; Satyres;
Elegies.*
JONSON, Benjamin (1572–1637). *Every Man in his humour* (produced 1598,
published 1601); *Every Man out of his humour* (1600); *Volpone: or the
Foxe* (1607); *The Alchemist* (1610, published 1612); *Bartholomew
Fayre* (1614, published 1631).
SHAKESPEARE, William (1564–1616). *Hamlet; Macbeth; Romeo and
Juliet; Julius Caesar; Henry V.*
HOBBES, Thomas (1588–1679). *Leviathan.*
HERRICK, Robert (1591–1674). *Hesperides.*

JOHN DONNE (above) tired of love
sonnets, including his own, and
began writing religious sonnets.

GEOFFREY CHAUCER (right)
wrote poetry that successfully
reconciled the bawdy and the delicate;
the realistic and the romantic; and
the earthy and the divine.

17th century

MILTON, John (1608–1674). *Paradise Lost*; *Lycidas*.
BUTLER, Samuel (1612–80). *Hudibras*.
BUNYAN, John (1628–88). *The Pilgrim's Progress*.
DRYDEN, John (1631–1700). *All For Love*.
LOCKE, John (1632–1704). *Essay Concerning Human Understanding*.
PEPYS, Samuel (1633–1703). *Memoirs* (Diary).
BEHN, Aphra (1640–1689). *Oroonoko*; *The Rover*.
NEWTON, Sir Isaac (1642–1727). *Philosophiae Naturalis Principia
Mathematica*; *Opticks*.
DEFOE, Daniel (1660–1731). *The Life and Adventures of Robinson
Crusoe*.
SWIFT, Jonathan (1667–1745). *Travels* (by Lemuel Gulliver).
OTWAY, Thomas (1669–85). *Venice Preserved*.
CONGREVE, William (1670–1729). *The Way of the World*.
ADDISON, Joseph (1672–1719). *The Spectator*.
POPE, Alexander (1688–1744). *An Essay on Criticism*; *The Rape of the
Lock*; *The Dunciad*; *An Essay on Man*.
RICHARDSON, Samuel (1689–1761). *Clarissa*.

18th century

FIELDING, Henry (1707–54). *Tom Thumb*; *The History of Tom Jones*.
JOHNSON, Dr. Samuel (1709–1784). *A Dictionary of the English Language*.
STERNE, Laurence (1713–68). *Life and Opinions of Tristram Shandy*.
GRAY, Thomas (1716–71). *An Elegy Written in a Country Churchyard*.
WALPOLE, Horace (1717–1797). *The Castle of Otranto*.
SMOLLETT, Tobias George (1721–71). *The Adventures of Peregrine Pickle*.

SAMUEL RICHARDSON
(top left) is generally
regarded as the father
of the novel.

ALEXANDER POPE (right,
above) made satirical poetry of his
critical principles, but is
best known for his
many quotable epigrams.

JONATHAN SWIFT
(lower left) carried Gulliver
on his *Travels* to several
imaginary lands in a novel
that satirized the imperfections
of 18th-century England.

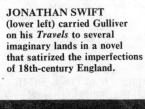

JAMES BOSWELL (right, above) became as famous as his subject, Dr. Samuel
Johnson, and "to be someone's Boswell" has come to mean "biographer par
excellence."

GOLDSMITH, Oliver (1728–74). *The Vicar of Wakefield*; *She Stoops to Conquer*.

BURKE, Edmund (1729–97). *Reflections on the Revolution*; *The Annual Register*.

COWPER, William (1731–1800). *Poems*.

GIBBON, Edward (1737–94). *A History of the Decline and Fall of the Roman Empire*.

PAINE, Thomas (1737–1809). *Rights of Man*.

BOSWELL, James (1740–95). *Life of Johnson*.

BURNEY, Frances "Fanny" (Madame D'Arblay) (1752–1840). *Evelina*.

SHERIDAN, Richard Brinsley (1751–1816). *The Rivals*; *The School For Scandal*.

BLAKE, William (1757–1827). *Songs of Innocence*; *Songs of Experience*.

BURNS, Robert (1759–96). *Poems chiefly in the Scottish dialect* (1786); *Tam O'Shanter* (1795); *The Cotters Saturday Night* (1795); *The Jolly Beggars* (1799).

COBBETT, William (1762–1835). *Rural Rides*.

RADCLIFFE, Ann (1764–1823). *The Mysteries of Udolpho*.

WORDSWORTH, William (1770–1850). *Lyrical Ballads*; *Prelude*.

SMITH, Rev. Sydney (1771–1845). *The Letters of Peter Plymley*; *Edinburgh Review*.

SCOTT, Sir Walter (1771–1832). *Waverley*; *Rob Roy*; *Ivanhoe*; *Kenilworth*; *Quentin Durward*; *Redgauntlet*; *Lady of the Lake*.

COLERIDGE, Samuel Taylor (1772–1834). *Lyrical Ballads* (*Ancient Mariner*).

SOUTHEY, Robert (1774–1843). *Quarterly Review* (contributions); *Life of Nelson*.

AUSTEN, Jane (1775–1817). *Sense and Sensibility* (1811); *Pride and Prejudice* (1813); *Mansfield Park* (1814); *Emma* (1816); *Northanger Abbey* and *Persuasion* (1818).

LAMB, Charles (1775–1834). *Tales from Shakespeare* [largely by his sister, Mary Lamb (1764–1847)]; *Essays of Elia*.

HAZLITT, William (1778–1830). *My First Acquaintance with Poets*; *Table Talk*; *The Plain Speaker*.

HUNT, James Henry Leigh (1784–1859). *The Story of Rimini*; *Autobiography*.

JOHN KEATS (left), lyrical poet, died young (26) but his work has lived on for a century and a half. SIR WALTER SCOTT (right) was most successful in blending history and human interest.

DE QUINCEY, Thomas (1785–1859). *Confessions of an English Opium Eater.*

PEACOCK, Thomas Love (1785–1866). *Headlong Hall; Nightmare Abbey.*

SHELLEY, Percy Bysshe (1792–1822). *Adonais; Prometheus Unbound.*

KEATS, John (1795–1821). *Endymion; Ode to a Nightingale; Ode on a Grecian Urn; Ode to Psyche; Ode to Autumn; Ode on Melancholy; La Belle Dame sans Merci; Isabella.*

CARLYLE, Thomas (1795–1881). *The French Revolution.*

BYRON, George Gordon, Lord (1788–1824). *Childe Harold; Don Juan.*

SHELLEY, Mary (1797–1851). *Frankenstein.*

HOOD, Thomas (1799–1845). *The Song of the Shirt; The Bridge of Sighs; To The Great Unknown.*

MACAULAY, Thomas Babington (Lord) (1800–59). *Lays of Ancient Rome.*

19th century

DISRAELI, Benjamin (Earl of Beaconsfield) (1804–81). *Coningsby; Sybil; Tancred.*

BROWNING, Elizabeth Barrett (1806–61). *Poems; Aurora Leigh.*

DARWIN, Charles Robert (1809–82). *On the Origin of Species; The Descent of Man.*

FITZGERALD, Edward (1809–83). *Rubáiyát of Omar Khayyám.*

TENNYSON, Alfred, Lord (1809–92). *In Memoriam; Charge of the Light Brigade.*

GASKELL, Mrs. (Elizabeth Cleghorn Stevenson) (1810–65). *Mary Barton; Cranford.*

THACKERAY, William Makepeace (1811–63). *Vanity Fair; The Newcomers.*

BROWNING, Robert (1812–89). *The Ring and the Book.*

LEAR, Edward (1812–88). *A Book of Nonsense; Nonsense Songs.*

TROLLOPE, Anthony (1815–82). *The Five Barsetshire Novels.*

BRONTE (later Nicholls), Charlotte (1816–55). *Jane Eyre.*

BRONTE, Emily Jane (1818–48). *Wuthering Heights.*

RUSKIN, John (1819–1900). *Praeterita.*

DICKENS, Charles (1812–70). *A Christmas Carol; A Tale of Two Cities.*

ELIOT, George (Mary Ann [or Marian] Evans, later Mrs. J. W. Cross) (1819–80). *Scenes of Clerical Life* (1858); *Adam Bede* (1859); *The Mill on the Floss* (1860); *Silas Marner* (1861); *Middlemarch* (1871–72).

KINGSLEY, Charles (1819–75). *Westward Ho!; The Water Babies.*

ARNOLD, Matthew (1822–88). *The Strayed Reveller* ("Sohrab and Rustum" and "Scholar Gypsy").

COLLINS, William Wilkie (1824–89). *The Woman in White; Moonstone.*

MEREDITH, George (1828–1909). *Modern Love.*

ROSSETTI, Dante Gabriel (1828–82). *Poems; Ballads and Sonnets.*

CARROLL, Lewis (Charles Lutwidge Dodgson) (1832–98). *Alice's Adventures in Wonderland; Through The Looking Glass.*

DU MAURIER, George (1834–96). *Trilby.*

GILBERT, Sir William Schwenck (1836–1911). *The Mikado; The Gondoliers; HMS Pinafore.*

SWINBURNE, Algernon Charles (1837–1909). *Rosamund.*

HARDY, Thomas (1840–1928). *Under The Greenwood Tree; Tess of the D'Urbervilles; Far From the Madding Crowd; The Return of the Native; The Mayor of Casterbridge; Jude the Obscure.*

JAMES, Henry (1843–1916). *Daisy Miller* (1879); *The Portrait of a Lady* (1881); *Washington Square* (1881); *The Turn of the Screw* (1898); *The Golden Bowl* (1904).

BRIDGES, Robert Seymour (1844–1930). *The Testament of Beauty.*

HOPKINS, Gerard Manley (1844–89). *The Notebooks and Papers of Gerard Manley Hopkins.*

STOKER, Bram (1847–1912). *Dracula.*

PINERO, Sir Arthur Wing (1855–1934). *The Profligate; The Second Mrs. Tanqueray.*

WILLIAM MAKEPEACE THACKERAY (left) wrote historical novels in which history was less important than human interest.   **GEORGE GORDON (LORD) BYRON** (right) was not only a Romantic poet but lived a romantic life. Lame from birth, he was a "record" swimmer.

STEVENSON, Robert Louis (1850–94). *Travels with a Donkey in the Cévennes* (1879); *New Arabian Nights* (1882); *Treasure Island* (1883); *Strange Case of Dr. Jekyll and Mr. Hyde* (1886); *Kidnapped* (1886); *The Black Arrow* (1888); *The Master of Ballantrae* (1889); *Weir of Hermiston* (unfinished) (1896).

WILDE, Oscar Fingal O'Flahertie Wills (1854–1900). *The Picture of Dorian Gray* (1891); *Lady Windermere's Fan* (1893); *The Importance of Being Earnest* (1899).

DOYLE, Sir Arthur Conan (1859–1930). *The White Company*; *The Adventures of Sherlock Holmes*; *The Hound of the Baskervilles*.

LEWIS CARROLL (left), pen name used by Charles L. Dodgson, a mathematics professor, originated a new genre of mad absurdity and subtle fantasy in his "Alice" stories. **ROBERT LOUIS STEVENSON** (right) was ill most of his life. His verses for the very young became as famous as his adventure books.

SHAW, George Bernard (1856–1950) (adjective Shavian). *Plays Pleasant and Unpleasant* (1893) (including *Mrs. Warren's Profession, Arms and the Man* and *Candida*); *Three Plays for Puritans* (1901) (*The Devil's Disciple, Caesar and Cleopatra* and *Captain Brassbound's Conversion*); *Man and Superman* (1903); *John Bull's Other Island* and *Major Barbara* (1907); *Androcles and the Lion;· Overruled* and *Pygmalion* (1916); *Saint Joan* (1924); *Essays in Fabian Socialism* (1932).

CONRAD, Joseph (*né* Jósef Teodor Konrad Nalecz Korzeniowski) (1857–1924). *Almayer's Folly; An Outcast of the Islands; The Nigger of the "Narcissus"; Lord Jim; Youth; Typhoon; Nostromo; The Secret Agent.*

THOMPSON, Francis (1859-1907). *The Hound of Heaven.*

HOUSMAN, Alfred Edward (1859–1936). *A Shropshire Lad.*

GRAHAME, Kenneth (1859–1932). *Wind in the Willows.*

BARRIE, Sir James Matthew (1860–1937). *Quality Street; The Admirable Crichton; Peter Pan.*

KIPLING, Rudyard (1865–1936). *Soldiers Three; Captains Courageous.*

QUILLER-COUCH, Sir Arthur ("Q") (1865–1944). *On the Art of Writing; Studies in Literature.*

YEATS, William Butler (1865–1939). *Collected Poems; The Tower; Last Poems; The Hour Glass.*

WELLS, Herbert George (1866–1946). *The Invisible Man; The History of Mr. Polly; Kipps; The Shape of Things to Come.*

MURRAY, Gilbert Amié (1866–1957). *Hippolytus; The Trojan Women.*

BENNETT, Enoch Arnold (1867–1931). *Anna of the Five Towns; The Old Wives' Tale; Clayhanger; The Card; Riceyman Steps.*

GALSWORTHY, John (1867–1933). *The Forsyte Saga; Modern Comedy; The White Monkey.*

BELLOC, Joseph Hilaire Pierre (1870–1953). *The Path to Rome; The Bad Child's Book of Beasts; Hills and the Sea.*

SYNGE, John Millington (1871–1909). *The Playboy of the Western World.*

BEERBOHM, Sir Max (1872–1956). *Zuleika Dobson.*

DE LA MARE, Walter (1873–1956). *Poems; Desert Islands* and *Robinson Crusoe.*

FORD, Ford Madox (1873–1939). *The Good Soldier; Parade's End.*

CHESTERTON, Gilbert Keith (1874–1936). *The Innocence of Father Brown; The Ballad of The White Horse.*

CHURCHILL, Sir Winston Spencer (1874–1965). *Marlborough; The Second World War; A History of The English-Speaking Peoples.*

BUCHAN, John (Baron Tweedsmuir) (1875–1940). *Montrose; The Thirty-Nine Steps; Greenmantle; Prester John.*

MASEFIELD, John (1878–1967). *Barrack-Room Ballads; Ballads and Poems.*

JOSEPH CONRAD, born in Russia, brought up in Poland, could not speak English until he was 21, yet he wrote some of the finest short sea novels in English literature.

JAMES JOYCE (2nd from left), the most successful practitioner of the stream of consciousness technique, is shown here surrounded by (left to right) writer Ford Madox Ford, poet Ezra Pound and John Quinn, a patron, in Paris in 1923.

MAUGHAM, William Somerset (1874–1965). *Of Human Bondage*; *The Moon and Sixpence*; *The Razor's Edge*.

TREVELYAN, George Macaulay (1876–1962). *History of England*; *English Social History*.

FORSTER, Edward Morgan (1879–1970). *Where Angels Fear to Tread*; *A Room with a View*; *Howards End*; *A Passage to India*.

WODEHOUSE, P. G. (Sir Pelham Grenville Wodehouse) (1881–1975). *The Inimitable Jeeves*.

JOYCE, James (1882–1941). *Ulysses*; *Finnegan's Wake*.

RUDYARD KIPLING, son of an artist in India, mastered both casual poetry and the short story form. His *Gunga Din* bent vernacular speech to poetry.

BRITISH AND IRISH WRITERS (continued)

WOOLF (*née* Stephen), Virginia (1882–1941). *The Voyage Out*; *Night and Day*; *Jacob's Room*; *The Years*.

KEYNES, John Maynard (Baron) (1883–1946). *The Economic Consequences of the Peace*; *The General Theory of Employment*.

MACKENZIE, Sir Compton (1883–1972). *Whisky Galore*.

FLECKER, James Elroy (1884–1915). *Thirty-Six Poems*; *Hassan*.

O'CASEY, Sean (1884–1964). *Juno and the Paycock*; *The Plough and the Stars*.

LAWRENCE, David Herbert (1885–1930). *Sons and Lovers*; *Love Poems and Others*.

SASSOON, Siegfried (1886–1967). *Memoirs of a Fox-Hunting Man*.

SITWELL, Dame Edith, D.B.E. (1887–1964). *Collected Poems*; *Aspects of Modern Poetry*.

BROOKE, Rupert Chawner (1887–1915). *1914 and Other Poems*; *Letters From America*.

CARY, Joyce (1888–1957). *The Horse's Mouth*.

ELIOT, Thomas Stearns, O.M. (1888–1965). *Murder in the Cathedral*; *The Wasteland*; *Ash Wednesday*; *Poems*.

LAWRENCE, Thomas Edward (later Shaw) (1888–1935). *Seven Pillars of Wisdom*.

TONYBEE, Arnold Joseph (1889–1975). *A Study of History*.

MANSFIELD, Katherine (1890–1923). *The Garden Party*; *Letters*.

CHRISTIE, Agatha (1891–1977). *And Then There Were None*; *The Mousetrap*.

COMPTON-BURNETT, Ivy (1892–1969). *A House and its Head*.

TOLKIEN, J. R. R. (1892–1973). *The Hobbit*; *The Lord of the Rings*.

OWEN, Wilfred (1893-1918) Poems.

SAYERS, Dorothy (1893–1957). *The Nine Tailors*.

PRIESTLEY, John Boynton (1894–   ). *The Good Companions*; *The Linden Tree*.

HUXLEY, Aldous Leonard (1894–1963). *Brave New World*; *Stories, Essays and Poems*.

GRAVES, Robert Ranke (1895–   ). *Poems and Satires*.

COWARD, Sir Noel (1899–1973). *Hay Fever*; *Private Lives*.

20th century

ORWELL, George (Eric Blair) (1903–50). *Animal Farm*; *1984*.

WAUGH, Evelyn (1903–66). *Scoop*; *Vile Bodies*; *Brideshead Revisited*; *The Loved One*; *The Ordeal of Gilbert Pinfold*.

DAY-LEWIS, Cecil (1904–72). *Collected Poems*; *Overture to Death and other poems*.

GREENE, Graham (1904–   ). *Brighton Rock*; *Our Man in Havana*; *The Power and the Glory*.

GREEN, Henry (Henry York) (1905–   ). *Nothing*; *Loving*.

POWELL, Anthony (1905–   ). *The Music of Time*.

BECKETT, Samuel (1906–   ). *Waiting for Godot*.

FRY, Christopher (1907–   ). *The Lady's Not for Burning*.

AUDEN, Wystan Hugh (1907–73). *Poems*; *Look Stranger*; *The Dance of Death*.

DuMAURIER, Daphne (1907–   ). *Rebecca*.

DURRELL, Lawrence (1912–   ). *The Alexandria Quartet*.

THOMAS, Dylan (1914–54). *Eighteen Poems*; *Twenty-Five Poems*; *Under Milk Wood*.

LESSING, Doris (1919–   ). *The Children of Violence*.

MURDOCH, Iris (1919–   ). *A Severed Head*.

AMIS, Kingsley (1922–   ). *Lucky Jim*.

BEHAN, Brendan (1923–64). *The Quare Fellow*; *The Hostage*.

OSBORNE, John (1929–   ). *Look Back in Anger*; *The Entertainer*; *Luther*.

PINTER, Harold (1930–   ). *The Caretaker*.

WESKER, Arnold (1932–   ). *Roots*; *Chips with Everything*.

American Writers

17th century
BRADSTREET, Anne (1612–1672). *The Tenth Muse Lately Sprung Up in America.*

18th century
BRACKENRIDGE, Hugh Henry (1748–1816). *Modern Chivalry.*
IRVING, Washington (1783–1859). *A History of New York; The Alhambra.*
COOPER, James Fenimore (1789–1851). *The Last of the Mohicans; The Deerslayer.*
BRYANT, William Cullen (1794–1878). *Thanatopsis; To a Waterfowl.*

19th century
EMERSON, Ralph Waldo (1803–82). *The Concord Hymn; Essays.*
HAWTHORNE, Nathaniel (1804–64). *Thv Scarlet Letter; The House of the Seven Gables.*
LONGFELLOW, Henry Wadsworth (1807–82). *Evangeline; The Song o Hiawatha.*
WHITTIER, John Greenleaf (1807–92). *Snow-bound.*
POE, Edgar Allan (1809–49). *The Raven; The Fall of the House of Usher; The City in the Sea.*
STOWE, Harriet Beecher (1811–96). *Uncle Tom's Cabin; Dred.*
THOREAU, Henry David (1817–62). *Walden; Civil Disobedience.*
LOWELL, James Russell (1819–91). *The Vision of Sir Launfal; The Bigelow Papers.*.
MELVILLE, Herman (1819–91). *Moby Dick; Billy Budd; Foretopman.*
WHITMAN, Walt (1819–92). *Leaves of Grass; Drum Taps.*
DICKINSON, Emily (1830–86). *Collected Poems.*
ALCOTT, Louisa May (1832–88). *Little Women.*
TWAIN, Mark (Samuel Langhorne Clemens) (1835–1910). *The Adventures of Huckleberry Finn; Tom Sawyer; The Prince and the Pauper.*
HARTE, Bret (Francis Brett Harte) (1836–1902). *The Outcasts of Poker Flat.*
HOWELLS, William Dean (1837–1920). *A Hazard of New Fortunes; A Modern Instance.*
ADAMS, Henry (1838–1918). *Mont St. Michel and Chartres.*
BIERCE, Ambrose (1842–1914?). *The Devil's Dictionary.*
LANIER, Sidney (1842–81). *Tiger-Lilies; Poems.*
CABLE, George Washington (1844–1925). *Gideon's Band; The Silent South.*
JEWETT, Sarah Orne (1849–1909). *A Country Doctor.*
BELLAMY, Edward (1850–98). *Looking Backward.*
GARLAND, Hamlin (1860–1940). *A Son of the Middle Border.*
HENRY, O. (William Sydney Porter) (1862–1910). *Cabbages and Kings; The Four Million.*
WHARTON, Edith (1862–1937). *The House of Mirth; The Age of Innocence.*
SANTAYANA, George (1863–1952). *The Last Puritan.*
ADE, George (1866–1944). *Fables in Slang.*
MASTERS, Edgar Lee (1869–1950). *Spoon River Anthology.*
ROBINSON, Edwin Arlington (1869–1935). *The Children of the Night; The Man Against the Sky.*
TARKINGTON, Booth (1869–1946). *The Magnificent Ambersons; Penrod.*
CRANE, Stephen (1871–1900). *The Red Badge of Courage; The Black Rider.*
DREISER, Theodore (1871–1945). *An American Tragedy.*
GLASGOW, Ellen (1873–1945). *Barren Ground; In This Our Life.*
FROST, Robert (1874–1963). *Collected Poems; A Witness Tree.*

MARK TWAIN (with white hair) was a deceptively profound writer. His *Huckleberry Finn*, although treated as a children's book, is a vivid and searching chronicle of life in 19th-century America. Twain, whose real name was Samuel L. Clemens, is shown here in 1906 at a young writers' club meeting in New York. The Russian short story writer, Maxim Gorky, is on Twain's right.

LOWELL, Amy (1874–1925). *Con Grande's Castle*; *What O'Clock?*

STEIN, Gertrude (1874–1946). *Three Lives*; *The Autobiography of Alice B. Toklas.*

ANDERSON, Sherwood (1876–1941). *Winesburg, Ohio.*

CATHER, Willa (1876–1947). *Death Comes for the Archbishop*; *Shadows on the Rock.*

LONDON, Jack (1876–1916). *The Call of the Wild*; *The Sea-Wolf.*

SANDBURG, Carl (1878–1967). *Complete Poems*; *Abraham Lincoln.*

SINCLAIR, Upton (1878–1968). *The Jungle*; *World's End.*

CABELL, James Branch (1879–1958). *Jurgen.*

ERSKINE, John (1879–1951). *The Private Life of Helen of Troy.*

LINDSAY, Vachel (1879–1931). *General William Booth Enters into Heaven*; *The Congo.*

STEVENS, Wallace (1879–1955). *Harmonium*; *Transport to Summer.*

MENCKEN, H(enry) L(ouis) (1880–1956). *Prejudices*; *The American Language.*

WILLIAMS, William Carlos (1883–1963). *Collected Poems*; *Paterson.*

LARDNER, Ring (Ringgold Wilmer Lardner) (1885–1933). *Treat 'Em Rough*; *What of It?*

LEWIS, Sinclair (1885–1951). *Main Street*; *Babbitt*; *Dodsworth.*

POUND, Ezra (1885–1972). *Hugh Selwyn Mauberley*; *The Cantos.*

BROOKS, Van Wyck (1886–1963). *Makers and Finders.*

DOOLITTLE, Hilda ("H.D.") (1886–1961). *The Sea Garden*; *The Walls Do Not Fall.*

JEFFERS, Robinson (1887–1962). *Medea*; *Roan Stallion.*

MOORE, Marianne (1887–1972). *Observations*; *Complete Poems.*

ANDERSON, Maxwell (1888–1959). *Winterset.*

CHANDLER, Raymond (1888–1959). *The Big Sleep*; *The Long Goodbye.*

O'NEILL, Eugene (1888–1953). *Strange Interlude*; *Desire under the Elms*; *Mourning Becomes Electra*; *The Iceman Cometh.*

RANSOM, John Crowe (1888–1974). *Chills and Fever; The New Criticism.*
AIKEN, Conrad (1889–1973). *Selected Poems.*
BENCHLEY, Robert (1889–1945). *My Ten Years in a Quandary.*
PORTER, Katherine Anne (1890–   ). *Pale Horse, Pale Rider; Ship of Fools.*
RICHTER, Conrad (1890–1968). *The Town; The Sea of Grass.*
MILLER, Henry (1891–   ). *Tropic of Cancer; The Colossus of Maroussi; Sexus.*
MILLAY, Edna St. Vincent (1892–1950). *Renascence; Fatal Interview.*
RICE, Elmer (1892–1967). *The Adding Machine; Street Scene.*
BEHRMAN, S(amuel) N(athaniel) (1893–1973). *No Time for Comedy.*
BODENHEIM, Maxwell (1893–1954). *Replenishing Jessica; Against This Age.*
MARQUAND, John P. (1893–1960). *The Late George Apley; Wickford Point.*
PARKER, Dorothy (1893–1967). *Death and Taxes; Here Lies.*
CUMMINGS, E(dward) E(stlin) (1894–1962). *The Enormous Room; Tulips and Chimneys.*
HAMMETT, Dashiell (1894–1961). *The Maltese Falcon; The Thin Man.*
THURBER, James (1894–1961). *The Male Animal; My Life and Hard Times.*
VAN DOREN, Mark (1894–1973). *Collected Poems, 1922–1938; The Noble Voice.*
WILSON, Edmund (1895–1972). *Axel's Castle; Patriotic Gore.*
DOS PASSOS, John (1896–1970). *U.S.A.; Manhattan Transfer.*
FITZGERALD, F. Scott (1896–1940). *The Great Gatsby; Tender is the Night.*
SHERWOOD, Robert E. (1896–1955). *Idiot's Delight; Abe Lincoln in Illinois.*
BOGAN, Louise (1897–1970). *Body of This Death; A Poet's Alphabet.*
FAULKNER, William (1897–1962). *The Sound and the Fury; As I Lay Dying.*
WILDER, Thornton (1897–1975). *Our Town; The Skin of Our Teeth.*
BENET, Stephen Vincent (1898–1943). *John Brown's Body.*
CATTON, Bruce (1899–1978). *A Stillness at Appomattox.*

SINCLAIR LEWIS (shown here in 1939 with Marcella Powers) was one of the foremost critics of American life through his 22 novels.

THOMAS WOLFE (left), American novelist, said of his own fiction that he could not escape biography. ARTHUR MILLER (right) in his modern tragedies such as *Death of a Salesman,* gives meaning to everyday problems.

CRANE, Hart (1899–1932). *White Building; The Bridge.*

HEMINGWAY, Ernest (1899–1961). *The Sun Also Rises; For Whom the Bell Tolls.*

NABOKOV, Vladimir (1899–1977). *The Real Life of Sebastian Knight; Lolita.*

WHITE, E(lwyn) B(rooks) (1899–1978). *One Man's Meat; Charlotte's Web.*

MITCHELL, Margaret (1900–1949). *Gone With the Wind.*

WOLFE, Thomas (1900–1938). *Look Homeward, Angel; Of Time and the River.*

20th century

HUGHES, Langston (1902–67). *Shakespeare in Harlem; Mulatto.*

STEINBECK, John (1902–68). *Of Mice and Men; The Grapes of Wrath.*

BOYLE, Kay (1903–   ). *Plagued by Nightingales.*

COZZENS, James Gould (1903–78). *By Love Possessed.*

WEST, Nathanael (Nathan Weinstein) (1903–40). *Miss Lonelyhearts; The Day of the Locust.*

BLACKMUR, R(ichard) P. (1904–65). *Lion and the Honeycomb; Primer of Ignorance.*

EBERHART, Richard (1904–   ). *Undercliff; Fields of Grace.*

FARRELL, James T. (1904–   ). *Young Lonigan; My Days of Anger.*

ISHERWOOD, Christopher (1904–   ). *Prater Violet; The Berlin Stories.*

HELLMAN, Lillian (1905–   ). *The Children's Hour; The Little Foxes.*

O'HARA, John (1905–70). *Appointment in Samarra; Butterfield 8.*

WARREN, Robert Penn (1905–   ). *Brother to Dragons; All the King's Men.*

ODETS, Clifford (1906–63). *Waiting for Lefty; Awake and Sing.*

SAROYAN, William (1908–   ). *The Time of Your Life; The Human Comedy.*

WRIGHT, Richard (1908–60). *Native Son; Uncle Tom's Children.*

AGEE, James (1909–55). *Let Us Now Praise Famous Men.*

ALGREN, Nelson (1909–   ). *The Man With the Golden Arm.*

WELTY, Eudora (1909–   ). *A Curtain of Green; Delta Wedding.*

BOWLES, Paul (1910–   ). *The Delicate Prey*; *The Sheltering Sky*.
BISHOP, Elizabeth (1911–   ). *North and South—A Cold Spring*.
GOODMAN, Paul (1911–72). *The Empire City*; *Growing Up Absurd*.
CHEEVER, John (1912–   ). *The Wapshot Chronicle*.
MCCARTHY, Mary (1912–   ). *The Groves of Academe*; *The Group*.
INGE, William (1913–73). *Come Back, Little Sheba*; *Picnic*.
SCHWARTZ, Delmore (1913–66). *Shenandoah*; *Genesis*.
BERRYMAN, John (1914–72). *77 Dream Songs*.
BURROUGHS, William (1914–   ). *The Naked Lunch*; *The Soft Machine*.
ELLISON, Ralph (1914–   ). *The Invisible Man*.
WILLIAMS, Tennessee (Thomas Lanier Williams) (1914–   ). *The Glass Menagerie*; *A Streetcar Named Desire*.
BELLOW, Saul (1915–   ). *Herzog*.
MILLER, Arthur (1915–   ). *Death of a Salesman*; *A View from the Bridge*.
MERTON, Thomas (1915–68). *Figures for an Apocalypse*; *The Seven Storey Mountain*.
CIARDI, John (1916–   ). *In the Stoneworks*.
AUCHINCLOSS, Louis (1917–   ). *The Rector of Justin*.
LOWELL, Robert (1917–77). *Lord Weary's Castle*; *The Dolphin*.
MCCULLERS, Carson (1917–67). *The Heart Is a Lonely Hunter*; *The Member of the Wedding*.
SALINGER, J(erome) D(avid) (1919–   ). *The Catcher in the Rye*; *Franny and Zooey*.
BRADBURY, Roy (1920–   ). *Fahrenheit 451*; *Dandelion Wine*.
HALEY, Alex (1921–   ). *Roots*.
JONES, James (1921–77). *From Here to Eternity*.
WILBUR, Richard (1921–   ). *Things of This World*; *Advice to a Prophet*.
KEROUAC, Jack (1922–69). *On the Road*.
VONNEGUT, Kurt (1922–   ). *Cat's Cradle*; *Slaughterhouse Five*.
DICKEY, James (1923–   ). *Deliverance*; *Buckdancer's Choice*.
MAILER, Norman (1923–   ). *The Naked and the Dead*; *The Armies of the Night*.
BALDWIN, James (1924–   ). *The Fire Next Time*.
CAPOTE, Truman (1924–   ). *Breakfast at Tiffany's*; *In Cold Blood*.
O'CONNOR, Flannery (1925–64). *Wise Blood*; *A Good Man Is Hard to Find*.
STYRON, William (1925–   ). *The Confessions of Nat Turner*.
VIDAL, Gore (1925–   ). *Myra Breckenridge*; *The City and the Pillar*.
GINSBERG, Allen (1926–   ). *Howl*; *The Fall of America*.
ALBEE, Edward (1928–   ). *Who's Afraid of Virginia Woolf?*
BARTH, John (1930–   ). *The Sot-Weed Factor*.
PLATH, Sylvia (1932–63). *Ariel*; *The Bell Jar*.
UPDIKE, John (1932–   ). *Rabbit Run*; *The Poorhouse Fair*.
ROTH, Philip (1933–   ). *Goodbye Columbus*; *Portnoy's Complaint*.
KESEY, Ken (1935–   ). *One Flew Over the Cuckoo's Nest*.
VAN ITALLIE, Jean-Claude (1936–   ). *America Hurrah*.
PYNCHON, Thomas (1937–   ). *V.*; *Gravity's Rainbow*.

European Writers

Austrian

Grillparzer, Franz (1791–1872). *Hero and Leander; The Poor Minstrel.*
Vogelweide, Walther von der (1170?–1230?). *Unter den Linden; Songs and Sayings.*
Wassermann, Jakob (1873–1934). *The World's Illusion; The Maurizius Case.*
Werfel, Franz (1890–1945). *The Forty Days of Musa Dagh; The Song of Bernadette.*
Zweig, Stefan (1881–1942). *Beware of Pity; The Tide of Fortune; Marie Antoinette.*

Belgian

Verhaeren, Emile (1855–1916). *La Ville Tentaculaire.*

Czech

Hasek, Jaroslav (1883–1923). *The Good Soldier Schweik.*

Danish

Andersen, Hans Christian (1805–75). *Fairy Tales.*
Dinesen, Isak (Baroness Karen Blixen) (1885–1962). *Out of Africa; Seven Gothic Tales.*

French

Apollinaire, Guillaume (1880–1918). *Alcools; Calligrammes.*
Aragon, Louis (1897–   ). *Le Paysan de Paris; Les Communistes.*
Balzac, Honoré de (1799–1850). *La Peau de chagrin; La Comédie humaine.*
Baudelaire, Charles (1821–67). *The Flowers of Evil.*
Beauvoir, Simone de (1908–   ). *The Mandarins; The Second Sex; The Coming of Age.*
Bernanos, Georges (1888–1948). *The Diary of a Country Priest; Dialogue des Carmelites.*
Camus, Albert (1913–60). *The Myth of Sisyphus; The Rebel; State of Siege.*
Céline, Louis Ferdinand (Louis Ferdinand Destouches) (1894–1961). *Death on the Installment Plan; Journey to the End of Night.*
Chateaubriand, François René de (1768–1848). *The Genius of Christianity; Mémoires d'outre-tombe.*
Colette (Sidonie Gabrielle Colette) (1873–1954). *Gigi; Chéri; The Vagrant.*
Daudet, Alphonse (1840–97). *Letters from My Mill; Les Aventures prodigieuses de Tartarin de Tarascon.*
Diderot, Denis (1713–84). *Lettre sur les aveugles; La Religieuse.*
Dumas, Alexandre (père) (1802–70). *The Three Musketeers; The Count of Monte Cristo; The Black Tulip.*
Duras, Marguerite (1914–   ). *The Sea Wall; The Sailor from Gibraltar.*
Flaubert, Gustave (1821–80). *Madame Bovary; Salammbô.*
France, Anatole (Jacques Anatole Thibault) (1844–1924). *Penguin Island; The Revolt of the Angels.*
Gide, André (1869–1951). *The Immoralist; The Counterfeiters.*
La Fontaine, Jean de (1621–95). *Fables choisies, mise en vers.*
Lamartine, Alphonse Marie Louis de (1790–1869). *Méditations poétiques; Harmonies.*
La Rochefoucauld, François, duc de (1613–80). *Maxims.*
Mallarmé, Stéphane (1842–98). *Hérodiade; The Afternoon of a Faun.*

ANDRE MALRAUX, author of novels, dipped into French politics and in 1959 became Minister of State for Cultural Affairs.

Malraux, André (1901–76). *Man's Fate*; *The Voices of Silence*.
Maupassant, Guy de (1850–93). *Tallow Ball*; *The Necklace*; *Bel Ami*.
Mauriac, François (1885–1970). *The Desert of Love*; *Thérèse*.
Maurois, André (Emile Herzog) (1885–1967). *Ariel*; *The Silence of Colonel Bramble*.
Mérimée, Prosper (1803–70). *Carmen*; *Letters to an Unknown*.
Mistral, Frédéric (1830–1914). *Mireille*; *Les Iles d'or*.
Musset, Alfred de (1810–57). *Rolla*; *Les Nuits*.
Nerval, Gérard de (Gerard Labrunie) (1808–55). *Daughters of Fire*; *Aurélia*.
Péguy, Charles (1873–1914). *Le Mystère de la charité de Jeanne d'Arc*.
Perrault, Charles (1628–1703). *Histoires ou contes du temps passé*.
Perse, St.-John (Alexis Saint-Léger Léger) (1887–1975). *Anabase*; *Winds*; *Seamarks*.
Proust, Marcel (1871–1922). *Remembrance of Things Past*.
Rabelais, François (1490–1533). *Gargantua*; *Pantagruel*.
Rimbaud, Arthur (1854–91). *Une Saison en enfer*; *Les Illuminations*.
Robbe-Grillet, Alain (1922–   ). *Jealousy*; *In the Labyrinth*.
Rolland, Romain (1866–1944). *Jean-Christophe*; *Above the Battle*.
Romains, Jules (Louis Farigoule) (1885–1972). *Men of Good Will*; *The Death of a Nobody*.
Ronsard, Pierre de (1524?–85). *Sonnets pour Hélène*; *Odes*; *Amours*.
Sagan, Françoise (Françoise Quoirez) (1935–   ). *Bonjour Tristesse*; *Un Certain Sourire*.
Sainte-Beuve, Charles Augustin (1804–69). *Causeries du lundi*; *Port-Royal*.
Saint-Exupéry, Antoine de (1900–44). *Night Flight*; *Wind, Sand and Stars*.
Sand, George (Amandine Aurore Dupin) (1804–76). *The Haunted Pool*; *Les Maîtres sonneurs*.
Sartre, Jean-Paul (1905–   ). *Being and Nothingness*; *Nausea*.
Stendhal (Marie Henri Beyle) (1783–1842). *The Red and the Black*; *The Charterhouse of Parma*.
Valéry, Paul (1871–1945). *La Jeune Parque*; *The Graveyard by the Sea*.
Verne, Jules (1828–1905). *Around the World in Eighty Days*; *Twenty Thousand Leagues Under the Sea*.
Villon, François (1431–63?). *Lais*; *Grand Testament*.
Voltaire, François Marie Arouet de (1694–1778). *Candide*; *Letters Concerning the English Nation*.
Zola, Emile (1840–1902). *The Dram Shop*: *Nana*; *Germinal*.

German

Böll, Heinrich (1917–   ). *Adam, Where Art Thou*; *Billiards at Half Past Nine.*
Feuchtwanger, Lion (1884–1958). *Power*; *Success.*
George, Stefan (1868–1933). *Das Jahr der Seele*; *Der siebente Ring.*
Grass, Günter (1927–   ). *The Tin Drum*; *Dog Years*; *Local Anaesthetic.*
Grimm, Jakob (1785–1863). *German Mythology*; *Grimm's Fairy Tales* (with his brother Wilhelm).
Grimm, Wilhelm (1786–1859). *Grimm's Fairy Tales* (with his brother Jakob).
Heine, Heinrich (1797–1856). *Book of Songs*; *Deutschland.*
Herder, Johann Gottfried von (1744–1803). *Outlines of the Philosophy of Man.*
Hesse, Hermann (1877–1962). *Steppenwolf*; *Magister Ludi*; *Siddartha.*
Hoffmann, Ernst Theodor Amadeus (1776–1822). *The Serapion Brethren*; *The Devil's Elixir.*
Hölderlin, Friedrich (1770–1843). *Hyperion*; *Der blinde Sanger.*
Kafka, Franz (1883–1924). *The Trial*; *The Castle*; *Amerika.*
Ludwig, Emil (1881–1948). *Goethe*; *Napoleon.*
Mann, Heinrich (1871–1950). *The Goddess*; *The Blue Angel.*
Mann, Thomas (1875–1955). *Death in Venice*; *The Magic Mountain*; *Joseph and His Brothers.*
Novalis (Friederich von Hardenberg) (1772–1801). *Heinrich von Ofterdingen*; *Hymns to the Night.*
Remarque, Erich Maria (1897–1970). *All Quiet on the Western Front*; *The Way Back.*
Rilke, Rainer Maria (1875–1926). *Poems from the Book of Hours*; *Duino Elegies.*
Schlegel, Friedrich von (1772–1829). *The Philosophy of History*; *The History of Literature.*
Spengler, Oswald (1880–1936). *The Decline of the West.*
Tieck, Ludwig (1773–1853). *Kaiser Octavianus*; *Tales from the Phantasius.*
Zweig, Arnold (1887–1968). *Education Before Verdun*; *The Case of Sergeant Grischa*; *The Crowning of a King.*

Greek

Kazantzakis, Nikos (1883–1957). *The Odyssey, a Modern Cycle*; *Zorba the Greek*; *The Greek Passion.*
Seferis, George (Giorgios Sefirides) (1900–71). *Strophe*; *On the Greek Style.*

Icelandic

Laxness, Halldor (1902–   ). *Independent People*; *The Light of the World.*

Israeli and Yiddish

Agnon, Shmuel Yosef (Samuel Josef Czaczkes) (1888–1970). *The Bridal Canopy*; *The Day Before Yesterday.*
Aleichem, Sholom (Solomon Rabinowitz) (1859–1916). *The Old Country*; *Tevye's Daughters.*
Asch, Sholem (1880–1957). *The Nazarene*; *The Prophet*; *Tales of My People.*
Singer, Isaac Bashevis (1904–   ). *The Family Moskat*; *Gimpel the Fool and Other Stories.*

Italian

Ariosto, Ludovico (1474–1533). *Orlando Furioso.*
Boccaccio, Giovanni (1313–75). *The Decameron*; *La Fiammetta*; *Corbaccio.*
Boiardo, Matteo Maria (1441?–94). *Orlando Innamorato.*
D'Annunzio, Gabriele (1863–1938). *Notturno*; *The Flame of Life.*
Dante Alighieri (1265–1321). *The Divine Comedy*; *La vita nuova.*

Italian Writers (continued)

Leopardi, Giacomo (1796–1837). *Canti.*
Lampedusa, Giusseppe di (1896–1957). *The Leopard.*
Machiavelli, Niccolò (1469–1527). *The Prince; On the Art of War; The Discourses.*
Manzoni, Alessandro (1785–1873). *Cinque maggio; The Betrothed.*
Moravia, Alberto (1907–   ). *The Indifferent Ones; Two Women; The Conformist.*
Pavese, Cesare (1908–50). *Among Women Only; The Devil in the Hills.*
Petrarch (Francesco Petrarca) (1304–74). *Italia mia; Secretum; Canzoniere.*
Silone, Ignazio (Secondo Tranquilli) (1900–   ). *Bread and Wine; The Seed Beneath the Snow.*
Tasso, Torquato (1544–95). *Rinaldo; Jerusalem Delivered.*

Norwegian

Bjornson, Bjornstjerne (1832–1910). *Sunny Hill; The Fisher Girl; The Bankrupt.*
Hamsun, Knut (1859–1952). *The Growth of the Soil; Hunger; Vagabonds.*
Rolvaag, Ole Edvart (1876–1931). *Giants in the Earth; Peder Victorious; Their Father's God.*
Undset, Sigrid (1882–1949). *Kristin Lavransdatter; The Master of Hestviken.*

Portuguese

Camoes, Luis de (1524?–80). *The Lusiads.*

Russian

Bunin, Ivan (1870–1953). *The Village; The Gentleman from San Francisco.*
Dostoyevsky, Feodor (1821–81). *Notes from the Underground; Crime and Punishment; The Idiot; The Brothers Karamazov.*
Ehrenburg, Ilya (1891–1967). *The Fall of Paris; The Stormy Life of Lasik Roitschwantz.*
Gogol, Nikolai (1809–52). *Dead Souls; The Overcoat; Taras Bulba.*

FEODOR DOSTOEVSKY: Freud is said to have learned from the psychological novels which this Russian wrote.

LEO TOLSTOI, in his difficult-to-classify novel *War and Peace* (a scene from the motion picture, above) re-evaluated Napoleon's attempt to capture Russia in 1812.

Lermontov, Mikhail (1814–41). *The Demon*; *The Circassian Boy*; *A Hero of Our Time*.

Mandelstam, Osip (1892–1940?). *Kamen*; *Tristia*.

Mayakovsky, Vladimir (1893–1930). *The Cloud in Trousers*.

Pasternak, Boris (1890–1960). *My Sister, Life*; *Spektorsky*; *Doctor Zhivago*.

Pushkin, Aleksandr (1799–1837). *Eugene Onegin*; *The Golden Cockerel*; *The Queen of Spades*.

Sholokhov, Mikhail (1905–   ). *And Quiet Flows the Don*; *The Don Flows Home to the Sea*.

Solzhenitzyn, Aleksandr (1918–   ). *One Day in the Life of Ivan Denisovich*; *The Gulag Archipelago*.

Yevtushenko, Yevgeny (1933–   ). *Babi Yar*; *Precocious Autobiography*; *Stolen Apples*.

Tolstoy, Leo (1828–1910). *War and Peace*; *Anna Karenina*; *The Kreutzer Sonata*; *Resurrection*.

Turgenev, Ivan (1818–83). *Fathers and Sons*; *First Love*; *The Torrents of Spring*.

Spanish

Alarcón, Pedro Antonio de (1833–91). *The Three-Cornered Hat*; *The Scandal*.

Baroja y Nessi, Pio (1879–1956). *The Quest*; *Red Dawn*.

Blasco Ibañez, Vicente (1867–1928). *Reeds and Mud*; *The Four Horsemen of the Apocalypse*.

Cervantes Saavedra, Miguel de (1547–1616). *Don Quixote*; *Novelas ejemplares*.

Ortega y Gasset, José (1883–1955). *The Modern Theme*; *The Revolt of the Masses*.

Pérez Goldos, Benito (1843–1920). *Dona Perfecta*; *La desheredada*.

Ruiz, Juan (1283–1351). *Libro de buen amor* (*The Book of Good Love*).

Unamuno, Miguel de (1864–1936). *The Tragic Sense of Life in Men and Nations*; *Three Exemplary Novels and a Prologue*.

Swedish

Lagerkvist, Pär (1891–1974). *The Dwarf*; *The Sybil*; *Barabbas*.

Lagerlof, Selma (1858–1940). *The Story of Gosta Berling*; *The Ring of the Lowenskjolds*.

Sachs, Nelly (1891–1970) (Wrote in German). *The Seeker and Other Poems*; *O the Chimneys*.

European Writers (continued)

Swiss

Burckhardt, Jakob Christoph (1818–97). *The Civilization of the Renaissance in Italy; Cicerone.*
Keller, Gottfried (1819–90). *Green Henry; People of Seldwyla.*
Rousseau, Jean Jacques (1712–78). *Julie, ou la Nouvelle Héloise; Confessions; Emile; Du contrat social.*
Spyri, Johanna (1827–1901). *Heidi.*
Staël, Germaine de (1766–1817). *Delphine; Corinne; De l'Allemagne.*

Yugoslav

Andric, Ivo (1892–1975). *The Bridge on the Drina; Bosnian Story; Young Miss.*
Djilas, Milovan (1911–). *Land Without Justice; Under the Colors.*

Latin—American Writers

Argentine

Borges, Jorge Luis (1899–). *In Praise of Darkness; Labyrinths; Extraordinary Tales.*
Cortazar, Julio, (1914–). *Hopscotch; The End of the Game; Sixty-two: A Model Kit.*

Brazilian

Amado, Jorge (1912–). *The Violent Land; Gabriela, Clove and Cinnamon; Dona Flor.*
Freyre, Gilberto (1900–). *The Masters and the Slaves; The Mansions and the Shanties.*
Machado de Assis, Joaquim Maria (1839–1908). *Epitaph of a Small Winner; Dom Casmurro: Philosopher or Dog?*

Chilean

Mistral, Gabriela (1889–1957). *Sonetos de la muerte; Desolación.*
Neruda, Pablo (1904–73). *Crepusculario; Twenty Love Poems and One Song of Despair.*

Nicaraguan

Dario, Rubén (Felix Rubén García Sarmiento) (1867–1916). *Azul; Poema del otono; Prosas profanas.*

Drama

Theatre

CLASSICAL DRAMATISTS

Greek

Aeschylus (525–426 B.C.). *The Oresteia.*
Sophocles (*c.* 496–406 B.C.). *Oedipus Rex; Oedipus at Colossus; Antigone.*
Euripides (*c.* 480–406 B.C.). *Iphigenia in Aulis; Iphigenia in Tauris; Electra; Medea.*
Aristophanes (*c.* 448–*c.* 388 B.C.). *Lysistrata; The Clouds; The Frogs; The Birds.*
Menander (342?–291?). *The Curmudgeon.*

Roman

Plautus (Titus Maccius Plautus) (*c.* 254–184 B.C.). *Menaechmi; Amphitryon; Curculio.*
Terence (Publius Terentius Afer) (*c.* 185–*c.* 159 B.C.). *Andria; Phormio; Adelphi.*
Seneca (Lucius Annaeus Seneca) (*c.* 3 B.C.–65 A.D.). *Hercules Furens.*

RENAISSANCE TO MODERN EUROPEAN DRAMATISTS

Austrian

Hoffmannsthal, Hugo von (1874–1929). *Der Turm; The Death of Titian.*
Schnitzler, Arthur (1862–1931). *The Lonely Way; The Vast Domain; Professor Bernhardi.*

Belgian

Ghelderode, Michel de (1898–1962). *Fastes d'enfer; Magie rouge.*
Maeterlinck, Maurice (1862–1949). *Pelléas et Mélisande; L'Oiseau bleu (The Blue Bird).*

British (not included in list of writers)

Beaumont, Francis (?1584–1616). *The Woman Hater; The Knight of the Burning Pestle.* (*see* Fletcher)
Centlivre, Susanna (*c.* 1667–1723). *The Perjured Husband; The Busy Body.*
Cibber, Colley (1671–1757). *The Careless Husband; Love's Last Shift; The Nonjuror.*
Chapman, George (1559–1634). *All Fools; Eastward Ho* (with Ben Jonson and John Marston); *Bussy d'Ambois.*
Davenant, Sir William (1606–68). *The Wits; The Platonic Lovers; Love and Honour.*
Dekker, Thomas (?1572–?1632). *The Shoemaker's Holiday.*
Etherege, George (*c.* 1635–91). *The Man of Mode.*
Farquhar, George (1678–1707). *The Beaux' Stratagem; The Constant Couple.*
Fletcher, John (1579–1625). *The Scornful Lady* (in collaboration with Francis Beaumont).
Ford, John (1586–*c.* 1640). *'Tis Pity She's a Whore; The Broken Heart; Love's Sacrifice.*
Garrick, David (1717–79). *Bon Ton; A Miss in Her Teens.*
Heywood, Thomas (?1574–1641). *A Woman Killed with Kindness; The London Traveller.*

BEN JONSON (left), a contemporary of Shakespeare, excelled in comedy. WILLIAM SHAKESPEARE (right) left a lasting imprint on the English language, developed blank verse to its greatest height, and has never been excelled in characterization.

Kyd, Thomas (1558–94). *The Spanish Tragedy.*
Marston, John (1576–1634). *The Malcontent; The Dutch Courtezan.*
Massinger, Philip (1583–1640). *A New Way to Pay Old Debts; The City Madam.*
Middleton, Thomas (1580–1627). *Michaelmas Term; A Trick to Catch the Old One.*
O'Keeffe, John (1746–1833). *Wild Oats; The Poor Soldier.*
Vanbrugh, Sir John (1664–1726). *The Provoked Wife.*
Webster, John (?1580–1634). *The White Devil; The Duchess of Malfi.*
Wycherly, William (1640–1716). *The Country Wife; The Plain Dealer.*

WILLIAM CONGREVE (left), the most polished of English dramatists of the late 17th century, attempted to dazzle the audience with his wit. GEORGE BERNARD SHAW (right) managed to hold the spotlight in late 19th and early 20th century drama with his Irish wit as he stuck his foil into all forms of stuffiness and social injustice.

DRAMATISTS (continued)

Czech

Capek, Karel (1890–1938). *R.U.R.*; *Power and Glory*.

French

Anouilh, Jean (1910–). *Antigone*; *The Waltz of the Toreadors*; *Becket*.

Arrabal, Fernando (1932–). *Guernica*; *Le Labyrinthe*.

Beaumarchais, Pierre Caron de (1732–99). *Le Barbier de Séville*; *Le Mariage de Figaro*.

Becque, Henri (1837–99). *Les Corbeaux*; *La Parisienne*.

Brieux, Eugène (1858–1932). *Les Avaries* (*Damaged Goods*); *La Robe rouge* (*The Red Robe*).

Claudel, Paul (1868–1955). *L'Annonce faite à Marie* (*The Tidings Brought to Mary*); *Le Soulier de satin* (*The Satin Slipper*).

Cocteau, Jean (1889–1963). *Orphée, La Machine Infernale*.

Corneille, Pierre (1606–84). *Le Cid*; *Cinna*; *Horace*.

Dumas, Alexandre (père) (1802–70). *Christine*; *Antony*; *La Tour de Nesle*.

Dumas, Alexandre (fils) (1824–95). *Camille*; *Le Demi-Monde*; *The Money Question*.

Feydeau, Georges (1862–1921). *Le Dindon*; *Occupe-toi d'Amélie*; *La Dame de chez Maxim*.

Genet, Jean (1910–). *The Maids*; *Deathwatch*; *The Balcony*.

Giraudoux, Jean (1882–1944). *The Madwoman of Chaillot*; *Amphitryon 38*; *La Guerre de Troie n'aura pas lieu* (*Tiger at the Gates*).

Hugo, Victor (1802–85). *Marion Delorme*; *Hernani*; *Ruy Blas*.

Ionesco, Eugéne (1912–). *The Bald Soprano*; *Rhinoceros*.

Jarry, Alfred (1873–1907). *Ubu Roi*; *Ubu enchaîné*.

Mauriac, François (1885–1970). *Asmodée*; *Les Mal-Aimés*.

Molière, Jean Baptiste Poquelin (1622–73). *L'Avare*; *Tartuffe*; *Le Bourgeois Gentilhomme*.

GUNTER GRASS first became well known in America for his novels, but is one of the foremost living German dramatists as well.

ALEKSANDR PUSHKIN
wrote "Boris Godunov,"
which later became
an opera.

Musset, Alfred de (1810–57). *Fantasio*; *On ne badine pas avec l'amour*.
Racine, Jean (1639–99). *Phedré*; *Britannicus*.
Rostand, Edmond (1868–1918). *Cyrano de Bergerac*; *L'Aiglon*.
Sardou, Victorien (1831–1908). *Fedora*; *La Tosca*; *Madame Sans-Gêne*.
Sartre, Jean-Paul (1905–). *The Flies*; *No Exit*; *The Respectful Prostitute*; *Dirty Hands*.
Scribe, Eugène (1791–1861). *Bataille de Dames*; *Adrienne Lecouvreur*.

German

Brecht, Berthold (1898–1956). *Mother Courage*; *The Good Woman of Setzuan*; *The Caucasian Chalk Circle*.
Goethe, Johann Wolfgang von (1749–1832). *Iphigenie auf Tauris*.
Grass, Günter (1927–). *Max*.
Hauptmann, Gerhart (1862–1946). *Before Dawn*; *The Weavers*; *The Sunken Bell*.
Hochhuth, Rolf (1931–). *The Deputy*; *Soldiers*.
Kaiser, Georg (1876–1945). *The Citizens of Calais*; *The Corals*.
Kleist, Heinrich von (1777–1811). *The Broken Pitcher*; *The Prince of Homburg*.
Lessing, Gotthold (1729–81). *Nathan the Wise*.
Schiller, Friedrich von (1759–1805). *Mary Stuart*; *William Tell*.
Sudermann, Hermann (1857–1928). *Magda*; *Morituri*.
Toller, Ernst (1873–1939). *Man and the Masses*; *The Machine-Wreckers*.

Hungarian

Molnar, Ferenc (1878–1952). *Liliom*; *The Guardsman*; *The Swan*.

Italian

Betti, Ugo (1892–1953). *La Padrona*; *Il Diluvio*.
Goldoni, Carlo (1707–93). *The Mistress of the Inn*; *The Fan*; *The Beneficent Bear*.
Pirandello, Luigi (1867–1936). *Six Characters in Search of an Author*; *Right You Are If You Think You Are*.

Norwegian
Ibsen, Henrik (1829–1906). *A Doll's House*; *Hedda Gabler*; *Peer Gynt*.

Portuguese
Vicente, Gil (1470?–1536). *Auto da fama*; *Auto da feira*; *Oviuvo*; *Amadis de Gaula*.

Russian
Andreyev, Leonid (1871–1919). *Anathema*; *He Who Gets Slapped*.
Chekov, Anton (1860–1904). *The Cherry Orchard*; *Uncle Vanya*; *The Three Sisters*.
Gogol, Nikolai (1809–52). *The Inspector-General*.
Gorki, Maxim (1869–1936). *The Lower Depths*.
Ostrovsky, Aleksandr (1823–86). *The Storm*; *The Snow Maiden*.
Pushkin, Aleksandr (1799–1837). *Boris Godunov*; *The Stone Guest*.
Tolstoy, Leo (1828–1911). *The Power of Darkness*; *The Living Corpse*.
Turgenev, Ivan (1818–83). *A Month in the Country*; *The Provincial Lady*.

Spanish
Alarcon y Mendoza, Juan Ruiz de (1581?–1639). *La verdad sospechosa*; *Las paredes oyen*; *El anticristo*.
Benevente, Jacinto (1866–1954). *The Passion Flower*; *Saturday Night*.
Calderon de la Barca, Pedro (1600–81). *El divino Orfeo*; *El magico prodigioso*.
García Lorca, Federico (1898–1936). *Yerma*; *Blood Wedding*; *The House of Bernarda Alba*.
Lope de Vega, Felix (1562–1635). *Punishment Without Vengeance*.
Martínez Sierra, Gregorio (1881–1947). *The Cradle Song*.
Tirso de Molina (Gabriel Téllez) (1584?–1648). *The Love Rogue*; *The Saint and the Sinner*.

Swedish
Strindberg, August (1849–1912). *The Father*; *Miss Julie*; *Creditors*.

Swiss
Dürrenmatt, Friedrich (1921–). *The Visit*; *The Physicist*; *Romulus der Grosse*.
Frisch, Max (1911–). *The Firebugs*; *Andorra*.

United States (not included in list of writers)
Akins, Zoe (1886–1958). *The Greeks Had a Word for It*; *The Old Maid*.
Connelly, Marc (1890–). *The Green Pastures*.
Gale, Zona (1874–1938). *Miss Lulu Bett*.
Hecht, Ben (1894–). *A Flag Is Born*; *The Front Page* (with Charles MacArthur).
Howard, Sidney (1891–1939). *They Knew What They Wanted*; *The Silver Cord*.
Kaufman, George S. (1889–1961). Wrote in collaboration with Edna Ferber (1887–1968): *The Royal Family*; *Stage Door*; *Dinner at Eight*. With Moss Hart (1904–61): *The Man Who Came to Dinner*.
Kelly, George (1887–1974). *Craig's Wife*; *The Show-Off*.
Kerr, Jean (1923–). *Mary, Mary*; *Poor Richard*.
Kingsley, Sidney (1906–). *Men in White*.

Motion Pictures

The milestones of the cinema industry are the first public showing in the Hotel Scribe, Boulevard des Capucines, Paris, on Dec. 28, 1895; and the earliest sound on film motion picture demonstrated in New York City on Mar. 13, 1923.

Development of the Cinema

1877   Eadweard Muybridge (1830–1904), English photographic experimenter, operated a series of still cameras to record the movements of a running horse. In 1881, Muybridge invented the zoopraxiscope, a device for projecting animated pictures on a screen.

1889   Thomas A. Edison (1847–1931), working with William K. Dickson and others, invented the kinetoscope, a peep show device featuring movement on film.

1895   Louis (1864–1948) and Auguste (1862–1954) Lumière, using an advanced kinetoscope called a cinematographe, showed the first motion pictures to paying audiences.

1900–   Georges Méliès (1861–1938), a French experimenter, developed
ca.   such film-making techniques as slow motion, dissolves, fade-ins
1905   and fade-outs in his films *Cinderella* (1900) and *A Trip to the Moon* (1902).

1903   Edwin S. Porter (1870–1941), an associate of Edison, introduced the close-up and abrupt scene changes in *The Great Train Robbery*, the first U.S. motion picture with a coherent plot.

1907–   David Wark Griffith (1880–1948), the first notable U.S. film
ca.   director, advanced the art of cinematography with such motion
1930   pictures as *Ben Hur* (1907), *The Birth of a Nation* (1914) and *Intolerance* (1916).

1912   Sarah Bernhardt (1844–1923), great French stage actress, appeared in the title role of *Queen Elizabeth*, a French-made film presented to audiences in the U.S. by Adolph Zukor, thus firmly establishing the "star system."

1912–   Adolph Zukor (1873–1976), U.S. film producer, pioneered in
ca.   the production of large-scale, full-length films featuring motion
1915   picture "stars" in the cast.

1913–   Mack Sennett (1884–1960), film actor and producer, advanced
1927   the art of film comedy with the slapstick antics of his Keystone Cops, and produced the first full-length motion picture comedy *Tillie's Punctured Romance* (1914), featuring Charlie Chaplin.

1913–   Advent of the first U.S. film stars, including:
ca.   Charlie Chaplin (1889–1977), brilliant motion picture comedian
1927   Mary Pickford (1893–   ), called "America's Sweetheart"
       Douglas Fairbanks (1883–1939), male lead in adventure films
       William S. Hart (1862–1946), first notable cowboy star
       Theda Bara (1890–1955), actress often cast in *femme fatale* rôles
       Rudolph Valentino (1895–1926), romantic matinee idol

1927   Al Jolson (1886–1950) was featured in the title role of *The Jazz Singer*, the first film with spoken dialogue.

1928   Walt Disney (1901–66) created the character of Mickey Mouse in the animated cartoon *Steamboat Willy*.

1920–   Film-making developed in Europe:

1939   Sergei Eisenstein (1898–1948), Russian director of early documentary-like epics, including *Potemkin* (1925) and *Ten Days That Shook the World* (1928).

INGMAR BERGMAN,
Swedish director, has
written and produced
milestone films like
"Wild Strawberries."

Jean Renoir (1894–   ), French director of *The Crime of Monsieur Lange* (1935), *Grand Illusion* (1937) and other profound films.

Luis Buñel (1900–   ), Spanish director of *An Andalusian Dog* with Salvador Dali) (1928), *Land Without Bread* (1932) and other surrealistic and irreverent films.

Salvador Dali (1904–   ), Spanish painter and sometime film director.

René Clair (1898–   ), French director of fantasies and satires, including *The Italian Straw Hat* (1927).

Marcel Pagnol (1895–1974), French director of the trilogy *Marius, Fanny* and *César* (1932–1933) and other comedies.

Jean Cocteau (1889–1963), director of sophisticated art films, including *The Blood of a Poet* (1930).

ca. 1930–   New era of U.S. motion picture stars, and heyday of dynamic directors and producers, including:

ca. 1950   Shirley Temple (1927–   ), child actress

Mae West (1893–   ), screen vamp and comedienne

Clark Gable (1901–60), male lead in romantic and adventure films

Cary Grant (1904–   ), male lead in sophisticated romantic comedies

Bette Davis (1908–   ), high-powered actress cast in melodramas

Humphrey Bogart (1899–1957), actor often cast in detective and other "tough guy" roles

MOTION PICTURES (continued)

Katharine Hepburn (1909–), accomplished actress of stage and screen

Cecil B. De Mille (1881–1959), director of theatrical, large-scale action films with elaborate sets

Samuel Goldwyn (1882–1974), producer who influenced the development of films and the modern motion picture corporation.

1939 Orson Welles (1915–), with his powerful film *Citizen Kane* expanded the horizons of serious film-making in the U.S.

1940–1950 Production of European films continued during and following World War II:

Vittorio de Sica (1901–74), Italian director: *Shoeshine* (1946), *The Bicycle Thief* (1948)

Roberto Rossellini (1906–77), Italian director: *Open City* (1946), *Paisan* (1946), *Stromboli* (1949)

Carl Dreyer (1889–1968), Danish director: *Day of Wrath* (1943)

Marcel Carné (1906–), French director: *Port of Shadows* (1938), *Children of Paradise* (1945)

1959–1970 Appearance in France of young "New Wave" directors, whose films featured ambiguous characterization and apparent formlessness of plot:

François Truffaut (1932–), *The 400 Blows* (1959), *Jules and Jim* (1961), *Stolen Kisses* (1968)

Jean-Luc Godard (1930–), *Breathless* (1959), *La Chinoise* (1967), *Weekend* (1968)

Alain Resnais (1922–), *Hiroshima Mon Amour* (1959)

Production of Full-length Films

The leading countries in the production of full-length films (1974 data) are:

India	435	France	234
Japan	405	USSR	162
Italy	237	USA	156

The United Kingdom produced 78 in the year ending Mar. 31, 1974.

Number of movie theatres

These figures for 1974 include, where known, mobile cinemas, drive-in cinemas and those only used in certain seasons.[1]

USSR	163 400	Italy	12 906
USA	14 950	India	8946[2]

The United Kingdom had 1535[5], Canada—1434[2], Australia—976[3], New Zealand—194.

Attendance

The highest attendances, by country[1] (1974 data) are:

USSR	4 566 900 000	Italy	546 100 000
India	2 424 000 000[2]	Philippines	318 000 000[4]

Comparative figures include the United Kingdom—138 500 000; Canada—89 000 000[2]; and New Zealand—13,100,000.

But some of the highest attendances per capita per annum are: USSR 18.1, Singapore 17.8, Hong Kong 14.8, Rwanda 14.6, and Cuba 14.2. By comparison India was 4.1, the United Kingdom 2.5 and Canada 3.9[2].

[1] No data available for China.
[2] 1973 data.   [3] 1972 data.
[4] 1975 data.   [5] 1977 data.

MOST POPULAR FILMS

VARIETY, bible of the entertainment industry, has compiled the following information, as of the end of 1978. Total rental means payments to the distributor for showings in U.S. and Canada only.

Title Director-Producer-Distributor	Total Rental
1. Star Wars (G. Lucas; G. Kurtz; 20th; 1977)	$164,765,000
2. Jaws (S. Spielberg (Zanuck/Brown); Universal; 1975)	121,254,000
3. The Godfather (F. Coppola; A. Ruddy; Par; 1972)	86,275,000
4. Grease (R. Kleiser; R. Stigwood/A. Carr; Par; 1978)	83,091,000
5. The Exorcist (W. Friedkin; W. P. Blatty; Warners; 1973)	82,200,000
6. The Sound of Music (R.Wise; 20th; 1965)	79,000,000
7. The Sting (G. R. Hill; T. Bill/M&J Phillips; Univ.; 1973)	78,889,000
8. Close Encounters of Third Kind (S. Spielberg; J&M Phillips; Col; 1977)	77,000,000
9. Gone With the Wind (V. Fleming; D. Selznick; MGM/UA; 1939)	76,700,000
10. Saturday Night Fever (J. Badham; R. Stigwood; Par; 1977)	71,463,000
11. One Flew Over Cuckoo's Nest (M. Forman; S. Zaentz/M. Douglas; UA; 1975)	59,000,000
12. Smokey and Bandit (H. Needham; M. Engelberg; Univ.; 1977)	57,259,000
13. American Graffiti (G. Lucas; F. Coppola; Univ.; 1973)	55,886,000
14. Rocky (J. Avildsen; Chartoff/Winkler; UA; 1976)	54,000,000
15. National Lampoon Animal House (J. Landis; M. Simmons/I.Reitman; Univ.; 1978)	52,368,000
16. Love Story (A. Hiller; H. Minsky; Par; 1970)	50,000,000
17. Towering Inferno (J. Guillermin; I. Allen; 20th; 1975)	50,000,000
18. Jaws II (J. Szwarc; Zanuck/Brown; Univ.; 1978)	49,299,000
19. The Graduate (M. Nichols; L. Turman; Avemb; 1968)	49,078,000
20. Doctor Zhivago (D. Lean; C. Ponti; MGM/UA; 1965)	46,550,000
21. Butch Cassidy and Sundance Kid (G. R. Hill; J. Foreman; 20th; 1969)	46,039,000
22. Airport (G. Seaton; R. Hunter; Univ; 1970)	45,300,000
23. The Ten Commandments (C. B. DeMille; Par; 1956)	43,000,000
24. Heaven Can Wait (W. Beatty; Par; 1978)	42,517,000
25. The Poseidon Adventure (R. Neame; I. Allen; 20th; 1972)	42,000,000

Radio and
Television

Radio and television can trace their origin to the same series of scientific investigations in the 19th century which discovered the use of electromagnetic waves as a means of "wireless" communication. Electromagnetic waves are similar to light and heat waves, but lower in frequency.

Radio

1865   English physicist James Clerk Maxwell (1831–79) postulates existence of electromagnetic waves.

1885–88   German physicist Heinrich Hertz (1857–94) verifies Clerk Maxwell's theories in a series of experiments.

1895   Italian physicist Guglielmo Marconi (1874–1937) improves and applies Hertz's inventions and sends a long-wave signal more than a mile.

1901   Marconi transmits messages across the Atlantic from England to Newfoundland.

1906   First advertised broadcast made at Brant Rock, Mass.

1920   First Scheduled radio broadcasts begin in the United States.

1920   David Sarnoff (1891–1971) becomes general manager of the Radio Corporation of America (RCA), and begins to transform radio into a mass medium.

1921   Over 300,000 U.S. listeners hear a report of the Dempsey–Carpentier fight.

1921   32 broadcasting stations are licensed by the U.S. Department of Commerce.

1922   The first U.S. commercial broadcast is presented.

1923   Chain broadcasting begins as stations hook up for simultaneous transmission of programs.

1926   The first nationwide network, the National Broadcasting Company (NBC) is organized by RCA.

1927   New Year's Day. The first coast-to-coast broadcast is presented: a play-by-play account of the Rose Bowl football game.

1927   NBC launches a second network called the Blue Network (the original being known as the Red).

1927   The Columbia Broadcasting System is established.

1930   Radio is now the great home entertainment, and second only to newspapers as the major medium of advertising.

1934   Mutual Broadcasting System established.

Radio (continued)

1938   The most famous incident of total audience involvement occurs when Orson Welles' convincing dramatization of H. G. Wells' novel, *The War of the Worlds*, peppered with "news bulletins" of the arrival on earth of Martians, caused thousands of people to grab their valuables and flee their homes.

1939   The outbreak of World War II spurs the development of radio as a major news medium, bringing to the fore such popular reporters as Eric Sevareid (1912–) and Edward R. Murrow (1908–65).

1943   NBC Blue Network becomes a separate company—the American Broadcasting Company (ABC)—after the Federal Communications Commission ruled that NBC could only own one network.

1950   Rise of television relegates radio to a minor position.

1960   As novelty of television wears off, radio recovers some ground, sparked to a considerable degree by the development of miniature, battery-operated sets usable where and when television is not feasible.

1974   World total of radio sets reaches 922,000,000 (no data available for China and Japan).

Television

1883   Paul Nipkow, a German scientist, begins experimenting with the transmission of pictures by wire.

1923   Vladimir Zworykin (1889–), Russian-born United States physicist, invents electronic scanner, the prototype of all scanning devices in use today.

1925   Short-range transmission of an image achieved by Francis Jenkins in Washington, D.C.

1926   Earliest public demonstration of television given by John Logie Baird in Great Britain.

1928   First trans-Atlantic transmission sent from Coulsdon, England, to New York.

1933   Experimental television transmission begins from Empire State Building, New York.

1936   November 2. World's first public television broadcasting service initiated at Alexandra Palace, London.

1939   Public programming in U.S. begins with the televising of the opening of the New York World's Fair.

1940   First television network set up by NBC on a limited scale between New York and Schenectady.

1941   Outbreak of World War II brings development of commercial television to a standstill.

1946   Beginning of rapid postwar growth of television industry in U.S.

1949   Sales of television sets in U.S. reach 250,000 a month.

1951   September 4. Coast-to-coast transmission begins in U.S. with address by President Truman from Japanese Peace Treaty Conference in San Francisco.

1958   Greatest total of TV prizes—$264,000—won on quiz programs by Teddy Nadler.

1962   First trans-Atlantic transmission by satellite *Telstar I*, from Andover, Maine, to Plumeur Bodou, France.

1975   Estimated world total of television receivers is 363,770,000, with 121,000,000 of these in the U.S. alone.

1976   An estimated 1,000,000,000 viewers throughout the world watch the Olympic Games held in Montreal.

MOST POPULAR TV PROGRAMS

Program	Date	Network	Avg. Audience
Roots	1/30/77	ABC	36,380,000
Super Bowl XII	1/15/78	CBS	34,410,000
Gone With The Wind, Pt. 1	11/7/76	NBC	33,960,000
Gone With The Wind, Pt. 2	11/8/76	NBC	33,750,000
Roots	1/28/77	ABC	32,680,000
Roots	1/27/77	ABC	32,540,000
Roots	1/25/77	ABC	31,900,000
Super Bowl XI	1/9/77	NBC	31,610,000
Roots	1/24/77	ABC	31,400,000
Roots	1/26/77	ABC	31,190,000
Roots	1/29/77	ABC	30,120,000
Super Bowl X	1/18/76	CBS	29,440,000
Super Bowl IX	1/12/75	NBC	29,040,000
Roots	1/23/77	ABC	28,840,000
Airport (movie)	11/11/73	ABC	28,000,000
Super Bowl VII	1/14/73	NBC	27,670,000
World Series Game 7	10/22/75	NBC	27,560,000
Super Bowl VIII	1/13/74	CBS	27,540,000
Super Bowl VI	1/16/72	CBS	27,450,000
Love Story (movie)	10/1/72	ABC	27,401,000
Laverne & Shirley	1/10/78	ABC	27,410,000
All In The Family	1/5/76	CBS	27,350,000
Bob Hope Christmas Show	1/15/70	NBC	27,260,000

According to A. C. Nielsen estimates these programs had the greatest audiences. These figures do not cover the last half of 1978.

BEETHOVEN wrote just 9 symphonies, one opera, one oratorio, one violin concerto and two masses, and lost his hearing at an early age.

BACH has been called "the colossal summit of centuries of musical energy." He wrote 150 chorale preludes, 200 cantatas and 40 organ fugues.

WAGNER's life was full of mystery. He carried out more ambitious projects in his operas than any other composer in history.

Music

History of Music

The following is a chart of the main works by historically important composers, with their music listed in generic columns. Lost and disputed works are ignored, as are those in sketch form, but important works which were not completed by the composer have been included (e.g.: Schubert's Symphony No. 8, *Unfinished*) where performances are possible.

Each of the categories should be regarded as covering its respective field in a wide sense. For example, Tchaikovsky's *Manfred*, although not numbered as a symphony, is included as one of his seven, and Berg's *Lyric Suite* for string quartet, even though not called a string quartet as such by the composer, is included in that column. Where totals are unknown or obscure, only the general outline of a corpus of works has been indicated using asterisks: one for a handful of such pieces, two for a significant contribution, and three indicating "very many." In some cases where the information might be useful, these vague symbols are amplified by details in the extreme right-hand column.

In all cases the figure in the "Concertos" columns include other major works (concertinos, rhapsodies, etc.) for the given instrument and orchestra.

Musical abbreviations used in this chart

arr	arranged	str	strings
clt	clarinet	str4	string quartet*
cor	horn	str5	string quintet*
fag	bassoon	tpt	trumpet
fl	flute	v d'a	viola d'amor
hps	harpsichord	vl	violin
instr	instruments	vla	viola
keyb'd	keyboard	w	wind (woodwind
misc	miscellaneous		and/or brass)
ob	oboe	w5	wind quintet*
orch	orchestra(l)		
pf	pianoforte		* and similar
pf4	piano quartet*		combination of
Rhap	Rhapsody		abbreviations.
Sinf Conc	Sinfonia Concertante		

Music

Dates (approx.)	Name of era	Musical developments	Principal composers
8th century B.C. to 4th century A.D. to 6th century A.D.	Prehistoric	Improvisatory music-making. Music and magic virtually synonymous.	
	Primitive (Ancient Greece and Rome; Byzantium)	Improvisatory music-making in domestic surroundings. Competitive music-making in the arena.	
4th century A.D.	Ambrosian	The beginnings of plainsong and the establishment of order in liturgical music.	Bishop Ambrose of Milan (c. 333–97) established four scales.
6th to 10th century	Gregorian	Church music subjected to strict rules, e.g.: melodies sung only in unison.	Pope Gregory I, The Great (540–604) extended the number of established scales to eight.
1100–1300	Medieval	Guido d'Arezzo (c. 980–1050) was called the inventor of music: his teaching methods and invention of a method of writing music transformed the art. Beginning of organized instrumental music; start of polyphony in church music.	Minstrels (10th–13th centuries). Goliards (traveling singers of Latin songs: 11th–12th centuries). Troubadours (c. 1100–1210) Trouvères (from 1100). Bernart de Ventadorn (c. 1150–95) encouraged singing in the vernacular.
1300–1600	Renaissance	The great age of polyphonic church music. Gradual emergence of instrumental music. Appearance of madrigals, chansons, etc.	Guillaume de Machaut (c. 1300–77) John Dunstable (d. 1453) Guillaume Dufay (c. 1400–74) Johannes Ockeghem (1430–95) Josquin des Pres (1450–1521) John Taverner (c. 1495–1545) Giovanni da Palestrina (c. 1525–94) Orlando di Lasso (c. 1530–94) Thomas Morley (1557–1603)

1600–1750	Baroque	The beginnings of true organization in music and instruments.	John Dowland (1563–1626) Michael Praetorius (1571–1621)
		Beginnings of opera and oratorio.	Giovanni Gabrieli (1557–1612) Claudio Monteverdi (1567–1633) Orlando Gibbons (1583–1625) Pietro Cavalli (1602–76)
		Rise of instrumental music; the first orchestras, used at first in the opera house but gradually attaining separate existence. Beginnings of sonata, concerto, suite, and symphony.	Jean-Baptiste Lully (1632–87) Arcangelo Corelli (1653–1713) Henry Purcell (1658–95) Alessandro Scarlatti (1660–1725) Reinhard Keiser (1674–1739) Georg Philipp Telemann (1681–1767) Jean Philippe Rameau (1683–1764) Domenico Scarlatti (1685–1757)
		The peak of polyphonic writing.	Johann Sebastian Bach (1685–1750) George Frideric Handel (1685–1759)
1750–1800+	Classical	The age of the concert symphony and concerto. Beginning of the string quartet and sinfonia concertante. Decline of church music.	Giovanni Battista Sammartini (c. 1700–75) Christoph Willibald von Gluck (1714–87) Carl Philipp Emanuel Bach (1714–88) Franz Joseph Haydn (1732–1809) Wolfgang Amadeus Mozart (1756–91)
		Important developments in opera.	Luigi Cherubini (1760–1842)
1800–50	Early Romantic	High maturity of the symphony and concerto, etc. in classical style. Romantic opera. The age of the piano virtuosi. Invention of the nocturne. Beginnings of the symphonic poem.	Ludwig van Beethoven (1770–1827) Nicolo Paganini (1782–1840) Carl Maria von Weber (1786–1826) Gioacchino Rossini (1792–1868) Franz Schubert (1797–1828) Hector Berlioz (1803–69) Jakob Ludwig Felix Mendelssohn (1809–47)
		Lieder. Beginnings of nationalism.	Frédéric François Chopin (1810–49) Robert Schumann (1810–56)

Dates (approx.)	Name of era	Musical developments	Principal composers
1850–1900	High Romanticism	The development of nationalism. Maturity of the symphonic and tone poems. Emergence of music drama.	Mikhail Glinka (1804–57) Franz Liszt (1811–86) Richard Wagner (1813–83) Bedřich Smetana (1824–84) Johannes Brahms (1833–97) Pyotr Il'ich Tchaikovsky (1840–93) Antonín Dvořák (1841–1904) Edvard Hagerup Grieg (1843–1907) Claude Debussy (1862–1918)
1900–	Modern	Impressionism and post-romanticism. Gigantism. Neo-classicism and other reactionary movements. Atonalism.	Richard Strauss (1864–1949) Carl Nielsen (1865–1931) Jean Sibelius (1865–1957) Alexander Scriabin (1872–1915) Ralph Vaughan Williams (1872–1958) Sergei Rachmaninoff (1873–1943) Arnold Schoenberg (1874–1951) Charles Ives (1874–1954) Béla Bartók (1881–1945) Igor Stravinsky (1882–1971) Anton Webern (1883–1945) Alban Berg (1885–1934) Samuel Barber (1910–) Benjamin Britten (1913–77)
Today	Avant-garde	Avant-garde is history in the making and any list of composers would be arbitrary since one cannot tell which of the many directions taken by modern music will prove most influential. There have always been avant-garde composers, without which the art of music would never have developed: many names from the above chart are good examples. Here are some names of avant-gardistes of prominence.	Luigi Dallapiccola (1904–75) John Cage (1912–) Iannis Xenakis (1922–) Luigi Nono (1924–) Hans Werner Henze (1926–) Karlheinz Stockhausen (1928–)

(Woodwinds 1–10; Brass 11–14; Percussion 15–24; Strings 25–29; Keyboard 30–33)

Name (earliest concerto)	Earliest orchestral use	History
1 Piccolo or Octave Flute (Vivaldi, c. 1735)	1717 (Handel's *Water Music*)	Name "piccolo" dates from 1856, but the origin goes back to prehistory via flute and sopranino recorder.
2 Recorder or Flûte-à-bec (c. 1690)	c. 1690	Earliest written mention 1388.
3 Flute—transverse or cross-blown (Vivaldi, c. 1729)	1672 (Lully)	Prehistoric (c. 18,000 B.C.); the modern Boehm flute dates from 1832.
4 Oboe (Marcheselli, 1708)	1657 (Lully's *L'amour malade*)	Originated Middle Ages in the schalmey (early double-reed woodwind) family. The name comes from Fr. *hautbois* (1511) = loud wood.
5 Clarinet (Vivaldi, c. 1740?: 2 clarinets; Molter, 1747: 1 clarinet)	1726 (Faber: *Mass*)	Developed by J. C. Denner (1655–1707) from the recorder and schalmey families.
6 Cor anglais (English Horn) (J. M. Haydn, c. 1775?)	1760 (in Vienna)	Purcell wrote for "tenor oboe" c. 1690: this *may* have originated the name English Horn. Alternatively, it may be from "angled horn," referring to its crooked shape.
7 Bass Clarinet	1838 (Meyerbeer's *Les Huguenots*)	Prototype made in 1772 by Gilles Lot of Paris. Modern Boehm form from 1838.
8 Bassoon (Vivaldi, c. 1730?)	c. 1619	Introduced in Italy c. 1540 as the lowest of the double-reed group.

9 Double Bassoon	c. 1730 (Handel)	"Borrowed" from military bands for elemental effects in opera.
10 Saxophone (Debussy's *Rhapsody*, 1903)	1844 (Kastner's *Last King of Judah*)	Invented by Adolphe Sax, c. 1840.
11 Trumpet (Torelli, before 1700) (Haydn, 1796: keyed trumpet)	c. 1800 (keyed) 1835 (valved, in Halévy's *La Juive*)	The natural trumpet is of prehistoric origin; it formed the basis of the earliest orchestras.
12 Trombone (Wagenseil, c. 1760)	c. 1600 (as part of bass-line)	From Roman *buccina* or slide trumpet, via the medieval sackbut to its modern form c. 1500.
13 Horn (Bach, 1717–21, or Vivaldi) (Bach . . . Vivaldi: 2 horns; Telemann, before 1721: 1 horn)	1639 (Cavalli)	Prehistoric. The earliest music horns were the German helical horns of the mid-16th century. Rotary valve horn patented in 1832.
14 Tuba (Vaughan Williams, 1954)	1830 (Berlioz' *Symphonie Fantastique*)	Patented by W. Wieprecht and Moritz, Berlin, 1835.
15 Timpani/Kettle drum (Mašek, c. 1790: 1 set; Tausch, c. 1870: 6 timpani)	1607 (Monteverdi's *Orfeo*)	Originated in the ancient Orient.
16 Bass Drum	1748 (Rameau's *Zaïs*)	As timpani.
17 Side or Snare drum	1749 (Handel's *Fireworks Music*)	Derived from the small drums of prehistory, via the medieval tabor. Achieved its modern form in the 18th century.
18 Tenor Drum	1842	
19 Tambourine	1820	Dates back to the medieval Arabs; prototype used by Assyrians and Egyptians. Earliest use of the word 1579.
20 Cymbals	1680 (Strungk's *Esther*)	From Turkish military bands of antiquity.

21 Triangle	1774 (Glantz: *Turkish Symphony*)	As cymbals.
22 Xylophone	1873 (Lumbye's *Traumbilder*)	Primitive; earliest "art" mention 1511.
23 Gong or Tam tam	1791 (Gossec's *Funeral March*)	Originating in the ancient Far East.
24 Glockenspiel	1739 (Handel's *Saul*)	Today strictly a keyboard instrument, in the 19th century the metal plates were struck by hand-held hammers. The original instrument dates from 4th century Rome.
25 Violin (Torelli, 1709)	c. 1600	Descended from the lyre via the 6th century crwth, rebec and fiddle. Modern instruments of Lombardic origin c. 1545. The words violin and fiddle derive ultimately from Roman *vitulari*. ("to skip like a calf").
26 Viola (Giranek or Telemann, "before 1762")	c. 1600	As violin.
27 Violoncello (Jacchini, 1701)	c. 1600	As violin.
28 Double bass (Vanhal, c. 1770)	c. 1600	Developed alongside the violin family, but is a closer relative to the bass viol or violone.
29 Harp (Handel, 1738)	c. 1600	Possibly prehistoric: attained its modern form by 1792.
30 Vibraphone	1934	First used in dance bands in the 1920s.
31 Celesta	1880 (Widor's *Der Korrigane*)	Invented by Mustel in 1880.
32 Pianoforte (J. C. Bach, 1776)	1776	Descended from the dulcimer. Invented by Cristofori c. 1709. Earliest printed music: 1732. First concert use 1767 in London.
33 Organ (Handel, c. 1730)	1886 (Saint-Saëns' *Symphony No. 3*)	Ultimate origin lies in the antique panpipes

Other Composers

Brazilian

Villa-Lobos, Heitor (1887–1959). *Chôros No. 7; Bachianas Brasileiras No. 1.*

Cuban

Lecuona, Ernesto (1869–1963). *Rapsodia Negra.*

English

Delius, Frederick (1862–1934). *A Village Romeo and Juliet* (opera); *Sea Drift* (choral work).

Elgar, Sir Edward (1857–1934). *The Dream of Gerontius* (cantata); *Violin Concerto in B Minor.*

Sullivan, Sir Arthur (1842–1900). *The Mikado; Trial by Jury; The Yeoman of the Guard,* etc. (all comic operas).

Vaughan Williams, Ralph (1872–1958). *A London Symphony; A Pastoral Symphony; Sir John in Love* (opera).

French

Bizet, Georges (1838–75). *Carmen* (opera); *The Pearlfishers* (opera).

Chaminade, Cécile (1857–1944). *Les Amazones* (symphony); *Callirhóé* (ballet).

Charpentier, Gustave (1860–1958). *Louise* (opera); *Impression d'Italie* (suite).

Delibes, Leo (1836–91). *Lakmé* (opera); *Coppélia* (ballet).

D'Indy, Vincent (1851–1931). *Symphony on a French Mountain Air.*

Dukas, Paul (1865–1935). *The Sorcerer's Apprentice* (symphonic poem).

Fauré, Gabriel (1845–1924). *Requiem; Claire de Lune* (song).

Franck, César (1822–90). Belgian-born. *Symphony in D Minor; Trois Chorals.*

Halévy, Jacques (1799–1862). *La Juive* (opera).

Honnegger, Arthur (1892–1955). Swiss-born. *King David* (oratorio); *Judith* (opera); *Antigone* (opera).

Lalo, Edouard (1832–92). *Le Roi d'Ys* (opera); *Symphonie Espagnole.*

Massenet, Jules (1842–1912). *Manon* (opera); *Thaïs* (opera).

Meyerbeer, Giacomo (1791–1864). German-born. *Les Huguenots* (opera); *Robert le Diable* (opera).

Milhaud, Darius (1892–1974). *Christophe Colombe* (opera); *The Nothing Doing Bar* (ballet).

Offenbach, Jacques (1819–80). German-born. *Orphée aux Enfers* (operetta); *La Vie Parisienne* (operetta); *Tales of Hoffmann* (opera).

Poulenc, Francis (1899–1963). *Les Biches* (ballet); *Dialogue des Carmélites* (opera).

Satie, Erik (1866–1925). *Sarabandes* (piano piece); *Socrate* (piece for four sopranos and chamber orchestra).

Thomas, Ambroise (1811–96). *Le Caïd* (opera); *Mignon* (opera); *Hamlet* (opera).

German

Humperdinck, Englebert (1854–1921). *Hänsel und Gretel* (opera).

Italian

Bellini, Vincenzo (1801–35). *La Sonnambula* (opera); *Norma* (opera).

Donizetti, Gaetano (1797–1848). *Lucia di Lammermoor* (opera); *The Daughter of the Regiment* (opéra comique).

Leoncavallo, Ruggiero (1858–1919). *Pagliacci* (opera).

Mascagni, Pietro (1863–1945). *Cavelleria Rusticana* (opera).

MAHLER (left) was a busy conductor but managed to compose many songs and 9 symphonies. CÉSAR FRANCK (right) is best known for his one symphony and a violin and piano sonata.

Spanish

Falla, Manuel de (1876–1946). *Wedded by Witchcraft* (ballet); *The Three-Cornered Hat* (ballet).

United States

Babbitt, Milton (1916–). *Three Compositions for Piano.*

Bernstein, Leonard (1918–). *The Jeremiah Symphony; Fancy Free* (ballet).

Copland, Aaron (1900–). *Third Symphony; Appalachian Spring* (ballet).

Creston, Paul (1906–). *Two Choric Dances.*

Floyd, Carlisle (1926–). *Susannah* (opera); *The Passion of Jonathan Wade* (opera).

Gershwin, George (1898–1937). *Rhapsody in Blue; Porgy and Bess* (folk opera); *An American in Paris* (tone poem).

Hanson, Howard (1896–). *Fourth Symphony; Hymn for the Pioneers* (for chorus and orchestra).

Harris, Roy (1898–). *First Symphony; Piano Quintet.*

MacDowell, Edward (1861–1908). *Tragica* (piano sonata); *Eroica* (piano sonata); *Indian Suite* (for orchestra).

Menotti, Gian-Carlo (1911–). Italian-born. *The Saint of Bleecker Street* (opera); *The Consul* (opera).

Piston, Walter (1894–). *Symphony No. 3.*

Rorem, Ned (1923–). *Air Music.*

Schuman, William (1910–). *Third Symphony; Symphony for Strings.*

Still, William Grant (1895–1978). *Troubled Island* (opera); *Afro-American Symphony.*

Thomson, Virgil (1896–). *Four Saints in Three Acts* (opera); *The Mother of Us All.*

Wuorinen, Charles (1938–). *Time's Encomium.*

Art

Painters

Some of the world's most renowned painters with well known examples of their work.

AUSTRIA
> KLIMT, Gustav (1862–1918). Leading painter of Art Nouveau.
> KOKOSCHKA, Oskar (1886–   ). "View of the Thames."

BELGIUM
> BRUEGHEL, Pieter (The Elder) (c. 1520–69). "The Adoration of the Kings," "The Peasant Dance."
> ENSOR, James (1860–1949). "Entry of Christ into Brussels."
> GOSSAERT, Jan (c. 1478–1533). "Adoration."
> JORDAENS, Jacob (1593–1678). "The Bean King."
> MAGRITTE, René (1898–1967). "The Red Model."
> MEMLING, Hans (c. 1430–94). "Mystic Marriage of St. Catherine."
> RUBENS, Peter Paul (1577–1640). "Adoration of the Magi," "Battle of the Amazons."
> TENIERS, David (The Younger) (1610–90). "Peasants Playing Bowls."
> VAN DER WEYDEN, Rogier (c. 1400–64). "Deposition," "The Magdalen Reading."
> VAN DYCK, Anthony (1599–1641). "Charles I of England."
> VAN EYCK, Hubert (c. 1370–c. 1426), Jan (c. 1390–1441). "Ghent Altarpiece." Jan alone "The Arnolfini Marriage."

FRANCE
> ARP, Hans (Jean) (1887–1966). "Berger et Nuage."
> BONNARD, Pierre (1867–1947). "The Window."
> BOUCHER, François (1703–70). "Diana Bathing."
> BRAQUE, Georges (1882–1963). "Vase of Anemones."
> CEZANNE, Paul (1839–1906). "Mont Sainte-Victoire," "Bathers."
> CHAGALL, Marc (1887–   ). "I and the Village," "Calvary."
> CHARDIN, Jean-Baptiste Siméon (1699–1779) "The Skate," "The Lesson."
> COROT, Jean-Baptiste Camille (1796–1875). "Pont de Mantes," "Sens Cathedral."

JAN VAN EYCK, Flemish Renaissance painter, is noted for his exploitation of the medium of oil and detailed realism seen here in "Giovanni Arnolfini and His Wife," 1434, in the National Gallery, London.

PAUL CÉZANNE "built" his paintings. He purified natural shapes to extract only the permanent qualities of ever-changing reality, as shown in this "Still Life," in the National Gallery of Art, Washington, D.C., Chester Dale Collection.

JEAN-BAPTISTE-CAMILLE COROT recorded the quality of a particular place at a particular time. This 19th-century French artist's fame rests on his landscapes and especially his trees. "A View Near Volterra" is in the National Gallery of Art, Washington, D.C., Chester Dale Collection.

COURBET, Gustave (1819–77). "Funeral at Ornans."
DAUMIER, Honoré (1808–79). "The Third-Class Carriage."
DAVID, Jacques Louis (1748–1825). "The Rape of the Sabines."
DEGAS, Hilaire-Germain-Edgar (1834–1917). "La Danseuse au Bouquet."

GEORGES BRAQUE was the co-developer of Cubism with Picasso. Objects are reconstructed on the canvas according to structural shapes, not natural forms, as in "Still Life: The Table," in the National Gallery of Art, Washington, D.C., Chester Dale Collection.

GUSTAVE COURBET believed that one must paint from his own experience. "The Stone Breakers," 1849, was the first painting to embody his programmatic Realism.

DELACROIX, Eugène (1798–1863). "The Massacre of Chios."
DUFY, Raoul (1877–1953). "The Palm."
DUNOYER DE SEGONZAC, André (1884–1974). Member of cubist group.
FOUQUET, Jean (c. 1420–c. 80). "Etienne Chevalier with St. Stephen."
FRAGONARD, Jean-Honoré (1732–1806). "The Love Letter," "Baigneuses."

EDOUARD MANET, a pioneer of French Impressionism, in his later work, directed his efforts toward a flattening of planes and increase in tonal values in "The Old Musician," in the National Gallery of Art, Washington, D.C., Chester Dale Collection.

CLAUDE MONET, a French Impressionist and leading exponent of "plein-air" painting, is most famous for his series of haystacks, Rouen Cathedral, and water lilies. This landscape is "Summer," in the Staatsgalerie, Stuttgart.

AUGUSTE RENOIR, a leader of the French Impressionist school, dappled patterns of sunlight and shadow to create warmth and happiness in "A Girl with a Watering Can," in the National Gallery of Art, Washington, D.C., Chester Dale Collection.

FRENCH PAINTERS (continued)

GAUGUIN, Paul (1848–1903). "Ta Matete."
GERICAULT, Jean Louis (1791–1824). "Raft of the Medusa."
GREUZE, Jean-Baptiste (1725–1805). "The Broken Pitcher."
INGRES, Jean-Auguste Dominique (1780–1867). "Odalisque."
LA TOUR, Georges de (1593–1652). "Job and His Wife."
LEGER, Fernand (1881–1955). "The City."
LORRAIN, Claude (1600–82). "Embarkation of St. Ursula."
MANET, Edouard (1823–83). "Déjeuner sur l'Herbe."
MATISSE, Henri (1869–1954). "Odalisque."
MILLET, Jean-François (1814–75). "Man with the Hoe," "Angelus."
MONET, Claude (1840–1926). "Rouen Cathedral," "Water Lilies."
MORISOT, Berthe (1841–95). "La Toilette."
PISSARRO, Camille (1830–1903). "The Harvest," "Montfoucault."
POUSSIN, Nicolas (1593/4–1665). "Worship of the Golden Calf."
PUVIS DE CHAVANNES, Pierre (1824–98). "War."
REDON, Odilon (1840–1916). "Les Yeux Clos."
RENOIR, Pierre Auguste (1841-1919). "Luncheon of the Boating Party."
ROUAULT, GEORGES (1871-1958). "Three Judges."
ROUSSEAU, Henri (1844–1910). "The Dream."
SEURAT, Georges (1859–91). "Sunday Afternoon on the Grande Jatte."
SIGNAC, Paul (1865–1935). "Port of St. Tropez."
SISLEY, Alfred (1839–99). "Flood at Port Marly."
TOULOUSE-LAUTREC, Henri de (1864–1901). "At the Moulin Rouge."
UTRILLO, Maurice (1883–1955). "Port St. Martin."
VIGEE-LEBRUN, Elisabeth (1755–1842). "Portrait of Marie Antoinette."
VLAMINCK, Maurice de (1876–1958). "Village in the Snow."
WATTEAU, Antoine (1684–1721). "The Embarkation for Cythera."

ALFRED SISLEY: A late 19th-century English landscape painter, Sisley joined the French Impressionist group. Most of his works are characterized by short brush strokes, as seen here in "The Tug Boat," Petit Palais, Paris.

MAURICE UTRILLO painted street scenes of Paris, particularly Montmartre and the suburbs. He depicted these views with a lyrical, sometimes hallucinatory vision. Note the lack of people in this scene, "Marizy-Sainte-Genevieve," in the National Gallery of Art, Washington, D.C., Chester Dale Collection.

MATTHIAS GRÜNEWALD couples Renaissance technique with Gothic intensity of emotion in the "Crucifixion" panel of his "Isenheim Altarpiece," Colmar, France.

PAINTERS (continued)

GERMANY

ALTDORFER, Albrecht (1480–1538). "Battle of Arbela."
BECKMANN, Max (1884–1950). "Departure."
CRANACH, Lucas (The Elder) (1472–1553). "Venus," "Rest on Flight into Egypt."
DURER, Albrecht (1471–1528). "The Four Apostles," "Apocalypse."
ERNST, Max (1891–1978). A founder of surrealism.
GROSZ, George (1893–1959). "Street Scene."
GRUNEWALD, Matthias (c. 1460–1528). "Isenheim Altarpiece."
HOLBEIN, Hans (The Younger) (1497–1543). "Henry VIII," "The Ambassadors."
KOLLWITZ, Kathe (1867–1945). "Death and the Mother."
NOLDE, Emil (1867–1956). "Christ among the Children."

GREAT BRITAIN

BONINGTON, Richard Parkes (1802–28). "A Sea Piece."
CONSTABLE, John (1776–1837). "The Hay Wain."
CROME, John (1768–1821). "The Slate Quarries."
GAINSBOROUGH, Thomas (1727–88). "Blue Boy."
HILLIARD, Nicholas (c. 1547–1619). "Elizabeth I," "Sir Walter Raleigh."
HOGARTH, William (1697–1764). "Rake's Progress," "Marriage à la Mode."
HUNT, William Holman (1827–1910). "The Scapegoat."
JOHN, Augustus Edwin (1878–1961). "The Smiling Woman."
LANDSEER, Sir Edwin (1802–73). "The Old Shepherd's Chief Mourner," "Shoeing."
MILLAIS, Sir John Everett (1829–96). "Order of Release."

WILLIAM HOGARTH was a painter of the realistic but florid Rococo school, and a strong social critic. Shown here is a scene from his "The Beggar's Opera," c. 1731, now in London's Tate Gallery.

JOSEPH TURNER, although he lived in 19th-century England, is recognized as a "modern" painter today. The swirling brush strokes blur the subject of nature's violence in his "Steamer in Snowstorm," described by a contemporary as "airy visions, painted with tinted steam." Tate Gallery, London.

BRITISH PAINTERS (continued)

RAEBURN, Sir Henry (1756–1823) "Sir John Sinclair."
REYNOLDS, Sir Joshua (1723–92). "Mrs. Siddons as the Tragic Muse," "The Three Graces."
ROSSETTI, Dante Gabriel (1828–82). "Beata Beatrix."
STUBBS, George (1724–1806). "Horse Frightened by a Lion."
SUTHERLAND, Graham (1903–). "Thorns."
TURNER, Joseph Mallord William (1775–1851). "The Grand Canal, Venice," "Shipwreck."
Wilson, Richard (1714–82). "Okehampton Castle."

LEONARDO DA VINCI, the genius of the Renaissance (left), is most famous for two paintings, "The Last Supper" (next page) a fresco in Milan, *c.* 1400, and the "Mona Lisa" in the Louvre, Paris.

Leonardo da Vinci's "The Last Supper."

ITALY

BELLINI, Giovanni (*c.* 1429–1516). "Pietá," "Coronation of the Virgin," "Agony in the Garden."

BOTTICELLI, Sandro (Alessandro di Mariano Filipepi) (1445–1510). "Birth of Venus," "Mystic Nativity."

CANALETTO, Giovanni Antonio Canal (1697–1768). "Venice: A Regatta on the Grand Canal."

CARAVAGGIO, Michelangelo Merisi (1573–1610). "St. Matthew," "Deposition."

CHIRICO, Giorgio di (1888–1978). Leading surrealist.

CORREGIO, Antonio Allegri (*c.* 1489–1534). "Jupiter and Io," "Assumption of the Virgin."

FRANCESCA, Piero della (*c.* 1410–92). "Nativity."

FRA ANGELICO, Giovanni da Fiesole (1387–1455). "Annunciation."

FRA FILIPPO LIPPI (*c.* 1406–69). "Tarquinia Madonna."

GIORGIONE, Giorgio da Castelfranco (1475–1510). "Sleeping Venus."

GIOTTO di Bondone (*c.* 1267–1337). "Life of St. Francis."

LEONARDO da Vinci (1452–1519). "Mona Lisa (La Gioconda)," "Last Supper."

MICHELANGELO (Buonarroti) (1475–1564). "Creation of Adam."

MODIGLIANI, Amadeo (1884–1920). "Portrait of Madame Zborowski."

RAPHAEL (1483–1520). "Sistine Madonna."

TIEPOLO, Giovanni Battista (1696–1770). "The Finding of Moses."

TINTORETTO, Jacopo Robusti (1518–94). "Last Supper," "Il Paradiso."

TITIAN (*c.* 1487–1576). "The Tribute Money," "Bacchus and Ariadne."

VERONESE, Paolo Caliari (1528–88). "Marriage at Cana."

FRA ANGELICO, a 15th-century Florentine monk, painted "The Annunciation," in the Diocesan Museum, Cortona. All of his works exude a pure, beautiful spirituality, and his figures are admired for their lyrical tenderness.

TINTORETTO, Venetian Mannerist master, contrasts the everyday setting with the supernatural by using unrealistic lights and shadows in his "Jesus with Mary and Martha," in the State Museum, Munich.

PIETER DE HOOCH, 17th-century Dutch genre painter, portrays an intimate domestic scene in his "A Dutch Courtyard," in the National Gallery of Art, Washington, D.C., Andrew Mellon Collection.

MEXICO

OROZCO, José Clemente (1883–1949). "Epic of Culture in the New World."

POSADA, José Guadalupe (1852–1913). First of the great 20th-century Mexican painters.

RIVERA, Diego (1886–1957). Foremost painter of murals of his generation.

SIQUEIROS, David Alfaro (1896–1974). "Liberation of Chile."

TAMAYO, Rufino (1899–   ). "Women of Tehuantepec."

NETHERLANDS

BOSCH, Hieronymus (c. 1450–1516). "Christ Crowned with Thorns," "The Garden of Earthly Delights."

HALS, Frans (c. 1580–1666). "Laughing Cavalier."

HOOCH, Pieter de (1629–83). "An Interior."

JAN VERMEER, 17th-century Dutch genre painter, most often chose intimate interior scenes. In "The Cook" in the Rijksmuseum, Amsterdam, can be seen the poetic serenity, mirror-like images, and luminous color for which Vermeer is famous.

REMBRANDT VAN RIJN was the greatest genius of Dutch art. His portraits of himself (as here) and others reveal both the intense individualism of the sitter and the psychological insight of the master.

JACOB VAN RUISDAEL: A Dutch painter and etcher, van Ruisdael (c. 1628-82) is the most celebrated of the Dutch landscape painters. This painting, "Windmill of Wijk," in the Rijksmuseum, Amsterdam, which displays a somber mood and precise accuracy in details, is characteristic of his work.

FRANS HALS, a Dutchman, used quick, deft brush strokes in his portraits to create a sense of spontaneity. This immediacy is seen in his "Malle Babbe," *c.* 1650, in the State Museum, Berlin-Dahlem.

MONDRIAN, Piet (1872–1944). "Composition."
REMBRANDT, Harmensz van Rijn (1606–69). "The Night Watch," "The Anatomy Lesson."
RUISDAEL, Jacob van (*c.* 1628–82). "View of Haarlem."
VAN GOGH, Vincent (1853–90). "Road with Cypresses," "Old Peasant."
VERMEER, Jan (1632–75). "Woman with a Water Jug."

VINCENT VAN GOGH: A Dutchman who did his best work in southern France, Van Gogh shows his talent for bright color, a bright sky and swirling brush strokes, in this work, "The Olive Orchard," in the National Gallery of Art, Washington, D.C., Chester Dale Collection.

DIEGO VELÁZQUEZ, one of the greatest Baroque artists, was a master of the use of direct and reflected light exemplified here by "The Maids of Honor," 1636, in The Prado, Madrid.

NORWAY

MUNCH, Edvard (1863–1944). "Dance of Death."

SPAIN

DALI, Salvador (1904–). "Crucifixion," "The Persistence of Memory."

EL GRECO (1541–1614). "The Burial of Count Orgaz," "View of Toledo."

FRANCISCO GOYA, Spanish Neo-Baroque painter, expresses with emotional intensity the gruesome reality of men dying for liberty in "The Third of May, 1808," in The Prado, Madrid.

SALVADOR DALI, Spanish surrealist painter, is best known for the melting watches in his artwork.

GOYA, Francisco de (1746–1828). "The Naked Maja," "The Shootings of May 3rd."

GRIS, Juan (1887–1927). Leader of cubist movement.

MIRO, Joan (1893–   ). "Dog Barking at the Moon."

MURILLO, Bartolomé Esteban (1617–82). "Virgin and Child," "Immaculate Conception."

PICASSO, Pablo (1881–1973). "Guernica," "Les Demoiselles d'Avignon."

RIBERA, José (1591–1652). "The Martyrdom of St. Bartholomew."

VELAZQUEZ, Diego (1599–1660). "Rokeby Venus," "The Water-Carrier."

BARTOLOME MURILLO was primarily a religious and portrait painter in 17th-century Spain. Here he uses everyday subject matter in his famous "A Girl and Her Duenna," in the National Gallery of Art, Washington, D.C., Widener Collection.

PAINTERS (continued)

SWITZERLAND

KAUFFMANN, Angelica (1741–1807). "Religion."
KLEE, Paul (1879–1940). "Twittering Machine."

UNITED STATES OF AMERICA

AUDUBON, John James (1785–1851). "Birds of America."
BELLOWS, George (1882–1925). "Stag at Sharkey's."
CASSATT, Mary (1845–1926). "Mother and Child."
CATLIN, George (1796–1872). Foremost painter of American Indians.
CHURCH, Frederick (1826–1900). Leading painter of the Hudson River School.
COLE, Thomas (1801–48). "Catskill Mountains."
EAKINS, Thomas (1844–1916). "The Swimming Hole."
HASSAM, Childe (1859–1935). "Fifth Avenue."
HARTLEY, Marsden (1877–1943). Abstract landscapist.
HOMER, Winslow (1836–1910). "The Gulf Stream."
JOHNS, Jasper (1930–   ). Leading abstract expressionist.
KENT, Rockwell (1882–1971). "Toilers of the Sea."
LUKS, George (1867–1933). "The Spielers."
MARIN, John (1870–1953). Famous for Maine seascapes.
MARSH, Reginald (1898–1954). "Why Not Use the El?"
MOTHERWELL, Robert (1915–   ). "Elegy for the Spanish Republic."
MOSES, Grandma (Anna Mary ˌRobertson) (1860–1961). "The Thanksgiving Turkey."
O'KEEFFE, Georgia (1887–   ). "Cow's Skull."
PEALE, Rembrandt (1778–1860). "The Court of Death."
POLLOCK, Jackson (1912–56). "Autumn Rhythm."
RAUSCHENBERG, Robert (1925–   ). "Gloria."
RAY, Man (1890–1978). "The Rope Dancer Accompanies Herself with Her Shadows."
REMINGTON, Frederic (1861–1909). Leading painter of U.S. West.

GEORGE BELLOWS worked in New York and portrayed the people and life of the city with a direct, unselfconscious realism. This painting is "Blue Morning," 1909, in the National Gallery of Art, Washington, D.C., gift of Chester Dale.

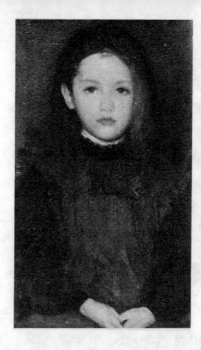

MARY CASSATT was an American who painted in France with Manet and Degas. Her pictures are pleasing because of their delicate simplicity and tone, and her favorite subject is a mother and child. "The Loge," National Gallery of Art, Washington, D.C., Chester Dale Collection.

JAMES McNEILL WHISTLER's portrait (above) of "Little Rose of Lyme Regis" in the Museum of Fine Arts, Boston, shows his extreme technical proficiency. He was most famous for the portrait of his mother.

CHILDE HASSAM was an American painter greatly influenced by Impressionism. Some of his paintings have a tapestry-like quality, as seen in "In the Rain," National Gallery of Art, Washington, D.C., gift of Chester Dale.

WINSLOW HOMER's "Breezing Up" is one of the most popular American paintings of the sea.

ROCKWELL, Norman (1894–1978). "Freedom from Want."
ROTHKO, Mark (1903–70). "Green on Blue."
RYDER, Albert Pinkham (1847–1917). "Death on a Pale Horse."

SARGENT, John Singer (1856–1925). "The Wyndham Sisters."
STUART, Gilbert (1755–1828). "Portrait of George Washington."
TRUMBULL, John (1786–1843). "Battle of Bunker's Hill."
WARHOL, Andy (1930?–). "Portrait of Marilyn Monroe."
WEIR, Julian Alden (1852–1919). "The Red Bridge."
WEST, Benjamin (1738–1820). "Death of General Wolfe."
WHISTLER, James Abbott McNeil (1834–1903). "Arrangement in Grey and Black—The Artist's Mother."
WOOD, Grant (1891–1942). "American Gothic."
WYETH, Andrew (1917–). "Christina's World."

GRANT WOOD's best-known painting, "American Gothic" in the Art Institute of Chicago, shows how he painted the American scene of the rural Midwest in a rigid, decorative style.

The Dance

Main Trends	Types of Dance Popular at the Time (*Basic rhythmic beat in parentheses*)
Pre-history Unorganized or loosely organized dances for warlike and communal purposes.	
c. 50 B.C. Mimes: dancing and singing spectacles Rome).	
14th Century Danse basse: low, slow gliding steps. Hault danse: with high fast steps.	Pavane (4); derived from instrumental music from Padua; possibly the first stylized dance. Galliard (3), also from Italy, where the name implies gaiety.
15th Century First true ballet, with settings by Leonardo da Vinci, danced at Tortona, 1489. Introduced at the court of Henry VIII of England as Masque.	Court ballet: Branle (2), English clog dance with circular figures. Allemande (2,4), i.e.: "from Germany," Courante (3), i.e.: "running," from It. *corrente* (current). Volta (3), very lively (It.: *volta*: vault).
16th Century Ballet comique. First complete printed account (Oct. 15, 1581), of a ballet to celebrate the marriage of Duke of Joyeuse and Marguerite of Lorraine. It was based on the story of Circe and choreographed by Baldassarino de Belgiojoso.	Morris dance, from Morocco.
17th Century Ballet Masquerade, often with hideous and elaborate masks.	Gigue (3,6,12), originally from English jig, the word from German *Geige*: "fiddle." Sarabande (3), slow and graceful, introduced to Spain *c.* 1588 from Morocco or West Indies.

Main Trends cont.	Types of Dance Popular at the Time cont.
	(Basic rhythmic beat in parentheses)

Playford's *English Dancing Master* published 1651: a collection of tunes and steps.

Bouree (4), lively dance, starting on the upbeat.
Chaconne (3), graceful dance introduced from Peru (*guacones, c.* 1580) via Spain.
Gavotte (2), medium pace, from Provençal *gavoto* (a native of the Alps).
Minuet (3), "smale steps"; rustic minuets occur in Strasbourg in 1682, but origin in the 15th century Branle.
Passacaglia (3), as chaconne above, but in minor key.

First waltz, developed from minuet and Landler in 1660; word "waltz" first used in 1754 in Austria.
Ballet systématique: Louis XIV established the Académie Royale de Danse 1661. 5 classic positions codified; first history of dancing published in 1682.

Rigaudon; Rigadoon (2,4), lively French dance.
Landler (3), rustic dance, from *Landl*: "small country."
Matelot (2) Dutch sailors' clog dance.
Contredanse (2,4) from Eng.: "country dance," but mistranslated as "counter-dance," i.e.: for opposing groups, and re-introduced into England in this form.
Cotillion (6), from French word for "petticoat," for 2 groups of 4 pairs each; developed into quadrille at the end of the 19th century.

18th Century
Ballet steps on toe-tips (on point) (*c.* 1800).

Reel (4), stylized form of Scottish dance.

19th Century
Square dance (*c.* 1815)
Can-can (*c.* 1835); high-kicking exhibitionist female dance popular on Parisian stages.

Quadrille (2,4).

Age of the great waltz composers: Josef Lanner; Johann Strauss; Emil Waldteufel, etc.

Polka (2), introduced to Paris in 1843 from Bohemian courtship dance (1-2-3-hop).
Cakewalk (2), graceful walking dance of competitive type with cakes as prizes, popular in Black America in 1872; introduced into ballrooms *c.* 1900.

20th Century
Ballet Russe established in Paris by Diaghilev, 1909.
New free dance forms emerging.

Samba (2), emerged from Brazil, 1885; known *c.* 1920 as Maxixe; resumed name "Samba" *c.* 1940.
Quickstep (2), invented in America 1900; reached peak of popularity in 1920's.
Tango (2), earliest contest in Nice, France, in 1907.
Barn dance (4), associated in America with festivities surrounding the completion of a new barn.
Two-step (2).
Boston (2), predecessor of the foxtrot.
Turkey Trot (2).

Ballroom dance craze, mostly couples dancing to small instrumental groups (*c.* 1920).

Foxtrot (4), slow and quick varieties, introduced in 1912 in America, allegedly named after Harry Fox. The slow foxtrot evolved *c.* 1927 into the "blues" dance.

Sadler's Wells (later the Royal) Ballet established in England by Ninette de Valois in 1931.

American Ballet founded by Lincoln Kirstein and Edward Warburg in 1934. Influenced development of American ballet style.

Growth of very energetic dancing, often to jazz or pseudo-jazz groups (from 1939).

Modern Discotheque style, i.e.: recorded music for dancing; originated in Parisian clubs (*c.* 1951).

Charleston (2), side kick from the knee. Named after a song about the town that saw the first ballet in America.

Pasodoble (2), Spanish-style two-step.

Rumba (8, i.e. 3 + 3 + 2), authentic Cuban dance.

Black Bottom (4), first mentioned in New York Times (Dec. 19, 1926), a type of athletic and jerky foxtrot.

Conga (4, i.e.: 1-2-3-kick), single-file dance developed in 1935 from Rumba and from aboriginal African dances.

Jitterbug and Jive (2,4).

Popularity of dances closely linked to the "hit-parade" progress of popular music and the consequent invention of many new dance styles.

Mambo (8), an off-beat Rumba of Cuban origin.

Rock 'n' Roll (2), introduced in 1953 by Bill Haley and his Comets in America; heavy beat and simple melody for energetic and free dancing.

Cha cha cha (2,4) (1954), a variation of the Mambo, couples dancing with lightly linked hands.

Twist (2) (1961), body-torsion and knee-flexing lively dance, with partners rarely in contact.

Bossa nova (2), lively Latin American dance.

Go-go (2,4) (1965), repetitious dance of verve, often exhibitionist.

Reggae (4) (1969), introduced from Jamaica, strong accentuations off-beat.

Pogo (2), introduced by "Punk Rockers" (1976). Dancers rise vertically from the floor in imitation of a pogo stick.

Philosophy

Branches of Philosophy

"Philosophy" is a word derived from the Greek word meaning "love of knowledge," and philosophy in the Western world began with the ancient Greeks. It is used to cover a wide area: the scientific arrangement of those principles which underlie all knowledge and existence. Needless to say, no one has yet covered the entire area.

The sphere of philosophy can be roughly delimited by stating how it is distinct from other areas of thought. It differs from religion since its quest for the underlying causes and principles of being and thinking does not depend on dogma and faith; and from science, since it does not depend solely on fact, but leans heavily on speculation. Its interrelation with both science and religion can be seen in the large number of philosophers who were also either theologians or scientists, and the few such as Blaise Pascal and Roger Bacon, who were all three. Philosophy developed from religion, becoming distinct when thinkers sought truth independent of theological considerations. Science in turn developed from philosophy, and all the branches of science from physics to psychology broke away from the all-embracing cover of philosophy—psychology being the last to do so, in the 20th century.

The vast number of works which have been written in what Bertrand Russell calls the "no-man's land" between theology and science make it especially difficult to generalize about the field. It may be somewhat easier if we break philosophy up into three spheres: ethics (the study of man's conduct), epistemology (the study of theories of knowledge) and metaphysics (the study of the universe). Such a division leaves out some important areas of philosophical speculation, but it will introduce a few of the most important writings.

1. ETHICS is the study of human conduct—as a rule with regard to what it *should be* rather than what it *is*. Philosophers have held many points of view about ideal human conduct but their opinions tend to resolve into an opposition between two main schools. One school, whom we may call the "Idealists," considers that the goodness or badness of a course of action must be judged by standards dictated from the other world—from God or from some force for good—external to man. The second school, who might be grouped under the term "Utilitarians," feels that the effect which a course of action produces in this world makes it good or bad.

The Idealist school was represented quite early in the history of Western philosophy by the Greek philosopher Plato, who wrote in the 4th century B.C. Plato, in a series of dialogues, has his ex-teacher Socrates discuss the problems of philosophy with friends and opponents.

These dialogues are important because they form a comprehensive system of philosophy which has probably never been bettered. They are also entertaining reading—if one does not become annoyed at the way in which Plato stacks the arguments in Socrates' favor.

Socrates' procedure is to draw out the wisdom from the gentleman with whom he is discussing the question. Socrates, in fact, rarely makes a statement. He prefers what advertising men call "the soft sell." That is to say, he asks questions which compel the others either to make the statements he wants them to make or to appear foolish.

In three of these dialogues especially—*The Protagoras, The Phaedo,* and *The Gorgias*—Plato develops a system of ethics which is essentially idealistic. Socrates propounds that the good comes from the realm of "ideas" or "forms." This is a sort of perfect other world which projects distorted copies of everything good down to the world we have to contend with. For Plato, individual conduct is good in so far as it is governed by the emanated spirit from above. Plato does not, of course, use the word "heaven" for the world of ideas, but he was adapted—after being modified by Aristotle, Plotinus, the church fathers, and all—for Christian purposes. One of the ways in which the knowledge from the realm of the "ideas" was communicated to mortals was by a voice or "demon." In the *Apology*, Socrates describes how this individual conscience has prevented him from wrongdoing.

Another important work which has to be classed with the idealists is Aristotle's *Nicomachean Ethics*. Aristotle was a pupil of Plato, and one would therefore expect him to be influenced by his master. Certainly, like Plato, he thinks of the good as a divine emanation, or overflow, but his ethics have a more "practical" bent. He equates happiness with the good and is responsible for the doctrine of the "golden mean." This states that every virtue is a mean, or middle-point, between two vices. Generosity, for instance, is the mean between prodigality and stinginess.

A more cynical approach was introduced by Niccolò Machiavelli, founder of the modern science of politics. In his famous book, *The Prince*, Machiavelli drew his conclusions from the very nature of man.

The same tendency to give idealism a practical bent is found in a more modern philosopher, Immanuel Kant. His idealistic aspect may be compared with Socrates' "demon." Kant maintains that there is in each man a still small voice which guides him as to right or wrong. It is as though each individual had a direct telephone to God.

But the part of Kant's ethics which is most famous is that connected with the phrase "categorical imperative." This phrase may seem a little difficult to decipher at first, but it rolls nicely on the tongue and its meaning is really quite simple—in Kant's own words: "Act only according to a maxim by which you can at the same time will that it shall become a general law." In other words, before acting in a certain way, the individual must ask himself: "If everybody did the same thing what would be the moral condition of the universe?" This is a practical consideration in the sense that it concerns the *result* of an action, but notice that Kant's concern is for the morality of the universe and not its happiness or earthly welfare. Kant's principal ethical works are *The Critique of Pure Reason, The Critique of Practical Reason, The Metaphysics of Morality*, and *The Metaphysics of Ethics*.

The opposing group of "utilitarian" ethics is concerned with the matter of earthly welfare. The earliest Western philosopher to represent this tradition is Epicurus, a Greek philosopher of the 4th century B.C. We have few of Epicurus' writings extant. What we do have—three letters, some aphorisms, and a few fragments—have been collected and translated into English by Cyril Bailey.

Instead of deriving ideas of right and wrong from above, as did the Socratics for example, Epicurus maintained that "we call pleasure the beginning and end of the blessed life." For this doctrine, Epicurus, and his disciples—especially the Roman poet Lucretius—were accused by the Christians of having a hog-philosophy. The term "Epicurean" was used—and often still is used—to describe one who indulges in excessive pleasure.

This usage is neither accurate nor just. Epicurus did not condone excesses. On the contrary, he said that pleasure was only good when moderate or "passive." "Dynamic" pleasure, which caused painful after-effects, was not good.

The utilitarian tradition has on the whole had more adherents than the idealistic tradition in modern philosophy. Jeremy Bentham, for example, writing in the 18th century, acknowledged his debt to Epicurus in his *Principles of Morals and Legislation.* Bentham agreed that pain and pleasure were the "sovereign masters" governing man's conduct. He added to this a doctrine of *utility* which argued that "the greatest happiness of the greatest number is the measure of right and wrong." On the whole, this is a likely theory to come from one who was as interested as Bentham was in government and legislation.

One of Bentham's disciples was James Mill, who founded the *Westminster Review* as an organ to express their opinions. James' son, John Stuart Mill, is perhaps the most famous of the Utilitarians. He extended Bentham's doctrines in a series of articles in *Frazer's Magazine.* Mill pointed out that there were different *qualities* of pleasure and pain, and that "some *kinds* of pleasure are more valuable than others." These articles were later put out in book form: *Utilitarianism.*

The Utilitarians have been enormously influential during the 20th century. In England their principles were a beacon which shone out a path for British Socialism. The Socialists professed to be concerned with the greatest good for the greatest number in the political sphere, and they found the ethics of the Utilitarians adaptable to their own ends.

In the U.S. the influence remained primarily philosophical and sociological. There the Utilitarians made an impact on the Pragmatists. The Pragmatists held that "the *right* is only the expedient in our way of thinking"—to quote William James, whose *Pragmatism* is the best-known book produced by this school. The idea that whatever works is right is not as shallow as it may seem at first. Much depends on the standards adopted in deciding what works. The philosophy of the Pragmatists has naturally been important to sociologists who are concerned with the science of social relations in a community. This is one more instance of the way in which philosophical speculation can overlap into other fields.

2. METAPHYSICS. The term "metaphysics" originated as the title of one of Aristotle's treatises. It probably meant only that he wrote it after his *Physics,* but it was once thought to signify study beyond the realm of physics. Today it is usually employed to describe the speculation as to the nature of true reality and the structure of the universe. This is vague and covers a lot of ground.

The sort of questions which metaphysicians have asked and attempted to answer are:

How was the universe conceived?

What is the relationship between God and the universe?—Did he simply wind it up like an eternal clock and then let it run, or is it like a top which he has to keep whipping?

Does the universe have any real substance or is it an illusion?

What is the true nature of matter?

Is it composed of separate atoms? If so, what is the nature of these atoms? Are they solid, etc.? . . .

These questions all concern the origin and condition of the universe in which man lives, and, as we might expect, they came up early in the

JOHN STUART MILL (left) pointed out the different qualities of pleasure and pain and formed the philosophy of Utilitarianism. Mill's father was a disciple of JEREMY BENTHAM (right) who measured utility as the greatest good for the greatest number.

history of philosophy. Before Aristotle had invented the term "metaphysics"—as early as the 6th century B.C.—pre-Socratic Greek philosophers were offering their solutions of the mysteries of the universe.

Much of the speculation of these pre-Socratic philosophers was centered on speculation about the four *elements* which they thought made up the universe. Empedocles, who, according to legend, threw himself into the volcano at Mt. Etna to prove his immortality—and failed—first defined earth, air, fire, and water as the four basic elements. Others attempted to make one of these the most important, or *primary*, element from which the others were derived. Thales—one of the seven wise men of Greece—thought water was on top. Heraclitus' primary element was fire. Anaximander reasoned that none of the four was primary. They must, he said, exist in perpetual balance.

The evidence with which these gentlemen backed their theories has some of the rashness of pioneer science. Thales reasoned that water must be the primary element because it comes from the sky (rain), out of the earth (springs), and is everywhere prevalent (seas and lakes).

The same elementary approach characterized the early atomic theories. Democritus maintained, in the 4th century B.C., that everything in the universe was made up of atoms. He had no idea of the structure of atoms and the sort of evidence that he offered for their existence was that, since substances were porous, they *must* be made up of separate atoms. Of course, neither he nor the later atomists such as Epicurus and Lucretius realized—even in an elementary form—the implications of atomic theory which have been forced on our attention.

All this fumbling after the facts of life by the early metaphysicians may seem clumsy by modern scientific standards, but such fumbling often anticipated later, more precise scientific work. This relationship has been stated poetically by Will Durant, who says in *The Story of Philosophy:*

"Philosophy seems to stand still, perplexed; but only because she leaves the fruits of victory to her daughters, the sciences, and herself passes on, divinely discontent, to the uncertain and unexplored."

123

3. EPISTEMOLOGY is the study of the nature, grounds, and validity of man's knowing:

To what extent is the evidence of the senses valid?

Is true knowledge *inductive*—to be gained by inducing evidence and construing this evidence into theories and laws—or is it *deductive*—to be gained by deducing facts from what appear to be self-evident truths?

Can we know God by reason, or by faith only? Obviously such questions must interest those concerned with the gathering of human knowledge.

One of the matters which epistemologists have debated most consistently concerns the learning process. One school of thought asserts that knowledge is born in the individual and has only to be drawn forth. The other point of view is that at birth the mind is a *tabula rasa*—blank sheet—on which knowledge is imprinted.

The first school is represented classically by Plato. In the *Theaetetus* especially, he discusses various theories of knowledge and discards those built on the shifting sands of sense perception. The senses are, he feels, too fallible. True knowledge comes from those general notions which are derived from the realm of the *ideas*—which the soul possesses prior to birth. This is the attitude reflected by Wordsworth when he says in the ode, "Intimations of Immortality":

> Our birth is but a sleep and a forgetting:
> The Soul that rises with us, our life's Star,
> Hath had elsewhere its setting,
> And cometh from afar:
> Not in entire forgetfulness,
> And not in utter nakedness,
> But trailing clouds of glory do we come
> From God, who is our home. . . .

Had Plato been reincarnated in the 19th century he would have agreed with the thought expressed in these lines. He would have pointed out that the Socratic method, with its leading questions, was intended

JOHN LOCKE believed that at birth our minds are a blank sheet on which our experiences are written. He propounded religious toleration and personal political liberty.

to recapture some of the "clouds of glory (true knowledge)" and to restore the soul to its condition before the "sleep and forgetting (birth)."

This is elaborated in *The Republic*, where Socrates draws the famous simile of the cave. This compares man to a prisoner, chained in a cave in such a way that he can only look at one wall of the cave. Behind the chained prisoner is a fire, and by its light, he can see the shadows of himself and other things behind him as they dance on the wall. He thinks that these shadows are real objects because he has never seen real objects. The philosopher-guardian—the ideal man of *The Republic*—is he who can break his chain, step out into the daylight, and see reality. He must then go back into the cave and try to communicate true knowledge to those still chained in the cave. His task is difficult because, having come in from the region of light, he will not be able to see the shadows as well as the people he is trying to convince.

The classic representative of the second school is John Locke—a 17th century philosopher. In his *Essay on Human Understanding*, Locke defines what is really the opposite point of view to Plato's. He is the pioneer proponent of the *tabula rasa*. Locke regards the mind at birth as comparable to an empty cabinet with two compartments. As we live, one compartment is filled with our *perceptions* and the other with our *sensations*. From these two combined we get our *idea*.

This theory tends to make knowledge a matter of experience and mental processing rather than one of religious insight. As one might expect, Locke's theories were important influences in those fields which investigate the processes of mental activity—such as psychology and education. This is one more example of the manner in which philosophy has invaded non-theoretical realms.

Theories of Philosophy

As we have seen, since the days of the early Greeks, philosophers have been divided into different schools and have advanced opposing theories. Among the many basic outlooks and theories not already discussed but which have developed since Thales of Miletus (624–550 B.C.) first questioned the nature of ultimate reality, the following may be listed:

1. *Absolutism:* the theory that there is an ultimate reality in which all differences are reconciled.

2. *Agnosticism:* the position that the ultimate answer to all fundamental inquiries is that we do not know.

3. *Altruism:* the principle of living and acting in the interest of others rather than oneself.

4. *Asceticism:* the belief that withdrawal from the physical world into the inner world of the spirit is the highest good attainable.

5. *Atheism:* rejection of the concept of God as a workable hypothesis.

6. *Atomism:* the belief that the entire universe is composed of distinct and indivisible units.

7. *Conceptualism:* the doctrine that universal ideas are neither created by finite (human) minds, nor entirely apart from absolute mind (God).

8. *Critical Idealism:* the concept that man cannot determine whether there is anything beyond his own experience.

9. *Critical Realism:* the theory that reality is tri-partite, that in addition to the mental and physical aspects of reality, there is a third aspect called essences.

10. *Criticism:* the theory that the path to knowledge lies midway between dogmatism and skepticism.

11. *Determinism:* the belief that the universe follows a fixed or pre-determined pattern.

12. *Dialectical Materialism:* the theory that reality is strictly material and is based on a struggle between opposing forces, with occasional interludes of harmony.

13. *Dogmatism:* assertion of a belief without authoritative support.

14. *Dualism:* the belief that the world consists of two radically independent and absolute elements, e.g., good and evil, spirit and matter.

15. *Egoism:* in ethics the belief that the serving of one's own interests is the highest end.

16. *Empiricism:* rejection of all *a priori* knowledge in favor of experience and induction.

17. *Evolutionism:* the concept of the universe as a progression of inter-related phenomena.

18. *Existentialism:* denial of objective universal values—man must create values for himself through action; the self is the ultimate reality.

19. *Hedonism:* the doctrine that pleasure is the highest good.

20. *Humanism:* any system that regards human interests and the human mind as paramount in the universe.

21. *Idealism:* any system that regards thought or the idea as the basis either of knowledge or existence; in ethics, the search for the best or the highest.

22. *Instrumentalism:* the concept of ideas as instruments, rather than as goals of living.

23. *Intuitionism:* the doctrine that the perception of truth is by intuition, not analysis.

24. *Materialism:* the doctrine that denies the independent existence of spirit, and asserts the existence of only one substance—matter; belief that physical well-being is paramount.

25. *Meliorism:* the belief that the world is capable of improvement, and that man has the power of helping in its betterment, a position between optimism and pessimism.

26. *Monism:* belief in only one ultimate reality, whatever its nature.

27. *Mysticism:* belief that the ultimate real lies in direct contact with the divine.

28. *Naturalism:* a position that seeks to explain all phenomena by means of strictly natural (as opposed to supernatural) categories.

29. *Neutral Monism:* theory that reality is neither physical nor spiritual, but capable of expressing itself as either.

30. *Nominalism:* the doctrine that general terms have no corresponding reality either in or out of the mind, and are, in effect, nothing more than words.

31. *Optimism:* any system that holds that the universe is the best of all possible ones, and that all will work out for the best.

32. *Pantheism:* the belief that God is identical with the universe.

33. *Personalism:* theory that ultimate reality consists of a plurality of spiritual beings or independent persons.

34. *Pessimism:* belief that the universe is the worst possible and that all is doomed to evil.

35. *Phenomenalism:* theory that reality is only appearance.

36. *Pluralism:* belief that there are more than two irreducible components of reality.

37. *Positivism:* the doctrine that man can have no knowledge except of phenomena, and that the knowledge of phenomena is relative, not absolute.

38. *Pragmatism:* a method that makes practical consequences the test of truth.

39. *Rationalism:* the theory that reason alone, without the aid of experience, can arrive at the basic reality of the universe.

40. *Relativism:* rejection of the concept of the absolute.

41. *Skepticism:* the doctrine that no facts can be certainly known.
42. *Theism:* acceptance of the concept of God as a workable hypothesis.
43. *Transcendentalism:* belief in an ultimate reality that transcends human experience.
44. *Voluntarism:* the theory that will is the determining factor in the universe.

Philosophers Through the Ages

PRE-SOCRATIC GREEKS

Thales (624–550 B.C.). Regarded as the starting point of Western philosophy; the first exponent of monism.

Anaximander (611–547 B.C.). Continued Thales' quest for universal substance, but reasoned that that substance need not resemble known substances.

Anaximenes (588–524 B.C.). Regarded air as the ultimate reality.

Pythagoras (572–497 B.C.). Taught a dualism of body and soul.

Parmenides (*c.* 495 B.C.). Formulated the basic doctrine of idealism; member of Eleatic school, so-called because based at Elea in southern Italy.

Heraclitus (533–475 B.C.). Opposed concept of a single ultimate reality; held that one permanent thing is change.

Zeno of Elea (490–430 B.C.). Argued that plurality and change are appearances, not realities.

Empedocles (*c.* 495–435 B.C.). Held that there were four irreducible substances (water, fire, earth and air) and two forces (love and hate).

Anaxagoras (500–428 B.C.). Believed in an indefinite number of basic substances.

Protagoras (481–411 B.C.). An early relativist and humanist; doubted human ability to attain absolute truth.

CLASSIC GREEK PHILOSOPHERS

Socrates (469–399 B.C.). Developed Socratic method of inquiry; teacher of Plato, through whose writings his idealistic philosophy was disseminated.

Democritus (460–370 B.C.). Began tradition in Western thought of explaining universe in mechanistic terms.

Antisthenes (*c.* 406 B.C.). Chief of group known as the Cynics; stressed discipline and work as the essential good.

Aristippus (*c.* 395 B.C.). Chief of Cyrenaic offshoot of Socratic school; taught that pleasure, from whatever source, is the greatest good.

Plato (427–347 B.C.). Founded the Academy at Athens; developed the idealism of his teacher Socrates; teacher of Aristotle.

Aristotle (384–322 B.C.). Taught that there are four factors in causation: the interrelated factors of form and matter; motive cause, which produces change; and the end, for which a process of change occurs.

HELLENISTIC PERIOD

Epicurus (341–270 B.C.). Taught that the test of truth is in sensation; proponent of atomism and hedonism.

Zeno of Citium (335–265 B.C.). Chief of Stoics, so called because they met in the Stoa Poikile or Painted Porch at Athens; proponent of pantheism, evolutionism; taught that man's role is to accept nature and all it offers, good or bad.

Lucretius (96–55 B.C.). Roman disciple of Epicurus; principal teacher of atomism.

Epictetus (60–117 A.D.). Developed Stoic teachings of Zeno of Citium.

Philosophers Through the Ages (continued)

Plotinus (205–270 A.D.). Chief expounder of Neo-Platonism, a combining of the teachings of Plato with Oriental concepts.

Augustine (354–430 A.D.). Known to history as St. Augustine; expounder of optimism and absolutism; believed that God transcends human comprehension; one of greatest influences on medieval Christian thought.

Boethius (480–524 A.D.). A Neo-Platonist, his great work, *The Consolations of Philosophy*, served to transmit Greek philosophy to medieval Europe.

MEDIEVAL PERIOD

John Scotus Erigena (810–877). Irish; first important philosopher of medieval Europe; taught that religion and philosophy were one; his pantheism led to condemnation of his works by the Church.

Avicenna (980–1037). Arabic follower of Aristotle and Neo-Platonism; his works led to a revival of interest in Aristotle in 13th-century Europe.

Anselm (1033–1109). Italian; known to history as St. Anselm; a realist, he is famous for his examination of the proof of God's existence.

Peter Abelard (1079–1142). Leading theologian and philosopher of medieval France; his nominalism caused him to be declared a heretic by the Church.

Averroes (1126–98). Great philosopher of Mohammedan Spain, and leading commentator on Aristotle; regarded religion as allegory for the common man, philosophy as the path to truth.

Moses Maimonides (1135–1204). Leading Jewish student of Aristotle in medieval Mohammedan world; sought to combine Aristotelian teaching with that of the Bible.

Roger Bacon (1214–94). English student of Aristotle, advocated return to Hebrew and Greek versions of Scripture; an empiricist.

St. Bonaventure (1221–74). Born John of Fidanza in Italy; friend of Thomas Aquinas; student of Plato and Aristotle; a mystic and ascetic.

St. Thomas Aquinas (1225–74). Italian; leading philosopher of the Scholastics or Christian philosophers of the Middle Ages; evolved a compromise between Aristotle and Scripture, based on the belief that faith and reason are in agreement; his philosophical system is known as Thomism.

THE RENAISSANCE

John Duns Scotus (*c.* 1270–1308). Scottish; student of Augustine and Anselm; stressed will rather than reason, in opposition to Aquinas; held that faith and reason cannot be fully reconciled.

Marsilo Ficino (1433–99). Protégé of Cosimo de'Medici, who had established a Platonic Academy in Florence, Ficino translated Plato's *Dialogues* in an effort to demonstrate that there was no conflict between Platonism and Christianity.

Desiderius Erasmus (1466–1536). Greatest of the humanists, he helped spread the ideas of the Renaissance in his native Holland and throughout northern Europe.

Niccolo Machiavelli (1469–1527). Italian; a realist, he placed the state as the paramount power in human affairs.

Giordano Bruno (1548–1600). Italian; a pantheist, he opposed Aristotelianism, and taught that God is all Being and the universe is his manifestation.

TRANSITION TO MODERN THOUGHT

Francis Bacon (1561–1626). English; in his major work, *Novum Organum*, he sought to replace the deductive logic of Aristotle with an inductive system in interpreting nature.

René Descartes (1596–1650). French; dualist, rationalist, theist, Descartes and his system, Cartesianism, are at the base of all modern knowledge. What he furnished is a theory of knowledge that underlies

FRANCIS BACON (left) sought to replace Aristotle's deductive logic with an inductive system. Another Englishman, THOMAS HOBBES (right), believed that the natural state of man is war.

modern science and philosophy. "All the sciences are conjoined with one another and interdependent," he wrote.

Thomas Hobbes (1588–1679). English materialist who believed the natural state of man is war; outlined a theory of human government in his book *Leviathan*, whereby the state and men's subordination to it form the sole solution to human selfishness and aggressiveness.

Blaise Pascal (1623–62). French theist who held that sense and reason are mutually deceptive; truth lies between dogmatism and skepticism.

Baruch Spinoza (1632–77). Dutch rationalist, parallelist, pantheist, monist, absolutist, he developed ideas of Descartes while rejecting his dualism.

John Locke (1632–1704). English dualist, empiricist; in his great *Essay Concerning Human Understanding* he sought to refute rationalist view that all knowledge derives from first principles.

18TH CENTURY

George Berkeley (1685–1753). Irish idealist and theist who taught that material things exist only in being perceived; his system of subjective idealism is called Berkeleianism.

Gottfried Wilhelm von Leibniz (1646–1716). German idealist, absolutist, optimist (his view that this is the best of all possible worlds was ridiculed by Voltaire in *Candide*); held that reality consisted of units of force called monads.

David Hume (1711–76). English empiricist who carried on ideas of Locke, but developed a system of skepticism (Humism) according to which human knowledge is limited to experience of ideas and sensations, whose truth cannot be verified.

Jean-Jacques Rousseau (1712–78). French political philosopher whose concepts have had a profound influence on modern thought; advocated a "return to nature" to counteract the inequality among men brought about by civilized society.

Immanuel Kant (1724–1804). German founder of critical philosophy. At first influenced by Leibniz, then by Hume, he sought to find an alternative approach to the rationalism of the former and the skepticism of the latter; in ethics, formulated the Categorical Imperative—which states that what applies to oneself must apply to everyone else unconditionally—a restatement of the Christian precept "Do unto others as you would have them do unto you."

Jeremy Bentham (1748–1832). Believed, like Kant, that the interests of the individual are one with those of society, but regarded fear of consequences rather than basic principle as the motivation for right action.

Johann Gottlieb Fichte (1762–1814). German; formulated a philosophy of absolute idealism based on Kant's ethical concepts.

19TH CENTURY

Georg Wilhelm Friedrich Hegel (1770–1831). German; his metaphysical system, known as Hegelianism, was rationalist and absolutist, based on the belief that thought and being are one, and nature is the manifestation of an Absolute Idea.

Arthur Schopenhauer (1788–1860). German; foremost expounder of pessimism, expressed in *The World as Will and Idea*. Rejected absolute idealism as wishful thinking, and taught that the only tenable attitude lay in utter indifference to an irrational world; an idealist who held that the highest ideal was nothingness.

Auguste Comte (1798–1857). French founder of positivism, a system which denied transcendant metaphysics and stated that the Divinity and man were one, that altruism is man's highest duty, and that scientific principles explain all phenomena.

John Stuart Mill (1806–73). English; utilitarian who differed from Bentham by recognizing differences in quality as well as quantity in pleasure.

Sören Kierkegaard (1813–1855). Danish religious existentialist, whose thought is the basis of modern (atheistic) existentialism; taught that "existence precedes essence," that only existence has reality, and the individual has a unique value.

Charles S. Peirce (1839–1914). American who founded philosophical school called pragmatism; regarded logic as the basis of philosophy and taught that the test of an idea is whether it works.

Ernst Mach (1838–1916). Austrian physicist and positivist who rejected *a priori* principles and sought to rid science of all metaphysical content. His work contributed largely to modern school of logical positivism.

Herbert Spencer (1820–1903). English evolutionist whose "synthetic philosophy" interpreted all phenomena according to the principle of evolutionary progress.

Friedrich Wilhelm Nietzsche (1844–1900). German evolutionist, egoist, who held that the "will to power" is basic in life, that the spontaneous is to be preferred to the orderly; attacked Christianity as a system that fostered the weak, whereas the function of evolution is to evolve "supermen."

William James (1842–1910). American pragmatist who held that reality is always in the making and that each man should choose the philosophy best suited to him.

20TH CENTURY

George H. Howison (1834–1916). American who developed system of "personal idealism" and taught that absolutism was incompatible with human freedom and responsibility.

Edmond Husserl (1859–1938). German who developed system called "phenomenology," which asserts that realities other than mere appearance exist—called essences.

Josiah Royce (1855–1966). American who developed "synthetic idealism"; held that four basic temperaments—realistic, mystical,

HERBERT SPENCER
interpreted all phenomena
according to the principle of
evolutionary progress.

critical rationalistic and synthetic idealistic—all approached ultimate attainment of the Real, but by different paths; thus all philosophies have a degree of truth, their differences lie in emphasis.

Bertrand Russell (1872–   ). English agnostic who adhered to many systems of philosophy before becoming chief expounder of scientism, the view that all knowledge is solely attainable by the scientific method.

George Santayana (1863–1952). An American born in Spain; a foremost critical realist who held that the ultimate substance of the world is matter in motion—and the mind itself is a product of matter in motion.

Henri Bergson (1859–1941). French evolutionist who asserted the existence of a "vital impulse" that carries the universe forward, with no fixed beginning and no fixed end—the future is determined by the choice of alternatives made in the present.

John Dewey (1859–1952). American; basically a pragmatist, he developed a system known as instrumentalism.

Martin Heidegger (1889–   ). German student of Husserl, he furthered development of phenomenology; an existentialist committed to destruction of existing philosophies arising from the Greek tradition.

Alfred North Whitehead (1861–1947). English evolutionist who held that reality must not be interpreted in atomistic terms, but in terms of events; that God is intimately present in the universe, yet distinct from it, a view called panentheism, as opposed to pantheism, which simply equates God and Nature.

Alfred J. Ayer (1910–   ). English; principal advocate of logical positivism, a modern extension of the thinking of Hume and Comte.

Jacques Maritain (1882–   ). French-American; a leading force in Neo-Thomism, the modern French Catholic movement based on the philosophy of Aquinas with modifications derived from Descartes and Kant.

Jean-Paul Sartre (1905–   ). French; developed existentialist thought of Heidegger; atheistic supporter of a subjective, irrational human existence, as opposed to an orderly overall reality.

131

Language

Origins of the English Language

The three Germanic dialects on which English is based are descended from the Indo-Germanic or Aryan family of languages, spoken since *circa* 3000 B.C. by the nomads of the Great Lowland Plain of Europe, which stretches from the Aral Sea in the Soviet Union to the Rhine in West Germany. Now only fragments of Old Lithuanian contain what is left of this ancestral tongue.

Of the three inherited Germanic dialects, the first was Jutish, brought into England in 449 A.D. from Jutland. This was followed 40 years later by Saxon, brought from Holstein, and Anglian, which came with the still later incursions from the area of Schleswig-Holstein.

These three dialects were superimposed on the 1,000-year-old indigenous Celtic tongue, along with what Latin had survived in the towns from nearly 15 generations of Roman occupation (43–410 A.D.). The next major event in the history of the English language was the first of many Viking invasions, beginning in 793, from Denmark and Norway. Norse and Danish left permanent influences on the Anglo-Frisian Old English, though Norse never survived as a separate tongue in England beyond 1035, the year of the death of King Canute (Cnut), who had then reigned for 19 years over England, 16 years over Denmark and 7 years over Norway.

The Scandinavian influence now receded before Norman French, though Norse still struggled on in remote parts of Scotland until about 1630 and in the Shetland Islands until *c.* 1750. The Normans were, however, themselves really Vikings, who in five generations had become converts to the Latin culture and language of northern France.

For three centuries after the Norman conquest of 1066 by William I, descendant of Rollo the Viking, England lived under a trilingual system. The mother tongue of all the first 12 Kings and Queens, from William I (1066–1087) until as late as Richard II (1377–1399), was Norman. English became the language of court proceedings only during the reign of Edward III, in October, 1362, and the language for teaching in the Universities of Oxford and Cambridge in *c.* 1380.

English did not really crystallize as an amalgam of Anglo-Saxon and Latin root forms until the 14th century, when William Langland (*c.* 1332–*c.* 1400), and Geoffrey Chaucer (?1340–1400) were the pioneers of a literary tradition, which culminated in William Shakespeare, who died in 1616, just four years before the sailing of the *Mayflower*.

Prefixes

a- or **an-** (Gk. *a-, an-*) without, lacking, not: anemia, lacking blood; aneroid, not wet (barometer without liquid); asymmetric, not symmetrical; amoral, without morals.

a-, ab- or **abs-** (L. *a, ab, abs*) away from: abrasion, a rubbing away; aboriginal, from the original, hence primitive; avert, turn away.

acro (Gk. *akros*) highest, at extremity of: acronym, a word formed from initial letters of other words, e.g. N.A.T.O.; acropolis, elevated city.

allo- or **all-** (Gk. *alos*) other, another: allergy, other (abnormal) sensitivity; allotrope, other form, *e.g.* graphite and diamond are allotropes of carbon.

alti- or **alto-** (L. *altus*) elevated, high: altitude, height; alto-cumulus, cloud form found only at an altitude of over 10,000 ft.

ambi- (L. *ambo*) on both sides: ambidextrous, able to use (or write with) both hands; ambivalent, having either or both of two different values; ambiguous, driving in both directions, hence of doubtful meaning.

amphi- (Gk. *amphi*) around, double, both sides of: amphitheatre, a circular or oval theatre; amphibian, animal living in both (*i.e.* on land and in water).

ampli- (L. *amplus*) large, wide: amplify, make wider (in electricity to make stronger); amplitude, width as applied particularly to wave motions.

an- or **ana-** (Gk. *ana*) up, throughout, up again: anabaptist, believer in being baptized again; anatomy, cutting up; analysis, breaking up (again).

andr- or **andro-** (Gk. *andros*) male: andrology, study of diseases peculiar to males (*cf.* gynaeco-); androgynous, having both male and female characteristics.

anomo- or **anomal-** (Gk. *anōmalos, anomos*) not even, irregular: anomalous, not in agreement with the usual order; anomodent, having irregular teeth.

ant- or **anti** (Gk. *ant-, anti-*) against, opposite to: anti-slavery, opposed to slavery; antipodes, opposite feet, hence opposite point on Earth, *e.g.* U.S. to China; antacid, substance which neutralizes (stomach) acid.

ante- (L. *ante*) before (in time or in position): antenatal, before birth; anteroom, room leading into larger room.

anthrop- (Gk. *anthrōpos*) man, human: anthropoid, manlike, as in anthropoid ape; philanthropist, lover of mankind: anthropologist, one who studies man scientifically.

apo- (Gk. *apo-*) away from, detached: apogee, the point on a satellite's orbit most distant from the Earth; apoplexy, struck away, paralysis, caused by blood leaving the brain; apologize, speaking away that which has caused offense.

arch-, arche- or **archi-** (Gk. *arch-*) first (in time), original, hence chief: archetype, original type or mode, *e.g.* Cristofori's pianoforte; architrave, principal beam across the top of columns.

archeo- (Gk. *archaios*) ancient: archeology, study of ancient history of artifacts; archean, rocks more ancient than Cambrian.

aut- or **auto-** (Gk. *autos*) self, by itself (hence independently): automatic, working by itself; autophagous, able to feed itself from birth.

bath-, batho- or **bathy-** (Gk. *bathos*, noun; *bathys*, adjective) depth, deep: bathyscaphe, depth boat or deep sea exploration vehicle; bathometer, instrument for measuring depth of the ocean.

bi- or **bin-** (L. *bis, bini*) twice, in twos: biped, animal with two legs; biennial, a plant producing seed in its second year, also any event occurring every two years; biceps, the upper arm muscle with two points of attachment; binocular, performed by, or adapted to, both eyes.

bio- (Gk. *bios*) life: biology, the study of living things; symbiotic, pertaining to a mutually helpful state of living together, *e.g.* rhinoceros (danger warning) and rhinoceros bird (feeding on nits).

cat-, cata-, cato-, kata- or **kato-** (Gk. *kata*) down, against: cataract, a falling down of water (shallow waterfalls) or of skin over the eye; cathedral, edifice containing a bishop's throne where he sits down; katabatic, a downward wind.

circum- (L. *circum*) around, about: circumstances, things standing about us; circumference, the line which forms a circle, hence the length of such a line.

cis- (L. *cis*) on *this* side: cis-Alpine, on this (the near) side of the Alps; similarly cis-Atlantic or cis-lunar.

co- (L. *cum*) with, together: cooperate, work together; co-champion, joint champion; coexist, exist at the same place and/or time.

com-, con- or **cor-** (L. *com, con-*) with, together: congenital, properties with which one is born; contagious, touching together, disease transmitted thus.

contra- or **counter-** (L. *contra*) against, opposite: contradict, say against or opposite; a contra, a bookkeeping entry which is entered on the opposite side to cancel another; counterattack, attack back or in response.

crypto- (Gk. *krytos*) hidden: crypt, underground or hidden cell; cryptogram, hidden message, code or cipher; crypto-Communist, a secretive or non-Party Communist.

cyclo- (Gk. *kyklos*) ring, circle: encyclopedia, work of all around knowledge; megacycles, millions of cycles; cyclic, a compound with a ring of atoms, *e.g.* benzene.

de- (L. *de*) down, away: deciduous (of trees), one whose leaves fall down; dehydrate, take water away from; denude, make completely bare.

dextro- (L. *dexter*) to, or on, the right side, right: dextrogyre, circling to the right; dexterous, right-handed, skilful in use of hands.

di- (Gk. *di-, dis*) two, twice, away: dicrotic, having a double beat; digress, to wander away.

dia- (Gk. *dia*) through, across: diameter, a line across circle passing through the center; diagnosis, knowing through.

dich-, dicha-, diche- or **dicho-** (Gk. *dicha*) apart, in two: dichotomy, cut in two; dichogamy, separate marriage, of plants in which self-fertilizing is impossible.

dipl- or **diplo-** (Gk. *diploos*) double, twofold: diploma, sheet folded in two; diploid, possessing a double set of chromosomes.

dis- (L. *dis*) apart, asunder, completely: dissociate, to become disconnected; distort, to twist asunder or twist thoroughly.

dupl- or **dupli-** (L. *duplex*) double, twofold: duplicate, make double or exact copy; duplex, a two-storied apartment or house.

dys- (Gk. *dys*) bad, ill, difficult: dyspepsia, weak digestion; dysentery, bad or disordered intestines; dysphagia, difficulty in swallowing.

e-, ef- or **ex-** (L. *ex-*) out of, free from: eject, thrown out; eviscerate, to disembowel; enucleate, to remove nucleus (as in tonsillectomy); effluent, outflowing.

ec- (Gk. *ek-*) out, out of: ectopic, displaced from normal position; eczema, an outboiling, eruption of the skin.

ect- or **ecto-** (Gk. *ektos*) outside: ectozoon, a parasitic insect infecting the surface of the body; ectoplasm, outer part of the protoplasm of a cell.

en- or **em-** (Gk. *en* L. *in*) in, into: embolism, "thrown in," hence blood vessel blockage; enclose, include or place into.

end-, endo-, ent- or **ento-** (Gk. *endon* or *entos*) within: endomorph, a mineral enclosed within another; endoscope, instrument for looking inside the body; endocrine, glands which secrete internally or within; entogastric, within the stomach or intestines.

ep- or **epi-** (Gk. *epi*) upon, over: epidemic, a disease spread over a wide area; epitaph, an inscription upon a tomb; epicenter, a point immediately over or above the focus of an earthquake.

equi- (L. *aequus*) equal: equinox, time of year when the length of daylight and darkness are equal; equator, the great circle dividing the Earth into two equal parts.

eu- or **ev-** (Gk. *eu*) good, well, true: eugenics, study of methods of improving human stock; euphoria, feeling of well being (often artificial); euthanasia, painless death.

exo- (Gk. *exō*) outside: exophthalmic (referring to goiter) in which the eyes stand out; exoskeletal, hard or bony covering on the outside of the body, *e.g.* fingernails.

extra- (L. *extra*) without, outside (scope): extragalactic, outside our own galaxy, beyond the Milky Way; extracurricular, outside the curriculum or normal course of study.

ge- or **geo-** (Gk. *gē*) the Earth: geography, Earth measurement, hence descriptive study of the Earth's surface; geoid, Earth shaped, *i.e.* a very slightly flattened sphere.

ger-, **gero-** or **gerat-** (Gk. *gēras*) old age: gerontocracy, rule by old men; geriatrics, medical care of the aged.

gyn-, **gyno-** or **gyneco-** (Gk. *gynē*, genitive *gynaikos*) a woman: gynecology, study of functions and diseases peculiar to women; misogynist, one who hates or professes to hate women.

hapl- or **haplo-** (Gk. *haploos*) single: haplodont, possessing single crowned molars; haploid, cells with a single set of chromosomes.

hemi- (Gk. *hēmi-*) half: hemiplegia, paralysis of one side of the body; hemisphere, half a sphere.

heter- or **hetero-** (Gk. *heteros*) other, different: heterogeneous, of different kinds; heterozygous, possessing both of a pair of contrasting genes, *e.g.* blue and brown eye genes from each parent.

hol- or **holo-** (Gk. *holos*) complete, whole: holocene, completely recent, *i.e.* current geochronological era; holocaust, wholesale sacrifice, hence massacre.

homo- (Gk. *homos*) same: homologous, possessing the same essential qualities; homosexual, having sexual interest towards one of the same sex.

homeo- (Gk. *homoios*) similar: homeopathy, similar suffering, *i.e.* a medical system based on the belief that cure is effected by inducing symptoms similar to the disease.

hydat-, **hydr-** or **hydro-** (Gk. *hydōr*) water: hydrosphere, layer of the Earth's oceans; hydatidiform, a sac containing watery liquid.

hygro- (Gk. *hygros*) damp, wet: hygroscopic, moisture-absorbing; hygrometer, humidity-measuring instrument.

hyp- or **hypo-** (Gk. *hypo*) less than usual, under: hypotension, low blood pressure; hypodermic, under the skin.

hyper- (Gk. *hyper*) above, beyond, over: hypertension, high blood pressure; hyperon, an atomic particle of greater weight than a proton; hypersensitive, more than usually sensitive.

in- (also **il-**, **im-**, **ir-**) (L. *in-*) (a) in, into, on, toward; (b) not: (a) innate, inborn; illuminate, sending light into; irradiate, sending radiations into; (b) insomnia, inability to sleep; irregular, not regular.

infra- (L. *infra-*) below: infra dig (*infra dignitatem*), beneath the dignity of; infrarenal, below the kidneys.

inter- (L. *inter*) between, among: interglacial, between ice ages; intercostal, between the ribs.

intr- or **intra-** (L. *intra*) within, inside: intradepartmental, between and within departments; intravenous, introduced inside a vein; intramural, inside the walls, or within the confines of an edifice.

intro- (L. *intro*) to the inside: introvert, a person given to self-inspection and sensitive to how he is regarded by others.

is- or **iso-** (Gk. *isos*) equal, similar: isosceles, equal-legged (of a triangle); isomer, chemical compound with equal parts (but different properties).

juxta- (L. *juxta*) near to: juxtaposition, placing two or more things close together.

Prefixes (continued)

lept- or lepto- (Gk. *leptos*) thin, small: leptodactylous, thin-fingered; leptodermatous, thin-skinned.

levo- (L. *laevus*) to the left: levotropism, a tending or turning toward the left; levorotatory, turning the polarization plane to the left.

lip- or lipo- (Gk. *lipos*) fat, lard: lipogenous, fat-producing; lipectomy, surgical removal of fatty tissue.

macr- or macro- (Gk. *makros*) large, long: macroscopic, visible to the unaided eye; macrocephalic, having a long or large head.

mega- or megalo- (Gk. *megas*) great: megaton, an explosive power equal to a million tons of TNT; megalomania, a delusion of grandeur, acting despotically.

mes- or meso- (Gk. *mesos*) middle, the half: Mesopotamia, the land in the middle of the rivers (Euphrates and Tigris); meson, a subatomic particle of a mass between an electron and a proton.

met- or meta- (Gk. *meta*) after, next after, following, hence indicating change: Metazoa, the subkingdom following Protozoa and Parazoa in complexity; metamorphosis, rapid and marked change in form.

micr- or micro- (Gk. *mikros*) small: microscope, optical instrument for examining very small items; microtome, instrument for cutting very thin slices.

neo- (Gk. *neos*) new, recent, young: neolithic, the new, hence later, phase of the Stone Age; neo-Fascism, relating to a new or late (post World War II) revival of Fascism.

non- (L. *non*) not: non-conductor, nondescript, non-ferrous (metal).

olig- or oligo- (Gk. *oligos*) few, small: oligarchy, rule by a few; oligopoly (*cf.* monopoly), financial control by a few; oligocarpous, bearing only a few fruit.

omni- (L. *omnis*) all: omnipotent, all powerful; omnivorous, indiscriminate eating.

onto- (Gk. *on*, genitive *ontos*) being, existing: ontology, study of individual development; ontogenesis, the origin of a being.

or-, oro- (L. *os*, genitive *oris*) mouth: oral, relating to the mouth; oronasal, the region of the mouth and nose.

orth- or ortho- (Gk. *orthos*) straight, upright, hence correct: orthodox, holding correct, *i.e.* currently accepted, opinions; orthogonal, at right angles; orthopedics, correction of body deformities, especially in children.

pach-, pachi-, pacho- or pachy- (Gk. *pachys*) thick: pachyderm, an animal with a thick skin, *e.g.* rhinoceros, hence a "thick-skinned" person; pachymeter, instrument for measuring thickness.

palin- (Gk. *palin*) again, back again: palindrome, a word which is spelt the same backwards as forwards, *e.g.* reviver; palingenesis, the reproduction of an ancestral characteristic.

pan-, panto- (also **pam-**) (Gk. *pan*, genitive *pantos*) all: pandermic, widespread disease; pantomime, all mimicry, hence a dumb show.

para- (a) beside, near: (b) wrong, disordered: (a) parabiotic, living side by side, *e.g.* Siamese twin; (b) paranoia, disordered mind.

para- (Italian *parare*) to ward off: parachute, chute to ward off effects of gravity; parasol, portable shade to protect from sun.

pen- or pene- (L. *paene*) almost: penultimate, almost last, *i.e.* one but last; peninsula, projection of land that is almost surrounded by water.

per- (L. *per*) through, completely: permeable, allowing itself to be penetrated; perspicacious, clear-sighted.

peri- (Gk. *peri*) around, round: perimeter, the measure around a closed figure; periscope, instrument for seeing around, *e.g.* as in submerged submarine.

plei-, pleio-, pleo- or plio- (Gk. *pleiōn*) more, more than usual: Pliocene, geological period which was more recent than the preceding Glacial epoch; pleion, an area in which the temperature, pressure or humidity is above usual.

poly- (Gk. *polys*) many: polyhedron, a solid figure with many facets, *e.g.* brilliant-cut diamond; polytechnic, a place where many subjects are taught.

post- (L. *post*) after (time), behind (in place): postcostal, behind the rib cage; post-humous, after being put in the ground, (of book) published after death of author, (of child) born after death of father and/or mother.

pre- (L. *prae-*) before (in importance, place or time): prenomen, first or personal name; prefabricated, fabricated off the site, ready made; prefrontal, in front of the frontal bone of the skull.

pro- (Gk. *pro-* and L. *pro*) Gk. before (in order, place or time); L. in front of, in favor of: prognosis, forecast of probable course of events; prognathous, with projecting jaws; prolapse, a slipping forward; pro- American, in favor of American aims and people.

prot- or **proto-** (Gk. *protos*) first, original, hence chief: Protozoa, first (*i.e.* premature) living beings; prototype, pioneer model.

re- (L. *re-*) (a) again, repeatedly; (b) in return, on each other; (c) opposing, acting against; (d) back, backwards: (a) recrystallize, to form into crystals again; research, to search again and again; (b) react, to act in return; (c) resist, to make a stand against; (d) regress, to step, or move, back.

retro- (L. *retro*) backwards, behind: retrograde, moving backwards; retrosternal, behind the sternum or breastbone.

semi- (L. *semi-*) half: semi-quaver, half a quaver; semi-conductor, substance part way between an electrical conductor and an insulator, *e.g.* germanium.

sesqui- (L. *sesqui-*) one and a half: sesqui-centennial, 150th anniversary; sesquipedalian, literally a foot and a half in length, but also (humorously) a very long word.

sinistr- or **sinistro-** (L. *sinister*) left, left-handed: sinistro-cerebral, pertaining to the left side of the brain; sinistrorse, left-handed spiral.

sten-, steneo or **steno-** (Gk. *stenos*) narrow: stenothermous, able to live within only a narrow range of temperature; stenography, narrow writing, hence shorthand.

sub- (L. *sub*) under, below, less than: subsonic, a speed below that of sound; subway, an underground passage especially an underground railway; subnormal, less than normal.

super- (L. *super*) above, over: supersonic, a speed above that of sound; supercharger, a fuel and air pump which supplies mixture for internal combustion engines above atmospheric pressure.

supra- (L. *supra-*) above, on upper side: supranational, above and beyond national interests; suprarenal, situated above the kidneys.

sym-, syn-, syr- or **sys-** (Gk. *sym-, syn-*) with, together: synchronize, to cause to coincide in time; syzygy, yoke together, *i.e.* when moon is new or full because it is in line with the Sun and the Earth.

tach- or **tachy-** (Gk. *tachys*) rapid, quick: tachycordia, unhealthily rapid heart beat; tachypnoea, unusually rapid breathing.

tele- or **teleo-** (Gk. *teleos*) complete, perfect: teleozoon, an animal of perfect or complete organization.

trans- (L. *trans*) across, through: transverse, turned crosswise; trans-Atlantic, across the Atlantic.

ultra- (L. *ultra*) beyond, on other side: ultrasonic, sound frequencies higher than those audible to human hearing.

xen- or **xeno-** (Gk. *xenos*) foreigner, stranger: xenophobia, morbid fear of foreigners; xenogamy, marriage of strangers.

xer- or **xero-** (Gk. *xēros*) dry: xerodermia, dryness of the skin; xerophilous, plant which flourishes in dryness.

Principal Languages

The total number of languages spoken (including dialects) is now estimated to be about 5,500. If Chinese is considered with all of its many dialects to be a single language, it is by far the most widely spoken in the world (about 800,000,000 people). Guoyu or Northern Chinese if considered a separate language from Cantonese, Wu, Min, etc., is spoken generally by 600,000,000 people.

The other languages in order of popularity are:

English (375,000,000)
Great Russian (210,000,000), with Ukrainian (40,000,000 more)
Hindustani (combination of Hindu and Urdu), foremost of India's 845
    languages (200,000,000)
Spanish (200,000,000)
German (125,000,000)
Bengali (120,000,000)
Arabic (120,000,000)
Portuguese (120,000,000)
Japanese (110,000,000)
Malay-Indonesian (95,000,000), with Javanese (45,000,000 more)
French (90,000,000)
Italian (60,000,000)
Korean (50,000,000)
Turkish (40,000,000)
Polish (35,000,000)
Vietnamese (35,000,000)

Alphabets

HEBREW

Letter(s)	Name
א	aleph
ב	beth
ג	gimel
ד	daleth
ה	he
ו	waw
ז	zayin
ח	heth
ט	teth
י	yodh
כ ך	kaph
ל	lamedh
מ ם	mem
נ ן	nun
ס	samekh
ע	ayin
פ ף	pe
צ ץ	sadhe
ק	qoph
ר	resh
שׂ	sin
שׁ	shin
ת	taw

ARABIC

alif
bā
tā
thā
jīm
ḥā
khā
dāl
dhāl
rā
zāy
sīn
shīn
ṣād
ḍād
ṭā
ẓā
ʿayn
ghayn
fā
qāf
kāf
lām
mīm
nūn
hā
wāw
yā

GREEK

A α	alpha
B β	beta
Γ γ	gamma
Δ δ	delta
E ε	epsilon
Z ζ	zeta
H η	eta
Θ θ	theta
I ι	iota
K κ	kappa
Λ λ	lambda
M μ	mu
N ν	nu
Ξ ξ	xi
O o	omicron
Π π	pi
P ρ	rho
Σ σ ς	sigma
T τ	tau
Υ υ	upsilon
Φ φ	phi
X χ	chi
Ψ ψ	psi
Ω ω	omega

RUSSIAN

Letters	Sound
А а	a
Б б	b
В в	v
Г г	g
Д д	d
Е е	e
Ж ж	zh
З з	z
И и Й й	i, ĭ
К к	k
Л л	l
М м	m
Н н	n
О о	o
П п	p
Р р	r
С с	s
Т т	t
У у	u
Ф ф	f
Х х	kh
Ц ц	ts
Ч ч	ch
Ш ш	sh
Щ щ	shch
Ъ ъ	"
Ы ы	y
Ь ь	'
Э э	e
Ю ю	yu
Я я	ya

CATHOLIC CHURCH: This altar in the Jesuit church named La Compania in Quito, Ecuador, is typical of the art and ornamentation of Catholic churches everywhere.

Religion

RELIGIONS OF THE WORLD (estimates in millions)

Christian	1,050	Confucian	312
Roman Catholic	630	Buddhist	160
Eastern Orthodox	160	Shinto	60
Protestant	260	Taoist	52
Moslem	600	Jewish	14.6
Hindu	437		

CHRISTIANITY

Christianity takes its name from Jesus Christ*, son of the Virgin Mary, whose subsequent husband, Joseph of Nazareth, was 27 generations descended from David. Jesus' birth is now regarded as occurring at Bethlehem in the summer of 4 B.C. or earlier. The discrepancy is due to an error in the 6th century by Dionysius Exiguus in establishing the dating of the Christian era.

The principles of Christianity are proclaimed in the New Testament which was written in Syriac-Aramaic and of which the earliest complete surviving manuscript dates from *c*. 350 A.D.

Christ was crucified in the reign of the Roman emperor Tiberius during the procuratorship in Judaea of Pontius Pilate in 29 A.D. or, according to the Roman Catholic chronology, April 7, 30 A.D.

The primary commandment of Jesus was to believe in God and to love Him. His second commandment (Mark xii, 31) was to "love thy neighbor" in a way that outward performance alone did not suffice. Hate was prohibited and not only adultery but evil lust (Matt. v, 21). Unselfishness and compassion are central themes in Christianity.

Jesus appointed twelve disciples; the following are common to the lists in the books of Matthew, Mark, Luke, and the Acts.
1. Peter, Saint Peter (brother of Andrew).
2. Andrew, Saint Andrew (brother of Peter).
3. James, son of Zebedee (brother of John).
4. John, Saint John (the Apostle) (brother of James).
5. Philip.
6. Bartholomew.
7. Thomas.
8. Matthew, Saint Matthew.
9. James of Alphaeus.
10. Simon the Cananaean (in Matthew and Mark) or Simon Zelotes (in Luke and the Acts).
11. Judas Iscariot (not an apostle).

In Matthew and Mark, Thaddaeus is the twelfth disciple, while in Luke and the Acts it is Judas of James. The former may have been a nickname or place name to distinguish Judas of James from the Iscariot. Matthias succeeded to the place of the betrayer Judas Iscariot.

---

*Jesus (the Saviour, from Hebrew root *yasha'*, to save) Christ (the anointed one, from Greek chrio, to anoint).

Roman Catholicism

Roman Catholic Christianity is practiced by those who acknowledge the supreme jurisdiction of the bishop of Rome (the Pope) and recognize him as the lawful successor of St. Peter who was appointed by Christ Himself to be head of the church. Peter visited Rome c. 42 A.D. and was martyred there c. 67 A.D. Pope Paul VI is his 261st successor.

The Roman Catholic Church claims catholicity inasmuch as it was charged (de jure) by Christ to "teach all nations" and de facto since its adherents are by far the most numerous among Christians. The Roman Catholic Church is regarded as the infallible interpreter both of the written (5 of the 12 apostles wrote) and the unwritten word of God. The organization of the Church is the Curia, the work of which is done by 11 permanent departments or congregations.

The great majority of Catholics are of the Roman rite and use the Roman liturgy. While acknowledging the hierarchical supremacy of the Holy See other Eastern Churches or Uniate Rites enjoy an autonomy. These include (1) the Byzantine rite, (2) the Armenian rite, and (3) the Coptic rite.

The doctrine of the Immaculate Conception was proclaimed on December 8, 1854, and that of Papal Infallibility was adopted by the Ecumenical Council by 547 votes to 2 on July 18, 1870. The 21st Council was convened by Pope John XXIII. The election of Popes is by the College of Cardinals, increased to over 80 by 1962.

Eastern Orthodox

The church officially described as "The Holy Orthodox Catholic Apostolic Eastern Church" consists of those churches which accepted all the decrees of the first seven General Councils and such churches as have since sprung up in that tradition.

The origin arises from the splitting of the old Roman Empire into a Western or Latin half, centered on Rome, and an Eastern or Greek half, centered on Constantinople.

The Orthodox Church has no succinctly stated creed, unlike the Western Churches. Some features of this branch of Christianity are that bishops must be unmarried; the dogma of the Immaculate Conception is not admitted: icons are in the churches but the only "graven image" is the crucifix; and fasts are frequent and vigorous.

Protestant

The term "protestant" had never been used officially in the style of any church until the Anglican community in North America called themselves the "Protestant Episcopal Church" during the 17th century.

The origin of the term specifically derives from the formal protestatio, entered in 1529 by the rulers of the evangelical states of the Holy Roman Empire against the repressive Diet of Spires, which forbade further innovations. The term was not used for some years and it later became a generic term for those followers of the teaching of the Reformation against what were regarded as doctrinal and administrative abuses of Rome, and in particular the Papacy's claim of universal supremacy.

JUDAISM

The word Jew is derived through the Latin Judaeus, from the Hebrew Yehudhi, signifying a descendant of Judah, the fourth son of Jacob whose tribe, with that of his half brother Benjamin, made up the peoples of the kingdom of Judah. This kingdom was separate from the remaining tribes of Israel. The exodus of the Israelites from Egypt is believed to have occurred c. 1400 B.C.

Judaism is monotheistic and based on the covenant that Israel is the bearer of the belief in the one and only God.

From 311 until 1790 Jews existed under severe disabilities and discrimination in both Christian and Moslem areas. Jewish emancipation began with the enfranchisement of Jews in France in September 1791.

It touched off anti-Semitism which in return fired Zionism, or the demand for a Jewish homeland. The first Zionist Congress was held in Basle, Switzerland, in August 1897.

The Balfour letter written on November 2, 1917, by Arthur Balfour, British foreign secretary to Lord Rothschild declared "His Majesty's Government view with favour the establishment of Palestine as a natural home for the Jewish people. . .".

On July 24, 1922 the League of Nations approved a British mandate over Palestine. These policies led to bitter Arab resistance with revolts in 1929 and 1936–39 claiming the right of self-determination. The irreconcilable aims of Arab nationalism and Zionism led to partition with the creation of Israel (*q.v.*) on May 14, 1948, and the internationalization of Jerusalem.

Jewish holidays including *Pesach* (Passover), celebrating the Exodus, *Shabuoth* (Pentecost), *Rosh Hashana* (New Year) and *Yom Kippur* (Day of Atonement) devoted to fasting, meditation and prayer.

ISLAM (Mohammedanism)

Mohammedanism is a religious system founded by Mohammed (Muhammad or Mahomet) (*c.* 575–632 A.D.) on July 16, 622 A.D. at Yathrib, now known as Al Madinah (Medina) in Saudi Arabia.

The religion was known by its founder as Islam (Arabic, submission) which is the term used today outside Europe. It is also known as Hanifism. Mohammed, a member of the Koreish tribe, was a caravan conductor and later became a shopkeeper in Mekkah (Mecca). There is some evidence that he was only semi-literate, at least in early manhood. He did not become a public preacher until 616. Soon after 622 [A.H. (anno Hegirae or the year of exile) 1] Mohammed turned the direction of his prayer southward from Jerusalem and an Israeli God to the pagan temple at Mecca and the God Allah. Mohammed soon became an administrator, general, judge and legislator in addition to being one through whom divine revelation was communicated.

Islam is based upon the word of God, the Koran (Arabic *Qur'an*, recitation) and the traditions (*hadith*) of the sayings and the life (*sunna*) of Mohammed. Other prophets are recognized including Jesus and his gospel (*injil*) but Mohammed is the last and greatest of the prophets.

BALI RELIGIOUS DANCE: Native men dance as they pray on the shores of the island.

143

Religion (continued)

Islam demands of Moslems worship five times daily, facing in the direction (*kiblah*) of Mecca, fasting in the month of Ramadan, payment of alms (*zakat*) and the pilgrimage (*hadj*) to Mecca.

HINDUISM

The origin of Hinduism, or *Arya-Dharma* (Religion of the Aryans), stems from the fears and ignorance which beset the early Indic civilization. There are no beliefs common to all Hindus but caste and certain deities are widespread. Caste is of ingrained importance and without this man has no place in society and cannot marry.

The *Veda*, or Divine Knowledge, was passed on by the Rishis, inspired men, to the people in the form of hymns or *Mantras*. Brahma is the spirit which gives life to the individual, the doctrine being that to be reunited with the spirit one should follow the path of knowledge, or *jnina*.

A Hindu believes that his caste in the next life (*karma*) is determined by his actions in the present life—if he leads a good life, he will be reborn into a good caste, but if he does evil, he will become of low caste or even reincarnated as an animal. Birth in a particular caste shows the relationship of one's soul with God—the perfect soul no longer has to go through the process of continual birth and death.

Hinduism is not an organized religion, since it assimilates ideas from other religions. It permits animal worship and that of numerous deities and even the animal or bird on which they are believed to ride. Orthodox Hindus object to the killing of cattle and peacocks. There is much stress on purification rites—particularly on the occasion of inter-marriage between castes and even on touching or going close to a member of a lower caste. They strive after *dharma* (good conduct), *kama* (satisfaction of desire), *arthra* (wealth) and *moksha* (salvation). Ceremonies for ancestors and pilgrimages to Holy Places occupy much time. The recent impact of Christianity has made the occidentally educated Hindus introspective about their religion and much of the original teaching has been modified in the last century.

BUDDHISM

Buddhism is the world's fourth largest religion. It is based on the teaching of the Indian prince, Siddhartha (later called Gautama) (*c.* 563–483 B.C.) of the Gautama clan of the Sakyas, later named Gautama Buddha (*buddha* meaning "the enlightened one"). After seeing in *c.* 534 B.C. for the first time a sick man, an old man, a holy man and a dead man, he wandered fruitlessly for six years, after which he meditated for 49 days under a Bodhi tree at Gaya in Magadha. He achieved enlightenment or *nirvana* and taught salvation in Bihar, west of Bengal, until he died, aged 80. Gautama's teaching was essentially a protesting offshoot of early Hinduism. It contains four Noble Truths: (1) Man suffers from one life to the next; (2) the Origin of suffering is craving; craving for pleasure, possessions and the cessation of pain; (3) the cure for craving is non-attachment to all things including self; (4) the way to non-attachment is the eight-fold path of right conduct, right effort, right intentions, right livelihood, right meditations, right mindfulness, right speech and right views.

Buddhism makes no provisions for God and hence has no element of divine judgment or messianic expectation. It provides an inexorable law or *dharma* of cause and effect which determines the individual's fate.

The vast body or *sangha* of monks and nuns practice celibacy, non-violence, poverty and vegetarianism. Under the *Hinayana*, or Lesser Vehicle tradition of India, only they have hope of attaining *nirvana*. Under the *Mahayana*, or Greater Vehicle, as practiced in Indo-China, China and Japan, laymen as well may attain the highest ideal of *bodhisattva*, the enlightened one who liberates himself by personal sacrifice. Under Zen Buddhism enlightenment or *satori* is achieved only by prolonged meditation and shock.

CONFUCIANISM

Confucius (551–479 B.C.) was not the sole founder of Confucianism but was rather a member of the founding group of *Ju* or meek ones. Confucius is the Latinized version of K'ung Fu-tzo or Master K'ung who was a keeper of accounts from the province of Lu. He became the first teacher in Chinese history to instruct the people of all ranks in the six arts: ceremonies, music, archery, charioteering, history and numbers.

Confucius taught that the main ethic is *jen* (benevolence), and that truth involves the knowledge of one's own faults. He believed in altruism and insisted on filial piety. He decided that people could be led by example and aimed at the rulers of his own time imitating those in a former period of history, where he attributed the prosperity of the people to the leadership of the Emperors. Confucianism included the worship of Heaven and revered ancestors and great men, though Confucius himself did not advocate prayer, believing that man should direct his own destiny.

Confucianism can be better described as a religious philosophy or code of social behavior than a religion in the accepted sense, since it has no church or clergy and is in no way an institution. For many years it had a great hold over education, its object being to emphasize the development of human nature and the person. During the early 19th century attempts were made by followers to promote Confucianism to being a state religion, and though this failed, a great deal of the Confucian teachings still remain.

TAOISM

Lao-tzu (Lao-tze or Lao-tse), the Chinese philosopher and founder of Taoism, was, according to tradition, born *c.* 600–500 B.C. Lao-tzu taught that Taoism (Tao = the Ultimate and Unconditioned Being) could be attained by virtue if thrift, humility and compassion were practiced.

Taoism has the following features—numerous gods (though Lao-tzu did not himself permit this); a still persisting though now decreasing body of superstition; and two now declining schools—the 13th-century Northern School with its emphasis on man's life, and the Southern School, probably of 10th-century origin, stressing the nature of man. Various Taoist societies have been formed more recently by laymen, who though worshipping deities of many religions, promote charity and moral culture. The moral principles of Taoism consist of simplicity, patience, contentment and harmony. Since the decline of its espousal by the T'ang dynasty (618–906 A.D.), it has proved to be chiefly the religion of the semi-literate.

Philosophical Taoism or Tao-chia advocates naturalism and is thus opposed to regulations and organization of any kind. After the 4th century B.C. when Buddhism and Taoism began to influence each other there was a weakening of this anarchical strain but the philosophy still has a strong hold over the way of life and culture in parts of China.

The religion imitates Buddhism in the matter of clergy and temple, the chief of which is the White Cloud temple in Peking.

SHINTO

Shinto ("the teaching" or "the way of the gods") came into practice during the 6th century A.D. to distinguish the Japanese religion from Buddhism which was reaching the islands by way of the mainland. The early forms of Shinto were a simple nature worship, and a religion for those who were not impelled by any complicated religious lore. The help of the deities was sought for the physical and spiritual needs of the people and there was great stress laid upon purification and truthfulness.

The more important national shrines were dedicated to well-known national figures, but there were also those set up for the worship of deities of mountain and forest.

During the 19th century, 13 Sect Shinto denominations were formed and these were dependent on private support for their teaching and organization. They had very little in common and varied widely in beliefs and practices. Some adhered to the traditional Shinto deities while others did not. Of the 13 denominations *Tenrikyo* is the one with the greatest following outside Japan.

Theories of Shinto have been greatly influenced by Confucianism, Taoism and Buddhism. In 1868, however, the Department of Shinto was established and attempts were made to do away with the Shinto and Buddhist coexistence, and in 1871 Shinto was proclaimed the Japanese national religion.

Holidays
Around the World

NATIONAL WEEKDAY HOLIDAYS

* Asterisks denote movable holidays.

ARGENTINA—January 1 (New Year's Day), January 6 (Epiphany), *February (Carnival), *March–April (Holy Thursday and Good Friday), May 1 (Labor Day), May 25 (Anniversary of 1810 Revolution), *June (Corpus Christi), June 20 (Flag Day), July 9 (Independence Day), August 15 (Assumption), August 17 (Death of Gen. San Martin), October 12 (Columbus Day), November 1 (All Saints' Day), November 6 (Bank Holiday), December 8 (Immaculate Conception), December 25 (Christmas).

AUSTRALIA—January 1 (New Year's Day), January 29 (Australia Day), *March–April (Good Friday and Easter Monday), April 25 (ANZAC Day), December 25 (Christmas), December 26 (Boxing Day). Regional holidays: January 2 (Additional New Year's Day), Victoria only; *March (Labor Day), Western Australia and Tasmania; *March (Labor Day), Victoria; *April (Bank Holiday) in Victoria, Western Australia and Tasmania; *May (Labor Day) in Queensland and Northern Territory; *June (Foundation Day) in Western Australia; *June (Queen's Birthday) except Western Australia; *August (Bank Holiday), Australian Capital Territory and New South Wales; *August (Bank Holiday) in Queensland; September 25 (Show Day) in Western Australia; *September (Show Day) in Melbourne, Victoria; *October (Labor Day) in Australian Capital Territory and New South Wales; *October (Queen's Birthday) in Western Australia; *October (Labor Day) in South Australia; *November (Cup Day), Victoria; *December (Proclamation Day), South Australia.

AUSTRIA—January 1 (New Year's Day), January 6 (Epiphany), *March–April (Easter Monday), May 1 (Labor Day), *May (Ascension Day), *June (Whit Monday), *June (Corpus Christi), August 15 (Assumption), October 26 (National Holiday), November 1 (All Saints' Day), Dec. 8 (Immaculate Conception), December 25 (Christmas), December 26 (St. Stephen's Day).

BELGIUM—January 1 (New Year's Day), *March–April (Easter Monday), May 1 (Labor Day), *May (Ascension Day), *June (Whit Monday), July 21–22 (National Holiday), August 15 (Assumption), November 1 (All Saints' Day), November 2 (All Souls' Day) November 11 (Armistice Day), November 15 (Dynasty—King's birthday), December 25–26 (Christmas).

BRAZIL: Coffee is Brazil's most important export and the major item in its economy. These cherries, which contain the coffee bean, are being spread out to dry.

BRAZIL—January 1 (New Year's Day), January 20 (St. Sebastian), *February (Carnival), *March–April (Good Friday), April 21 (Tiradentes), May 1 (Labor Day), *June (Corpus Christi), September 7 (Independence Day), November 2 (All Souls' Day), November 15 (Proclamation of the Republic), December 25 (Christmas). Regional holiday: January 25 (Sao Paulo Anniversary) is celebrated in Sao Paulo.

CANADA—January 1 (New Year's Day), *March–April (Good Friday and Easter Monday), *May (Queen's Birthday), July 1 (Dominion Day), *September (Labor Day), *October (Thanksgiving Day), December 25 (Christmas). *Regional holidays:* the following are celebrated only in Quebec province—January 6 (Epiphany), *February (Ash Wednesday), *May (Ascension Day), June 24 (St. John the Baptist's Day), November 1 (All Saints' Day), December 8 (Feast of Immaculate Conception); January 11 (Sir John Macdonald's Day) is celebrated only in Nova Scotia; the following are celebrated only in Newfoundland: March 17 (St. Patrick's Day), April 23 (St. George's Day), *June (Discovery Day), July 12 (general holiday), *August (St. John's Regatta); *August (Civic Holiday) is celebrated only in Manitoba and Ontario; December 26 (Boxing Day) is celebrated in Alberta, British Columbia, Manitoba, New Brunswick, Newfoundland and Prince Edward Island.

CHILE—January 1 (New Year's Day), *March–April (Good Friday), May 1 (Labor Day), *May (Ascension Day), *June (Corpus Christi), June 29 (Sts. Peter and Paul), August 15 (Assumption), September 18–19 (Independence Day), October 12 (Columbus Day), November 1 (All Saints' Day), December 8 (Immaculate Conception), December 25 (Christmas).

COLOMBIA—January 1 (New Year's Day), January 6 (Epiphany), March 19 (St. Joseph's Day), *March–April (Holy Thursday and

Good Friday), May 1 (Labor Day), *May (Ascension Day), *June (Corpus Christi), *June (Sacred Heart), June 29 (Sts. Peter and Paul), July 20 (Independence Day), August 7 (Battle of Boyaca), August 15 (Assumption), October 12 (Columbus Day), November 1 (All Saints' Day), November 11 (Independence of Cartagena), December 8 (Immaculate Conception), December 25 (Christmas).

COSTA RICA—January 1 (New Year's Day), March 19 (St. Joseph), *March–April (Holy Week), May 1 (Labor Day), *June (Corpus Christi), August 2 (Our Lady of the Angels), August 15 (Assumption), September 15 (Independence Day), October 12 (Columbus Day), December 8 (Immaculate Conception), December 25 (Christmas). Although the week after Christmas is not a holiday, practically no business is carried on then.

DENMARK—January 1 (New Year's Day), *March–April (Maundy Thursday, Good Friday, and Easter Monday), *May (Prayer Day), *May (Ascension Day), *June (Whit Monday), June 5 (Constitution Day), December 25 (Christmas), December 26 (Second Christmas Day). Many industries close at noon on May 1. Banks are closed April 13 and December 24.

DOMINICAN REPUBLIC—January 1 (New Year's Day), January 21 (Day of LaAltagracia), January 26 (Duarte Day), February 27 (Independence Day), *March–April (Good Friday), *June (Corpus Christi), August 16 (National Restoration Day), September 24 (Our Lady of Mercy), December 25 (Christmas).

ECUADOR—January 1 (New Year's Day), January 6 (Epiphany), *February (Carnival), *March–April (Holy Thursday and Good Friday), May 1 (Labor Day), May 24 (Battle of Pichincha), July 24 (Simón Bolívar's Birthday), August 10 (Independence Day), October 9 (Guayaquil Independence), October 12 (Columbus Day), November 2 (All Souls' Day), November 3 (Cuenca Independence), December 6 (Founding of Quito), December 25 (Christmas).

COLOMBIA: Boys in the village of Sylvia in typical Colombian country garb, ponchos and felt hats.

* Asterisks denote movable holidays.

Holidays (continued)

FIJI—January 1 (New Year's Day), *March–April (Good Friday, Holy Saturday and Easter Monday), First week in June (Queen Elizabeth's Birthday), *August (Bank Holiday), October 9 (Cession Day), November 14 (Prince of Wales' Birthday), December 25 (Christmas), December 26 (Boxing Day).

FINLAND—January 1 (New Year's Day), January 6 (Epiphany), *March–April (Good Friday and Easter Monday), May 1 (May Day), *May (Ascension Day), *June (Whit Monday), June 22 (Midsummer's Day), November 2 (All Saints' Day), December 6 (Independence Day), December 25–26 (Christmas).

FRANCE—January 1 (New Year's Day), *March–April (Easter Monday), May 1 (Labor Day), *May (Ascension Day), *June (Whit Monday), July 14 (Bastille Day), *August (Assumption), November 1 (All Saints' Day), November 11 (Armistice Day), December 25 (Christmas).

GERMANY—January 1 (New Year's Day), *March–April (Good Friday and Easter Monday), May 1 (Labor Day), *May (Ascension), *June (Whit Monday), June 17 (Day of German Unity), *November (Repentance Day), December 24—after 4 p.m.—(Christmas Eve), December 25–26 (Christmas).

GREAT BRITAIN—*March–April (Good Friday and Easter Monday), *June (Whitsuntide or Spring Bank Holiday), *September (Late Summer Bank Holiday), December 25 (Christmas), December 26 (Boxing Day).

GREECE—January 1 (New Year's Day), January 6 (Epiphany), *March (Kathara Deftera), March 25 (Independence Day), *March–April (Good Friday and Easter Monday), *April (half-holiday after Easter Monday), May 21 (King's Name Day), *June (Whit Monday), August 15 (Assumption), October 28 (Ohi Day), December 25 (Christmas), December 26 (Boxing Day), December 31 (New Year's Eve—half-holiday).

GUATEMALA—January 1 (New Year's Day), *March–April (Holy Thursday and Good Friday), May 1 (Labor Day), June 30 (Army Day), August 15 (Assumption), September 15 (Independence Day), October 12 (Columbus Day), October 20 (Revolution Day), Nov. 1 (All Saints' Day), December 24–25 (Christmas).

HAITI—January 1 (New Year's Day, Independence Day), January 2 (Ancestors Day), *February (Mardi-Gras), *March–April (Holy Thursday and Good Friday), May 1 (Agriculture and Labor Day), May 18 (Haitian Flag and University Day), May 22 (National Sovereignty Day), *May (Ascension Day), *June (Corpus Christi), August 15 (Assumption), October 17 (Anniversary of death of Dessalines), October 22 (Anniversary of Pres. Duvalier taking oath), October 24 (U.N. Day), November 1 (All Saints' Day), November 2 (All Souls' Day), November 18 (Anniversary of Battle of Vertieres, Armed Forces Day), December 5 (Anniversary of Discovery of Haiti by Columbus), December 25 (Christmas).

HONG KONG—*January (First weekday in January), *January–February (Chinese New Year), *April (Ching Ming Festival), *March–April (Good Friday, Holy Saturday and Easter Monday), *May (Dragon Boat Festival), *July (First weekday in July), *August (First Monday in August), *August (Liberation Day—last Monday in

* Asterisks denote movable holidays.

August), *October (day after Chinese Mid-Autumn Festival Day), *October (Chung Young Festival), December 25 (Christmas), December 26 (or first weekday after Christmas). A holiday observing Queen Elizabeth's Birthday will be announced.

INDIA—January 1 (New Year's Day), *January (Id-ul-Fitr), January 26 (Republic Day), *February (Basant Panchami), *February (Shiv Ratri), *March (Holi), *March (Dulhendi), *April (Durga Ashtmi), *April (Muharram), *April (Mahavir Jayanti), *March–April (Good Friday), April 13 (Baisakhi), *August (Raksha Bandhan), August 15 (Independence Day), *August (Janmashtami), *September (Anant Choudas), *October (Dusehra), October 2 (Mahatma Gandhi's Birthday), *October (Diwali), *October (Bhaiya Dooj), *November (Guru Nanak's Birthday), December 25 (Christmas), *December (Guru Gobind Singh's Birthday), December 31 (Bank Holiday).

INDONESIA—January 1 (New Year's Day), *January (End of Lebaran Fast), *March (End of Fasting Period of Pilgrims), March 30 (Moslem New Year), *March–April (Good Friday), May 1 (Labor Day), May 23 (Ascension Day of Christ), June 1 (Birth of Pantjasila), June 8 (Mohammed's Birthday), August 17 (Independence Day), October 19 (Ascension of Mohammed), *December (End of Lebaran Fast), December 25 (Christmas).

IRELAND—March 18 (Monday after St. Patrick's Day), *March–April (Good Friday and Easter Monday), *June (Bank Holiday), *August (Bank Holiday), December 25 (Christmas), December 26 (St. Stephen's Day).

ISRAEL—*March–April (last day of Passover), May 2 (Independence Day), June 2 (Pentecost), *September (1st and 2nd Days of Rosh Hashanah), *October (Yom Kippur), *October (1st and last Days of Succoth). All Holy Days are movable, since the Hebrew calendar differs from the Gregorian. Saturdays are not regular working days in Israel, but Sundays are.

ITALY—January 1 (New Year's Day), January 6 (Epiphany), March 19 (St. Joseph's Day), *March–April (Easter Monday), April 25 (Liberation Day), May 1 (Labor Day), *May (Ascension Day), *June (Corpus Christi), June 2 (Founding of the Republic Day), June 29 (Sts. Peter and Paul), August 15 (Assumption), November 1 (All Saints' Day), November 4 (National Unity Day), December 8 (Immaculate Conception), December 25–26 (Christmas).

JAMAICA—January 1 (New Year's Day), *February (Ash Wednesday), *March–April (Good Friday and Easter Monday), May 23 (Labor Day), *June (Queen's Birthday), August 5 (Independence Day), December 25 (Christmas), December 26 (Boxing Day).

JAPAN—January 1 (New Year's Day), January 15 (Adult's Day), February 11 (National Foundation Day), *March (Vernal Equinox Day), April 29 (Emperor's Birthday), May 3 (Constitution Day), May 5 (Children's Day), September 15 (Respect for the Aged Day), *September (Autumnal Equinox Day), October 10 (Physical Culture Day), November 3 (Culture Day), November 23 (Labor Thanksgiving).

KOREA—January 1–3 (New Year's Day), March 1 (Independence Movement Day), April 5 (Arbor Day), June 6 (Memorial Day), July 17 (Constitution Day), August 15 (Independence Day), October 3 (National Foundation), *October (Korean Thanksgiving Day), October 9 (Korean Alphabet Day), October 24 (U.N. Day), December 25 (Christmas). March 10 (Labor Day) is observed by banks.

MONACO: This tiny principality on the Mediterranean is a popular resort area. The world-famous casino is in the town of Monte Carlo.

MEXICO—January 1 (New Year's Day), February 5 (Promulgation of Constitution), March 21 (Juarez's Birthday), *March–April (Holy Week), May 1 (Labor Day), May 5 (Victory of Gen. Zaragosa), September 16 (Independence Day), October 12 (Columbus Day), November 2 (All Souls' Day), November 20 (Anniversary of the Revolution), December 12 (Our Lady of Guadalupe's Day), December 25 (Christmas).

MONACO—January 27 (Sainte Devote), *February (Shrove Tuesday), March 21 (Mie-Careme), *March–April (Holy Thursday, Good Friday and Easter Monday), May 1 (May Day), *May (Ascension Day), *June (Pentecost), June 13 (Fete-Dieu), August 15 (Assumption), November 1 (All Saints' Day), November 19 (National Holiday), December 8 (Immaculate Conception), December 25 (Christmas Day).

NETHERLANDS—January 1 (New Year's Day), *March–April (Good Friday and Easter Monday), April 30 (Queen's Birthday), *May (Ascension Day), *June (Whit Monday), December 25–26 (Christmas).

NEW ZEALAND—January 1–2 (New Year's Day), *March–April (Good Friday and Easter Holiday), *April 25 (ANZAC Day), *June (Queen's Birthday), *October 28 (Labor Day), December 25–27 (Christmas Holiday). *Regional holidays*: *January (Wellington Day), *January (Auckland Day) *December (Canterbury Day). December 25–January 12, businesses operate with a minimal staff.

NICARAGUA—January 1 (New Year's Day), *March–April (Holy Week), May 1 (Labor Day), May 27 (Army Day), August 1 and 10 (St. Domingo), September 14 (Battle of San Jacinto), September 15 (Independence Day), October 12 (Columbus Day), December 8 (Immaculate Conception), December 25 (Christmas).

NIGERIA—January 1 (New Year's Day), *January (Id-El-Fitr) *March (Id-El-Kabir) *March–April (Good Friday and Easter Monday) *June (Id-El-Maulud) October 1 (National Day), December 25 (Christmas) December 26 (Boxing Day).

Holidays (continued)

NORTHERN IRELAND—March 18 (day after St. Patrick's Day), *March–April (Good Friday and Easter Monday), *June (Spring Bank Holiday), July 12 (Orangeman's Day), *September (Late Summer Bank Holiday), December 25 (Christmas), December 26 (Boxing Day). Banks, schools and government offices are closed for St. Patrick's Day (March 17), but most businesses remain open.

PAKISTAN—*January (Eid-ul-Fitr), March 10–11 (Eid-ul-Azha), March 23 (Pakistan Day), April 9 (Ashura), June 10 (day following Eid-i-Milad-un-Nabi), August 14 (Independence Day), September 6 (Defense of Pakistan Day), September 11 (Anniversary of death of Quaid-i-Azam), October 28 (day following Revolution Day), December 20 (Jamatul Wida), *December (Eid-ul-Fitr), December 25 (Quaid-i-Azam's Birthday and Christmas). Bank holidays: January 1, July 1, December 31. Eid-ul-Fitr occurred twice in 1968 as the Islamic calendar is shorter than the Gregorian.

PANAMA—January 1 (New Year's Day), *February (Carnival), March 1 (Constitution Day), *March–April (Good Friday), May 1 (Labor Day), November 3 (Independence from Colombia), November 10 (Cry of Independence from Spain), November 28 (Independence from Spain), December 8 (Mother's Day), December 25 (Christmas). October 1 (Presidential Inauguration) is observed every 4 years.

PERU—January 1 (New Year's Day), *March–April—half-day (Holy Thursday), *March–April (Good Friday), May 1 (Labor Day), June 29 (Sts. Peter and Paul), July 28–29 (Independence Day), August 30 (St. Rose of Lima), November 1 (All Saints'), December 8 (Immaculate Conception), December 25 (Christmas).

PERU: Cuzco, the sacred city of the Incas, lies in a valley almost 11,000 feet above sea level. Cuzco cathedral (left) is a superb example of the best Spanish colonial architecture.

* Asterisks denote movable holidays.

153

SOUTH AFRICA: Bird's-eye view of huge gold mine dumps just outside the city of Johannesburg. Gold is South Africa's major export.

PHILIPPINES—January 1 (New Year's Day), *March–April (Holy Thursday and Good Friday), May 1 (Labor Day), June 12 (Independence Day), June 19 (Rizal Day), November 30 (National Heroes' Day), December 25 (Christmas), December 30 (Rizal Day).

POLAND—January 1 (New Year's Day), *April (Easter Monday), May 1 (Labor Day), *June (Corpus Christi), July 22 (National Day), November 1 (All Saints' Day), December 25–26 (Christmas).

PORTUGAL—January 1 (New Year's Day), *March–April (Good Friday), June 10 (Portugal Day), *June (Corpus Christi, St. Antonio's Day), August 15 (Assumption), October 5 (Proclamation of Portuguese Republic), November 1 (All Saints' Day), December 1 (Restoration of Portuguese Independence), December 8 (Feast of Immaculate Conception), December 25 (Christmas).

SINGAPORE—January 1 (New Year's Day), *January (Hari Raya Puasa), *January–February (Chinese New Year), February 12 (Thaipusam), *March (day following Hari Raya Haji), *March–April (Good Friday and day following and Easter Monday), May 1 (Labor Day), May 11 (Vesak Day), *June (day following Prophet's Birthday), August 9 (National Day), October 21 (Deepavali), December 25 (Christmas).

SOUTH AFRICA—January 1 (New Year's Day), April 6 (Van Riebeeck Day), *March–April (Good Friday and Easter Monday), *May (Ascension Day), May 31 (Republic Day), *July (Family Day), *September (Settlers Day), October 10 (Kruger Day), December 16 (Day of the Covenant), December 25 (Christmas Day), December 26 (Boxing Day). *Regional holiday:* January 2 in Cape Province.

SPAIN—January 1 (New Year's Day), January 6 (Epiphany), March 19 (St. Joseph's Day), April 1 (Victory Day), *March–April—after 2 p.m.—(Maundy Thursday), *March–April (Good Friday), May 1 (Labor Day), *May (Ascension Day), *June (Corpus Christi), June

Holidays (continued)

29 (Sts. Peter and Paul Day), July 18 (National Day), July 25 (St. James Day), August 15 (Assumption), October 1 (Day of the Caudillo), October 12 (Columbus Day), November 1 (All Saints' Day), December 8 (Immaculate Conception), December 25 (Christmas). *Local holidays:* May 15 (St. Isidro) is celebrated in Madrid only; *April (Easter Monday), June 24 (St. John the Baptist Day), September 24 (Our Lady of Mercy), and December 26 (St. Stephen's Day) are celebrated in Barcelona only.

SWEDEN—January 1 (New Year's Day), January 6 (3 Kings Day), *March–April (Good Friday and Easter Monday), May 1 (Labor Day), *May (Ascension Day), *June (Whit Monday), *June (Midsummer Eve), November 1 (All Saints' Day), December 25 (Christmas), December 26 (Second Day of Christmas).

SWITZERLAND—January 1 (New Year's Day), *March–April (Good Friday and Easter Monday), *May (Ascension Day), *June (Whit Monday), December 25 (Christmas), December 26 (St. Stephen's Day). Thirty other days are observed locally in various areas.

TAIWAN—January 1–2 (New Year's Day), *January–February (Chinese New Year—Spring Festival), March 29 (Youth Day), September 28 (Confucius' Birthday—Teachers' Day), October 10 (Founding of Republic of China), October 25 (Restoration Day), November 12 (Dr. Sun Yat-sen's Birthday), December 25 (Constitution Day). October 31 (President Chaing Kai-shek's Birthday) is not an official holiday, but widely observed.

THAILAND—January 1 (New Year's Day), *February (Makha Bucha Day), May 1 (May Day), May 6 (Substitute for Coronation), *May (Wisakha Bucha Day), *July (Asalaha Bucha Day), *July (Buddhist

THAILAND: The Temple of the Emerald Buddha in the middle of other shrines in Bangkok, capital of Thailand. The legendary Emerald Buddha is a 22-inch-high statue carved out of green jasper that sits upon a golden throne.

* Asterisks denote movable holidays.

155

Holidays (Thailand) (continued)

Lent), August 12 (Queen's Birthday), October 23 (Chulalongkorn Day), December 5 (King's Birthday), December 10 (Constitution Day), December 31 (New Year's Eve). Business firms are closed, government offices open *January–February (Chinese New Year), July 1 is a bank holiday. December 25 (Christmas) is a holiday observed by banks and foreign business firms only.

TRINIDAD & TOBAGO—January 1 (New Year's Day), *March–April (Good Friday and Easter Monday), May 1 (Labor Day), *June (Whit Monday), *June (Corpus Christi), August 5 (Discovery Day), August 31 (Independence Day), December 25 (Christmas), December 26 (Boxing Day).

U.S.S.R.—January 1 (New Year's Day), March 8 (Women's Day), May 1–2 (May Day), May 9 (Victory over Fascism), November 7–8 (October Revolution), December 5 (Constitution Day).

VENEZUELA—January 1 (New Year's Day), January 6 (Epiphany), *February (Carnival), *March–April (Holy Week), April 19 (Declaration of Independence), May 1 (Labor Day), *May (Ascension), *June (Corpus Christi), June 29 (Sts. Peter and Paul), July 5 (Independence Day), July 24 (Simón Bolívar's Birthday), August 15 (Assumption), October 12 (Columbus Day), November 1 (All Saints' Day), December 24 (Christmas Eve—half holiday), December 25 (Christmas), December 31 (New Year's Eve—half holiday).

U.S.S.R.: Red Square in Moscow. On the left is the Kremlin wall (with the Kremlin behind it). On the right is the G.U.M. department store.

Nations
of the World

Ranking by size	Country	Area Miles²	U.S. = 100	Population Latest Estimates	U.S. = 100	Rank-ing
1	Union of Soviet Socialist Republics	8,649,540	239.26	258,932,000	119.42	3
2	Canada	3,851,809	106.55	23,316,000	10.75	31
3	China (Mainland)	3,691,500	102.11	849,688,000	391.89	1
4	United States of America	3,615,122	100.00	216,817,000	100.00	4
5	Brazil	3,286,488	90.91	112,259,000	51.78	7
6	Australia	2,966,150	82.05	14,215,000	6.56	45
7	India	1,269,346	35.11	625,818,000	288.64	2
8	Argentina	1,072,163	29.65	26,056,000	12.02	29
9	Sudan	967,500	26.76	16,953,000	7.82	37
10	Algeria	919,595	25.43	17,910,000	8.26	36
11	Zaire	905,365	25.04	26,376,000	12.17	27
12	Saudi Arabia	830,000	22.96	7,013,000	3.23	69
13	Mexico	761,605	21.07	64,594,000	29.79	11
14	Indonesia	735,272	20.33	143,282,000	66.08	5
15	Libya	679,363	18.79	2,444,000	1.13	108
16	Iran	636,296	17.60	34,274,000	15.81	24
17	Mongolia	604,250	16.71	1,531,000	0.71	118
18	Peru	496,525	13.73	16,358,000	7.54	40
19	Chad	495,750	13.71	4,197,000	1.96	90
20	Niger	489,191	13.53	4,859,000	2.24	85
21	Angola	481,354	13.32	6,761,000	3.12	70
22	Mali	478,767	13.24	5,994,000	2.76	77
23	Ethiopia	471,800	13.05	28,981,000	13.37	26
24	South Africa	471,445	13.04	26,129,000	12.05	28
25	Colombia	439,737	12.16	25,048,000	11.55	30
26	Bolivia	424,164	11.73	5,950,000	2.74	78
27	Mauritania	397,955	11.01	1,481,000	0.68	119
28	Egypt	386,662	10.70	38,741,000	17.87	20
29	Tanzania	364,900	10.09	16,073,000	7.41	41
30	Nigeria	356,669	9.87	66,628,000	30.73	10
31	Venezuela	352,144	9.74	12,737,000	5.87	49
32	Pakistan	310,404	9.59	75,278,000	34.72	9
33	Mozambique	302,330	8.36	9,678,000	4.46	58
34	Turkey	301,392	8.34	42,134,000	19.43	19
35	Chile	292,258	8.08	10,656,000	4.91	54
36	Zambia	290,586	8.04	5,347,000	2.47	80
37	Burma	261,218	7.23	31,512,000	14.53	25
38	Afghanistan	250,000	6.92	20,339,000	9.38	34
39	Somalia	246,201	6.81	3,354,000	1.55	97
40	Central African Empire	240,535	6.65	2,370,000	1.09	109
41	Botswana	231,805	6.41	710,000	0.33	128
42	Madagascar	226,658	6.27	8,520,000	3.81	63
43	Kenya	224,961	6.22	14,337,000	6.61	44
44	France	211,208	5.84	53,196,000	24.53	15
45	Thailand	198,457	5.49	44,039,000	20.31	18
46	Spain	194,897	5.39	36,672,000	16.91	21
47	Cameroon	183,569	5.08	7,663,000	3.53	66
48	Papua New Guinea	178,704	4.94	2,905,000	1.34	102

Ranking by size	Country	Area Miles²	U.S. =100	Population Latest Estimates	U.S. =100	Rank-ing
49	Sweden	173,732	4.81	8,271,000	3.81	64
50	Morocco	172,414	4.77	18,245,000	8.41	35
51	Iraq	167,925	4.65	12,171,000	5.61	52
52	Paraguay	157,048	4.34	2,805,000	1.30	105
53	Rhodesia	150,804	4.17	6,740,000	3.11	71
54	Japan	143,751	3.98	113,863,000	52.52	6
55	Congo	132,047	3.65	1,440,000	0.66	120
56	Finland	130,120	3.60	4,746,000	2.19	86
57	People's Democratic Republic of Yemen	128,560	3.57	1,797,000	0.83	115
58	Viet-Nam	128,402	3.55	47,872,000	22.08	16
59	Malaysia	127,315	3.52	12,600,000	5.81	50
60	Norway	125,182	3.46	4,051,000	1.87	92
61	Ivory Coast	124,504	3.44	6,671,000	3.08	72
62	Poland	120,725	3.34	34,945,000	16.12	23
63	Italy	116,317	3.22	56,601,000	26.11	13
64	Philippines	115,831	3.20	45,028,000	20.77	17
65	Ecuador	109,484	3.03	7,556,000	3.48	67
66	Upper Volta	105,869	2.93	6,319,000	2.91	75
67	New Zealand	103,736	2.87	3,152,000	1.45	100
68	Gabon	103,347	2.86	534,000	0.25	133
69	Yugoslavia	98,766	2.73	21,912,000	10.11	32
70	Germany (West)	95,993	2.66	61,371,000	28.31	12
71	Guinea	94,926	2.63	4,646,000	2.14	88
72	United Kingdom	94,214	2.61	55,852,000	25.76	14
73	Ghana	92,100	2.55	10,475,000	4.83	55
74	Romania	91,699	2.54	21,658,000	9.99	33
75	Uganda	91,452	2.53	12,353,000	5.70	51
76	Laos	91,400	2.53	3,427,000	1.58	96
77	Guyana	83,000	2.30	827,000	0.38	126
78	Oman	83,030	2.27	817,000	0.38	127
79	Sénégal	75,750	2.10	5,115,000	2.36	82
80	Yemen Arab Republic	75,290	2.08	5,238,000	2.42	81
81	Syria	71,498	1.98	7,845,000	3.62	65
82	Cambodia	69,898	1.93	8,606,000	3.97	62
83	Uruguay	68,536	1.90	2,814,000	1.30	104
84	Tunisia	63,170	1.74	6,065,000	2.80	76
85	Surinam	63,037	1.74	448,000	0.21	135
86	Bangladesh	55,598	1.54	80,558,000	37.15	8
87	Nepal	55,362	1.50	13,136,000	6.06	48
88	Greece	50,944	1.41	9,284,000	4.28	60
89	Nicaragua	50,193	1.39	2,312,000	1.07	112
90	Czechoslovakia	49,373	1.37	15,090,000	6.96	43
91	Korea (North)	46,540	1.29	16,651,000	7.68	39
92	Malawi	45,747	1.27	5,572,000	2.57	79
93	Benin	43,484	1.20	3,286,000	1.52	98
94	Honduras	43,277	1.20	2,831,000	1.31	103
95	Liberia	43,000	1.19	1,796,000	0.83	116
96	Cuba	42,827	1.18	9,474,000	4.37	59
97	Bulgaria	42,823	1.18	8,804,000	4.06	61
98	Guatemala	42,042	1.16	6,436,000	2.97	73
99	Germany (East)	41,768	1.15	16,765,000	7.73	38
100	Iceland	39,769	1.10	222,000	0.10	144
101	Korea (South)	38,131	1.05	36,436,000	16.80	22
102	Jordan	37,738	1.04	2,779,000	1.28	106
103	Hungary	35,920	0.99	10,678,000	4.92	53
104	Portugal	35,553	0.98	9,733,000	4.49	57
105	Austria	32,375	0.90	7,506,000	3.46	68
106	United Arab Emirates	32,278	0.89	236,000	0.11	143
107	Panama	29,209	0.81	1,771,000	0.82	117
108	Sierra Leone	27,699	0.77	3,470,000	1.60	95
109	Ireland	27,136	0.75	3,192,000	1.47	99
110	Sri Lanka	25,332	0.70	13,971,000	6.44	46
111	Togo	21,622	0.60	2,348,000	1.08	110
112	Costa Rica	19,600	0.54	2,071,000	0.96	114
113	Dominican Republic	18,816	0.52	4,978,000	2.30	84
114	Bhutan	18,000	0.50	1,232,000	0.57	121
115	Denmark	16,629	0.46	5,099,000	2.35	83
116	Switzerland	15,941	0.44	6,327,000	2.92	74
117	Netherlands	15,770	0.43	13,912,000	6.42	47
118	Guinea-Bissau	13,948	0.39	544,000	0.25	132

Ranking by size	Country	Area Miles²	U.S. =100	Population Latest Estimates	U.S. =100	Ranking
119	China (Taiwan)	13,893	0.38	15,989,000	7.37	42
120	Belgium	11,781	0.33	9,837,000	4.54	56
121	Lesotho	11,720	0.32	1,214,000	0.56	122
122	Solomon Islands	11,498	0.32	210,000	0.97	146
123	Albania	11,101	0.31	2,616,000	1.21	107
124	Equatorial Guinea	10,831	0.30	322,000	0.15	139
125	Burundi	10,747	0.30	3,966,000	1.83	93
126	Haiti	10,714	0.30	4,749,000	2.19	87
127	Rwanda	10,169	0.28	4,368,000	2.01	89
128	Djibouti	8,500	0.23	111,000	0.05	149
129	El Salvador	8,124	0.22	4,123,000	1.90	91
130	Israel	8,019	0.22	3,643,000	1.68	94
131	Fiji	7,055	0.20	600,000	0.28	130
132	Kuwait	6,880	0.19	1,129,000	0.52	123
133	Swaziland	6,704	0.19	497,000	0.23	134
134	Bahamas	5,382	0.15	220,000	0.10	145
135	Gambia	4,361	0.12	553,000	0.26	131
136	Qatar	4,247	0.12	98,000	0.05	150
137	Jamaica	4,244	0.11	2,085,000	0.96	113
138	Lebanon	3,950	0.11	3,056,000	1.41	101
139	Cyprus	3,572	0.10	640,000	0.30	129
140	Trinidad & Tobago	1,980	0.05	1,098,000	0.51	124
141	Cape Verde	1,557	0.04	306,000	0.14	140
142	Western Samoa	1,097	0.03	153,000	0.07	147
143	Luxembourg	999	0.03	356,000	0.16	137
144	Comoros	838	0.02	370,000	0.17	136
145	Mauritius	790	0.02	909,000	0.42	125
146	Sao Tomé & Principe	372	0.01	82,000	0.04	153
147	Dominica	290	0.008	70,302	0.32	154
148	Tonga	270	0.007	91,000	0.04	152
149	Bahrain	240	0.007	267,000	0.12	141
150	Singapore	232	0.006	2,322,000	1.07	111
151	Andorra	175	0.005	24,000	0.01	157
152	Barbados	166	0.005	254,000	0.11	142
153	Seychelles	156	0.004	62,000	0.03	155
154	Grenada	133	0.004	97,000	0.04	151
155	Malta	122	0.003	326,000	0.15	138
156	Maldives	115	0.003	141,000	0.07	148
157	Liechtenstein	62	0.002	23,000	0.01	158
158	San Marino	23.4	0.0006	21,000	0.01	159
159	Tuvalu	10	0.0003	6,000	0.003	161
160	Nauru	8	0.0002	8,000	0.004	160
161	Monaco	0.73	0.00002	25,000	0.01	156
162	Vatican City	0.17		723	0.0003	162

Proper Names

Germany (West) = Germany, Federal Republic of
    ”   (East) = German Democratic Republic
Cambodia = Democratic Kampuchea
Korea (South) = Republic of Korea
    ”   (North) = Democratic People's Republic of Korea
Laos = Lao People's Democratic Republic
Cameroon = United Republic of Cameroon
Tanzania = United Republic of Tanzania
Syria = Syrian Arab Republic

History

Important Dates

---

c. 3000–2000 B.C.	Greeks enter Peloponnesian peninsula from Asia
2900–2700 B.C.	Egyptian dynasties I-II
2700–2200 B.C.	The Old Kingdom (Egypt)
2700–2650 B.C.	Dynasty III
2650–2500 B.C.	Dynasty IV. Pyramids at Gizeh built
2500–2350 B.C.	Dynasty V
2350–2200 B.C.	Dynasty VI
2200–2100 B.C.	Egyptian dynasties VIII-X
2100–1788 B.C.	The Middle Kingdom (Egypt)
2100–2000 B.C.	Dynasty XI
2000–1788 B.C.	Dynasty XII
c. 2000 B.C.	Building of palace at Cnossus, Crete
c. 2000 B.C.	Invasion of Italian peninsula by first Indo-Europeans
c. 2000–1225 B.C.	Patriarchs of the sagas in Genesis
c. 1900–1600 B.C.	First Dynasty of Babylon (Hammurabi *c.* 1800 B.C.)
1788–1580 B.C.	Dynasties XIII-XVII
c. 1750–1500 B.C.	Old Hittite Kingdom
c. 1600 B.C.	Palace at Cnossus destroyed, rebuilt. Spread of Cretan civilization to Greece
1580–1090 B.C.	The New Kingdom (Egypt)
1580–1350 B.C.	Dynasty XVIII. Hatshepsut (1520–1480); Thutmosis III (1501–1447); Amenophis IV or Ikhnaton (1375–1358)
1350–1200 B.C.	Dynasty XIX. Ramses II (1292–1225)
1200–1090 B.C.	Dynasty XX. Ramses III (1198–1167)
1479 B.C.	Thutmosis III of Egypt conquers Palestine at battle of Megiddo
c. 1225–1200 B.C.	Moses leads Israelites out of Egypt
1200–600 B.C.	Invasion of England by Celts
c. 1184 B.C.	Sack of Illium (Troy)
c. 1150 B.C.	Judges written
1090–945 B.C.	Dynasty XXI (Egypt)
1026–1013 B.C.	Saul, king of Israelites
1013–973 B.C.	David, king of Judah
973–933 B.C.	Solomon, king of Judah
950 B.C.	Books of Samuel written
945–712 B.C.	Dynasties XXII-XXIV (Egypt)
933–722 B.C.	Kingdom of Israel
933–586 B.C.	Kingdom of Judah
c. 900 B.C.	First appearance of Etruscans in Italy
c. 800 B.C.	*Iliad* and *Odyssey* written by Homer
c. 800–600 B.C.	Colonization of Mediterranean by Greeks
814 B.C.	Carthage founded by colonists from Tyre (Phoenicia)
c. 760 B.C.	First Greek colonization of Italy, in Bay of Naples
753 B.C.	Traditional founding of Rome by Romulus
c. 750 B.C.	Amos the prophet
750–550 B.C.	Prophets active

CNOSSUS, CRETE: Minoan Palace built in 2000 B.C., destroyed in 1600 B.C., and rebuilt.

712–663 B.C.   Dynasty XXV (Egypt)
663–525 B.C.   Dynasty XXVI (Egypt)
660 B.C.   Traditional date of ascension of first emperor of Japan, Jimmu
660 B.C.   Zarathustra (Zoroaster) born
625–538 B.C.   Chaldean Empire
621 B.C.   Deuteronomy published
c. 610 B.C.   Spartans reorganize themselves into military state
c. 600–300 B.C.   *Upanishads* written
586–538 B.C.   Nebuchadnezzar destroys Jerusalem (586); the Babylonian exile
563?–483? B.C.   Siddhartha, founder of Buddhism
551–479 B.C.   Confucius (K'ung Ch'iu)
c. 550 B.C.   Isaiah written
538–532 B.C.   Jews return to Judah under Persians
520–516 B.C.   Temple rebuilt
525–404 B.C.   Persians conquer Egypt. Dynasty XXVII
509 B.C.   Traditional founding of Roman Republic
490 B.C.   Battle of Marathon
480 B.C.   Battle of Thermopylae and battle of Salamis
460–451 B.C.   First Peloponnesian War
450 B.C.   Twelve Tables published, fundamental law of Rome
447–432 B.C.   Parthenon built on Acropolis, Athens
431–404 B.C.   Great Peloponnesian War
420–408 B.C.   Erechtheum built on Acropolis
400 B.C.   Pentateuch published
404–332 B.C.   Dynasties XXVIII-XXX
399 B.C.   Death of Socrates
337–323 B.C.   Alexander III, the Great, king of Macedon
332–331 B.C.   Alexander founds Alexandria
332–323 B.C.   Egypt under Alexander the Great
327 B.C.   Alexander the Great invades India
323 B.C.   June 13. Death of Alexander at Babylon
323–30 B.C.   Egypt under the Ptolemies

264–241 B.C.   First Punic War, Rome vs. Carthage
218–201 B.C.   Second Punic War
218 B.C.   Hannibal crosses the Alps
216 B.C.   Battle of Cannae
215–205 B.C.   First Macedonian War, Philip V and Carthaginians vs. Rome
214 B.C.   Great Wall of China begun
201 B.C.   Rome acquires Spain from Carthaginians
168–63 B.C.   Maccabean rebellion of Jews
149–146 B.C.   Third Punic War
146 B.C.   Destruction of Carthage
c. 130 B.C.   Esther written
63 B.C.   Palestine under Roman rule
58–51 B.C.   Conquest of Gaul by Caesar
54 B.C.   Invasion of Britain by Caesar
49 B.C.   January 10–11. Caesar crosses the Rubicon
47–30 B.C.   Reign of Cleopatra VII of Egypt
44 B.C.   March 15. Assassination of Caesar
37–4 B.C.   Herod, king of Judea
31 B.C.   September 2. Battle of Actium
31 B.C.–14 A.D.   Reign of Imperator Caesar Octavianus (Augustus)
29 B.C.   Temple of Janus closed for first time since 235 B.C.
4 B.C.   Jesus of Nazareth born
6 A.D.   In China, all candidates for office required to take civil service examinations
30 A.D.   Crucifixion of Jesus ordered by Pontius Pilate
c. 60 A.D.   Buddhism introduced into China
61 A.D.   Revolt of Boadicea (Boudicca)
61 A.D.   St. Paul arrested by Felix, procurator of Judea
64 A.D.   Great fire of Rome while Emperor Nero watches
66–73 A.D.   War of Jews against Rome
69 A.D.   Destruction of Temple in Jerusalem by Titus
70 A.D.   Jerusalem destroyed by Titus
79 A.D.   Eruption of Mt. Vesuvius buries Pompeii and Herculaneum
   Colosseum completed in Rome
c. 105   Paper invented in China
107   Forum of Trajan built in Rome
117   Revolt of the Jews
122–127   Hadrian's Wall built in Scotland
132–135   Revolt of Jews under Eleazar and Simon Bar-Cocheba. Beginning of *Diaspora* (the Dispersion)
166–175   Danube crossed by invading Marcomanni. Beginning of invasions by barbarian hordes
249–251   C. Messius Quintus Traianus Decius emperor
   First systematic persecution of Christians begun
271–276   Existing walls of Rome built
300–350   Height of Roman influence in England
303   February 23. General persecution of Christians proclaimed. Until 313
325   First ecumenical council of the Church, at Nicaea
330   May 11. Constantinople established as capital of Empire. Built on site of Byzantium
340   Introduction of monasticism in west by Athanasius
340–420   St. Jerome, translator of Bible into Latin (the *Vulgate*)
354–430   St. Augustine, Bishop of Hippo Regius
378   August 9. Visigoths defeat Romans at battle of Adrianople, establishing supremacy of cavalry over infantry
395   January 17. Division of the Roman Empire into eastern and western parts
407   Evacuation of Britain by Romans
407–553   First Mongol empire established in Mongolia by Avars

JERUSALEM: The hills of this city, center of three religions, have seen many structures rise and be destroyed. This is the Church of All Nations.

410   August 14. Sack of Rome by Alaric the Visigoth
410–442   Invasion of British Isles by Jutes, Angles and Saxons
422–432   Petrine doctrine enunciated by Pope Celestine I
432   St. Patrick arrives in Ireland
c. 450   Huns, under Attila, invade Empire
451   June. Visigoth king, Theodoric I defeats Huns under Attila at battle of Châlons
455   June 2–16. Sack of Rome by Vandals
481–511   Clovis, first king of the Franks
529   *Codex Justinianus* published
532–537   St. Sophia (later a Mosque) built in Constantinople
c. 552   Introduction of Buddhism into Japan
570–632   Mohammed

590–604	Pope Gregory the Great
597	Arrival of St. Augustine in England
605	Grand Canal (China) built
622	July 15. *Hegira* (flight) of Mohammed to Medina. Traditional date of beginning of Moslem era
634–641	Arab conquests
638	Arab conquest of Jerusalem
687	Election of the first doge of Venice
711–715	Moslem conquest of Spain
732	Battle of Tours, Moslem invasion of Gaul halted by Charles Martel
756	*Donation of Pepin* establishes Papal States and papacy as temporal power
771–814	Charles the Great (Charlemagne), king of the Franks
778	*Song of Roland*
785–809	Harun al-Rashid
787	Danes first raid England
795	First Norse attack on Ireland
800	December 25. Charlemagne crowned Roman Emperor by Pope Leo III
840	Dublin founded
841	Norsemen invade Gaul (Normandy)
871–899	Alfred the Great
874	Norsemen settle in Iceland
c. 880–912	Prince Oleg, ruler of Kiev
c. 900	Apogee of kingdom of Ghana
900	Magyars begin invasion of eastern Europe
910	Abbey of Cluny founded
c. 940	Printing from wood blocks, in China
966	Conversion of the Poles to Roman Catholicism
981	Norsemen discover Greenland
987–996	Hugh, king of France, founder of the Capetian dynasty
c. 990	Russians converted to Greek Orthodoxy
992–1025	Boleslav I, organizer of first Polish state
997–1038	St. Stephen of Hungary
1000	Leif Ericsson lands on American coast, probably at Nova Scotia
1017–1035	King Canute
1034–1040	Duncan I, king of Scotland. Murdered by Macbeth.
1035	William I becomes duke of Normandy
1037	Appearance of Seljuk Turks in Middle East
1040–1057	Macbeth, king of Scotland
1042–1066	Edward the Confessor
1043	Church of St. Mark (Venice) begun
1054	Final schism between Rome and Constantinople
1054	Arabs begin conquest of West Africa
1066	October 14. Battle of Hastings
1066–1087	William I (the Conqueror), king of England
1073–1085	Pope Gregory VII (Hildebrand) enunciates infallibility of Pope
1086	Domesday survey of England
1096–1099	First Crusade
1099	Death of *el Cid* (Rodrigo Diaz of Bivar), Spanish national hero
1099	Sack of Jerusalem by Crusaders
1100–1125	Use of tea spreads throughout China
1147–1149	Second Crusade
1147	First mention of Moscow
1161	Chinese use explosives in battle
1162	Thomas Becket named Archbishop of Canterbury
1167–1171	Norman conquest of Ireland
1169–1250	Saladin, founder of Ayyubid dynasty

NORSEMEN who conquered all of Northern Europe in the 8th-10th centuries were the first to land in America. Wherever they went they left "rune stones" marking their conquests.

1170	Thomas Becket murdered
1175	Canterbury cathedral begun
1179	Portugal becomes independent
c. 1181	Alcazar, in Seville, begun
1187	Capture of Jerusalem by Saladin
1189–1192	Third Crusade
1190–1294	Creation of Mongol empire in central Asia
c. 1194	Chartres cathedral begun
1200	University of Paris founded
1202–1204	Fourth Crusade
1204	Capture and sacking of Constantinople by Crusaders
1206	Temujin, Mongol chief, proclaimed *Genghiz Khan*
1208–1213	Albigensian-Waldensian Crusade
1209	Cambridge University founded
1210	Reims (Rheims) cathedral begun
1211–1222	Mongols begin conquest of China
1212	Children's Crusade
1214–1294	Kublai Khan
1215	Magna Carta
1218–1221	Fifth Crusade
1222	First appearance of Mongols in Europe
1228–1229	Sixth Crusade
1236–1263	Alexander Nevski, prince of Novgorod
1237–1240	Mongol conquest of eastern Europe
1242	Battle of Lake Peipus, defeat of Teutonic Knights by Alexander Nevski

Important Dates in History (continued)

1248–1254   Seventh Crusade
1249   University College founded at Oxford
1255–1266   First journey of Nicolo and Maffeo Polo to China
1257   Sorbonne endowed
1258   Capture and sacking of Baghdad by Mongols
1267   Peking founded
1270–1291   Eighth Crusade
1271–1295   Second journey of Nicolo and Maffeo Polo to China, accompanied by 17-year-old Marco
1273–1291   Rudolf I, Holy Roman Emperor, founder of Hapsburg dynasty
1274   Thomas Aquinas dies
c. 1275   Walls of Carcassonne built
1275–1292   Marco Polo's journeys to China
1282   Title, Prince of Wales, given to heir to English throne
1284   First ducat coined by Venice
1290   Expulsion of Jews from England
1290–1326   Osman I, traditional founder of Ottoman Turk dynasty
1294–1328   John of Montecorvino, Catholic missionary to China
1305   Beginning of the papal Babylonian Captivity at Avignon
1306   Expulsion of the Jews from France
1307–1332   Apogee of Mandingo empire in West Africa
1324–1328   Travels of Friar Oderic of Pordenone through China
1326   Rise of Ottoman Turks
1334   Privileges granted to Jews by Casimir III, of Poland
1337   Beginning of 100 Years' War
1339–1349   Emergence of Commons in English Parliament
c. 1340   Hanseatic League established
c. 1344   Order of the Garter (English) founded
1346–1351   Conquest of Macedonia and Greece by Serbs
1346   August 26. Battle of Crécy
1348–1349   Black Death
1351   Rise of condottieri starts
1252   First gold florin coined
1354   Ottoman Turks first invade Europe, at Gallipoli
1358   Revolt of the *Jacquerie*
c. 1360   Organization of Janissary corps by Turks
c. 1362   *Piers Plowman* published
1368–1644   Ming Dynasty in China
1371–1390   Robert II, King of Scotland, establishes Stuart dynasty
c. 1376   Wiclif (Wycliffe) Bible published
1394–1460   Henry (the Navigator), of Portugal
1401   Cathedral of Seville begun
1412   Jeanne d'Arc (Joan of Arc) born at Domrémy
1415   Establishment of Hohenzollerns in Brandenburg
1415   October 25. Battle of Agincourt
1416   First war of Venice against Ottoman Turks
1420–1433   Hussite Wars
1431   Death of Joan of Arc
1433   Portuguese begin slave-raiding in West Africa
1434–1494   Dominance of Medici family in Florence
1439   Beginning of separate Russian Orthodox Church
1442   Turks invade Hungary
1453   Capture of Constantinople by Ottoman Turks
1454   Invention of printing from movable type by Johann Gutenberg
1455–1485   Wars of the Roses
1461   Final expulsion of English from France
1476   Caxton sets up printing press at Westminster
1478   Establishment of Inquisition in Spain
1484   Malory's *Morte d'Arthur* published
1485   August 22. Battle of Bosworth Field

COLUMBUS first set foot on American soil at this spot on San Salvador Island in the Bahamas.

1486	Maximilian, king of the Romans, establishes Hapsburg dynastic empire in Germany
1492	Expulsion of the Jews from Spain
1492	September 6. Columbus sails from Canary Islands
1492	October 12. Columbus lands in West Indies (San Salvador Island)
1493–1496	Second voyage of Columbus
1496	Expulsion of the Jews from Portugal
1497	Voyage of John Cabot to Newfoundland
1497	July 8. Vasco da Gama begins voyage to India
1498–1500	Third voyage of Columbus
1498	May 22. Vasco da Gama reaches Calicut (India)
1499	May. Voyage of Amerigo Vespucci and Alonso de Ojeda to the New World; discovered mouth of Amazon. Until June, 1500
1500–1501	Portuguese establish trade route to India
1501	Negro slavery introduced into West Indies by Spaniards
1501–1502	Second voyage of Amerigo Vespucci to South America
1502–1504	Fourth voyage of Columbus
1505	Portuguese establish trading posts on Malabar coast
1505–1507	Portuguese found Mozambique
1507	Martin Waldseemüller proposes calling New World *America*
1508–1511	San Juan, Puerto Rico, founded; Jamaica settled by Spaniards
1508–1512	Sistine Chapel painted
1509–1547	Henry VIII, of England

Wives	From	To
Catharine of Aragon	June 3, 1509	March 30, 1533
Anne Boleyn	January 25, 1533	May 19, 1536
Jane Seymour	May 20, 1536	October 24, 1537
Anne of Cleves	October 24, 1537	June 24, 1540
Catharine Howard	August 8, 1540	February 12, 1542
Catherine Parr	July 10, 1543	Widowed

1517	Discovery of Yucatan civilization by Francisco Hernández de Córdoba

167

Important Dates in History (continued)

1517   October 17. Luther nails 95 theses to church door at Wittenberg
1517   Slave trade established by Charles V of Spain
1518–1522   Conquest of Mexico by Hernándo Cortes
1519   Election of Charles I, of Spain, as Charles V, as Holy Roman Emperor
1519–1522   Circumnavigation of Earth by Ferdinand Magellan
1520   Luther excommunicated
1521   April 25. Magellan killed in Philippines
1524   Giovanni de Verrazano explores east coast of N. America
1526–1761   Mogul empire established in India
1531–1536   Conquest of Peru by Francisco Pizarro
1533–1584   Ivan IV (the Terrible), of Russia
1534–1541   Voyages of Jacques Cartier to St. Lawrence River
1536   Buenos Aires founded by Pedro de Mendoza
1540   September 27. Society of Jesus (Jesuits) established
1540–1542   Grand Canyon discovered by Francisco Vásquez de Coronado
1541   Calvin introduces Reformation into Geneva
1541   Mississippi River discovered by Hernando de Soto
1542   Ireland made kingdom
1542   Portuguese reach coast of Japan
1547   Dome of St. Peter's, Rome, built
1547   Ivan IV assumes title of *Tsar* (Czar)
1559   First index of forbidden books drawn up
1562–1598   Religious wars against the Huguenots
1562   John Hawkins initiates British slave trade to West Indies
1563   Escorial started
1563   Establishment of Anglican Church
1565–1567   Rio de Janeiro founded by Mem de Sá
1568–1648   Revolt of the Netherlands from Spain
1569   Spanish Inquisition introduced into New World
1571   October 7. Battle of Lepanto. Venetian victory ends threat of Turks
1572   August 23–24. Massacre of St. Bartholomew
1576   Martin Frobisher seeks Northwest Passage
1577–1580   Sir Francis Drake circumnavigates world
1582   Calendar reformed by Pope Gregory XIII
1584   Sir Walter Raleigh establishes colony on Roanoke Island (Virginia)
1587   Execution of Mary, queen of Scots
1588   July 21–29. Defeat of the Spanish Armada
1589   Russian Orthodox Church becomes independent of Greek Orthodox Church
1595   First Dutch settlements on coast of W. Africa
1598–1605   Boris Godunov, Tsar of Russia
1600   East India Company chartered
1602   Dutch East India Company established
1603–1625   James I, of England (James VI, of Scotland)
1603   March 24. Union of Scotland and England
1605   *Don Quixote* published
1605   November 5. Gunpowder Plot
1607   May. Jamestown (R.I.) founded by Christopher Newport
1608   July 3. Quebec founded
1609   Galileo Galilei first observes planets through telescope
1609   Dutch establish trading post at Hirado, Japan
1609   Henry Hudson explores river named after him
1610   Henry Hudson discovers bay named after him
1611   Authorized (King James) version of *Bible* completed
1612   Tobacco first cultivated in N. America
1612   Trading post established on Manhattan Island by Dutch

NEW AMSTERDAM's governor, Peter Stuyvesant, in 1664, surrendered this city to the British without a shot being fired.

1613–1645	Michael Romanov, Tsar of Russia, founder of the dynasty
1618–1648	Thirty Years' War
1620	November. Pilgrims arrive at Cape Cod
1626	Manhattan Island purchased from Indians by Peter Minuit
1630	Boston founded
1632–1653	Taj Mahal built by Shah Jahan for his wife Mumtaz Mahal
1636	Japanese forbidden to travel abroad
1636	June. Providence (R.I.) founded by Roger Williams
1637	Harvard College established, first in American colonies
1642	August 22. English Civil War begins
1642	Montreal founded by de Maisonneuve
1649–1660	Commonwealth in England under Oliver Cromwell
1653	December 16. Cromwell declared Lord Protector
1655	English capture Jamaica from Spanish
1657	Slaves introduced in Cape Colony by Dutch
1661	English acquire Bombay
1663	Carolina granted to eight proprietors
1664	August 27. New Amsterdam surrenders to English. Name changes to New York
1666	September 2–9. Great Fire in London
1668	Hudson's Bay Company founded
1681	March 4. Charter of Pennsylvania granted to William Penn
1682	Philadelphia founded
1683	July 17–September 12. Siege of Vienna by Ottoman Turks. High point of Turkish advance
1685	October 18. Revocation of the Edict of Nantes
1689–1702	William III and Mary, of England
1689–1725	Peter I (the Great), Tsar of Russia
1690	Calcutta founded by British
1692	Salem witchcraft trials
1694	July 27. Bank of England established
1701	Yale College founded

Important Dates in History (continued)

1701   Detroit founded
1701   January 18. Frederick III, Elector of Brandenburg, assumes title, King of Prussia
1702–1713   Queen Anne's War in N. America
1703   Russian capital established at St. Petersburg
1704   August 4. British occupy Gibraltar
1707   May 1. Union of England and Scotland as Great Britain. Union Jack adopted
1713   British receive right to import African slaves into Spanish colonies in New World
1714–1727   George I, first of the house of Hanover
1718   New Orleans founded
1725   Vitus Bering discovers strait named after him
1729   North and South Carolina established by Act of Parliament
1733   Georgia founded
1740–1786   Frederick II (the Great), king of Prussia
1749   Halifax, Nova Scotia, founded
1755   November 1. The great Lisbon earthquake
1755   University of Moscow founded
1755–1763   French and Indian war in N. America
1756–1763   Seven Years' War in Europe
1756   June 20. Calcutta captured, English imprisoned in *Black Hole*
1757   June 22. Battle of Plassey. French influence in India destroyed
1759   September 13. Battle of the Plains of Abraham
1760   September 8. Surrender of Montreal. All Canada now British
1762–1796   Catherine II (the Great), of Russia
1765   Passage of Stamp Act by Parliament
1765   May 29. Patrick Henry: "Give me liberty or give me death"
1766   March. Repeal of Stamp Act
1767   Mason and Dixon survey border between Pennsylvania and Maryland
1770   Marriage of Louis XVI to Marie Antoinette
1770   March 5. Boston massacre
1773   December 16. Boston Tea Party
1774   Regulating Act by Parliament establishes British India
1775–1783   War of American Independence
1775   April 19. Battles of Lexington and Concord
1775   May 10. Second Continental Congress meets in Philadelphia
1775   May 10–12. Ticonderoga captured by Ethan Allen
1775   June 15. George Washington appointed commander-in-chief
1775   June 17. Battle of Bunker Hill
1775   July. Siege of Boston begins
1776   March 17. British evacuate Boston
1776   July 4. Declaration of Independence adopted
1776   August 27. Battle of Long Island
1776   September 15. British occupy New York
1776   December 26. Battle of Trenton
1777   November 15. Articles of Confederation adopted by Continental Congress
1779   February 14. Captain James Cook killed by natives on Hawaiian Islands
1779   June. Spain enters war of U.S. independence
1780   September 23. Major André captured, Benedict Arnold escapes
1780   October 2. Major André hanged
1781   October 19. Cornwallis surrenders at Yorktown, Va.
1783   January 20–September 3. Treaty of Paris ends War of American Independence
1784   India Act places English East India Company under government control
1787   Northwest Ordinance enacted by Congress
1787   May. Constitutional Convention meets in Philadelphia

TREATY OF PARIS in 1783, ending the Revolutionary War, was signed by John Jay, John Adams, Ben Franklin, and others for America. They are shown on the left in this unfinished painting by Benjamin West.

1787	September 17. Constitution of U.S. adopted in Philadelphia
1788	January 26. First convict transport arrives at Sydney, Australia
1789	March 4. First Congress meets at New York
1789	April 30. George Washington inaugurated President
1789	May 5. Meeting of Estates-General at Versailles
1789	June 17. First meeting of French National Assembly
1789	July 14. Storming of the Bastille
1789	August 27. Declaration of the Rights of Man by French National Assembly
1790	Mutineers from *Bounty* settle on Pitcairn Island
1791	June 10. Passage of Canada Act by Parliament
1791	June 20–25. Flight of Louis XVI
1792	Denmark prohibits slave trade
1792	Storming of Tuilleries
1792	September 21. National Convention meets. Monarchy abolished, France declared a republic
1793	January 21. Louis XVI executed
1793	July 13. Marat assassinated by Charlotte Corday
1793	October 16. Marie Antoinette executed
1794	May 6. Slave revolt in Haiti under Toussaint L'Ouverture, Jean-Jacques Dessalines, and Henri Christophe
1794	Sheep raising begins in Australia
1795	August 22. Constitution of 1795 adopted in France. Formation of the Directory
1796	September 18. Washington's farewell address
1798	Ceylon becomes British crown colony
1798	Eli Whitney manufactures guns using interchangeable parts— first use of this principle
1798	Malthus' *Essay on Population* published
1798	August 1. Battle of the Nile
1796	November 9. Coup d'état de Brumaire. Napoleon seizes power as first consul
1800	Russia annexes kingdom of Georgia
1801	January 1. Union of Great Britain and Ireland as United Kingdom
1802	Cuneiform writing deciphered by Georg Friedrich Grotefeud
1802	Legion of Honor created in France

Important Dates in History (continued)

1802	August 2. Napoleon becomes consul for life
1803	April 30. Louisiana Territory purchased from France
1804	May 18. Napoleon proclaimed Emperor of French
1804	July. Duel between Aaron Burr and Alexander Hamilton. Hamilton dies from wounds next day
1804	October 8. Dessalines proclaims self emperor Jacques I, of Haiti. Assassinated October 17, 1806
1804	Lewis and Clark Expedition; until 1806
1805–1812	Russians expand into Alaska and N. California
1805	October 21. Naval battle of Trafalgar off Spanish coast
1806	August 6. End of the Holy Roman Empire
1806	October 27. Napoleon occupies Berlin
1807	Slavery abolished in British dominions
1807	August 17. Robert Fulton's steamboat, the *Claremont*, travels from New York to Albany
1808	February 2. French occupy Rome
1808	March. Spain invaded by French
1808	May. Spanish insurrection against French
1809	January 1. U.S. prohibits African slave trade
1809	May 13. French occupy Vienna
1810	April. Marriage of Napoleon to Marie Louise
1810	Kingdom of Holland established
1810	August 12. French abandon Madrid
1812	June. French begin invasion of Russia
1812	June 18. U.S. declares war on Great Britain
1812	September 7. Battle of Borodino won by Napoleon
1812	September 14. French occupy Moscow
1812	September 15–19. Burning of Moscow
1812	October 19. Retreat from Moscow by French
1813	September 10. Battle of Lake Erie
1814	April 11. Napoleon abdicates
1814	May 30. British obtain Cape Colony by Treaty of Paris
1814	August 7. Inquisition re-established in Rome by Papacy
1814	September. Congress of Vienna begins

NAPOLEON dominated history in Europe, North Africa and had large tracts of land in America from 1796 to his final abdication in 1815.

1814	December 24. Treaty of Ghent ends War of 1812.
1815	January 8. Battle of New Orleans
1815	June 18. Battle of Waterloo
1815	June 22. Napoleon abdicates again
1819	February 22. Spain cedes Florida to U.S.
1819	Sir Stamford Raffles founds Singapore
1819	Steamship *Savannah* crosses Atlantic
1820	First British colonists settle in South Africa
1821	March 6. Alexander Ypsilanti starts Greek revolt against Turks. Beginning of Greek war of independence
1821	Egyptian hieroglyphics deciphered by Jean François Champollion
1821	May 5. Death of Napoleon on St. Helena
1822	Liberia founded as haven for freed American slaves
1825	September 27. First railroad line placed in operation in England, the Stockton and Darlington
1825	December 26. Decembrist Rising in Russia
1826	Erie Canal completed
1827	June 5. Turks capture Acropolis
1828–1829	Russo-Turkish war. Russia secures mouth of Danube and east coast of Black Sea
1829	British outlaw *Suttee* in India
1830–1833	Lyell's *Principles of Geology* published
1830	July 5. French occupy Algiers
1830	July 30. Louis Philippe proclaimed king of France
1830	Mormon Church established in America by Joseph Smith
1833	General Trades' Union organized in N.Y.
1833	August 23. Slavery abolished in British colonies
1833–1835	Voyage of the *Beagle*, with Charles Darwin, to the Pacific
1834	Cyrus McCormick invents reaping machine
1835	Great Trek of the Boers from Cape Colony to the Transvaal. Until 1837
1836	Samuel Colt invents revolver
1836	March 2. Republic of Texas proclaimed
1837	June 20. Victoria, queen of Great Britain
1838	Underground Railroad established
1839	February 10. Victoria marries Albert of Saxe-Coburg-Gotha
1840	January 22. First British colonists land in New Zealand
1844	Nitrous oxide first used as anaesthetic in dentistry by Horace Wells
1845	March 1. Texas annexed by U.S.
1846	U.S.-Mexican War
1847	July 26. Republic of Liberia founded
1847	September 14. Winfield Scott captures Mexico City
1848	*Communist Manifesto* published
1848	January 24. Gold discovered at Coloma, California
1848	February 2. Treaty of Guadalupe Hidalgo ends Mexican War. California, New Mexico ceded to U.S.
1848	February 22. Insurrection begins in Paris
1848	February 24. Louis Philippe abdicates. French Republic proclaimed
1848	March 15. Insurrection in Berlin
1848	September 12. Adoption of new federal constitution by Switzerland, modeled on U.S. example
1848	November 16. Popular insurrection in Rome against Papacy
1848	November 25. Pope flees Rome
1848	December 20. Prince Louis Napoleon, President of French Republic
1850	April 12. Pope returns to Rome
1851	May 1–October 15. The Great Exhibition in London
1851	August 9. Gold discovered in Australia
1851	December 2. Coup d'état by Louis Napoleon
1852	November 2. French empire re-established. Napoleon III, emperor

1854	March 28. England, France declare war on Russia: Crimean War
1854	March 31. Commodore Matthew C. Perry signs Treaty of Kanagawa with Japanese
1854	September 14. French, English troops land in Crimea
1854	October 25. Battle of Balaklava (Charge of the Light Brigade)
1854	November 30. Egyptians grant Suez Canal concession to Ferdinand de Lesseps
1854	December 8. Promulgation of dogma of the immaculate conception
1856	March 30. Treaty of Paris ends Crimean War
1857	March 7. Dred Scott decision by Supreme Court
1858	June 29. Treaties of Tientsin permits foreign legations at Peking, Christian missions in interior, establishes maritime customs service under British control, legalizes importation of opium
1858	July 23. Parliament gives civil rights to Jews
1858	August. Lincoln-Douglas debates
1858	August 5. Transatlantic cable completed
1858	September 1. End of East India Company. British crown assumes authority
1859	Darwin's *Origin of Species* published
1859	Oil discovered at Titusville, Pa.
1859	April 29. Work begins on Suez Canal
1859	October 19. John Brown raids Harper's Ferry
1860	May 11. Garibaldi lands at Marsala, Sicily
1860	September 7. Garibaldi captures Naples
1860	Oliver F. Winchester invents repeating rifle
1860	Vladivostok founded
1861	February 4. Formation of Confederate States of America
1861	February 8. Jefferson Davis elected president of Confederacy
1861	March 3. Emancipation of serfs in Russia
1861	March 4. Abraham Lincoln inaugurated President
1861	March 17. Kingdom of Italy proclaimed. Victor Emmanuel king
1861	April 12–13. Fort Sumter shelled
1861	May 13. Great Britain recognizes Confederacy
1861	July 21. First battle of Bull Run
1861	December 14. Albert, Victoria's prince consort, dies
1862	Slavery abolished in Dutch West Indies
1862	March 9. Battle of *Monitor* vs. *Merrimac*
1862	June 1. Robert E. Lee, commander-in-chief of Confederate army
1862	June 3. U.S. recognizes Republic of Liberia
1862	August 30. Second battle of Bull Run
1862	September. Otto von Bismarck becomes minister-president of Prussia
1862	September 17. Battle of Antietam
1862	December 13. Battle of Fredericksburg
1863	January 1. Emancipation Proclamation by Abraham Lincoln
1863	May 1–4. Battle of Chancellorsville
1863	June. French troops occupy Mexico City. Archduke Maximilian proclaimed emperor
1863	July 1–3. Battle of Gettysburg
1863	July 4. Surrender of Vicksburg
1863	September 19–20. Battle of Chickamauga
1863	November 23–25. Battle of Chattanooga
1864	George Pullman builds first railroad sleeping car
1864	Marx founds first International Workingmen's Association
1864	March 9. Ulysses S. Grant, commander-in-chief, Union forces
1864	May 5–6. Battle of the Wilderness

JEFFERSON DAVIS was sworn in as president of the Confederate States in the capitol building (center of photo) in Montgomery, Alabama, in 1861.

1864	May 5. Sherman begins march to sea from Chattanooga
1864	July 22. Battle of Atlanta
1864	September 2. Atlanta evacuated by Confederate forces
1865	Gregor Mendel establishes laws of genetic inheritance
1865	April 3. Surrender of Richmond
1865	April 9. Lee surrenders at Appomattox Court House
1865	April 14. Lincoln assassinated; dies April 15.
1865	December 18. Ratification of 13th amendment abolishing slavery
1866	July 27. Atlantic cable successfully completed
1867	Formation of North German Confederation under Prussia
1867	Last convicts arrive in Australia
1867	Marx's *Das Kapital* published
1867	Diamonds discovered in South Africa, on Orange River
1867	March 2. Passage of Basic Reconstruction Act
1867	March 29. British North America Act passed by Parliament; formation of Dominion of Canada effective July 1
1867	March 30. Alaska purchased for $7,200,000
1867	June 19. Maximilian executed by Mexicans
1868	January 3. Emperor assumes direct rule of Japan, beginning of Meiji period
1868	February 24. Andrew Johnson impeached
1868	May 26. Johnson acquitted
1868	July 28. Ratification of 14th amendment
1869	November 16. Suez Canal opens
1870	July 18. Promulgation of the dogma of papal infallibility
1870	July 19. France declares war on Prussia
1870	September 1. Defeat of French army at Sedan
1870	September 2. Capitulation of Napoleon III at Battle of Sedan
1870	September 4. Republic proclaimed in Paris
1870	September 19. Siege of Paris by Germans
1870	October 2. Rome annexed to Italy, becomes capital
1871	Henry M. Stanley finds David Livingstone
1871	January 18. German empire proclaimed. William I emperor
1871	January 28. Paris capitulates to Germans
1871	March 1–3. Establishment of Paris Commune
1873	Silver discovered in Nevada

Important Dates in History (continued)

1874	March 15. Indo-China becomes French protectorate
1875	November 25. Britain purchases Suez Canal shares
1876	February 15. Barbed wire patented
1876	June 25. Massacre of Gen. Custer at Little Big Horn by Plains Sioux under Sitting Bull
1877	January 1. Victoria proclaimed empress of India
1878	May 18. Colombian govt. grants de Lesseps right to construct Panamanian canal
1880	January 1. Construction starts on sea-level canal across Panama
1880	December 30. Boers revolt in Transvaal, proclaim republic
1881	Pasteur develops vaccination for rabies
1881	Pogroms begin in Ukraine
1881	July 2. Garfield shot, dies September 19
1882	Koch discovers tuberculosis germ
1882	May 6. Phoenix Park murders, Dublin
1882	September 15. British occupy Cairo
1883	January 16. Passage of Pendleton Act initiates civil service examinations
1884	Koch discovers cholera germ
1885	Pasteur develops innoculation against hydrophobia
1885	January 26. Mahdi captures Khartum. General Charles Gordon killed
1885	May 2. Congo Free State established by Leopold II of Belgium
1886	Gold discovered on Witwatersrand in S. Transvaal
1886	May 4. Haymarket Square riot in Chicago
1886	September. Johannesburg founded
1887	February 4. Passage of Interstate Commerce Act
1889	January 30. Suicide of Archduke Rudolf, heir to the Austrian throne, at Mayerling
1889	February. Collapse of the Compagnie du Canal Interocéanique (the Panama scandal)
1890	March 18. Bismarck dismissed by William II
1891–1903	Trans-Siberian Railway built
1891	April 15. Katanga Company formed by Leopold of Belgium to exploit copper deposits
1892	June 30. Start of steelworkers strike at Homestead Plant of Carnegie Steel Co.
1892	December 5. Forced labor introduced in Congo by King Leopold
1893	Laos becomes French protectorate
1893	January. Independent Labour Party founded in Great Britain
1893	January 14. Hawaiian coup d'état. U.S. Marines land January 16
1894	Principle of general strike adopted by French labor movement
1894	July 4. Republic of Hawaii proclaimed
1894	October 15. Captain Alfred Dreyfus arrested for treason
1894	December 22. Dreyfus convicted of treason
1895–1896	Italians invade Ethiopia
1895	December 29. Jameson Raid into Transvaal
1896	April. Revival of Olympic Games
1896	August. Klondike gold rush starts
1898	Count Ferdinand von Zeppelin builds first rigid airship
1898	Curies discover radium
1898	January 13. Émile Zola publishes denunciation of French army general staff: *J'accuse*
1898	February 15. U.S.S. *Maine* destroyed in Havana harbor
1898	March 27. Russia obtains 25-year lease of Port Arthur from Chinese
1898	April 10. France obtains 99-year lease of Kwangchow Bay from Chinese
1898	April 25. U.S. declares war against Spain
1898	May 1. Battle of Manila Bay

1898	June 9. Britain obtains 99-year lease of Kowloon (opposite Hong Kong Island)
1898	August 12. Hawaii annexed by U.S.
1898	August 13. Manila captured
1898	December 10. Treaty of Paris ends Spanish-American War. U.S. obtains Philippines, Puerto Rico, Guam
1899	French abandon work on Panama Canal
1899	September 6. Open Door policy in Far East suggested by U.S.
1899	October 12. Boer War begins. Until May 31, 1902
1900	Planck introduces quantum theory
1900	May 28. Boxer rebellion begins
1900	June 20. Chinese begin siege of Peking legations. Until August 14
1901	Marconi transmits radio signals across Atlantic
1901	September 14. McKinley assassinated. Theodore Roosevelt succeeds to Presidency
1902	January 30. Anglo-Japanese Alliance signed
1903	November 3. Panama declares independence from Colombia. U.S. and Panama sign canal treaty November 18
1903	Split in Russian Social Democrat Party into *Mensheviks* and *Bolsheviks*
1903	December 17. First aircraft flight by Wilbur and Orville Wright
1904	February 8. Japan attacks Port Arthur
1904	February 10. Russia declares war on Japan
1905	Einstein's *Special Theory of Relativity* published
1905	January 2. Fall of Port Arthur to Japanese
1905	January 22. Russian troops fire on procession of workers in St. Petersburg: Bloody Sunday
1905	May 27–29. Battle of Tsushima. Japanese annihilate Russian fleet
1905	September 5. Treaty of Portsmouth ends Russo-Japanese war
1905	October 20–30. General strike in St. Petersburg
1905	October 26. First soviet formed by St. Petersburg workers

ALASKA, purchased for $7,200,000 from Russia in 1867, became one of the biggest bargains in history when gold was discovered there in 1896. This is an Alaskan totem pole.

1905	October 30. Tsar issues October Manifesto granting constitution
1906	Wasserman test for syphilis introduced
1906	February 10. Launching of the *Dreadnought*
1906	July 12. Guilty finding against Dreyfus set aside
1907	September 26. New Zealand becomes British Dominion
1908	Congo ceded to Belgium by Leopold II
1908	April 20. F. A. Cook claims he reached North Pole on this date
1908	December 28. Severe earthquake strikes S. Italy; 150,000 killed
1909	Anglo-Persian Oil Company founded
1909	April. Armenian massacres; provoked by Armenian demonstrations
1909	April 6. Robert E. Peary claims he reached the North Pole on this date
1910	May 31. South Africa Act (approved by Parliament September 20, 1909), becomes effective. Union of South Africa established
1911	May 1. Supreme Court orders dissolution of Standard Oil and American Tobacco
1911	October. Chinese Revolution begins
1911	December 16. Roald Amundsen reaches South Pole
1912	January 16. R. F. Scott reaches South Pole
1912	August. U.S. Marines land in Nicaragua
1913	February 25. Ratification of 16th amendment permitting personal income tax
1913	December 23. Passage of Federal Reserve Bank Act
1914	April 21. U.S. Marines land at Vera Cruz
1914	June 28. Archduke Francis Ferdinand assassinated at Sarajevo by Garrilo Princip
1914	July 28. Austria declares war on Serbia
1914	August 1. French mobilization; German mobilization. Germany declares war on Russia
1914	August 2. Germans invade Luxembourg
1914	August 3. Germany declares war on France; invades Belgium
1914	August 4. England declares war on Germany
1914	August 6. Austria declares war on Russia
1914	August 15. Panama Canal opens
1914	August 23. Japan declares war on Germany
1914	September 5. Battle of the Marne. Until September 12
1914	October 15. Passage of Clayton Anti-Trust Act
1914	November 2. Russia declares war on Turkey
1914	November 5. England and France declare war on Turkey
1914	December 18. British declare protectorate over Egypt
1915	January 19. First German airship raid on England
1915	February 18. Germans begin submarine blockade of Britain.
1915	April 25. British land at Gallipoli, Turkey
1915	May 7. *Lusitania* sunk
1915	May 23. Italy declares war on Austria-Hungary
1915	October 14. Bulgaria enters World War I
1915	December 19. British begin withdrawal from Gallipoli. Completed January 9, 1916
1916	February 21. Battle of Verdun begins. Until July 11
1916	March 15. General John J. Pershing invades Mexico in search of Francisco (Pancho) Villa. Withdraws February 5, 1917
1916	April 24. Easter Rebellion begins in Ireland. Suppressed May 1
1916	May 31. Naval Battle of Jutland, off Danish coast
1916	June 5. Arab revolt against Turkey begins
1916	July 1. Battle of the Somme begins. Until November 18
1916	August 27. Romania declares war on Austria
1916	August 28. Italy declares war on Germany
1916	September 15. First use of tanks in battle. By the British

RUSSIAN REVOLUTION: The Red Guard enters the Kremlin in Moscow in 1918. Painting by E. Lissner.

1916	November 28. First German airplane raid on London
1916	December 7. David Lloyd George, Prime Minister, forms war cabinet
1916	December 30. Rasputin assassinated by Prince Felix Yussupov
1917	January 31. Germans begin unrestricted submarine warfare
1917	February 3. U.S. severs relations with Germany
1917	March 10. Russian troops mutiny in Petrograd
1917	March 12. Provisional government formed in Russia
1917	March 12. Russian socialists organize Council of Workers' and Soldiers' Deputies (Soviet) in Petrograd
1917	March 15. Tsar Nicholas II abdicates
1917	March 31. U.S. obtains Virgin Islands from Denmark for $25,000,000
1917	April 6. U.S. declares war on Germany
1917	April 16. Lenin arrives in Petrograd
1917	May. Beginning of mutiny in French armies
1917	May 10. British begin use of convoy system to counter heavy losses at sea
1917	November 2. Balfour Declaration published
1917	November 6. Bolshevik revolution begins in Petrograd (St. Petersburg)
1917	December 5. Armistice concluded between Russia and Germany
1917	December 8. British capture Jerusalem
1917	December 9. Don Cossacks under Kornilov revolt. Beginning of Russian civil war
1917	December 15. Armistice concluded on eastern front between Bolsheviks and Germans
1918	March 3. Russians sign treaty of Brest-Litovsk
1918	March 9. Russian government moves from Petrograd (St. Petersburg) to Moscow
1918	June 23. Allied expeditionary force lands at Murmansk
1918	July 16. Tsar, Tsarina, and their children murdered at Ekaterinburg
1918	October 21. Czechoslovaks proclaim independence
1918	October 29. Yugoslavs proclaim independence
1918	October 30. Turks sign armistice
1918	November 3. Mutiny in the German fleet at Kiel
1918	November 7. Revolution breaks out in Munich

179

Important Dates in History (continued)

1918	November 8. Bavarian republic proclaimed
1918	November 9. William II of Germany abdicates. German republic proclaimed
1918	November 11. Armistice on western front
1918	November 13. Austrian Republic proclaimed
1918	November 16. Hungarian Republic proclaimed
1919	January 5–15. Spartacist revolt in Berlin.
1919	January 18. Peace conference opens at Paris
1919	March 22. Bolshevik *coup d'état* in Hungary led by Bela Kun. Until August 1
1919	March 23. Benito Mussolini founds Italian fascist party
1919	April 4. Soviet republic established in Bavaria. Until May 1
1919	April 13. Amritsar Massacre in India
1919	June 15. John Alcock and Arthur W. Brown first to cross Atlantic in airplane
1919	June 21. Entire German fleet scuttled at Scapa Flow
1919	June 28. Treaty of Versailles signed
1919	July 31. Weimar Constitution adopted
1919	September 4. Turkish nationalist congress meets under Mustapha Kemal. Wins control of Turkish parliament
1919	September 10. Treaty of St. Germain signed, ending war with Austria
1919	October 28. Passage of National Prohibition Act (Volstead Act) in U.S.
1919	November 26. Sinn Fein suppressed by British government. Insurrection begins
1919	November 27. Treaty of Neuilly signed, ending war with Bulgaria
1920	January 10. Official birth of League of Nations
1920	January 20. British assume mandate over German East Africa; rename it Tanganyika
1920	March 19. U.S. Senate rejects Treaty of Versailles
1920	April 23. Mustapha Kemal becomes president of provisional Turkish government at Angora
1920	May 15. Arrival of British troops ("Black and Tans") in Ireland
1920	June 4. Treaty of Trianon, ending war with Hungary
1920	July 20. British East Africa renamed Kenya
1920	August 20. Treaty of Sèvres signed, ending war with Turkey
1920	September 8. Gandhi launches first non-cooperation campaign
1920	December 23. Government of Ireland Act passed by Parliament. Establishes N. and S. Ireland
1921	March 17. New economic policy initiated by Soviet government
1921	August 24–25. U.S. signs peace treaties with Germany and Austria
1921	December 6. Sinn Fein sign agreement with British government establishing Irish Free State as Dominion. Ratified by Irish Dail January 14, 1922
1921	December 24. Gandhi introduces first civil disobedience campaign
1922	August. German mark collapses
1922	October 28. Fascist March on Rome
1922	October 31. Mussolini becomes Italian prime minister
1922	December 30. Formation of Union of Socialist Soviet Republics (USSR)
1923	January 11. French troops occupy Ruhr after Germany defaults on reparations
1923	September. Height of German hyperinflation
1923	September 1. Great earthquake in Japan
1923	October 14. Angora (Ankara) becomes new Turkish capital
1923	October 29. Turkish republic proclaimed
1923	November 8. Beer Hall Putsch in Munich, led by Gen. Erich Ludendorff and Adolf Hitler

CHARLES A.
LINDBERGH made
the first solo crossing
of the Atlantic in this
plane in 1927.

1924	January 21. Lenin dies
1924	January 26. Petrograd (St. Petersburg) renamed Leningrad
1924	May 26. New immigration act severely limits immigration into U.S.
1924	November 18. French evacuate Ruhr
1925	November. Wearing of fez forbidden in Turkey
1926	May 3. General strike begins in England. Lasts 9 days
1926	May 9. Richard Byrd and Floyd Bennett fly over North Pole
1927	May 21. Charles A. Lindbergh makes first solo crossing of Atlantic in airplane
1927	December 27. Final victory of Stalin over opponents
1928	July 2. Universal female suffrage in England
1928	October 7. Ras Tafari becomes king of Ethiopia
1929	February 11. Italy and papacy sign Lateran Treaties creating state of Vatican City
1929	October 29. Stock market crashes
1930	February 23. Rafael Leonidas Trujillo becomes president of Dominican Republic
1930	March 28. Name of Constantinople changed to Istanbul
1930	June 30. Last French troops evacuate Rhineland
1930	November 2. Ras Tafari crowned with title of Haile Selassie I
1931	May 11. Failure of Austrian Credit-Anstalt
1931	June. Wiley Post and Harold Gatty first to fly around world (8 days, 15 hours, 51 minutes)
1931	August 12. Republicans win elections in Spain. King Alfonso goes into exile August 14
1931	September 18. Japanese begin conquest of Manchuria
1931	September 21. Britain goes off gold standard
1932	July 5. Oliveira Salazar becomes prime minister of Portugal
1933	January 30. Hitler appointed German chancellor
1933	February 27. *Reichstag* fire
1933	March 4. Franklin D. Roosevelt inaugurated President
1933	March 6. Four-day bank holiday proclaimed
1933	April 1. Official persecution of Jews begins in Germany
1933	May 18. Passage of Tennessee Valley Authority Act
1933	June 5. U.S. goes off gold standard
1933	June 16. Passage of National Industrial Recovery Act. (Declared unconstitutional, May 27, 1935)
1933	September 5. Cuban *coup d'état* by Fulgencio Batista
1933	November 17. U.S. recognizes Soviet Union
1933	December 5. Ratification of 21st amendment, repealing prohibition
1934–35	Long trek of Chinese communists under Mao Tse-tung into northern Shensi
1934	June 6. Passage of Securities Exchange Act establishing Securities and Exchange Commission
1934	July 25. Attempted Nazi *coup d'état* of Austria. Austrian chancellor, Engelbert Dollfuss, killed

1934	August 19. Hitler becomes president of Germany and assumes sole executive power; approved by plebiscite
1934	December 1. Serge Kirov assassinated in Leningrad. Widespread reign of terror in Russia begins
1935	January 13. Plebiscite reunites Saar to Germany
1935	March 16. Germany begins universal compulsory military service
1935	March 21. Persia officially renamed Iran
1935	August 14. Passage of Social Security Act
1935	September 15. Passage of Nurnberg Laws against Jews in Germany
1935	October 3. Italians begin invasion of Ethiopia
1936	March 7. Germany reoccupies Rhineland
1936	April 28. Farouk becomes king of Egypt
1936	May 9. Italy annexes Ethiopia
1936	June 5. Popular Front led by Léon Blum forms French government. Until June 18, 1937
1936	July 18. Beginning of Spanish Civil War
1936	October 1. Gen. Francisco Franco named chief of Spanish state by insurrectionists
1936	November 6. Beginning of siege of Madrid
1936	December 5. New constitution promulgated in Soviet Union
1936	December 10. Edward VIII abdicates
1937	July 1. Pastor Martin Niemöller arrested in Germany
1937	July 7. Japan begins conquest of China
1937	October 16. Beginning of Sudetan German agitation in Czechoslovakia
1938	March 2–15. Trial of Bukharin, Rykov, Yagoda in Moscow; executed
1938	March 12. Germany invades and annexes Austria
1938	July 10–14. Howard Hughes flies around world in 3 days, 19 hours, 17 minutes
1938	September 15. Chamberlain and Hitler meet at Berchtesgaden on Sudetan crisis
1938	September 22–23. Chamberlain and Hitler meet at Godesberg on Sudetan crisis
1938	September 29. Munich Agreement signed by Hitler, Chamberlain, Daladier. Czechoslovakia dismembered
1939	February 27. England and France recognize Franco government in Spain
1939	March 16. Czechoslovakia annexed by Germany
1939	March 28. Madrid surrenders. End of Spanish Civil War
1939	April 7. Italy invades Albania
1939	August 23. German-Russian mutual non-aggression pact
1939	September 1. Germany invades Poland
1939	September 3. England and France declare war on Germany
1940	April 9. German troops invade Denmark and Norway
1940	April 30. Germans complete invasion of Norway
1940	May 10. German troops invade Belgium, Luxembourg, the Netherlands. Neville Chamberlain resigns; Winston Churchill becomes Prime Minister
1940	June 4. Evacuation of British and French troops from Dunkerque completed
1940	June 10. Italy declares war on France and Great Britain
1940	June 13. German troops occupy Paris
1940	June 22. Germany, France sign armistice
1940	September 16. Passage of Selective Training and Service Act in U.S.
1941	March 11. Passage of Lend-Lease Act
1941	June 22. Germans invade Russia
1941	September 4. Germans begin siege of Leningrad. Until January 1943

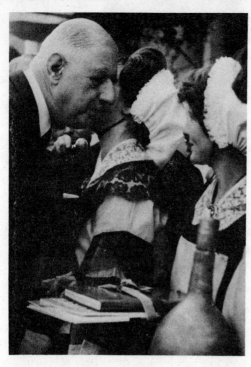

CHARLES DE GAULLE set up a government in exile when France signed an armistice with Germany in 1940, then returned in 1944 to head the French government. Here he is being greeted by girls in southeastern France.

1941	December 7. Japanese make surprise attack on Pearl Harbor
1941	December 8. U.S. declares war on Japan
1941	December 11. Germany and Italy declare war on U.S.
1942	January 2. Manila captured by Japanese
1942	February 15. Japanese capture Singapore
1942	May 6. Corregidor surrenders
1942	May 7. Battle of the Coral Sea
1942	June 4–7. Naval battle near Midway Island
1942	August 7. U.S. Marines invade Solomon Islands
1942	October 23. Battle of El Alamein, Egypt
1942	November 8. U.S. troops land in North Africa
1942	November 12. Naval battle of the Solomon Islands
1942	November 27. French fleet scuttled by crews in Toulon
1943	January 3. Russian troops lift siege of Leningrad
1943	January 14. Casablanca conference. Until January 24
1943	February 2. German forces at Stalingrad surrender
1943	May 12. Fighting ends in North Africa
1943	July 10. Allied forces invade Sicily
1943	August 11. Quebec conference. Until August 24
1943	September 2. Allied troops land in southern Italy
1943	September 9. Italian government under Badoglio surrenders. German forces seize control of country
1943	November 28. Tehran conference. Until January 12, 1944
1944	January 22. Allied troops land at Anzio, south of Rome
1944	June 6. Invasion of Normandy
1944	June 17. Germans launch first V-1 aircraft against England
1944	July 11. de Gaulle forces recognized as *de facto* government of France
1944	August 24. Allied army enters Paris
1944	October 19. U.S. troops invade Philippine Islands at Leyte
1944	December 16. Battle of the Bulge. Until December 25
1945	February 7. Yalta conference. Until February 12
1945	February 19. U.S. Marines invade Iwo Jima. Until March 17

Important Dates in History (continued)

1945	April 1. U.S. troops invade Okinawa
1945	April 12. F. D. Roosevelt dies. Harry S. Truman becomes President
1945	April 20. Russian troops enter Berlin
1945	April 25. U.N. conference at San Francisco. Until June 26
1945	April 28. Mussolini killed by Italian partisans
1945	May 1. Hitler commits suicide
1945	May 7. German army surrenders at Reims
1945	May 8. VE Day proclaimed
1945	July 17. Potsdam conference. Until August 2
1945	August 6. First atomic bomb dropped on Hiroshima
1945	August 8. Russia declares war on Japan
1945	August 9. Atomic bomb dropped on Nagasaki
1945	August 14. Japan surrenders
1945	September 2. Formal surrender of Japan on board U.S.S. *Missouri*
1947	February 10. Peace treaties signed at Paris
1946	January 1. Emperor Hirohito disclaims his divinity.
1946	March 5. Churchill warns of Communist "Iron Curtain" at Fulton, Missouri.
1946	June 2. Italy becomes republic.
1946	July 4. Philippines given independence by U.S.
1946	October 16. Nazi leaders hanged at Nuremberg.
1946	October 23. First meeting of General Assembly of United Nations to be held in New York.
1947	June 23. Taft-Hartley Act passed.
1947	August 14–15. India and Pakistan given independence by Britain.
1948	April 3. Marshall Plan for European recovery enacted.
1948	August. Whittaker Chambers accuses Alger Hess of spying.
1948–49	June 24–May 12. Berlin blockade and airlift.
1948	November 2. Harry Truman defeats Thomas E. Dewey in presidential election.

JAWAHARLAL NEHRU contributed significantly to India's efforts for independence and was his nation's first prime minister.

FRANKLIN ROOSEVELT (left) meeting with WINSTON CHURCHILL during WW II.

1948–49	First Arab-Israeli war.
1949	April 4. North Atlantic Treaty Organization signed.
1949	August 29. U.S.S.R. explodes first atomic bomb.
1949	December 7. Communists win control of mainland China.
1950	February 9. Sen. Joseph McCarthy charges that State Department is infiltrated by Communists.
1950	June 25. Korean war begins.
1952	November 4. Dwight D. Eisenhower wins presidential election.
1953	July 27. Korean Armistice signed.
1954	May 7. Fall of Dienbien Phu, French Indo-China.
1954–62	Algerian war of independence.
1955	February 12. U.S. aid to Vietnam begins.
1955	March 25. East Germany given sovereignty by U.S.S.R.
1955	May 5. West Germany becomes independent under Adenauer.
1956	October 23–November 4. Hungarian uprising against U.S.S.R. occupation.
1956	October 29–November 6. Second Arab-Israeli war; France and Britain land troops in Suez Canal area.
1957	March 27. Treaty of Rome signed, establishing European Economic Community.
1957	October 4. First man-made satellite orbits earth, launched by U.S.S.R.
1958	January 8. Gen. de Gaulle becomes president of France.
1958	January 31. First U.S. earth satellite launched.
1958	July 15. U.S. troops land in Lebanon, withdraw October 25.
1959	January 1. Castro overthrows Batista.

Important Dates in History (continued)

1959	January 3. Alaska admitted to the Union.
1959	August 21. Hawaii admitted to the Union.
1960	May 1. U-2 reconnaissance plane piloted by Gary Powers shot down.
1960	June 30. Belgian Congo becomes independent.
1960	November 8. John F. Kennedy elected president.
1961	April 12. Yuri Gagarin becomes first man to orbit Earth.
1961	August 13. Erection of Berlin wall starts.
1962	October 20–November 22. China invades and then withdraws from disputed border area of northern India.
1962	October 22–28. Cuban missile crisis.
1963	August 5. Nuclear Test Ban Treaty between U.S., U.S.S.R. and Britain.
1963	November 22. John F. Kennedy assassinated; Lyndon Johnson becomes President.
1964	March 27. U.N. troops land in Cyprus.
1964	August 7. U.S. Congress votes president authority "to prevent further aggression" by North Vietnam.
1964	November 3. Lyndon Johnson wins presidential election.
1967	June 5–10. Third Arab-Israeli war—Six Day War.
1967–70	Nigerian civil war—attempted Biafran secession.
1968	April 4. Rev. Martin Luther King assassinated.
1968	June 6. Sen. Robert F. Kennedy assassinated.
1968	August 20–21. Invasion and occupation of Czechoslovakia by U.S.S.R.
1968	November 5. Richard Nixon elected president.
1969	July 20. First men on the Moon, Neil A. Armstrong and Edwin E. Aldrin Jr. in Apollo XI.
1971	October 25. United Nations voted to admit Communist China.
1973	January 1. Britain, Denmark and Ireland join Common Market.
1973	October 6–24. Fourth Arab-Israeli war.
1974	July 15–August 16. War in Cyprus.
1974	August 8. President Nixon resigns, replaced by Gerald R. Ford.
1975	April 30. End of Vietnam War.

When JOHN KENNEDY (left) became the fourth U.S. president to be assassinated, his vice president LYNDON JOHNSON succeeded him in office.

ANWAR SADAT visits Israel and is greeted by MENACHIM BEGIN.

1975–76 Civil war in Lebanon.
1976   September 9. Mao-Tse-Tung dies.
1976   November 2. James E. Carter, Jr. defeats Gerald R. Ford in presidential election.
1977   November 20. Sadat addresses Israeli Parliament.
1978   October 16. Pope John-Paul II elected—first from Communist country.
1979   January 16. Months of rioting in Iran culminate in the expulsion of the Shah.

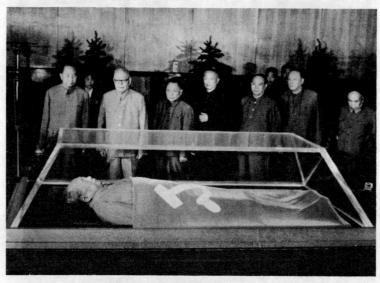

Chinese leaders paying their respects to the remains of MAO TSE-TUNG.

THE ATOMIC AGE:
The employment of
nuclear energy has been
a source of controversy.
The destructive power of
the first atomic bombs
(left) shocked the people
of the world. Opposition
to domestic reactors was
intensified by an accident
at Pennsylvania's
THREE MILE ISLAND
(below).

THE SPACE AGE:
Rockets such as
the SATURN V (right)
have lifted man beyond
the pull of gravity and
taken him all the way to
the moon, offering a new
perspective of our planet
EARTH (below).

Inventions and Inventors

ADDING MACHINE, 1623. *Inventor:* Wilhelm Schickard (Ger.) Earliest commercial machine invented by William Burroughs (U.S.) in St. Louis, Missouri, in 1885.

ADDRESSOGRAPH, 1860. *Inventor:* Christopher Sholes (U.S.), Milwaukee. First manufactured in Madison, Wisconsin.

AIRPLANE, 1903. *Inventors:* Orville (1871–1948) and Wilbur Wright (1867–1912) (U.S.). Kitty Hawk, N.C. (Dec. 17).

AIRSHIP (non-rigid), 1852. *Inventor:* Henri Giffard (Fr.) (1825–82). Steam-powered propeller, near Paris (Sept. 24).

AIRSHIP (rigid), 1900. *Inventor:* Graf Ferdinand von Zeppelin (Ger.) (1838–1917). Bodensee (July 2).

AUTOMOBILE (steam), *c.* 1769. *Inventor:* Nicolas Cugnot (Fr.) (1725–1804). Three-wheeled military tractor. Oldest surviving is Italian Bordino (1854) in Turin.

AUTOMOBILE (gasoline), 1888. *Inventor:* Karl Benz (Ger.) (1844–1929). Earliest internal combustion automobile built 1826 by Samuel Brown (G.B.). First run, Benz Motorwagen, Mannheim, Germany, Nov. or Dec. 1885. Patented Jan. 29, 1886. First powered hand cart with internal combustion engine was by Siegfried Marcus (Austria) (*c.* 1864).

BAKELITE, 1907. *Inventor:* Leo H. Baekeland (Belg./U.S.) (1863–1944). First use, electrical insulation by Loando and Co., Boonton, New Jersey.

BALLOON, 1783. *Inventors:* Jacques (1745–99) and Joseph Montgolfier (Fr.) (1740–1810). Tethered flight, Paris (Oct. 15) manned free flight, Paris (Nov. 21), by François de Rozier and Marquis d'Arlandes. Father Bartolomeu de Gusmão (né Lourenço) (b. Brazil 1685) demonstrated hot air balloon in Portugal on Aug. 8, 1789.

ORIGINAL MODEL T FORD built in 1905. The 4-cylinder, 20-horsepower engine was capable of propelling the car at 40 miles per hour. The car carried 10 gallons of gas—sufficient for 225 miles, weighed 1,200 pounds, and cost $850.

THOMAS A. EDISON spent much of his life in his laboratory. More than 1,000 of his inventions were patented.

BALL-POINT PEN, 1888. *Inventor:* John J. Loud (U.S.). First practical models by Lazlo and Georg Biro (Hungary) in 1938.

BARBED WIRE, 1867. *Inventor:* Lucien B. Smith (U.S.) (patentee) (June 25).

BAROMETER, 1644. *Inventor:* Evangelista Torricelli (It.) (1608–47).

BICYCLE, 1839–40. *Inventor:* Kirkpatrick Macmillan (Scot.) (1810–78). Pedal-driven cranks. First direct drive in March, 1861 by Ernest Michaux (Fr.).

BICYCLE TIRES (pneumatic), 1888. *Inventor:* John Boyd Dunlop (G.B.) (1840–1921). Principle patented but undeveloped by Robert William Thomson (G.B.), June 10, 1845. First motor car pneumatic tires adapted by André and Edouard Michelin (Fr.), 1895 (see Rubber tires).

BIFOCAL LENS, 1780. *Inventor:* Benjamin Franklin (1706–90) (U.S.). His earliest experiments began *c.* 1760.

INVENTIONS AND INVENTORS (continued)

BUNSEN BURNER, 1855. *Inventor:* Robert Wilhelm von Bunsen (Ger.) (1811–99) at Heidelberg. Michael Faraday (1791–1867) (U.K.) had previously designed an adjustable burner.

BURGLAR ALARM, 1858. *Inventor:* Edwin T. Holmes (U.S.). Electric installed, Boston, Mass. (Feb. 21).

CARBURETOR, 1876. *Inventor:* Gottlieb Daimler (Ger.) (1834–1900). Carburetor spray: Charles E. Duryea (U.S.) 1892).

CARPET SWEEPER, 1876. *Inventor:* Melville R. Bissell (U.S.). Grand Rapids, Mich. (Patent, Sept. 19).

CASH REGISTER, 1879. *Inventor:* James Ritty (U.S.). (Patent Nov. 4). Built in Dayton, Ohio. Taken over by National Cash Register Co. 1884.

CELLOPHANE, 1908. *Inventor:* J. E. Brandenberger (Switz.) at Zurich. Machine production not before 1911.

CELLULOID, 1861. *Inventor:* Alexander Parkes (G.B.) (1813–90). Invented in Birmingham, Eng.; developed and trade marked by J. W. Hyatt (U.S.) in 1870.

CEMENT, 1824. *Inventor:* Joseph Aspdin (G.B.). Wakefield, Yorkshire (Oct. 21).

CHRONOMETER, 1735. *Inventor:* John Harrison (G.B.) (1693–1776). Received in 1772 Government's £20,000 prize on offer since 1714.

CINEMA, 1895. *Inventors:* Auguste Marie Louis Nicolas Lumière (1862–1954) and Louis Jean Lumière (Fr.) (1864–1948). Development pioneers were Etienne Jules Marey (Fr.) (1830–1903) and Thomas A. Edison (U.S.) (1847–1931). First public showing, Blvd. des Capucines, Paris (Dec. 28, 1895).

CLASSIFICATION OF DATA FOR LIBRARIES. *Inventor:* Melvil Dewey (U.S.) (1851–1931). Introduced his decimal classification in 1873.

CLOCK (mechanical), 725. *Inventors:* I-Hsing and Liang Ling-Tsan (China). Earliest escapement, 600 years before Europe.

CLOCK (pendulum), 1656. *Inventor:* Christaan Huygens (Neth.) (1629–95).

THE FIRST AUTOMOBILE built by Henry Ford was constructed in this workshop behind his home in a section of what is now downtown Detroit.

FIRST CALCULATOR (above)
by William Burroughs of
St. Louis in 1885. THE FIRST
PRACTICAL TYPEWRITER in
America (right) was built by
Remington in 1873. The carriage
was returned by the foot treadle.
An early 27-key machine was
invented in 1808 in Italy.

DACRON, 1941. *Inventors:* J. R. Whinfield (1901–66), J. T. Dickson
(G.B.) at Accrington, Lancashire, Eng. First available 1950,
marketed in U.S.

DENTAL PLATE, 1817. *Inventor:* Anthony A. Plantson (U.S.) (1774–
1837).

DENTAL PLATE (rubber), 1855. *Inventor:* Charles Goodyear (U.S.)
(1800–60).

DIESEL ENGINE, 1895. *Inventor:* Rudolf Diesel (Ger.) (1858–1913).
Lower pressure oil engine patent by Stuart Akroyd, 1890. Diesel's
first commercial success, Augsberg, 1897.

DISC BRAKE, 1902. *Inventor:* Dr. F. Lanchester (G.B.) First used on
aircraft 1953 (Dunlop Rubber Co.).

ELECTRIC BLANKET, 1883. Exhibited Vienna, Austria Exhibition. Marketed in 1946 by Simmons Co. (U.S.), Petersburg, Virginia.

ELECTRIC FLAT IRON, 1882. *Inventor:* H. W. Seeley (U.S.). New York
City. Patent June 6.

ELECTRIC LAMP, 1879. *Inventor:* Thomas Alva Edison (U.S.) (1847–
1931). First practical demonstration at Menlo Park, New Jersey
(Dec. 20).

ELECTRIC MOTOR (D.C.), 1873. *Inventor:* Zénobe Gramme (Belg.)
(1826–1901). Exhibited in Vienna. Patent by Thomas Davenport
(U.S.) of Vermont, Feb. 25, 1837.

ELECTRIC MOTOR (A.C.), 1888. *Inventor:* Nikola Tesla (U.S.) (1856–
1943).

ELECTROMAGNET, 1824. *Inventor:* William Sturgeon (G.B.) (b. 1783).
Improved by Joseph Henry (U.S.), 1831.

ELECTRONIC COMPUTER, 1942. *Inventors:* J. G. Brainerd, J. P. Eckert,
J. W. Mauchly (U.S.). ENIAC (Electronic numerical integrator and
calculator), University of Pennsylvania, Philadelphia. Point-
contact transistor announced by John Bardeen and Walter Brattain
July, 1948. Junction transistor announced by R. L. Wallace,
Morgan Sparks and Dr. William Shockley in early 1951.

ELEVATOR, 1852. *Inventor:* Elisha G. Otis (U.S.) (1811–61). Earliest
elevator at Yonkers, N.Y.

FIRST MOTION PICTURE STUDIO: Built by Thomas A. Edison at West Orange, New Jersey, in 1892, the studio was mounted on a circular track to follow the sun, the only source of light.

FILM (Moving outlines). 1885. *Inventor:* Louis le Prince (Fr.) Institute for the Deaf, Washington Hts., N.Y.C.

FILM (Musical Sound), 1923. *Inventor:* Dr. Lee de Forest (U.S.). New York demonstration (March 13).

FILM (Talking), 1926. *Inventor:* Warner Bros. (U.S.). First release "Don Juan," Warner Theatre, New York (Aug. 5).

FOUNTAIN PEN, 1884. *Inventor:* Lewis E. Waterman (U.S.) (1837–1901). Patented by D. Hyde (U.S.), 1830, undeveloped.

GAS LIGHTING, 1792. *Inventor:* William Murdock (G.B.) (1754–1839). Private house in Cornwall, 1792; Factory, Birmingham, 1798; London Streets, 1807.

GENERATOR, 1832. *Inventor:* Hippolyte Pixii (Fr.) demonstrated Paris, Sept. 3. Rotative dynamo demonstrated by Joseph Saxton, Cambridge, England, June, 1833.

GLASS (Stained), *c.* 1080. *Inventor:* Augsberg, Germany. Earliest English, *c.* 1170, York Minster.

GLASSWARE, *c.* 1500 B.C. *Inventor:* Egypt and Mesopotamia. Glass blowing Syria, *c.* 50 B.C.

GLIDER, 1853. *Inventor:* Sir George Cayley (G.B.) (1773–1857). Near Brompton Hall, Yorkshire, England. Passenger possibly John Appleby. Emanuel Swedenborg (1688–1772) sketches dated *c.* 1714.

GYRO-COMPASS, 1911. *Inventor:* Elmer A. Sperry (U.S.) (1860–1930). Tested on U.S.S. *Delaware* (Aug. 28). Gyroscope devised 1852 by Foucault (Fr.).

HELICOPTER, 1924. *Inventor:* Etienne Oehmichen (Fr.). First FAI world record set on April 14, 1924. Earliest drawing of principle, Le Mans Museum, France, *c.* 1460. First serviceable machine by Igor Sikorsky (U.S.), 1939.

HOVERCRAFT, 1955. *Inventor:* C. S. Cockerell (G.B.). Patented Dec. 12. Earliest air-cushion vehicle patent was in 1877 by J. I. Thornycroft (1843–1928) (G.B.). First "flight" Saunders Roe SR-N1 at Cowes, England, May 30, 1959.

IRON WORKING, *c.* 1200 B.C. *Inventor:* Cyprus and Northern Israel. Introduced into Britain, *c.* 550 B.C.

JET ENGINE, 1937. *Inventor:* Sir Frank Whittle (G.B.) (*b.* 1907). First test bed run (April 12). Principles announced by Merconnet (Fr.) 1909 and Maxime Guillaume (Fr.) 1921. First flight Aug. 27, 1939, by Heinkel He-178.

INVENTIONS AND INVENTORS (continued)

LASER, 1960. *Inventor:* Dr. Charles H. Townes (U.S.). First demonstration by Theodore Maiman (U.S.). Demonstrated at Hughes Research, Malibu, California, in July. Abbreviation for Light amplification by stimulated emission of radiation.

LAUNDERETTE, 1934. *Inventor:* J. F. Cantrell (U.S.). Fort Worth, Texas (April 18).

LIGHTNING CONDUCTOR, 1752. *Inventor:* Benjamin Franklin (U.S.) (1706–90). Philadelphia, in Sept.

LINOLEUM, 1860. *Inventor:* Frederick Walton (G.B.).

LOCOMOTIVE, 1804. *Inventor:* Richard Trevithick (G.B.) (1771–1833). Penydarren, Wales, 9 miles (Feb. 21).

LOOM (Power), 1785. *Inventor:* Edmund Cartwright (G.B.) (1743–1823).

LOUDSPEAKER, 1900. *Inventor:* Horace Short (G.B.) Patentee in 1898. A compressed air Auxetophone. First used atop the Eiffel Tower, Paris, Summer 1900. Earliest open-air electric public address system used by Bell Telephone on Staten Island, N.Y., on June 30, 1916.

MACHINE GUN, 1718. *Inventor:* James Puckle (G.B.) patentee, May 15, 1718. White Cron Alley factory in use 1721. Richard Gatling (U.S.) (1818–1903) model dates from 1861.

MAPS, *c.* 3800 B.C. *Inventor:* Sumerian (clay tablets of river Euphrates). Earliest world map by Eratosthenes, *c.* 220 B.C. Earliest printed map printed in Bologna, Italy 1477.

MARGARINE, 1869. *Inventor:* Hippolyte Mège-Mouries (Fr.). Patented July 15.

MATCH (Safety), 1826. *Inventor:* John Walker (G.B.) Stockton, Teesside, Eng.

A 360-DEGREE LASER PHOTOGRAPH called a hologram: Made by laser light this is remarkable in many ways; one being the laser's ability to present several views of a stationary object on the same piece of film without shooting through a lens. In the multiple holographic photograph shown here, each exposure was made on the same negative with the camera being shifted slightly between exposures. The figurine was not moved. The result is that even the back of the figurine (the side hidden from the direct view of the lens) can be seen.

INVENTIONS AND INVENTORS (continued)

MICROPHONE, 1876. *Inventor:* Alexander Graham Bell (U.S.) (1847–1922). Name coined 1878 by David Hughes who gave demonstrations in London in Jan., 1878.

MICROSCOPE, 1590. *Inventor:* Zacharias Janssen (Neth.). Compound convex-concave lens.

MICROSCOPE (Electron), 1933. *Inventor:* M. Knoll and E. Ruska in Berlin.

MOTORCYCLE, 1885. *Inventor:* Gottlieb Daimler of Candstatt, Germany, patent Aug. 29. First rider Paul Daimler (Nov. 10, 1885); first woman rider Mrs. Edward Butler near Erith, Kent, Eng. 1888.

MOTOR SCOOTER, 1915. *Inventor:* Auto-Ped Co. of New York. It was powered by a 2 hp engine and had a top speed of 35 mph.

NEON LAMP, 1910. *Inventor:* Georges Claude (Fr.) (1871–1960). First installation at Paris Motor Show (Dec. 3).

NIGHT CLUB, 1843. *Inventor:* Paris, France. First was Le Bal des Anglais, Paris, 5me. (Closed *c.* 1960).

NYLON, 1937. *Inventor:* Dr. Wallace H. Carothers (U.S.) (1896–1937) at Du Pont Labs., Seaford, Delaware, U.S. (Patent Feb. 16). First stockings made about 1937. Bristle production Feb. 24, 1938. Yarn production Dec. 1939.

PAPER, *c.* A.D. 105. *Inventor:* Mulberry based fiber, China. Introduced to West *via* Samarkand, 14th century.

PARACHUTE, 1797. *Inventor:* André-Jacques Garnerin (Fr.) (1769–1823). First descent (from 2,230 ft. over Paris) Oct. 22. Earliest jump from aircraft March 1, 1912, by Albert Berry (U.S.) St. Louis, Missouri.

PARCHMENT, *c.* 1300 B.C. *Inventor:* Egypt. Modern name from Pergamam, Asia Minor, *c.* 250 B.C.

PARKING METER, 1935. *Inventor:* Carlton C. Magee (U.S.). Oklahoma City (July 16).

PHONOGRAPH, 1878. *Inventor:* Thomas Alva Edison (U.S.) (1847–1931). Hand-cranked cylinder at Menlo Park, N.J. Patent, Feb. 19. First described on April 30, 1877, by Charles Cros (Fr.) (1842–88).

PHOTOGRAPHY (on Metal), 1826. *Inventor:* J. Nicéphore Niépce (Fr.) (1765–1833). Sensitized pewter plate, 8 hr. exposure at Chalon-sur-Saône, France.

PHOTOGRAPHY (on Paper), 1835. *Inventor:* W. H. Fox Talbot (G.B.) (1807–77). Lacock Abbey, Wiltshire, England (August).

PHOTOGRAPHY (on Film), 1888. *Inventor:* John Carbutt (U.S.). Kodak by George Eastman (U.S.) (1854–1932), Aug. 1888.

PORCELAIN, 851. *Inventor:* Earliest report from China. Reached Baghdad *c.* 800.

POTTER'S WHEEL, *c.* 6500 B.C. *Inventor:* Asia Minor. Used in Mesopotamia *c.* 3000 B.C.

PNEUMATIC TIRE, *see* Bicycle Tires.

PRINTING PRESS, *c.* 1455. *Inventor:* Johann Gutenberg (Ger.) (*c.* 1400–68). Hand printing known in India in 868.

PRINTING (Rotary), 1846. *Inventor:* Richard Hoe (U.S.) (1812–86). Philadelphia Public Ledger rotary printed, 1847.

PROPELLER (Ship), 1837. *Inventor:* Francis Smith (G.B.) (1808–74).

PYRAMID, *c.* 2685 B.C. *Inventor:* Egypt. Earliest was Djoser step pyramid, Saqqâra.

RADAR, 1922. *Inventors:* Dr. Albert H. Taylor and Leo C. Young (U.S.). Radio reflection effect first noted. First harnessed by Dr. Rudolph Kühnold, Kiel, Germany Mar. 20, 1934. Word coined in 1940 by Cdr. S. M. Tucker, U.S.N.

RADIO TELEGRAPHY, 1864. *Inventor:* Dr. Mahlon Loomis (U.S.) demonstrated over 14 miles Bear's Den, Loudoun County, Virginia (October). First advertised radio broadcast by Prof. R. A. Fessenden (b. Canada 1868–1932) at Brant Rock, Mass., on Dec. 24, 1906.

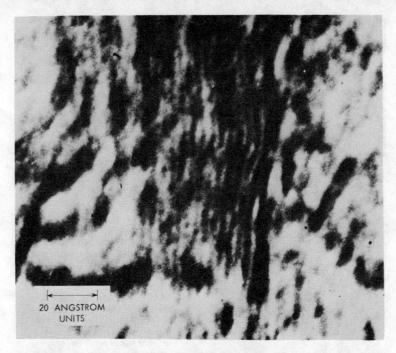

VIEW THROUGH AN ELECTRON MICROSCOPE: The lines in the center are layers of carbon atoms, each layer one atom thick. Individual atoms are not visible because they overlap each other throughout each plane. The layers are about 3.4 angstrom units—about 13,000,000,000th of an inch—apart.

RADIO TELEGRAPHY (Transatlantic), 1901. *Inventor:* Guglielmo Marconi (It.) (1874–1937). Morse signals from Poldhu, Cornwall, to St. John's, Newfoundland (Dec. 12).

RAYON, 1883. *Inventor:* Sir Joseph Swan (G.B.) (1828–1917). Production at Courtauld's Ltd., Coventry, England, Nov. 1905. Name "Rayon" adopted in 1924.

RAZOR (Electric), 1931. *Inventor:* Col. Jacob Schick (U.S.). First manufactured Stamford, Conn. (March 18).

RAZOR (Safety), 1895. *Inventor:* King C. Gillette (U.S.). Patented Dec. 2, 1901. First throw-away blades. Earliest fixed safety razor by Kampfe.

RECORD (Long-playing), 1948. *Inventor:* Dr. Peter Goldmark (U.S.). Microgroove developed in the C.B.S. Research Labs and launched June 21, so ending the 78 rpm market supremacy.

REFRIGERATOR, 1850. *Inventor:* James Harrison (G.B.) and Alexander Catlin Twining (U.S.). Simultaneous development at Rodey Point, Victoria, Australia, and in Cleveland, Ohio. Earliest domestic refrigerator in 1913 in Chicago, Illinois.

REVOLVER, 1822. *Inventor:* Elisha Hayden Collier (U.S.) of Fountain Court, London; five-shot flintlock.

RUBBER (Latex Foam), 1928. *Inventor:* Dunlop Rubber Co. (G.B.) Team led by E. A. Murphy at Fort Dunlop, Birmingham, England.

RUBBER (Tires), 1846. *Inventor:* Thomas Hancock (G.B.) (1786–1865). Introduced solid rubber tires for vehicles (1847) (*see also* Bicycle).

RUBBER (Vulcanized), 1841. *Inventor:* Charles Goodyear (U.S.) (1800–60).

RUBBER (Waterproof), 1823. *Inventor:* Charles Macintosh (G.B.) (1766–1843). Patent. First experiments in Glasgow with James Syme. G. Fox in 1821 had marketed a Gambroon cloak of which no detail has survived.

THE FIRST INCANDESCENT LIGHT BULB that worked was invented by Thomas A. Edison on October 21, 1879. Shown on the left is a replica. **THE SEWING MACHINE** (above) patented in the U.S. in 1864 by Elias Howe of Spencer, Mass., was preceded by an English machine patented in 1790 but never developed.

SAFETY PIN, 1849. *Inventor:* Walter Hunt (U.S.). First manufactured New York City, N.Y. (April 10).

SELF-STARTER, 1911. *Inventor:* Charles F. Kettering (U.S.) (1876–1958). Developed at Dayton, Ohio, sold to Cadillac.

SEWING MACHINE, 1829. *Inventor:* Barthélemy Thimmonnier (Fr.) (1793–1854). A patent by Thomas Saint (G.B.) dated July 17, 1790 for an apparently undeveloped machine was found in 1874. Earliest practical domestic machine by Isaac M. Singer (1811–75) of Pittstown, N.Y., in 1851.

SHIP (Sea-going), *c.* 7250 B.C. *Inventor:* Grecian ships. Traversed from Mainland to Melos.

SHIP (Steam), 1775. *Inventor:* J. C. Périer (Fr.) (1742–1818). On the Seine, near Paris. Propulsion achieved on River Saône, France, by Marquis d'Abbans, 1783.

SHIP (Turbine), 1894. *Inventor:* Hon. Sir Charles Parsons (G.B.) (1854–1931). S.S. *Turbinia* attained 34.5 kts. on first trial. Built at Heaton, County Durham, Eng.

SILK MANUFACTURE, *c.* 50 B.C. *Inventor:* Reeling machines devised, China. Silk mills in Italy, *c.* 1250, world's earliest factories.

SKYSCRAPER, 1882. *Inventor:* William Le Baron Jenny (U.S.). Home Insurance Co. Building, Chicago, Ill. 10 story (top 4 steel beams).

SLIDE RULE, 1621. *Inventor:* William Oughtred (G.B.) (1575–1660). Earliest slide between fixed stock by Robert Bissaker, 1654.

SPECTACLES, 1289. *Inventor:* Venice, Italy (convex). Concave lens for myopia not developed till *c.* 1450.

SPINNING FRAME, 1769. *Inventor:* Sir Richard Arkwright (G.B.) (1732–92).

SPINNING JENNY, 1764. *Inventor:* James Hargreaves (G.B.) (*d.* 1778).

SPINNING MULE, 1779. *Inventor:* Samuel Crompton (G.B.) (1753–1827).

STEAM ENGINE, 1698. *Inventor:* Thomas Savery (G.B.) (*c.* 1650–1715). Recorded on July 25.

STEAM ENGINE (Piston), 1712. *Inventor:* Thomas Newcomen (G.B.) (1663–1729).

INVENTIONS AND INVENTORS (continued)

STEAM ENGINE (Condenser), 1765. *Inventor:* James Watt (G.B.) (1736–1819).

STEEL PRODUCTION, 1855. *Inventor:* Henry Bessemer (G.B.) (1813–98). At St. Pancras, London. Cementation of wrought iron bars by charcoal contact known to Chalybes people of Asia Minor *c.* 1400 B.C.

STEEL (Stainless), 1913. *Inventor:* Harry Brearley (G.B.) First cast at Sheffield, England (Aug. 20). Krupp patent, Oct. 1912 for chromium carbon steel; failed to recognize corrosion resistance.

STETHOSCOPE, 1837. *Inventor:* Rene Laënnec (Fr.) at the Hôpital Necker, Paris.

STREETCAR (Electric), 1879. *Inventor:* E. Werner von Siemen (Ger.) (1816–92). Earliest permanent self-propelled public streetcar at Lichterfelde, Germany, 1881. Public service began May 16.

SUBMARINE, 1776. *Inventor:* David Bushnell (U.S.), Saybrook, Conn. Hand propelled screw, one man crew, used off New York. A twelve man wooden and leather submersible devised by Cornelius Drebbel (Neth.) demonstrated in Thames in 1624.

TANK (Military), 1914. *Inventor:* Sir Ernest Swinton (G.B.) (1868–1951). Built at Leicester, England. Designed by William Trilton. Tested Sept. 1915.

TELEGRAPH, 1787. *Inventor:* M. Lammond (Fr.) demonstrated a working model, Paris.

TELEGRAPH CODE, 1837. *Inventor:* Samuel F. B. Morse (U.S.) (1791–1872). The real credit belonged largely to his assistant Alfred Vail (U.S.) who first transmitted at Morristown, N.J. on Jan. 8, 1838.

FIRST LONG-DISTANCE TELEPHONE: Alexander Graham Bell opening the service between New York and Chicago in 1892.

199

TELEPHONE, 1849. *Inventor:* Antonio Meucci (It.) in Havana, Cuba. Caveat not filed until 1871. Instrument worked imperfectly by electrical impulses.

TELEPHONE, 1876. *Inventor:* Alexander Graham Bell (U.S.) (1847–1922). Patented Mar. 9, 1876. First exchange at Boston, Mass., 1878.

TELESCOPE, 1608. *Inventor:* Hans Lippershey (Neth.) (Oct. 2.).

TELEVISION, 1926. *Inventor:* John Logie Baird (G.B.) (1888–1946). First public demonstration Jan. 27, of moving image with gradations of light and shade at 22 Frith Street, London. First successful experiment on Oct. 30, 1925. First transmission in color on July 3, 1928 at 133 Long Acre, London.

THERMOMETER, 1593. *Inventor:* Galileo Galilei (It.) (1564–1642).

TRACTOR (Gasoline engined), 1889. *Inventor:* Charter Engine Co. of Chicago, Illinois and named the Burger.

TRACTOR (Crawler), 1904. *Inventor:* Benjamin Holt (U.S.). First commercially practical tractor named Holt Steam Traction Engine No. 77 built at Stockton, California, and first tested on Nov. 24.

TRANSFORMER, 1831. *Inventor:* Michael Faraday (G.B.). Built at Royal Institution, London (Aug. 29).

TRANSISTOR, 1948. *Inventors:* John Bardeen, William Shockley and Walter Brattain (U.S.). Researched at Bell Telephone Laboratories. First application for a patent was by Dr. Julius E. Lilienfeld in Canada in Oct. 1925. (*see* Electronic Computer).

TYPEWRITER, 1808. *Inventor:* Pellegrine Tarri (It.). First practical 27 character keyed machine with carbon paper built in Reggio Emilia, Italy.

WASHING MACHINE (Electric). 1907. *Inventor:* Hurley Machine Co. (U.S.). Marketed under name of "Thor" in Chicago, Illinois.

WATCH, 1462. *Inventor:* Bartholomew Manfredi (It.). Earliest mention of a named watchmaker (November) but in reference to an earlier watchmaker.

REPLICA OF THE FIRST TELEPHONE, including some parts of the original instrument. Thomas A. Watson and Alexander Graham Bell first spoke to each other over the original system on June 3, 1875.

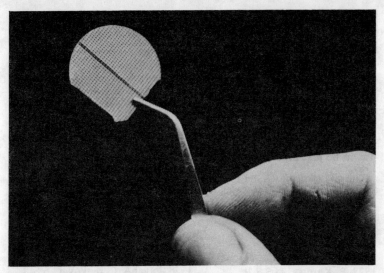

MINIATURE ELECTRONIC CIRCUITS: The wafer held by the tweezers contains about 1,000 separate electronic circuits. Even though an individual circuit is barely visible to the eye, each contains 5 transistors, 13 diodes, and 8 resistors.

WELDER (Electric), 1877. *Inventor:* Elisha Thomson (U.S.) (1853–1937).

WHEEL, *c.* 3500 B.C. *Inventor:* Sumerian civilization. Spoked as opposed to solid wheels intro. *c.* 1900 B.C.

WINDMILL, *c.* 600 A.D. *Inventor:* Persian corn grinding. Oldest known English port mill, 1191, Bury St. Edmunds, England.

WRITING, *c.* 3500 B.C. *Inventor:* Sumerian civilization. Earliest evidence found in S.E. Iran in 1970.

XEROGRAPHY, 1938. *Inventor:* Chester F. Carlson (U.S.) on Oct. 22. First copying machines marketed in U.S. in 1950 by the Haloid Co., Rochester, N.Y.

X-RAY, 1895. *Inventor:* Wilhelm von Röntgen (Ger.). University of Würzburg (Nov. 8).

ZIGGURATS, *c.* 2000 B.C. *Inventor:* Sumerian civilization. Earliest staged towers at Ur in Iraq.

ZIP FASTENER, 1891. *Inventor:* Whitcomb L. Judson (U.S.). Exhibited 1893 at Chicago Exposition. First practical fastener invented in U.S. by Gideon Sundback (Sweden) in 1913.

Nobel Prizes

Nobel Prizes are awarded after annual consideration to a person (or persons) in each of five categories "to those who shall have conferred the greatest benefit on mankind." The awards, which are to be without regard to nationality, are made under the will of the Swedish inventor of dynamite, Alfred Bernhard Nobel (1833–1896). The awards started in 1901.

On May 15, 1968, it was announced that a sixth category—Economic Sciences—was established by funds from the Swedish *Riksbank* and was to be first awarded by the Royal Swedish Academy of Sciences in 1969.

The value of the Nobel Prizes varies, but those for 1978 were worth about $165,000 for each category. The winners:

PHYSICS

Year Name and Country
1978 P. Kapitsa, U.S.S.R.
     A. Penzias, U.S.
     R. Wilson, U.S.
1977 Sir Nevill Mott, U.K.
     J. Van Vleck, U.S.
     P. Anderson, U.S.
1976 B. Richter, U.S.
     S. Ting, U.S.
1975 J. Rainwater, U.S.
     A. Bohr, Denmark
     B. Mottelson, Denmark
1974 Sir Martin Ryle, U.K.
     A. Hewish, U.K.
1973 B. D. Josephson, U.K.
     L. Esaki, Japan
     I. Giaever, U.S.
1972 J. Bardeen, U.S.
     L. N. Cooper, U.S.
     G. R. Schrieffer, U.S.
1971 Dennis Gabor, U.K.
1970 Louis Neel, France
     Hannes Alfven, Sweden
1969 Murray Gell-Mann, U.S.
1968 Luis W. Alvarez, U.S.
1967 Hans A. Bethe, U.S.
1966 Alfred Kastler, France
1965 Richard P. Feynman, U.S.
     Julian S. Schwinger, U.S.
     Shinichiro Tomanaga, Japan
1964 Nikolai G. Basov, U.S.S.R.
     Aleksander M. Prochorov, U.S.S.R.
     Charles H. Townes, U.S.
1963 Maria Goeppert-Mayer, U.S.
     J. Hans D. Jensen, Germany
     Eugene P. Wigner, U.S.
1962 Lev. D. Landau, U.S.S.R.
1961 Robert Hofstadter, U.S.
     Rudolf L. Mössbauer, Germany
1960 Donald A. Glaser, U.S.

1959 Owen Chamberlain, U.S.
     Emilio G. Segrè, U.S.
1958 Paval A. Cerenkov, U.S.S.R.
     Ilya M. Frank, U.S.S.R.
     Igor J. Tamm, U.S.S.R.
1957 Tsung-Dao Lee, U.S.
     Chen Ning Yang, U.S.
1956 John Bardeen, U.S.
     Walter H. Brattain, U.S.
     William Shockley, U.S.
1955 Polykarp Kusch, U.S.
     Willis E. Lamb, U.S.
1954 Max Born, U.K.
     Walther Bothe, Germany
1953 Frits Zernike, Netherlands
1952 Felix Bloch, U.S.
     Edward M. Purcell, U.S.
1951 Sir John D. Cockroft, U.K.
     Ernest T. S. Walton, Ireland
1950 Cecil F. Powell, U.K.
1949 Hideki Yukawa, Japan
1948 Patrick M. S. Blackett, U.K.
1947 Sir Edward V. Appleton, U.K.
1946 Percy Williams Bridgman, U.S.
1945 Wolfgang Pauli, U.S.
1944 Isidor Isaac Rabi, U.S.
1943 Otto Stern, U.S.
1942 No award
1941 No award
1940 No award
1939 Ernest O. Lawrence, U.S.
1938 Enrico Fermi, U.S.
1937 Clinton J. Davisson, U.S.
     George P. Thomson, U.K.
1936 Carl D. Anderson, U.S.
     Victor F. Hess, Austria
1935 James Chadwick, U.K.
1934 No award
1933 Paul A. M. Dirac, U.K.
     Erwin Schrödinger, Austria
1932 Werner Helsenberg, Germany
1931 No award

ALFRED NOBEL is doubly famous. First, he invented dynamite in 1866. Then he left the funds to start the prizes for pacifism and sciences in 1901.

Physics (continued)

1930 Sir Chandrasekhara Raman, India
1929 Prince Louis-Victor de Broglie, France
1928 Owen W. Richardson, U.K.
1927 Arthur H. Compton, U.S.
     Charles T. R: Wilson, U.K.
1926 Jean B. Perrin, France
1925 James Franck, Germany
     Gustav Hertz, Germany
1924 Karl M. G. Siegbahn, Sweden
1923 Robert A. Millikan, U.S.
1922 Niels Bohr, Denmark
1921 Albert Einstein, U.S.
1920 Charles E. Guillaume, France
1919 Johannes Stark, Germany
1918 Max K. E. L. Planck, Germany
1917 Charles G. Barkia, U.K.
1916 No award
1915 Sir William H. Bragg, U.K.
     William L. Bragg, U.K.
1914 Max von Laue, Germany
1913 Heike Kamerlingh-Onnes, Netherlands
1912 Nils G. Dalén, Sweden
1911 Wilhelm Wien, Germany
1910 Johannes D. van der Waals, Netherlands
1909 Carl F. Braun, Germany
     Guglielmo Marconi, Italy
1908 Gabriel Lippmann, France
1907 Albert A. Michelson, U.S.

1906 Sir Joseph J. Thomson, U.K.
1905 Philipp E. A. von Lenard, Germany
1904 Rayleigh, Lord (John W. Strutt), U.K.
1903 Antoine Henri Becquerel, Marie Curie, Pierre Curie, France
1902 Hendrik A. Lorentz, Pieter Zeeman, Netherlands
1901 Wilhelm C. Röntgen, Germany

MEDICINE OR PHYSIOLOGY

1978 H. O. Smith, U.S.
     W. Arber, Switzerland
     D. Nathans, U.S.
1977 Rosalyn Yalow, U.S.
     R. Guillemin, U.S.
     A. Schally, U.S.
1976 B. S. Blumberg, U.S.
     D. G. Gajdusek, U.S.
1975 D. Baltimore, U.S.
     R. Dulbecco, U.S.
     H. M. Temin, U.S.
1974 A. Claude, U.S.
     C. de Duve, Belgium
     G. E. Palade, Belgium
1973 K. Lorenz, Austria
     N. Tinbergen, Netherlands
     K. von Frisch, Austria
1972 G. M. Edelman, U.S.
     R. R. Porter, U.K.
1971 Earl W. Sutherland, Jr., U.S.

1970 Julius Axelrod, U.S.
Sir Bernard Katz, U.K.
Ulf von Euler, Sweden
1969 Max Delbruck, U.S.
Alfred D. Hershey, U.S.
Salvador Luria, U.S.
1968 Robert W. Holley, U.S.
H. Gobind Khorana, U.S.
Marshall W. Nirenberg, U.S.
1967 Ragnar Granit, Sweden
Haldan Keffer Hartline, U.S.
George Wald, U.S.
1966 Charles B. Huggins, U.S.
Francis Peyton Rous, U.S.
1965 Francois Jacob, France
André Lwoff, France
Jacques Monod, France
1964 Konrad E. Bloch, U.S.
Feodor Lynen, Germany
1963 Sir John Eccles, Australia
Alan L. Hodgkin, U.K.
Andrew F. Huxley, U.K.
1962 Francis H. C. Crick, U.K.
James D. Watson, U.S.
Maurice H. F. Wilkins, U.K.
1961 Georg von Bekesy, U.S.
1960 Sir F. Macfarlane Burnet,
Australia
Peter B. Medawar, U.K.
1959 Arthur Kornberg, U.S.
Severo Ochoa, U.S.
1958 George W. Beadle, U.S.
Edward L. Tatum, U.S.
Joshua Lederberg, U.S.
1957 Daniel Bovet, Italy
1956 André F. Cournand, U.S.
Werner Forssmann, Germany
Dickinson W. Richards, Jr.,
U.S.
1955 Alex H. T. Theorell, Sweden
1954 John F. Enders, U.S.
Frederick C. Robbins, U.S.
Thomas H. Weller, U.S.
1953 Hans A. Krebs, U.K.
Fritz A. Lipmann, U.S.
1952 Selman A. Waksman, U.S.
1951 Max Theiler, U.S.
1950 Philip S. Hench, U.S.
Edward C. Kendall, U.S.
Tadeus Reichstein, Switzerland
1949 Walter R. Hess, Switzerland
Antonio Moniz, Portugal
1948 Paul H. Müller, Switzerland
1947 Carl F. Cori, U.S.
Gerty T. Cori, U.S.
Bernardo A. Houssay,
Argentina
1946 Hermann J. Muller, U.S.

1945 Ernst B. Chain, U.K.
Sir Alexander Fleming, U.K.
Sir Howard W. Florey, U.K.
1944 Joseph Erlanger, U.S.
Herbert S. Gasser, U.S.
1943 Henrik C. P. Dam, Denmark
Edward A. Doisy, U.S.
1942 No award
1941 No award
1940 No award
1939 Gerhard Domagk, Germany
1938 Corneille J. F. Heymans,
Belgium
1937 Albert Szent-Györgyi von
Nagyrapolt, U.S.
1936 Sir Henry Dale, U.K.
Otto Loewi, U.S.
1935 Hans Spemann, Germany
1934 George R. Minot, U.S.
William P. Murphy, U.S.
George H. Whipple, U.S.
1933 Thomas H. Morgan, U.S.
1932 Edgar D. Adrian (now
Lord), U.K.
Sir Charles S. Sherrington,
U.K.
1931 Otto H. Warburg, Germany
1930 Karl Landsteiner, U.K.
(Austrian-born)
1929 Christiaan Eijkman,
Netherlands
Sir Frederick G. Hopkins,
U.K.
1928 Charles J. H. Nicolle,
France
1927 Julius Wagner-Jauregg,
Austria
1926 Johannes A. G. Fibiger,
Denmark
1925 No award
1924 Willem Einthoven, Netherlands
1923 Frederick G. Banting,
Canada
John J. R. Macleod, Canada
1922 Archibald V. Hill, U.K.
Otto F. Meyerhof, Germany
1921 No award
1920 Schack A. S. Krogh,
Denmark
1919 Jules Bordet, Belgium
1918 No award
1917 No award
1916 No award
1915 No award
1914 Robert Bárány, Hungary
1913 Charles R. Richet, France
1912 Alexis Carrel, U.S.
1911 Allvar Gullstrand, Sweden

1910 Albrecht Kossel, Germany
1909 Emil T. Kocher, Switzerland
1908 Paul Ehrlich, Germany
     Elle Metchnikoff, France
1907 Charles L. A. Laveran,
     France
1906 Camillo Golgi, Italy
     Santiago Roman y Cajal,
     Spain
1905 Robert Koch, Germany
1904 Ivan P. Pavlov, U.S.S.R.
1903 Niels R. Finsen, Denmark
1902 Sir Ronald Ross, U.K.
1901 Emil A. von Behring,
     Germany

CHEMISTRY

1978 P. Mitchell, U.K.
1977 I. Prigogine, Belgium
1976 W. M. Lipscomb, U.S.
1975 J. W. Cornforth, Australia
     V. Prelog, Switzerland
1974 P. J. Flory, U.S.
1973 G. Wilkinson, U.K.
     E. O. Fischer, Germany
1972 C. B. Anfinsen, U.S.
     S. Moore, U.S.
     W. H. Stein, U.S.
1971 Gerhard Herzberg, Canada
1970 Luis A. Leloir, Argentina
1969 Derek H. R. Barton, U.K.
     Odd Hassel, Norway
1968 Lars Onsager, U.S.
1967 Manfred Eigen, Germany
     Ronald G. W. Norrish,
     U.K.
     George Porter, U.K.
1966 Robert S. Mulliken, U.S.
1965 Robert B. Woodward, U.S.
1964 Dorothy Crowfoot
     Hodgkin, U.K.
1963 Giulio Natta, Italy
     Karl Ziegler, Germany
1962 John C. Kendrew, U.K.
     Max F. Perutz, U.K.
1961 Melvin Calvin, U.S.
1960 Willard F. Libby, U.S.
1959 Jaroslav Heyrovsky,
     Czechoslovakia
1958 Frederick Sanger, U.K.
1957 Sir Alexander R. Todd,
     U.K.
1956 Sir Cyril N. Hinshelwood,
     U.K.
     Nikolai N. Semenov,
     U.S.S.R.
1955 Vincent du Vigneaud, U.S.
1954 Linus C. Pauling, U.S.
1953 Hermann Staudinger,
     Germany
1952 Archer J. P. Martin, U.K.
     Richard L. M. Synge, U.K

1951 Edwin M. McMillan, U.S.
     Glenn T. Seaborg, U.S.
1950 Kurt Alder, Germany
     Otto P. H. Diels, Germany
1949 William F. Giauque, U.S.
1948 Arne W. K. Tiselius, Sweden
1947 Sir Robert Robinson, U.K.
1946 James B. Sumner, U.S.
     John H. Northrop, U.S.
     Wendell M. Stanley, U.S.
1945 Artturi I. Virtanen, Finland
1944 Otto Hahn, Germany
1943 Georg de Hevesy, Hungary
1942 No award
1941 No award
1940 No award
1939 Adolf F. J. Butenandt,
     Germany
     Leopold Ruzicka, Switzer-
     land
1938 Richard Kuhn, Germany
1937 Walter N. Haworth, U.K.
     Paul Karrer, Switzerland
1936 Peter J. W. Debye, Nether-
     lands
1935 Frédéric Joliot, France
     Iréne Joliot-Curie, France
1934 Harold C. Urey, U.K.
1933 No award
1932 Irving Langmuir, U.S.
1931 Friedrich Bergius, Germany
     Carl Bosch, Germany
1930 Hans Fischer, Germany
1929 Arthur Harden, U.K.
     Hans K. A. S. von Euler-
     Chelpin, Sweden
1928 Adolf O. R. Windaus,
     Germany
1927 Heinrich O. Wieland,
     Germany
1926 Theodor Svedberg, Sweden
1925 Richard A. Zsigmondy,
     Germany
1924 No award
1923 Fritz Pregl, Austria
1922 Francis W. Aston, U.K.
1921 Frederick Soddy, U.K.
1920 Walther H. Nernst, Ger-
     many
1919 No award
1918 Fritz Haber, Germany
1917 No award
1916 No award
1915 Richard M. Willstätter,
     Germany
1914 Theodore W. Richards, U.S.
1913 Alfred Werner, Switzerland
1912 Victor Grignard, France
     Paul Sabatier, France
1911 Marie Curie, France
1910 Otto Wallach, Germany
1909 Wilhelm Ostwald, Germany
1908 Ernest Rutherford, U.K.
1907 Eduard Buchner, Germany

Chemistry (continued)

1906 Henri Moissan, France
1905 Johann F. W. A. von
     Baeyer, Germany
1904 Sir William Ramsay, U.K.
1903 Svante A. Arrhenius,
     Sweden
1902 Hermann E. Fischer,
     Germany
1901 Jacobus H. van't Hoff,
     Netherlands

LITERATURE

1978 I. B. Singer, U.S.
1977 V. Aleixandre, Spain
1976 Saul Bellow, U.S.
1975 E. Montale, Italy
1974 E. Johnson, Sweden
     H. Martinson, Sweden
1973 P. V. M. White, Australia
1972 Heinrich Boll, Germany
1971 Pablo Neruda, Chile
1970 Aleksandr Solzhenitsyn,
     U.S.S.R.
1969 Samuel Beckett, Republic
     of Ireland
1968 Yasunari Kawabata, Japan
1967 Miguel Angel Asturias,
     Guatemala
1966 Samuel Joseph Agnon,
     Israel
     Nelly Sachs, Sweden
1965 Mikhail Sholokhov,
     U.S.S.R.
1964 Jean Paul Sartre, France
     (Prize declined)
1963 Giorgos Seferis, Greece
1962 John Steinbeck, U.S.
1961 Ivo Andrîc, Yugoslavia
1960 Saint-John Perse, France
1959 Salvatore Quasimondo,
     Italy
1958 Boris L. Pasternak, U.S.S.R.
     (Prize declined)
1957 Albert Camus, France
1956 Juan Ramón Jiménez,
     Puerto Rico
1955 Halldör K. Laxness, Iceland
1954 Ernest Hemingway, U.S.
1953 Sir Winston Churchill, U.K.
1952 François Mauriac, France
1951 Pär F. Lagerkvist, Sweden
1950 Bertrand Russell, U.K.
1949 William Faulkner, U.S.
1948 T. S. Eliot, U.K.
1947 André Gide, France
1946 Herman Hesse, Switzerland
1945 Gabriela Mistral, Chile

1944 Johannes V. Jensen,
     Denmark
1943 No award
1942 No award
1941 No award
1940 No award
1939 Frans E. Sillanpäa, Finland
1938 Pearl S. Buck, U.S.
1937 Roger Martin du Gard,
     France
1936 Eugene O'Neill, U.S.
1935 No award
1934 Luigi Pirandello, Italy
1933 Ivan A. Bunin, France
1932 John Galsworthy, U.K.
1931 Erik A. Karlfeldt, Sweden
1930 Sinclair Lewis, U.S.
1929 Thomas Mann, Germany
1928 Sigrid Undset, Norway
1927 Henri Bergson, France
1926 Grazia Deledda, Italy
1925 George Bernard Shaw, U.K.
1924 Wladyslaw S. Reymont,
     Poland
1923 William Butler Yeats, Ireland
1922 Jacinto Benavente, Spain
1921 Anatole France, France
1920 Knut Hamsun, Norway
1919 Carl F. G. Spitteler,
     Switzerland
1918 No award
1917 Karl A. Gjellerup, Denmark
     Henrik Pontoppidan,
     Denmark
1916 Carl G. von Heidenstam,
     Sweden
1915 Romain Rolland, France
1914 No award
1913 Rabindranath Tagore, India
1912 Gerhart Hauptmann, Ger-
     many
1911 Count Maurice Maeterlinck,
     Belgium
1910 Paul J. L. Heyse, Germany
1909 Selma Lagerlof, Sweden
1908 Rudolf C. Eucken, Germany
1907 Rudyard Kipling, U.K.
1906 Giosuè Carducci, Italy
1905 Henryk Sienkiewicz, Poland
1904 Frédéri Mistral, France
     José Echegaray, Spain
1903 Björnsterne Björnson,
     Norway
1902 C. M. T. Mommsen,
     Germany
1901 Sully-Prudhomme (René F.
     A. Prudhomme), France

PEACE

1978 Anwar el-Sadat, Egypt
    Menachem Begin, Israel
1977 Amnesty International,
    London
1976 Mairead Corrigan, U.K.
    Betty Williams, U.K.
1975 A. D. Sakharov, U.S.S.R.
1974 S. McBride, Republic of
    Ireland
    E. Sato, Japan
1973 Henry A. Kissinger, U.S.
1972 No award
1971 Willy Brandt, W. Germany
1970 Norman E. Borlaug, U.S.
1969 International Labor
    Organization
1968 Rene Cassin, France
1967 No award
1966 No award
1965 The United Nations Children's Fund (UNICEF)
1964 Martin Luther King, Jr.,
    U.S.
1963 International Committee of
    the Red Cross
    Red Cross Societies League
1962 Linus C. Pauling, U.S.
1961 Dag Hammarskjöld,
    Sweden (Awarded
    posthumously)
1960 Albert J. Luthuli, South
    Africa
1959 Philip J. Noel-Baker, U.K.
1958 Georges Pire, Belgium
1957 Lester B. Pearson, Canada
1956 No award
1955 No award
1954 Office of the United Nations
    High Commissioner for
    Refugees
1953 Gen. George C. Marshall,
    U.S.
1952 Albert Schweitzer, France
1951 Léon Jouhaux, France
1950 Ralph J. Bunche, U.S.
1949 Lord Boyd Orr of Brechin,
    U.K.
1948 No award
1947 Friends Service Council,
    U.K.
    American Friends Service
    Committee, U.S.
1946 Emily G. Balch, U.S.
    John R. Mott, U.S.
1945 Cordell Hull, U.S.
1944 International Committee of
    the Red Cross
1943 No award
1942 No award
1941 No award
1940 No award

DAG HAMMARSKJOLD
served as Secretary-General of the
United Nations from 1957 until his
death in a plane crash in 1961. He was
posthumously awarded the Nobel
Peace Prize.

1939 No award
1938 Nasen International Office
    for Refugees
1937 Viscount Cecil of Chelwood,
    U.K.
1936 Carlos de Saavedra Lamas,
    Argentina
1935 Carl von Ossietzky,
    Germany
1934 Arthur Henderson, U.K.
1933 Sir Norman Angell, U.K.
1932 No award
1931 Jane Addams, U.S.
    Nicholas Murray Butler,
    U.S.
1930 Lars O. N. Söderblom,
    Sweden
1929 Frank B. Kellogg, U.S.
1928 No award
1927 Ferdinand E. Buisson,
    France
    Ludwig Quidde, Germany
1926 Aristide Briand, France
    Gustav Stresemann,
    Germany
1925 Sir Austen Chamberlain,
    U.K.
    Charles G. Dawes, U.S.
1924 No award
1923 No award
1922 Fridtjof Nansen, Norway
1921 Karl H. Branting, Sweden
    Christian L. Lange, Norway

Peace (continued)

1920 Léon V. A. Bourgeois, France
1919 Woodrow Wilson, U.S.
1918 No award
1917 International Committee of the Red Cross
1916 No award
1915 No award
1914 No award
1913 Henri La Fontaine, Belgium
1912 Elihu Root, U.S.
1911 Tobias M. C. Asser, Netherlands
     Alfred H. Fried, Austria
1910 Permanent International Peace Bureau
1909 Auguste M. F. Beernaert, Belgium
     Paul H. B. B. d'Estournelles de Constant, France
1908 Klas P. Arnoldson, Sweden
     Fredrik Bajer, Denmark
1907 Ernesto T. Moneta, Italy
     Louis Renault, France
1906 Theodore Roosevelt, U.S.
1905 Baroness Bertha von Suttner, Austria
1904 Institute of International Law
1903 Sir William Cremer, U.K.

1902 Élie Ducommun, Switzerland
     Charles A. Gobat, Switzerland
1901 Jean H. Dunant, Switzerland
     Frédéric Passy, France

ECONOMICS

1978 H. A. Simon, U.S.
1977 J. E. Meade, U.K.
     B. Ohlin, Sweden
1976 M. Friedman, U.S.
1975 L. V. Kantorovich, U.S.S.R.
     T. C. Koopmans, U.S.
1974 F. von Hayek, U.K. (Austrian-born)
     G. Myrdal, Sweden
1973 W. Leontief, U.S.
1972 Sir John Hicks, U.K.
     Kenneth G. Arrow, U.S.
1971 Simon Kuznets, U.S.
1970 Paul A. Samuelson, U.S.
1969 Ragnar Frisch, Norway
     Jan Tinbergen, Netherlands

International Organizations

The United Nations

The United Nations grew out of the alliance of nations throughout the world against Nazi Germany in World War II. In the summer of 1941, a meeting between Franklin D. Roosevelt, President of the United States, and Winston Churchill, Britain's Prime Minister, resulted in the phrasing of the Atlantic Charter—a set of principles for world peace and cooperation among nations. Two years later (October, 1943), the leaders again conferred—this time with Joseph Stalin, Premier of Russia—in Teheran, Iran, and agreed on the need for an effective instrument for maintaining international peace.

"A general international organization . . . for the maintenance of international peace and security" was recognized as desirable in Clause 4 of the proposals of the Four-Nation Conference of Foreign Ministers signed in Moscow on Oct. 30, 1943, by R. Anthony Eden, later the Earl of Avon (1897–1977) (U.K.), Cordell Hull (1871–1955) (U.S.), Vyacheslav M. Skryabin, *alias* Molotov (U.S.S.R.), (b. 1893) and Ambassador Foo Ping-Sheung (China).

Ways and means were resolved at the mansion of Dumbarton Oaks, Washington, D.C., between Aug. 21 and Oct. 7, 1944. A final step was taken at San Francisco, California, between Apr. 25 and June 26, 1945, when delegates of 50 participating states signed the Charter (Poland signed on Oct. 15, 1945). This came into force on Oct. 24, 1945, when the four above-mentioned states, plus France and a majority of the other 46 states, had ratified the Charter. The first regular session was held in London on Jan. 10–Feb. 14, 1946.

The U.N. was to be a world organization which would give member nations a workable international forum for peaceful cooperation in every field of human enterprise toward the prevention of war. It was to be a place where member nations could meet and exchange ideas in freedom, where great and small, rich and poor, weak and strong would have a voice. The Charter recognizes that the U.N.'s authority does not extend to matters within the "domestic jurisdiction" of member states.

The specific purposes of the U.N., as outlined in the Charter, are to:

1. Maintain international peace and security.

2. Work towards improved relations among nations, based on respect for the principle of equal rights and self-determination of peoples.

UNITED NATIONS HEADQUARTERS in New York City. The Dag Hammarskjold Library building (center) faces the circular drive and the main entrance to the U.N., which is in the Secretariat building, to the left.

3. Cooperate in finding a solution for international social, economic, cultural and humanitarian problems and in advancing respect for human rights and basic freedoms.

4. Serve as a base for coordinating the actions of nations to attain these common goals.

MEMBERS

The original signers were:

The U.N. consists of six major divisions or organs: the Security Council, General Assembly, Economic and Social Council, Trusteeship Council, International Court of Justice, and Secretariat. There were 51 nations among the original signatories to the U.N. Charter in 1945:

Argentina	El Salvador	Norway
Australia	Ethiopia	Panama
Belgium	France	Paraguay
Bolivia	Greece	Peru
Brazil	Guatemala	Philippines
Byelorussia	Haiti	*Poland
Canada	Honduras	Saudi Arabia
Chile	India	South Africa
(Nationalist) China	Iran	Syria
Colombia	Iraq	Turkey
Costa Rica	Lebanon	Ukraine
Cuba	Liberia	U.S.S.R.
Czechoslovakia	Luxembourg	United Kingdom
Denmark	Mexico	United States
Dominican Republic	Netherlands	Uruguay
Ecuador	New Zealand	Venezuela
Egypt	Nicaragua	Yugoslavia

* Although Poland was unable to attend the United Nations Conference on International Organization held at San Francisco, it was agreed that it should sign the Charter as an original member.

Of the 163 *de facto* sovereign states of the world 150 are now in membership plus the two U.S.S.R. republics of Byelorussia and the Ukraine which have separate membership.

The non-members are:

Andorra	Rhodesia
China (Taiwan)	San Marino
Korea, North	Switzerland
Korea, South	Tonga
Liechtenstein	Tuvalu
Monaco	Vatican City (Holy See)
Nauru	

The members decided that New York City would be the permanent home for the U.N. However, preparations were made to hold the first meeting of the General Assembly in London.

From the start, the United Nations concerned itself with various problems: political ones, outgrowths of the war, as well as economic and social problems. Specialized agencies and commissions, related to various U.N. activities, developed within the U.N. family to help carry on the important and difficult work of keeping international peace.

The United Nations' principal organs are:

The General Assembly consisting of all member nations, each with up to five delegates but one vote, and meeting annually in regular sessions with provision for special sessions. The Assembly has seven main committees, on which there is the right of representation by all member nations. These are (1) Political Security, (2) Economic and Financial, (3) Social, Humanitarian and Cultural, (4) Trust and Non-Self-Governing Territories, (5) Administration and Budgetary, (6) Legal, and the Special Political.

The Security Council, consisting of 15 members, each with one representative, of whom there are five permanent members (China, France, U.K., U.S.A. and U.S.S.R.) and ten elected members serving a two-year term. Apart from procedural questions, an affirmative majority vote of at least nine must include that of all five permanent members. It is from this stipulation that the so-called veto arises.

The Economic and Social Council, consisting of 54 members elected for three-year terms, is responsible for carrying out the functions of the General Assembly's second and third Committees, viz. economic, social, educational, health and cultural matters. It has the following Functional Commissions: (1) Statistical, (2) Population, (3) Social Development, (4) Narcotic Drugs, (5) Human Rights (and its sub-commission on the Prevention of Discrimination and the Protection of Minorities), (6) Status of Women. The Council has also established Economic Commissions, as follows: (1) for Europe (ECE), (2) for Asia and the Far East (ESCAP), (3) for Latin America (ECLA), (4) for Africa (ECA) and (5) for Western Asia (ECWA).

The International Court of Justice, comprising 15 Judges (quorum of nine) of different nations, each serving a nine-year term and meeting at 's Gravenhage (The Hague), Netherlands. Only states may be parties in contentious cases. In the event of a party's failing to adhere to a judgment, the other party may have recourse to the Security Council. Judgments are final and without appeal, but can be reopened on grounds of a new decisive factor within ten years.

The Secretariat. The principal administrative officer is the Secretary General who is appointed by the General Assembly for a five-year term. This office has been held thus:

SECURITY COUNCIL in session at the U.N. The 25 members (5 of which are permanent) are gathered around the horseshoe-shaped conference table working in an attempt to keep world peace.

Trygve Halvdan Lie (1896–1968) (Norway) Feb. 1, 1946–Nov. 10, 1952.

Dag Hjalmar Agne Carl Hammarskjöld (1905–61) (Sweden) Apr. 10, 1953–Sept. 18, 1961.

U. Maung Thant (1909–1974) (Burma) (acting) Nov. 3, 1961–Nov. 30, 1962, (permanent) Nov. 30, 1962–Dec. 31, 1971.

Kurt Waldheim (b. Dec. 21, 1918) (Austria) Jan. 1, 1972 (in office).

The **Trusteeship Council** administers territories under U.N. trusteeship. Twelve territories have been under U.N. trusteeship:

Original Trust Territory	*Subsequent Status*
Tanganyika (U.K.)	Independent, Dec. 9, 1961; merged with Zanzibar, Apr. 26, 1964 as Tanzania
Ruanda–Urundi (Belgium)	Two independent states, July 1, 1962
Somaliland (Italy)	Independent, July 1, 1960
Cameroons (U.K.)	Northern part joined Nigeria, June 1, 1961; southern part joined Cameroon, Oct. 1, 1961
Cameroons (France)	Independent republic of Cameroon, Jan. 1, 1960
Togoland (U.K.)	United with Gold Coast, to form Ghana, Mar. 6, 1957
Togoland (France)	Independent republic of Togo, Apr. 27, 1960
Western Samoa (N.Z.)	Independent, Jan. 1, 1962
Nauru (Australia, N.Z. and U.K.)	Independent, Jan. 31, 1968
Papua New Guinea (Australia)	Self-Government, Sept. 16, 1975
Pacific Islands (U.S.) comprising the Carolines, Marshalls and Marianas (excepting Guam)	

Note: South West Africa (Namibia), under jurisdiction of South Africa was claimed as a protectorate by the United Nations when in November, 1977, South Africa refused to grant independence to this former League of Nations mandated territory.

AGENCIES IN RELATIONSHIP WITH THE UNITED NATIONS

There are 14 specialized agencies, which in order of absorption or creation are as follows:

ILO

International Labor Organization (Headquarters—Geneva). Founded Apr. 11, 1919, in connection with The League of Nations. Re-established as the senior U.N. specialized agency, Dec. 14, 1946. Especially concerned with social justice, hours of work, unemployment, wages, industrial sickness, and protection of foreign workers.

FAO

Food and Agriculture Organization of the United Nations (Headquarters—Rome). Established, Oct. 16, 1945. Became U.N. agency, Dec. 14, 1946. Objects: to raise levels of nutrition and standards of living; to improve the production and distribution of agricultural products. FAO provides an Intelligence Service on Agriculture, Forestry and Fisheries.

UNESCO

United Nations Educational, Scientific and Cultural Organization (Headquarters—Paris). Established, Nov. 4, 1946. Objects: to stimulate popular education and the spread of culture, and to diffuse knowledge through all means of mass communication; to further universal respect for justice, the rule of law, human rights, and fundamental freedoms. Became a U.N. agency, Dec. 14, 1946.

ICAO

International Civil Aviation Organization (Headquarters—Montreal). Established Apr. 4, 1947. Objects: to study the problems of international civil aviation; to encourage safety measures and co-ordinate facilities required for safe international flight. A U.N. agency from May 13, 1947.

IBRD

International Bank For Reconstruction and Development (The World Bank) (Headquarters—Washington). Established, Dec. 27, 1945. Objects: to assist in the reconstruction and development of territories of members by aiding capital investment. Became a U.N. agency, Nov. 15, 1947. The *International Development Association* (Headquarters—Washington) is affiliated to the IBRD. Established, Sept. 24, 1960. Object: Making special term loans to less developed countries. Membership limited as in IFC.

IMF

International Monetary Fund (Headquarters—Washington). Established, Dec. 27, 1945. Objects: to promote international monetary co-operation, the expansion of international trade and stability of exchange rates. A U.N. agency from Nov. 15, 1947.

GATT

General Agreement on Tariffs and Trade (Headquarters—Geneva). Established, Jan. 1, 1948. Objects: to reduce or stabilize customs duties and assist the trade of developing countries. A major advancement of its aims was the establishment of the European Economic Community (EEC) or Common Market by The Treaty of Rome (signed, Mar. 21, 1957).

UPU

Universal Postal Union (Headquarters—Berne, Switzerland). Established, July 1, 1875, became U.N. specialized agency July 1, 1948. Objects: to unite members in a single postal territory.

U.N. HEADQUARTERS facing the East River in New York City. The permanent home for the United Nations was completed in 1962. Before that time, the U.N. held sessions in London, Hunter College in the Bronx, New York, and then in Lake Success, Long Island. Pictured here are the 39-story Secretariat (right), the General Assembly building (background) and the Dag Hammarskjold Library (foreground).

WHO
World Health Organization (Headquarters—Geneva). Established, Apr. 7, 1948. Objects: to promote the attainment by all peoples of the highest possible standard of health. Its services are both advisory and technical. A U.N. agency from July 10, 1948.

ITU
International Telecommunication Union (Headquarters—Geneva). Founded May 17, 1865; incorporated in the United Nations, Jan. 10, 1949. Objects: to seek the standardization of procedures concerning greater efficacy of telecommunications and to allocate frequencies.

WMO
World Meteorological Organization (Headquarters—Geneva). Established Mar. 23, 1950. Objects: to standardize meteorological observations; to secure their publication, and apply the information for the greater safety of aviation and shipping and benefit of agriculture, etc. A U.N. agency from Dec. 20, 1951.

IFC
International Finance Corporation (Headquarters—Washington). Established July 24, 1956. Objects: to promote the flow of private capital internationally and to stimulate the capital markets. Membership is open only to those countries that are members of the World Bank. A U.N. agency from Feb. 20, 1957.

IAEA
International Atomic Energy Agency (Headquarters—Vienna). Established July 29, 1957. Objects: to accelerate and enlarge the contribution of non-military atomic energy to peace, health and prosperity. A U.N. agency from Nov. 14, 1957.

IMCO
Inter-Governmental Maritime Consultative Organization (Headquarters —London). Established Mar. 17, 1958. Objects: to co-ordinate safety at sea and to secure the freedom of passage. A U.N. agency from Jan. 13, 1959.

NORTH ATLANTIC TREATY ORGANIZATION (NATO)

NATO, an idea first broached by the Secretary of State for External Affairs for Canada on Apr. 28, 1948, came into existence on Apr. 4, 1949 and into force on Aug. 24, 1949, with Belgium, Canada, Denmark, France, Iceland, Italy, Luxembourg, the Netherlands, Norway, Portugal, the United Kingdom and the U.S. In February, 1952, Greece and Turkey were admitted and West Germany on May 5, 1955 bringing the total of countries to 15. In 1966 France withdrew from NATO's military affairs and the headquarters was moved from Paris to Brussels. Greece withdrew its military forces in August, 1974.

ORGANIZATION FOR ECONOMIC CO-OPERATION AND DEVELOPMENT (OECD)

Founded as a European body on Sept. 30, 1961 (OEEC) the Organization after 14 years was reconstituted to embrace other Western countries. It now comprises 24 countries: Australia, Austria, Belgium, Canada, Denmark, Finland, France, Greece, Iceland, Ireland, Italy, Japan, Luxembourg, the Netherlands, New Zealand, Norway, Portugal, Spain, Sweden, Switzerland, Turkey, United Kingdom, U.S. and West Germany, with Yugoslavia (special status).

Headquarters are in Paris. The aims are to achieve the highest sustainable economic growth and level of employment with a rising standard of living compatible with financial stability.

EUROPEAN FREE TRADE ASSOCIATION (EFTA)

With the departure of the United Kingdom and Denmark, EFTA comprised six countries viz. Austria, Iceland, Norway, Portugal, Sweden and Switzerland, with Finland as an associate member. EFTA was established on Mar. 27, 1961.

The EFTA countries (except Norway) signed a free trade agreement with the EEC on July 22, 1972 and Norway did so on May 14, 1973.

ORGANIZATION OF AFRICAN UNITY (OAU)

In Addis Ababa, Ethiopia, on May 25, 1963, 30 African countries established the organization for common defense of independence, the elimination of colonialism and co-ordination of economic policies.

U.N. GENERAL ASSEMBLY in session. Often called the "town meeting" of the world, it is the discussion body of the United Nations where all U.N. members are represented. Constantly in rapport with the other councils, the General Assembly can begin studies on, and offer plans for international cooperation in politics, law, economics, social welfare, education, health and human rights.

U.N. TRUSTEESHIP COUNCIL supervises the administration of various territories governed by nations designated by the U.N. as trustees. Although the Council cannot determine or enforce laws, it helps prepare people for self-government and independence by keeping reports and making suggestions in regard to social, economic and educational progress. Permanent members of the Security Council plus those nations who administer trust territories are represented here.

United Nations (continued)

English and French are recognized as official languages in addition to African languages. By July, 1977, there were 48 African nation members.

EUROPEAN ECONOMIC COMMUNITY (EEC)

The EEC (or Common Market) was established by the treaty signed in Rome (the Treaty of Rome) on Mar. 25, 1957 by Belgium, France, West Germany, Luxembourg, Italy and the Netherlands (known as The Six). Denmark, the Irish Republic and the United Kingdom became members on Jan. 1, 1973, having signed the Treaty of Accession to the Community on Jan. 22, 1972. On Sept. 25, 1972 a referendum in Norway rejected membership with a vote of 53.5% in a 77.7% poll.

The object was to weld a complete customs union between The Nine (as was forged by July 1, 1968 between The Six) by July 1, 1977. A common transport and external trade policy and co-ordination of financial, commercial, economic and social policy is a future target. Economic and monetary union was scheduled for the end of 1980 and the Common Agricultural Policy was extended to The Nine by Jan. 1, 1978. In July, 1977, full free trade between the countries of the EEC and those of EFTA was achieved.

OTHER INTERNATIONAL ORGANIZATIONS
(with number of members)

International Development Association (IDA) (117)
Council of Europe (CE) (18)
League of Arab States (Arab League) (LAS) (20)
Council for Mutual Economic Assistance (COMECON) (9)
Organization of American States (OAS) (25)
Organization of Petroleum Exporting Countries (OPEC) (13)
Organization of Central American States (OCAS) (5)
Colombo Plan for Co-operative Economic Development in South and South East Asia (C-PLAN) (27)
European Atomic Energy Community (EURATOM) (9)
European Coal and Steel Community (ECSC) (9)
Inter-American Development Bank (IDB) (24)
Latin American Free Trade Association (LAFTA) (11)
Commonwealth of Nations (CN) (35)
World Intellectual Property Organization (WIPO) (91)
Common African and Mauritian Organization (OCAM) (10)
Warsaw Treaty Organization (WTO) (7)
African Financial Community (CFA) (14)
South Pacific Commission (SPC) (8)

The Earth

MASS, DENSITY AND VOLUME

The Earth has an estimated mass of 5,882,000,000,000,000,000,000 long tons and a density 5.517 times that of water. The volume of the Earth has been estimated at 259,875,620,000 cubic miles.

DIMENSIONS

Its equatorial circumference is 24,901.47 miles with a polar or meridional circumference of 24,859.75 miles, indicating that the Earth is not a true sphere but flattened at the poles and hence an ellipsoid. The Earth also has a slight ellipticity at the equator since its long axis (about longitude 0°) is 174 yards greater than the short axis. Artificial satellite measurements have also revealed further departures from this biaxial ellipsoid form in minor protuberances and depressions varying between extremes of 244 ft. in the area of Papua New Guinea and a depression of 354 ft. south of Sri Lanka (formerly Ceylon) in the Indian Ocean. The equatorial diameter of the Earth is 7,926.385 miles and the polar diameter 7,899.809 miles.

LAND AND SEA SURFACES

The estimated total surface area of the Earth is 196,937,600 square miles of which the sea (hydrosphere) covers 5/7ths, or more accurately 71.43%, and the land or lithosphere 2/7ths, or 28.57%. The mean depth of the hydrosphere is 11,660 ft. The total volume of the oceans is 308,400,000 cubic miles or 0.21% by weight of the whole Earth, *viz.* 1.2×10^{18} long tons.

EARTH'S STRATA BY DEPTH

Miles Below
the Surface

0–9	crust or granitic shell	
9–560 }	upper mantle	{ basaltic shell / peredotitic shell
560–1800 }	lower mantle	{ perrosporic shell / lithosporic shell
1800–3100	Outer core	
3100–3200	Transition region	
3200–3958	Inner core or siderosphere	

The Earth's crust is sometimes referred to as the lithosphere, comparable to the hydrosphere and the atmosphere. The inner core, assumed to be nickel-iron, has been termed the siderosphere and its boundary has been established by a discontinuity detected in seismic waves. The temperature of the core was reassessed in February, 1966, at 3,700°C. (previously 7,500°C.). The pressure is estimated to be 3,400 kilobars or 22,000 tons per sq. inch.

GEOPHYSICS

There have been two principal theories on the cause for the mountainous surface of the Earth's crust, or lithosphere:

(1) The contractionists used to maintain that the hot Earth shrank as it cooled. This, however, could explain only a loss of 9 kilometers in the radius of the Earth whereas a shrinkage of 80 kilometers is required to explain the existing terrain. The contraction theory is discredited by the majority of cosmologists, who now believe in a cold origin of the Earth.

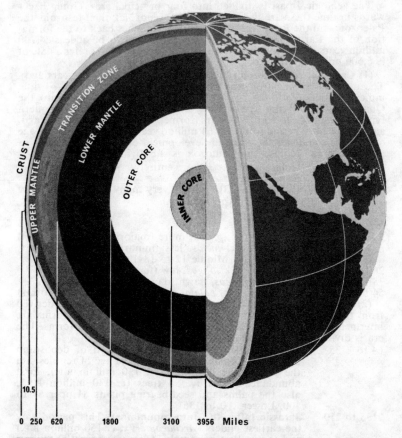

INTERIOR OF THE EARTH: The three main sections are the crust, mantle, and core. The crust constitutes about 1 per cent of the Earth's total volume and about 0.4 per cent of its mass. The materials of the mantle and core are much heavier, and are thought to be primarily iron and nickel.

Geophysics (continued)

(2) The expansionists maintain that a cold primeval Earth grew gradually by the accretion of planetary debris and was heated up by the radioactivity of some of its constituent elements until after one thousand million years the core became liquid.

According to the Lyttleton theory, the Earth once had a diameter much larger than at present and an area sixty million square kilometers larger. Since at high pressure the core is less incompressible than the mantle, as the core grows so the Earth shrinks. The inward contraction rate is of the order of 0.1 millimeter per annum, a centimeter per century, or 100 meters per 1,000,000 years.

GEO-CHRONOLOGY

The time scale of the Earth's geological evolution and that of the Plant and Animal Kingdoms is being continually revised. Modern dating techniques, relying on the half-lives of radioisotopes, have contributed greatly to recent revisions.

The table below is based on the Fitch, Forster and Miller revised Potassium-Argon time scale published in 1974 and the Geological Society Phanerozoic Time Scale, 1964, as amended by Lambert (1971).

The geological past is divided into four principal eras. Going backwards in time these are the Cainozoic (or Cenozoic), the Mesozoic, the Paleozoic and the Precambrian, which last stretches back to the formation of the Earth. This is now generally believed to be at least 4,700 million years ago, except by a few recent authorities who prefer a date of c. 6,500 million years ago.

(1) **Cainozoic (or Cenozoic) Era** (the present to 64 million years ago). The name is derived from the Gk. *kainos*, new or recent; *zo-os*, life, indicating that life-forms are all recent. The era is divided into the Quaternary Period (the Age of Man, and animals and plants of modern type), dating back to 2 million years (formerly only 1 million years) ago, and the Tertiary Period from 2 to 64 million years ago. This was the age of mammals and saw the rise and development of the highest orders of plants such as orchids. The Cainozoic is sub-divided thus:

Present to 50,000 B.C.	**Holocene**—Gk. *holos*, entirely; *kainos*, recent (all forms recent)
50,000 B.C. to c. 1,750,000 B.C.	**Pleistocene**—Gk. *pleisto*, very many (great majority of forms recent)

millions of years before the present (B.P.)

2 to c. 7	**Pliocene**—Gk. *pleion*, more (majority of forms recent)
c. 7 to 26	**Miocene**—Gk. *meios*, less (minority of forms recent) (Upper 7–12, Middle 12 to 18–19)
26 to 38	**Oligocene**—Gk. *oligos*, few (few forms recent)
38 to 54	**Eocene**—Gk. *eos*, dawn (dawn of recent forms)
54 to 64	**Paleocene**—Gk. *palaios*, ancient (earliest recent forms)

(2) **Mesozoic Era** (65 to 225 million years ago). The name is derived from the Gk. *mesos*, middle; *zo-os*, life, indicating that life-forms are intermediate between the recent evolutions and the ancient forms. The era is divided into 3 periods thus:

64 to ?135	**Cretaceous** (Latin *creta*, chalk; period of deposition and chalk formation). This was the age of reptiles and the fall of the dinosaurs (c. 120 million B.P.). First abundance of hardwood trees (c. 130 million B.P.), also the palms and seed-bearing plants. (Upper 65 to 100, Lower 100 to 136)
?135 to 210	**Jurassic** (after the Jura mountains). This period saw the earliest gliders (*Archaeopteryx*, c. 150 million B.P.) and the earliest mammals (*Megazostrodon* 190 million B.P.). (Upper 135 to 162, Middle 162 to 172, Lower 172 to 210)
c. 210 to 235	**Triassic** (adj. of *trias*, the old three-fold German division). First appearance of dinosaurs (c. 210 million B.P.).

(3) **Paleozoic Era** (235 to <597 million years ago). The name is derived from the Gk. *palaios*, ancient; *zo-os*, life, indicating that fossilized life-forms are of ancient forms. The era is broadly divided into the Upper Paleozoic (235–395 million B.P.) and the Lower Paleozoic from 395–570 million years B.P. The sub-divisions are as follows:

235 to 280	**Permian** (named in 1841 after the Russian province Perm). Earliest land reptiles dated from 290 million B.P.
280 to 360	**Carboniferous** (carbon-bearing, so named in 1822). Earliest spider (*Palaeoteniza crassipes*) (370 million B.P.) and the earliest quadruped, the amphibian, *Ichthyostega*, dating from 350 million B.P. The earliest conifers, great coal forests, tree ferns and huge mosses date from *c*. 340 million B.P. In North America the Late Carboniferous is called the Pennsylvanian and the Early Carboniferous the Mississippian Period.
c.360 to *c*. 405	**Devonian** (named after the English county). The earliest insects (*Rhyniella procursor*) date from 370 million B.P. Molluscs abundant.
c. 405 to ?435–460	**Silurian** (named after the ancient British tribe, *Silures*). The earliest land plants date from the late Silurian. Reef-building corals active.
?435–460 to *c*. 510	**Ordovician** (named after the Welsh border tribe, *Ordovices*). Earliest known fish, *Anatolepis* (510 million B.P.) and molluscs (the still living *Neopilina*).
>510 to <597	**Cambrian** (from the Latin, *Cambria* for Wales, scene of pioneer rock investigations). Marine invertebrates were abundant *c*. 550 million B.P. (Upper *c*. 510–515, Middle 515–540, Lower 540–570)

(4) **Precambrian Era** (earlier than 597 million years before the present). The name indicates merely all time pre (from Latin, *prae*, before) the Cambrian period (see above). This era includes such events as the earliest dated metazoan traces (1050 million B.P.); the earliest life form (blue-green algae from 3,400 million B.P.) and the earliest certainly dated rock formations of 3,980 $\pm$170 million B.P.

The Precambrian is divided into the Late Precambrian (<597 to 2,400 million B.P.); the Middle Precambrian (2,400 to 3,500 million B.P.) and Early Precambrian (3,500 to *c*. 4,600 million B.P.).

GEOCHEMICAL ABUNDANCES
OF THE ELEMENTS

Element	Lithosphere* (Parts per Mill. ‰)	Hydrosphere† (Parts per Mill. ‰)	Atmosphere (Parts per Mill. ‰)
Oxygen	466.0	857.0	209.5
Silicon	277.2	0.003 to 0.00002	—
Aluminum	81.3	0.00001	—
Iron	50.0	0.0001	—
Calcium	36.3	0.40	—
Sodium	28.3	10.50	—
Potassium	25.9	0.38	—
Magnesium	20.9	1.35	—
Hydrogen	1.4	103.0	0.0005
Titanium	4.4	—	—
Manganese	0.95	0.00001 to 0.000001	—
Phosphorus	0.7	0.00007	—
Fluorine	0.65	0.0013	—
Sulfur	0.26	0.88	—
Carbon	0.25	0.028	0.30 (as CO_2) 0.0015 (as CH_4)
Chlorine	0.13	19.0	—
Zirconium	0.17	—	—
Rubidium	0.09	0.0001	—
Chromium	0.01	0.00000005	—
Nitrogen	0.002	0.0007 to 0.00001	780.90

* Assessment based on crustal rock.
† Sea water is 35% saline.

Ice Ages

Climatic variations occur in many time scales ranging from day to day weather changes in the shortest term and seasonal cycles up to major meteorological variations known as "fourth order climatological changes."

Weather is the present state of the climate in which temperature has been known to change 49°F. (27.2°C.) in 2 minutes. Second order temperature changes are those trends which now show that the mean temperature in the Northern Hemisphere which peaked in the period 1940–45 has dropped sharply by 2.7°F. (1.5°C.) to a point lower than the 1900 average when the world was emerging from the so called "Little Ice Age" of the period 1595–1898.

Third order climatological changes are now being measured by the ratio of oxygen isotopes found in seashells. These reveal 8 Ice Ages in the last 700,000 years thus:

Ice Age	Duration	Nadirs
	B.C.	B.C.
Last Ice Age	75,000–9,000	60,000
		& 18,000
Penultimate	130,000–105,000	115,000
Pre-penultimate	285,000–240,000	250,000
Fourth	355,000–325,000	330,000
Fifth	425,000–400,000	410,000
Sixth	520,000–500,000	510,000
Seventh	620,000–580,000	605,000
Eighth	685,000–645,000	670,000

Many theories have been advanced on the causes of Ice Ages which most profoundly affect human, animal and plant life. The most recent is that the Solar System which is revolving round the center of the Milky Way at 480,000 mph (772,500 km/h) passes through dust belts which dim the Sun's heating and lighting powers.

Fourth order climatological change will be determined by the Sun's conversion from a yellow dwarf to a red giant as it burns 4 million tons of hydrogen per second. Thus in 5,000 million years the oceans will boil and evaporate.

Volcanoes

It is estimated that there are about 535 active volcanoes of which 80 are submarine. Vulcanologists classify volcanoes as extinct, dormant or active (which includes rumbling, steaming or erupting). Areas of volcanoes and seismic activity are well defined, notably around the shores of the N. Pacific and the eastern shores of the S. Pacific, down the Mid-Atlantic range, the Africa Rift Valley and across from Greece and Turkey into Central Asia, the Himalayas and Heghalaya (Assam).

Cerro Aconcagua (22,834 feet), the highest Andean peak, is an extinct volcano, while Kilimanjaro (19,340 feet) in Africa and Volcán Llullaillaco in Chile (22,057 feet) are classified as dormant. Among the principal volcanoes active in recent times are:

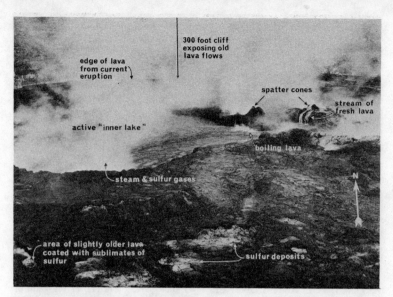

VOLCANIC ERUPTION: The ¾-mile-diameter firepit of Halemaumau, on the island of Hawaii, during its 1967-68 eruption. This volcano is one of several under the active surveillance of the U.S. Geological Survey's Hawaiian Volcano Observatory.

LARGEST ACTIVE VOLCANO: Extending 13,680 feet above the Pacific Ocean, Mauna Loa on the island of Hawaii has slopes covered with solidified lava flows. In the background is Mauna Kea, a 13,780-foot-high dormant volcano.

EXTINCT VOLCANIC CONE: Crater Grande (Sykes Crater), in the state of Sonora, Mexico. Note other extinct cones surrounding it.

Volcanoes (continued)

Height (feet)	Name and Location	Date of Last Notified Eruption
19,882	Guallatiri—Andes, Chile	1959
19,652	Lascar—Andes, Chile	1951
19,347	Cotopaxi—Andes, Ecuador	1942– Steams
19,167	Volcán Misti—Andes, Peru	—
18,504	Tupungatito—Andes, Chile	1959
17,887	Popocatépetl—Altiplano de Mexico, Mexico	1932– Steams
17,159	Sangay—Andes, Ecuador	1946
16,197	Cotacachi—Andes, Ecuador	1955
15,913	Klyuchevskaya—Sredinnyy Khrebet (Kamchatka Peninsula), U.S.S.R.	1962
15,604	Puracé—Andes, Colombia	1950
13,812	Tajumulco—Guatemala	Rumbles
13,680	Mauna Loa—Hawaii	1950
13,350	Cameroon Mt.—(Monarch Range), Cameroon	1959
13,333	Tacama—Sierra Madre, Guatemala	—
12,582	Fuego—Sierra Madre, Guatemala	1973
12,450	Erebus—Ross Is., Antarctica	Steams
12,224	Rindjani—Lombok, Indonesia	1964
12,198	Pico de Tiede—Teneriffe, Canary Is.	—
12,080	Tolbachik—U.S.S.R.	1941
12,060	Semeru—Java, Indonesia	1963
11,385	Nyiragongo—Virunga, Zaire (Kinshasa)	1972
11,339	Koryakskaya—Kamchatka Peninsula, U.S.S.R.	1957
11,268	Irasu—Cordillera Central, Costa Rica	1963
11,253	Chiriqui—Cadelia de Talamanca, Panama	—
11,247	Slamat—Java, Indonesia	1953
11,070	Mt. Spurr—Alaska Range	1953
10,705	Mt. Etna—Sicily, Italy	1974
10,453	Lassen Peak—Cascade Range, Calif.	1915
9,351	Tambora—Sumbawa, Indonesia	—

Earthquakes

It was not until as recently as 1874 that subterranean slippage along faults became generally accepted as the cause of tectonic earthquakes. The collapse of caverns, volcanic action, and also possibly the very rare event of a major meteoric impact can also cause tremors. The study of earthquakes is called seismology.

The two great seismic zones are the Alps-Himalaya great circle and the circum-Pacific belt. The foci below the epicenters are classified as shallow (<50 km. deep), intermediate (50–200 km.) and deep (200–700 km.).

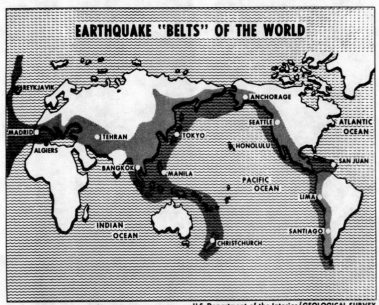

U.S. Department of the Interior/GEOLOGICAL SURVEY

EARTHQUAKE BELTS OF THE WORLD: Most earthquakes occur in seismically active "belts" that coincide with zones in which tectonic plates are impinging upon one another. Four-fifths of all earthquakes, as well as most volcanic eruptions occur in an enormous belt surrounding the Pacific Ocean.

SAN ANDREAS FAULT: These two photographs of the San Francisco Bay area were not made by ordinary photographic techniques but by radar, which can penetrate surface vegetation to show the underlying geologic structure.

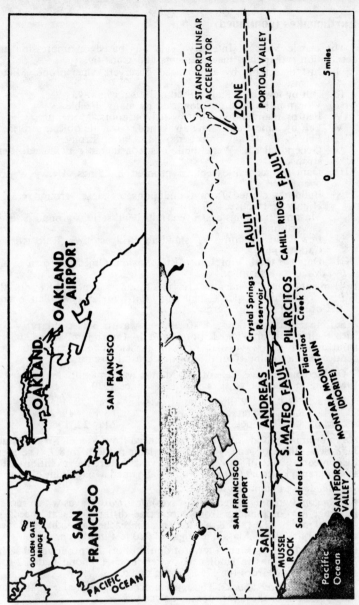

AREA covered in the two photographs opposite. The long scar of the San Andreas fault is clearly visible in the bottom photograph, as are the subsidiary San Mateo and Pilarcitos faults just below it. Earth movements along the San Andreas fault were responsible for the major earthquake of 1906 as well as the persistent minor quakes to which the area is subject.

227

Earthquakes (continued)

The classic Mercalli Intensity Scale was based on impression and description rather than measurements and reads thus:

I   Just detectable by experienced observers when prone. Microseisms.

II   Felt by few. Delicately poised objects may sway.

III   Vibration but still unrecognized by many. Feeble.

IV   Felt by many indoors but by few outdoors. Moderate.

V   Felt by almost all. Many awakened. Unstable objects moved.

VI   Felt by all. Heavy objects moved. Alarm. Strong.

VII   General alarm. Weak buildings considerably damaged. Very strong.

VIII   Damage general except in proofed buildings. Heavy objects overturned.

IX   Buildings shifted from foundations, collapse, ground cracks. Highly destructive.

X   Masonry buildings destroyed, rails bent, serious ground fissures. Devastating.

XI   Few if any structures left standing. Bridges down. Rails twisted. Catastrophic.

XII   Damage total. Vibrations distort vision. Objects thrown in air. Major catastrophe.

Instrumental measurements are made on seismographs on the Gutenberg-Richter scale. Cataclysmic earthquakes have an energy of the order of 3×10^{19} ergs.

Seismographs can denote P (primary) waves, S (secondary) waves with their reflections, and L (long) and M (maximum) waves. It was from a double P wave that A. Mohorovicic (Croatia) in 1909 first deduced a discontinuity in the Earth's crustal structure.

On the comparative scale of the Mantle wave magnitudes (defined in 1968) the most cataclysmic earthquakes since 1930 have been:

Mag. 8.9 Prince William Sound, Alaska   Mar. 28, 1964
Mag. 8.8 Kamchatka, U.S.S.R.   Nov. 4, 1952
Mag. 8.8 Concepción, Chile   May 22, 1960

An interim magnitude of 8.9 was announced from Vienna for the South Java Sea 'quake of Aug. 18, 1977 but later reduced to 8.7. The great Lisbon earthquake of Nov. 1, 1755, 98 years before the invention of the seismograph, killed 60,000, and would have rated a magnitude of $8\frac{3}{4}$ to 9.

Attendant phenomena include:

(i) *Tsunami* (wrongly called tidal waves) or gravity waves which radiate in long, low oscillations from submarine disturbances at speeds of 450–490 m.p.h. The 1883 Krakatoa *tsunami* reached a height of 135 feet and that off Valdez, Alaska, a height of 220 feet in March, 1964.

(ii) *Seiches* (a Swiss-French term of doubtful origin, pronounced sāsh). Seismic oscillations in landlocked water. Loch Lomond had a 2-foot *seiche* for 1 hour from the 1755 Lisbon quake.

(iii) *Fore and After Shocks*. These often occur before major quakes and may persist after these for months or years.

(iii) *Fore and After Shocks*. These often occur before major 'quakes and may persist after these for months or years.

HISTORIC EARTHQUAKES

The five earthquakes in which the known loss of life has exceeded 100,000 have been:

830,000	Shensi Province, China	Jan. 24, 1556
750,000	Tangshan, China	July 27, 1976
300,000	Calcutta, India	Oct. 11, 1737
180,000	Kansu Province, China	Dec. 16, 1920
142,807	Kwanto Plain, Honshu, Japan	Sept. 1, 1923

The material damage done in the Kwanto Plain, which includes Tokyo, was estimated at $3,000,000,000.

Other notable earthquakes during this century, with loss of life (in parentheses), have been:

1906 San Francisco, Calif. (Apr. 18) (452)

1908 Messina, Italy (Dec. 28) (75,000)

1915 Avezzano, Italy (Jan. 13) (29,970)

1932 Kansu Province, China (Dec. 26) (70,000)

1935 Quetta, India (May 31) (60,000)

1939 Erzingan, Turkey (Dec. 27) (23,000)

1960 Agadir, Morocco (Feb. 29) (12,000)

1964 Anchorage, Alaska (Mar. 28) (131)

1970 Northern Peru (May 31) (66,800)

1972 Nicaragua (Dec. 23) (10,000)

1975 Lice, Turkey (Sept. 6) (2,312)

1976 Guatemala (Feb. 4) (22,419)

1976 Southern Philippines (Aug. 17) (8,000)

1976 Van Province, Turkey (Nov. 24) (4,000)

1977 Bucharest, Romania (Mar. 4) (1,570)

1978 Tabriz, Iran (Sept. 17) (22,000)

U.S. EARTHQUAKES

The earliest recorded U.S. earthquake was one *c.* 1568 near Providence, Rhode Island, reported as a recollection by some aged Indians to Roger Williams in 1638.

The most extensive earthquakes in the U.S. were those of 1811–12 centered on New Madrid, Missouri. The major shocks occurred on Dec. 15, 1811, Jan. 23, and probably the greatest on Feb. 7, 1812. This last was felt from New Orleans to Canada over an area of at least 2,000,000 square miles. Owing to the sparseness of the population at the

METEORITE CRATER: Meteor Crater (Barrington Crater), Arizona, is a depression resulting from the collision of a meteor with the earth.

time near the epicenters the loss of life was insignificant. The San Francisco 'quake of Apr. 18, 1906, killed 452 and focussed attention on the San Andreas fault line. The Los Angeles 'quake of Feb. 9, 1971, killed 64. The states most free from seismic activity are North Dakota, West Virginia and Wisconsin.

Meteorites

The term meteorite must now be confined to a fallen meteor, a meteoric mass of stone (aerolite) or nickel-iron (siderite). It is loosely and incorrectly used of a meteor or shooting star which is usually only the size of a pinhead. The existence of meteorites was not admitted, owing to a religious bias, until as late as Apr. 26, 1803, after a shower of some 2,500 aerolites fell around L'Aigle, near Paris, France.

Name	Location	Approximate tonnage
Hoba	nr. Grootfontein, South-West Africa	67
Tent (Abnighito)	Cape York, west Greenland	34½
Bacuberito	Mexico	30
Mbosi	Tanganyika	29
Williamette (1902)	Oregon	16
Chupaero	Chihuahua, Mexico	16
Campo de Cielo	Argentina	14½
Morito	Chihuahua, Mexico	12

The largest recorded in other continents are:

Australia	Cranbourne	3.8
Asia	Sikhote-Alin, U.S.S.R.	1.9
Europe	Magura, Czechoslovakia	1.6

The majority of meteorites inevitably fall into the sea (71.4% of the Earth's surface) and are not recovered. Only eight meteorites exceeding 10 tons have been located. All these are of the iron-nickel type. The largest recorded stone meteorite is the 3,894 lb. stone which fell in the Kirin Province, Manchuria on Mar. 8, 1976.

METEORITE CRATERS

The most spectacular of all dry craters is the Coon Butte or Barringer crater near Canyon Diablo, Winslow, Arizona, discovered in 1891, which is now 575 feet deep and 4,150 feet in diameter. The next largest crater is Wolf's Creek, Western Australia (2,785 feet diameter, 170 feet deep) discovered in 1947. The New Quebec (formerly Chubb) "crater" in North Ungava, Canada, first located in June, 1943, is 1,325 feet deep and 2.1 miles in diameter, but is now regarded as a water-filled vulcanoid.

Ancient and oblique meteoric scars are much less spectacular though of far greater dimensions. These phenomena are known as astroblemes (Gk. *astron*, a star; *blemma*, a glance).

ANCIENT METEORITE CRATER: Deep Bay, about 10 miles in diameter, and a part of Reindeer Lake in northern Saskatchewan, Canada, was formed by the impact of a meteorite striking the earth millions of years ago.

Name	Diameter (miles)
Vredefort Ring, South Africa (meteoric origin first disputed, 1963) (discernible scar 43 miles wide)	24.8
Nordlinger Ries, Germany	15.5
Deep Bay, Saskatchewan, Canada (disc. 1956)	8.5
Lake Bosumtwi, Ghana	6.2
Serpent Mound, Ohio	3.98
Wells Creek, Tennessee	2.97
Brent, Ontario, Canada	2.3
Al Umchaimin, Iraq	1.98

Other Major Natural Disasters

Landslides caused by earthquakes in the Kansu Province of China on December 16, 1920, killed 200,000 people. The highest toll from an eruption was 60,000 killed around Mt. Etna, Sicily, on Jan. 11, 1693.

The Peruvian snow avalanches at Huarás (Dec. 13, 1941) and from Huascarán (Jan. 10, 1962) killed 5,000 and 3,000 people, respectively. The Huascarán alluvion flood triggered by the earthquake of May 31, 1970, wiped out 25,000.

Disasters (continued)

Both floods and famines have wreaked a greater toll of human life than have earthquakes. The greatest river floods on record are those of the Hwang-ho, China. From September into October in 1887 some 900,000 people were drowned. The flood of August 1931 killed some 3,700,000. A typhoon flood at Haiphong in North Vietnam (formerly Indo-China) on Oct. 8, 1881, killed an estimated 300,000 people. The cyclone of Nov. 12–13, 1970, which struck the Ganges Delta islands, Bangladesh drowned an estimated 1,000,000. The Mont Pelée eruption on Martinique destroyed the city of St. Pierre and killed more than 30,000 on May 8, 1902. Auguste Ciparis, a prisoner, survived.

History's worst famines have occurred in Asia. In 1770 nearly one third of India's total population died, with 10,000,000 in Bengal alone. From February 1877 to September 1878 an estimated 9,500,000 people died of famine in China.

The Oceans and Seas

The strictest interpretations permit of only three oceans—the Pacific, Atlantic and Indian. The so-called Seven Seas would require the three undisputed oceans to be divided by the equator into North and South and the addition of the Arctic Sea. The term Antarctic Ocean is not recognized by the International Hydrographic Bureau.

Ocean with adjacent seas	Area in millions sq. miles	Percentage of world area	Greatest depth (feet)	Location*
Pacific	69.3	35.25	35,760	Mariana Trench
Atlantic	41.0	20.9	27,498	Puerto Rico Trench
Indian	28.9	14.65	26,400	Diamantina Trench
Total	139.2	70.8		

If the adjacent seas are detached and the Arctic Sea regarded as an ocean, the oceanic areas may be listed thus:

	Area (sq. miles)	Percentage of sea area
Pacific	63,800,000	45.7
Atlantic	31,800,000	22.8
Indian	28,400,000	20.3
Arctic	5,400,000	3.9
Other Seas	10,270,000	7.3
	139,670,000	100%

Ocean depths are zoned by oceanographers as bathyl (down to 2,000 m. or 6,560 feet); abyssal (between 2,000 and 6,000 m. [19,685 feet]); and hadal (below 6,000 m.).

PRINCIPAL SEAS

	Area (sq. miles)	Average depth (feet)
Malay Sea (inc. South China Sea and Malacca Straits)	3,144,000	4,000
Caribbean Sea	1,063,000	8,000
Mediterranean Sea	966,750	4,875
Bering Sea	875,750	4,700
Gulf of Mexico	595,750	5,000
Sea of Okhotsk	589,800	2,750
East China Sea	482,300	600
Hudson Bay	475,800	400
Sea of Japan	389,000	4,500
Andaman Sea	308,000	2,850
North Sea	222,125	300
Black Sea	178,375	3,600
Red Sea	169,000	1,610
Baltic Sea	163,000	190
Persian Gulf*	92,200	80
Gulf of St. Lawrence	91,800	400
Gulf of California	62,530	2,660
English Channel	34,700	177
Irish Sea	34,200	197
Bass Strait	28,950	230

Note: The largest inland bay in the 50 States is Chesapeake Bay, between Maryland and Virginia, with an area of 3,237 square miles.

* Also referred to as the Arabian Gulf.

OCEAN CURRENTS

Oceanography is a science of comparatively recent origin. The word was first used in 1883. One of its aspects is the study of ocean currents.

The Gulf Stream is the most famous of all oceanic currents. It derives its name from being fed by water from the Gulf of Mexico, though it is much reinforced by water from the trade-wind currents off Florida. The Gulf Stream travels clockwise around the North Atlantic west of the 46th meridian and has a maximum velocity greater than 4 knots (4.60 m.p.h.) and a maximum flow of 7,500,000,000 cubic feet of water per second—or about 1,000 times greater than the mean discharge rate of the Mississippi River.

Beyond Cape Hatteras, the relatively deep and narrow pattern breaks down to a broader, and consequently slacker, stream. On reaching the Grand Banks off Newfoundland it mixes to some extent with the Labrador Current, which is an inshore counter current. The resultant northeasterly and westerly flow is directed across the ocean towards the British Isles and is henceforward more properly known as the North Atlantic Current. Thus the coasts of the Hebrides and western Scotland receive the benefit of its relatively higher temperatures. The current eventually meets the coast of Norway at about latitude 62°N.

The major North Atlantic Ocean currents are clockwise. Their sectors may be discribed thus:

Gulf Stream—North Atlantic Drift	9 o'clock to	2 o'clock
Canary Current	3 o'clock to	6 o'clock
North Equatorial Current	6 o'clock to	9 o'clock

In the South Atlantic, the major currents are counterclockwise, thus:

South Equatorial Current (east to west)	1 o'clock to	11 o'clock
Brazil Current (southward off South America)	11 o'clock to	9 o'clock
West Wind Drift (west to east)	9 o'clock to	5 o'clock
Benguela Current (northward off southwest Africa)	5 o'clock to	1 o'clock

Ocean Currents (continued)

Similarly, the great current of the Pacific Ocean flows clockwise round the North Pacific basin and counterclockwise around the Southern Pacific basin, thus:

North Pacific:

Kuroshio Current (northeast along Japanese coast)	9 o'clock to 11 o'clock
North Pacific Drift	11 o'clock to 1 o'clock
California Current (south and east along U.S. west coast)	1 o'clock to 3 o'clock
North Equatorial Current (east to west)	3 o'clock to 9 o'clock

South Pacific:

Humboldt Current (northward along South America's west coast)	4 o'clock to 1 o'clock
South Equatorial Current (east to west)	1 o'clock to 10 o'clock
West Wind Drift (west to east)	7 o'clock to 4 o'clock

This pattern of currents is in accordance with the coriolis force caused by the Earth's rotation and named for the French engineer, M. Coriolis, who first derived it in 1835.

DEEP SEA TRENCHES

Length (miles)	Name	Deepest Point	Depth (feet)
2,200	Peru-Chile (Atacama) Trench, E. Pacific	Bartholomew Deep	26,454
2,000	Aleutian Trench, N. Pacific	—	26,574
1,600	Tonga-Kermadec Trench, S. Pacific	Vityaz II (Tonga)	35,598

DEEPEST SPOT IN THE OCEAN was reached by this bathyscaphe, the "Trieste," designed by Auguste Piccard. In 1960, Piccard's son, Jacques, and Lieutenant Donald Walsh, U.S.N., descended in the "Trieste" to 35,800 ft. below sea level, the bottom of the Marianas Trench.

Length (miles)	Name	Deepest Point	Depth (feet)
1,400	Kuril-Kamchatka Trench*, W. Pacific	—	34,587
1,400	Java (Sunda) Trench, Indian Ocean	Planet Deep	25,344
1,400	Mariana Trench*, W. Pacific	Challenger Deep	35,760†
1,000	Japan Trench*, (including Idzu-Bonin) W. Pacific	Ramapo Deep	32,196
825	Philippine Trench, W. Pacific	Galathea Deep	34,578
650	Nansei Shoto (Ryukyu) Trench, W. Pacific	—	24,630
600	Cayman Trench, Caribbean	—	24,720
600	Romanche Trench, N.-S. Atlantic	—	25,800
600	South Sandwich Trench, S. Atlantic	Meteor Deep	27,112
500	Guatemala Trench, E. Pacific	—	21,288
500	Puerto Rico Trench, W. Atlantic	Milwaukee Deep	28,374
400	Solomon Trench, S. Pacific	—	29,988
350	Yap Trench*, W. Pacific	—	27,976
300	Vityaz Trench, S.W. Pacific	—	20,142
200	Diamantina Fracture, Indian Ocean	Ob Trench	22,553

* These four trenches are sometimes regarded as a single 4,600-mile-long system.

† Subsequent visits to the Challenger Deep since 1951 have produced claims for greater depths in this same longitude and latitude. In March, 1959, the U.S.S.R. research ship *Vityaz* claimed 36,198 feet using echo-sounding only.

SEA LEVEL

Mean sea level has long been regarded as an equipotential geodetic surface and a foolproof basis for measuring land altitudes. The British Ordnance Survey datum level is based on levels at Newlyn, Cornwall, in the period 1915–20. In fact average sea levels vary with time (century by century) and from place to place over the Earth. The English cross-channel slope Ramsgate to Dunkerque was about 8 cms. in 1957–58.

Factors affecting sea levels are: (1) Surf beat (long waves superimposed on wind generated waves); (2) Tsunami (from submarine earthquakes); (3) Seiches resonant wave oscillations across bays and bights); (4) Atmospheric pressures; (5) Storm surges; (6) Thermal effects (1° C. over all oceans would raise the level by 60 mm.); (7) Perihelion-Aphelion (sun distance).

Since 1900 a rise in the world's temperature and the melting of polar ice has raised sea levels by 6 cm. This has increased the Earth's radius of gyration and hence slowed down our rate of rotation. Tidal friction would be expected to lengthen the day by 2.3 milliseconds per century, thus indicating some as yet unidentified compensatory accelerating force.

TIDES

Tides are caused by the gravitational attraction of the Moon and the Sun. The Sun's power, because its greater mass is not fully outweighed by its greater distance, is only 46% that of the Moon.

Normally the interval between high waters is 12 hours 25 minutes of half that of the Moon's apparent revolution around the Earth. There are wide variations in the intervals, *e.g.* at Southampton, England, high waters are often doubled while at places in the China Sea the interval often extends to over 24 hours.

The range also varies very widely being 53½ feet in the Minas Basin of the Bay of Fundy, Nova Scotia and a matter of inches in the Mediterranean.

SEA CLIFFS

No comprehensive survey has yet been published of the world's greatest sea cliffs. Great sea cliffs exist in the Philippines and on the coast of N.W. Greenland. The tallest in Europe are probably those on Achill Island off County Mayo, Ireland, which rise 2,192 feet sheer above the Atlantic. The tallest on the coast of the 48 U.S. mainland States are at Cape Flattery, Washington and Cape Mendocino, California, both 700 feet high. The highest on the east coast are at Somerset Sound, Mount Desert Island, Maine, and are 640 feet high.

The Continents

There is ever increasing evidence that the Earth's land surface once comprised a single primeval land mass, now called Pangaea, and that this split during the Upper Cretaceous period (65,000,000 to 100,000,000 years ago) into two super-continents, called Laurasia in the north and Gondwanaland in the south.

The Earth's land surface embraces seven continents, each with their attendant islands. Europe, Africa and Asia, though politically distinct, physically form one land mass known as Afro-Eurasia. Central America is often included in North America (Canada, the U.S. and Greenland). Europe includes all the U.S.S.R. territory west of the Ural Mountains. Oceania embraces Australasia (Australia and New Zealand) and the non-Asian Pacific Islands.

Continent	Area in sq. miles	Greatest overland distance between extremities of land masses	
		North to South (miles)	East to West (miles)
Asia	16,993,000	4,000	4,700
America	16,233,000		
North America	8,301,000	2,900	2,900
Central America	1,062,000	820	950
South America	6,870,000	4,500	3,200
Africa	11,673,000	4,400	3,750
Antarctica	c. 5,250,000	—	2,700*
Europe†	4,063,000	1,800	2,500
Oceania§	3,450,000	1,870‡	2,300‡
	57,270,000		

* Greatest transit from coast to coast.
† Includes 2,151,000 sq. miles of U.S.S.R. territory west of the Urals.
§ Includes 159,376 sq. miles in West Irian (West New Guinea), politically part of Indonesia, which is largely in Asia.
‡ Figures applicable only to Australian mainland (2,941,526 sq. miles).

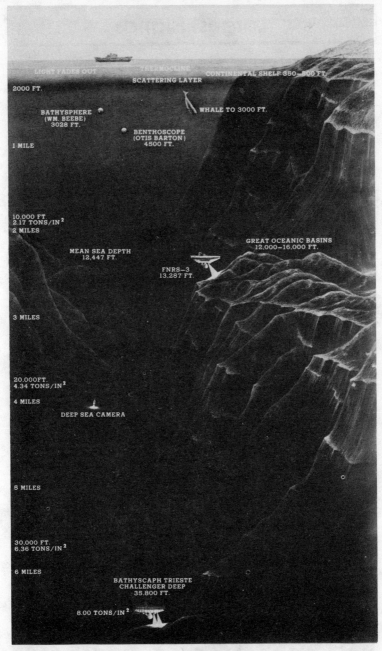

DEPTHS OF THE SEA: an artist's drawing. The figures in tons per sq. in. indicate the pressures at different depths.

Largest Islands

World's Largest Islands

Name	Area in sq. miles	Location
* Australia	2,941,526	—
1. Greenland	840,000	Arctic Ocean
2. New Guinea	300,000	W. Pacific
3. Borneo	287,100	Indian Ocean
4. Madagascar	227,800	Indian Ocean
5. Baffin Island	183,810	Arctic Ocean
6. Sumatra	182,860	Indian Ocean
7. Honshu	88,031	N.W. Pacific
8. Great Britain	84,186	North Atlantic
9. Victoria Island	81,930	Arctic Ocean
10. Ellesmere Island	75,767	Arctic Ocean
11. Celebes (Sulawezi)	72,987	Indian Ocean
12. South Island, New Zealand	58,093	S.W. Pacific
13. Java	48,763	Indian Ocean
14. North Island, New Zealand	44,281	S.W. Pacific
15. Newfoundland	43,359	North Atlantic
16. Cuba	42,827	Caribbean Sea
17. Luzon	40,420	W. Pacific
18. Iceland	39,768	North Atlantic
19. Mindanao	36,381	W. Pacific
20. Ireland (Northern Ireland and the Republic of Ireland)	31,839	North Atlantic
21. Hokkaido	30,077	N.W. Pacific
22. Hispaniola (Dominican Republic and Haiti)	29,418	Caribbean Sea
23. Sakhalin	28,597	N.W. Pacific
24. Tasmania	26,215	S.W. Pacific
25. Sri Lanka (formerly Ceylon)	25,332	Indian Ocean

* Geographically regarded as a continental land mass, as are Antarctica, Afro-Eurasia, and America.

THIRTEENTH LARGEST ISLAND: Java in Indonesia has many temples with Buddhist statues like this.

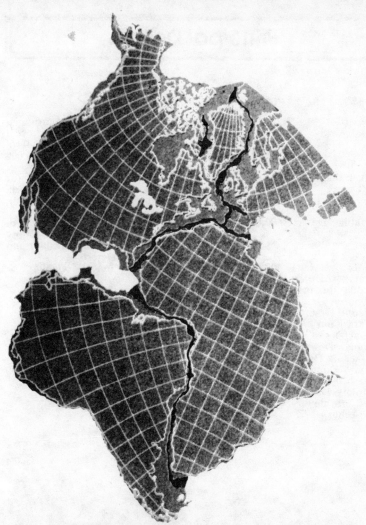

CONTINENTAL DRIFT: The close fit that can be made between the continental shelves of the Western Hemisphere, Europe, and Africa is one of the reasons that geologists accept that the continents were once part of a single land mass that has since been slowly drifting apart. This theory was first set forth in detail in 1912 by a German geologist, Alfred Wegener, who called the original land mass Pangaea.

Largest Peninsulas

	Sq. miles
Arabia	1,250,000
Southern India	800,000
Alaska	580,000
Labrador	500,000
Scandinavia	309,000
Iberian Peninsula	225,500

Principal Deserts

Name	Approx. area in sq. miles	Territories
Sahara	3,250,000	Algeria, Chad, Libya, Mali, Mauritania, Niger, Sudan, Tunisia, Egypt, Morocco. Includes the Libyan Desert (600,000 sq. miles) and the Nubian Desert (100,000 sq. miles)
Australian Desert	600,000	Australia. Includes the Great Sandy (or Warburton) (160,000), Great Victoria (125,000), Simpson (Arunta) (120,000), Gibson (85,000) and Sturt Deserts
Arabian Desert	500,000	Saudi Arabia, North and South Yemen. Includes the Ar Rub'al Khali or Empty Quarter (250,000), Syrian (125,000) and An Nafud (50,000) Deserts
Gobi	400,000	Mongolia and China (Inner Mongolia)
Kalahari Desert	200,000	Botswana
Takla Makan	125,000	Sinkiang, China
Sonoran Desert	120,000	Arizona, California and Mexico
Namib Desert	120,000	S.W. Africa (Namibia)
Kara Kum	105,000	Turkmenistan, U.S.S.R.
Thar Desert	100,000	Northwestern India and West Pakistan
Somali Desert	100,000	Somalia
Atacama Desert	70,000	Northern Chile
Kyzyl Kum	70,000	Uzbekistan–Kazakhstan, U.S.S.R.
Dasht-i-Lut	20,000	Eastern Iran (Iranian Desert)
Mojave Desert	13,500	Southern California
Desierto de Sechura	10,000	Northwest Peru

DENIZENS OF THE DESERT: Camels store more water in their stomachs than they can immediately use, and can withstand the heat rising from arid sands.

Highest Mountains

The 55 mountains in the world over 25,000 feet high are listed below. In addition three other peaks are given (in *italic* type) which many authorities do not regard as separate mountains.

	Mountain	Height in feet	Range	Date of First Ascent (if any)
1.	Mount Everest*	29,028	Himalaya	May 29, 1953
2.	K 2 (Chogori)	28,250	Karakoram	July 31, 1954
3.	Kangchenjunga I	28,208	Himalaya	May 25, 1955
4.	Lohtse I	27,923	Himalaya	May 18, 1956
—	Yalung Kang	27,894	Himalaya	May 14, 1973
—	Kangchenjunga S. Peak	27,828	Himalaya	May 19, 1978
5.	Makalu I	27,824	Himalaya	May 15, 1955
	Kangchenjunga (Middle Peak)	*27,806*	*Himalaya*	*Unclimbed*
	Lhotse Shar (Lhotse II)	*27,504*	*Himalaya*	*May 12, 1970*
6.	Dhaulagiri I	26,795	Himalaya	May 13, 1960
7.	Manaslu I (Kutang I)	26,760	Himalaya	May 9, 1956
8.	Cho Oyu I	26,750	Himalaya	Oct. 19, 1954
9.	Nanga Parbat (Diamir)	26,660	Himalaya	July 3, 1953
10.	Annapurna I	26,546	Himalaya	June 3, 1950
11.	Gasherbrum I (Hidden Peak)	26,470	Karakoram	July 5, 1958
12.	Broad Peak I	26,400	Karakoram	June 9, 1957
13.	Gasherbrum II	26,360	Karakoram	July 7, 1956
—	Broad Peak (Middle)	26,300	Karakoram	July 28, 1975
14.	Shisha Pangma (Gosainthan)	26,291	Himalaya	May 2, 1964
15.	Gasherbrum III	26,090	Karakoram	Aug. 11, 1975
16.	Annapurna II	26,041	Himalaya	May 17, 1960
17.	Gasherbrum IV	26,000	Karakoram	Aug. 6, 1958
18.	Gyachung Kang	25,990	Himalaya	Apr. 10, 1964
19.	Kangbachen	25,925	Himalaya	May 26, 1974
20.	Disteghil Sar I	25,868	Karakoram	June 9, 1960
21.	Himal Chuli	25,801	Himalaya	May 24, 1960
22.	Khinyang Chhish	25,762	Karakoram	Aug. 26, 1971
23.	Nuptse	25,726	Himalaya	May 16, 1961
24.	Peak 29 (Manaslu II)	25,705	Himalaya	Oct. —, 1970
25.	Masherbrum East	25,660	Karakoram	July 6, 1960
26.	Nanda Devi	25,645	Himalaya	Aug. 29, 1936
27.	Chomo Lönzo	25,640	Himalaya	Oct. 30, 1954
28.	Ngojumba Ri (Cho Oyu II)	25,610	Himalaya	May 5, 1965
—	Masherbrum West	25,610	Karakoram	Unclimbed
29.	Rakaposhi	25,550	Karakoram	June 25, 1958
30.	Batura Muztagh (Hunza Kunji I)	25,542	Karakoram	June 30, 1976
31.	Zemu Peak	25,526	Himalaya	Unclimbed
—	Gasherbrum II East	25,500	Karakoram	Unclimbed
32.	Kanjut Sar	25,460	Karakoram	July 19, 1959
33.	Kamet	25,447	Himalaya	June 21, 1931
34.	Namcha Barwa	25,445	Himalaya	Unclimbed
35.	Dhaulagiri II	25,429	Himalaya	May 18, 1971
36.	Saltoro Kangri I	25,400	Karakoram	July 24, 1962
37.	Batura Maztagh II (Hunza Kunji II)	25,361	Karakoram	Unclimbed

* Discovered to be world's highest in 1852 and named for Sir George Everest (1790-1866). Tibetan name was Chu-mu-lang-ma.

Highest Mountains (continued)

Mountain	Height in feet	Range	Date of First Ascent (if any)
38. Gurla Mandhata	25,355	Himalaya	Unclimbed
39. Ulugh Muztagh	25,340	Kunlun Shan	Unclimbed
40. Qungur II	25,326	Pamir	Unclimbed
41. Dhaulagiri III	25,318	Himalaya	Oct. 23, 1973
42. Jannu	25,294	Himalaya	Apr. 27, 1962
43. Tirich Mir	25,282	Hindu Kush	July 21, 1950
44. Saltoro Kangri II	25,280	Karakoram	Unclimbed
45. Disteghil Sar E. Pk.	25,262	Karakoram	Unclimbed
Tirich Mir, East Peak	*25,236*	*Hindu Kush*	*July 25, 1963*
46. Saser Kangri I	25,170	Karakoram	Unclimbed
47. Chogolisa II	25,148	Karakoram	Aug. 2, 1975
48. Phola Gangchhen	25,135	Himalaya	Unclimbed
49. Dhaulagiri IV	25,134	Himalaya	May 9, 1975
50. Shahkang Sham	25,131		Unclimbed
51. Makalu II (Kangshungtse)	25,120	Himalaya	Oct. 22, 1954
52. Chogolisa I (Bride Peak)	25,110	Karakoram	Aug. 9, 1958
53. Trivor	25,098	Karakoram	Aug. 17, 1960
54. Ngojumba Ri II	25,085		Unclimbed
55. Khinyang Chhish (South)	25,000		Unclimbed

NORTH AMERICAN MOUNTAINS

Mt. McKinley (first ascent 1913) is the only peak in excess of 20,000 feet in the entire North American continent.

Name	Height (feet)	Country or state
1. McKinley, South Peak	20,320	Alaska
2. Logan	19,850	Canada
McKinley, North Peak	*19,470*	*Alaska*
3. Citlaltepetl or Orizaba	18,700	Mexico
4. St. Elias	18,008	Alaska–Canada
5. Popocatépetl	17,887	Mexico
6. Foraker	17,400	Alaska
7. Lucania	17,150	Canada
8. King Peak	17,130	Canada
9. Ixtaccihuatl	17,000	Mexico
10. Steele	16,625	Alaska
11. Bona	16,500	Alaska
12. Blackburn	16,390	Alaska
13. Sanford	16,237	Alaska
14. South Buttress	15,885	Alaska
15. Wood	15,885	Canada
16. Vancouver	15,700	Alaska–Canada
17. Churchill	15,638	Alaska
18. Fairweather	15,300	Alaska
19. Zinantecatl (Toluca)	15,016	Mexico
20. Hubbard	14,950	Alaska–Canada
21. Bear	14,831	Alaska
22. Walsh	14,780	Canada
23. East Buttress	14,730	Alaska
24. Matlalcueyetl	14,636	Mexico
25. Hunter	14,573	Alaska
26. Browne Tower	14,530	Alaska
27. Alverstone	14,500	Alaska–Canada
28.*Whitney	14,495	California

* The highest mountain in the 48 contiguous states of the United States was first climbed in 1872. It was first surveyed in 1864 by Josiah Dwight Whitney.

HIGHEST PEAK in North America is Mt. McKinley in Alaska. It is also the only mountain in excess of 20,000 feet on the whole continent. Known during the Russian occupation of Alaska before 1867 as Bolshaya (meaning large), it was first climbed in 1913.

29. Elbert	14,431	Colorado
30. Harvard	14,420	Colorado
31. Massive	14,418	Colorado
32. Rainier	14,410	Washington

SOUTH AMERICAN MOUNTAINS

The mountains of the Cordillera de los Andes are headed by Aconcagua at 22,834 feet (first climbed on Jan. 14, 1897), which has the distinction of being the highest mountain in the world outside the great ranges of Central Asia. The following list contains the 22 Andean summit peaks in excess of 21,000 feet above sea level, as given in the *American Alpine Journal*, 1963.

Name	Height (feet)	Country
1. Cerro Aconcagua	22,834	Argentina
2. Ojos del Salado	22,598	Argentina–Chile
3. Nevado de Pissis	22,241	Argentina
4. Huascarán, South Peak	22,205	Peru
5. Llullaillaco, Volcan	22,057	Argentina–Chile
6. Mercedario	21,884	Argentina
7. Huascarán, North Peak	21,834	Peru
8. Yerupajá	21,758	Peru
9. Cerro Tres Cruces, Central Peak	21,720	Argentina–Chile
10. Coropuna	21,705	Peru
11. Nevado Incahuasi	21,657	Argentina–Chile
12. Tupungato	21,490	Argentina–Chile
13. Sajama	21,427	Bolivia
14. Nevado González	21,326	Argentina
15. Cerro del Nacimiento	21,302	Argentina
16. Illimani	21,260	Bolivia

Highest Mountains (continued)

17.	El Muerto	21,253	Argentina–Chile
18.	Illimani, South Peak	21,201	Bolivia
19.	Anto Falla	21,162	Argentina
20.	Ancohuma (Sorata North)	21,086	Bolivia
21.	Nevado Bonete	21,031	Argentina
22.	Cerro de la Ramada	21,031	Argentina

EUROPEAN MOUNTAINS

The Caucasus range, along the spine of which runs the traditional geographical boundary between Asia and Europe, includes the following peaks which are higher than Mont Blanc (15,771 feet). El'brus is often rendered Elbruz in atlases.

Name	Height (feet)	Name	Height (feet)
1. El'brus, West Peak	18,481	8. Dzhangi Tau	16,565
El'brus, East Peak	18,356	9. Kazbek	16,558
2. Shkara	17,060	10. Katuintau (Adish)	16,355
3. Dych Tau	17,054	11. Mishirgitau,	
4. Pik Shota		West Peak	16,148
Rustaveli	17,028	*Mishirgitau,*	
5. Koshtantau	16,880	*East Peak*	*16,135*
6. Pik Pushkin	16,732	12. Kunjum Mischikji	16,001
7. Janga, West Peak	16,572	13. Gestola	15,940
Janga, East Peak	*16,529*	14. Tetnuld	15,938

ANTARCTIC MOUNTAINS

Some areas of eastern Antarctica remain unsurveyed. Immense areas of the ice cap around the Pole of Inaccessibility lie over 12,000 feet above sea level, rising to 14,000 feet in 82° 25′ S 65° 30′ E.

	Name	Height (feet)	Location
1.	Vinson Massif*	16,863	Sentinel Range, Ellsworth Mts.
2.	Mt. Tyree	16,298	Sentinel Range, Ellsworth Mts.
3.	Mt. Shinn (volcanic)	15,750	Sentinel Range, Ellsworth Mts.
4.	Mt. Gardner	15,374	Sentinel Range, Ellsworth Mts.
5.	Mt. Kirkpatrick	14,860	Queen Alexandra Range
6.	Mt. Elizabeth	14,698	
7.	Mt. Markham	14,250	Queen Elizabeth Range
8.	Mt. MacKellar	14,082	Queen Alexandra Range
9.	Mt. Kaplan	13,960	Queen Maud Range
10.	Mt. Sidley (volcanic)	13,850	Executive Committee Range
11.	Ostenso	13,711	Sentinel Range, Ellsworth Mts.
12.	Mt. Minto	13,648	
13.	Long Gables	13,622	Sentinel Range, Ellsworth Mts.
14.	Mt. Miller	13,600	Queen Elizabeth Range
15.	Mt. Falla	13,500	Queen Alexandra Range
16.	Mt. Fridtjof Nansen	13,350	Queen Maud Range
17.	Mt. Fisher	13,340	Queen Maud Range
18.	Mt. Wade	13,330	Queen Maud Range
19.	Mt. Lister	13,205	Royal Society Range
20.	Mt. Huggins	12,870	

* Range first sighted from the air on Nov. 23, 1935. The Vinson Massif was not sighted till 1957 and was first surveyed in December of that year. It was first climbed by a National Geographical Society expedition on Dec. 18, 1966.

AFRICAN MOUNTAINS

All the peaks listed in Zaïre and Uganda are in the Ruwenzori group.

Name	Height (feet)	Location
1. Kilimanjaro (Uhuru Point*, Kibo)	19,340	Tanzania
Hans Meyer Peak, Mawenzi	*16,890*	
2. Mount Kenya (Batian)	17,058	Kenya
Nelion	*17,022*	
Point Piggott	*16,265*	
Point John	*16,020*	
3. Mount Stanley (Margherita Peak)	16,763	Zaïre–Uganda
Albert Peak	*16,735*	*Zaïre*
Alexandra Peak	*16,726*	*Zaïre–Uganda*
Elena Peak	*16,388*	*Uganda*
Great Tooth	*16,290*	*Uganda*
Savoia Peak	*16,269*	*Uganda*
Philip Peak	*16,239*	*Uganda*
Elizabeth Peak	*16,236*	*Uganda*
Moebius	*16,134*	*Uganda*
Unnamed peak	*c. 15,500*	*Uganda*
Unnamed peak	*c. 15,100*	*Uganda*
4. Duwoni or Mt. Speke (Vittorio Emmanuele Peak)	16,042	Uganda
Ensonga Peak	*15,961*	*Zaïre–Uganda*
Johnston Peak	*15,906*	*Uganda*
5. Mount Baker (Edward Peak)	15,889	Uganda
Semper Peak	*15,843*	*Uganda*
Wollaston Peak	*15,286*	*Uganda*
Moore Peak	*15,269*	*Uganda*
6. Mount Emin (Umberto Peak)	15,797	Zaïre
Kraepelin Peak	*15,720*	*Zaïre*
7. Mount Gessi (Iolanda Peak)	15,470	Uganda
Bottego Peak	*15,418*	*Uganda*
8. Mount Luigi di Savoia (Sella Peak)	15,179	Uganda
Weismann Peak	*15,157*	*Uganda*

* Formerly called Kaiser Wilhelm Spitze

OCEANIA MOUNTAINS

Name	Height (feet)	Location
1. *Putjak Djaja	c. 16,500	Irian Jaya (W. New Guinea)
2. Idenburg Peak	15,748	Irian Jaya (W. New Guinea)
3. *Mt. Mohammed Yamin (Wilhelmina Top)	15,525	Irian Jaya (W. New Guinea)
4. *Mt. Trikora (Juliana Top)	15,420	Irian Jaya (W. New Guinea)
5. Mt. Wilhelm	15,400	N.E. New Guinea
6. Mt. Kubur	14,300	N.E. New Guinea
7. Mt. Herbert	14,000	N.E. New Guinea
8. Mt. Leonard Darwin	13,887	Irian Jaya (W. New Guinea)
9. †Mauna Kea	13,796	Hawaii, Hawaiian Is.
10. †Mauna Loa	13,680	Hawaii, Hawaiian Is.

* Politically regarded as in Asian territory. Putjak Djaja (formerly Ngga Pulu, Mt. Sukarno, and Carstensz Pyramide) is the tallest island mountain in the world.
† Since Aug. 21, 1959, politically part of the U.S.

World's Greatest Mountain Ranges

The greatest mountain system is the Himalaya–Karakoram–Hindu Kush–Pamir range with 73 peaks over 24,606 feet (7,500 meters).
The second greatest range is the Andes with 54 peaks over 20,000 feet.

Length (miles)	Name	Location	Culminating Peak	Height (feet)
4,500	Cordillera de Los Andes	W. South America	Aconcagua	22,834
3,750	Rocky Mountains	W. North America	Mt. Robson	12,972
2,400	Himalaya–Karakoram–Hindu Kush	S. Central Asia	Mt. Everest	29,028
2,250	Great Dividing Range	E. Australia	Kosciusko	7,316
2,200	Trans-Antarctic Mts.	Antarctica	Mt. Kirkpatrick	14,860
1,900	Brazilian Atlantic Coast Range	E. Brazil	Pico da Bandeira	9,482
1,800	West Sumatran Java Range	W. Sumatra and Java	Kerintji	12,484
1,650*	Aleutian Range	Alaska and N.W. Pacific	Shishaldin	9,387
1,400	Tien Shan	S. Central Asia	Pik Pobeda	24,406
1,250	Central New Guinea Range	New Guinea	Putjak Djaja	c. 16,500
1,250	Altai Mountains	Central Asia	Gora Belukha	14,783
1,250	Uralskiy Khrebet	Russian S.F.S.R.	Gora Narodnaya	6,214
1,200	†Kamchatka Range	Eastern Russian S.F.S.R.	Klyuchevskaya Sopka	15,584
1,200	Atlas Mountains	N.W. Africa	Jebel Toubkal	13,665
1,000	Verkhoyanskiy Khrebet	Eastern Russian S.F.S.R.	Gora Mas Khaya	9,708
1,000	Western Ghats	W. India	Anai Madi	8,841
950	Sierra Madre Oriental	Mexico	Citlaltepec (Orizaba)	18,865
950	Kuhha-ye-Zagros	Iran	Zard Kuh	14,921
950	Scandinavian Range	W. Norway	Galdhopiggen	8,104
900	Ethiopian Highlands	Ethiopia	Ras Dashan	c. 15,100
900	Sierra Madre Occidental	Mexico	Nevado de Colima	13,993
850	Malagasy Range	Madagascar	Maromokotro	9,436
800	Drakensberg (edge of plateau)	S.E. Africa	Thabana Ntlenyana	11,425
800	Khrebet Cherskogo	Eastern Russian S.F.S.R.	Gora Pobeda	10,325
750	Caucasus	Georgia, U.S.S.R.	El'brus	18,481
700	Alaska Range	Alaska	Mt. McKinley	20,320
700	Assam–Burma Range	Assam–W. Burma	Hkakado Razi	19,296
700	Cascade Range	Northwest U.S.–Canada	Mt. Rainier	14,410

* Continuous mainland length (excluding islands) 450 miles.   † Comprises the Sredinnyy and Koryaskiy Khrebets.

700	Central Borneo Range	Central Borneo	13,455
700	Tihamat ash Sham	S.W. Arabia	12,336
700	Apennines	Italy	9,617
700	Appalachians	Eastern U.S.	6,684
650	Alps	Central Europe	15,771

Highest Alps (Europe)

The highest point in Italian territory is a shoulder of the main summit of Mont Blanc (Monte Bianco) through which a 15,616-foot contour passes. The highest top exclusively in Italian territory is Picco Luigi Amedeo (14,632 feet) to the south of the main Mont Blanc peak, which is itself exclusively in French territory.

Subsidiary peaks or tops on the same massif have been omitted except in the case of Mont Blanc and Monte Rosa, where they have been indented in *italic* type.

	Country	Feet	First Ascent
1. Mont Blanc	France	15,771	1786
Mont Blanc de Courmayeur	France	15,577	1877
2. Monte Rosa			
Dufourspitze	Switzerland	15,203	1855
Nordend	Swiss–Italian border	15,121	1861
Ostspitze	Swiss–Italian border	15,078	1854
Zumsteinspitze	Swiss–Italian border	14,970	1820
Signal Kuppe	Swiss–Italian border	14,947	1842
3. Dom	Switzerland	14,912	1858
4. Lyskamm (Liskamm)	Swiss–Italian border	14,853	1861
5. Weisshorn	Switzerland	14,781	1861
6. Täschhorn	Switzerland	14,733	1862
7. Matterhorn	Swiss–Italian border	14,683	1865
Le Mont Maudit (Mont Blanc)	Italy–France	14,649	1878
Picco Luigi Amedeo (Mont Blanc)	Italy	14,632	1901
8. La Dent Blanche	Switzerland	14,293	1862
9. Nadelhorn	Switzerland	14,196	1858
10. Le Grand Combin de Grafaneire	Switzerland	14,153	1859
Dôme du Goûter (Mont Blanc)	France	14,120	1784
11. Lenspitze	Switzerland	14,087	1871
12. Finsteraarhorn	Switzerland	14,021	1829*

* Also reported climbed in 1812 but evidence lacking.

MT. KILIMANJARO in Tanzania, a dormant volcano, is the tallest mountain in Africa, at 19,340 feet.

GRAND CANYON in Arizona has been cut away by the narrow, rapid-flowing Colorado River.

ANGEL FALLS in the jungles of Venezuela is the tallest waterfalls in the world with a total drop of 3,212 feet. Note the relative size of the plane passing by in this unusual shot by Ruth Robertson.

NIAGARA FALLS (Canadian side) or Horseshoe Falls (named for its shape) has 94 per cent of the Niagara River water flow over it, or about 200,000 cu. ft./sec.

WORLD'S GREATEST WATERFALLS (by Height)

	Name	Total Drop (feet)	River	Location
1.	Angel (highest fall—2,648 ft.)	3,212	Carrao, an upper tributary of the Caroni	Venezuela
2.	Tugela (5 falls, highest fall—1,350 ft.)	3,110	Tugela	Natal, S. Africa
3.	Utigård (highest fall—1,970 ft.)	2,625	Jöstedal Glacier	Nesdale, Norway
4.	Mongefossen	2,540	Monge	Mongebekk, Norway
5.	Yosemite (Upper Yosemite—1,430 ft.; Cascades in middle section—675 ft.; Lower Yosemite—320 ft.)	2,425	Yosemite Creek, a tributary of the Merced	Yosemite Valley, Yosemite National Park, Calif.
6.	Østre Mardøla Foss (highest fall—974 ft.)	2,154	Mardals	Eikisdal, W. Norway
7.	Tyssestrengane (highest fall—948 ft.)	2,120	Tysso	Hardanger, Norway
8.	Kukenaom (or Cuquenán)	2,000	Arabopó, upper tributary of the Caroni	Venezuela
9.	Sutherland (highest fall—815 ft.)	1,904	Arthur	nr. Milford Sound, Otago, S. Island, New Zealand
10.	Kile* (or Kjellfossen) (highest fall—490 ft.)	1,841	Naeröfjord feeder	nr. Gudvangen, Norway
11.	Takkakaw (highest fall—1,200 ft.)	1,650	A tributary of the Yoho	Daly Glacier, British Columbia, Canada
12.	Ribbon	1,612	Ribbon Fall Stream	3 miles west of Yosemite Falls, Yosemite Nat. Park, Calif.
13.	King Geroge VI	1,600	Utshi, upper tributary of the Mazaruni	Guyana
			an upper tributary of the Mazaruni	
14.	Roraima	1,500	—	Guyana
15.	Cleve-Garth	1,476		New Zealand
16.	Kalambo	1,400	S.E. feeder of Lake Tanganyika	Tanzania–Zambia
17.	Gavarnie	1,384	Gave de Pau	Pyrénées Glaciers, France

* Some authorities would regard this as no more than a "Bridal Veil" waterfall, i.e., of such low volume that the fall atomizes.

Waterfalls (continued)

Name	Total Drop (feet)	River	Location
18. Glass	1,325	Iguazú	Brazil
19. Krimmler Fälle (4 falls, upper fall 460 ft.)	1,280	Krimml Glacier	Salzburg, Austria
20. Lofoi	1,259	—	Zaïre

By Volume of Water

Name	Maximum Height (feet)	Width (feet)	Mean Annual Flow (cu. ft. per sec.)	Location
Boyóma (formerly Stanley) (7 cataracts)	200 (total)	2,400 (7th)	c. 600,000	Zaïre River, near Kisangani
Guaíra (or Salto das Sete Quedas) ("Seven Falls")	374	15,900	470,000*	Alto Paraná River, Brazil–Paraguay
Khône	70	35,000	400,000 to 420,000	Mekong River, Laos
Niagara:				
Horseshoe (Canadian)	160	2,500	212,000 (Horseshoe—94%)	Niagara River, Lake Erie to Lake Ontario
American	167	1,000		Niagara River, Lake Erie to Lake Ontario
Paulo Afonso	192	—	100,000	São Francisco River, Brazil
Urubu-punga	40		97,000	Alto Paraná River, Brazil
Cataratas del Iguazú (or Iguacu)	308	c. 13,000	61,660	Iguazú (or Iguacu) River, Brazil–Argentina
Patos-Maribondo	115	—	53,000	Rio Grande, Brazil
Victoria (Mosi-oa-tunya):				Zambezi River, nr. Livingstone, Zambia–Rhodesia
Leaping Water	{ 355 (maximum)	{ 108	{ 38,430	
Main Fall		2,694		
Rainbow Falls		1,800		
Churchill (formerly Grand)	245		30,000 to 40,000	Churchill (formerly Hamilton) River, Labrador, Canada
Kaieteur (Köituök)	741	300 to 350	23,400	Potaro River, Guyana

* The peak flow has reached 1,750,000 cu. ft. per sec.

251

THE DEAD SEA between Israel and Jordan is not only a source of salt but one of the world's largest potash beds. This is a potash research station.

Deepest Depressions

Maximum depth below sea level (feet)

Dead Sea, Jordan–Israel	1,296
Turfan Depression, Sinkiang, China	505
Munkhafad el Qattâra (Qattâra Depression), Egypt	436
Poluostrov Mangyshlak Kazakh S.S.R., U.S.S.R.	433
Danakil Depression, Ethiopia	383
Death Valley, California	282
Salton Sink, California	235
Zapadnyy Chink Ustyurta, Kazakh S.S.R.	230
Prikaspiyskaya Nizmennost', Russia S.F.S.R. and Kazakh S.S.R.	220
Ozera Sarykamysh, Uzbek and Turkmen S.S.R.	148
El Faiyûm, Egypt	147
Peninsula Valdiéz Lago Enriquillo, Dominican Republic	131

Note: Immense areas of west Antarctica would be below sea level if stripped of their ice sheet. The deepest estimated crypto-depression is the bed rock on the Hollick-Kenyon plateau beneath the Marie Byrd Land ice cap (84° 37′ S 110° W) at −8,100 feet. The bed of Lake Baikal (U.S.S.R.) is 4,871 feet below sea level and the bed of the Dead Sea is 2,600 feet below sea level. The ground surface of large areas of central Greenland under the overburden of ice up to 11,190 feet thick are depressed to 1,200 feet below sea level. The world's largest exposed depression is the Prikaspiyskaya Nizmennost' stretching the whole northern third of the Caspian Sea (which is itself 92 feet below sea level) up to 250 miles inland. The Qattâra Depression extends for 340 miles and is up to 80 miles wide.

Deepest Caves

Feet

1. 4,370   Gouffre de la Pierre
   St. Martin   Basses-Pyrénées, Spain–France
2. 4,258   Gouffre Jean Bernard   Savoie Alps, France
3. 3,743   Gouffre Berger   Vercors, France
4. 3,214   Chouran des Aguillea   Dauphiné Alps, France
5. 3,182   Sumidero de Cellagua   Cantabria, Spain
6. 3,118   Kievskaya   U.S.S.R.
7. 3,117   Antro di Corchia   Italy
8. 3,117   Gouffre André Touya   Western Pyrénées, France
9. 3,025   Grotta del Monte Cucco   Perugia, Italy
10. 3,018   Abisso Michele Gortani   Italy

Note: The most extensive cave system is the Mammoth system, Kentucky (first discovered by Indians before 1190 B.C.). It was linked with the Flint Ridge System in 1972 so giving a charted passageway length of 181.44 miles. The largest known cavern is the Big Room in the Carlsbad Caverns, New Mexico, which has maximum measurements of 4,720 feet in length, 328 feet high and 656 feet across.

CARLSBAD CAVERNS in New Mexico has the largest single cave room in the world. The ceiling here ranges from 255 to 328 feet at its highest.

253

Glaciers

LONGEST GLACIERS

Miles

Miles	
c. 320	Lambert–Fisher Ice Passage, Antarctica (disc. 1956–7)
260	Novaya Zemlya, North Island, U.S.S.R. (area, 1,160 sq. miles)
225	Arctic Institute Ice Passage, Victoria Land, E. Antarctica
180	Nimrod–Lennox–King Ice Passage, E. Antarctica
150	Denman Glacier, E. Antarctica
140	Beardmore Glacier, E. Antarctica (disc. 1908)
140	Recovery Glacier, W. Antarctica
124*	Petermanns Gletscher, Knud Rasmussen Land, Greenland
120	Unnamed Glacier, S.W. Ross Ice Shelf, W. Antarctica
115	Slessor Glacier, W. Antarctica

* Longest in N. Hemisphere extending 24.8 miles out to sea.

GLACIATED AREAS OF THE WORLD

It is estimated that 6,050,000 sq. miles or about 10.5% of the world's land surface is permanently covered with ice, thus:

	sq. miles		*sq. miles*
South Polar Regions	5,250,000	Asia	14,600
North Polar Regions (inc. Greenland with 695,500)	758,500	South America	4,600
		Europe	4,128
		New Zealand	380
Alaska–Canada	22,700	Africa	92

Notable glaciers in other areas include:

		Length *(miles)*	Area *(sq. miles)*
Iceland	Vatnajökull	88	3,400
Alaska	Malaspina Glacier	26	1,480
Alaska	Nabesna Glacier	43½	770
Pamirs	Fedtschenko	47	520
Karakoram	Siachen Glacier	47	444
Norway	Jostedalsbre	62	415
Karakoram	Hispar-Biafo Ice Passage	76	125–240
Himalaya	Kanchenjunga	12	177
New Zealand	Tasman Glacier	18	53
Alps	Aletschgletscher	16½	44

ALASKA has many glaciers like this.

LAKE TITICACA is the lake at the highest altitude in the world at 12,506 feet. It separates Peru from Bolivia.

Lakes

HIGHEST LAKES

The highest steam-navigated lake in the world is the 130 mile long Lago Titicaca in Peru and Bolivia at an altitude of 12,506 feet. There is an unnamed glacial lake near Mount Everest at an altitude of 19,300 feet. The highest lake in the United States is Lake Waiau (13,020 feet) on Hawaii Island and the highest in the 48 coterminous States is Tulainyo (12,865 feet) in California.

LAKES UNDER 3,000 BUT OVER 2,000 SQ. MILES

Area (sq. miles)	Name	Country
2,473	Turkana (formerly Rudolf)	Kenya and Ethiopia
2,465	Reindeer	Canada
2,355	Issyk Kul'*	U.S.S.R.
2,230	Torrens	Australia
2,149	Vänern	Sweden
2,105	Winnipegosis	Canada
2,075	Mobuto Sese Seko (formerly Albert)	Uganda and Zaïre
2,050	Kariba (dammed)	Rhodesia and Zambia

* Has a maximum depth of 2,303 feet and an average depth of 1,050 feet. The height of the surface above sea level is 5,279 feet.

LAKES OF THE WORLD (by Area)

	Name	Country	Area (sq. miles)	Length (miles)	Maximum Depth (ft.)	Average Depth (ft.)	Height of Surface above sea level (ft.)
1.	Kaspiskoye More (Caspian Sea)	U.S.S.R. and Iran	143,550	760	3,215	675	−92
2.	Superior	Canada and U.S.	31,800	350	1,333	485	602
3.	Victoria Nyanza	Uganda, Tanzania, and Kenya	26,828	225	265	130	3,720
4.	Aral'skoye More (Aral Sea)	U.S.S.R.	25,300	280	223	52	174
5.	Huron	Canada and U.S.	23,010	206	750	196	579
6.	Michigan	U.S.	22,400	307	923	275	579
7.	Tanganyika	Zaire, Tanzania, and Zambia	12,700	450	4,708	1,900	2,534
8.	Great Bear	Canada	12,275	232	270	240	390
9.	Ozero Baikal	U.S.S.R.	11,780	385	6,365	2,300	1,493
10.	Malawi (formerly Nyasa)	Tanzania, Malawi, and Mozambique	11,430	360	2,226	895	1,550
11.	Great Slave	Canada	10,980	298	535	240	512
12.	Erie	Canada and U.S.	9,930	241	210	60	572
13.	Winnipeg	Canada	9,464	266	120	50	713
14.	Ontario	Canada and U.S.	7,520	193	780	260	246
15.	Ozero Ladozhskoye (Lake Ladoga)	U.S.S.R.	6,835	120	738	170	13
16.	Ozero Balkhash	U.S.S.R.	6,720	300	85	—	1,112
17.	Lac Tchad (Chad)	Niger, Nigeria, Chad, and Cameroon	6,300*	130	13–24	5	787
18.	Ozero Onezhskoye (Onega)	U.S.S.R.	3,710	145	361	105	108
19.	Eyre	Australia	3,700†	115	65	—	−39
20.	Lago Titicaca	Peru and Bolivia	3,200	130	1,000	338	12,506
21.	Athabasca	Canada	3,120	208	407	—	699
22.	Saimaa complex‡	Finland	c. 3,100	203	—	—	249
23.	Lago de Nicaragua	Nicaragua	3,089	100	200	—	110

* Highly variable area between 4,250 and 8,500 sq. miles.

† Highly variable area between 3,100 and 5,800 sq. miles.

‡ The Saimaa proper (The Lake of a Thousand Isles) is, excluding the islands, c. 500 sq. miles.

256

LAKES OF THE WORLD (by Volume)

Name	Salt or Fresh	Estimated Volume in cubic miles
1. Kaspiskoye More (Caspian Sea)	Salt water (0.6%)	21,500
2. Ozero Baykal (Lake Baikal)	Fresh	5,520
3. Superior*	Fresh	5,400
4. Tanganyika	Fresh	4,500
5. Michigan*	Fresh	2,600
6. Huron*	Fresh	2,100
7. Malawi (formerly Nyasa)	Fresh	1,900
8. Victoria Nyanza	Fresh	1,200
9. Ontario*	Fresh	770
10. Great Bear	Fresh	525
11. Great Slave	Fresh	510
12. Aral'skoye More (Aral Sea)	Salt water (1.1%)	260

* Adding Lake Erie (240 cubic miles), the total volume of the Great Lakes is 11,110 cubic miles.

DEEPEST LAKES

The Olkhon Crevice in Lake Baikal (see 2 above) was measured in 1957 to be 6,365 feet deep and hence 4,872 feet below sea level. The deepest lake in the U.S. is Crater Lake, Oregon, which is 1,932 feet deep.

LAKE BAIKAL in Siberia is both large (5,520 cubic miles in volume) and deep (6,365 feet). It is slightly bigger than Lake Superior.

Greatest Rivers

The importance of rivers still tends to be judged on their length rather than by the more significant factors—their basin areas and volume of flow. In the following compilation all the world's river systems with a watercourse of a length of 2,000 miles or more are listed with all three criteria where ascertainable.

BASIN OF THE AMAZON RIVER covers 2,722,000 square miles, an area three-fourths the size of the conterminous United States.

Length (miles)	Name of Watercourse	Source	Basin Area (sq. miles)
1. 4,145	Nile (Bahr-el-Nîl)– White Nile (Bahr el Jabel)–Albert Nile– Victoria Nile– Victoria Nyanza– Kagera–Luvironza	Rwanda: Luvironza branch of the Kagera, a feeder of the Victoria Nyanza	1,293,000
2. 4,007	Amazon (Amazonas)	Peru: Lago Villafro, head of the Apurimac branch of the Ucayali, which joins the Marañon to form the Amazonas	2,722,000

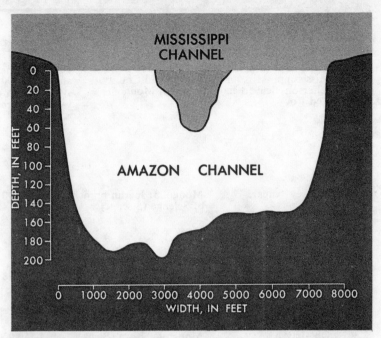

AMAZON COMPARED TO THE MISSISSIPPI: A channel cross-section of the Amazon at Obidos, Brazil, dwarfs a similar Mississippi River channel area at Vicksburg. The water flowing out of the Amazon is purer than tap water in most places in the United States. This is because all of the soluble salts in the basin of the Amazon have long ago been washed out of the soil, and because sediment has a chance to settle out of the water before it reaches the main channel.

Course and Outflow	Mean Discharge Rate (cu. ft. per sec.)	Notes
Through Tanzania (Kagera), Uganda (Victoria Nile and Albert Nile), Sudan (White Nile), U.A.R. (Egypt) to eastern Mediterranean	110,000	Navigable length to first cataract (Aswan) 960 miles. Egyptian Irrigation Dept. states length as 4,164 miles. Discharge 93,200 cu. ft./sec. near Aswan. Delta is 9,250 sq. miles
Through Colombia to Equatorial Brazil (Solimões) to South Atlantic (Canal do Sul)	6,350,000	Total of 15,000 tributaries, ten over 1,000 miles including Madeira (2,100 miles). Navigable 2,300 miles up stream. Delta extends 250 miles inland. The full flood discharge is more than 7,000,000 cu. ft./sec.

Length (miles)	Name of Watercourse	Source	Basin Area (sq. miles)
3. 3,710	Mississippi–Missouri–Jefferson–Beaverhead–Red Rock	Beaverhead County, southern Montana	1,245,000
4. 3,442	Yenisey–Angara–Selenga	Mongolia: Ideriin branch of Selenga (Selenge)	996,000
5. 3,436	Yangtze Kiang (Ch'ang Chiang)	Western China, Kunlun Shan Mts. (as Dre Che and T'ungt'ien)	756,498
6. 3,362	Ob'–Irtysh	Mongolia: Kara (Black) Irtysh via northern China (Sin Kiang) feeder of Ozero Zaysan	1,150,000
7. 3,000	Hwang Ho (Yellow River)	China: Tsaring-nor, Tsinghai Province	378,000

MISSISSIPPI RIVER:
Fog often encroaches on the ships entering the huge delta of 13,900 sq. miles which is near New Orleans, Louisiana.

Course and Outflow	*Mean Discharge Rate (cu. ft. per sec.)*	*Notes*
Through N. Dakota, S. Dakota, Nebraska–Iowa, Missouri–Kansas, Illinois, Kentucky, Tennessee, Arkansas, Mississippi, Louisiana, South West Pass into Gulf of Mexico	650,000	Missouri is 2,315 miles, the Jefferson–Beaverhead–Red Rock is 217 miles, Lower Mississippi is 1,171 miles. Total Mississippi from Lake Itasca, Minn., is 2,348 miles. Longest river in one country. Delta is 13,900 sq. miles
Through Buryat A.S.S.R. (Selenga feeder) into Ozero Baikal, thence *via* Angara to Yenisey confluence at Strelka to Kara Sea, northern U.S.S.R.	670,000	Estuary 240 miles long. Yenisey is 2,200 miles long and has a basin of 792,000 sq. miles. The length of the Angara is 1,150 miles
Begins at T'ungt'ien, then Chinsha, through Yünnan, Szechwan, Hupeh, Anhwei, to Yellow Sea	770,000	Flood rate (1931) of 3,000,000 cu. ft./sec. Estuary 120 miles long
Through Kazakhstan into Russian S.F.S.R. to Ob' confluence at Khanty Mansiysk, thence Ob' to Kara Sea, northern U.S.S.R.	550,000	Estuary (Obskaya Guba) is 450 miles long. Ob' is 2,286 miles long, Irtysh 1,840 miles long
Through Kansu, Inner Mongolia, Hunan, Shantung to Po Hai (Gulf of Chili), Yellow Sea, North Pacific	100,000 to 800,000	Changed mouth by 250 miles in 1852. Only last 25 miles navigable. Longest river in one country in Asia

AMAZON RIVER: The source of this great river is in the jungles of Peru, where headhunters using curare-tipped arrows still exist.

Length (miles)	Name of Watercourse	Source	Basin Area (sq. miles)
8. 2,920	Zaïre (Congo)	Zambia–Zaïre border, as Lualaba	1,314,000
9 2,734	Lena–Kirenga	U.S.S.R. hinterland of west central shores of Ozero Baikal as Kirenga	960,000
10. 2,700	Amur–Argun' (He lung Chiang)	Northern China in Khingan Ranges (as Argun')	787,000
11. 2,653	Mackenzie–Peace	Tatlatui Lake, Skeena Mts., Rockies, British Columbia, Canada (as River Findlay)	711,000
12 2,600	Mekong (Me Nam Kong)	Central Tibet (as Lants'ang), slopes of Dza-Nag-Lung-Mong, 16,700 ft.	381,000
13 2,600	Niger	Guinea: Loma Mts. near Sierra Leone border	580,000
14. 2,485	Rió de la Plata–Paraná	Brazil: as Paranáiba. Flows south to eastern Paraguay border and into eastern Argentina	1,600,000
15. 2,330	Murray–Darling	Queensland, Australia: as the Culgoa continuation of the Condamine, which is an extension of the Balonne branch of the Darling	408,000

Course and Outflow	Mean Discharge Rate (cu. ft. per sec.)	Notes
Through Zaïre as Lualaba along to Congo border to N.W. Angola mouth into the South Atlantic	1,450,000	Navigable for 1,075 miles from Kisangari to Kinshasa (formerly Léopoldville). Estuary 60 miles long
Northwards through eastern Russia to Laptu Sea, Arctic Ocean	575,000	Lena Delta (17,375 sq. miles) extends 110 miles inland, frozen Oct. 15 to July 10. Second longest solely Russian river
North along Inner Mongolian–U.S.S.R. and Manchuria–U.S.S.R. borders for 2,326 miles to Tarter Strait, Sea of Okhotsk, North Pacific	438,000	Amur is 1,771 miles long (711,600 basin and 388,000 flow). *China Handbook* claims total length to be 2,903 miles of which only 575 miles is exclusively in U.S.S.R. territory
Flows as Findlay for 250 miles to confluence with Peace. Thence 1,050 miles to join Slave (258 miles) which feeds Great Slave Lake, whence flows Mackenzie (1,077) to Beaufort Sea	400,000	Peace 1,195 miles
Flows into China, thence south to form Burma–Laotian and most of Thai–Laotian frontiers, thence through Cambodia to Vietnam into South China Sea	388,000	Max. flood discharge 1,700,000 cu.ft./sec.
Flows through Mali, Niger and along Dahomey border into Nigeria and Atlantic	500,000	Delta extends 80 miles inland and 130 miles in coastal length
Emerges into confluence with River Uruguay to form Río de la Plata, South Atlantic	970,000	After the 75-mile-long delta estuary, the river shares the 210-mile-long estuary of the Uruguay
Balome (intermittent flow) crosses into New South Wales to join Darling, which itself joins the Murray on the New South Wales–Victoria border and flows west into Lake Alexandrina, in South Australia	14,000	Darling *c.* 1,700 miles, Murray 1,609 miles or 1,160 miles

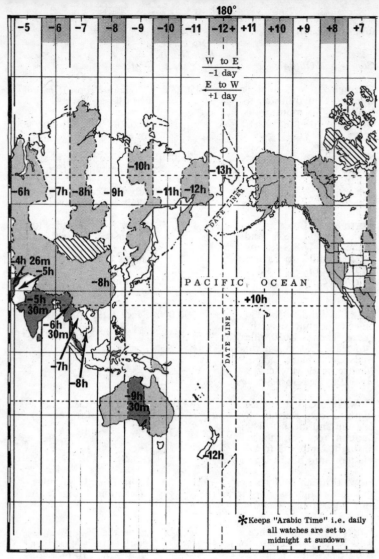

⁕ Keeps "Arabic Time" i.e. daily all watches are set to midnight at sundown

TIME AROUND THE WORLD: Standard time (based on the time at Greenwich, England), in which the world is divided into 24 equal zones, was established by an international commission in 1884. There are a great many deviations from this basic system, as can be seen by referring to the map.

U.S. GEOGRAPHICAL FACTS

Areas	Sq. miles
Area of the 50 States (incl. 66,237 sq. miles inland water)	3,615,211
Area of the 49 North American U.S. States (incl. inland water)	3,608,787
Area of the 48 coterminous U.S. States (incl. 50,893 sq. miles inland water)	3,022,387
Most Northerly Point	
(50 States) Point Barrow, Alaska	71° 23′ N
(48 States) Lake of the Woods, Minnesota	49° 23′ N

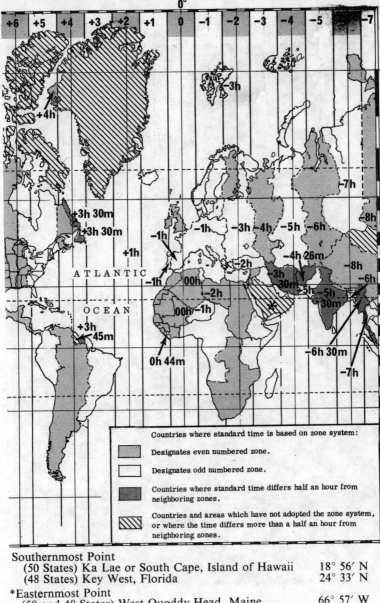

| +6 | +5 | +4 | +3 | +2 | +1 | 0 | −1 | −2 | −3 | −4 | −5 | −7 |

−3h

+4h

−7h

−8h

+3h 30m
+3h 30m

−1h −3h −4h −5h −6h

+1h

−4h 26m −8h

ATLANTIC −2h −6h

−1h 00h
30h

OCEAN −2h −5h −5h
30h

00h −1h
+3h
45m

0h 44m −6h 30m

−7h

Countries where standard time is based on zone system:

Designates even numbered zone.

Designates odd numbered zone.

Countries where standard time differs half an hour from neighboring zones.

Countries and areas which have not adopted the zone system, or where the time differs more than a half an hour from neighboring zones.

Southernmost Point
    (50 States) Ka Lae or South Cape, Island of Hawaii   18° 56′ N
    (48 States) Key West, Florida   24° 33′ N
*Easternmost Point
    (50 and 48 States) West Quoddy Head, Maine   66° 57′ W
*Westernmost Point
    (50 States) Cape Wrangell, Attu Island, Aleutians   172° 27′ E
    (48 States) Cape Alava, Washington   124° 44′ W

* Care should be taken of terminology. The world reference for longitude is based on the Prime Meridian (0°) running through Greenwich Observatory, London, England, and the International Date Line (180°) running through the Aleutian Islands, Alaska. It may be contended the points of U.S. territory with the highest value longitude east of Greenwich and west of Greenwich are thus:
Highest value of Easterly Longitude:—
    Semisopochnoi Island (52° N) 179° 45′ E.
Highest value of Westerly Longitude:—
    Little Diomede Island (65° 45′ N) 179° 58′ W.

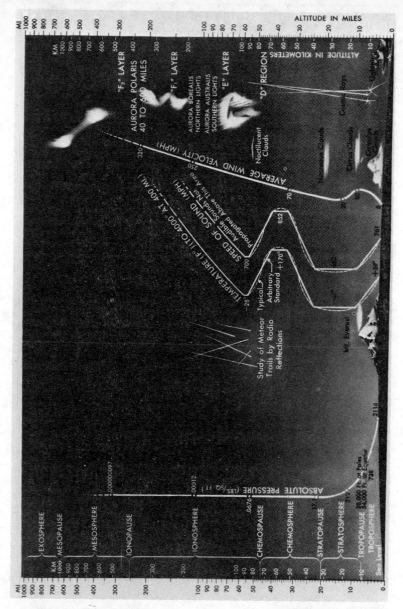

EARTH'S ATMOSPHERE: The chart above shows the layers of the Earth's atmosphere, together with physical characteristics of the atmosphere at different altitudes. On the left side of the chart (when turned readable) is the nomenclature used by physical scientists to describe different layers; on the right side is the nomenclature used by early investigators of radio propagation in the atmosphere.

Meteorology

LAYERS OF THE ATMOSPHERE

Troposphere	up to between 32,800 ft. (at poles) and 55,700 ft. (at equator).
Tropopause	Layer joining tropo- and stratospheres between 10 and 17 km. (32,800 and 55,700 ft.).
Stratosphere	from 30,000 to 60,000 ft. up to the ozone bands at from 100,000 to 250,000 ft.
Stratopause	Layer at *c.* 45 km. (147,000 ft.).
Mesosphere (lower Ionosphere)	the airglow and ozone band, lower layer of the Ionosphere.
Mesopause	Layer at 75–85 km. (246,000 to 278,000 ft.).
Ionosphere	above the 250,000 ft. mesopause, extending to 400–500 miles. The radio mirror layer.
Magnetosphere	from 400–500 miles outward to 40,000 miles (Van Allen Belts).

CLOUD CLASSIFICATION

Genus (with abbreviation)	Ht. of base (ft.)	Temp. at base level (° C.)
CIRRUS (Ci)	16,500 to 45,000	−20 to −60

Detached clouds in the form of white delicate filaments or white or mostly white patches or narrow bands. They have a fibrous (hair-like) appearance or a silky sheen, or both.

CIRROCUMULUS (Cc)	16,500 to 45,000	−20 to −60

Thin, white patch, sheet or layer of cloud without shading, composed of very small elements in the form of grains, ripples, etc., merged or separate, and more or less regularly arranged.

CIRROSTRATUS (Cs)	16,500 to 45,000	−20 to −60

Transparent, whitish cloud veil of fibrous or smooth appearance, totally or partly covering the sky, and generally producing halo phenomena.

ALTOCUMULUS (Ac)	6,500 to 23,000	+10 to −30

White or gray, or both white and gray, patch, sheet or layer of cloud, generally with shading, composed of laminae, rounded masses, rolls, etc., which are sometimes partly fibrous or diffuse, and which may or may not be merged.

ALTOSTRATUS (As)	6,500 to 23,000	+10 to −30

Grayish or bluish cloud sheet or layer of striated, fibrous or uniform appearance, totally or partly covering the sky, and having parts thin enough to reveal the sun at least vaguely.

NIMBOSTRATUS (Ns)	3,000 to 10,000	+10 to −15

Gray cloud layer, often dark, the appearance of which is rendered diffuse by more or less continually falling rain or snow which in most cases reaches the ground. It is thick enough throughout to blot out the sun. Low, ragged clouds frequently occur below the layer with which they may or may not merge.

STRATOCUMULUS (Sc)	1,500 to 6,500	+15 to −5

Gray or whitish, or both gray and whitish, patch, sheet or

layer of cloud which almost always has dark parts, composed of tessellations, rounded masses, rolls, etc., which are non-fibrous (except for virga) and which may or may not be merged.

STRATUS (St) surface to 1,500 +20 to −5

Generally gray cloud layer with a fairly uniform base, which may give drizzle, ice prisms or snow grains. When the sun is visible through the cloud its outline is clearly discernible. Stratus does not produce halo phenomena (except possibly at very low temperatures). Sometimes stratus appears in the form of ragged patches.

CUMULUS (Cu) 1,500 to 6,500 +15 to −5

Detached clouds, generally dense and with sharp outlines, developing vertically in the form of rising mounds, domes or towers, of which the bulging upper part often resembles a cauliflower. The sunlit parts of these clouds are mostly brilliant white; their bases are relatively dark and nearly horizontal.

CUMULONIMBUS (Cb) 1,500 to 6,500 +15 to −5

Heavy and dense cloud, with a considerable vertical extent, in the form of a mountain or huge towers. At least part of its upper portion is usually smooth, or fibrous or striated, and nearly always flattened; this part often spreads out in the shape of an anvil or vast plume. Under the base of this cloud, which is often very dark, there are frequently low ragged clouds either merged with it or not, and precipitation, sometimes in the form of virga.

CONSTITUENTS OF AIR

Gas	Formula	% By volume
Invariable component gases of dry carbon dioxide-free air:		
Nitrogen	N_2	78.110
Oxygen	O_2	20.953
Argon	A	0.934
Neon	Ne	0.001818
Helium	He	0.000524
Methane	CH_4	0.0002
Krypton	Kr	0.000114
Hydrogen	H_2	0.00005
Nitrous oxide	N_2O	0.00005
Xenon	Xe	0.0000087
		99.9997647%
Variable components:		
Water vapor	H_2O	0 to 7.0*
Carbon dioxide	CO_2	0.01 to 0.10, average 0.034
Ozone	O_3	0 to 0.000007
Contaminants:		
Sulfur dioxide	SO_2	up to 0.0001
Nitrogen dioxide	NO_2	up to 0.000002
Ammonia	NH_3	trace
Carbon monoxide	CO	trace

* This percentage can be reached at a relative humidity of 100% at a shade temperature of 40° C (104° F.).

FOG

A convenient meteorological definition of fog is a "cloud touching the ground and reducing visibility to less than one kilometer (1,100 yards)."

Fog requires the coincidence of three conditions:

(i) Minute hygroscopic particles to act as nuclei. The most usual source over land is from factory or domestic chimneys, whereas at sea salt particles serve the same purpose. Such particles exist everywhere, but where they are plentiful the fog is thickest.

(ii) Condensation of water vapor by saturation.

(iii) The temperature at or below dew point. The latter condition may arise in two ways. The air temperature may simply drop to dew point, or the dew point may rise because of increased amounts of water vapor.

Sea fog persists for up to 120 days in a year on the Grand Banks, off Newfoundland. London, once famous for "pea-soupers" was last beset by 114 hours continuous fog on Nov. 26 to Dec. 1, 1948, and Dec. 5–9, 1952.

PHENOMENA

Ball Lightning
A very rare phenomenon. A spheroid glowing mass of energized air, usually about one foot in diameter. On striking an earthed object it seems to disappear, hence giving the impression that it has passed through it. It was successfully photographed in August, 1961.

"Blue Moon"
The defraction of light through very high clouds of dust or smoke, as might be caused by volcanic eruptions (notably Krakatoa, Aug. 27, 1883) or major forest fires (notably in British Columbia, Sept. 26, 1950), can change the color of the Sun (normally white overhead and yellow or reddish at sunrise or sunset) and the Moon (normally whitish) on such rare occasions to other colors, notably green and even blue.

Brocken Specter
A person standing with his back to the Sun and looking down from higher ground onto a lower bank of fog or cloud, casts a shadow known by this name.

Corona
When the Sun's or Moon's light is defracted by water droplets in some types of cloud, a ring of light (sometimes two or more) may be seen closely and concentrically around the Sun or Moon.

Cyclone
The local name given to a tropical depression that results in a violent circular storm in the northern part of the Indian Ocean (see also Hurricane and Typhoon). The term can also be used for a low-pressure system, in contrast to the anticyclone or high-pressure system.

Flachenblitz
A rare form of lightning which strikes upwards from the top of Cumulonimbus clouds and ends in clear air.

Fogbow
In rainbow conditions, when the refracting droplets of water are very small, as in fog or clouds, the colors of the rainbow may overlap and so the bow appears white. Alternative names for this phenomenon are a cloudbow, or Ulloa's Ring.

Glory
At the anti-solar point, from an observer in the situation that gives a Brocken specter (see above) a corona is seen round the head of the observer. When several people are standing side by side, each can only see a glory round the shadow of his own head.

Halo
When the Sun's light is refracted by ice crystals in Cirrus or Cirrostratus clouds, a bright ring of light, usually reddish on the inside and white on the outside, may be seen round the Sun with a 22° radius. Much more rarely a 46° halo may appear, and, very rarely indeed, halos of other sizes with radii of 7° upwards. Halo phenomena may also be seen round the Moon.

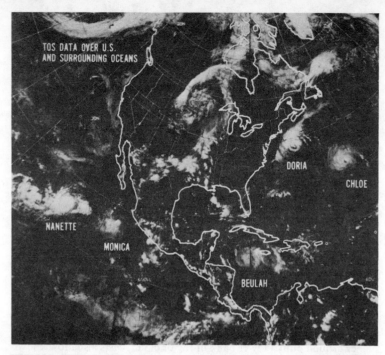

HURRICANES: Photographic mosaic assembled from photographs transmitted by the ESSA V weather satellite on Sept. 14, 1967, showing five severe tropical storms simultaneously.

HURRICANE FORCE is demonstrated by this fence picket which has been driven through the trunk of a palm tree by the fury of the wind.

Hurricane

The local name given to a tropical depression that results in a violent circular storm in the southern part of the North Atlantic, notably the Caribbean Sea (see also Cyclone and Typhoon).

Iridescence (or Irisation)

When conditions giving rise to coronas illuminate clouds, the phenomena is so described.

Mirage

Mirages are caused by the refraction of light when layers of the atmosphere have sharply differing densities (due to contrasting temperature). There are two types of mirages: with the *inferior mirage*—the more common of the two—an object near the horizon appears to be refracted as in a pool of water; with the *superior mirage* the object near—or even beyond—the horizon appears to float above its true position.

Mock Sun

In halo conditions the ice crystals when orientated in a particular way can refract light so as to produce one or more *mock suns* or *parhelia* on either or both sides of the Sun and usually 22° away from it.

Nacreous Clouds and Noctilucent "Clouds"

Nacreous, or mother-of-pearl, clouds occasionally appear after sunset over mountainous areas, at a height of from 60,000 to 80,000 feet. These are lit by sunlight from below the horizon, so may be seen hundreds of miles away, for example in Scotland from Scandinavia.

Noctilucent "clouds" are a rare phenomena, possibly formed by cosmic dust, that appear bluish in color at a very great height of 300,000 feet or nearly 60 miles. This phenomenon is very frequently reported from Arctic regions and in 1967 33 times even from the Shetlands, N. of Scotland.

Rainbow

If an observer stands with his back to the Sun and looks out on a mass of falling raindrops lit by the Sun, he will see a *rainbow*. A *primary bow* is vividly colored with violet on the inside, followed by blue, green, yellow, orange, and red. A *secondary bow*, which, if visible, is only about a tenth of the intensity of its primary, has its color sequence reversed. Further bows, even more feeble, can on very rare occasions be seen.

Saint Elmo's Fire (or Corposants)

A luminous electrical discharge in the atmosphere which emanates from protruding objects, such as ships' mastheads, lightning conductors and windvanes.

Sun Pillar

In halo conditions, when the ice crystals are oriented in a particular way, a *sun pillar*, which is a bright image of the Sun extending both above and below it, may appear.

Thunderbolt

These do not in fact exist, but the effect of the intense heating of a lightning strike may fuse various materials and so give the false impression that a solid object in fact hit the ground. A lightning strike may boil water almost instantaneously and so, for example, shatter damp masonry, giving it the appearance of having been struck by a solid object.

Tornado

A *tornado* is the result of intense convection which produces a violent whirlwind extending downwards from a storm cloud base, often reaching the ground. The width varies between about 50 yards and a quarter of a mile and it moves across country at speeds varying from 10 to

TORNADO APPROACHING: Most tornadoes are about 300 to 400 yards in width and rotate counterclockwise. Wind speeds in the cone have been estimated to be as high as 500 m.p.h. The destructiveness of a tornado is due not only to the force of the winds but also to the enormous drop in barometric pressure that occurs within the cone, which causes houses to explode outward as the tornado passes over them.

Tornado (continued)

30 m.p.h., causing great damage. (See photograph, above.) On Mar. 18, 1925, tornadoes in the south central states killed 689. On Apr. 2, 1958, a wind speed of 280 m.p.h. was recorded at Wichita Falls, Texas.

Typhoon

The local name given to a tropical depression that results in a violent circular storm in the southwestern part of the North Pacific and especially the China Sea (see also Cyclone and Hurricane).

Waterspout

The same phenomenon as a tornado, except that it occurs over the sea, or inland water. These may reach an extreme height of 5,000 feet.

Whiteout

When land is totally covered by snow, the intensity of the light refracted off it may be the same as that refracted off overhead clouds. This results in the obliteration of the horizon, and makes land and sky indistinguishable.

NORTHERN AND SOUTHERN LIGHTS

Polar lights are known as Aurora Borealis in the northern hemisphere and Aurora Australis in the southern hemisphere. These luminous phenomena are caused by electrical solar discharges in the upper atmosphere and are usually visible only in the higher latitudes.

It is believed that in an auroral display some 100 million protons (hydrogen nuclei) strike each square centimeter of the upper atmosphere each second. Colors vary from yellow-green (attenuated oxygen), reddish (very low pressure oxygen), red below green (molecular nitrogen below ionized oxygen) or bluish (ionized nitrogen). Displays, which may occur up to 240 nights in the year in some places (*e.g.* northern Canada), vary in frequency with the 11-year sunspot cycle. Edinburgh may expect perhaps 25 displays a year against 7 in London, and Malta once a decade. In September, 1909, a display was reported from just above the equator at Singapore. The height range varies between extremes of 45 miles (lower) and 620 miles (upper).

WORLD AND U.S. METEOROLOGICAL ABSOLUTES COMPARED

	World	U.S.
Highest Temperature	136.4° F. Al'Aziziyah, Libya, Sept. 13, 1922	134.0° F. Death Valley, California, July 10, 1913
Hottest Place (Annual Mean)	94° F. Dallol, Ethiopia (1960–66)	78.2° F. Death Valley, California (1941–70)
Lowest Temperature	−126.9° F. Vostok, Antarctica, Aug. 24, 1960	−80° F. Prospect Creek, Alaska, Jan. 23, 1971
Coldest Place (Annual Mean)	−72° F. Pole of Cold, Antarctica, 78° S, 96° E	9.3° F. Barrow, Alaska (1941–70)
Highest Wind Strength	231 m.p.h. Mt. Washington, New Hampshire, April 12, 1934	World record Averaged 188 m.p.h. for 5 minutes
Greatest Barometric Pressure	1,079 mb (31.86 ins.) Barnaul, U.S.S.R., Jan. 23, 1900	31.29 ins. Lander, Wyoming, Dec. 20, 1924
Least Barometric Pressure	877 mb (25.91 ins.) *c.* 600 miles N.W. off Guam, Sept. 24, 1958	26.35 ins. Long Key, Florida, Sept. 2, 1935
Highest Rainfall (24 hours)	73.62 ins. Cilaos, La Réunion, March 15–16, 1952	38.70 ins. Yankeetown, Florida, Sept. 5–6, 1950
(Month)	366.14 ins. Cherrapunji, India, July 1861	107 ins. Kukui, Hawaii, Mar. 1942
(Year)	1,041.78 ins. Cherrapunji, India, 1860–61	624.10 ins. Mt. Waialeale, Hawaii, 1947–48
Longest Drought	Unrecorded in Calama, Desierto de Atacama, Chile	767 days, Bagdad, Calif., Oct. 3, 1912— Nov. 8, 1914
Wettest Place (annual average)	451 ins. Mt. Waialeale, Kauai, Hawaii Is. (av. 1920–72)	World record Note: rainy days average 335 per year
Highest Snowfall (12 months)	1,224.5 ins. Paradise Ranger station, Mt. Rainier, Washington 1971–72	World record Note: annual average at this station is 575 inches
Highest Sunshine (Annual)	>4,300 hours (97% of possible) eastern Sahara (frequently)	95.78% of possible Yuma, Arizona, 1924
Most Thunder (Year)	322 thunder days Bogor, Java, Indonesia, 1916–19	101 thunder days Lakeland, Florida (annual average)

LIGHTNING: Lightning occurs when differential electrical charges between the ground and clouds build up to an excessive level. A leader stroke then descends from the cloud, breaking down the electrical resistance of the air. This leader stroke is usually invisible to the eye and reaches the ground in about 1/100th to 1/1000th of a second. A series of strong, main strokes, perhaps with secondary branches, then travel upwards to the clouds at a speed of about 87,000 miles per second, giving the appearance of one continuous lightning stroke. A single stroke of this series lasts about 1/500th of a second.

METEOROLOGICAL AVERAGES

The world's overall average annual day-side temperature is 59° F. (15° C.). The average barometric pressure is 1,013 millibars. It has been estimated that at any given moment there are 2,200 thunderstorms taking place in the world. These can be heard up to a range of 18 miles.

In historical times since the birth of Christ it would appear that the world's peak for warmth was about 650 A.D. and its nadir for coldness about 1430 A.D.

THUNDER AND LIGHTNING

At any given moment there are some 2,200 thunderstorms on the Earth's surface, which are audible at ranges of up to 18 miles. The world's most thundery location is Bogor (formerly Buitenzorg), Java, Indonesia, which in 1916–19 averaged 322 days per year with thunder.

Thunder arises after the separation of electrical charges in cumulonimbus (q.v.) clouds. In the bipolar thundercloud the positive charge is in the upper layer. Thunder is an audible compression wave, the source of which is the rapid heating of the air by a return lightning stroke.

Lightning: The speed of lightning varies greatly. The downward leader strokes vary between 100 and 1,000 miles per second. In the case of the

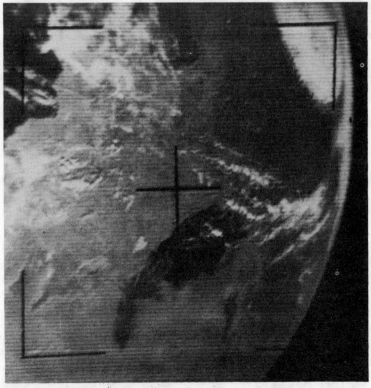

WEATHER SATELLITE: A photograph of the Caspian and Aral Seas taken from the Tiros X. Iran is in the lower part of the photograph, and a corner of the Black Sea is in the upper left-hand corner.

Meteorology (continued)

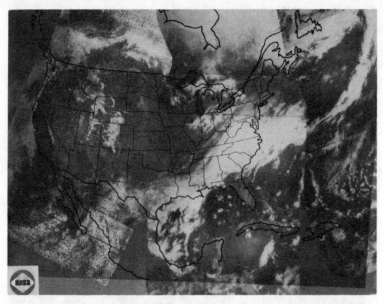

WEATHER FORECASTING BY SATELLITE: A mosaic made up of photographs taken from a weather satellite. It was assembled by meteorologists of the Environmental Science Services Administration.

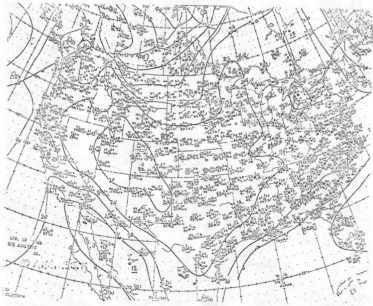

WEATHER MAP for the same day as above made on the basis of satellite photographs and the reports of ground stations.

Thunder and Lightning (continued)

powerful return stroke a speed of 87,000 miles per second (nearly half the speed of light) is attained. The length of stroke varies with cloud height and thus between 300 feet and 4 miles though lateral strokes as long as 20 miles have been recorded. The central core of a lightning channel is extremely narrow—perhaps as little as a half-inch. In the case of the more "positive giant" stroke the temperature reaches c. 30,000° C. or over five times that of the Sun's surface.

BEAUFORT SCALE

A scale of numbers, designated Force 0 to Force 12, was originally devised in 1806 by Commander Francis Beaufort (1774–1857) (later Rear-Admiral Sir Francis Beaufort of the British Royal Navy).

Force No.	Descriptive term	Wind speed (m.p.h.)
0	Light	Less than 1
1	Light	1–3
2	Light	4–7
3	Gentle	8–12
4	Moderate	13–18
5	Fresh	19–24
6	Strong	25–31
7	Strong	32–38
8	Gale	39–46
9	Gale	47–54
10	Whole gale	55–63
11	Whole gale	64–72
12	Hurricane	73–82
13	Hurricane	83–92
14	Hurricane	93–103
15	Hurricane	104–114
16	Hurricane	115–125
17	Hurricane	126–136

FARSIDE OF THE MOON: A topographic map prepared from photographs taken by Moon-orbiting spacecraft. Grid lines are about 150 miles apart.

The Universe

Astronomy

DISCOVERY THAT THE EARTH IS ROUND

The first of the great Greek astronomers was Thales of Miletus (*c.* 624–546 B.C.). Though he may have realized that the Earth is a globe, there is no surviving evidence of this. The first definite argument against the assumption that the Earth was flat was advanced by Aristotle (*c.* 385–325 B.C.). He pointed out that the ascension of the Pole Star (Polaris) and Canopus varied according to whether one viewed them from Greece or Egypt and that the Earth's shadow in a lunar eclipse is curved.

THE CIRCUMFERENCE OF THE EARTH DISCOVERED

Eratosthenes (*c.* 276–194 B.C.) of Cyrene who, as librarian of the Alexandria library, had access to the writings of both Thales and Aristotle, made the earliest estimate of the Earth's circumference. He learnt from a reference that at Syene (the modern Aswan) in Egypt on the summer solstice (longest day in northern hemisphere) the Sun was vertically overhead because it shone down a well without casting a shadow. He determined that on the same day the Sun's zenith at Alexandria was 83°. He thus concluded that, since a circle contains 360° the Earth's circumference was $\frac{360}{7}$ × the distance down the Nile from

Alexandria to Aswan. This gave him the remarkably accurate result of 24,662 miles (*cf.* modern polar value of 24,859.75 miles).

PTOLEMY'S FALSE THEORY

Astronomical progress largely ceased with the death of Claudius Ptolemaeus (Ptolemy) in *c.* 180 A.D. His book, which survived only as an 8th-century Arab translation, *Almagest* (the greatest), from Baghdad, had established the so-called Ptolemaic System in that the Earth was the center of the Universe with the Moon, Mercury, Venus, the Sun, Mars, Jupiter, Saturn, and the stars in that order of remoteness revolving around it in a complex series of deferred epicycles.

The Chinese adopted a 365-day calendar year as early as 1600 B.C. but it mattered little to them whether the Sun went round the Earth or vice versa. Early Chinese records describe a comet in 467 B.C.

The false Ptolemy theory held sway for the next $13\frac{1}{2}$ centuries until in 1533 the Polish priest Nicolaus Koppernigk (1473–1543), known as Copernicus, wrote his *De Revolutionibus Orbium Coelestium* in which he explained that the apparent retrograde movement of Mars was due to the fact that both the Earth and Mars orbit round the Sun. His work was not published, for the justified fear of persecution by the Roman Catholic church, until 1543. He received the first copy, printed in Nürnberg, Germany, shortly before his death.

KEPLER'S LAWS

The next major contribution to astronomy came from Johannes Kepler, born in Württemberg, Germany, in 1571. Cursed with very poor eyesight, he was nonetheless able to use the wonderfully accurate lifetime observations of the Dane, Tycho Brahe (1546–1601). In 1609 he published Kepler's first and second laws.

The first law stated that the planets move round the Sun in elliptical orbits with the center of the Sun at one focus, the other being vacant. The second law stated that the radius vector of a planet sweeps out equal areas in equal times, *i.e.* that a planet's orbiting speed must be higher at perihelion. In the case of the Earth its orbital speed is highest above the mean of 66,620 m.p.h. on Jan. 6 when we are closest to the sun, namely 67,750 m.p.h. The minimum at aphelion is 65,520 m.p.h.

Kepler's third law, published in 1619, was the brilliant conclusion that for any planet the sideral period (time taken to complete one orbit round the Sun) is related to the cube of the planet's distance from the Sun. Kepler died in 1630 when travelling to collect an unpaid salary from Emperor Rudolph II, who kept him as his Imperial Mathematician to indulge his interest in astrology.

GALILEO'S TELESCOPIC DISCOVERIES

The year 1609 was doubly renowned, for it was then that the Italian genius Galileo Galilei (1564–1642) learned of the principle of the telescope discovered by the Dutchman Hans Lippershey. Claims have been advanced that the Britons Roger Bacon (*c.* 1214–92) and Leonard Digges (died *c.* 1571) had priority over Lippershey but it was the Dutchman who was the effective discoverer of the refracting telescope.

Armed with the new instrument, Galileo quickly found that the Moon's surface was mountainous and that the Pleiades, which apparently numbered six when seen by the naked eye, contained at least 40 stars. On the night of Jan. 7, 1610, he found that Jupiter had three moons and soon he saw another (actually there are now identified 13). In 1611 he observed sun-spots, which had been recorded by a Chinese astronomer. Along with Christopher Scheiner, he made the first estimate of the mean solar period of revolution.

In 1633 Galileo challenged the dogma of the Roman church, and was summoned to Rome to abjure his herèsy that the Earth revolved round the Sun and not vice versa. Galileo, doubtless remembering the death at the stake of Giordano Bruno on Feb. 17, 1600, did not protest at this dictum. Despite being forbidden to use his telescopes and although going blind, he made a final great discovery—that the Moon's period of rotation on its own axis coincides with its period of revolution round the Earth, hence we have presented to us the same face at all times. In fact, because of its slightly elliptical orbit, we can see some way round its alternate edges and could directly map 59% of its surface from the Earth. This effect is called the moon's libration.

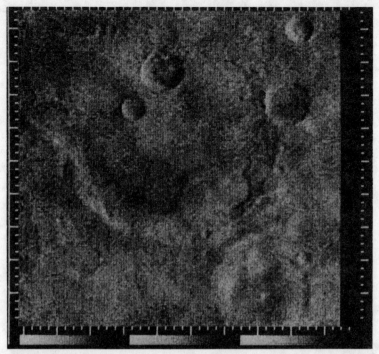

CLOSEUP OF MARS: An enhanced photograph taken originally by Mariner IV, on July 14, 1965, when the spacecraft was 7,800 miles from Mars. The original data transmitted from Mariner IV was passed through an electronic computer, which produced the photograph. The area shown is about 150 miles by 170 miles.

TRANSITS OF MERCURY AND VENUS

The first observational evidence that Mercury and Venus orbit inside (*i.e.* are nearer to the Sun than) the Earth came from Kepler's posthumous prediction that the two planets would cross the face of the Sun on Nov. 7 and Dec. 6, 1631. The Frenchman Pierre Gassendi saw Mercury flitting across as a dark speck as calculated but missed Venus as it was later proved it crossed during the time the Sun was below the horizon. The Rev. Jeremiah Horrocks (1619–41), curate of Hoole, Cheshire, England, calculated that a Venus transit would occur on Nov. 24 (O.S.), or Dec. 4 (N.S.), 1639. Horrocks had the thrill of becoming the first man ever to spot the tiny black object. It was last seen in transit in 1882 and will not again be seen on the solar photosphere until June 8, 2004.

IMPROVED TELESCOPES

Telescopes grew more powerful and more cumbersome to the point that the great Dutch astronomer Christiaan Huygens (1629–95), inventor of the pendulum clock, at one time built a refractor 210 feet in length. It was he who in 1655 first clearly described the nature of Saturn's rings which had so puzzled Galileo.

In the 17th century other major observational advances included the discovery of the largest of Saturn's satellites, Titan (Huygens, 1655), the markings on Mars (Huygens, 1659), and the finding of four more Saturn satellites by Giovanni Cassini (1625–1712), who also fixed the rotation of Mars at 24 hours 40 min. compared with the modern value of 24 hours 37 min. 22.654 sec. In 1663 the Scot, James Gregory, put forward the principle of the reflecting telescope and in 1668 Sir Isaac Newton (Eng.) built the first one, with a metal mirror one inch in diameter.

THE SPEED OF LIGHT CALCULATED

Two other great achievements of this period were the recalculation of the Sun's distance by Cassini (from Kepler's 14-million-mile figure to 86 million miles) and the brilliant achievement of his colleague, the Dane Ole Rømer, who in 1675 measured the velocity of light. Rømer was intrigued by the fact that Jupiter's satellites were eclipsed behind Jupiter at intervals that were not regular. The eclipses occurred too early when Jupiter was at its closest and later when at its farthest from the Earth. The reason, of course, was that the light had taken longer to reach us. Rømer's calculations gave the inspired answer that light traveled at 186,000 miles per second compared with the modern value of 186,282.397 miles per second.

THE PEERLESS NEWTON AND HALLEY

In 1686 Newton (1642–1727) completed 15 months' intense labor in producing his *Philosophiae Naturalis Principia Mathematica* (published 1687), which has been called the greatest scientific treatise ever published. The invention of calculus and the enunciation of the principles of artificial satellites were seemingly incidental in this amazing *tour de force*.

Halley, who had paid to have the irascible and retiring Newton's work published, predicted in 1705 that a great comet would appear in 1758. He had realized that the comets of 1531, 1607, and 1682 were one and the same. Sure enough, on Christmas Day, 1758, the German amateur Johann Palitzsch spotted, from near Dresden, the arrival of this comet and Halley earned immortality.

HERSCHEL'S GREAT CONTRIBUTIONS

On March 13, 1781, Friedrich Wilhelm (later Sir William) Herschel (1738–1822) spotted a curious greenish disc moving in the constellation Gemini. The Finn, Prof. Anders Lexell, at St. Petersburg (Leningrad) proved that what Herschel thought was a comet was in fact a totally unsuspected planet outside Saturn—it was named Uranus. It had in fact been seen as early as 1690 by Flamsteed but it was Herschel, with his homemade reflector, who found the key because of its proper motion.

Herschel first deduced that our Milky Way galaxy is lens-shaped and in 1783 announced that the Solar System is in fact moving towards the star Vega. Herschel, who worked from his garden in Slough, Buckinghamshire, England, also made the inspired deduction that the dim patches of light which Halley had seen and identified as six in number were extragalactic nebulae. Herschel's subsequent observations raised this number from 100 to 1,500. In 1802 Herschel announced the existence of binary stars.

ASTEROIDS AND MORE PLANETS

The first minor planet or asteroid to be spotted was by the Sicilian Guiseppe Piazzi on Jan. 1, 1801. It was confirmed in 1802, and was named Ceres. Its diameter is 623 miles. It is now believed that the total number of asteroids is more than 40,000 of which the orbits of over 3,100 have been published. The only one which is visible to the naked eye is Vesta. The earth-grazer, Hermes, on Oct. 30, 1937, came within 485,000 miles of Earth.

THE VISIBLE UNIVERSE: Almost every object in this photograph, taken through the 200-inch Hale telescope, is a galaxy, a system of millions upon millions of stars much like our own Milky Way. There are probably as many galaxies in the universe as there are stars in an individual galaxy.

In 1834 the Rector of Hayes, Kent, England, the Rev. T. J. Hussey, suggested that the perturbations in the orbit of Uranus might be due to another still more remote planet. In 1845 John Adams worked out where this notional planet should be and in 1846 similar calculations by the Frenchman, U. Le Verrier, were published. The search was on.

Prof. James Challis of Cambridge University, England, on Aug. 4 and 12 recorded the planet. On Sept. 25 Galle and d'Arrest pinpointed the new planet from Le Verrier's calculations. Neptune's first moon, Triton, was found within a month and its second, Nereid, not until 1949. The ninth planet, Pluto, was discovered by Clyde Tombaugh from Flagstaff, Arizona, on Feb. 18, 1930, and announced on March 13.

MEASURING THE DISTANCE OF THE STARS

The vastness of our galaxy was not realized until 1838 when Friedrich Bessel of Königsberg Observatory used the parallax method to determine the distance of the 5th magnitude star *61 Cygni*. The method relies on the apparent shift of a "near" star against its distant background when comparing observations in January and July from the opposite extremities of the base of the Earth's orbit. Bessel announced that *61 Cygni* was 60 million million miles distant, because the shift was only 0.3 second of arc.

Because of the vastness of the distances, the light-year unit came into use in March, 1888. Light travels 5,878,499,814,000 miles in a year so *61 Cygni* was nearly 11 light-years away. The modern value is 10.7 light-years, which ranks this star fourteenth in closeness to the Sun. In Capetown, South Africa, Scot Thomas Henderson (1798–1844) had in fact made parallax measurements on *Alpha Centauri* earlier than Bessel but he did not complete his calculations until later. Henderson had picked the closest of all star systems at a distance of 4.3 light-years.*

GALAXIES BEYOND OUR OWN

The earliest mention of bodies now known to be outside our galaxy goes back 10 centuries when Al-Sûfi recorded the most distant of all naked-eye bodies, the Spiral Galaxy in Andromeda. This was later catalogued as Messier 31.

Herschel's suspicions that here was an "island universe" far beyond the edge of our own system was not, however, confirmed until 1923. The necessary preliminary discoveries had, of course, come much earlier. In 1784 the deaf and dumb English astronomer, John Goodriche (1764–85), noted that the variable star *Delta Cephei* had a regular fluctuation of brightness every 5 days, 9 hours. Stars of fluctuating luminosity were termed Cepheid variables and it was found that the slower the bright-dull-bright cycle the higher the luminosity. By comparison of luminosity with apparent magnitude, distances of a star can be estimated. This proved a basic tool in astronomical measurement.

In 1923 Edwin P. Hubble (U.S.) discovered six Cepheid variables in the Andromeda Spiral. His calculation showed this body to be a staggering 750,000 light-years away—10 times further than the furthest star on the edge of our own galaxy. He later raised this to 900,000 years. Even this second estimate in 1952 was found by W. Baade (U.S.) to be greatly undercalculated. The Cepheids used by Hubble were of a different type or population from that assumed. In fact the Spiral was, according to Baade, about 2.2 to 2.3 million light-years distant.

The impossibility of resolving Cepheid variables and hence of estimating the distance of the really distant extragalactic nebulae was overcome by another device. In 1920 V. M. Slipher, working from Flagstaff, Arizona, found that light from these galaxies all exhibited Doppler shifts to the red end of the spectrum, *i.e.* they must be receding. It was then postulated that the more distant the galaxy the higher the speed of recession. Using this relationship it has now been estimated that the Quasi Stellar Object QSO 0Q172 observed by Dr. Margaret Burbidge from the Lick Observatory, California in April, 1973, was receding at 95.5% the speed of light, thus indicating a distance close to 15,000 million light years or 90,000,000,000,000,000,000,000 (90 sextillion) miles.

In November, 1962, Dr. John G. Bolton (Australia) pinpointed a radio source of immensely high luminosity but of very small diameter. By March, 1967, more than 200 such bodies, named "quasars" (quasi-stellar radio sources) had been detected. Among the most puzzling is the quasar 3C 446, which has a diameter of only 90 light-days but which exhibits a measurable increase in luminosity in less than one day.

Three main rival theories of the universe have been postulated.

1. The Steady State (or Continuous Creation) Theory: This was postulated in 1948 by Profs. Hermann Bondi and Thomas Gold (both Eng.). It maintains that the universe has always existed (infinite) and must appear essentially the same at whatever distance or point of time. Creation of new matter (matter is created, according to the Heisenberg principle, at the rate of 62 atoms of hydrogen per cubic inch per 1 billion years) to form new galaxies fills in gaps created by expansion such that a constant density of space and matter is preserved. This theory has been undermined by subsequent observations and has been modified by Prof. Fred Hoyle (Eng.) and others.

2. The "Big Bang" (or Superdense) Theory: This was first postulated in 1957 by Prof. Martin Ryle (Eng.). It held that some 10 billion years ago all detectable galaxies were packed into one superdense body which exploded. A cubic inch of superdense matter may weigh up to 1.8 billion tons. Fragments of the explosion—now galaxies—will continue, like spots on an expanding balloon, to move away from each other indefinitely.

3. The Oscillating Theory: This was first expounded in 1965 by Prof. Allan Sandage (U.S.), and is a refinement of the "Big Bang" theory. It maintained that the universe was 10 billion years advanced in the expansive stage of an 80-billion-year cycle of expansion and contraction. Thus, the speculation is that in 30 billion years' time gravitational attraction between galaxies will begin to overcome their centrifugal motions and that they will begin rushing back together for a cataclysmic implosion. This event should occur in a finite 70 billion years, when another "Big Bang" would mark the start of the next 80-billion-year oscillation of an infinite series of explosion-implosion cycles.

COMPARISON OF THE SUN AND PLANETS: From left to right, Mercury, Venus, Earth (with its satellite, the Moon), Mars, Jupiter, Saturn, Uranus, Neptune, and Pluto. The sun fills the upper part of the illustration.

PHYSICAL PARAMETERS OF THE SUN AND PLANETS

Sun or Planet		Diameters miles	Equatorial Rotation Period d h m s			Sidereal Period	Equatorial Inclination	Mass tons	Density g/cm.³
Sun		864,940	25	09	07		7° 15'	1.958×10^{27}	1,049
Mercury		3,031	58	15	30	32	0°	3.250×10^{20}	5,433
Venus		7,519	*243	00			178°	4.792×10^{21}	5.249
Earth	Equ.	7,926		23	56	04.091	23° 27'	5.880×10^{21}	5.515
	Polar	7,900							
Mars	Equ.	4,221		24	37	22.655	25° 12'	6.318×10^{20}	3.934
	Polar	4,196							
Jupiter	Equ.	88,780		9	50	30.003	3° 04'	1.869×10^{24}	1,330
	Polar	82,980							
Saturn	Equ.	74,600		10	14		26° 44'	5.596×10^{23}	0,705
	Polar	66,400							
Uranus	Equ.	31,600	*10	49			97° 53'	8.602×10^{22}	1,31
	Polar	30,700							
Neptune	Equ.	30,200		15	48		28° 48'	1.013×10^{23}	1,75
	Polar	29,500							
Pluto		3,400	6	09	17		0°	2.6×10^{20}	3,0

* Retrograde

ELEMENTS OF THE PLANETARY ORBITS

Planet	Mean Distance From Sun miles km.	Perihelion Distance miles km.	Aphelion Distance miles km.	Orbital Eccentricity
Mercury	35,983,100	28,584,000	43,382,000	0.205 630
	57,909,100	46,001,000	69,817,000	
Venus	67,237,900	66,782,000	67,694,000	0.006 783
	108,208,900	107,475,000	108,943,000	
Earth	92,955,800	91,402,000	94,510,000	0.016 718
	149,597,900	147,097,000	152,099,000	
Mars	141,635,700	128,410,000	154,862,000	0.093 380
	227,940,500	206,656,000	249,226,000	
Jupiter	483,634,000	460,280,000	506,990,000	0.048 286
	778,333,000	740,750,000	815,920,000	
Saturn	886,683,000	837,000,000	936,370,000	0.056 037
	1,426,978,000	1,347,020,000	1,506,940,000	
Uranus	1,783,951,000	1,701,660,000	1,866,230,000	0.046 125
	2,870,991,000	2,738,560,000	3,003,400,000	
Neptune	2,794,350,000	2,766,270,000	2,822,430,000	0.010 050
	4,497,070,000	4,451,880,000	4,542,270,000	
Pluto	3,674,490,000	2,761,600,000	4,587,300,000	0.248 432
	5,913,510,000	4,444,400,000	7,382,600,000	

Escape Velocity m.p.s.	Surface Temperature °C	Equatorial Diameter	Surface Gravity	Mean Apparent Magnitude	
383.73	5,530	109.12	27.90	−26.8	*On Scale*
2.64	−180 to +420	0.3824	0.3771	0.0	
6.44	475	0.9486	0.9038	− 4.4	*Earth = 1*
6.95	− 88 to + 58	1.0000	1.0000	——	
3.12	−125 to + 30	0.5325	0.3795	−2.0	
37.42	−25	11.201	2.644	−2.6	
22.52	−110	9.407	1.159	+0.7	
13.38	−160	3.98	0.938	+5.5	
14.82	−160	3.81	1.200	+7.8	
2.21	−220	0.43	0.235	+15.0	

Orbital Inclination ° ′ ″	Sidereal Period days	Orbital Velocity Mean m.p.h. km./h.	Maximum m.p.h. km./h.	Minimum m.p.h. km./h.
7 00 15	87.9693	105,950 *170,500*	131,930 *212,310*	86,920 *139,890*
3 23 39	224.7008	78,340 *126,070*	78,870 *126,930*	77,810 *125,220*
———	365.2564	66,620 *107,220*	67,750 *109,030*	65,520 *105,450*
1 50 59	686.9797	53,860 *86,680*	59,270 *95,390*	49,150 *79,100*
1 18 16	4,332.62	29,210 *47,000*	30,670 *49,360*	27,840 *44,810*
2 29 21	10,759.06	21,560 *34,700*	22,820 *36,730*	20,400 *32,830*
0 46 23	30,707.79	15,200 *24,460*	15,930 *25,630*	14,520 *23,370*
1 46 20	60,199.63	12,150 *19,560*	12,270 *19,750*	12,030 *19,360*
17 08 22	90,777.61	10,430 *16,790*	13,660 *21,980*	8,220 *13,230*

A GUIDE TO THE SCALE OF THE SOLAR SYSTEM AND THE UNIVERSE

The utter remoteness of the solar system from all other heavenly bodies is stressed by the fact that if the Sun were on the scale of a beach ball two feet in diameter atop the Empire State Buiding, New York City, the nearest stars, the triple Centauri system, would lie 10,950 miles away, say in the region of Melbourne, Australia with the largest member also having a two-foot diameter. Only the next three nearest stars in our Milky Way galaxy could, even on this scale, be accommodated on the Earth's surface.

Human imagination must boggle at distances greater than these, so it is necessary to switch to a much vaster scale of measurement.

Light travels at 186,282.397 miles per second *in vacuo*. Thus, in the course of a solar year (*i.e.* 365.24219878 mean solar days at January 0, 12 hours Ephemeris time in 1900 A.D.) light will travel 5,878,499,814,000 miles. This distance is conveniently called a light-year.

Light will thus travel to the Earth from the following heavenly bodies in the approximate times given:

From the Moon (reflected light)	1.25 sec.
From the Sun (at perihelion)	8 min. 10.6 sec.
From Pluto (variable)	about 6 hrs.
From nearest star (excepting the Sun)	4.28 yrs.
From Rigel	900 yrs.
From most distant star in Milky Way	75,000 yrs.
From nearest extragalactic body (Larger Magellanic cloud)	160,000 yrs.
From Andromeda (limit of naked eye vision)	2,200,000 yrs.
By radio telescope, Quasars may be detectable up to about	15,500,000,000 yrs.

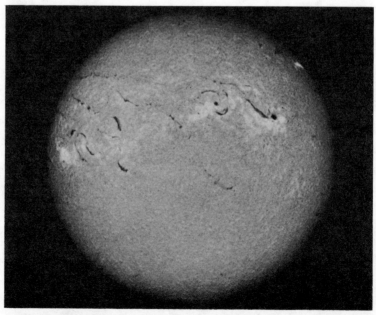

SUNSPOT ACTIVITY: This photograph taken in the light of the red hydrogen line, shows sunspots and the granular appearance of the Sun's surface clearly.

THE SUN

The Sun (for statistics see Solar System table) is a Yellow Dwarf star with a luminosity of 3×10^{27} candle power such that each square inch of the surface emits 1.5×10^6 candle power. Sun spots appear to be darker because they are 2,700° F. (1,500° C.) cooler than the surface temperature of 10,220°F (5660°C). These may measure up to 7×10^9 sq. miles and have to be 5×10^8 sq. miles to be visible to the (*protected*) naked eye. During 1957 a record 263 were noted. Solar prominences may flare out to some 300,000 miles from the Sun's surface.

Stars

There are 5,776 stars visible to the naked eye. It is estimated that our own galaxy, the Milky Way galaxy, contains some 100 billion (10^{11} stars) and that there are between 100 billion and 1 trillion (10^{11} to 10^{12}) galaxies in the detectable universe. This would indicate a total of 10^{22} to 10^{23} stars in the detectable universe. The Milky Way galaxy is of a lens-shaped spiral form with a diameter of some 100,000 light-years. The Sun is some 32,000 light-years from the center and hence the most distant star in our own galaxy is about 75,000 light-years distant.

AGE OF STARS

Being combustible, stars have a limited life. The Sun, which is classified as a Yellow Dwarf, functions like a controlled hydrogen bomb, losing 4 million tons in mass each second. It has been estimated that it has less than 10 billion years to burn. The concept of the age of the Universe is a difficult one because of the conflict of basic theories of its creation (see below). In November, 1976, an estimate of between 17,500 and 21,300 million years was published but in August, 1978 this was reduced to between 13,500 and 15,500 million years. The oscillation theory requires some 84 billion years for each explosion-implosion cycle.

Magnitude—is a measure of stellar brightness such that the light of a star of any magnitude bears a ratio of 2.511886 to that of a star of the next magnitude. Thus a fifth magnitude star is 2.512 times as bright as a sixth magnitude star, while one of the first magnitude is exactly one hundred or $(2.512)^5$ times brighter. In the case of such exceptionally bright bodies as Sirius, Venus, the Moon (Mag. -12.71) or the Sun (Mag. -26.78), the magnitude is expressed as a minus quantity.

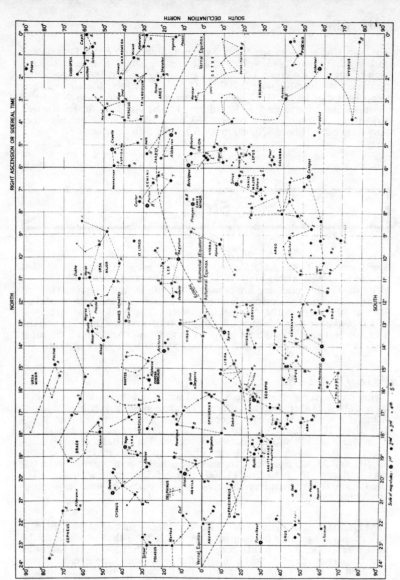

WORLD STAR CHART: The constellations, showing their approximate appearance and relation to each other.

CONSTELLATIONS

There are 31 accepted constellations in the northern and 52 in the southern hemispheres and 5 which appear at times in both hemispheres, making 88 in all. Such groupings are believed to be of Sumerian origin in the 4th millennium B.C. The International Astronomical Union completed the now accepted arc codification in 1945. The rectangular constellation Orion includes 3 of the 24 brightest stars in its great quadrilateral—Rigel (bottom left, Mag. 0.1), Betelgeuse (top right, Mag. 0.85) and Bellatrix (top left, Mag. 1.7).

BRIGHTEST STARS

Name	Magnitude Apparent	Magnitude Absolute	Distance Light years	Distance Parsecs
Sirius	−1.46	+1.4	8.7	2.7
Canopus*	−0.73	−4.6	200	60
Alpha Centauri*	−0.29	+4.1	4.4	1.3
Arcturus	−0.06	−0.3	36	11
Vega	+0.04	+0.5	26	8.1
Capella	+0.08	−0.5	42	13
Rigel	+0.10	−7.0	850	250
Procyon	+0.35	+2.6	11	3.5
Achernar*	+0.48	−2.5	127	39
Beta Centauri*	+0.60	−4.6	360	110
Altair	+0.77	+2.3	16	5.0
Betelgeuse	+0.85 v	−5.7 v	650	200
Aldebaran	+0.85	−0.7	65	21
Alpha Crucis	+0.90	−3.7	270	85
Spica	+0.96	−3.6	260	80
Antares	+1.08	−4.5	430	130
Pollux	+1.15	+1.0	35	11
Fomalhaut	+1.16	+1.9	23	7.0
Deneb	+1.25	−7.1	1500	500
Beta Crucis	+1.25	−5.1	530	160
Regulus	+1.35	−0.7	85	26
Adhara	+1.50	−4.4	490	150

* Not visible from northern America.
v = very variable apparent magnitude, average figure.

NEAREST STARS

Name	Distance Light-years	Parsecs	Magnitude Apparent			Magnitude Absolute		
Proxima Centauri	4.28	1.31		11.0			15.4	
Alpha Centauri	4.38	1.34	A	0.0	B 1.3	A 4.4		B 5.7
Barnard's Star	5.91	1.81		9.5			13.2	
Wolf 359	7.60	2.33		13.5			16.7	
Lalande 21185	8.13	2.49		7.5			10.5	
Sirius	8.65	2.65	A	−1.5	B 8.7	A 1.4		B 11.6
Luyten 726–8**	8.89	2.72	A	12.5	B 13.0	A 15.3		B 15.8
Ross 154	9.45	2.90		10.6			13.3	
Ross 248	10.3	3.15		12.3			14.8	
Epsilon Eridani	10.8	3.30		3.7			6.1	
Luyten 789–6	10.8	3.30		12.2			14.6	
Ross 128	10.8	3.32		11.1			13.5	
61 Cygni	11.1	3.40	A	5.2	B 6.0	A 7.6		B 8.4
Epsilon Indi	11.2	3.44		4.7			7.0	
Procyon	11.4	3.50	A	0.4	B 10.7	A 2.6		B 13.0
Sigma 2398	11.5	3.53	A	8.9	B 9.7	A 11.2		B 11.9
Groombridge 34	11.6	3.55	A	8.1	B 11.0	A 10.3		B 13.3
Lacaille 9352	11.7	3.58		7.4			9.6	
Tau Ceti	11.8	3.62		3.5			5.7	
Luyten's Star	12.2	3.73		9.8			12.0	
Luyten 725–32	12.5	3.83		11.5			13.6	
Lacaille 8760	12.5	3.85		6.7			8.8	
Kapteyn's Star	12.7	3.91		8.8			10.8	
Kruger 60	12.9	3.95	A	9.9	B 11.3	A 11.9		B 13.3
Ross 614	13.0	4.00	A	11.2	B 14.8	A 13.2		B 16.8

** The B star component is known as UV Ceti.

The Earth—Moon System

CREATION OF THE MOON

The latest theory on the origin of the moon is that it was (a) not part of the Earth, and (b) once a small free planet and not the Earth's satellite. This theory was propounded by the Swedish physicist Hannes Alfven in April 1963. Alfven believes that *c.* 2.5 billion years ago the Earth's gravitational field captured the passing Moon. The Moon closed to the point where its gravitational pull caused tides miles high. When the Moon reached Roche's limit of satellite entity, *i.e.* 3,700 miles away, it began to be torn to pieces by the vast gravitational forces. In the ensuing disintegration the Moon lost half its mass, much of which churned into the Earth to form our present continental land masses. The remaining diminished Moon was now just outside Roche's limit but revolving in the same direction as the Earth and began to recede slowly towards its present mean distance of 238,866 miles (center to center).

CREATION OF THE EARTH

The long-popular theory that the Earth and other planets were globules thrown out from a molten Sun has long been discarded. Spectroscopic analysis has shown that the Sun consists of 98% hydrogen and helium whereas the planets are a composite of heavy non-gaseous elements.

It has been suggested that *c.* 10 billion years ago the Sun, like so many stars, was a binary system with a companion star 500 million miles distant. This star, Sun B, could have been the one from which the planets agglomerated. Alternatively the Earth may have been formed by accretion from a cloud of material from a solar nebula formerly associated with the Sun.

THE 20 LARGEST ASTEROIDS

Size of Asteroids Relative to the Moon
(Diameter 2,160 miles 3,476 km.)

Asteroid		Diameter		Year of Discovery
		miles	*km.*	
(1)	Ceres	593	*955*	1801
(2)	Pallas	347	*558*	1802
(4)	Vesta	313	*503*	1807
(10)	Hygiea	237	*382*	1849
(15)	Eunomia	168	*270*	1851
(511)	Davida	165	*265*	1903
(16)	Psyche	158	*254*	1852
(324)	Bamberga	143	*230*	1892
(3)	Juno	140	*226*	1804
(19)	Fortuna	137	*221*	1852
(624)	Hektor	130	*210*	1907
(6)	Hebe	122	*197*	1847
(7)	Iris	120	*193*	1847
(29)	Amphitrite	116	*187*	1854
(747)	Winchester	116	*187*	1913
(9)	Metis	105	*169*	1848
(22)	Kalliope	104	*168*	1852
(68)	Leto	95	*153*	1861
(89)	Julia	95	*153*	1866
(8)	Flora	93	*150*	1847

MOON CRATER: The position of the crater Tycho as seen from the Earth.

FROM LUNAR ORBITER V: The area marked out by white line in the photograph above is seen more clearly from the spacecraft. Tycho is about 56 miles in diameter.

CLOSE-UP: The area marked out by white lines in the photograph above (about 7 by 8 miles).

293

Eclipses

An eclipse (derived from the Greek *ekleipsis* "failing to appear") occurs when the sight of a celestial body is either obliterated or reduced by the intervention of a second body.

There are two main varieties of eclipse.

(i) Those when the eclipsing body passes between the observer on Earth and the eclipsed body. Such eclipses are those of the Sun by the Moon; occultations of various stars by the Moon; transits of Venus or Mercury across the face of the Sun; and the eclipses of binary stars.

(ii) Those when the eclipsing body passes between the Sun and the eclipsed body. These can only affect planets or satellites which are not self-luminous. Such are eclipses of the Moon (by the Earth's shadow); and the eclipses of the satellites of Jupiter.

There is nothing in all the variety of natural phenomena that is quite so impressive as a total eclipse of the Sun.

Eclipses of the Sun (by the Moon) and of the Moon (by the Earth) have caused both wonder and sometimes terror throughout recorded history.

The element of rarity enhances the wonder of this event, which should be seen on average from a given city or town only once in about four hundred years. Eclipses of the Sun are in fact commoner than those of the Moon but the area from which they can be seen is so much smaller that the number of possible spectators is infinitely smaller.

The places from which and the times at which solar eclipses have been seen have been worked out back as far as the year 4200 B.C. and can be worked out far into the future, with of course an increasing, but still slight, degree of inaccuracy, for centuries ahead. The precise date of actual historical events in the Assyrian, Chinese, Greek and Roman empires have been fixed or confirmed by eclipses. For example, the battle between the Lydians and the Medes, which is reported by Herodotus, can be fixed exactly as occurring on May 28, 585 B.C., because a solar eclipse caused such awe that it stopped the fight. Modern astronomy has benefited from the study of ancient eclipses because they help to determine "secular accelerations," that is, the progressive changes in celestial motions.

SOLAR ECLIPSES
(i.e. of the Sun by the Moon)

Solar eclipses are of three sorts—total, partial and annular. A *total* eclipse occurs when the Moon, which, of course, must be new, comes completely between the Sun's disc and the observer on Earth. The Moon's circular shadow—its umbra—with a maximum diameter of only 170 miles, sweeps across the face of the Earth. The maximum possible duration of totality is 7 minutes 31 seconds.

The dramatic events at the moment of totality are: sunlight vanishes in a few seconds; sudden darkness (but *not* as intense as that during a night even under a full moon); the brightest stars become visible; the Sun's corona is seen; there is a hush from the animal and bird world; cocks have been noted to crow when the light floods back.

The Moon's partial shadow—its penumbra—which forms a much larger circle of about 2,000 miles in diameter, causes a *partial* eclipse. Partial eclipses, of course, vary in their degree of completeness. There must be a minimum of two Solar eclipses each year.

An *annular* eclipse occurs when—owing to variations in the Sun's distance—the Moon's disc comes inside the Sun's orbit. In other words, the Moon's umbra stops short of the Earth's surface and an outer rim of the Sun surrounds the Moon. The maximum possible duration of containment is 12 minutes 24 seconds.

PREDICTION OF ECLIPSES

The prediction of the exact time and the path of totality of solar eclipses once was an extremely laborious mathematical exercise. With the availability since World War II of numerous computers, the drudgery of the work has been eliminated. Not only can eclipses of the distant future now be pinpointed, but also eclipses of the distant past. For instance, a Babylonian tablet of 568 B.C. recording that a predicted eclipse of the moon failed to materialize has been investigated. The verdict is that there *was* an eclipse, but it was not visible from that part of southern Iraq.

Looking to the future there are going to be 13 more total solar eclipses this century visible from the inhabited regions of the Earth, excluding eclipses of fleeting duration.

The list, with land areas crossed by the path of totality, reads thus:

February 16, 1980	Central Africa and India
July 31, 1981	Northeast U.S.S.R. and Sakhalin Island
June 11, 1983	Indonesia (Java and West Irian)
November 22, 1984	New Guinea, Chile and Argentina
March 29, 1987	Central Africa
March 18, 1988	Indonesia (Sumatra) and Philippines
July 22, 1990	Finland
July 11, 1991	Hawaii, Central America and Brazil
November 3, 1994	Chile, Argentina, Paraguay and Brazil
October 4, 1995	Iran, India, Southeast Asia
March 9, 1997	Northeast U.S.S.R.
February 26, 1998	Central America
August 11, 1999	Cornwall (England), central Europe, central Asia and India

LUNAR ECLIPSES
(i.e. of the Moon by the Earth's Shadow)

Lunar eclipses are caused when the Moon—which, of course, must be full—passes through the shadow of the Earth and so loses its bright direct illumination by the Sun. A lunar eclipse is *partial* until the whole Moon passes into the Earth's umbra and so becomes *total*. After the Moon leaves the umbra it passes through the Earth's penumbra, which merely dims the moonlight so little that it is scarcely visible and is not even worth recording.

ECLIPSES OF THE SATELLITES OF JUPITER

The four principal "moons" of Jupiter frequently and rapidly provide a remarkable series of eclipse phenomena, but these of course require telescopic observation. To the aided eye of the observer on Earth, the following events occur in order with practically every circuit of a satellite.

(a) The disappearance of the satellite in the shadow of Jupiter, *i.e.* an eclipse of type (ii) above.

(b) The disappearance of the satellite behind Jupiter, *i.e.* "an occultation."

(c) The appearance of the shadow of the satellite (small dark spot) on the disc of Jupiter.

(d) The sight of the satellite itself crossing the disc of Jupiter, *i.e.* a "transit."

The timing of these events and the prediction of the behavior of these satellites can be very accurately established. The practical value of observing this sequence was demonstrated in 1675 when Ole Rømer noticed a discrepancy between predicted and actual performance. He brilliantly and correctly surmised that this was due to the varying distance between Jupiter and the Earth and was accounted for by the time that light took to travel to his eye. Thus he calculated with wonderful accuracy nearly three hundred years ago that the speed of light is 186,000 miles per second but did not himself believe in his own answer.

OTHER OBSERVABLE ECLIPSES

I. The Moon occasionally masks a star for about 30 minutes. The star "immerses" on the eastern limb of the Moon (which is only faintly visible while the Moon is still waxing) and remarkably suddenly and without a flicker "emerses" on the western limb, thus providing an early confirmation that there is no appreciable atmosphere round the Moon.

II. The two planets—Mercury and Venus—which are nearer the Sun than is the Earth, occasionally can be seen (with proper protection to the eyes) to pass slowly across the face of the Sun. These so-called Transits of Mercury occur on average about 14 times every century; Transits of Venus are far rarer with the last in 1882 and the next two on June 8, 2004, and June 6, 2012.

III. Some apparently single stars have been observed to vary sharply in brightness. They have been found in fact to be twin stars, revolving around each other and so eclipsing one another. Such stars are called *eclipsing binaries*, and the best-known examples are Algol and β Persei.

Comets

Comets are Solar System bodies moving in orbits about the Sun. Records go back to the 7th century B.C. The speeds of the estimated 2,000,000 comets vary from only 700 m.p.h. in the outer reaches of the solar system to 1,250,000 m.p.h. when near the Sun. The periods of revolution vary, according to the ellipticity of orbit, from 3.3 years (Encke's comet) to millions of years as in the case of Comet 1910a (the letter *a* indicating that it was the first classified during that year).

Comets are tenuous to the point that 10,000 cubic miles of tail might embrace only a cubic inch of solid matter. Comets are not self-luminous, hence only visible when in the inner part of the Solar System. They consist mainly of a head of dirty ice particles and a tail which always points more or less away from the Sun. In May, 1910, the Earth probably passed through the tail of the famous Halley's Comet which is next due to return in April, 1986.

Telescopes

The prototype of modern refracting telescopes was that made in 1608 by the Dutchman Hans Lippershey (or Lippersheim) after an accidental discovery of the magnifying power of spectacle lens when held apart. The principle of the reflecting telescope was expounded by the Scot James Gregory in 1633 and the first reflector was built with a one-inch diameter mirror by Sir Isaac Newton in 1672.

The principle of the reflecting telescope was expounded by the Scot, James Gregory in 1633 and the first reflector was built with a one-inch diameter mirror by Sir Isaac Newton in 1671.

200-INCH TELESCOPE: Located on Mount Palomar, California, part of the facilities of the Mt. Palomar and Mt. Wilson Observatories, itself a part of the California Institute of Technology, the 200-inch Hale telescope has its mirror (at the lower end of the open tube) covered by a protective shield.

The world's most powerful astronomical telescopes are now:

236.2	Mount Semirodriki, Caucasus, U.S.S.R.	1976
200	Hale, Mt. Palomar, nr. Pasadena, Calif.	1948
158	Kitt Peak National Observatory, Tucson, Ariz.	1970
158	Cerró Tololo, Chile	1970
153	Siding Spring, Australia	1974
150	Mount Strumlo Observatory, Canberra, Australia	1972
120	Lick, Mt. Hamilton, Calif.	1959
107	McDonald, Fort Davis, Texas	1968
104	Crimean Astrophysical Lab., Nauchny, U.S.S.R.	1960
100	Hooker, Mt. Wilson, Calif.	1917
98	Newton, Herstmonceux, Sussex, England	1967
88	Mauna Kea Observatory, Hawaii	1970

The Russian 236.2 in. reflector is now the largest in the world; it may well remain so as it is quite likely that future emphasis will be upon telescopes in space.

Object Glass (in.)	Diameter of Refractors (Lens)	Completion Date
40.0	Yerkes, Williams Bay, Wis.	1897
36.0	Lick, Mt. Hamilton, Calif.	1888
32.7	Paris Observatory, Meudon, France	1893
32.0	Astrophysical Observatory, Potsdam, Germany	1899
30.0	Nice Observatory, Nice, France	1880
30.0	Alleghany Observatory, Pittsburgh, Pa.	1914

RADIO ASTRONOMY

Radio astronomy became possible with the discovery in 1887 of radio waves by Heinrich Hertz (Germany). The earliest suggestion that extra-terrestrial radio waves might exist and be detected came from Thomas Edison (U.S.), whose collaborator, Prof. A. E. Kennelly, corresponded on the subject on Nov. 2, 1890.

It was not until 1932 that Karl Guthe Jansky (1905–49), a U.S. scientist of Czech descent, first detected radio signals from the Sagittarius constellation at Holmdel, New Jersey. This "cosmic static" was recorded on a 15-meter wave length. The pioneer radio astronomer was Grote Reber (U.S.) (*b.* 1911), who built the world's first radio telescope, a 31-feet 5-inch parabolic dish, in his backyard at Wheaton, Illinois, in 1937. His first results were published in 1940.

Dr. J. S. Hey (G.B.) discovered during war-time radar jamming research that sun spots emitted radio waves; that radio echoes come from meteor trails; and that the extragalactic nebula Cygnus A was a discreet source of immense power.

In 1947 from the Radio Physics Laboratory in Sydney, Australia, Dr. John G. Bolton found that the Crab Nebula (M.1), a supernova remnant, was a strong radio source. Since then many more discrete sources have been found; some are supernova remnants in our Galaxy, while others are external Galaxies and the mysterious, very remote Quasars. Young science though it may be, radio astronomy is of fundamental importance in our studies of the Universe, and it has provided information which could never have been obtained in any other way.

RADIO TELESCOPES

The world's largest dish radio telescope is the non-steerable $10-million ionospheric apparatus at Arecibo, Puerto Rico, completed in November, 1963. It utilizes a natural crater which is spanned by a dish 1,000 feet in

FIRST PARABOLIC RADIO TELESCOPE: Grote Reber of Wheaton, Ill., in the 1930's constructed this telescope single-handedly and established the science and technology of radio astronomy.

WORLD'S LARGEST RADIO TELESCOPE: Located at Arecibo, Puerto Rico, this 1,000-foot-wide telescope is "aimed" by shifting the receiving equipment suspended from the three towers.

diameter, covering an area of $18\frac{1}{2}$ acres. Improvements and re-plating cost a further $1,000,000 in 1974. The RATAN-600 radio telescope being built in the northern Caucasus, U.S.S.R., will have mirror dishes on a 1,968.5 ft. perimeter. The world's largest radio telescopic installation is the U.S. National Science Foundation V.L.A. (Very Large Array) being built 50 miles west of Socorro in New Mexico and due for completion in 1981 at an estimated cost of $78 million. It is Y-shaped with each arm 13 miles long with 27 mobile antennae (each of 82 ft. in diameter) on rails.

The Sciences

The word Science, derived from the Latin *scientia*, meaning knowledge, is often used in a restricted sense in that it traditionally includes certain departments of knowledge and excludes others. Thus, scientific studies exclude what are generally regarded as human and social studies, sometimes loosely called "the Arts" but include such branches of knowledge as mathematics and anthropology.

This distinction is not, however, in any way precise, because the arts, for example music, can be studied in a scientific way. A scientific study is generally held to mean one that is conducted precisely, systematically and quantitatively. Musical appreciation and criticism are qualitative and non-scientific, while the measurement of the frequency and volume of musical sounds is scientific.

The "-ologies"/Studies of:

The suffix -logy derives from the Greek *legō*, to speak, or *logos*, a discourse. The earliest branch of science given this suffix was anthropology in 1593. Since the end of the 18th century, the application of the suffix has become widespread.

The following list excludes words ending in *-ology* when the first part of the word is similar to the usual English word for the subject, *e.g.* weatherology, the study of weather. Words referring to minutely specialized branches of knowledge have also been excluded.

abiology—inanimate things
acarology—lice and ticks
acology—therapeutic agents (remedies)
acrology—initial sounds or signs
acyrology—use of language
adenology—glands
aesthophysiology—organs of sensation
alethiology—truth
algology—seaweeds
ambrology—amber
amphibology—ambiguity
anatripsology—friction
andrology—diseases of maleness
angiology—blood vessels
anorganology—inorganic objects
anthology—literary collection
anthropology—man
anthropomorphology—pertaining to the deity
apiology—bees

arachnology (araneology)—spiders
archelogy—principles
archeology—antiquities
archology—government, philosophy of origins
areology—Mars
aristology—dining
arthrology—joints
asthenology—diseases arising from debility
astrolithology—meteorites
astrology—influence of stars
astrometeorology—alleged influence of planetary phenomena on weather
atmology—aqueous vapor
audiology—hearing
auxology—growth
azoology—inanimate nature
balneology—medicinal baths
barology—weight

batology—brambles
battology—needless repetition in speaking and writing
bibliology—books
bioecology—plant and animal interrelationship
biology—living things
biometeorology—inter-relationship of atmosphere and organisms
bromatology—food
brontology—thunder
bryology—mosses
cacology—mispronunciation
caliology—birds' nests
campanology—bells
carcinology—crustaceans
cardiology—heart
caricology—sedges
carphology—plucking of bed-clothes in delirium
carpology—fruits
cartology—maps
cephalology—head
cerebrology—brains
cetology—whales
chirology—speaking on the fingers
chiropodology—corns, warts and bunions
chiropterology—bats
chololology (choledology)—bile
chondrology—cartilage
chorology—geographical limits
chronology—dating
coleopterology—beetles
conchology—shells
coprology—pornography
cosmology—universe
craniology—skull
crustaceology—crustaceans
cryptology—code
curiology—picture writing
cyesiology—pregnancy
cytology—cells
cytopathology—pathology of cells
dactylology—speaking with the fingers
deltiology—picture postcards
demology—human activities
dendrochronology—tree ring dating
dendrology—trees
deontology—moral obligation
dermatology—skin
desmology—ligaments
diabology—devil-lore
dipterology—flies
dittology—double interpretation
docimology—metal assaying
dosiology (dosology)—dosage
dysteleology—purposelessness in nature
ecclesiology—church building and church history

ecology—environment
edaphology—soils
eidology—mental imagery
electrology—electricity
endocrinology—endocrine glands
enterology—intestines
entomology—insects
epiphytology—false parasites
epistemology—origin and nature of origins
eremology—deserts
ergology—effect of work on mind and body
eschatology—last things (death judgment, heaven and hell)
ethnology—races, peoples
ethology—character
etiology—causes
etymology—parts of speech
eulogy—praise
exobiology—life on other planets
faunology—animal distribution
fungology—fungi
gastrology—catering for the stomach
geology—Earth's crust
geratology—extinction
gerontology—old age
glossology—language
gnomology—sententious litera-ture
gnosiology—theory of knowledge
graphology—handwriting, graphs
gynecology—female functions and diseases
hagiology—lives and legends of saints
hamartiology—sin
haplology—vocal contraction of word
helcology—ulcers
heliology—sun
helminthology—intestinal worms
hematology—blood
heortology—religious festivals
hepatology—liver
heresiology—heresies
herpetology—reptiles
heterology—diversity
hierology—sacred literature
hippology—horses
hippopathology—equine disease
histology (histiology)—organic tissues
historiology—history
homology—correspondence (sameness of relation)
horology—clock making, time measurement
hydrology—water
hyetology—rainfall
hygiology—health and hygiene
hygrology—humidity

hymenology—membranes
hymenopterology—ants, wasps, etc.
hypnology—sleep
hysterology—uterus
iatrology—medicine
ichnolithology—fossil footprints
ichnology—fossil footprints
ichthyology—fishes
ideology—ideas
immunology—immunity from disease
kalology—beauty
laryngology—larynx
lexicology—word derivation
limnology—lakes, pondlife
lithology (lithoidology)—stones, rocks
loimology—infectious diseases
macrology—prolixity of speech
malacology—molluscs
malacostracology—crustaceology
mantology—divination
mastology—mammals
mataeology—vain, unprofitable matters
meteorology—atmosphere, weather
menology—months
metrology—weights and measures
microbiology—micro-organisms
micrology—minute objects
microseismology—minute earth tremors
misology—hatred of knowledge, discussion, etc.
monology—monologue
morology—foolish talking
morphology—form and shape of living things
muscology—mosses
mycology (mycetology)—fungi
myology—muscles
myriology—funeral songs
myrmecology—ants
naology—sacred buildings
nasology—nose
necrology—obituaries
neology—new words, views
neontology—organisms not yet extinct
nephology—clouds
nephrology—kidneys
neurology—nervous system
neuropathology—pathology of nervous system
neurophysiology—physiology of nervous system
neurypnology—hypnotism
nomology—law
noology—understanding

nosology—classification of disease
numismatology—coins
nyctology—night-blindness
odontology—teeth
oenology—wines
olfactology—smells
ombrology—rain
oncology—tumors
oneirology—dreams
onomatology—terminology
ontology—origins, developments
oology—birds' eggs
ophiology—snakes
ophthalmology—eyes
optology—sight testing
organology—bodily organs
orismology—terminology
ornithology—birds
orology (oreology)—mountains
orthology—correct use of words
oryctology—fossils
osmology—odors
osteology—bones
otology—ears
ovology—origin of eggs
paleobiology—fossil life
pale(o)ichthyology—extinct fossil fish
paleoethnology—primitive races
paleology—archeology
paleontology—past history of life
paleopedology—prehistoric soil
paleornithology—extinct and fossil birds
paleozoology—extinct or fossil animals
palil(l)ology—emphasis
palynology—pollen
pantheology—all deities and religions
pantology—universal knowledge
paroemiology—proverbs
paromology—partial admission (fact)
pathology—cause, nature, effect of disease
pedology—children
pedology—soils
penology—prevention and punishment of crime
perissology—redundancy (speech)
petrology—rocks
pharmacology—drugs
phenology—times of recurring natural phenomena
phenomenology—phenomena (as distinct from 'being' [ontology])
philology—linguistics
phlebology—veins
phonology—vocal sounds
photology—light, optics
phrenology—mental faculties

phycology—seaweed
physico-theology—theology founded on the facts of nature
physiology—living body
phytology—botany
phytopathology—plant diseases
phytophysiology—plant physiology
piscatology—fishing
plasmology—corpuscles of living matter
pneumatology—spiritual beings
pomology—fruit
ponerology—evil
posology—dosage
potamology—rivers
proctology—rectum, hemorrhoids
promorphology—morphology of fundamental forms
psephology—election statistics
pseudology—art of lying
psychology—behavior of mind
psychonosology—mental diseases
pyschopathology—insanity
psychophysiology—experimental psychology
pteridology—ferns
pterology—insect wings
pterylology—feathers
pyretology—fever
pyrgology—towers
pyritology—pyrites
pyrology—fire and heat
radiology—X-rays
rhabdology—divination with the divining rod
rheology—flow and deformation of matter
rhinology—nose
Röntgenology—Röntgen rays
runology—runes
sarcology—flesh
satanology—devil worship
scatology—fossil excrement
seismology—earthquakes
selenology—moon
semasiology—meaning of words
sematology—signs in relation to thought and knowledge
semeiology—symptoms
serology—serum
sinology—China, Chinese
sitiology—diet
sociology—human society
somatology—organic bodies
sophiology—activities designed to give instruction
soteriology—salvation
speciology—nature and origin of species
spectrology—spectres or spectra

speleology—caves
spermatology—sperm
spermology—seeds
sphygmology—pulse
splanchnology—viscera
splenology—spleen
stoichiology—elements
stomatology—mouth diseases
storiology—folklore
synchronology—comparative chronology
systematology—methodical arrangements
tautology—repetition in different words
taxology—scientific classification
technology—useful arts
tecnology—children
tectology—structural morphology
tegestology—beer mats
teleology—final causes
teratology—(med.) monstrosities
terminology—correct use of words
thanatology—death
thaumatology—miracles
theology—divinity
thermology—heat
thermatology—heat
therology—mammals
thremmatology—animal or plant breeding
threpsology—nutrition
tidology—tides
timbrology—philately
tocology—obstetrics
topology—mnemonics based on association of ideas with places
toxicology—poisons
traumatology—wounds, shock
trichology—hair
tropology—figurative language
typhlology—blindness
typology—scriptural interpretation
typtology—spirit-rapping
uranology—astronomy
urology—urinary system
vermiology—worms
vulcanology—volcanoes
xylology—structure of wood
zoogeology—fossil animal remains
zoology—natural history of animals
zoonosology—animal diseases
zoophysiology—animal physiology
zymology—fermentation
zymotechnology—fermentation

(See next pages for the reverse of this table.)

Studies of/The "-ologies"

Abnormalities (monsters)	Teratology
Activities designed to give instruction	Sophiology
Admission, partial (of fact)	Paramology
Aged, study of	Gerontology
Amber	Ambrology
Ambiguity	Amphibology
Animal breeding	Thremmatology
Animal diseases	Zoonosology
Animal distribution	Faunology
Animal natural history	Zoology
Animal physiology	Zoophysiology
Animal remains (fossil)	Zoogeology
Antiquities	Archeology, paleology
Ants	Myrmecology
Ants, wasps, etc.	Hymenopterology
Aqueous vapor	Atmology
Archeology	Paleology
Arranging methodically	Systematology
Assaying metals	Docimology
Astronomy	Uranology
Atmosphere	Meteorology
Atmospheric interrelationship with organisms	Biometeorology
Bats	Chiropterology
Beauty	Kalology
Bedclothes plucking in delirium	Carphology
Beer mats	Tegestology
Bees	Apiology
Beetles	Coleopterology
Behavior of the mind	Psychology
Bells	Campanology
Bile	Cholology, choledology
Birds	Ornithology
Birds nests	Caliology
Blindness (see also Night-blindness)	Typhlology
Blood	Hematology
Blood vessels	Angiology
Bodily organs	Organology
Body; effects of work	Ergology
Bones	Osteology
Books	Bibliology
Botany	Phytology
Brains	Cerebrology
Brambles	Batology
Breeding (plants and animals)	Thremmatology
Cartilage	Chondrology
Catering for the stomach	Gastrology
Causes	Etiology
Caves	Speleology
Cell pathology	Cytopathology
Cells	Cytology
Character	Ethology
Children	Pedology, tecnology
China; Chinese	Sinology
Church building	Ecclesiology, naology
Church history	Ecclesiology
Classification (scientific)	Taxology
Classification of disease	Nosology
Clock making	Horology
Clouds	Nephology

Code	Cryptology
Coins	Numismatology
Comparative chronology, or dating	Synchronology
Corns, warts and bunions	Chiropodology
Corpuscles of living matter	Plasmology
Correct word usage	Orthology, terminology
Correspondence (sameness of relation)	Homology
Crime; punishment and prevention	Penology, criminology
Crustaceans	Carcinology, crustaceology, malacostracology
Dating	Chronology
Dating comparatively	Synchronology
Dating tree rings	Dendrochronology
Death	Thanatology
Debility, causing disease	Asthenology
Deformation of matter	Rheology
Deities and religions (all)	Pantheology
Deity, pertaining to	Anthropomorphology
Deserts	Eremology
Development; origins	Ontology
Devil-lore	Diabology
Devil worship	Satanology
Diet	Sitiology
Dining	Aristology
Diseases of animals	Zoonosology
Disease (cause, nature and effect)	Pathology
Disease, causes of	Etiology
Disease classification	Nosology
Disease, immunity from	Immunology
Diseases, infectious	Loimology
Diseases, mental	Psychonosology
Diseases, mouth	Stomatology
Diseases of plants	Phytopathology, epiphytology
Distribution of animals	Faunology
Diversity	Heterology
Divination	Mantology
Divination (with divining rod)	Rhabdology
Divinity	Theology
Dosage	Dosiology, dosology, posology
Double interpretation	Dittology
Dreams	Oneirology
Drugs	Pharmacology
Ears	Otology
Earthquake tremors	Seismology, microseismology
Earth's crust	Geology
Effort of work on mind and body	Ergology
Eggs (birds)	Oology
Eggs, origin of	Ovology
Election statistics	Psephology
Electricity	Electrology
Elements	Stoichiology
Emphasis	Palilology, palillology
Endocrine glands	Endocrinology
Environment	Ecology
Equine diseases	Hippopathology
Experimental psychology	Psychophysiology
Extinct and fossil animals	Paleozoology
Extinct and fossil birds	Paleornithology
Extinct fossil fish	Pale(o)ichthyology
Extinction	Geratology
Evil	Ponerology
Eyes	Ophthalmology

Facts of nature applied to theology	Physicotheology
False parasites	Epiphytology
Feathers	Pterylology
Female functions (and diseases)	Gynecology
Fermentation	Zymology, zymotechnology
Ferns	Pteridology
Festivals, religious	Heortology
Fever	Pyretology
Figurative language	Tropology
Final causes	Teleology
Fingers, speaking with	Dactylology
Fingers, speaking with	Chirology
Fire	Pyrology
Fishes	Ichthyology
Fishing	Piscatology
Flesh	Sarcology
Flies	Dipterology
Flow of matter	Rheology
Folklore	Storiology
Food	Bromatology
Foolish talking	Morology
Form (and shape) of living things	Morphology
Fossil animal remains	Zoogeology
Fossil excrement	Scatology
Fossil and extinct animals	Paleozoology
Fossil and extinct birds	Paleornithology
Fossil fish (extinct)	Pale(o)ichthyology
Fossil footprints	Ichnolithology, ichnology
Fossil life	Paleobiology
Fossils	Oryctology
Friction	Anatripsology
Fruits	Carpology, pomology
Fundamental form and shape	Promorphology
Funeral songs	Myriology
Fungi	Fungology, mycology, mycetology
Geographical limits	Chorology
Glands	Adenology
Glands, endocrine	Endocrinology
Government (philosophy of origin)	Archology
Graphs (see also Handwriting)	Graphology
Growth	Auxology
Hair	Trichology
Handwriting	Graphology
Hatred of knowledge, discussion, etc.	Misology
Head	Cephalology
Health (see also Hygiene)	Hygiology, soteriology
Hearing	Audiology
Heart	Cardiology
Heat	Pyrology, thermology, thermatology
Hemorrhoids	Proctology
Heresies	Heresiology
History	Historiology
History of life (past)	Paleontology
Horse diseases	Hippopathology
Horses	Hippology
Human activities	Demology
Human (and animal) diseases	Nosology
Human (and animal) old age	Gerontology
Human society	Sociology
Humidity	Hygrology

Hygiene (see also Health)	Hygiology, soteriology
Hypnotism	Neurypnology
Ideas	Ideology, sophiology
Immunity from disease	Immunology
Inanimate nature	Azoology
Inanimate things	Abiology
Incorrect use of language	Acyrology
Infant monstrosities	Teratology
Infectious diseases	Loimology
Influence of planetary phenomena on weather (alleged)	Astrometeorology
Influence of stars	Astrology
Initial sounds (or signs)	Acrology
Inorganic objects	Anorganology
Insanity	Psychopathology
Insects	Entomology
Insect wings	Pterology
Intestinal worms	Helminthology
Intestines	Enterology
Joints	Arthrology
Kidneys	Nephrology
Knowledge, theory of	Gnosiology
Knowledge, universal	Pantology
Lakes	Limnology
Language	Glossology, glottology
Language, figurative	Tropology
Larval form	Silphology
Larynx	Laryngology
Last things (death, judgment, heaven and hell)	Eschatology
Law	Nomology
Lice and ticks	Acarology
Life on other planets	Exobiology
Ligaments	Desmology
Light	Photology
Linguistics	Philology
Literary collection	Anthology
Literature of sententious nature	Gnomology
Liver	Hepatology
Living body	Physiology
Living species (as opposed to extinct)	Neontology
Living things	Biology
Living things (form and shape)	Morphology
Lying	Pseudology
Male diseases	Andrology
Mammals	Mastology, therology
Man	Anthropology
Maps	Cartology
Mars	Areology
Matter, flow and deformation of	Rheology
Medicinal baths	Balneology
Medicine	Iatrology
Membranes	Hymenology
Mental diseases	Psychonosology
Mental faculties	Phrenology
Mental imagery	Eidology
Metal assaying	Docimology
Meteorites	Astrolithology
Methodical arrangement	Systematology
Micro-organisms	Microbiology
Mind, behavior of	Psychology
Mind, effects of work upon	Ergology
Minute objects	Micrology

Miracles	Thaumatology
Mispronunciation	Cacology
Mnemonics (based upon association of ideas with places)	Topology
Molluscs	Malacology
Monologues	Monology
Monsters (abnormalities) and infant monstrosities	Teratology
Months	Menology
Moon	Selenology
Moral obligation	Deontology
Mosses	Bryology, muscology
Mountains	Orology, oreology
Muscles	Myology
Natural history (of animals)	Zoology
Natural phenomena recurring in time	Phenology
Natural purposelessness	Dysteleology
Nature, inanimate	Azoology
Nature of origins	Epistemology
Nature's facts (as applied to theology)	Physico-theology
Needless repetition in speaking and writing	Battology
Nervous system	Neurology
Nervous system pathology	Neuropathology
Nervous system physiology	Neurophysiology
Nests, birds'	Caliology
New words, views	Neology
Night-blindness	Nyctology
Nose	Nasology, rhinology
Nutrition	Threpsology
Obituaries	Necrology
Obstetrics	Tocology
Odors	Osmology
Old age	Gerontology, nostology
Optics	Photology
Organic bodies	Somatology
Organic tissues	Histology, histiology
Organisms and atmosphere	Biometeorology
Organs of the body	Organology
Organs of sensation	Aesthophysiology
Origin	Epistemology
Origin and nature of species	Speciology
Origins; developments	Ontology
Partial admission (fact)	Paromology
Past history of life	Paleontology
Pathology of nervous system	Neuropathology
People, races	Ethnology
Phenomena (as distinct from being [Ontology])	Phenomenology
Phenomena (natural) recurring in time	Phenology
Philately	Timbrology
Physiology of animals	Zoophysiology
Physiology of nervous system	Neurophysiology
Physiology of plants	Phytophysiology
Picture-writing	Curiology
Picture postcards	Deltiology
Planets, life on other	Exobiology
Plant and animal interrelationship	Bioecology
Plant breeding	Thremmatology

Plant diseases	Phytopathology
Plant physiology	Phytophysiology
Poisons	Toxicology
Pollen	Palynology
Pond life	Limnology
Pornography	Coprology
Pregnancy	Cyesiology
Prehistoric soil	Paleopedology
Prevention of crime	Penology
Primitive races	Paleoethnology
Principles	Archelogy
Prolixity of speech	Macrology
Proverbs	Paroemiology
Pulse	Sphygmology
Punishment of crime	Penology
Purposelessness in nature	Dysteleology
Pyrites	Pyritology
Races; peoples	Ethnology
Rain	Ombrology
Rainfall	Hyetology
Rectum	Proctology
Recurrence in time of natural phenomena	Phenology
Redundancy (speech)	Perissology
Religions and deities (all)	Pantheology
Religious festivals	Heortology
Remedies (therapeutic)	Acology
Reptiles	Herpetology
Rings	Dactyliology
Rivers	Potamology
Rocks	Lithology, petrology, stromatology
Röntgen rays	Röntgenology
Runes	Runology
Sacred buildings	Naology
Sacred literature	Hierology
Saints, lives and legends	Hagiology
Salvation	Soteriology
Scientific classification	Taxology
Scriptural interpretations	Typology
Seaweed	Phycology, algology
Sedges	Caricology
Seeds	Spermology
Sententious literature	Gnomology
Serum	Serology
Shape of living things	Morphology
Shells	Conchology
Shock	Traumatology
Sight testing (see also Eyes)	Optology
Signs (in relation to thought and knowledge)	Sematology
Sin	Hamartiology
Skin	Dermatology
Skull	Craniology
Skull reading	Phrenology
Sleep	Hypnology
Smells	Olfactology
Snakes	Ophiology
Society (human)	Sociology
Soil, prehistoric	Paleopedology
Soils	Edaphology, pedology
Sounds, vocal	Phonology
Speaking on the fingers	chirology
Species, nature and origin of	Speciology

Studies of/the "-ologies" (continued)

Specters or spectra	Spectrology
Speech, parts of	Etymology
Speech, wordy or lengthy	Macrology
Sperm	Spermatology
Spirit rapping	Typtology
Spleen	Splenology
Stamps (see also Philately)	Timbrology
Stars, influence of	Astrology
Statistics of elections	Psephology
Stomach, catering for	Gastrology
Stones	Lithology
Structural morphology	Tectology
Sun	Heliology
Symptoms	Semeiology
Teeth	Odontology
Terminology	Orismology, onomatology
Theory of knowledge	Gnosiology
Therapeutic agents (remedies)	Acology
Thunder	Brontology
Ticks and lice	Acarology
Tides	Tidology
Time measurement	Horology
Tissues (organic)	Histology, histiology
Towers	Pyrgology
Tree-ring dating	Dendrochronology
Trees	Dendrology
Truth	Alethiology
Tumors	Oncology
Ulcers	Helcology
Understanding	Noology
Universal knowledge	Pantology
Universe	Cosmology
Urinary system	Urology
Useful arts	Technology
Uterus	Hysterology
Vain, unprofitable matters	Mataeology
Values	Timology
Veins	Phlebology
Viscera	Splanchnology
Vocal contraction of words	Haplology
Vocal sounds	Phonology
Volcanoes	Vulcanology
Wasps, ants, etc.	Hymenopterology
Water	Hydrology
Weather	Meteorology
Weather (alleged influence of planetary phenomena upon)	Astrometeorology
Weight (see also Weights and measures)	Barology
Weights and measures	Metrology
Whales	Cetology
Wines	Oenology
Wings of insects	Pterology
Wood, structure of	Xylology
Word derivation	Lexicology
Word meanings	Semasiology
Words, correct usage	Orthology, terminology
Words, vocal contraction of	Haplology
Work, its effect on mind and body	Ergology
Worms	Vermiology
Worms, intestinal	Helminthology
Wounds	Traumatology
X-rays	Radiology

Measurements

Length, mass and time are the three fundamental quantities in measurement. The three systems most generally used are the centimeter-gram-second (C.G.S.) and meter-kilogram-second (M.K.S.) metric systems, and the older foot-pound-second (F.P.S.) Imperial or United States system.

Small differences between the yard and the pound as defined in the Imperial and the United States systems were rationalized for scientific use on July 1, 1959, and for legal use on Jan. 31, 1964. These differences were resolved thus:

	. Unit	
	Yard	Pound
United States	0.914 401 83m	0.453 592 427 7kg
Canada	0.914 4m	0.453 592 338kg
United Kingdom	0.914 398 41m	0.453 592 338kg
Factor Adopted	0.914 4m	0.453 592kg

The minor differences which had existed between units of capacity and volume *within* the metric system were themselves eliminated in November 1964 by the 12th International Congress on Weights and Measures in New Dehli, India. Previously 1 liter had been equated with 1.000 028 cubic decimeters. The relationship between capacity and volume was there rationalized whereby 1 liter became equal to 1 cubic decimeter (1 dm³) exactly.

LENGTH

The Imperial Standard Yard was established in the United Kingdom by the Weights and Measures Act 1856. It is of Baily's metal (16 Cu, 2½ Sn, 1 Zn). By an Act of 1878 the yard is defined as the distance between two graduation lines engraved on gold plugs recessed into this bar at 62° F. This bar is preserved at the Standard Weights and Measures Department of the Board of Trade. Five "parliamentary copies" exist, of which four are inter-compared every decade and with the Imperial Standard at least every 20 years, by the National Physical Laboratory, Teddington, England.

The yard is now, of course, only a comparative standard, namely 91.44 per cent precisely of the length of the Standard Meter.

MASS

The international prototype kilogram is in the custody of Le Bureau International des Poids et Mesures et Sèvres, near Paris, France.

TIME

The second is the interval occupied by 9,192,631,770 cycles of the radiation corresponding to the transition of the caesium-133 atom, when unaffected by exterior fields.

WEIGHTS AND MEASURES

The United States system of weights and measures is fundamentally the British foot-pound-second system modified by usage. Most of the modifications were rationalized by agreement in 1959 under which both the U.S. and the Imperial Yard and Pound became equated to a metric comparison of 0.914 4m exactly and 0.453 592kg exactly. The National Bureau of Standards, a department of the U.S. Department of Commerce, was set up in 1901.

The use of the metric system was legalized in the United Kingdom in 1897. The Halsbury Committee there recommended the introduction of decimal currency in September 1963. The intention to switch to the metric system was declared on May 24, 1965, by the President of the Board of Trade "within ten years." In practice the transition was protracted and in 1978 there was increased public pressure to preserve the more familiar and versatile Imperial system.

METRIC SYSTEM

Following the adoption of decimal coinage by the United States in 1785, Thomas Jefferson and others advocated adoption of the metric system also. However, it was not until 1866 that the Congress legalized the use of the metric system in the United States.

The United States was one of the original adherents to the Treaty of the Meter in 1875, which established the International Bureau of Weights and Measures. Despite this, little was done by the government to spread the use of the metric system until 1968, when the Congress passed legislation calling for a study of the question.

The study, completed in 1971, found metric measurements already in wide use in United States industry and government, and recommended a 10-year program for a coordinated nationwide switch to the metric system. The program failed to get through the Congress, but the use of metrics continued to spread through industry, the media, educational systems and at the local level.

MACH NUMBERS

A Mach number is the ratio of the speed of a body to the local speed of sound in similar surrounding conditions. The term was introduced in 1887 by Ernst Mach (1838–1916), a professor of physics at Prague.

Mach 1.0 at sea level at $15.0°$ C. and 1013.2 millibars, *i.e.* at standard pressure and temperature, is 1116.1 ft./sec., 660.85 knots, 1,224.6 km./h. or 760.98 m.p.h.

The figure falls to the constant 967.7 ft./sec., 572.97 knots, 1,061.8 km./h. or 659.78 m.p.h. in the stratosphere, *i.e.* above 11,000 meters or 36,089 feet. Thus stratospheric Mach numbers, together with the date they were first achieved or surpassed in fixed-wing aircraft, read as follows:

Mach 1.0	659.78 m.p.h.	Oct. 14, 1947
Mach 2.0	1,319.56 m.p.h.	Nov. 20, 1953
Mach 2.5	1,649.45 m.p.h.	Dec. 12, 1953
Mach 3.0	1,979.34 m.p.h.	Sept. 27, 1956
Mach 3.5	2,309.23 m.p.h.	Mar. 7, 1961
Mach 4.0	2,639.12 m.p.h.	Mar. 7, 1961
Mach 5.0	3,298.9 m.p.h.	June 23, 1961
Mach 6.0	3,958.68 m.p.h.	Nov. 9, 1961
Mach 7.0	4,618.46 m.p.h.	not yet attained

The maximum speed attained by a fixed-wing aircraft is 4,534 m.p.h. (Mach 6.72) piloted by Major William J. Knight (U.S.) on Oct. 3, 1967.

The maximum speed computed for any manned satellite is 24,791 m.p.h. by the U.S. astronauts Col. Thomas P. Stafford and Cdrs. Eugene A. Cernan and John W. Young on Apollo 10 on 29 May, 1969.

The terms subsonic (below the speed of sound), transonic (at or about the speed of sound), supersonic (above but not significantly above it) and hypersonic (significantly above it) are not precise.

OTHER UNITS OF LENGTH

animal stature	the hand = 4 inches. *N.B.*—a horse of 14 hands 3 inches to the withers is often written 14.3 hands.
surveying	the link = 7.92 inches or a hundredth part of a chain.
approximate	the span = 9 inches from the span of the hand.
biblical	the cubit = 18 inches.
approximate	the pace = 30 inches (from the stride).
navigation	the International nautical mile (adopted also by the U.S. on July 1, 1954) = 6,076.1 feet (0.99936 of a U.K. nautical mile).
historical	the league = 3 statute miles.

Conversion Tables

To Convert	Into	Multiply by
	A	
acre	sq chain (Gunters)	10.0
acre	rods	160.0
acre	sq links (Gunters)	1×10^5
acre	hectare or sq hectometer	0.4047
acres	sq feet	43,560.0
acres	sq meters	4,047.0
acres	sq miles	1.562×10^{-3}
acres	sq yards	4,840.0
acre-feet	cu feet	43,560.0
acre-feet	gallons	3.259×10^5
ampere-hours	coulombs	3,600.0
ampere-hours	faradays	0.03731
ampere-turns	gilberts	1.257
angstrom unit	inch	$3,937 \times 10^{-9}$
angstrom unit	meter	1×10^{-10}
angstrom unit	micron	1×10^{-4}
astronomical unit	kilometers	1.495×10^8
atmospheres	ton/sq inch	0.007348
atmospheres	cms of mercury	76.0
atmospheres	ft of water (at 4°C)	33.90
atmospheres	in. of mercury (at 0°C)	29.92
atmospheres	kgs/sq cm	1.0333
atmospheres	kgs/sq meter	10,332.0
atmospheres	pounds/sq in	14.70
atmospheres	tons/sq ft	1.058
	B	
barrels (U.S., dry)	cu inches	7,056.0
barrels (U.S., dry)	quarts (dry)	105.0
barrels (U.S., liquid)	gallons	31.5
barrels (oil)	gallons (oil)	42.0
bars	atmospheres	0.9869
bars	dynes/sq cm	1×10^6
bars	kgs/sq meter	1.020×10^4
bars	pounds/sq ft	2,089.0
bars	pounds/sq in	14.50
bolt (U.S. cloth)	meters	36.576
Btu	ergs	1.0550×10^{10}
Btu	foot-lbs	778.3
Btu	gram-calories	252.0
Btu	horsepower-hrs	3.931×10^{-4}
Btu	joules	1,054.8
Btu	kilogram-calories	0.2520

To Convert	Into	Multiply by
Btu	kilogram-meters	107.5
Btu	kilowatt-hrs	2.928×10^{-4}
Btu/hr	foot-pounds/sec	0.2162
Btu/hr	gram-cal/sec	0.0700
Btu/hr	horsepower-hrs	3.929×10^{-4}
Btu/hr	watts	0.2931
Btu/min	foot-lbs/sec	12.96
Btu/min	horsepower	0.02356
Btu/min	kilowatts	0.01757
Btu/min	watts	17.57
Btu/sq ft/min	watts/sq in	0.1221
bucket (Br. dry)	cubic cm	1.818×10^{4}
bushels	cu ft	1.2445
bushels	cu in.	2,150.4
bushels	cu meters	0.03524
bushels	liters	35.24
bushels	pecks	4.0
bushels	pints (dry)	64.0
bushels	quarts (dry)	32.0

C

To Convert	Into	Multiply by
calories, gram (mean)	Btu (mean)	3.9685×10^{-3}
candle/sq cm	lamberts	3.142
candle/sq inch	lamberts	0.4870
centares (centiares)	sq meters	1.0
centigrade	Fahrenheit	$(C° \times 9/5) + 32$
centigrams	grams	0.01
centiliter	ounce fluid (U.S.)	0.3382
centiliter	cubic inch	0.6103
centiliter	drams	2.705
centiliters	liters	0.01
centimeters	feet	3.281×10^{-2}
centimeters	inches	0.3937
centimeters	kilometers	1×10^{-5}
centimeters	meters	0.01
centimeters	miles	6.214×10^{-6}
centimeters	millimeters	10.0
centimeters	mils	393.7
centimeters	yards	1.094×10^{-2}
centimeter-dynes	cm-grams	1.020×10^{-3}
centimeter-dynes	meter-kgs	1.020×10^{-8}
centimeter-dynes	pound-feet	7.376×10^{-8}
centimeter-grams	cm-dynes	980.7
centimeter-grams	meter-kgs	1×10^{-5}
centimeter-grams	pound-feet	7.233×10^{-5}
centimeters of mercury	atmospheres	0.01316
centimeters of mercury	feet of water	0.4461
centimeters of mercury	kgs/sq meter	136.0
centimeters of mercury	pounds/sq ft	27.85
centimeters of mercury	pounds/sq in	0.1934
centimeters/sec	feet/min	1.1969
centimeters/sec	feet/sec	0.03281
centimeters/sec	kilometers/hr	0.036
centimeters/sec	knots	0.1943
centimeters/sec	meters/min	0.6
centimeters/sec	miles/hr	0.02237
centimeters/sec	miles/min	3.728×10^{-4}
centimeters/sec/sec	feet/sec/sec	0.03281
centimeters/sec/sec	kms/hr/sec	0.036
centimeters/sec/sec	meters/sec/sec	0.01
centimeters/sec/sec	miles/hr/sec	0.02237
chain	inches	792.00
chain	meters	20.12

To Convert	Into	Multiply by
chains (surveyors' or Gunter's)	yards	22.00
circular mils	sq cms	5.067×10^{-6}
circular mils	sq mils	0.7854
circumference	radians	6.283
circular mils	sq inches	7.854×10^{-7}
cords	cord feet	8.0
cord feet	cu feet	16.0
coulomb	statcoulombs	2.998×10^{9}
coulombs	faradays	1.036×10^{-5}
coulombs/sq cm	coulombs/sq in	64.52
coulombs/sq cm	coulombs/sq meter	1×10^{4}
coulombs/sq in	coulombs/sq cm	0.1550
coulombs/sq in	coulombs/sq meter	1,550.0
coulombs/sq meter	coulombs/sq cm	1×10^{-4}
coulombs/sq meter	coulombs/sq in	6.452×10^{-4}
cubic centimeters	cu feet	3.531×10^{-5}
cubic centimeters	cu inches	0.06102
cubic centimeters	cu meters	1×10^{-6}
cubic centimeters	cu yards	1.308×10^{-6}
cubic centimeters	gallons (U.S. liq.)	2.642×10^{-4}
cubic centimeters	liters	0.001
cubic centimeters	pints (U.S. liq.)	2.113×10^{-3}
cubic centimeters	quarts (U.S. liq.)	1.057×10^{-3}
cubic feet	bushels (dry)	0.8036
cubic feet	cu cms	28,320.0
cubic feet	cu inches	1,728.0
cubic feet	cu meters	0.02832
cubic feet	cu yards	0.03704
cubic feet	gallons (U.S. liq.)	7.48052
cubic feet	liters	28.32
cubic feet	pints (U.S. liq.)	59.84
cubic feet	quarts (U.S. liq.)	29.92
cubic feet/min	cu cms/sec	472.0
cubic feet/min	gallons/sec	0.1247
cubic feet/min	liters/sec	0.4720
cubic feet/min	pounds of water/min	62.43
cubic feet/sec	million gals/day	0.646317
cubic feet/sec	gallons/min	448.831
cubic inches	cu cms	16.39
cubic inches	cu feet	5.787×10^{-4}
cubic inches	cu meters	1.639×10^{-5}
cubic inches	cu yards	2.143×10^{-5}
cubic inches	gallons	4.329×10^{-3}
cubic inches	liters	0.01639
cubic inches	mil-feet	1.061×10^{5}
cubic inches	pints (U.S. liq.)	0.03463
cubic inches	quarts (U.S. liq.)	0.01732
cubic meters	bushels (dry)	28.38
cubic meters	cu cms	1×10^{6}
cubic meters	cu feet	35.31
cubic meters	cu inches	61,023.0
cubic meters	cu yards	1.308
cubic meters	gallons (U.S. liq.)	264.2
cubic meters	liters	1,000.0
cubic meters	pints (U.S. liq.)	2,113.0
cubic meters	quarts (U.S. liq.)	1,057.0
cubic yards	cu cms	7.646×10^{5}
cubic yards	cu feet	27.0
cubic yards	cu inches	46,656.0
cubic yards	cu meters	0.7646
cubic yards	gallons (U.S. liq.)	202.0
cubic yards	liters	764.6

To Convert	Into	Multiply by
cubic yards	pints (U.S. liq.)	1,615.9
cubic yards	quarts (U.S. liq.)	807.9
cubic yards/min	cubic ft/sec	0.45
cubic yards/min	gallons/sec	3.367
cubic yards/min	liters/sec	12.74

D

days	seconds	86,400.0
decigrams	grams	0.1
deciliters	liters	0.1
decimeters	meters	0.1
degrees (angle)	quadrants	0.01111
degrees (angle)	radians	0.01745
degrees (angle)	seconds	3,600.0
degrees/sec	radians/sec	0.01745
degrees/sec	revolutions/min	0.1667
degrees/sec	revolutions/sec	2.778×10^{-3}
dekagrams	grams	10.0
dekaliters	liters	10.0
dekameters	meters	10.0
drams (apothecaries' or troy)	ounces (avoirdupois)	0.1371429
drams (apothecaries' or troy)	ounces (troy)	0.125
drams (U.S., fluid or apothecaries')	cubic cm	3.6967
drams	grams	1.7718
drams	grains	27.3437
drams	ounces	0.0625
dyne/cm	erg/sq millimeter	0.01
dyne/sq cm	atmospheres	9.869×10^{-7}
dyne/sq cm	inch of mercury at 0°C	2.953×10^{-5}
dyne/sq cm	inch of water at 4°C	4.015×10^{-4}
dynes	grams	1.020×10^{-3}
dynes	joules/cm	1×10^{-7}
dynes	joules/meter (newtons)	1×10^{-5}
dynes	kilograms	1.020×10^{-6}
dynes	poundals	7.233×10^{-5}
dynes	pounds	2.248×10^{-6}
dynes/sq cm	bars	1×10^{-6}

E

ell	cm	114.30
ell	inches	45.0
em, pica	inch	0.167
em, pica	cm	0.4233
erg/sec	dyne-cm/sec	1.000
ergs	Btu	9.480×10^{-11}
ergs	dyne-centimeters	1.0
ergs	foot-pounds	7.3670×10^{-8}
ergs	gram-calories	0.2389×10^{-7}
ergs	grams-cms	1.020×10^{-3}
ergs	horsepower-hrs	3.7250×10^{-14}
ergs	joules	1×10^{-7}
ergs	kg-calories	2.389×10^{-11}
ergs	kg-meters	1.020×10^{-8}
ergs	kilowatt-hrs	0.2778×10^{-13}
ergs	watt-hours	0.2778×10^{-10}
ergs/sec	Btu/min	$5,688 \times 10^{-9}$
ergs/sec	ft-lbs/min	4.427×10^{-6}
ergs/sec	ft-lbs/sec	7.3756×10^{-8}
ergs/sec	horsepower	1.341×10^{-10}
ergs/sec	kg-calories/min	1.433×10^{-9}
ergs/sec	kilowatts	1×10^{-10}

To Convert	Into	Multiply by
	F	
farads	microfarads	1×10^6
faraday/sec	ampere (absolute)	9.6500×10^4
faradays	ampere-hours	26.80
faradays	coulombs	9.649×10^4
fathoms	meter	1.828804
fathoms	feet	6.0
feet	centimeters	30.48
feet	kilometers	3.048×10^{-4}
feet	meters	0.3048
feet	miles (naut.)	1.645×10^{-4}
feet	miles (stat.)	1.894×10^{-4}
feet	millimeters	304.8
feet	mils	1.2×10^4
feet of water	atmospheres	0.02950
feet of water	in. of mercury	0.8826
feet of water	kgs/sq cm	0.03048
feet of water	kgs/sq meter	304.8
feet of water	pounds/sq ft	62.43
feet of water	pounds/sq in	0.4335
feet/min	cms/sec	0.5080
feet/min	feet/sec	0.01667
feet/min	kms/hr	0.01829
feet/min	meters/min	0.3048
feet/min	miles/hr	0.01136
feet/sec	cms/sec	30.48
feet/sec	kms/hr	1.097
feet/sec	knots	0.5921
feet/sec	meters/min	18.29
feet/sec	miles/hr	0.6818
feet/sec	miles/min	0.01136
feet/sec/sec	cms/sec/sec	30.48
feet/sec/sec	kms/hr/sec	1.097
feet/sec/sec	meters/sec/sec	0.3048
feet/sec/sec	miles/hr/sec	0.6818
feet/100 feet	per cent grade	1.0
foot-candle	lumen/sq meter	10.764
foot-pounds	Btu	1.286×10^{-3}
foot-pounds	ergs	1.356×10^7
foot-pounds	gram-calories	0.3238
foot-pounds	hp-hrs	5.050×10^{-7}
foot-pounds	joules	1.356
foot-pounds	kg-calories	3.24×10^{-4}
foot-pounds	kg-meters	0.1383
foot-pounds	kilowatt-hrs	3.766×10^{-7}
foot-pounds/min	Btu/min	1.286×10^{-3}
foot-pounds/min	foot-pounds/sec	0.01667
foot-pounds/min	horsepower	3.030×10^{-5}
foot-pounds/min	kg-calories/min	3.24×10^{-4}
foot-pounds/min	kilowatts	2.260×10^{-5}
foot-pounds/sec	Btu/hr	4.6263
foot-pounds/sec	Btu/min	0.07717
foot-pounds/sec	horsepower	0.818×10^{-3}
foot-pounds/sec	kg-calories/min	1.01945
foot-pounds/sec	kilowatts	1.356×10^{-3}
furlongs	miles (U.S.)	0.125
furlongs	rods	40.0
furlongs	feet	660.0
	G	
gallons	cu cms	3,785.0
gallons	cu feet	0.1337
gallons	cu inches	231.0

To Convert	Into	Multiply by
gallons	cu meters	3.785×10^{-3}
gallons	cu yards	4.951×10^{-3}
gallons	liters	3.785
gallons (liq. Br. imp.)	gallons (U.S. liq.)	1.20095
gallons (U.S.)	gallons (imp.)	0.83267
gallons of water	pounds of water	8.3453
gallons/min	cu ft/sec	2.228×10^{-3}
gallons/min	liters/sec	0.06308
gallons/min	cu ft/hr	8.0208
gausses	lines/sq in	6.452
gausses	webers/sq cm	1×10^{-8}
gausses	webers/sq in	6.452×10^{-8}
gausses	webers/sq meter	1×10^{-4}
gilberts	ampere-turns	0.7958
gilberts/cm	amp-turns/cm	0.7958
gilberts/cm	amp-turns/in	2.021
gilberts/cm	amp-turns/meter	79.58
gills (British)	cubic cm	142.07
gills	liters	0.1183
gills	pints (liq.)	0.25
grains	drams (avoirdupois)	0.03657143
grains (troy)	grains (avoirdupois)	1.0
grains (troy)	grams	0.06480
grains (troy)	ounces (avoirdupois)	2.0833×10^{-3}
grains (troy)	pennyweight (troy)	0.04167
grains/U.S. gal	parts/million	17.118
grains/U.S. gal	pounds/million gal	142.86
grains/imp gal	parts/million	14.286
grams	dynes	980.7
grams	grains	15.43
grams	joules/cm	9.807×10^{-5}
grams	joules/meter (newtons)	9.807×10^{-3}
grams	kilograms	0.001
grams	milligrams	1,000.0
grams	ounces (avoirdupois)	0.03527
grams	ounces (troy)	0.03215
grams	poundals	0.07093
grams	pounds	2.205×10^{-3}
grams/cm	pounds/inch	5.600×10^{-3}
grams/cu cm	pounds/cu ft	62.43
grams/cu cm	pounds/cu in	0.03613
grams/cu cm	pounds/mil-foot	3.405×10^{-7}
grams/liter	grains/gal	58.417
grams/liter	pounds/1,000 gal	8.345
grams/liter	pounds/cu ft	0.062427
grams/liter	parts/million	1,000.0
grams/sq cm	pounds/sq ft	2.0481
gram-calories	Btu	3.9683×10^{-3}
gram-calories	ergs	4.1868×10^{7}
gram-calories	foot-pounds	3.0880
gram-calories	horsepower-hrs	1.5596×10^{-6}
gram-calories	kilowatt-hrs	1.1630×10^{-6}
gram-calories	watt-hrs	1.1630×10^{-3}
gram-calories/sec	Btu/hr	14.286
gram-centimeters	Btu	9.297×10^{-8}
gram-centimeters	ergs	980.7
gram-centimeters	joules	9.807×10^{-5}
gram-centimeters	kg-cal	2.343×10^{-8}
gram-centimeters	kg-meters	1×10^{-5}

H

hand	cm	10.16
hectares	acres	2.471

To Convert	Into	Multiply by
hectares	sq feet	1.076×10^5
hectograms	grams	100.0
hectoliters	liters	100.0
hectometers	meters	100.0
hectowatts	watts	100.0
henries	millihenries	1,000.0
hogsheads (British)	cubic ft	10.114
hogsheads (U.S.)	cubic ft	8.42184
hogsheads (U.S.)	gallons (U.S.)	63.0
horsepower	Btu/min	42.44
horsepower	foot-lbs/min	33,000.0
horsepower	foot-lbs/sec	550.0
horsepower (metric) (542.5 ft lb/sec)	horsepower (550 ft lb/sec)	0.9863
horsepower (550 ft lb/sec)	horsepower (metric) (542.5 ft lb/sec)	1.014
horsepower	kg-calories/min	10.68
horsepower	kilowatts	0.7457
horsepower	watts	745.7
horsepower (boiler)	Btu/hr	33,479.0
horsepower (boiler)	kilowatts	9.803
horsepower-hrs	Btu	2,547.0
horsepower-hrs	ergs	2.6845×10^{13}
horsepower-hrs	foot-lbs	1.98×10^6
horsepower-hrs	gram-calories	641,190.0
horsepower-hrs	joules	2.684×10^6
horsepower-hrs	kg-calories	641.1
horsepower-hrs	kg-meters	2.737×10^5
horsepower-hrs	kilowatt-hrs	0.7457
hours	days	4.167×10^{-2}
hours	weeks	5.952×10^{-3}
hundredweights (long)	pounds	112.0
hundredweights (long)	tons (long)	0.05
hundredweights (short)	ounces (avoirdupois)	1,600.0
hundredweights (short)	pounds	100.0
hundredweights (short)	tons (metric)	0.0453592
hundredweights (short)	tons (long)	0.0446429

I

inches	centimeters	2.540
inches	meters	2.540×10^{-2}
inches	miles	1.578×10^{-5}
inches	millimeters	25.40
inches	mils	1,000.0
inches	yards	2.778×10^{-2}
inches of mercury	atmospheres	0.03342
inches of mercury	feet of water	1.133
inches of mercury	kgs/sq cm	0.03453
inches of mercury	kgs/sq meter	345.3
inches of mercury	pounds/sq ft	70.73
inches of mercury	pounds/sq in	0.4912
inches of water (at 4°C)	atmospheres	2.458×10^{-3}
inches of water (at 4°C)	inches of mercury	0.07355
inches of water (at 4°C)	kgs/sq cm	2.540×10^{-3}
inches of water (at 4°C)	ounces/sq in	0.5781
inches of water (at 4°C)	pounds/sq ft	5.204
inches of water (at 4°C)	pounds/sq in	0.03613
international ampere	ampere (absolute)	0.9998
international volt	volts (absolute)	1.0003
international volt	joules (absolute)	1.593×10^{-19}
international volt	joules	9.654×10^4

J

joules	Btu	9.480×10^{-4}
joules	ergs	1×10^{7}
joules	foot-pounds	0.7376
joules	kg-calories	2.389×10^{-4}
joules	kg-meters	0.1020
joules	watt-hrs	2.778×10^{-4}
joules/cm	grams	1.020×10^{4}
joules/cm	dynes	1×10^{7}
joules/cm	joules/meter (newtons)	100.0
joules/cm	poundals	723.3
joules/cm	pounds	22.48

K

kilograms	dynes	980,665.0
kilograms	grams	1,000.0
kilograms	joules/cm	0.09807
kilograms	joules/meter (newtons)	9.807
kilograms	poundals	70.93
kilograms	pounds	2.205
kilograms	tons (long)	9.842×10^{-4}
kilograms	tons (short)	1.102×10^{-3}
kilograms/cu meter	grams/cu cm	0.001
kilograms/cu meter	pounds/cu ft	0.06243
kilograms/cu meter	pounds/cu in	3.613×10^{-5}
kilograms/cu meter	pounds/mil-foot	3.405×10^{-10}
kilograms/meter	pounds/ft	0.6720
kilograms/sq cm	dynes	980,665.0
kilograms/sq cm	atmospheres	0.9678
kilograms/sq cm	feet of water	32.81
kilograms/sq cm	inches of mercury	28.96
kilograms/sq cm	pounds/sq ft	2,048.0
kilograms/sq cm	pounds/sq in	14.22
kilograms/sq meter	atmospheres	9.678×10^{-5}
kilograms/sq meter	bars	98.07×10^{-6}
kilograms/sq meter	feet of water	3.281×10^{-3}
kilograms/sq meter	inches of mercury	2.896×10^{-3}
kilograms/sq meter	pounds/sq ft	0.2048
kilograms/sq meter	pounds/sq in	1.422×10^{-3}
kilograms/sq mm	kgs/sq meter	1×10^{6}
kilogram-calories	Btu	3.968
kilogram-calories	foot-pounds	3,088.0
kilogram-calories	hp-hrs	1.560×10^{-3}
kilogram-calories	joules	4,186.0
kilogram-calories	kg-meters	426.9
kilogram-calories	kilojoules	4.186
kilogram-calories	kilowatt-hrs	1.163×10^{-3}
kilogram-meters	Btu	9.294×10^{-3}
kilogram meters	ergs	9.804×10^{7}
kilogram meters	foot-pounds	7.233
kilogram meters	joules	9.804
kilogram meters	kg-calories	2.342×10^{-3}
kilogram meters	kilowatt-hrs	2.723×10^{-6}
kilolines	maxwells	1,000.0
kiloliters	liters	1,000.0
kilometers	centimeters	1×10^{5}
kilometers	feet	3,281.0
kilometers	inches	3.937×10^{4}
kilometers	meters	1,000.0
kilometers	miles	0.6214
kilometers	millimeters	1×10^{6}
kilometers	yards	1,094.0

To Convert	Into	Multiply by
kilometers/hr	cms/sec	27.78
kilometers/hr	feet/min	54.68
kilometers/hr	feet/sec	0.9113
kilometers/hr	knots	0.5396
kilometers/hr	meters/min	16.67
kilometers/hr	miles/hr	0.6214
kilometers/hr/sec	cms/sec/sec	27.78
kilometers/hr/sec	ft/sec/sec	0.9113
kilometers/hr/sec	meters/sec/sec	0.2778
kilometers/hr/sec	miles/hr/sec	0.6214
kilowatts	Btu/min	56.92
kilowatts	foot-lbs/min	4.426×10^4
kilowatts	foot-lbs/sec	737.6
kilowatts	horsepower	1.341
kilowatts	kg-calories/min	14.34
kilowatts	watts	1,000.0
kilowatt-hrs	Btu	3,413.0
kilowatt-hrs	ergs	3.600×10^{13}
kilowatt-hrs	foot-lbs	2.655×10^6
kilowatt-hrs	gram-calories	859,850.0
kilowatt-hrs	horsepower-hrs	1.341
kilowatt-hrs	joules	3.6×10^6
kilowatt-hrs	kg-calories	860.5
kilowatt-hrs	kg-meters	3.671×10^5
kilowatt-hrs	pounds of water evaporated from and at 212°F	3.53
kilowatt-hrs	pounds of water raised from 62° to 212°F	22.75
knots	feet/hr	6,080.0
knots	kilometers/hr	1.8532
knots	nautical miles/hr	1.0
knots	statute miles/hr	1.151
knots	yards/hr	2,027.0
knots	feet/sec	1.689

L

To Convert	Into	Multiply by
league	miles (approx)	3.0
light-year	miles	5.9×10^{12}
light-year	kilometers	9.46091×10^{12}
lines/sq cm	gausses	1.0
lines/sq in.	gausses	0.1550
lines/sq in.	webers/sq cm	1.550×10^{-9}
lines/sq in.	webers/sq in	1×10^{-8}
lines/sq in.	webers/sq meter	1.550×10^{-5}
links (engineer's)	inches	12.0
links (surveyor's)	inches	7.92
liters	bushels (U.S. dry)	0.02838
liters	cu cm	1,000.0
liters	cu feet	0.03531
liters	cu inches	61.02
liters	cu meters	0.001
liters	cu yards	1.308×10^{-3}
liters	gallons (U.S. liq.)	0.2642
liters	pints (U.S. liq.)	2.113
liters	quarts (U.S. liq.)	1.057
liters/min	cu ft/sec	5.886×10^{-4}
liters/min	gals/sec	4.403×10^{-3}
lumens/sq ft	foot-candles	1.0
lumen	spherical candle power	0.07958
lumen	watt	0.001496
lumen/sq ft	lumen/sq meter	10.76
lux	foot-candles	0.0929

To Convert	Into	Multiply by
M		
maxwells	kilolines	0.001
maxwells	webers	1×10^{-8}
megalines	maxwells	1×10^{6}
megohms	microhms	1×10^{12}
megohms	ohms	1×10^{6}
meters	centimeters	100.0
meters	feet	3.281
meters	inches	39.37
meters	kilometers	0.001
meters	miles (nautical)	5.396×10^{-4}
meters	miles (statute)	6.214×10^{-4}
meters	millimeters	1,000.0
meters	yards	1.094
meters/min	cms/sec	1.667
meters/min	feet/min	3.281
meters/min	feet/sec	0.05468
meters/min	kms/hr	0.06
meters/min	knots	0.03238
meters/min	miles/hr	0.03728
meters/sec	feet/min	196.8
meters/sec	feet/sec	3.281
meters/sec	kilometers/hr	3.6
meters/sec	kilometers/min	0.06
meters/sec	miles/hr	2.237
meters/sec	miles/min	0.03728
meters/sec/sec	cms/sec/sec	100.0
meters/sec/sec	ft/sec/sec	3.281
meters/sec/sec	kms/hr/sec	3.6
meters/sec/sec	miles/hr/sec	2.237
meter-kilograms	cm-dynes	9.807×10^{7}
meter-kilograms	cm-grams	1×10^{5}
meter-kilograms	pound-feet	7.233
microfarad	farads	1×10^{-6}
micrograms	grams	1×10^{-6}
microhms	megohms	1×10^{-12}
microhms	ohms	1×10^{-6}
microliters	liters	1×10^{-6}
microns	meters	1×10^{-6}
miles (nautical)	feet	6,080.27
miles (nautical)	kilometers	1.853
miles (nautical)	meters	1,853.0
miles (nautical)	miles (statute)	1.1516
miles (nautical)	yards	2,027.0
miles (statute)	centimeters	1.609×10^{5}
miles (statute)	feet	5,280.0
miles (statute)	inches	6.336×10^{4}
miles (statute)	kilometers	1.609
miles (statute)	meters	1,609.0
miles (statute)	miles (nautical)	0.8684
miles (statute)	yards	1,760.0
miles/hr	cms/sec	44.70
miles/hr	feet/min	88.0
miles/hr	feet/sec	1.467
miles/hr	kms/hr	1.609
miles/hr	kms/min	0.02682
miles/hr	knots	0.8684
miles/hr	meters/min	26.82
miles/hr	miles/min	0.1667
miles/hr/sec	cms/sec/sec	44.70
miles/hr/sec	feet/sec/sec	1.467
miles/hr/sec	kms/hr/sec	1.609
miles/hr/sec	meters/sec/sec	0.4470

To Convert	Into	Multiply by
miles/min	cms/sec	2,682.0
miles/min	feet/sec	88.0
miles/min	kms/min	1.609
miles/min	knots/min	0.8684
miles/min	miles/hr	60.0
mil-feet	cu inches	9.425×10^{-6}
milliers	kilograms	1,000.0
millimicrons	meters	1×10^{-9}
milligrams	grains	0.01543236
milligrams	grams	0.001
milligrams/liter	parts/million	1.0
millihenries	henries	0.001
milliliters	liters	0.001
millimeters	centimeters	0.1
millimeters	feet	3.281×10^{-3}
millimeters	inches	0.03937
millimeters	kilometers	1×10^{-6}
millimeters	meters	0.001
millimeters	miles	6.214×10^{-7}
millimeters	mils	39.37
millimeters	yards	1.094×10^{-3}
million gals/day	cu ft/sec	1.54723
mils	centimeters	2.540×10^{-3}
mils	feet	8.333×10^{-5}
mils	inches	0.001
mils	kilometers	2.540×10^{-8}
mils	yards	2.778×10^{-5}
minims (British)	cubic cm	0.059192
minims (U.S., fluid)	cubic cm	0.061612
minutes (angles)	degrees	0.01667
minutes (angles)	quadrants	1.852×10^{-4}
minutes (angles)	radians	2.909×10^{-4}
minutes (angles)	seconds	60.0

N

nepers	decibels	8.686
newton	dynes	1×10^5

O

ohm (international)	ohm (absolute)	1.0005
ohms	megohms	1×10^{-6}
ohms	microhms	1×10^6
ounces	drams	16.0
ounces	grains	437.5
ounces	grams	28.349527
ounces	pounds	0.0625
ounces	ounces (troy)	0.9115
ounces	tons (long)	2.790×10^{-5}
ounces	tons (metric)	2.835×10^{-5}
ounces (fluid)	cu inches	1.805
ounces (fluid)	liters	0.02957
ounces (troy)	grains	480.0
ounces (troy)	grams	31.103481
ounces (troy)	ounces (avoirdupois)	1.09714
ounces (troy)	pennyweights (troy)	20.0
ounces (troy)	pounds (troy)	0.08333
ounce/sq inch	dynes/sq cm	4,309.0
ounces/sq in.	pounds/sq in	0.0625

P

parsec	miles	19×10^{12}
parsec	kilometers	3.084×10^{13}

To Convert	Into	Multiply by
parts/million	grains/U.S. gal	0.0584
parts/million	grains/imperial gal	0.07016
parts/million	pounds/million gal	8.345
pecks (British)	cubic inches	554.6
pecks (British)	liters	9.091901
pecks (U.S.)	bushels	0.25
pecks (U.S.)	cubic inches	537.605
pecks (U.S.)	liters	8.809582
pecks (U.S.)	quarts (dry)	8.0
pennyweights (troy)	grains	24.0
pennyweights (troy)	ounces (troy)	0.05
pennyweights (troy)	grams	1.55517
pennyweights (troy)	pounds (troy)	4.1667×10^{-3}
pints (dry)	cu inches	33.60
pints (liquid)	cu cm	473.2
pints (liquid)	cu feet	0.01671
pints (liquid)	cu inches	28.87
pints (liquid)	cu meters	4.732×10^{-4}
pints (liquid)	cu yards	6.189×10^{-4}
pints (liquid)	gallons	0.125
pints (liquid)	liters	0.4732
pints (liquid)	quarts (liquid)	0.5
Planck's quantum	erg-second	6.624×10^{-27}
poise	gram/cm sec	1.00
pounds (avoirdupois)	ounces (troy)	14.5833
poundals	dynes	13,826.0
poundals	grams	14.10
poundals	joules/cm	1.383×10^{-3}
poundals	joules/meter (newtons)	0.1383
poundals	kilograms	0.01410
poundals	pounds	0.03108
pounds	drams	256.0
pounds	dynes	44.4823×10^{4}
pounds	grains	7,000.0
pounds	grams	453.5924
pounds	joules/cm	0.04448
pounds	joules/meter (newtons)	4.448
pounds	kilograms	0.4536
pounds	ounces	16.0
pounds	ounces (troy)	14.5833
pounds	poundals	32.17
pounds	pounds (troy)	1.21528
pounds	tons (short)	0.0005
pounds (troy)	grains	5,760.0
pounds (troy)	grams	373.24177
pounds (troy)	ounces (avoirdupois)	13.1657
pounds (troy)	ounces (troy)	12.0
pounds (troy)	pennyweights (troy)	240.0
pounds (troy)	pounds (avoirdupois)	0.822857
pounds (troy)	tons (long)	3.6735×10^{-4}
pounds (troy)	tons (metric)	3.7324×10^{-4}
pounds (troy)	tons (short)	4.1143×10^{-4}
pounds of water	cu feet	0.01602
pounds of water	cu inches	27.68
pounds of water	gallons	0.1198
pounds of water/min	cu ft/sec	2.670×10^{-4}
pound-feet	cm-dynes	1.356×10^{7}
pound-feet	cm-grams	13,825.0
pound-feet	meter-kgs	0.1383
pounds/cu ft	grams/cu cm	0.01602
pounds/cu ft	kgs/cu meter	16.02
pounds/cu ft	pounds/cu in	5.787×10^{-4}
pounds/cu ft	pounds/mil-foot	5.456×10^{-9}

To Convert	Into	Multiply by
pounds/cu in	gms/cu cm	27.68
pounds/cu in	kgs/cu meter	2.768×10^4
pounds/cu in	pounds/cu ft	1,728.0
pounds/cu in	pounds/mil-foot	9.425×10^{-6}
pounds/ft	kgs/meter	1.488
pounds/in	gms/cm	178.6
pounds/mil-foot	gms/cu cm	2.306×10^6
pounds/sq ft	atmospheres	4.725×10^{-4}
pounds/sq ft	feet of water	0.01602
pounds/sq ft	inches of mercury	0.01414
pounds/sq ft	kgs/sq meter	4.882
pounds/sq ft	pounds/sq in	6.944×10^{-3}
pounds/sq in	atmospheres	0.06804
pounds/sq in	feet of water	2.307
pounds/sq in	inches of mercury	2.036
pounds/sq in	kgs/sq meter	703.1
pounds/sq in	pounds/sq ft	144.0

Q

To Convert	Into	Multiply by
quadrants (angle)	degrees	90.0
quadrants (angle)	minutes	5,400.0
quadrants (angle)	radians	1.571
quadrants (angle)	seconds	3.24×10^5
quarts (dry)	cu inches	67.20
quarts (liquid)	cu cms	946.4
quarts (liquid)	cu feet	0.03342
quarts (liquid)	cu inches	57.75
quarts (liquid)	cu meters	9.464×10^{-4}
quarts (liquid)	cu yards	1.238×10^{-3}
quarts (liquid)	gallons	0.25
quarts (liquid)	liters	0.9463

R

To Convert	Into	Multiply by
radians	degrees	57.30
radians	minutes	3,438.0
radians	quadrants	0.6366
radians	seconds	2.063×10^5
radians/sec	degrees/sec	57.30
radians/sec	revolutions/min	9.549
radians/sec	revolutions/sec	0.1592
radians/sec/sec	revs/min/min	573.0
radians/sec/sec	revs/min/sec	9.549
radians/sec/sec	revs/sec/sec	0.1592
revolutions	degrees	360.0
revolutions	quadrants	4.0
revolutions	radians	6.283
revolutions/min	degrees/sec	6.0
revolutions/min	radians/sec	0.1047
revolutions/min	revs/sec	0.01667
revolutions/min/min	radians/sec/sec	1.745×10^{-3}
revolutions/min/min	revs/min/sec	0.01667
revolutions/min/min	revs/sec/sec	2.778×10^{-4}
revolutions/sec	degrees/sec	360.0
revolutions/sec	radians/sec	6.283
revolutions/sec	revs/min	60.0
revolutions/sec/sec	radians/sec/sec	6.283
revolutions/sec/sec	revs/min/min	3,600.0
revolutions/sec/sec	revs/min/sec	60.0
rod	chain (Gunter's)	0.25
rod	meters	5.029
rods (surveyor's meas.)	yards	5.5
rods	feet	16.5

To Convert	Into	Multiply by
	S	
scruples	grains	20.0
seconds (angle)	degrees	2.778×10^{-4}
seconds (angle)	minutes	0.01667
seconds (angle)	quadrants	3.087×10^{-6}
seconds (angle)	radians	4.848×10^{-6}
slug	kilogram	14.59
slug	pounds	32.17
sphere	steradians	12.57
square centimeters	circular mils	1.973×10^5
square centimeters	square feet	1.076×10^{-3}
square centimeters	square inches	0.1550
square centimeters	square meters	0.0001
square centimeters	sq miles	3.861×10^{-11}
square centimeters	sq millimeters	100.0
square centimeters	sq yards	1.196×10^{-4}
square feet	acres	2.296×10^{-5}
square feet	circular mils	1.833×10^8
square feet	sq cms	929.0
square feet	sq inches	144.0
square feet	sq meters	0.09290
square feet	sq miles	3.587×10^{-8}
square feet	sq millimeters	9.290×10^4
square feet	sq yards	0.1111
square inches	circular mils	1.273×10^6
square inches	sq cms	6.452
square inches	sq feet	6.944×10^{-3}
square inches	sq millimeters	645.2
square inches	sq mils	1×10^6
square inches	sq yards	7.716×10^{-4}
square kilometers	acres	247.1
square kilometers	sq cms	1×10^{10}
square kilometers	sq ft	10.76×10^6
square kilometers	sq inches	1.550×10^9
square kilometers	sq meters	1×10^6
square kilometers	sq miles	0.3861
square kilometers	sq yards	1.196×10^6
square meters	acres	2.471×10^{-4}
square meters	sq cms	1×10^4
square meters	sq feet	10.76
square meters	sq inches	1,550.0
square meters	sq miles	3.861×10^{-7}
square meters	sq millimeters	1×10^6
square meters	sq yards	1.196
square miles	acres	640.0
square miles	sq feet	27.88×10^6
square miles	sq kms	2.590
square miles	sq meters	2.590×10^6
square miles	sq yards	3.098×10^6
square millimeters	circular mils	1,973.0
square millimeters	sq cms	0.01
square millimeters	sq feet	1.076×10^{-5}
square millimeters	sq inches	1.550×10^{-3}
square mils	circular mils	1.273
square mils	sq cms	6.452×10^{-6}
square mils	sq inches	1×10^{-6}
square yards	acres	2.066×10^{-4}
square yards	sq cms	8,361.0
square yards	sq feet	9.0
square yards	sq inches	1,296.0
square yards	sq meters	0.8361
square yards	sq miles	3.228×10^{-7}
square yards	sq millimeters	8.361×10^5

To Convert	Into	Multiply by

T

temperature (°C) + 273	absolute temperature (°C)	1.0
temperature (°C) + 17.78	temperature (°F)	1.8
temperature (°F) + 460	absolute temperature (°F)	1.0
temperature (°F) − 32	temperature (°C)	5/9
tons (long)	kilograms	1,016.0
tons (long)	pounds	2,240.0
tons (long)	tons (short)	1.120
tons (metric)	kilograms	1,000.0
tons (metric)	pounds	2,205.0
tons (short)	kilograms	907.1848
tons (short)	ounces	32,000.0
tons (short)	ounces (troy)	29,166.66
tons (short)	pounds	2,000.0
tons (short)	pounds (troy)	2,430.56
tons (short)	tons (long)	0.89287
tons (short)	tons (metric)	0.9078
tons (short)/sq ft	kgs/sq meter	9,765.0
tons (short)/sq ft	pounds/sq in	2,000.0
tons of water/24 hrs	pounds of water/hr	83.333
tons of water/24 hrs	gallons/min	0.16643
tons of water/24 hrs	cu ft/hr	1.3349

V

volt inch	volt/cm	0.39370
volt (absolute)	statvolts	0.003336

W

watts	Btu/hr	3.4129
watts	Btu/min	0.05688
watts	ergs/sec	107.0
watts	foot-lbs/min	44.27
watts	foot-lbs/sec	0.7378
watts	horsepower	1.341×10^{-3}
watts	horsepower (metric)	1.360×10^{-3}
watts	kg-calories/min	0.01433
watts	kilowatts	0.001
watts (absolute)	Btu (mean)/min	0.056884
watts (absolute)	joules/sec	1.0
watt-hours	Btu	3.413
watt-hours	ergs	3.60×10^{10}
watt-hours	foot-pounds	2,656.0
watt-hours	gram-calories	859.85
watt-hours	horsepower-hrs	1.341×10^{-3}
watt-hours	kilogram-calories	0.8605
watt-hours	kilogram-meters	367.2
watt-hours	kilowatt-hrs	0.001
watt (international)	watt (absolute)	1.0002
webers	maxwells	1×10^{8}
webers	kilolines	1×10^{5}
webers/sq in.	gausses	1.550×10^{7}
webers/sq in.	lines/sq in	1×10^{8}
webers/sq in.	webers/sq cm	0.1550
webers/sq in.	webers/sq meter	1,550.0
webers/sq meter	gausses	1×10^{4}
webers/sq meter	lines/sq in	6.452×10^{4}
webers/sq meter	webers/sq cm	1×10^{-4}
webers/sq meter	webers/sq in	6.452×10^{-4}

Y

yards	centimeters	91.44
yards	kilometers	9.144×10^{-4}
yards	meters	0.9144
yards	miles (nautical)	4.934×10^{-4}
yards	miles (statute)	5.682×10^{-4}
yards	millimeters	914.4

CELSIUS AND FAHRENHEIT COMPARED

The three principal temperature scales are Celsius, Fahrenheit and Kelvin. The first was devised in 1743 by J. P. Christen (1683–1755) but is referred to as Celsius although not truly invented by Anders Celsius (1701–44). The latter is named after Gabriel Daniel Fahrenheit (1686–1736), a German physicist. The name Centigrade was generally abandoned for the Celsius scale in 1948 except in the United Kingdom.

Temperature in °C. = (Temp. in °F. -32) $\times$ 5/9
Temperature in °F. = Temp. in °C. $\times$ 9/5 + 32

Useful comparisons are:

(1)	Absolute Zero	=	$-273.16°$ C. =	$-459.69°$ F.
(2)	Point of Equality	=	$-40.0°$ C. =	$-40.0°$ F.
(3)	Zero Fahrenheit	=	$-17.8°$ C. =	$0.0°$ F.
(4)	Freezing Point of Water	=	$0.0°$ C. =	32° F.
(5)	Normal Human Blood Temperature	=	37.0° C. =	98.6° F.
(6)	100 Degrees F.	=	37.8° C. =	100° F.
(7)	Boiling Point of Water at standard pressure	=	100.0° C. =	212° F.

On the Kelvin scale zero K is absolute zero and the zero of the Celsius scale is 273.16 K.

GRAVITY AND ACCELERATION

The internationally accepted value of standard gravity is 9.80665 meters/per sec./per sec. (32.1740 ft./sec.²). The formulas used in mechanics for free falling bodies are:

$$v = u + gt \qquad s = ut + \tfrac{1}{2}gt^2 \qquad v^2 = u^2 + 2gs$$

where u = initial velocity, v = final velocity, g = acceleration in ft./sec./sec., t = elapsed time in secs., s = distance traveled in feet.

The relation between the length and periodicity of a pendulum is expressed by:

$$t = 2\pi \sqrt{\frac{1}{g}} \text{ where } 1 = \text{the length.}$$

Measuring Instruments

Below is a list of the principal scientific measuring devices. The suffix "meter" derives from the Greek *metron*, a measure. Entries marked with a star possess a "-meter" suffix but are not *instruments* of measurement.

acid—acidimeter
air inhaled or exhaled at one breath—pneumatometer
alcohol content—alcoholometer
altitude—altimeter
altitude (by boiling point)—hypsometer
amperage—amperemeter (ammeter)
angles—graphometer
angles (esp. crystals)—goniometer
atmospheric pressure—barometer
atmospheric tint—cyanometer
atmospheric transparency—diaphanometer
bleaching power—chlorometer
blood circulation (force of)—rheometer
blood pressure—sphygmomanometer
body (volume of solid)—stereometer
boundary (outer) of a figure—perimeter*
brine (marine engine boiler)—salinometer
calculation—arithmometer
calculation—comptometer
chemical equivalents—logometer
circles, cycles—cyclometer
color hue and brightness—colorimeter
constant quantity (equations)—parameter*
crystal (form, angles and planes)—halometer
crystal (hardness)—sclerometer
curve of a chart—cyrtometer
depth (ocean)—bathometer
depth (ocean)—bathymeter
depth (sea, in fathoms)—fathometer
dew—drosometer
distance (between stars)—heliometer
distance covered by wheeled vehicles—hodometer
distance covered by vehicle—trechometer
distance of inaccessible objects—macrometer
distance over ground—odometer
distance travelled—viameter
distance walked—pedometer
distance (small, vertical)—cathetometer
distance (on a map)—rotometer
distant object—telemeter
ductibility—extensometer
dust—konometer
earthquake—seismometer
eggs (birds')—oometer
electric current—ammeter
electric current (small)—galvanometer
electric power in watts—wattmeter
electrical force—electrometer
electrical pressure (potential difference of)—potentiometer
elevation (angle of)—clinometer
energy—dynamometer

"everything" (angles, elevations, distances)—pantometer
expansion—dilatometer
fermentation—zymometer
fiber diameter—eriometer
flood level—floodometer
gas (volume of)—volumeter
gas (or vapor) pressure—manometer
gas (density of)—dasymeter
gas (pressure of) vaporimeter
gas storage container—gasometer*
geometrician—geometer*
glacier (motion of)—glaciometer
gradient—gradiometer
grain (balance for weighing)—chondrometer
gravity—gravimeter
head (fetal)—labidometer
hearing—audiometer
heat—bolometer
heat (quantity)—calorimeter
humidity (air or gas)—hygrometer
humidity (atmospheric)—psychrometer
light (polarization of)—polarimeter
light (relative intensity)—photometer
line consisting of one meter—monometer*
line of eight metrical feet—octameter*
line (straight) passing through center of circle or sphere, each end
    terminating at circumference—diameter*
line (curved)—opisometer
liquid (pipette for counting drops)—stactometer
liquid (viscosity of)—viscometer
liquid—araometer
liquid (density)—hydrometer
liquid (specific gravity)—litrameter
liquid (specific gravity)—pycnometer (pyknometer)
liquid (specific gravity)—stereometer
lung capacity—pulmometer
lung capacity—spirometer
magnetic force (terrestrial)—inclinometer
magnetic force (variations of)—variometer
magnetic force—magnetometer
magnetic needle (declination of)—declinometer
measures (two)—dimeter*
mental state (duration and intensity of)—psychometer
milk (flow of)—galactometer
milk (specific gravity of)—lactometer
moisture (rate of exhalation)—atmometer
moth—geometer*
mountain (height of)—orometer
nitrogen content—nitrometer
ohm (electrical resistance)—ohmmeter
oil (specific gravity of)—alaometer
organ (bodily, size variation)—oncometer*
oxygen—eudiometer
paint (weather resistance of)—weatherometer
photographic plate (sensitivity of)—sensitometer
plant growth—auxanometer
pressure (minute variations in)—tasimeter
pressure (or compression) of liquids—piezometer
purity—oleometer
pulse rate—pulsimeter
radiation—radiometer
rain—hyetometer
rain—ombrometer

rain—pluviometer
rain—udometer
ray (deflection of ray by prism)—spectrometer
refraction—refractometer
respiration (leaf)—porometer
respiration (movement of chest)—stethometer
respiration (movement of chest wall)—thoracometer
river level—fluviometer
river rise and fall (esp. Nile)—nilometer
roll (ship or spacecraft)—iscillometer
salinity—salimeter
ship's speed—sillometer
silver solution (strength of)—argentometer
skull—craniometer
sliding friction—tribometer
smell (accuracy)—osmometer
smoke content—reflectometer
sounds—sonometer
sound (duration of)—echometer
space (non-Euclidean)—metageometer
speed—tachometer
speed (of machinery)—speedometer
speed range—torquemeter
specific gravity—densimeter
sphere (radius and curve of)—spherometer
strain (structural)—taseometer
star (apparent relative magnitude)—astrometer (astrophanometer)
starlight (intensity)—astrophotometer
stellar scintillation—scintillometer
sugar (by polarized light)—saccharimeter
sugar (amount of solution by specific gravity)—saccharometer
sun's rays (heat of)—actinometer
sun's heat—pyrheliometer
surface (plane)—planometer (planimeter)
surveying (rapid)—tachymeter (tacheometer)
telescope (magnifying power)—dynameter
temperature—thermometer
temperature (high)—pyrometer
temperature (low)—cryometer (kryometer)
theodolite—stadometer
thickness—micrometer
thickness—pachymeter
time (with high accuracy)—chronometer
time and distance (taxis)—taximeter
tint—tintometer
tree—dendrometer
tuning-fork—tonometer
urine (specific gravity)—urinometer
vacuum pump for raising water—pulsometer*
verse of four measures—tetrameter*
verse of five metrical feet—pentameter*
verse of six metrical feet—hexameter*
verse of seven metrical feet—heptameter*
velocity—velocimeter
vibration—vibrometer
vision (range of)—optometer
voltage (voltmeter)—voltimeter
water intake—potometer
wave length (early)—cymometer
wine (alcoholic strength)—vinometer
wind speed—anemometer
work (quantity of power)—ergometer

(See next pages for the reverse of this table.)

---

* indicates -meter suffix, but not an instrument of measurement.

acidimeter—acids
actinometer—heat of sun's rays
alcoholometer—alcohol contents
altimeter—altitudes
ammeter—electric currents
amperemeter (ammeter)—amperages
anemometer—wind speeds
araeometer—liquids
argentometer—strength of silver solutions
arithmometer—calculation
astrometer (astrophanometer)—apparent relative magnitude of stars
astrophotometer—intensity of star's light
atmometer—rates of exhalation of moisture
audiometer—hearing
auxanometer—plant growths
barometer—atmospheric pressures
bathometer—ocean depths
bathymeter—ocean depths
bolometer—heat
calorimeter—heat (quantity)
cathetometer—small vertical distances
chlorometer—bleaching powers
chondrometer—balance for weighing grain
chronometer—time (with high accuracy)
clinometer—angles of elevation
colorimeter—color hues and brightnesses
comptometer—calculation
craniometer—skulls
cryometer—low temperatures
cyanometer—atmospheric tints
cyclometer—circles, cycles
cymometer—wavelengths (early)
cyrtometer—curves of a chart
dasymeter—density of gases
declinometer—declination of magnetic needles
dendrometer—trees
densimeter—specific gravities
*diameter—straight line passing through center of circle or sphere, each end terminating at circumference
diaphanometer—atmospheric transparency
dilatometer—expansions
*dimeter—two measures
drosometer—dew
dynameter—magnifying power of telescopes
dynamometer—energy

echometer—duration of sounds
elaeometer—specific gravity of oils
electrometer—electrical forces
ergometer—quantity or power of work done
eriometer—fiber diameters
eudiometer—oxygen
extensometer—ductility
fathometer—sea depths (fathoms)
floodometer—flood levels
fluviometer—river levels
galactometer—flow of milk
galvanometer—small electric currents
*gasometer—gas storage container
*geometer—a geometrician; a moth
glaciometer—motion of glaciers
goniometer—angles (esp. crystals)
gradiometer—gradients
graphometer—angles
gravimeter—gravity
halometer—form, angles, and planes of crystals
heliometer—delicate astronomical measurement
*heptameter—verse of seven metrical feet
*hexameter—verse of six metrical feet
hodometer—distance covered by wheeled vehicles
hydrometer—density of liquids
hyetometer—rain
hygrometer—humidity of air or gas
hypsometer—altitude by boiling point
inclinometer—terrestrial magnetic force
konometer—dust
labidometer—the fetal head
lactometer—specific gravity of milk
litrameter—specific gravities in liquid
logometer—chemical equivalents
macrometer—distance of inaccessible objects
magnetometer—magnetic forces
manometer—gas or vapor pressures
metageometer—non-Euclidean space
micrometer—thickness
*monometer—line consisting of one meter

---

* indicates -meter suffix, but not an instrument of measurement.

nilometer—rise and fall of river (esp. Nile)
nitrometer—nitrogen content
*octameter—a line of eight metrical feet
odometer—distance over ground
ohmmeter—ohms (electrical resistance)
oleometer—purity
ombrometer—rain
*oncometer—size variation of bodily organs
oometer—birds' eggs
opisometer—curved lines
optometer—range of vision
orometer—height of mountains
oscillometer—roll of a ship or spacecraft
osmometer—accuracy of sense of smell
pachymeter—thickness
pantometer—angles, elevations, distances
*parameter—constant quantity (equations)
pedometer—distance walked
*pentameter—a verse of five metrical feet
*perimeter—the outer boundary of a figure
photometer—relative intensity of light
piezometer—pressure or compressibility of liquids
planometer (planimeter)—plane surfaces
pluviometer—rain
pneumatometer—quantity of air inhaled or exhaled at one breath
polarimeter—polarization of light
porometer—leaf respiration
potentiometer—potential difference of electrical pressure
potometer—water intake
psychrometer – atmospheric humidity
pulmometer—lung capacity
pulsimeter—pulse rate
*pulsometer—vacuum pump for raising water
pycnometer (pyknometer)— specific gravity of liquids
pyrheliometer—sun's heat
pyrometer—high temperatures
psychometer—duration and intensity of mental states
radiometer—radiation
reflectometer—smoke content
refractometer—refraction
rheometer—force of blood circulation
rotometer—map distances
saccharimeter—sugars by polarized light
saccharometer—amount of sugar solution by specific gravity
salinometer—brine (marine engine boilers)
salimeter—salinity
scintillometer—stellar scintillation
sclerometer—hardness of crystals
seisometer—earthquakes
sensitometer—sensitivity of photographic plates
sillometer—speed of ships
sonometer—sounds
spectrometer—deflection of rays by prisms
speedometer—speed
spherometer—radii and curves of spheres
sphygmomanometer—blood pressure
spirometer—lung capacity
stactometer—pipette for counting drops of liquid
stadometer—theodolite
stereometer—volume of solid bodies; specific gravity of liquids
stethometer—chest movement during respiration
tachymeter (tacheometer)—rapid surveying
tachometer—speed
taseometer—structural strains
tasimeter—minute variations in pressure
taximeter—time and distance (taxis)
telemeter—distant objects
thermometer—temperature
thoracometer—movement of chest-wall in respiration
tintometer—tints
tonometer—a tuning-fork
torquemeter—speed ranges
trechometer—distance covered by a vehicle
tribometer—sliding friction
udometer—rain
urinometer—specific gravity of urine
vaporimeter—pressure of gases
variometer—variations of magnetic force
velocimeter—velocity
viameter—distance traveled
vibrometer—vibrations
vinometer—alcoholic strength of wine
viscometer—viscosity of liquids
voltimeter—voltage (voltmeter)
volumeter—volume of gas
wattmeter—electric power
weatherometer—weather resistance of paint
zymometer—fermentation

Microscopes

The optical parts of the ordinary compound microscope consist of an objective and an eyepiece mounted rigidly in a tube. The objective enlarges the object mounted on the stage of the microscope and focuses an image of this object in front of the eyepiece. The eyepiece further enlarges this image and brings it to a focus just at the viewer's eye. The total magnification of the object being viewed is thus the magnification of the objective times the magnification of the eyepiece.

The principal optical defects that limit the useful magnification are spherical and chromatic aberration. Spherical aberration prevents all the light rays coming to a focus at the same point or plane; this results in fuzzy, out-of-focus images. Chromatic aberration prevents light of different wavelengths coming to a focus at the same point or plane; this results in color fringes that degrade the image. Both defects can largely be corrected for by using complex and expensive lens systems.

Assuming a highly corrected optical system, the limiting magnification of a microscope is determined by diffraction effects. The smallest distance between any two points that can be resolved by any corrected optical system is given by the formula $n \sin \alpha$, where n is the index of refraction of the medium between the objective and the object and α is the angle between the axis of the optical system and the limiting rays of light that can pass through the optical system into the eye. The quantity $n \sin \alpha$ is called the numerical aperature (N.A.) of the microscope. The higher this figure, the better the resolution of the microscope. In an oil-emersion system, the air space between the objective and object is filled with a liquid that increases the N.A. and hence the total useful magnification of the microscope. Resolution is also affected by the wavelength of light passing through the optical system. The smaller the wavelength, the better the resolution. Therefore, the limiting resolution of any microscope is determined by the formula $\lambda/2n \sin \alpha$, where λ is the wavelength of light.

Most objects are viewed by transmitted light. In less expensive microscopes, natural or artificial light is focused on the object by a curved mirror. In more expensive systems, a lens system designed as part of the overall optical path serves as a condenser, gathering and focusing a corrected beam of light upon the object. In dark-field illumination, the central cone of light from the condenser is blocked off, leaving only a thin ring of light to illuminate the object. The rays of light strike the object at fairly large angles and the object is observed from the rays of light as they are refracted off the object.

Electron microscopes operate on identical principles to light microscopes but use beams of electrons rather than rays of light. Because of the extremely short wavelengths of the electrons the resolution of the microscope is greatly increased. In an electron microscope electrical and magnetic fields replace the condensers, objectives and eyepieces used to focus the beam. The resulting image is then focused upon a fluorescent screen or photographed. In one recent development, the electron beam scans the object being viewed much as a beam of electrons inside a television camera scans a scene being televised. The beam is reflected off the object and enlarged onto a fluorescent screen much as in a television receiver. This technique enables a much greater depth of field to be achieved than is otherwise possible. Examples of objects photographed with this scanning technique are shown throughout the encyclopedia.

CRYSTALS of rhenium trioxide, a rare metal heavier than gold, photographed here through a Cambridge Scientific Instruments Company scanning electron microscope. This new instrument has a remarkable depth of field and a "zoom" device. The illustration shown is about 200 × life size.

POLLEN GRAIN of the common mallow plant, *Malva sylvestris*, a member of the family Malvaceae. This photograph taken through a Cambridge scanning electron microscope is shown about 1000 × life size.

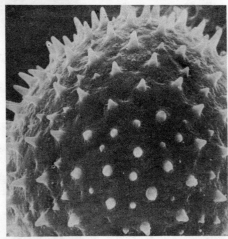

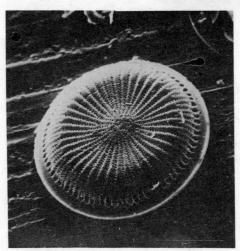

SKELETON of an Auckland diatom, a unicellular algae, photographed at about 2000 x life size through a Cambridge scanning electron microscope.

Predicting Human Stature

The height of ambition can often be measured in inches. A boy who sees himself leaving school to become a fearless police officer must grow to 5 feet 8 inches to get into the force at all. A girl who dreams of fame as a ballerina will be rejected as too tall if she stretches to more than 5 feet 6 inches.

An inch in height can mean the difference between an exhilarating start to a long-planned career and bitter disappointment at the most vulnerable period of a young person's life.

Now the height a child will attain as an adult need no longer be numbered with all the other uncertainties of his future. Records of the growth of children reveal an extraordinary regularity and it is now possible to predict from an early age, with increasing accuracy, the ultimate height of a boy or girl.

The length of a baby at birth, which averages fractionally over 20 inches (18 inches among pygmies in Africa), is of no value. Predictability begins to rise sharply at the age of only 8 weeks, and by the second birthday reaches a level of mathematical respectability. From the age of 3 until the onset of the adolescent spurt (in boys usually around $12\frac{1}{2}$ to 15, in girls $10\frac{1}{2}$ to 13) the reliability of prediction remains high. Peak reliability is at the eighth birthday for girls and the tenth birthday for boys.

In Great Britain, a professor of medicine, John Mourilyan Tanner, well known for his work at the Institute of Child Health at the University of London, set himself the task some years ago of bringing together all the material on child growth scattered over the world in medical literature. He found the pioneer was a French count named de Montbeillard, whose recordings on his own son (1759–1777) are still of value.

Professor Tanner, aided by his wife, also a doctor, finally brought some order into this highly mathematical and complex subject with the appearance of his classic work *Growth of Adolescence* (Blackwell Scientific Publications). Dr. Tanner regards the prediction table devised from the painstaking work of the Americans Bayley and Pinneau, as the best working guide so far published.

Our simplified version shows, in effect, the percentage of mature height reached at each age from one to seventeen years.

Records show that boys reach half their most likely final height at 2 years 5 weeks, whereas little girls, true perhaps to the song in *Gigi*, reach this point nearly 13 weeks before their second birthday.

Quite apart from a curiosity and entertainment value, height prediction tables have practical use in what is termed vocational disorientation. They provide an "early warning system" for parents with daughters who are going to be too tall for ballet or sons too short for the police force.

With the advent of anabolic steroid drugs, the growth of markedly undersized children can sometimes now be nudged towards the average.

It is interesting to reflect on the tremendous impact that human stature or the lack of it has had on history. Many men are extremely sensitive to physical height. If such little men as Attila the Hun, Ghengis Khan, Napoleon or the 5-foot-4-inch Joseph Stalin had not lacked the inches which could now both be predicted and to an extent controlled, the world might have suffered less from their tyrannies.

AVERAGE HEIGHT AND WEIGHT AT BIRTH

Nationality	Boys Length in ins.	Weight lb.	Weight oz.	Girls Length in ins.	Weight lb.	Weight oz.
United Kingdom	20.1	7	6.4	20.0	7	4.8
German	20.0	7	11.2	19.8	7	4.8
Swiss	20.0	7	4.8	19.7	6	12.8
U.S. (White)	19.9	7	12.8	19.7	7	9.6
Japanese	19.7	6	11.5	19.4	6	8.6
French	19.6	6	12.8	19.3	6	12.8
U.S. (Black)	19.5	7	1.6	19.1	6	12.8
U.S.S.R.	19.1	7	8	19.1	7	4.8
China	18.9	6	12.8	18.9	6	9.6
Africa (Pygmy)	18.0	7	14.4	18.2	8	3.2

In humans the musculature normally accounts for some 40% of the total body weight. There are 639 named muscles in the human anatomy.

PREDICTIONS

The table below shows the average mean percentage of mature height for both boys and girls at each age from birth to 18 years.

Age in Years	Boys	Girls
Birth	28.6%	30.9%
$\frac{1}{4}$	33.9%	36.0%
$\frac{1}{2}$	37.7%	39.8%
$\frac{3}{4}$	40.1%	42.2%
1	42.2%	44.7%
$1\frac{1}{2}$	45.6%	48.8%
2	49.5%	52.8%
$2\frac{1}{2}$	51.6%	54.8%
3	53.8%	57.0%
4	58.0%	61.8%
5	61.8%	66.2%
6	65.2%	70.3%
7	69.0%	74.0%
8	72.0%	77.5%
9	75.0%	80.7%
10	78.0%	84.4%
11	81.1%	88.4%
12	84.2%	92.9%
13	87.3%	96.5%
14	91.5%	98.3%
15	96.1%	99.1%
16	98.3%	99.6%
17	99.3%	100.0%
18	99.8%	100.0%

Thus a boy measuring 4 ft. 6 in. (54 in.) on his ninth birthday could be expected to be:

$$54 \times \frac{100}{75.0} = 72 \text{ in. or } 6 \text{ ft. } 0 \text{ in. as a man.}$$

In practice because of maternal factors, the prediction of adult stature becomes of value only after the age of 2 or $2\frac{1}{2}$ years. After the age of $9\frac{1}{2}$ prediction is more accurately based on skeletal rather than chronological age. The accuracy tends to be greater throughout for girls than for boys who, at 14, are subject to a standard deviation of error of 4%, viz. the 91.5% figure can be 95.8% for a physically advanced boy, and 87.6% for a retarded one.

NORMAL WEIGHTS

Men

Height (inches)	Low Pounds	Median Pounds	High Pounds
63	(118)	(129)	(141)
64	(122)	(133)	(145)
65	126	137	149
66	130	142	155
67	134	147	161
68	139	151	166
69	143	155	170
70	147	159	174
71	150	163	178
72	154	167	183
73	158	171	188
74	162	175	192
75	165	178	195

Women

Height (inches)	Low Pounds	Median Pounds	High Pounds
60	100	109	118
61	104	112	121
62	107	115	125
63	110	118	128
64	113	122	132
65	116	125	135
66	120	129	139
67	123	132	142
68	126	136	146
69	130	140	151
70	133	144	156
71	(137)	(148)	(161)
72	(141)	(152)	(166)

Weights were based on those of college men 25 to 29 years old and college women 20 to 24 years old. Measurements were made without shoes and other clothing. The range from "low" to "high" at a given height included the middle 50 per cent of the cases. Half the weights were below the median and half above. Body build will determine where, within the ranges given, normal weight should be. Weight at any age probably should not exceed these values by more than 5 pounds for the shorter adults and 10 pounds for the taller ones.

WEIGHT CHANGES THROUGH THE YEARS

Men

Dates	Age in years	Height in inches			
		65	68	70	73
		Weight in pounds			
1885–1900	25–29	142	154	163	171
	35–39	148	162	172	191
	40–49	152	166	177	197
1955	25–29	156	161	167	172
	35–39	152	166	172	186
	40–49	151	168	170	181

Women

Dates	Age in years	Height in inches			
		60	63	65	68
		Weight in pounds			
1885–1908	25–29	122	132	140	152
	35–39	129	140	148	159
	40–49	136	146	155	166
1955	25–29	116	124	133	146
	35–39	132	133	140	149
	40–49	135	142	151	154

Calories and Body Weight

CALORIE ALLOWANCES FOR INDIVIDUALS OF VARIOUS BODY WEIGHTS

[At mean environmental temperature of 68° F. and assuming moderate physical activity]

MEN

Calorie allowances

Desirable weight Pounds	25 years	45 years	65 years
110	2,500	2,350	1,950
121	2,700	2,550	2,150
132	2,850	2,700	2,250
143	3,000	2,800	2,350
154	3,200	3,000	2,550
165	3,400	3,200	2,700
176	3,550	3,350	2,800
187	3,700	3,500	2,900

WOMEN

88	1,750	1,650	1,400
99	1,900	1,800	1,500
110	2,050	1,950	1,600
121	2,200	2,050	1,750
128	2,300	2,200	1,800
132	2,350	2,200	1,850
143	2,500	2,350	2,000
154	2,600	2,450	2,050
165	2,750	2,600	2,150

100–CALORIE PORTIONS OF COMMONLY-EATEN FOODS

Cereals and Breads
biscuit or plain muffin	$\frac{3}{4}$ medium
bread, white, enriched	$1\frac{1}{2}$ slices
corn flakes	1 cup
crackers, saltines	6 crackers
oatmeal, cooked	$\frac{3}{4}$ cup
rice, white, cooked	$\frac{1}{2}$ cup
roll, plain	$\frac{5}{8}$ medium
wheat, puffed	$2\frac{1}{3}$ cups

Dairy Products
butter	1 tbsp.
buttermilk	$1\frac{1}{8}$ cups
cheese, Cheddar	$\frac{7}{8}$ oz.
cheese, cottage	$3\frac{2}{3}$ oz.
cream, heavy	2 tbsp.
ice cream, plain	$\frac{1}{3}$ cup
milk, nonfat solids	$3\frac{1}{2}$ tbsp.
milk, whole	$4\frac{1}{8}$ oz.

Fats and Oils
French dressing	$1\frac{2}{3}$ tbsp.
mayonnaise	1 tbsp.
salad oil	$\frac{7}{8}$ tbsp.

100-Calorie Portions (continued)

Fruit
apple, raw .... $1\frac{1}{3}$ medium
apricot, canned .... $\frac{1}{2}$ cup
banana .... $1\frac{1}{8}$ medium
grapefruit juice, canned .... $1\frac{1}{10}$ cups
orange juice, fresh .... $\frac{9}{10}$ cups
peaches or pears, canned .... $\frac{3}{8}$ cup
pineapple, canned, crushed .... $\frac{1}{2}$ cup
strawberries, raw .... $1\frac{5}{8}$ cups

Meat, Fish, Poultry, and Nuts
bacon .... 2 slices
beef .... 1 oz.
chicken breast .... $3\frac{1}{8}$ oz.
egg, whole .... $1\frac{1}{4}$
frankfurter .... $\frac{4}{5}$
haddock .... $\frac{2}{3}$ fillet
ham .... $\frac{9}{10}$ oz.
liver, beef .... $1\frac{3}{4}$ oz.
luncheon meat .... $1\frac{1}{8}$ oz.
peanut butter .... $1\frac{1}{10}$ tbsp.
pork .... $1\frac{1}{10}$ oz.
tuna fish, canned .... $1\frac{1}{8}$ oz.

Sugars and Sweets
cake, plain, iced .... $\frac{5}{8}$ medium
candy bar, chocolate .... $\frac{3}{4}$ oz.
carbonated beverages .... 8 oz.
cookies, plain .... $\frac{9}{10}$ medium
jellies .... 2 tbsp.
pie, apple .... $\frac{1}{21}$ medium
syrup, corn .... $1\frac{3}{4}$ tbsp.
sugar .... $6\frac{1}{4}$ tbsp.

Vegetables
beans, green, canned .... $2\frac{2}{3}$ cups
beans, lima, canned .... $\frac{4}{5}$ cup
broccoli, cooked .... $2\frac{1}{4}$ cups
cabbage, shredded, raw .... $4\frac{1}{5}$ cups
carrots, raw .... $4\frac{3}{4}$ medium
cauliflower, cooked .... $3\frac{1}{3}$ cups
celery, diced, raw .... $5\frac{1}{2}$ cups
corn, canned .... $\frac{3}{4}$ cup
lettuce .... $1\frac{1}{2}$ lb. head
onion, cooked .... $1\frac{1}{4}$
peas, green, canned .... $\frac{2}{3}$ cup
pepper, green, raw .... $5\frac{7}{8}$ medium
potato, white, baked .... 1 medium
potato, white, mashed .... $\frac{2}{3}$ cup
spinach, cooked .... $2\frac{1}{6}$ cups
sweet potato, baked .... $\frac{1}{2}$ medium
tomatoes, canned .... $2\frac{1}{6}$ cups

PROTEIN—RECOMMENDED DAILY DIETARY ALLOWANCES

Person	Age, years	Weight Pounds	Height Inches	Protein Grams
Men	25	154	69	70
	45	154	69	70
	65	154	69	70
Women	25	128	64	58
	45	128	64	58
	65	128	64	58
Pregnant (2d. half)				+20
Lactating (28 ounces daily)				+40
Children	1–3	27	34	40
	4–6	40	43	50
	7–9	60	51	60
	10–12	79	57	70
Boys	13–15	108	64	85
	16–19	139	69	100
Girls	13–15	108	63	80
	16–19	120	64	75

DESIRABLE WEIGHTS FOR HEIGHT

Height in inches	Weight in pounds Men	Women
58		112 ± 11
60	125 ± 13	116 ± 12
62	130 ± 13	121 ± 12
64	135 ± 14	128 ± 13
66	142 ± 14	135 ± 14
68	150 ± 15	142 ± 14
70	158 ± 16	150 ± 15
72	167 ± 17	158 ± 16
74	178 ± 18	

SOMATOTYPES

One of the systems used for classifying human physique is somatotyping (from the Greek *soma*, body) first published in 1940 by Sheldon (U.S.).

The three components used, some degree of which is present in everyone, are: (1) Endomorphy (a tendency to globularity); (2) Mesomorphy (a tendency to muscularity); and (3) Ectomorphy (a tendency to linearity). The degrees of tendency range from 1 to an extreme of 7.

Humpty Dumpty types would be 7—1—1; Hercules would have been 1—7—1, and the extreme in "weediness" would be 1—1—7. In practice such extremes are rarely encountered. The commonest somatotypes are 3—4—4, 4—3—3, and 3—5—2. The components are oblique, not orthogonal, *i.e.* not independent of each other to the point where it would be impossible to have a 5—5—5 or a 7—7—1.

Research (Tanner, 1964) into a sample of Olympic athletes shows that mean Endomorphy varies between 2.0 (steeplechasers) and 3.8 (shot putters); Mesomorphy between 4.1 (high jumpers) and 6.2 (discus throwers); and Ectomorphy between 4.5 (steeplechasers) and 2.0 (shot and discus throwers). Sprinters averaged 2.5—5.5—2.9 while milers have a mean rating of 2.5—4.3—4.3.

Medical Science

BONES IN THE HUMAN BODY
Number

Skull

Occipital	1
Parietal—1 pair	2
Sphenoid	1
Ethmoid	1
Inferior Nasal Conchae— 1 pair	2
Frontal—1 pair, fused	1
Nasal—1 pair	2
Lacrimal—1 pair	2
Temporal—1 pair	2
Maxilla—1 pair	2
Zygomatic—1 pair	2
Vomer	1
Palatine—1 pair	2
Mandible—1 pair, fused	1
Hyoid	1
	23

The Ears

Malleus	2
Incus	2
Stapes	2
	6

Vertebrae

Cervical	7
Thoracic	12
Lumbar	5
Sacral—5, fused to form the Sacrum	1
Coccyx—between 3 and 5, fused	1
	26

Vertebral Ribs

Ribs, "true"—7 pairs	14
Ribs, "false"—5 pairs of which 2 pairs are floating	10
	24

Sternum

Manubrium	1
"The Body" (Sternebrae)	1
Xiphisternum	1
	3

Pectoral Girdle

Clavicle—1 pair	2
Scapula—(including Coracoid)—1 pair	2
	4

Upper Extremity (each arm)

Humerus	1
Radius	1
Ulna	1
Carpus:	
Scaphoid	1
Lunate	1
Triquetral	1
Pisiform	1
Trapezium	1
Trapezoid	1
Capitate	1
Hamate	1
Metacarpals	5
Phalanges:	
First Digit	2
Second Digit	3
Third Digit	3
Fourth Digit	3
Fifth Digit	3
	30

Lower Extremity (each leg)

Femur	1
Tibia	1
Fibula	1
Tarsus:	
Talus	1
Calcaneus	1
Navicular	1
Cuneiform, medial	1
Cuneiform, inter- mediate	1
Cuneiform, lateral	1
Cuboid	1
Metatarsals	5
Phalanges:	
First Digit	2
Second Digit	3
Third Digit	3
Fourth Digit	3
Fifth Digit	3
	29

Bones in the Human Body (continued)

Pelvic Girdle
Ilium, Ischium and Pubis
  (combined)—1 pair
  of hip bones, innom-
  inate   2
               —

Total	
Skull	22
The Ears	6
Vertebrae	26
Vertebral Ribs	24
Sternum	4
Pectoral Girdle	4
Upper Extremities (arms)—2 × 30	60
Lower Extremities (legs)—2 × 29	58
Pelvic Girdle	2
	206

HUMAN DENTITION

Man normally has two sets of teeth during his life span. The primary
(milk or deciduous) set of 20 that is usually acquired between the ages

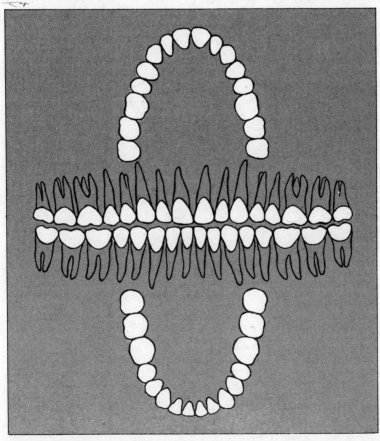

ADULT DENTITION: From left to right (top and bottom rows are identical):
L. wisdom tooth, L. 12-yr. molar, L. 6-yr. molar, two L. bicuspids, L. canine, two L.
incisors, two R. incisors, R. canine, two R. bicuspids, R. 6-yr. molar, R. 12-yr. molar,
R. wisdom tooth.

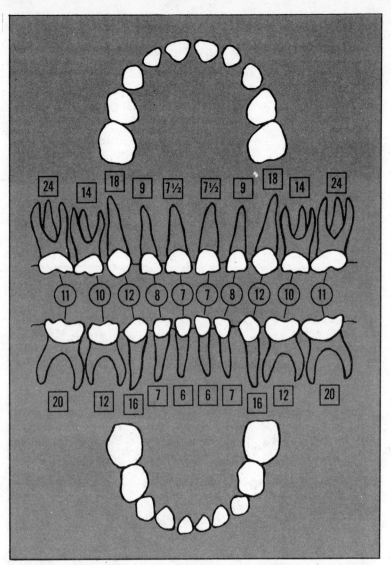

CHILDHOOD DENTITION: From left to right (top and bottom rows are identical): 2nd L. molar, 1st L. molar, L. cuspid, L. lateral incisor, L. central incisor, R. central incisor, R. lateral incisor, R. cuspid, 1st R. molar, 2nd R. molar. ☐ Average age in months at which teeth usually appear. Actual time of eruption can vary widely from the average. ○ Average age in years at which childhood teeth usually fall out. This average time can also vary widely.

of 6 and 24 months. The secondary (or permanent) dentition of 32 teeth grows in usually from about the sixth year.

The four principal types of teeth are:

Incisors (Lat. *incidere*—to cut into) total 8. Two upper central, flanked by two upper lateral with 4 lower.

Canine (Lat. *canis*—a dog) total 4. These are next to the lateral incisors and are thus the third teeth from the mid-line in each quadrant of the mouth. These are also referred to as *cuspids* (Lat. *cuspis*—a point).

Pre-Molars (Lat. *molare*—to grind) total 8. These are next in line back from the incisors, two in each quadrant. Because these have two cusps these are alternatively known as bicuspids.

Molars (see above) total 12. These are the teeth furthest back in the mouth—three in each quadrant. The upper molars often have four cusps and the lower five cusps for grinding. The third (hindermost) molars are known also as "wisdom teeth" and do not usually appear until the age of 18 to 20.

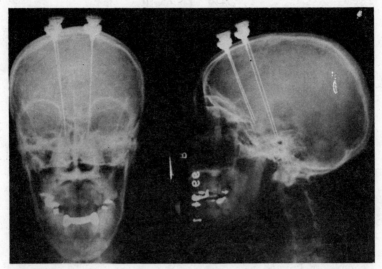

THE BRAIN: Probes inserted deep into the brain are used to locate brain tumors and diagnose and treat epilepsy.

THE HUMAN BRAIN

It is estimated that a human brain, weighing about 3 lbs., contains 10,000,000,000 nerve cells. Each of these deploys a potential 25,000 interconnections with other cells making a total of 250 trillion (2.5 × 10^{14}) permutations. Compared with this the most advanced computers are giant electronic morons.

SKIN

The skin is by far the largest single organ of the human body. It weighs about 16 per cent of the total body weight and in an average adult male has a surface area of 2,800 square inches. The three main groups into which man is divided by the color of his skin are *Leukoderms* (white-skinned), *Melanoderms* (black-skinned) and *Xanthoderms* (yellow-skinned). Pigment-producing cells in the basal layers of the epidermis are called melanoblasts (Greek *melas*—black, *blastos*—bud).

The number of cells (up to 4,000 per sq. cm.) and their size do not vary significantly in white and black skin but are more active and productive in the latter so protecting the iris and the retina against the brightness of the sun.

NORMAL PULSE RATES

	Beats per minute		Beats per minute
Embryo 5 months	156	30–35	70
6 months	154	35–40	72
7 months	150	40–45	72
8 months	142	45–50	72
9 months	145	50–55	72
Newborn (premature)	110–185	55–60	75
Newborn (full term)	135	60–65	73
2 years	110	65–70	75
4 years	105	70–75	75
6 years	95	75–80	72
8 years	90	>80	78
10 years	87	Lying down (adult)	66
15 years	83	Sitting (adult)	73
20 years	71	Standing (adult)	82
21–25	74	Sleeping (adult)	♂59 ♀65
25–30	72	Waking (adult)	♂78 ♀84

SENSE OF SMELL

According to the stereochemical theory of olfaction there are for man seven primary odors each associated with a typical shape of molecule.

1. camphoraceous — spherical molecules
2. ethereal — very small or thin molecules
3. floral — kite-shaped molecules
4. musky — disc-shaped molecules
5. peppermint — wedge-shaped molecules
6. pungent — undetermined
7. putrid — undetermined

Other smells are complexes of the above basic seven, *e.g.* almonds are a complex of 1, 3 and 5.

HUMAN GENETICS

The normal human cell has 46 chromosomes. The chromosomes are the microscopic thread-like bodies within cells which carry hereditary factors or genes. These are classified as 22 pairs of non-sex chromosomes or autosomes (one of each pair derived from the father and one from the mother) and 2 sex chromosomes or gonosomes, making 46. In a female both gonosomes are Xs, one from the father and one from the mother. In a male they are an X from the mother and a Y from the father. The X chromosome is much larger than the Y, thus women possess 4% more deoxyribonucleic acid than males. This may have a bearing on their greater longevity. The cell sometimes exhibits 47 chromosomes.

One such instance is the XXX female in which the supernumerary is an extra X. In some cases of hermaphroditism the supernumerary is a Y.

Chimpanzees, gorillas, and orang-outangs have 48 chromosomes. It has been suggested that man's emergence from the primitive man-ape population may have occurred by a process known as "reciprocal translocation." This is a mechanism whereby two dissimilar chromosomes break and two of the four dissimilar parts join with the possible net loss of one chromosome. It is possible that 47 and 46 chromosome hominoids enjoyed a bipedal advantage on forest edges over brachiating apes and thus the evolution of man began from this point.

The term genetics for the scientific study of heredity and variation in plant and animal life was invented in 1906 by Prof. William Bateson of Cambridge University, England, but the subject dates from 1866 when an Austrian monk, Johann Gregor Mendel (1822–1884), discovered the general laws of heredity.

Mendel taught in the Brno (now in Czechoslovakia) technical high school from 1854 until 1868, but never succeeded in passing the examinations for a formal license to teach. His leisure was devoted to working on experiments, openly with plants in the monastery garden, but secretly with mice. On February 8 and March 8, 1865, he delivered a paper on his work to the newly formed *Naturforschenden Verein in Brunn* (The Brno Natural History Society). The paper was published in detail in 1866 under the title *"Versuche uber Pflanzen hybriden."* It created not a single ripple among the scientists of the world until 1900, 16 years after his death. Then, three European botanists, K. E. Correns, H. de Vries and E. Eschermak von Sysenegg found that their discoveries of the general laws of genetics had already been published over a third of a century before.

The branch of genetics which fascinates most people is identifying the various dominant and recessive characteristics of their own children, and even predicting how their first or next child will look.

Color of Eyes

Dark eyes are dominant and pale or light-colored eyes recessive. Thus, if there are *all* dark eyes on one side of a family (*i.e.*, say among the husband's ascendants) then *almost all* the children will be dark-eyed regardless of having a blue-eyed mother. If, however, both parents are light-eyed, *almost all* the children will be light-eyed. Geneticists, however, always caution that occasionally legitimate brown-eyed children have been born to two blue-eyed parents. In genetics there is a saying *"Pater est semper incertus"*—the true identity of the father is always uncertain.

Hair Form

Curly or wavy hair forms are dominant.

Parentage and Ascendants	Result in Children
1. Two straight-haired parents	Almost all straight-haired
2. All curly-haired on one side	Almost all curly-haired regardless of hair form of the other side
3. Both parents curly-haired but each with some straight-haired relatives	Odds are 3:1 that children will have curly hair
4. A curly-haired parent with straight-haired relatives and the other parent straight-haired	A 50-50 chance between curly-haired and straight-haired children

Hair Color

Dark hair *tends* to be dominant and light hair recessive.

1. All dark-haired on one side	Almost all dark-haired
2. Both parents blond	Almost all children blond
3. Both parents dark-haired but each with some fair-haired relatives	Odds are 3:1 on dark-haired children
4. A dark-haired parent with light-haired relatives and the other parent fair-haired	A 50-50 chance between dark and fair hair

Note: Red hair genes are often masked by dark hair. Two red-headed parents will almost always produce red-haired children.

If all the human female eggs which produced the population of the world of close to 4,000,000,000 people were put together they would not fill an empty chicken's egg. All the sperm needed to fertilize those eggs could rest on a pin's head. Such is the miniscule world of genetics.

SEX RATIO

In the United States about 1,054 boys are born to every 1,000 girls.

At the time of the 1970 census there were 1,169 females to every 1,000 males in the U.S.S.R. In 1972 in Pakistan there were only 885 enumerated females to each 1,000 males.

THE HIPPOCRATIC OATH

A form of the following oath, attributed to Hippocrates (*c.* 460–377 B.C.), the Greek physician called the "Father of Medicine," is sworn to at some medical schools on the occasion of taking a degree.

"I swear by Apollo the healer, invoking all the gods and goddesses to be my witnesses, that I will fulfill this oath and this written covenant to the best of my ability and judgment.

"I will look upon him who shall have taught me this art even as one of my own parents. I will share my substance with him, and I will supply his necessities if he be in need. I will regard his offspring even as my own brethren, and I will teach them this art, if they would learn it, without fee or covenant. I will impart this art by precept, by lecture and by every mode of teaching, not only to my own sons but to the sons of him who has taught me, and to disciples bound by covenant and oath, according to the law of medicine.

"The regimen I adopt shall be for the benefit of the patients according to my ability and judgment, and not for their hurt or for any wrong. I will give no deadly drug to any, though it be asked of me, nor will I counsel such, and especially I will not aid a woman to procure abortion. Whatsoever house I enter, there will I go for the benefit of the sick, refraining from all wrongdoing or corruption, and especially from any act of seduction, of male or female, of bond or free. Whatsoever things I see or hear concerning the life of men, in my attendance on the sick or even apart therefrom, which ought not to be noised abroad, I will keep silence thereon, counting such things to be as sacred secrets. Pure and holy will I keep my life and my art."

Medicine and Drugs

Below is listed a selection of the most used and important drugs in medical practice. These are listed in order of the date of their introduction so that the weakness or strength of the pharmacological armory can be seen at a glance at any point in time.

2100 B.C.
> *Ethyl alcohol* (C_2H_5OH). One of the earliest drugs used to stupefy.

— B.C.
> *Marijuana* (Marihuana), derived from Indian hemp plant (*Cannabis sativa*). Prohibited by U.S. Govt. in 1937. Illegally used in cigarettes, also snuffed and swallowed. Addiction to morphine drugs is common sequel. Causes euphoria and alters perception. Effects last 4 hours. Slang names: grass, hash(ish), Mary Jane, pot, tea, and reefers. In Hindi, *bhang*.

c. 1550
> *Digitalis*, from the leaf of the foxglove (*Digitalis purpurea L.*) Myocardial stimulant, used by herbalists since *c.* 1550 and introduced into scientific medicine by William Withering (Eng.) in 1785. Still used in cardiac treatment.

DIGITALIS PURPUREA, growing here, has been used by herbalists since about 1550 as a stimulant.

1805   *Morphine* (hydrochloride is $C_{17}H_{19}NO_3HCl \cdot 3H_2O$ and the sulfate is $[C_{17}H_{19}NO_3]_2 \cdot H_2SO_4 \cdot 5H_2O$). Narcotic analgesic, an alkaloid of opium which is the dried latex from the unripe capsules of the poppy (*Papaver somniferum*). First recognized by Friedrich Sertürner (Germany) in 1805 but not used in medical practice till 1821. Not totally synthesized until 1952 by Gates and Tschadi. Usual dose 15 mg., causing euphoria and drowsiness lasting 6 hours. Addictive. Slang names: white stuff, dreamer, and Miss Emma. *Heroin* is the derivative diacetyl-morphine and is analgesically 4 to 8 times more potent than the sulfate. Causes untractable addiction, constipation, loss of appetite, and convulsions in overdose. Slang names: Harry, horse, joy powder, junk, scag, snow, stuff.

1818   *Quinine hydrochloride* ($C_{20}H_{24}N_2O_2HCl \cdot 2H_2O$). Obtained from cinchona tree bark. Separated by P. J. Pelletier and J. B. Caventou (France) 1818 to 1820. Anti-malarial use.

1819   *Atropine* ($C_{17}H_{23}NO_3$). A parasympatholytic. First isolated in 1819 by Rudolph Brandes from belladonna (*Atropa belladonna*). Related drug for motion-sickness is hyoscine.

1820   *Colchicine* ($C_{22}H_{25}NO_6$). Analgesic derived from meadow saffron (*Colchicum Autumnale*), used particularly in the treatment of gout. Isolated in 1820 by P. J. Pelletier and J. B. Caventou.

1821   *Codeine* or *methylmorphine* (phosphate is $2[C_{18}H_{12}NO_3H_3PO_4 \cdot]H_2O$). Occurs naturally in opium and is a derivative of morphine (*q.v.*). Anti-tussive, weak analgesic. Usual dose 30 mg., causing drowsiness 4 hours. Addictive. Slang name: schoolboy.

1842   *Ether*. Diethyl [$(C_2H_5)_2O$]. General anesthetic. First administered by Dr. Crawford W. Long (1815–78) in Jefferson, Georgia, on March 30, 1842, for a cystectomy.

Medicine and Drugs (continued)

1844   *Nitrous Oxide* (N_2O) (Dinitrogen Monoxide, or Laughing Gas). Anaesthetic in operations of short duration as prolonged inhalation can cause death. Discovered in 1776 by Joseph Priestley. First used as anaesthetic in 1844 by an American dentist, Horace Wells.

1846   *Glyceryl Trinitrate* (nitroglycerin, $C_3H_5N_3O_9$). Known mainly as an explosive. Used as a vasolidator in easing cardiac pains in angina pectoris. First prepared in 1846 by Ascanio Sobrero of Italy.

1847   *Chloroform.* Introduced as an anesthetic by Sir James Simpson (Scot.).

1859   *Cocaine*, from the Peruvian coca bean (*Erythroxylon coca*). First separated by Niemann. Formula established by Wöhler in 1860. Used as local anesthetic 1884. Used for local anesthesia. As stimulant drug causes mental dependence and convulsions in long run. Slang names: coke, flake, gold dust, star dust.

1867   *Phenol* (carbolic acid C_6H_5OH). Earliest germicidal disinfectant, discovered by Lister in 1867. Antiseptic and antipruritic.

1891   *Thyroid Extract.* First use as injection in treatment for Myxoedema by George Murray in 1891. The active principles are *tri-iodothyronine* and *thyroxine*.

1893   *Aspirin* (a trade name of acetylsalicylic acid, $C_9H_8O_4$). An analgesic, and the earliest antiuretic. Introduced in 1893 by Hermann Dresser.

1901   *Adrenaline* (*epinephrine*) ($C_9H_{13}NO_3$). A sympathomimetic. The active principles are secreted by the medulla of the adrenal glands of domesticated animals. A vasco-constrictor. First isolated in 1901 by J. Takamine (1854–1922) and T. B. Aldrick (*b*. 1861) and synthesized in 1904 by Friedrich Stolz (1860–1936).

1903   *Phenobarbitone* (luminal) is 5-ethyl-5-phenylbarbituric acid ($C_{12}H_{12}N_2O_3$). A hypnotic, long-acting sedative, anti-convulsant, and relieves high blood pressure. Usual dose 50–100 mg., causing drowsiness and muscular relaxation for 4 hours. Long term symptoms are addiction with severe withdrawal symptoms and convulsions. Slang names: barbs, blue devils or blue heavens, candy, peanuts, phennies, and yellow jackets. Chemical and trade names include *Seconal*.

1905   *Procaine* (novocaine) (Procainamide hydrochloride, $C_{13}H_{22}$-N_2O_2, HCl). Local anesthetic, introduced as a substitute for cocaine by Alfred Einhorn. Non-habit forming but low penetrating power.

1907   *Histamine* (β-iminoazolylethylamine). Isolated by Adolf Windus (1876–1959) and Karl Vogt (*b*. 1880). The earliest anti-histamine was 933F discovered by G. Ungar (France) *et al.* in 1937.

1912   *Acriflavine.* Introduced as an antiseptic by Paul Ehrlich.

1893   *Paracetamol* (Acetaminophen) ($C_8H_9NO_2$). First used in medicine by Joseph von Mering in 1893, but only gained popularity as an antipyretic analgesic in 1949.

1917   *Oxygen* (O). The most plentiful element in the Earth's crust. Essential to life as we know it. Discovered *c.* 1772 by the

Swede, Carl Wilhelm Scheele and independently in 1774 by Joseph Priestley. First used therapeutically by J. S. Haldane in 1917.

1921   *Ergotmetrine maleate* ($C_{19}H_{23}N_3O_2$, $C_4H_4O_4$). Used as a uterine stimulant. First isolated by K. Spiro and A. Stoll (Germany) in 1921. Ergot in rye grain infected with the fungus *Claviceps purpurea*.

1921   *Insulin*, the specific antidiabetic principle from the mammalian pancreas. Isolated by Sir Frederick Banting (1891–1941) and Dr. C. H. Best (*b.* 1899) at Toronto, Canada, in 1921. First synthesized in 1964.

1929   *Progesterone* ($C_{21}H_{30}O_2$). Female steroid hormone secreted by ovary following ovulation to prepare uterus for, and to maintain pregnancy. Isolated by G. Corner and W. Allen in 1929. Related compounds are used with estrogen, or alone, in oral contraceptives.

1929   *Testosterone* ($C_{19}H_{28}O_2$). Androgenic (masculanizing) hormone. First obtained in 1929 by C. Moore, T. Gallagher and F. Koch. Related anabolic (muscle-building) steroids used by participants in sporting activities.

1930   *Pentobarbitone sodium* (nembutal) ($C_{11}H_{17}N_2NaO_3$). Hypnotic; sedative. See *Phenobarbitone* (above).

1930   *Mepacrine* (or *quinacrine* or *atebrin*). Now replaced by chloroquine. Antimalarial.

1933   *Adrenocorticotropic hormone* (ACTH). First isolated by J. B. Collip (*b.* 1892) *et al.* Active against arthritis.

1935   *Pentothal* (thiopentone sodium, $C_{11}H_{18}N_2O_2S$ + Na). Intravenous anesthetic.

1935   *Tubocurarine*. Crystalline alkaloid isolated from curare in 1935 by Harold King, used as a skeletal-muscle relaxant.

1936   *Oestradiol* ($C_{25}H_{28}O_3$). The principal estrogenic hormone, isolated by D. MacCorquodale in 1936.

1937   *Dapsone* ($C_{12}H_{12}N_2O_2S$). Bacteriostatic drug, effects in treatment of leprosy noted in 1937.

1938   *Sulfanilamide*. The sulfa drug prototype, Prontosil Red, was discovered in 1935 by G. Domagk (1899–1964). The most used early sulfa drug was sulfapyridine (May and Baker 693), $C_{11}H_{14}N_3O_2S$ from 1937 (Dr. Arthur Ewins).

1938   *Phenytoin* ($C_{15}H_{12}N_2O_2$). Anticonvulsant introduced in 1938 by Merritt and Pulman for all types of epilepsy except absence seizures.

1939   *D.D.T.* (dichloro-diphenyl-trichloro-ethane). A powerful insecticide developed by Dr. Paul Müller which has vastly lowered the malarial death rate and increased world population.

1939   *Pethidine hydrochloride* ($C_{15}H_{21}NO_2$, HCl). A narcotic analgesic particularly for childbirth. Introduced 1939 from Hoechst. Synthesized by Eisleb and Schaumann.

1940   *Penicillin* (penicillin G, the benzyl derivative, $C_{16}H_{17}N_2Na$ [or K]O_4S). Antibiotic. Discovered in 1928 by Sir Alexander Fleming (1881–1955) by the chance contamination of a petri dish at St. Mary's Hospital, London. First concentrated in 1940 by Howard (later Lord) Florey (1898–1968) and E. B. Chain (*b* 1906.) Not identified as *Penicillium notatum* until 1930. Penicillin G introduced, 1946.

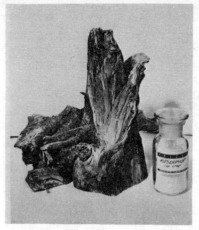

TRANQUILIZER IN THE RAW: *Rauwolfia heterophylla*, a small, woody shrub found in the tropic and semi-tropic regions of the world, is the natural source of reserpine, which is used as a tranquilizer.

c. 1943   *Dimercaprol* (*BAL*) (Formerly British Anti-Lewisite) ($C_3H_8OS_2$). Developed during the war by L. Stocken and R. Thompson, to combat lethal war gas, lewisite. Later uses discovered as antidote to poisoning by arsenic, gold or mercury.

1943   *LSD-25*. Dextro-lysergic acid diethylamide. A hallucinogen, discovered by Albert Hoffman (Switzerland) in April 1943. Now has no therapeutic use. May intensify existing psychosis but not proved to cause physical dependence. Slang names: acid, big D, sugar, and trips.

1944   *Amphetamine* (commercial name for the sulfate is benzedrine). Dextro-amphetamine is marketed as Dexedrine. A fatigue-inhibiting mildly addictive synthetic drug. Usual medical dose 2½–5 mg., causing increased activity and alertness for 4 hours but, in the long run, delusions, hallucinations, and mental dependence. Other chemical and trade names include *Preludin*, *Dexogyn*, and *Methedrine*. Slang names: bennies, co-pilots, dexies, hearts (purple), lid poppers, wake-ups, speed.

1944   *Mepyramine* (*Pyrilamine*). First acceptable antihistamine.

1944   *Streptomycin* (sulfate is $[C_{21}H_{39}N_7O_{12}]_2, 3H_2SO_4$). An antibiotic discovered by S. A. Waksman (Russian born, U.S.). Important in treatment of tuberculosis.

c. 1944   *Paludrine* (proguanil hydrochloride). An anti-malarial drug.

1947   *Chloramphenicol* ($C_{11}H_{12}Cl_2N_2O_5$). An antibiotic from *Streptomyces venezuelae* used for treatment of typhoid. First isolated by Buckholder (U.S.) in 1947 and first synthesized in 1949.

1948   *Aureomycin* (*Chlortetracycline*) *Hydrochloride* ($C_{22}H_{24}N_2O_8$, HCl). An antibiotic first isolated in 1948 at Pearl River, N.Y., by Dr. Benjamin M. Duggar.

1948   *Impramine* ($C_{11}H_{24}N_2$). A dibenzazepine derivative, synthesized by Häfliger in 1948. An antidepressant.

1949   *Cortisone acetate* ($C_{23}H_{30}O_6$). A steroid hormone from adrenal cortical extracts so named in 1939. First used in treatment of rheumatoid arthritis in 1949. Use with vitamin E by Kira and Morotomi (Japan) found to eliminate some serious side effects in March 1967.

1951   *Halothane* ($C_2HBrClF_3$). General anesthetic first synthesized in 1951 by Suckling.

Medicine and Drugs (continued)

1952   *Chlorpromazine* ($C_{17}H_{19}ClN_2S$). Potent synthetic tranquillizer first synthesized by Charpentier in 1952. Acts selectively upon higher centers in brain as a central nervous system depressant.

1952   *Isoniazide* (Isotonic Acid Hydrazide-INH) ($C_6H_7N_3O$). Use in the treatment of tuberculosis reported on by Edward Robitzek in 1952.

1954   *Methyldopa.* Use in treatment of hypertension. Effects first noted in 1954 by Sourkes.

1954   *Reserpine* ($C_{33}H_{40}N_2O_9$). Tranquillizer from Rauwolfia, a genus of plant in the dogbane family, used in treatment of high blood pressure and hypertension. Effects noted in modern times by Kline in 1954.

1955   *Oral Contraceptives.* The first reported field studies of a pill containing synthetic hormones that prevent ovulation were those by Pincus using Enovid in 1955, in Puerto Rico.

1955   *Metronidazole* ($C_6H_9N_3O_3$). Based on discovery of Azomycin in 1955 by Nakamura. Used in treatment of trichomoniasis, and other protozoal infections.

1956   *Amphotericin.* An antifungal antibiotic used typically. Elucidated in 1956 by Vandeputte *et al.*

1957   *Interferon.* A group of proteins produced on virus-infected cells. They inhibit the multiplication of viruses.

c. 1960   *Tolbutamide* ($C_{12}H_{18}N_2O_3S$). Reduces blood sugar level in diabetics.

1960   *Chlordiazepoxide* (Librium). Tranquillizer for treatment of anxiety and tension states, convulsive states and neuromuscular and cardio-vascular disorders. Effects first noted in 1960 by Randall *et al.* Related drug *Diazepam* (Valium) also used in anxiety states and as pre-medication for surgery.

c. 1960   *Frusemide* ($C_{12}H_{11}ClN_2O_5S$). A diuretic.

1961   *Thiabendazole* ($C_{10}H_7N_3S$). Efficacy in dealing with intestinal tract infestations noted by Brown *et al* in 1961. Used to treat various worm infections.

1962–3   *Clofibrate* ($C_{12}H_{15}ClO_3$). Lowers the fatty acid and cholesterol levels in the blood. Effects noted in 1962–3 by Thorp and Waring.

1963   *Allopurinol* ($C_5H_4N_4O$). Used in treatment of gout, it slows rate at which body forms uric acid. Reported on by Hitchings, Elion *et al* in 1963.

1963   *Cephalosporin*, antibiotic discovered in 1945 in Sardinia by Prof. Brotzu. First utilized in 1963. Developed by Howard (later Lord) Florey and Glaxo Laboratories.

1964   *Tolnaftate*, an anti-fungal agent announced October 1964. Highly effective against epidermiphytosis (athlete's foot) which infected some 40% of adult males in U.S.

1965   *Niridazole.* Disovered 1961 (announced December 1965) by Dr. Paul Schmidt of CIBA, Basle. Treatment of debilitating liver-infestation disease bilharzia (250 million world incidence).

1966   *Pralidoxime.* Antidote for poisoning by cholinesterase inhibitors, particularly organophosphorus compounds, which are used as insecticides and "nerve gases."

1966   *Trometamol* (Tromethamine). A diuretic used to treat acidosis, for example during organ transplantation.

1967   *Nitrazepam* (Trade name—Mogadon) ($C_{15}H_{11}N_3O_3$). Tranquillizer and hypnotic.

Vitamins

Vitamins	Deficiency Symptoms	Natural Sources	Requisite Adult Daily Dosage
A axerophthol	nyctalopia (night blindness), xerophthalmia, cornification of the epithelial tissue, stunting of growth	dairy produce, fish-liver oils, carotene	1,500 mg (5,000 iu) mixed carotene and Vitamin A alcohol; or 2,250 mg (7,500 iu) carotene
B_1 aneurin or thiamine	beriberi, impaired metabolism of carbohydrate	meat, yeast, eggs, cereal germ, pulses	1 mg (3 + iu)
B_2 riboflavin	ariboflavinosis, cheilitis, glossitis, angular stomatitis	yeast, eggs, cereal germ, pulses, milk, cheese	1.8 mg (6 iu)
B_6 pyridoxal, pyridoxamine and pyridoxine	severe reddening and erosion of the skin, convulsions in infants	rice, corn and yeast	
B_{12} cyanocobalamin	inability to absorb, causes pernicious anemia (found in vegans)	meat, liver, kidney	Total requirement < 3 mg
C ascorbic acid	scurvy, first controlled in 1928	fruit and vegetables	30 mg (100 iu)
D calciferol	rickets in infants, osteomalacia in adults	fish-liver oils, egg yolk, milk, butter, cheese	150 mg (500 iu) (unless synthesized from sunshine)
K phylloquinone	blood fails to clot in bleeding, used against jaundice since 1934	normally synthesized in the intestine	
M folacin (folic acid or pteroylglutamic acid)	inability to absorb causes macrocytic anemia	yeast, liver, cheese, fruit, vegetables	c. 100 mg (300 iu)
PP (pellagra preventive) nicotinic acid (niacin)	pellagra, intestinal disorders, dermatitis, mental disturbance	yeast, meat, liver, cereal germ	10 mg (30 iu)

mg = microgram
iu = international unit

354

Medicine and Drugs (continued)

1967 *Laevo-dopa* (L-Dopa) ($C_9H_{11}NO_4$). Naturally occurring amino acid reported on by Cotzias and others in 1967. Used in treatment of Parkinson's Disease.

1968 *Propanolol* (A β-adrenergic blocking drug) ($C_{16}H_{21}NO_2$). Affects rate and rhythm of the heart and may be helpful in angina pectoris.

1969 *Salbutamol.* Useful in asthma for its selective bronchodilator effects, whereas earlier unselective drugs were more dangerous in elevating the heart rate.

1976 *Cimetidine.* Pioneer antihistamine which prevents excessive acid secretion in the stomach, often the cause of ulcers.

Notes to Vitamin table

The term Vitamin A_2 has been used for axerophthol from fresh-water fish-liver oils.

Vitamin B_3 is a name given to pantothenic acid; B_4 to a mixture of arginine, glycine and cystine; B_5 is now presumed to be identical to B_6 ($C_8H_{11}O_3N$), B_7, B_8 and B_9 never existed.

B_{10} and B_{11} (variously known as Vitamin T or torulitine) now known to be a mixture of Vitamins B_{12} and M.

Vitamin B_{12} was first isolated by Glaxo Laboratories in May, 1948. Its ultra-complex structure ($C_{53}H_{86}O_{13}N_{14}$ PCo) long defined synthesis. It is used to combat pernicious anemia.

Vitamin D, commercially synthesized by ultra-violet irradiation of ergosterol, is sometimes termed Vitamin D_2, and was first manufactured at Evansville, Indiana, in 1927.

Vitamin D, naturally formed subcutaneously by sunlight, is sometimes termed Vitamin D_3, formula is $C_{28}H_{44}O$.

A deficiency of a substance termed Vitamin E was believed to contribute to human infertility. First reported in 1922, first isolated (as α Tocopherol) in 1935.

Vitamin F is an obsolete name for unsaturated fatty acids (linoleic, linolenic and arachidonic), a deficiency of which causes no known symptoms.

Vitamin H, or biotin, is not now regarded as a human vitamin.

Vitamin L was once regarded as essential to proper human lactation.

Vitamin P (citrin or rutin) is no longer considered a dietary essential.

Vitamin T or torulitine, see Vitamin B_{12} above.

Medical Specialties

There are in medicine a great number of specialties. It is possible to have Departments of Neurology, Pediatrics and Pediatric-Neurology in the same hospital. This list provides an explanation of medical departments.

Allergy—reaction of a patient to an outside substance, e.g. pollen or penicillin, producing symptoms which may vary between being inconvenient e.g. hay fever or rashes to fatal, e.g. asthma.

Anesthetics—the skill of putting a patient to sleep with drugs.

Anatomy—the study of the structure of the body.

Anthropology—the study of man in his environment.

Apothecary—a pharmacist or, in its old-fashioned sense, a general practitioner was once described as an apothecary.

Audiology—the assessment of hearing.

Aurology—the study of ear disease.

Bacteriology—the study of bacterial infections. This usually includes viruses as well.

Biochemistry—the study of the variation of salts and chemicals on the body.

Bio-engineering—the study of the mechanical workings of the body, particularly with reference to artificial limbs and powered appliances which the body can use.

Biophysics—the study of electrical impulses from the body. This can be seen with assessment of muscle disease etc.

Cardiology—the study of heart disease.

Community medicine—the prevention of the spread of disease and the increase of physical and mental well being within a community.

Cryo-surgery—the use of freezing techniques in surgery.

Cytogenetics—the understanding of the particles within a cell which help to reproduce the same type of being again.

Cytology—the microscopic study of body cells.

Dentistry—the treatment and extraction of teeth.

Dermatology—the treatment of skin diseases.

Diabetics—the treatment of diabetes.

Embryology—the study of the growth of the baby from the moment of conception to about the 20th week.

Endocrinology—the study of the diseases of the glands which produce hormones.

E.N.T. *see* Otorhinolaryngology.

Entomology—the study of insects, moths, with particular reference to their transmission of disease.

Epidemiology—the study of epidemics and the way that diseases travel from one person to another.

Forensic medicine—the study of injury and disease caused by criminal activity and the detection of crime by medical knowledge.

Gastro-enterology—the study of stomach and intestinal diseases.

Genetics—the study of inherited characteristics, disease and malformations.

Genito-urinary disease—the study of diseases of the sexual and urine-producing organs.

Geriatrics—the study of diseases and condition of elderly people.

Gerontology—the study of diseases of elderly people and in particular the study of the ageing process.

Gynecology—the study of diseases of women.

Hematology—the study of blood diseases.

Histochemistry—the study of the chemical environment of the body cells.

Histology—the microscopic study of cells.

Histopathology—the microscopic study of diseased or abnormal cells.

Homeopathy—is a form of treatment by administering minute doses which in larger doses would reproduce the symptoms of the disease that is being treated. The theory is that the body is thereby stimulated into coping with the problem by itself.

Immunology—the study of the way the body reacts to outside harmful diseases and influences, e.g. the production of body proteins to overcome such diseases as diphtheria or the rejection of foreign substances like transplanted kidneys.

Laryngology—the study of throat diseases.

Metabolic disease—diseases of the interior workings of the body, e.g. disorders of calcium absorption etc., thyroid disease or adrenal gland disease.

Microbiology—the study of the workings of cells.

Nephrology—the study of kidney disease.

Neurology—the study of a wide range of diseases of the brain or nervous system.

Neurosurgery—operations on the brain or nervous system.

Nuclear medicine—treatment of diseases with radio-active substances.

Obstetrics—the care of the pregnant mother and the delivery of the child.

Oncology—study of cancer.

Ophthalmology—the study of diseases of the eye.

Optician—the measurement of disorders of the lens of the eye done by a medically unqualified but trained practitioner so that spectacles can be given to correct the disorder.

Orthodontology—a dental approach to producing teeth that are straight.

Orthopedics—fractures and bone diseases.

Orthoptics—medically unqualified but trained practitioner treatment of squints of the eye.

Orthotist—an orthopedic appliance technician.

Otology—the study of diseases of the ear.

Otorhinolaryngology—the study of diseases of the ear, nose and throat, often referred to as E.N.T.

Pediatrics—diseases of children.

Parisitology—the study of infections of the body by worms.

Pathology—the study of dead disease by *post mortem* examination either under the microscope or the whole organ.

Pharmacology—the study of the use of drugs in relation to medicine.

Physical Medicine—the treatment of damaged parts of the body with exercises, electrical treatments etc. or the preparation of the body for surgery, e.g. breathing exercises and leg exercises.

Medical Specialties (continued)

Physiology—the study and understanding of the normal workings of the body.

Physiotherapist—a trained person who works in the physical medicine department.

Plastic surgery—the reconstruction and alteration of damaged or normal parts of the body.

Proctology—the study of diseases of the rectum or back passage.

Prosthetics—the making of artificial limbs and appliances.

Psychiatry—the study and treatment of mental disease.

Psycho-analysis—the investigation of the formation of mental illness by long-term repeated discussion.

Psychology—the study of the mind with particular reference to the measurement of intellectual activity.

Psychotherapy—treatment of mental disorder.

Radiobiology—the treatment or investigation of disease using radio-active substances.

Radiography—the taking of X-rays.

Radiology—the study of X-rays.

Radiotherapy—the treatment of disease with X-rays.

Renal diseases—the diseases of the kidney or urinary tract.

Rheumatology—the study of diseases of muscles and joints.

Rhinology—the study of diseases of the nose.

Therapeutics—curative medicine, the healing of physical and/or mental disorder.

Thoracic surgery—surgery on the chest or heart.

Toxicology—the understanding and analysis of poisons.

Urology—the study of diseases of the kidney or urinary tract.

Vascular disease—diseases of the blood vessels.

Venereology—the study of sexually transmitted disease.

Virology—the study of virus diseases.

Inflammatory Conditions

The suffix -itis is the feminine adjectival form of the Greek *-ites*, meaning connected with. Originally, for example, carditis was termed *carditis nosus*, meaning the disease connected with the heart. Soon the *nosus* was dropped and the -itis suffix was used to indicate, more narrowly, an inflammation of a part of the body.

adenitis—lymphatic glands
appendicitis—vermiform appendix
arthritis—joints
blepharitis—eyelid
bronchitis—bronchial tubes
bursitis—bursa
carditis—heart
cephalitis—brain (not now used)
cerebritis—brain (rare)
cervicitis—neck of the uterus
cheilitis—lip
cholecystitis—gall bladder
chondritis—cartilage
colitis—colon
conjunctivitis—conjunctiva
coxitis—hip joint
cystitis—bladder
dermatitis—skin
diaphragmatitis—diaphragm
diverticulitis—diverticulae of colon
duodenitis—duodenum
encephalitis—brain
encystitis—"an encysted tumor"
endocarditis—endocardium
enteritis—bowels
enterocolitis—colon and small intestine
epididymitis—epididymis
esophagitis—esophagus
fibrositis—fibrous tissues
gastritis—stomach
gingivitis—gums
glossitis—tongue
gnathitis—upper jaw or cheek
hepatitis—liver
hyalitis—vitreous humor of the eye
hysteritis—uterus
iritis—iris
keratitis—cornea
laminitis—part of a vertebra
laryngitis—larynx
mastitis—the breast (female)
meningitis—meninges
meningomyelitis—meninges and spinal cord
mephitis—a noxious emanation (especially from the earth)
mesenteritis—mesentery

metritis—uterus
myelitis—spinal cord
myelomeningitis—(see meningomyelitis)
myocarditis—myocardium
myositis—muscle
nephritis—kidneys
neuritis—nerves
omphalitis—navel
oophoritis—ovary
ophthalmitis—whole eye
orchitis—testes
osteitis—bone
otitis—ear
ovaritis—ovaries
pancreatitis—pancreas
parotitis—parotid glands (*e.g.* mumps)
pericarditis—pericardium
periodontitis—jaw (part around the tooth)
periostitis—periosteum
peritonitis—peritoneum (or of the bowels)
perityphlitis—tissue surrounding the caecum
pharyngitis—pharynx
phlebitis—vein
phrenitis—brain (rare)
pleuritis—pleura
pneumonitis—lungs
poliomyelitis—inflammation of gray matter of spinal cord (or paralysis due to this)
pyelitis—pelvis of the kidney
rachitis—spine
rectitis—rectum
retinitis—retina
rhinitis—nose
salpingitis—salpinx
sclerotitis—sclerotic
scrotitis—scrotum
sinusitis—sinus
sphenoiditis—air cavity in the sphenoid bone
splenitis—spleen
spondylitis—vertebrae
stomatitis—mouth
synovitis—synovial membrane
tonsillitis—tonsils

Inflammatory Conditions (continued)

tracheitis—trachea
tympanitis—ear-drum
typhilitis—caecum
ulitis—gums
ureteritis—ureter
urethritis—urethra
uteritis—womb
vaginitis—vagina
vulvitis—vulva

---

appendix (vermiform)—
  appendicitis
bladder—cystitis
bone—osteitis
bowels—enteritis
bowels—peritonitis
brain—encephalitis
brain (not now used)—cephalitis
brain (rare)—cerebritis
brain (rare)—phrenitis
breast (female)—mastitis
bronchial tubes—bronchitis
bursa—bursitis
caecum—typhlitis
caecum (tissue surrounding)—
  perityphlitis
cartilage—chondritis
cheek or upper jaw—gnathitis
colon—colitis
colon (diverticulae of)—
  diverticulitis
colon (and small intestine)—
  enterocolitis
conjunctiva—conjunctivitis
cornea—keratitis
diaphragm—diaphragmatitis
duodenum—duodenitis
ear—otitis
eardrum—tympanitis
endocardium—endocarditis
epididymis—epididymitis
esophagus—esophagitis
eye (vitreous humor of)—hyalitis
eye (whole)—ophthalmitis
eyelid—blepharitis
gall bladder—cholecystitis
gums—gingivitis
gums—ulitis
heart—carditis
hip joint—coxitis
iris—iritis
jaw (upper)—gnathitis
jaw (part around the tooth)—
  periodontitis
joints—arthritis
kidney (pelvis)—pyelitis
kidneys—nephritis

larynx—laryngitis
lip—cheilitis
liver—hepatitis
lungs—pneumonitis
lymphatic glands—adenitis
meninges—meningitis
meninges—meningomyelitis
meninges—myelomeningitis
mesentery—mesenteritis
mouth—stomatitis
muscle—myositis
myocardium—myocarditis
naval—omphalitis
nerves—neuritis
nose—rhinitis
ovary (ovaries)—oophoritis
ovary (ovaries)—ovaritis
pancreas—pancreatitis
parotid glands (*e.g.* mumps)—
  parotitis
pericardium—pericarditis
periosteum—periostitis
peritoneum—peritonitis
pharynx—pharyngitis
pleura—pleuritis
rectum—rectitis
retina—retinitis
salpinx—salpingitis
sclerotic—sclerotitis
scrotum—scrotitis
sinus—sinusitis
skin—dermatitis
sphenoid bone (in the air cavity)
  —sphenoiditis
spinal cord—meningomyelitis
spinal cord—myelitis
spinal cord (inflammation of grey
  matter, or paralysis due to this)
  —poliomyelitis
spine—rachitis
spleen—splenitis
stomach—gastritis
synovial membrane—synovitis
testes—orchitis
tissues (fibrous)—fibrositis
tongue—glossitis
tonsils—tonsillitis
trachea—tracheitis
tumor (encysted)—encystitis
ureter—ureteritis
urethra—urethritis
uterus (neck of)—cervicitis
uterus—hysteritis
uterus—metritis
vagina—vaginitis
vein—phlebitis
vertebra—spondylitis
vertebra (part of)—laminitis
vulva—vulvitis
womb—uteritis

Communicable Diseases

Chicken Pox (or Varicella)

Incubation period: 13–17 days. Communicable 1 day before and 6 days after onset. Age group 2–6 most susceptible. In urban areas 70 per cent have had disease by 15 years. Caused by the filtrable virus *Briareus varicellae*. Symptoms: slight fever (up to 102° F.), rash of raised red papules, which become in 12–24 hours tense vesicles and in another 36 hours turn opalescent. During fourth day they shrivel to scabs. Treatment: isolation, 3–4 days in bed, light diet, prevention from scratching, which would lead to scarring and possibly ulceration. First identified by G. F. Ingrassia (Italy) in 1553.

Cholera, Asiatic

Incubation period: from under 24 hours to a maximum of 5 days. Communicable up to 14 days from onset. Caused by the intestinal infection of the bacillus *Vibrio cholerae* first isolated by R. Koch (Germany) in 1883. Symptoms: abrupt onset with purging diarrhea followed by vomiting, exhaustive retching, cramps and prostration (2–12 hours), cyanosis, low blood pressure, apathy and circulatory failure. Mortality: 40–60 per cent (untreated), 10–20 per cent (treated). Treatment: intravenous administration of alkaline hypotonic saline solutions, atropene, pitressin. Also use of sulphaguanidine. Earliest description: J. Bontius in 1642. First pandemic began in India in 1817. Arrived Eng. Oct., 1831 (22,000 d.); further epidemics 1848–49 (53,300 d.) and 1853–54. Died out by 1866. Still endemic in India and E. Pakistan.

Common Cold (or Coryza)

Incubation period: usually about 48 hours (some strains up to 4 days). Caused by a virus, *Tarpeia premens*, 0.05μ (half-millionth inch) in diameter which is unaffected by antibiotics. Symptoms: sneezing, nasal discharge and stuffiness and in more severe cases headaches, muscular pain. Treatment: warm temperature, rest in more severe cases with measures to relieve symptoms. Colds afflict 75 per cent of the population of N. America and Europe annually and 25 per cent have 4 or more colds per annum. The loss to the U.S. economy has been put at $3 billion per annum.

Dengue Fever

Incubation period: 4–10 days. Caught from mosquito bite (usually *Aedes aegypti*) which transmits the filterable virus *Sabinia ashburnii*. Symptoms: chills, excruciating pain in the joints, loins and behind the eyeballs, facial puffiness, high pulse and a fever (103–104° F.) lasting 4–7 days. Convalescence is very slow and unsteady. Mortality is very low. Treatment: no specific therapy but the relief of symptoms. D.D.T. has proved a fundamental preventative. Earliest description by D. Bylon (Netherlands) in Java in 1779.

Diphtheria

Incubation period: usually 2–5 days, occasionally longer. Communicable—rarely beyond four weeks. An acute febrile infection. The agent *Corynebacterium diphtheriae* was first isolated by E. Klebs in 1883. Symptoms: sore throat, obstruction of the layrnx. First described by Aretaeus (?81–138 A.D.). Recorded in Plymouth, England, 1751, wave in 1855 and 1859 (9,600 died). Anti-toxin introduced 1895, prophylactic 1913.

Communicable Diseases (continued)

Dysentery, Bacillary (Shigellosis)
Incubation period: 1–7 days, usually less than four. Susceptibility: general but disease is more common and more severe in children. Caused by various kinds of the genus *Shigella* (dysentery bacillus), *Shigella sonnei*. Bacillus discovered by K. Shiga (Japan) in 1898. Symptoms: diarrhea, colic and tenesmus. Treatment: isolation (if illness acute); tetracyclines or chloramphenicol.

German Measles (Rubella)
Incubation period: 14–21 days, usually 14–18. Susceptibility: general among young children. Cause: virus *Morbillifex embryorum*. First described by Wagner (Germany) in 1829. Symptoms: mild fever, pink rash spreading from above down the body and fades the same way. Treatment: isolation (especially from women in the first 3 months of pregnancy).

Hepatitis, Infectious (Epidemic Hepatitis, Epidemic Jaundice or Catarrhal Jaundice)
Incubation period: generally 25 days but can be 10–40 days. Disease is most common among children and young adults. Caused by virus *Reedella trigenta*. Symptoms: fever, anorexia, nausea, malaise, abdominal discomfort, followed by yellowing. The classical description of interstitial hepatitis was by G. Hayem (France) in 1874.

Impetigo Contagiosa
Incubation period: 2–5 days. Common among children in conditions of overcrowding. Caused by *Staphylococcus aureus*. Symptoms: an infection of the skin causing vesicular lesions which later become crusted sero-purulent plaques, most commonly of the face and hands. Treatment: prompt isolation of infected infants until lesions heal; antibiotics. The classical description was by W. T. Fox (Eng.) in 1864.

Influenza
Incubation period: usually 24 to 72 hours. Communicable: from briefly before clinical onset to seven days thereafter. Caused by the virus *Tarpeia taylorii*, first isolated by Andrews, Laidlaw and Wilson Smith in 1933. Types include A (1934), A1 (1947), A2 (1957, Asian strain) and two varieties B and C, so far known only in localized outbreaks. Symptoms: abrupt onset, fever up to six days, chills, aches (back and leg pains) and general malaise with symptoms of coryza (see above). First described in Eng. in 1510. Earliest use of the word was by John Huxham in 1750. Highly fatal pandemics termed Russian Flu 1889–92 and one termed Spanish Flu April–November 1918 (deaths estimated at 21.6 million) have occurred. Pandemic of influenza A2, termed Asian Flu, occurred in 1957–58.

Leprosy
Incubation period: undetermined but prolonged from a few months to several years. A chronic wasting disease caused by the bacillus *Mycobacterium leprae* first identified by G. H. A. Hansen in 1871. Disease first described by Aretaeus *c.* 120 A.D. Symptoms: skin lesions, anesthia of peripheral nerves, muscular weakness, paralysis and trophic changes in muscle and bone. Treatment: Sulphone therapy. Other drugs under evaluation, notably streptomycin. Estimated incidence now four million. Low endemicity in Europe (Greece and Spain only). Probably the least infectious of all communicable diseases.

Malaria

Incubation period: 12 days (falciparum malaria); up to 30 days (quartum malaria). Some strains of vivax malaria have a delay of 10 months. A disease caused by *Plasmodium falciporum, P. malariae, P. ovale,* or *P. vivax.* Protozoa isolated by C. A. L. Laveran (France) in 1880. Earliest extensive account was by A. v. d. Spieghel in 1624. Transmission by female *Anopheles* mosquito proved by Sir Ronald Ross (Scot.) in 1895. Symptoms: shaky chill, high fever, headache, nausea, profuse sweating. Cyclical paroxysms sometimes over a month. Fatality rarely above 10 per cent (untreated), $\frac{1}{2}$ per cent (treated). Treatment: Choroquine diphosphate, mepacrine methane sulphonate intramuscularly. Incidence much reduced by D.D.T. insecticide.

Measles (Rubeola)

Incubation period: 10 days to onset or 14 days to appearance of rash. Communicable from 4 days before rash to 5 days after. An acute viral disease caused by the virus *Morbillifex morbillorum.* Symptoms: catarrhal symptoms, fever, blotchy red rash on third to fourth day. Incidence: 80–90 per cent of persons surviving to 20 years. Recorded in London, 1670.

Meningitis (Cerebrospinal Fever)

Incubation period: 2–10 days, commonly 3–4 days. An acute bacterial infection by *Neisseria meningitidis,* isolated by A. Weichelbaum in 1887. Symptoms: sudden fever, intense headache, vomiting, meningeal inflammation, sometimes delirium. Treatment: Sulphadiazine with proper hydration, penicillin, etc. Fatality thus reduced from 40–50 per cent to under 5 per cent. Recorded in Geneva in 1805; in Great Britain 1939–43 (34,700 cases).

Mumps (Infectious Parotitis)

Incubation period: 12–26 days, commonly 18 days. Communicable 7 days before and up to 9 days after distinctive symptoms. An acute viral infection from *Rubula inflans.* First isolated in 1934. Earliest modern description by R. Hamilton (G.B.) in 1773. Symptoms: fever and swelling of the salivary glands (usually the parotid, hence its alternative name). Involvement of ovaries or testicles occurs in patients past puberty.

Paratyphoid

Incubation period: 1–3 weeks.

Transmission, diagnosis, clinical course, pathology, and prophylaxis are all similar to typhoid (*q.v.*). The disease was first described by Emile Achard in 1896.

The organisms responsible are *Salmonella paratyphi* (paratyphoid A), *S. schottmülleri* (paratyphoid B) and *S. hirschfeldii* for the Type C, which is mainly limited to man. Salmonella is named after Dr. Daniel E. Salmon (1850–1914). Mild infection requires only symptomatic treatment but severe infection requires treatment as for the much rarer typhoid.

Plague

Incubation $1\frac{1}{2}$–7 days (bubonic), $2\frac{1}{2}$–5 days (pneumonic). Communicability: the pneumonic form is intensely infectious. A severe disease caused by the bite of the rat flea (usually *Xenopsylla cheopis*) infected with the bacillus *Pasteurella pestis.* Symptoms: severe toxemia, raging fever, fall in blood pressure, rapid pulse, mental confusion, prostration, delirium and coma; intense pain in the groin, neck or armpit with swelling of the lymph nodes and the appearance of bubo. Untreated fatality up to 50 per cent (bubonic), over 95 per cent (pneumonic). Modern treatment: Streptomycin and chloramphenicol with penicillin for secondary pneumonia. The great pandemics have been those of 542–43 A.D., the Black Death of 1347–51 (an estimated 75 million deaths) and 1894.

Communicable Diseases (continued)

Pneumonia

There are three main forms (*a*) acute lobar, (*b*) bacterial, (*c*) virus. Incubation period: believed to be 1–3 days for *a* and *b* but 7–21 (commonly 12) for *c*. An acute infection caused by: in *a*—*Diplococcus pneumoniae* (types I to XXXII) in *b*—*Streptococcus pyogenes, Klebsiella, pneumoniae, Haemophilus influenzae* or *Staphylococcus aureus*; in *c*—by viruses as yet unisolated. Symptoms: onset with chill, then fever, chest pains, coughing, bronchial or lobar inflammation. Fatality in *a* formerly as high as 40 per cent now vastly reduced by intramuscular penicillin injection and oral penicillin G. In some forms of *b* and *c* tetracyclines and chloramphenicol also used.

Poliomyelitis (Infantile Paralysis)

Incubation period: 3–21 days, usually 7–12. An acute viral illness caused by *Legio debilitans* first isolated in 1908 by Landsteiner and E. Popper. First described by M. Underwood (Eng.) 1789. Three types of virus now distinguished. Symptoms: fever, malaise, headache, stiffness of neck and back. Paralysis often of lower extremities in severer cases. Incidence greater (though now less markedly) among 1–16 year age group. Preventative measures include active immunization with formalinized vaccine by inoculation in 3 injections with the first and second at a four-week interval and a third some 7 months later.

Rabies (Hydrophobia)

Incubation, depending on laceration, usually 2–6 weeks. An almost invariably fatal disease contracted from the saliva of biting mammals which are rabid (infected with *Formido inexorabilis*), *viz.* bat, cat, dog, fox or wolf. Symptoms: headache, fever, malaise, paralysis, inability to drink, delirium, convulsions, and death from respiratory paralysis usually in 2–6 days.

Scarlet Fever (Streptococcal Pharyngitis with rash or Scarlatina)

Incubation period: usually 2–5 days. Communicable normally for about 10 days (penicillin treatment can reduce this to 24 hours) but in some untreated cases, patients can spread infection for months. Carrier state is well known. A streptococcal infection caused by *Streptococcus pyogenes*. Symptoms: fever, sore throat, strawberry tongue, exudative tonsillitis (if present), rash desquamation. Fatality varies from 3 to 50 per 1,000 in different countries, 5–9 year group most affected. First described by G. F. Ingrassia (Italy) in 1553.

Smallpox (Variola major)

Incubation period: 7–16 (commonly 12) days. Communicable until the disappearance of scabs. A virus (*Briareus variolae*) infection. Symptoms: sudden fever, chills, head and back aches, prostration continuing for 3–4 days, a rash progressing from macule, papule, vesicle to pustule, forming crusts and scabs which drop off in the third week. First described in *c*. 910 by Abu-Bakr Muhammad ibn Zakariya ar-Razi (Rhazes) (*c*. 865–?923), an Arab physician. Recorded in Britain since 1610. Inoculation was practiced in England as early as 1720. Free vaccination was available from 1840 and made compulsory 1853–68 and effectively so from 1868 until about 1900.

Syphilis

Incubation period: 10 days to 10 weeks, usually 3 weeks. Communicability variable, but if treated can be terminated within 24 hours. Normally transmitted by sexual intercourse or kissing. The virus *Treponema pallidum* was first isolated by Schaudinn in 1905. Symptoms: an acute and chronic disease involving long periods of latency between primary, secondary and tertiary stages. A primary lesion appears at about 3 weeks as a papule. The two principal theories of its origin are (*a*) introduced via Columbus' crew into Palos, Spain, from the Caribbean on March 15, 1493; (*b*) already rife in Europe but a new virulent strain from France and Spain became rampant in 1493. Name first accorded by Niccolò Leoniceno in 1497.

Tuberculosis

Incubation period (from infection to demonstrable symptoms): 4–6 weeks. Communicable by coughing, sneezing or alimentary contamination by a patient—some remain sputum-positive for years. A chronic bacterial disease caused by *Mycobacterium tuberculosis*, first isolated by Koch. Disease diagnosed in Egyptian mummy from 10th century B.C. Modern treatments include isoniazid (INH) and para-aminosalicyclic acid (PAS) given orally. Vaccination disaster at Lübeck, Germany, in 1930 (30 children died).

Typhoid (Enteric Fever)

Incubation period: 1–3 weeks, averaging 13–15 days. Communicable from second week and throughout convalescence. Transmitted by contaminated water or food by patient or carrier. Flies are sometimes vectors. First described in 1659 by T. Willis (Eng.). A bacterial infection by *Salmonella typhi*. Symptoms: a continued fever, enlargement of spleen, rose spots on trunk. Fatality rate now reduced from 10 per cent to 2–3 per cent by antibiotic treatment, notably chloramphenicol or a tetracycline.

Typhus

Incubation period: 6–15 days, commonly 12 days. Communicated by the infective rat flea, *Xenopsylla cheopis* through the agency of *Rickettsia prowazeki*. First isolated by H. de Roche-Lima in 1916. Earliest description by Cardano in 1576. Symptoms: headache, chills, chronic fever with a macular eruption after 5–6 days. Fatality, if untreated, 10–40 per cent. Modern treatment includes tetracyclines or chloramphenicol.

Whooping Cough (Pertussis)

Incubation period: commonly 7–10 days but up to a limit of 21 days. Communication by direct contact over a period from 7 days after contact's exposure to 3 weeks after onset of whooping. A bacterial infection by *Haemophilus pertussis*. First isolated by J. Bordet and O. Gengoa (France). First described by G. de Baillou (France) in 1598. Symptoms: catarrhal onset followed by cough which often becomes paroxysmal. Overall fatality is only 0.5 per cent but among infants under 6 months this may reach 30 per cent. The disease has declined since 1880.

Psychology

Psychology, the study of human behavior and the functioning of the mind, shares its field of interest with psychiatry (a branch of medicine devoted to the study and treatment of mental diseases and emotional disorders) and neurology (a branch of medicine devoted to the study and treatment of diseases of the nervous system). In contrast to these medical disciplines, however, psychology concentrates on the study of normal patterns of thought and behavior.

EXPERIMENTAL PSYCHOLOGY studies sensations, perceptions, and behavior of individuals under laboratory or controlled conditions. Animals as well as humans are used as subjects.

PHYSIOLOGICAL PSYCHOLOGY studies functioning of the nervous system insofar as it has a bearing on behavior. Animals are chiefly used as subjects.

EDUCATIONAL PSYCHOLOGY studies the nature of the learning process, motivation, memory, and differences in innate learning ability.

COMPARATIVE PSYCHOLOGY studies similarities and differences between the behavior of man and animals.

ABNORMAL PSYCHOLOGY studies variances from average behavior and attempts to find the causes for such behavior.

CLINICAL PSYCHOLOGY applies findings of other fields of psychology to the treatment of aberrations and mental disorders in individuals.

SOCIAL PSYCHOLOGY studies behavior of individuals as members of a group, behavior of groups as groups, and the relationships existing between groups.

Schools of Psychology. The founder of modern experimental psychology was Wilhelm Wundt (Ger., 1832–1930), who established a psychological testing laboratory at the University of Leipzig in 1879. Wundt's studies were in reaction against philosophic schools that attempted to discuss human behavior and mental qualities in terms of intuitive definitions.

STRUCTURALISM. The school that believed rational study of introspective thoughts could unravel the nature of the thought processes. Followers used themselves as test subjects. Founded by Edward Bradford Titchener (Eng., 1867–1927). Declined in importance during 1920's, although the principle of introspection is still important in psychoanalysis.

FUNCTIONALISM. Adherents believed that the way in which the mind functioned could be understood by studying how individuals reacted to outside stimuli. The mind was thought to seek an equilibrium position in which the individual was in harmony with his environment. Founded by John Dewey (U.S., 1859–1949), functionalism flourished from about 1896. Though it declined as a school of psychological thought from about 1915, its pragmatic bias had a great influence in the U.S., where psychology has concentrated on the testing of abilities and aptitudes and the grading of individuals as "normal," "average," "successful" or "unsuccessful."

BEHAVIORISM. Founded in 1913 by John Broadus Watson (U.S., 1879–1958). Adherents believed that "consciousness" was an unmeasurable abstraction and should be eliminated from psychological theory if psychology were ever to be a science; and that the subject matter of psychology should be restricted to measurable and observable behavior. Watson was strongly influenced in his opinions by Ivan Petrovich Pavlov (1849–1936), the Russian physiologist whose studies on the reactions of dogs to various stimuli had led him to the concept of the conditioned reflex. Behaviorism dominated U.S. psychology until about 1925, after which time Gestalt psychology increased in importance. Behaviorism, its original dogmatic rigidity much muted, is still an important school of thought in psychology. Its principles underly current programmed learning techniques.

GESTALT PSYCHOLOGY. Founded about 1912 by Max Wertheimer (Ger., 1880–1943), and named after the German word, *Gestalten*, meaning form or shape. Adherents stress the fact that an individual is more than an innumeration of his characteristics, no matter how complete. Gestalt psychologists emphasize the unity of an individual or a group and attempt to study the whole rather than the parts.

PSYCHOANALYSIS. Founded as a school of psychological thought by Sigmund Freud (Aust., 1856–1939). Adherents believe that overt patterns of behavior and thought are the expression of unconscious thoughts of which the individual is unaware. The unconscious thoughts are in turn derived from elemental emotions that are largely instinctual. In contrast to other schools of psychological thought, psychoanalysis emphasizes motivations and eschews experimentation.

Precursors of psychoanalysis include:
Anton Mesmer (Fr., 1733–1815) who first developed the technique of hypnotism, which he used to treat mental illnesses. He attributed his success to his ability to change the magnetic forces which he believed emanated from his patients and were the cause of their distress.
James Braid (Eng., 1795–1861) who gave hypnosis its name and concluded that the basis for its effectiveness was the suggestability of the subjects.
Ambroise-August Liebault (Fr., 1823–1904) and *Hippolyte Bernheim* (Fr., 1840–1919) who concluded that the symptoms of hysterical patients were due to their suggestability. In this respect, hysterics and hypnotic subjects were similar.
Pierre Janet (Fr., 1859–1947) who developed the first psychological explanation for neuroses using hypnosis as his basic experimental technique.
Joseph Breuer (Aust., 1842–1925) who was the first to successfully treat a hysterical patient using hypnosis. He observed that the release of emotion removed the symptoms of the patient.

FREUDIAN PSYCHOANALYSIS Freud also tried to treat hysteria using hypnosis but with less success, which led him eventually to a theraputic technique in which free association of thoughts and the analysis of the patient's dreams were the methods used to probe for the causes of the patient's illness.

According to Freudian theory, there are three levels of activity in the mind. The most elemental level consists of our instinctual urges and desires, such as our sexual drive (or libido), our life force, and our desire for constant pleasure and complete self-indulgence. This level of mental activity is unconscious, *.ie.*, we are never consciously aware of these urges and desires nor do we have any conscious control over them. This level of mental activity is called the "id."

At the opposite extreme is the level of conscious thought. At this level we are aware of powerful social pressures. We are aware of ourselves as social beings with social responsibilities. We feel a need to earn and maintain a reputation for selflessness, moral rectitude, and sexual moderation. This level of mental activity is the "superego."

Betweed the id and the superego, and subject to the pressures of both, is the third level of mental activity, the "ego." This is a preconscious level of thought; we are barely aware of it. It is the unthinking mental level of early childhood with its unquestioned assumption that "I" is the center of the universe. At this preconscious level of thought, the brute sexual drives of the id are modified by the social pressures of the super-ego into more socially acceptable customs of courtship and "dating." Our urge for constant self-indulgence exerted by the id is modified by the superego into more socially acceptable forms of behavior.

There is a constant struggle between the id and the superego for control of the ego. Neither can win finally (in any normal person), but neither will lose this struggle finally either. If some sort of *modus vivandi* is reached between the id and superego, a person is considered to be "normal" or "well-balanced." If the struggle tips persistently more to one contender rather than the other, the result is the development of a neurosis or eccentricity.

NEUROSES

Neuroses are classified according to the general class of symptoms exhibited:

ANXIETY. Manifests itself as a chronic, unjustified feeling of apprehension, which may become acute at times. One is constantly preoccupied with past errors, future calamities, threats to one's defensive shield. Occurs in those having an excessively overprotective or overly insecure childhood.

CONVERSION HYSTERIA. Rare. Manifests itself as some sort of a physical ailment which incapacitates the sufferer. An extremely wide selection of disabilities may be simulated, including blindness, partial or complete paralysis, heart disease, or gastro-intestinal disorders. Occurs in very immature, exhibitionist personalities who try to escape from their problems by simulating an illness.

DISASSOCIATION HYSTERIA. Rare. Similar to conversion hysteria (above) but symptoms take the form of a mental rather than a physical disability. Amnesia, multiple (split) personalities, sleep-walking are principle symptoms. Personality of sufferer is similar to those having conversion hysteria but is more withdrawn, suggestible, with a greater tendency to indulge in fantasies and daydreams.

PHOBIA. Manifests itself as an irrational fear of an object, person, event, or act—in fact, almost anything at all. (See list of phobias, p. 371.) Occurs in those who were excessively timid or fearful as children. Function of the phobia is to protect one against expression of forbidden thoughts or feelings.

OBSESSION-COMPULSION. Obsession manifests itself as an irrational thought that persistently obtrudes itself upon the mind of the sufferer to the point where his overt behavior is dominated by the obsession. A common obsession is the desire to use obscenities in public (and the fear that one might really do it). Compulsion manifests itself as an irrational act that the sufferer feels compelled to perform, such as continually washing one's hands. Obsessions and compulsions are often combined into a single pattern of behavior. Occurs in those who were repressively and rigidly toilet trained during childhood.

DEPRESSION. Manifests itself as prolonged periods of depression following an emotional shock or family bereavement; sufferers find it difficult or impossible to snap out of it. Other symptoms include restlessness, inability to sleep, continual feeling of tension and inability to concentrate. Occurs in those predisposed to melancholia, whose childhoods were insecure and fearful.

NEURASTHENIA. The most common form of neurosis. Manifests itself as a succession of minor physical complaints—upset stomachs, headaches, backaches, dizzy spells, aching joints and muscles, nervousness, etc.—and a chronic feeling of fatigue and disinterest. In a severe case, the complaints become hypochondriacal and the sufferer's behavior is dominated by imaginary ailments. Occurs in those in whom an excessive parental concern over health was evident and/or where there has been a long history of frustrated plans and ambitions.

EMOTIONAL DEVELOPMENT

In Freudian psychology, an individual passes through several stages of emotional development before reaching maturity.

In infancy, there is an oral stage during which the infant is chiefly interested in sucking, biting, and swallowing, and derives his principal sexual pleasures from these actions.

At about 2 years, the child's attention shifts to his excretory processes and he finds these processes sexually pleasurable.

At about 4 years, he discovers and begins to derive pleasure from playing with his genitals. At the same time, the child's sexual attention shifts from an exclusive attention upon his own body to the outside world. His attention fixes upon his parents, about whom he develops fantasies and from whom he derives his first external emotional satisfactions. A boy becomes emotionally attached to his mother and looks upon his father as a rival for her affections. This is the Oedipus complex. Similarly, a girl becomes emotionally attached to her father and looks upon her mother as a rival for his affections. This is the Electra complex.

From about 6 years to the onset of puberty the child's sexual interests become dormant and they go underground. With puberty, they rise to the surface again and the adolescent begins the emotional transformations that, if successfully completed, will lead to emotional maturity and a normally happy sex life. The resurrection of the sexual drive at puberty arouses again all the stages of sexual interest the adolescent passed through as an infant. At that time they were subverted; now they are somewhat more overt. Whether he does pass through these stages satisfactorily depends on innumerable circumstances, chief of which is his relationship with his parents and the sexually significant experiences he may have had as a child. Failure to pass through these stages successfully means a more-or-less arrested sexual development and the appearance of neurotic symptoms. Success means an emotionally healthy life with one's sexual interest fixed upon mature examples of the opposite sex.

In his early writings, Freud expressed the belief that neuroses were exclusively the result of arrested sexual development and an unresolved conflict between the id and the superego. He later began to emphasize the influence of the immediate environment in predisposing a person towards a neurosis. Freud had a great many disciples and followers, most of whom depreciated Freud's inelegant emphasis upon sex and therefore developed other interpretations about the causes of neurotic behavior and what to do about it.

FREUD'S FOLLOWERS

Alfred Adler (Aust., 1870–1937), an early associate of Freud, disagreed with Freud's emphasis on sexual instincts and substituted for them a will to power. Adler believed that feelings of inferiority were fostered when a child attempted to compare himself to his parents and other adults. The will to power was a reaction against the feelings of inferiority that resulted. Males were afraid of not being sufficiently masculine; females were unhappy they weren't males. Neurotic symptoms were the result of an unsuccessful attempt to compensate for the feelings of inferiority.

Carl Jung (Swiss, 1875–1961) modified Freud's emphasis on sex into a generalized life force. He also modified Freud's strict psychological determinism into a generalized racial unconscious from which an individual could draw specific emotional attitudes without coming into contact with his parents. Jung also introduced the concept of inherent introverted or extroverted personalities—one is born with a tendency towards shyness, openness, drive, etc. He also invented word-association tests.

Otto Rank (Aust., 1884–1939), an early disciple of Freud, later reacted strongly against his theories. Rank emphasized the process of being born as the principal cause of most of the anxieties suffered in life, not the Oedipus complex, which Freud emphasized. If one had not been born, one would not need to become neurotic. Rank also stressed the importance of will. The neurotic was one who had a weak will or was unable to assert himself; he therefore developed neurotic symptoms.

Erich Fromm (Ger., 1900–   ) emphasized the importance of social influences on emotional development. Man is a social being and the social setting in which he lives is as important as the biological and instinctual forces acting on him. Neurotic symptoms can develop because of an inability to win fame and power as well as an inability to achieve a satisfactory internal balance between the id and superego.

Karen Horney (Ger., 1885–1952) emphasized the importance of cultural influences on emotional development. To Horney, the chief cause of neurotic behavior was a basic anxiety fostered by the child's feeling of hostility towards his parents when he discovered he could not have his way entirely at all times.

Harry Stack Sullivan (U.S., 1892–1949) also emphasized the importance of cultural and social influences upon the personality which, he said, develops ultimately from the way in which an individual meets and deals with other individuals in the same society, not merely because he has a particular biologic heritage.

Phobias and Morbid Fears

A phobia can concern a dislike, morbid fear, horror, or unreasoning dread of an object, condition, place, action, state of affairs, abstract idea, sense, natural phenomenon or class of persons. Some of those listed come from early 20th century psychological literature and are now rarely seen. The use of the term *phobia* dates only from 1801.

acerophobia	sourness	dendrophobia	trees
acrophobia	sharpness (pinnacles)	dermatophobia	skin
		dikephobia	justice
agoraphobia	open spaces	doraphobia	fur
aichurophobia	points	eisoptrophobia	mirrors
ailourophobia	cats	elektrophobia	electricity
akousticophobia	sound	eleutherophobia	freedom
algophobia	pain	enetephobia	pins
altophobia	heights	entomophobia	insects
amathophobia	dust	eosophobia	dawn
ancraophobia	wind	eremitophobia	solitude
androphobia	men	ergophobia	work
anginophobia	narrowness	erythrophobia	blushing
Anglophobia	England or things English	Gallophobia	France or things French
anthropophobia	human beings	gametophobia	marriage
antlophobia	flood	genophobia	sex
apeirophobia	infinity	gephyraphobia	bridges
apiphobia	bees	Germanophobia	Germany or things German
arachnophobia	spiders		
asthenophobia	weakness	geumatophobia	taste
astraphobia	lightning	graphophobia	writing
atephobia	ruin	gymnophobia	nudity
atelophobia	imperfection	gynophobia	women
aulóphobia	flute	haptophobia	touch
auroraphobia	auroral lights	harpaxophobia	robbers
bacilliphobia	microbes	hedonophobia	pleasure
barophobia	gravity	hematophobia	blood
bathyphobia	deep water	hippophobia	horses
batophobia	walking	hodophobia	travel
batrachophobia	reptiles	homichlophobia	fog
belonephobia	needles	hormephobia	shock
bibliophobia	books	hydrophobia	water (also applied to rabies)
blennophobia	slime		
brontophobia	thunder	hygrophobia	dampness
carcinophobia	cancer	hypegiaphobia	responsibility
cardiophobia	heart condition	hypnophobia	sleep
cheimatophobia	cold	hypsophobia	heights
chaetophobia	hair	ideophobia	ideas
chionophobia	snow	kakorraphia-phobia	failure
chrometophobia	money		
chromophobia	color	katagelophobia	ridicule
chronophobia	duration	kenophobia	void
claustrophobia	enclosed spaces	kinesophobia (kinetophobia)	motion
clinophobia	going to bed		
cnidophobia	stings	kleptophobia	stealing
coprophobia	feces	koniphobia	dust
cryophobia	ice, frost	kopophobia	fatigue
crystallophobia	crystals	kyphophobia	stooping
cymophobia	sea swell	lalophobia	speech
cynophobia	dogs	limnophobia	lakes
demophobia	crowds	linonophobia	string
demonophobia	demons		

Phobias (continued)

logophobia	words	pnigerophobia	smothering
lyssophobia	insanity	pogonophobia	beards
maniaphobia	insanity	poinephobia	punishment
mastigophobia	flogging	polyphobia	many things
mechanophobia	machinery	potophobia	drink
metallophobia	metals	pteronophobia	feathers
meteorophobia	meteors	pyrophobia	fire
monophobia	one thing	Russophobia	Russia or things
musophobia	mice		Russian
musicophobia	music	rypophobia	soiling
mysophobia	dirt	satanophobia	satan
myxophobia	slime	sciophobia	shadows
necrophobia	corpses	selaphobia	flashes
negrophobia	Negroes	siderophobia	stars
nelophobia	glass	sinophobia	China or things
neophobia	new		Chinese
nephophobia	clouds	sitophobia	food
nosophobia	disease	spermophobia	
nyctophobia	darkness	(spermato-	
ochophobia	vehicles	phobia)	germs
odontophobia	teeth	stasophobia	standing
oikophobia	home	stygiophobia	
olfactophobia	smell	(hadephobia)	hell
ommetaphobia	eyes	syphilophobia	syphilis
oneirophobia	dreams	tachophobia	speed
ophiophobia	snakes	taphophobia	burial alive
ornithophobia	birds	teratophobia	monsters
ouranophobia	heaven	terdekaphobia	number 13
panphobia		thaasophobia	sitting idle
(pantophobia)	everything	thalassophobia	sea
parthenophobia	young girls	thanatophobia	death
pathophobia	disease	theophobia	God
patroiophobia	heredity	thermophobia	heat
peccatophobia	sinning	thixophobia	touching
pediculophobia	lice	tocophobia	childbirth
peniaphobia	poverty	toxiphobia	poison
phagophobia	swallowing	traumatophobia	wounds, injury
pharmacophobia	drugs	tremophobia	trembling
phasmophobia	ghosts	trypanophobia	inoculations
phobophobia	fears	xenophobia (zenophobia) foreigners	
phonophobia	speaking aloud	zelophobia	jealousy
photophobia	strong light	zoophobia	animals
phyllophobia	leaves		

Animals	Zoophobia
Auroral lights	Auroraphobia
Beards	Pogonophobia
Bees	Apiphobia
Birds	Ornithophobia
Blood	Hematophobia
Blushing	Erythrophobia
Books	Bibliophobia
Burglars	Harpaxophobia
Burial alive	Taphophobia
Cancer	Carcinophobia
Cats	Ailourophobia
Childbirth	Tocophobia
China, or things Chinese	Sinophobia
Clouds	Nephophobia
Cold	Cheimatophobia

Color	Chromaphobia
Corpses	Necrophobia
Crowds	Demophobia
Crystals	Crystallophobia
Dampness	Hygrophobia
Darkness	Nyctophobia
Dawn	Eosophobia
Death	Thanatophobia
Depth	Bathophobia
Demons	Demonophobia
Dirt	Mysophobia
Disease	Nosophobia; Pathophobia
Dogs	Cynophobia
Dreams	Oneirophobia
Drink	Potophobia
Drugs	Pharmacophobia
Duration	Chronophobia
Dust	Amathophobia; Koniphobia
Electricity	Elektrophobia
Enclosed spaces	Claustrophobia
England, or things English	Anglophobia
Everything	Panphobia or Pantophobia
Eyes	Ommetaphobia
Failure	Kakorraphiaphobia
Fatigue	Kopophobia
Fears	Phobophobia
Feathers	Pteronophobia
Feces	Coprophobia
Fire	Pyrophobia
Flashes	Selaphobia
Flogging	Mastigophobia
Flood	Antlophobia
Flutes	Aulophobia
Fog	Homichlophobia
Food	Sitophobia
Foreigners	Xenophobia or Zenophobia
France, or things French	Gallophobia or Francophobia
Freedom	Eleutherophobia
Frost	Cyrophobia
Fur	Doraphobia
Germany, or things German	Germanophobia
Germs	Spermophobia (Spermatophobia)
Ghosts	Phasmophobia
Glass	Nelophobia
God	Theophobia
Going to bed	Clinophobia
Gravity	Barophobia
Hair	Chaetophobia
Heart condition	Cardiophobia
Heat	Thermophobia
Heaven	Ouranophobia
Heights	Altophobia
Hell	Stygiophobia (or Hadephobia)
Heredity	Patroiophobia
High places	Hypsophobia
Home	Oikophobia
Horses	Hippophobia
Human beings	Anthropophobia
Ice	Cryophobia
Ideas	Ideophobia
Imperfection	Atelophobia
Infinity	Apeirophobia
Injections	Trypanophobia
Injury	Traumatophobia
Inoculations	Trypanophobia

Phobias (continued)

Insanity	Lyssophobia; Maniaphobia
Insects	Entomophobia
Jealousy	Zelophobia
Justice	Dikephobia
Lakes	Limnophobia
Leaves	Phyllophobia
Lice	Pediculophobia
Light, strong	Photophobia
Lightning	Astraphobia
Machinery	Mechanophobia
Many things	Polyphobia
Marriage	Gametophobia
Men	Androphobia
Metal	Metallophobia
Meteors	Meteorophobia
Mice	Musophobia
Microbes	Bacilliphobia
Mirrors	Eisoptrophobia
Money	Chrometophobia
Monsters	Teratophobia
Motion	Kinesophobia or Kinetophobia
Music	Musicophobia
Narrowness	Anginophobia
Needles	Belonephobia
Negroes	Negrophobia
New	Neophobia
Nudity	Gymnophobia
Number 13	Terdekaphobia
One thing	Monophobia
Open spaces	Agoraphobia
Pain	Algophobia
Paints	Aichurophobia
Pins	Enetephobia
Pleasure	Hedonophobia
Poison	Toxiphobia
Poverty	Peniaphobia
Punishment	Poinephobia
Reptiles	Batrachophobia
Responsibility	Hypegiaphobia
Ridicule	Katagelophobia
Robbers	Harpaxophobia
Ruins	Atephobia
Russia, or things Russian	Russophobia
Satan	Satanophobia
Sea	Thalassophobia
Sea swell	Cymophobia
Sex	Genophobia
Shadows	Sciophobia
Sharpness	Acrophobia
Shock	Hormephobia
Sinning	Peccatophobia
Sitting idle	Thaasophobia
Skin	Dermatophobia
Sleep	Hypnophobia
Slime	Blennophobia; Myxophobia
Smell	Olfactophobia
Smothering	Pnigerophobia
Snakes	Ophiophobia
Snow	Chionophobia
Soiling	Rypophobia
Solitude	Eremitophobia

Sound	Akousticophobia
Sourness	Acerophobia
Space	Agoraphobia
Speaking aloud	Phonophobia
Speech	Lalophobia
Speed	Tachophobia
Spiders	Arachnophobia
Standing	Stasophobia
Stars	Siderophobia
Stealing	Kleptophobia
Stings	Cnidophobia
Stooping	Kyphophobia
String	Linonophobia
Strong light	Photophobia
Swallowing	Phagophobia
Syphilis	Syphilophobia
Taste	Geumatophobia
Teeth	Odontophobia
Thunder	Brontophobia
Touch	Haptophobia
Touching	Thixophobia
Travel	Hodophobia
Trees	Dendrophobia
Trembling	Tremophobia
Vehicles	Ochophobia
Voidness	Kenophobia
Walking	Batophobia
Water	Hydrophobia (also a specific disease)
Weakness	Asthenophobia
Wind	Ancraophobia
Women	Gynophobia
Words	Logophobia
Work	Ergophobia
Writing	Graphophobia
Wounds	Traumatophobia
Young girls	Parthenophobia

PSYCHOSES

A neurosis represents a conflict in the mind of a fundamentally healthy person: the neurotic exists in the real world. A psychosis, on the other hand, represents a distortion in the personality. A psychotic sees neither himself, others, nor events as they actually exist.

There are three main groups of psychotics—schizophrenics, manic-depressives, and paranoids. Within each group there are various classifications based on the symptoms exhibited and the degree of disturbance, whether mild or severe.

Schizophrenia is a term first used in 1911. It means "split personality." Schizophrenia replaced the term *dementia praecox*, "insanity of youth," which had been widely used before.

A person suffering from a mild degree of this disease, or having a tendency towards it, is said to have a schizoid personality. As a child, such a person was excessively obedient, shy, and hypersensitive to criticism. As an adult, he is very shy and withdrawn, and finds it difficult, if not impossible, to meet and get along with others. He tends, therefore, to retreat into Walter Mitty-like daydreams and fantasies. He is hostile when thwarted or upset, but suppresses all feelings of violence. Intellectually, a schizoid personality tends to be over-idealistic and will pursue schemes that are impossible of realization. If he writes a book it will be unpublishable; if he invents anything, it will be impracticable.

Organic Psychoses

In distinction to the psychoses listed above, which are purely mental disturbances without any accompanying physical disease or incapacitation, there are a number of physical diseases that can affect the functioning of the brain. These are generally classified as organic psychoses:

If the schizoid personality slides into full-blown schizophrenia, his symptoms sharpen. The schizophrenic is unable to exhibit any emotion: he is apathetic and distant towards others. Any emotional response he does make is out of all proportion to the stimulus and resembles a disorganized panic more than a normal response. His thought processes are highly disorganized and erratic and an outsider finds it impossible to discern any trend in his conversation or thought processes.

A schizophrenic may suffer also from delusions and hallucinations. He may believe himself possessed of supernatural powers, the victim of persecution, or another person entirely (Napoleon, the Virgin Mary, the Czar of Russia, etc.), or he may claim to hear, see, and smell things that are not present.

Overtly, a schizophrenic can behave either in a passive, withdrawn and childlike manner; in an infantile, irresponsible and bizarre manner (such as playing with his own feces); or become catatonic—remaining immobile and apparently unaware of himself and his surroundings for days at a time. A violent form of schizophrenia—paranoid schizophrenia—is a state in which the sufferer believes himself to be the victim of an organized persecution and this delusion leads him to take murderous revenge on his imagined persecutors.

Manic-Depressive (Cyclothymic). The person having a mild form of this disease is said to have a cyclothymic personality. His childhood was frequently very disciplined and morally strict. On the manic side, such a person is an energetic extrovert who gets along easily with others and knows how to get things done. He is an enthusiast, ambitious, a hard worker, and tends to become highly successful in our society. He is frequently an object of envy or admiration, and pointed out as a person to emulate. He also drinks too much, relaxes too hard, and is unfaithful to his wife. On the depressive side, he is subject to inexplicable swings in mood and will suffer from periods of depression, which he snaps out of spontaneously to resume his energetic course.

In the full-blown psychosis, the symptoms are the same but more so—to the point of irrationality. The elation and energy become extreme, his mind works at high speed but erratically, shooting out grandiose and impossible ideas. If blocked, he becomes angry and abusive. The depressions are also extreme, to the point where he feels extremely melancholy and defeated; even his pulse and blood pressure may decline. He has feelings of unworthiness and guilt, can't think or reason clearly, and may suffer from hallucinations in which voices call him names and berate him for his supposed crimes.

Paranoia. The distinguishing characteristics of the paranoid personality are suspiciousness, jealousy, and envy. As a child, he developed a strong sense of inferiority. Such a person is acutely sensitive to others and tends to read hostility and rejection into their behavior toward him. He has learned to disguise his sense of inferiority by pretending gruffness and toughness, and is generally difficult to get along with. Paranoid personalities are found in large numbers among social reformers, moralists, and supporters of unpopular causes. They are also prolific instigators of law suits.

The full-blown paranoid suffers from an intense and overwhelming conviction that he is being persecuted. His outstanding symptom is suspiciousness. He may also develop highly-organized delusions built around his feeling of inadequacy, believing that others are systematically attempting to betray and humiliate him. Aside from his delusion, a paranoid acts and behaves as rationally as anyone else: he has become exceptionally skilled at disguising or dissembling the fact that he is controlled by his delusion.

Senility is a deterioration in mental powers that often appears in old age. The characteristics of senility are well known: loss of memory about recent events, garrulousness about the long-distant past, crankiness and irritability, inability to concentrate on any one subject for any length of time or to associate correctly names with faces, increasing inability to control one's bladder or bowels or to take care of oneself, one's life coming to an end in a vegetable-like existence. The primary cause (or causes) is unknown. Chief theories include the breaking down of large numbers of brain cells with increasing age, hereditary influences, a chronic lifelong deficiency in some necessary vitamin or mineral, the gradual crumbling of one's defenses against the persistent emotional blows of life, and long-term imbibing of alcohol.

Cerebral Arteriosclerosis. Arteriosclerosis, a thickening of the walls of the arteries, can lead to high blood pressure and eventual heart failure. If this disease occurs in the arteries that supply the brain with blood, it can affect the mental processes. The symptoms of cerebral arteriosclerosis come on rapidly and include a lessened ability to concentrate and an impaired memory for recent events; common objects cannot be named or their purpose recollected; there is an exaggerated emotional response to trivial irritations, and often, an increased feeling of depression or paranoia.

Paresis is the end result of a syphilitic infection that may have been acquired years before. Its specific cause is the attack upon the central nervous system by the microorganism, *Treponema pallidum.* The symptoms are distinctive: the sufferer gradually loses the ability to speak clearly or write distinctly, followed by the loss of ability to think clearly and logically. Great gaps appear in his memory, he becomes increasingly less capable of caring for himself and ends by becoming permanently bedridden and totally disoriented, recognizing neither time, place, nor himself.

Alcoholism. Persistent and uncontrolled use of alcohol may finally affect the brain. If it does, the alcoholic may suffer spells of amnesia while drunk, during which time he may commit a crime, get married, sign away all his money, or whatever, and have no recollection of having done so when next sober. He may suffer spells of *delirium tremens,* experiencing frightening hallucinations or delusions during which he believes he is being persecuted or threatened. Lapses in memory appear and in time there is a gradual loss in his mental and physical abilities. The cause of alcoholism is unknown, though it is more probably a symptom of some deeper psychological disturbance in the personality than a distinctive disease of itself.

Brain tumors frequently interfere with normal brain function as they increase in size and press upon the brain tissue. Symptoms include persistent, pulsating headaches, vomiting at odd times (that is, with no relation to the food eaten), stupor, depression, and general mental disorientation.

Epilepsy appears to be hereditary. It is about 5 times more prevalent among family groups than in individuals having no previous family history. The predisposing cause is apparently a brain injury or abnormality that leaves the brain sensitive to endocrine or metabolic disorders that do not affect a normal brain.

There are two principal types of epileptic seizure: grand mal and petit mal. The symptoms of a grand mal seizure are an initial muscular rigidity or tension, during which consciousness is lost, followed immediately by a series of convulsions. Consciousness is then gradually regained. The epileptic has a premonitory warning: he may feel dizzy or nauseous or feel a tingling or numbness in his arms and legs. Grand mal seizures can occur several times in one day or once a year or even less frequently.

The petit mal seizure consists of a temporary loss in consciousness (a fainting spell) that lasts from a few seconds to a minute or so. Seizures may occur several times in one day.

Organic Psychoses (continued)

Migraine, a violent and incapacitating headache, appears to be related to epilepsy since the two ailments appear frequently in the same person, and families in which epilepsy occurs also have a high percentage of migraine sufferers. Migraine headaches can be treated by taking ergotamine tartrate.

Drug Use

Drug addiction affects both the mind and body, different types of addictive drugs having different effects.

Morphine and heroin are both opium derivatives and their effects on the body and mind are similar. Basically, both are depressant drugs. They relax the addict, decrease his sex drive, induce a state of passive reverie. The addict does not continue taking the drug to prolong these effects, but because failure to do so leads to extremely painful withdrawal symptoms, including sweating, vomiting, diarrhea, cramps, and a general sense of impending doom accompanied by hallucinations and delusions.

Cocaine acts as a stimulant, the addict feeling euphoric and hyperactive for 4 to 6 hours. Prolonged use of the drug induces paranoid feelings, depressions, and hallucinations. The addict becomes physically addicted to the drug and suffers the same withdrawal symptoms as the user of morphine or heroin.

Marijuana is not physically addictive, but the habitual user becomes emotionally addicted and discovers in time he is more comfortable with the drug than without and incapable of stopping its use even if he wanted to. In many ways, he resembles a chronic drinker who is not yet an alcoholic. Marijuana induces a state of euphoria during which the user's ordinary awareness of time and space become distorted. The user may at times feel enormously expanded physically, at other times shrunk to a minute size. Marijuana relaxes the user's usual moral code, he feels sexually uninhibited and free to act in ways he would not act otherwise. Again, this resembles an alcoholic's taking a few drinks to give him courage. Under the influence of marijuana, however, as with alcohol, there is a great difference between what one thinks one is capable of doing and one's actual abilities.

HALLUCINOGENIC DRUGS

These include mescaline, psilocybin, and lysergic acid diethylamide (LSD). Substances containing mescaline (obtained chiefly from peyote [*Lophophora williamsii*], a cactus plant growing in southwest U.S. and in Mexico) have been used by the Tarahumara and Huichol Indians of Mexico, the Aztecs before them, and by various Indian tribes in the U.S. Aldous Huxley, in his book, *Doors of Perception*, described the hallucinatory effects of mescaline, which are similar to those reported from users of LSD.

LSD first came to the attention of medical researchers in 1943 when a Swiss researcher, Albert Hoffman, unknowingly swallowed a small amount of the substance while investigating its properties and experienced bizarre hallucinations as a result.

Extremely small amounts, 50 micrograms taken orally, will affect the minds of most people. The effects of the drug will vary to some extent with the amount swallowed and also with the individual's personality and state of mind at the time of ingestion.

Subjective effects occur about 20 to 30 minutes after swallowing the drug. A numbness is felt around the mouth, followed by various symptoms, which may include dizziness, nausea, headaches, or palpitations. Perceptual changes then gradually occur. Walls and ceilings may appear to tilt, advance, or recede, and brilliant-colored patterns may appear on the walls. The body feels as if it were changing shape, expanding or contracting. The senses become intensified—colors appear more brilliant, tastes more exquisite, sounds more lovely, sexual pleasure more acute. The perception of time changes. The mood of the person can vary between calm contemplation to feelings of extreme fear and depression. The thought processes become less concrete and more abstract, there is a loss of ability to think logically and coherently. In some persons, paranoid delusions or schizophrenic distortions may occur.

The effects of LSD begin to lessen in 4 to 6 hours, although they may last as long as 48 hours. Therapeutically, LSD appears to have some value in treating disturbed or neurotic persons, though it may also intensify a state of depression to the point of suicide, and schizoid personalities can be precipitated into states of acute schizophrenia. Manic states and aggressive psychopathic behavior can also be precipitated by indiscriminate use of the drug. For these reasons, and because of the widespread publicity LSD has received in recent years, the U.S. Food and Drug Administration has severely restricted the manufacture and use of the drug by medical researchers, and the drug has been classified as a narcotic, users being subject to the same legal penalties as users of opium derivatives, cocaine, and marijuana.

Intelligence

Psychologists have had a great deal of difficulty establishing definitions of intelligence and testing individuals for their particular level of intelligence. Individuals differ not only in their "raw" intelligence but also in the degree to which they have aptitudes in particular fields. An otherwise dull-minded person may have an extreme aptitude for chess or mathematics; a person accounted a genius in one of the arts is not necessarily gifted in more mundane pursuits, especially politics. In addition, there appear to be innumerable reasons that prevent an inherently intelligent person from developing that intelligence—social, economic, or emotional reasons, for example.

Nevertheless, there are a great many tests in existence that attempt to measure general intelligence or some aspect of intelligence. The two most widely used tests of general intelligence are Terman's and Wechsler's:

TERMAN'S CLASSIFICATION OF INTELLIGENCE

Classification	I.Q. Range
Genius	Above 140
Very Superior	120–140
Superior	110–120
Normal, or Average	90–110
Dull	80– 90
Borderline	70– 80
Feebleminded: Moron	50– 70
Imbecile	25– 50
Idiot	Below 25

WECHSLER'S CLASSIFICATION OF INTELLIGENCE

Classification	I.Q. Range	Per cent of Population
Very Superior	128 and over	2.2
Superior	120–127	6.7
Bright Normal	111–119	16.1
Average	91–110	50.0
Dull Normal	80– 90	16.1
Borderline	66– 79	6.7
Defective	65 and below	2.2

Morons can complete an education equivalent to the 4th or 5th grade of most American public school systems. They can learn to perform simple, routine tasks, can be toilet-trained, and learn to avoid dangerous situations.

Imbeciles do not develop beyond the stage of mental development reached by a normal 6- or 8-year-old child. That is, they can tell others what they want and if they are sick, and they can discuss the world about them on a very simple level, but they cannot learn to read or write. With effort, they can be toilet-trained and taught to recognize obvious dangers.

Idiots are incompetent to take care of their simplest needs nor do they learn to avoid obvious dangers. They are usually placed in institutions for their own protection.

Mongoloids are born mentally defective because of an unfortunate prenatal environment, usually an endocrine deficiency in the mother. They are usually classified as imbeciles. Mongoloids are very affectionate and lovable creatures.

Anthropology

ORIGIN OF THE RACES

In his *Origin of the Races* (1964) Dr. Carlton S. Coon (U.S.) makes the hypothesis that man has devolved into five basic races thus:

Australoid	from	Java Man *c*. 400,000 B.C.
Capoid	from	Ternifine-Tangier Man *c*. 500,000 B.C.
Caucasoid	from	Heidelberg Man *c*. 450,000 B.C.
Congoid	from	Rhodesian Man *c*. 50,000 B.C.
Mongoloid	from	Peking Man *c*. 400,000 B.C.

The classification of the various races of mankind is intensely complex. There is much debate as to whether the best criterion for classification is the cranial form, skin color, stature and nose form, or hair form.

The most modern research indicates that there are possibilities in another basis of classification—namely the blood group.

There are obvious objections to any method of classification. The main reason for difficulty is that, with the possible exception of the people inhabiting the Andaman Islands in the Indian Ocean, there is no such thing as a pure race. The inter-breeding between racial types blurs every boundary distinction so far devised. Probably the most convenient method of classification is still based on hair form.

There are three main types: the straight haired groups, the wooly haired groups and the curly haired groups.

THE STRAIGHT HAIRED GROUPS

The straight haired peoples correspond mainly to the Mongoloid or "yellow-brown" races. In general these people possess prominent cheek bones, flat faces, and are brachycephalic. The main two divisions of straight haired people are: (1) the Asiatic groups and (2) the Amerinds (*i.e.* the American aborigines).

The Asiatic Groups

There are three main sub-divisions:

(1) The north or arctic group, who inhabit the circumpolar regions stretching from the Lapps in the west to the Koreans in the east.

(2) The central group known as the Pareoeans, who are distinguishable by their less prominent cheek bones and their broader noses. In the north of China they are often tall but lose stature the further south they live. The Japanese, who have mixed with the distinctive Ainu type, are a special variety of the Pareoean people.

(3) The third group is known as the southern Mongoloids, "Oceanic Mongols" or Indonesians and are considerably mixed, but their broader heads sometimes distinguish them. An outcrop of the straight haired Asiatic group are the Polynesians who live in the Pacific islands, including New Zealand. Their origins are believed to be an ancient mixture of proto-Malays with Nesiots (see below).

The Amerinds

This group consists of the Eskimos, stretching from the northern coasts of Asia across Canada to Greenland. They have exceptionally long skulls and surprisingly broad faces but with narrow noses.

The Races (continued)

Coming further south there are the various Red Indian people with the Sioux being a well-known example. The Aztecs and the Mayas were from this group. The ethnology of the South American aborigines is still in dispute but there are similarities with the Maya people and a distinctive round headed type of tall stature is observed in Patagonia. The Fuegians are a branch of the latter division. The picture is confused by traces of curly haired types in this area.

THE WOOLLY HAIRED GROUPS

The woolly haired groups are divided into two, an eastern group that inhabit parts of Asia and Oceania and a western group who populate the greater part of Africa. The common characteristic, besides woolly hair, is dark, often almost black, skin, broad noses, and a tendency to a small brain in relation to physical height. Both groups contain Pygmy divisions.

Eastern Group

The taller members are Papuans and Melanesians and the shorter the Negritos. This latter group is in four separate areas: the Andaman Is.; central Malaya and eastern Sumatra, with the Semang; parts of the Philippine Islands (the people commonly known as the Aeta), the western mountains of New Guinea and parts of Melanesia inhabited by the Tapiro people. The Papuans and Melanesians have narrower heads than the Negritos. The extinct Tasmanian aboriginals (but not Australian aboriginals) seem to have been connected with this Eastern group.

Western Group

This group is dominated by the [Negroes. True Negroes come from the Guinea coast where they are tall with black or dark brown skin, long narrow heads, retreating foreheads and pronounced jaws. The lips are thickened and everted and the nose is strikingly broad. The negroes have mixed with other races, a notable example being the Nilotes, who inhabit the Upper Nile Valley. The African Pygmies or Negrillos, besides their smallness of stature, have lightly colored skins and even broader noses than the negroes.

A striking division is the Bushmen and their close allies the Hottentots. Bushmen are now only found in the Kalahari Desert. They have yellowish skin and a massive development of the buttocks (steatopygia).

THE CURLY HAIRED GROUPS

All the remaining races of the world come from this group, which has a world-wide distribution and includes both highly differentiated groups and undifferentiated groups. The hair color varies strikingly from jet black to light blond. This group is mainly large brained, with a prominent forehead, but the skin color is fairly variable. The range of civilization also differs widely, from the more primitive Australian aboriginals up to the most sophisticated white people in the world.

Other primitive peoples in this group are the proto-Nordics, who include the inhabitants of the Turkoman steppes, and the Ainu, who survive in the most northern parts of Japan and are totally distinct from the Japanese, especially in that they lack their epicanthic fold.

The proto-Indics are in four divisions, as follows: first, the jungle tribes of southern India; secondly, the most primitive inhabitants of Ceylon, known as the Vedda; thirdly, the primitive peoples of Malaya known as the Sakai; and fourthly, some scattered tribes in Sumatra and the Celebes. The Australian aboriginals are believed to stem from this proto-Indic stock, but their long isolation has produced some special characteristics, such as their massive skulls, and the Cherisots (the mainlanders) are scattered throughout southern Asia, including India where they are rounder headed. The curly haired races populate the horn of Africa, the Nile and Red Sea areas and some have surprisingly pale skins. Three groups of these are the Eurafricans, the Bedouin Arabs and the Mediterranean races. The Nordic people predominate in Scandinavia but form a strong element of the British Isles, northern France, the Low Countries, and northern parts of Germany.

Finally, the round headed, wavy haired people conveniently called Eurasiatic, stretch across Europe and Asia from central France to the Himalayas in the east. An important branch of this group are the Alpine people, distinguishable by the extreme flatness and height of the head. A separate branch are the Pamiri, who inhabit the high areas of Asia and India. Locally, in western Europe, there are isolated groups of Beaker Folk.

Population

Progressive Estimates of World Population in Millions

10,000 B.C.	c.	5	1940	2,295
4,000 B.C.	c.	80	1950*	2,533
A.D. 1	c.	200	1960	3,049
1000		275	1970	3,704
1250		375	1975	4,090
1500		420	1976	4,163
1650		500	1977	4,314
1750		720	1978	4,395
1800		900	1979	4,435
1900		1,625	1980	4,470
1920		1,862	2000	6,350
1930		2,070		

If this trend continues, the world has only 15 generations left before the human race breeds itself to an overcrowded extinction. By 2600 A.D. there would be one person per square yard of habitable land surface.

Increasing food production, it is argued could aggravate the problem by broadening the base of the expansion. However, higher living standards often result in lower birth rates as well as death rates. History's greatest war (World War II with 54,800,000 killed) made the merest dent in the inexorable advance between 1940 and 1950 (see table).

The intractable problem is that with 17,150 births and only 6,850 deaths per hour the world's natural increase would run at 247,200 per day. Some demographers now maintain that the figure will (or must) stabilize at 10 to 15,000 million but above 8,000 million in the 21st century.

THE 26 CIVILIZATIONS OF MAN

If the duration of man's evolution, now estimated at 1,750,000 years, is likened to a single year, then the earliest of all recorded civilizations began after 5 p.m. on December 30. Put another way, 289/290ths of man's existence has been uncivilized.

Few historians have attempted to classify the world's civilizations

---

* All figures after this date are based on U.S. Bureau of Census medium variant data. The mid-1977 U.N. figure was 190 million lower at 4,124 million.

because of the natural tendency to specialize. An early attempt was that of the Frenchman, Count de Gobineau, in his four-volume *L'Inégalité des races humaines* (Paris, 1853–55). His total was ten. Since that time Western archeologists have rescued five more ancient civilizations from oblivion—the Babylonic, the Hittite, the Mayan, the Minoan, and the Sumeric. This would have brought his total to fifteen compared with a more modern count of twenty-six.

The most authoritative classification now available is the revised twelve-volume life work of Professor Arnold Toynbee, *A Study of History*, published between 1921 and 1961. This concludes that there have been twenty-one civilizations of which seven still survive. Those surviving are the Arabic (Islamic), the Far Eastern (begun in 910 A.D and now split into two), the Orthodox Christian (now also split into two), the Hindu (begun *c.* 775 A.D.) and the Western civilization.

No.	Name	Dawn	Final Collapse	Duration in Centuries
1.	Egyptiac	before 4000 B.C.	*c.* 280 A.D.	*c.* 43
2.	Sumeric or Sumerian	before 3500 B.C.	*c.* 1700 B.C.	*c.* 18
3.	Indic	before 3000 B.C.	*c.* 500 A.D.	35
4.	Minoan	before 2000 B.C.	*c.* 1400 B.C.	6
5.	Mayan[1]	before 2000 B.C.	1550 A.D.	*c.* 35?
6.	Hittite	2000 B.C.	*c.* 1200 B.C.	8
7.	Sinic	*c.* 1600 B.C.[3]	220 A.D.	18
8.	Babylonic	*c.* 1500 B.C.	538 B.C.	10
9.	Hellenic	*c.* 1300 B.C.	558 A.D.	18½
10.	Syriac	*c.* 1200 B.C.	970 A.D.	22

Notes

1. Toynbee regards a Yucatec civilization (*c.*1075–1680 A.D.) as a separate entity. Archeological discoveries in 1960 indicate that Dzibilchaltan, on the Yucatan Peninsula, was in fact the cradle of the whole Mayan civilization.

2. There is increasing evidence of links with the Egyptiac. The early classic period at Tikal dates from *c.* 250–550 A.D.

3. The earliest archeologically acceptable dynasty was that of Shang, variously dated 1766–1558 B.C. The historicity of the First or Hsia dynasty, allegedly founded by Yü in 2205 B.C., is in decided doubt.

Cradle	Dominant States	Religion and Philosophy	Derivation
Lower Nile	Middle Empire *c.* 2065–1660 B.C.	Osiris-worship Philosophy of Atonism	Spontaneous
Euphrates-Tigris Delta	Sumer and Akkad Empire *c.* 2298–1905 B.C.	Tammuz-worship	Spontaneous
Mohenjo-Daro, Harappa Indus and Ganges valleys	Mauryan Empire 322–185 B.C. Gupta Empire 390–475 A.D.	Hinduism Jainism Hinayana Buddhism	Possibly of Sumeric origin
Knossus, Crete and the Cyclades	Thalassocracy of Minos *c.* 1750–1400 B.C.	?Orphism	Spontaneous
Guatemalan forests	First Empire *c.* 300–690 A.D.	Human sacrifice and human penitential self-mortification	Related to Egyptiac[2]
Boghazköi, Anatolia, Turkey	—	Pantheonism	Related to Minoan
Yellow River Basin	Ts'in and Han Empire 221 B.C.–172 A.D.	Mahayana Buddhism, Taoism, Confucianism	Believed unrelated
Lower Mesopotamia	Babylonian Empire 610–539 B.C.	Judaism, Zoroastrianism Astrology	Related to Sumeric
Greek mainland and Aegean Is.	Roman Empire 31 B.C.–378 A.D.	Mithraism, Platonism Stoicism Epicureanism Christianity	Related to Minoan
Eastern Cilicia	Achaemenian Empire *c.* 525–332 B.C.	Islam and Philosophy of Zervanism	Related to Minoan

The 26 Civilizations of Man (continued)

No.	Name	Dawn	Final Collapse	Duration in Centuries
11.	Eskimo	c. 1100 B.C.	c. 1850 A.D.	c. 30
12.	Spartan	c. 900 B.C.	396 A.D.	13
13.	Polynesian	c. 500 B.C.	c. 1775 A.D.	22½
14.	Andean	c. 100 B.C.	1783 A.D.	19
15.	Khmer⁴	c. 100 A.D.	1432 A.D.	13
16.	Far Eastern (main)	589 A.D.	Scarcely survives	14 to date
17.	Far Eastern (Japan and Korea)	645 A.D.	Survives	13 to date
18.	Western	c. 675 A.D.	Flourishes	13 to date
19.	Orthodox Christian (main)	c. 680 A.D.	Survives	13 to date
20.	Hindu	c. 810 A.D.	Survives	11 to date
21.	Orthodox Christian (Russia)	c. 950 A.D.	Oppressed	10 to date
22.	Arabic	c. 975 A.D.	1525 A.D.	5½
23.	Mexic	c. 1075 A.D.	1821 A.D.	7½
24.	Ottoman	c. 1310 A.D.	1919 A.D.	6
25.	Iranic (now Islamic)	c. 1320 A.D.	Survives	6½ to date
26.	Communist	1848	Flourishes	1 to date

4. Not regarded by Toynbee as a separate civilization but as an offshoot of the Hindu civilization. Modern evidence shows, however, that the Khmer origins predate those of the Hindu civilization by seven centuries.

Cradle	Dominant States	Religion and Philosophy	Derivation
Umnak Aleutian Islands	Thule c. 1150–1850 A.D.	Includes Sila, sky god; Sedna, seal goddess	—
Laconia	620–371 B.C.	—	Hellenic
Samoa and Tonga	— —	Ancestor spirits Mana—supernatural power	—
Chimu, N. Peru and Nazca, S. Peru	Inca Empire 1430–1533 A.D.	Philosophy of Viracochaism	Spontaneous
Cambodian coast	Ankor Kingdom 802–1432 A.D.	—	Possibly related to Indic and Sinic
Si Ngan (Sian-fu) Wei Valley	Mongol Empire 1280–1351 A.D. Manchu Empire 1644–1912 A.D.	Muhayaniah Buddhism	Related to Sinic
Yamato, Japan via Korea	Tokugawa Shogunate 1600–1868 A.D.	Mikado-worship; Shintoism; Buddhism and Zen Philosophy	Related to Sinic
Ireland	Habsburg Monarchy 1526–1918 A.D. and Napoleonic Empire 1797–1815 A.D.	Philosophy of Christianity	Related to Hellenic
Anatolia, Turkey	Byzantine Empire A.D. 395–1453	Bedreddinism, Orthodox Church, Imami	Related to Hellenic and Western
Kanauj, Jumna-Ganges Duab	Mughal Raj c. 1572–1707 A.D. British Raj 1818–1947	Hinduism Sikhism	Related to Indic
Upper Dnieper Basin	Muscovite Empire 1478–1918 A.D.	Orthodox Church Sectarianism	Related to Hellenic
Arabia, Iraq, Syria	Abbasid Caliphate of Baghdad	Islam (after 1516 A.D.)	Related to Syriac
Mexican Plateau	Aztec Empire 1375–1521 A.D.	Quetzalcoatl	Related to Mayan
—	—	Islam	—
Oxus-Jaxartes Basin	—	Islam (after 1516 A.D.)	Related to Syriac
Western Europe	U.S.S.R. and China	Atheism; Marxist-Leninism; Maoism	—

MAJOR ANTHROPOLOGICAL DISCOVERIES

Year	Scientific Name	Period and Estimated Date B.C.	Location	Description	Anthropologist
1856[1]	Homo neanderthalensis	Late middle Paleolithic 120,000	Neander Valley, nr. Düsseldorf, Germany	skull, bones	Fuhlrott
1868[2]	Homo sapiens (Cromagnon)	Upper Paleolithic 35,000	Cromagnon, Les Eyzies, France	4 skeletons, 1 fetus	Lartet
1890	Pithecanthropus erectus	Upper Pleistocene 400,000	Kedung Brebus, Java	mandible, tooth	Dubois
1907	Homo heidelbergensis	Lower Paleolithic 450,000	Mauer, nr. Heidelberg, Germany	lower jaw	Schoetensack
1912[3]	Eoanthropus dawsonii	Holocene (Recent) (fraud)	Piltdown, Sussex	composite skull	Dawson
1921	Homo rhodesiensis	Upper Gamblian c. 50,000	Broken Hill, Zambia	skull	Armstrong
1924	Australopithecus africanus	Early Pleistocene 1,000,000	Taung, Botswana	skull	Dart (Izod)
1926[4]	Proconsul nyanzae	Miocene c. 25,000,000	Koru, Kenya	fragments (non-hominoid)	Hopwood
1927	Pithecanthropus pekinensis	Lower Paleolithic 400,000	Choukoutien, nr. Peking, China	tooth	Bohlin
1929–34	Neanderthaloid man	Middle Paleolithic or Mousterian 120,000	Mt. Carmel, Israel	part 16 skeletons	Garrod
1935[6]	Homo sapiens fossilis	Lower Paleolithic 250,000	Boyn Hill, Swanscombe, Kent	parts skull	Marston
1935[7]	Gigantopithecus blacki	Middle Pleistocene 450,000	from Kwangsi, China (Hong Kong druggist)	teeth only	von Koenigswald
1936	Pleistanthropus transvaalensis	Early Pleistocene 1,000,000	Sterkfontein, Transvaal	skull, part femur	Broom (Barlow)
1938	Paranthropus robustus	Early Pleistocene 700,000	Kromdraai, Transvaal	skull part, bones	Broom (Terblanche)
1947	Homo sapiens fossilis	Middle Paleolithic or Mousterian 125,000	Fontéchevade, France	2 calottes	Martin
1949	Australopithecus prometheus	Early Pleistocene 900,000	Makapansgat, Transvaal	fragments	Dart
1953	Telanthropus capensis	Early Pleistocene 800,000	Swartkrans, Transvaal	jaw, skull parts	Broom
1954	Atlanthropus	Chelleo-Acheulian 500,000	Ternifine, Algeria	parietal, 3 mandibles	Arambourg
1957	Neanderthaloid man	Upper Paleolithic 45,000	Shanidar, Iraq	skeletons	Solecki
1959	Zinjanthropus boisei	Late Pliocene c. 1,750,000	Olduvai, Tanzania	skull	Leakey (Mrs. Leakey)
1960	Homo habilis	Late Pliocene ante supra	Olduvai, Tanzania	fragments	Leakey
1961	Kenyapithecus wickeri	Mid Miocene c. 14,000,000	Fort Ternan, Kenya	palate, teeth (non-hominoid)	Leakey (Mukiri)
1963	Australopithecus robustus	Middle Pleistocene 450,000	Chenchiawo, Lantien, N.W. China	jaw	—
1964	Sinanthropus lantianensis	Middle Pleistocene c. 500,000	Kungwangling, Lantien, Shensi, China	skull cap and female jaw in 1963	Wu Ju Kang
1965	Homo sapiens fossilis	Middle Paleolithic	Grotte du Lazaret, Nice, France	skull (male)	Octobon
1965	Homo sapiens paleo-hungaricus	Middle Pleistocene c. 450,000	Vertesszöllös, Hungary	occipital	Vértes

Major Anthropological Discoveries (continued)

1969	*Homo erectus*	Middle Pleistocene 500,000–1,000,000	Sangiran, Java	skull	Sartono
1972	*Homo?*	Plio–Pleistocene 2,000,000	East Turkana, Kenya	mandibular, cranial and limb bones	Richard Leakey
1974/5	*Australopithecus* or *Homo*	Plio–Pleistocene 3,000,000	Hadar Afar region, Ethiopia	skull parts, jaws, teeth, skeleton	Johanson and Taieb
1975	*Homo erectus*	Plio–Pleistocene 1,500,000	Turkana, Kenya	skull**	Richard Leakey
1976	*Homo?*	Pleistocene 400,000	Halkidiki, Greece	complete skeleton	Greek Anthropological Society
1978	*Australopithecus afarensis*	Plio–Pleistocene 3,500,000	Ethiopia, Tanzania	skull, bones	Johanson, Mary Leakey

[1] Female skull discovered in Gibraltar in 1848 but unrecognized till 1864.
[2] Earliest specimen found at Engis, near Liège, Belgium, in 1832 by Schmerling.
[3] Exposed by X-Ray and radio-activity tests in Nov., 1953, as an elaborate fraud.
[4] Non-hominoid. Complete skull discovered 1948 by Mrs. Leakey.
[5] Further part discovered 1955.
[6] Since 1957, evidence is that these relate to a non-hominoid giant ape.
[7] Complete skull in 1958 (Kitching).

**Of great importance because of its uncanny resemblance to Peking man which Leakey believes is more correctly datable to triple the age advanced by the Chinese.

Geology

Rocks of the Earth's crust are grouped in three principal classes:

(1) Igneous rocks have been solidified from molten *magma* and are divided into extrusive rock, *viz.* lava and pumice, or intrusive rock, such as some granites or gabbro which is high in calcium and magnesium and low in silicon. It should be noted that extreme metamorphism (transformation) can also produce granitic rocks from sediment.

(2) Sedimentary rocks are formed by the deposition of sediment in water, *viz.* conglomerates (*e.g.* gravel, shingle, pebbles), sandstones and shales (layered clay and claystone). Peat, lignite, bituminous coal and anthracite are the result of the deposition of organic matter. Gypsum, chalk and limestone are examples of chemical sedimentation.

(3) Metamorphic rocks were originally igneous or sedimentary but have been metamorphosed by the action of intense heat, pressure or the action of water. Gneiss is metamorphosed granite, marble is metamorphosed limestone, and slate is highly pressurized shale. Metamorphic rocks made cleavable by intense heat and pressure are known generically as schist. Their foliate characteristics are shared by both gneiss and slate.

Gemstones

Gemstones are minerals possessing a rarity and usually a hardness, color or translucency which gives them strong aesthetic appeal. Diamond, emerald, ruby and sapphire were once classed as "precious stones" and all other gemstones as "semi-precious". This distinction is no longer generally applied. The principal gemstones in order of hardness are listed below with data in the following order:—name; birthstone (if any); chemical formula; classic color; degree of hardness on Mohs' Scale 10–1; principal localities where found; brief notes on outstanding specimens. A metric carat is ⅕th of a gramme. It should be noted that most gems are found in many colors and that only the classic color is here described. In 1937 the National Association of Goldsmiths (G.B.) unified the various national lists of birthstones; their list, which completely agrees with an earlier U.S. version, is followed here.

Diamond: (birthstone for April); C (pure crystalline isotope); fiery bluish-white; Mohs 10.0; S., S.W. and E. Africa and India with alluvial deposits in Australia, Brazil, Zaïre, India, Indonesia, Liberia, Sierra Leone and U.S.S.R. (Urals). Largest uncut: *Cullinan* 3,106 carats (over

DIAMOND MINING: When diamonds were found in Kimberley, South Africa, in 1871, a shanty town sprang up (see surface) and mining began in earnest. By 1875, primitive methods of digging by an army of prospectors had produced this large excavation.

20 oz.), by Capt. M. F. Wells, Premier Mine, Pretoria, S. Africa on Jan. 26, 1905. Cut by Jacob Asscher of Amsterdam 1909. Largest cut: *Cullinan I*, or *Star of Africa*, from the above in British Royal Sceptre at 530.2 carats. *Koh-i-nor* originally 186 carats now re-cut to 106 carats; also in British Crown Jewels. The largest colored diamond is the 44.4 carat vivid blue *Hope diamond* from Killur, Golconda, India (*before* 1642) in the Smithsonian Institution, Washington, D.C. since November, 1958.

Ruby: (birthstone for July); Al_2O_3 (corundum with reddening trace of chromic oxide); dark red; 9.0; Brazil, Burma, Sri Lanka, Thailand. Largest recorded gem is 1,184 carat stone from Burma; broken red corundum originally of 3,421 carats (not gem quality) July, 1961.

Sapphire: (birthstone for September); Al_2O_3 (corundum with bluish trace of iron or titanium); dark blue; 9.0; Australia, Burma, Sri Lanka, Kashmir, U.S.A. (Montana). Largest cut: *Star of India*, 563.5 carats from Sri Lanka now in American Museum of Natural History, New York City. Largest uncut: 1,200 carats (white stone) from Anakie, Queensland, May, 1956.

Alexandrite: $BeAl_2O_4$ (chrysoberyl); dull green in daylight but blood red by artificial light; 8.5; Brazil, Moravia, U.S.A. (Connecticut), U.S.S.R. (Urals).

Cat's Eye: $BeAl_2O_4$ (chrysoberyl, variety cymophane); yellowish to brownish-green with narrow silken ray; 8.5.

Topaz: (birthstone for November); $Al_2(F, OH)_2SiO_4$; tea colored; 8.0; Australia, Brazil, Sri Lanka, Germany, Namibia, U.S.S.R. The largest recorded is one of 596 lb. from Brazil.

Spinel: $MgAl_2O_4$ with reddening trace of Fe_2O_3; red; 8.0; mainly Sri Lanka and India.

Gemstones (continued)

Emerald: (birthstone for May); $Be_3Al_2(SiO_3)_6$ (beryl); vivid green; 7.5–8.0; Austria, Colombia, Norway, U.S.A. (N. Carolina), U.S.S.R. (Urals); largest recorded beryl prism (non-gem quality) 135 lb. from Urals; largest gem: Devonshire stone of 1,350 carats from Muso, Colombia.

Aquamarine: (birthstone for March); $Be_3Al_2(SiO_3)_6$ (beryl), pale limpid blue; 7.5–8.0; found in emerald localities and elsewhere, including Brazil; largest recorded 229 lb. from near Marambaia, Brazil, 1910.

Garnet: (birthstone for January); silicates of Al, Ca, Cr, Fe, Mg, Ti; purplish-red (almandine, Fe_3 $Al_2[SiO_4]_3$; 7.5–8.0; India, Sri Lanka, U.S.A. [Arizona]); green (andradite, $Ca_3Fe_2[SiO_4]_3$; 6.5–7.0; U.S.S.R. [Siberia and Urals]; black (mal, $TiCa_3$) $(Fe, Ti, Al)_2[SiO_4]_3$; 6.5.

Zircon: $ZrSiO_4$; colorless but also blue and red-brown (hyacinth); 7.0–7.5; Australia (N.S.W.), Burma, Sri Lanka, India, North America, Thailand, U.S.S.R. (Siberia).

Tourmaline: complex boro-silicate of Al, Fe, Mg alkalis; notably deep green, bluish green, deep red; 7.0–7.25; Brazil, Sri Lanka, U.S.S.R. (Siberia).

Rock Crystal: (birthstone for April, alternative to diamond); SiO_2; Colorless; 7.0; Brazil, Burma, France, Madagascar, Switzerland, U.S.A. (Arkansas). The largest recorded crystal ball is one of 106 lb. from Burma now in the U.S. National Museum, Washington, D.C.

Rose quartz: SiO_2; coarsely granular pale pink; 7.0; Bavaria, Brazil, Finland, Namibia, U.S.A. (Maine), U.S.S.R. (Urals).

Cairngorm: (smoky quartz); SiO_2; smoky yellow to brownish; 7.0; Brazil, Madagascar, Manchuria, Scotland (Cairngorm Mountains), Switzerland, U.S.A. (Colorado), U.S.S.R. (Urals).

Amethyst: (birthstone for February); SiO_2; purple; 7.0; Brazil, Sri Lanka, Germany, Madagascar, Uruguay, U.S.S.R. (Urals).

Chrysoprase (chalcedony form): (birthstone for May, alternative to emerald); SiO_2 with nickel hydroxide impurity; apple green (opaque); 6.5–7.0; Germany, U.S.A.

Jade: $NaAlSi_2O_6$; dark to leek green; 6.5–7.0; Burma, China, Tibet (pale green and less valuable form is nephrite, $Na_2Ca_4(Mg, Fe)_{10}$ $[(OH)_2O_2Si_{16}O_{44}]$).

Cornelian (chalcedony form); often (wrongly) spelt carnelian; (birthstone for July, alternative to ruby); SiO_2 with ferric oxide impurity; blood red to yellowish-brown; 6.5–7.0; widespread, including Great Britain.

Agate (striped chalcedony): SiO_2; opaque white to pale gray, blue; 6.5–7.0; a variety is moss agate (milky white with moss-like inclusions, often green); Brazil, Germany, India, Madagascar, Scotland.

Onyx: a black and white banded agate (see Agate).

Sardonyx (birthstone for August, alternative to peridot); a reddish-brown and white-banded agate (see Agate).

Jasper (chalcedony): SiO_2 with impurities; brown (manganese oxide), red (ferric oxide), yellow (hydrated ferric oxide); opaque; 6.5–7.0; Egypt, India.

Peridot (green olivine): (birthstone for August); $(Mg, Fe)_2SiO_4$; green; 6.0–7.0; Australia (Queensland), Brazil, Burma, Norway, St. John's Island (Red Sea).

Bloodstone or Blood Jasper (chalcedony): (birthstone for March, alternative to aquamarine); SiO_2; dark green with red spots (oxide of iron); 6.0–7.0.

Moonstone (feldspar): (birthstone for June, alternative to pearl); $(K, Na)AlSi_3O$; white to bluish iridescent; 6.0–6.5; Brazil, Burma, Sri Lanka.

Opal: (birthstone for October); $SiO_2 \cdot nH_2O$; rainbow colors on white background; other varieties include fire opal, water opal, black opal; 5.0–6.5; Australia, Mexico and formerly Hungary. The largest recorded is one of 143 oz. named *Olympic Australis* from near Coober Pedy, S. Australia in August, 1956.

Turquoise: (birthstone for December); $CuAl_6(Po_4)_4(OH)_8 4H_2O$; sky blue; 5.5–6.0; Egypt (Sinai Peninsula), Iran, Turkey, U.S.A. (California, Nevada, New Mexico, Texas).

Lapis Lazuli: (birthstone for September, alternative to sapphire); $(Na, Ca)_8[(S, Cl, SO_4)_2(AlSiO_4)_6]$; deep azure blue, opaque; 5.5–5.75; Afghanistan, Chile, Tibet, U.S.S.R. (Lake Baikal area).

Obsidian: (glassy lava); green or yellowish-brown; 5.0–5.5; volcanic areas.

NON-MINERAL GEM MATERIAL

Amber (organic): about $C_{40}H_{64}O_4$; honey yellow, clear, or paler yellow, cloudy; 2.0–2.5; mainly Baltic and Sicily coasts. A variety is fly amber in which the body of an insect is encased.

Coral (polyps of *Coelenterata*): varied colorations including Blood or Red Coral; Australasia, Pacific and Indian Oceans.

Pearl: (birthstone for June); (secretions of molluscs, notably of the sea-water mussel, genus *Pinctada*, and the fresh-water mussel, *Quadrula*); western Pacific; largest recorded is the *Hope Pearl* weighing nearly 3 oz., circumference $4\frac{1}{2}$ inches. A nacreous mass of 14 lb. 2 oz. from a giant clam (*Tridacna gigas*) was recovered in the Philippines in 1934 and is known as the "Pearl of Allah."

PETROLEUM

Most deposits of petroleum are found in sedimentary rocks representing deposition in shallow new seas which once supported flora and fauna. The assumption that oil is a downward migration of such organic decay is now modified by the abiogenic theory, which maintains that some of the heavy hydrocarbons may have sprung, already polymerized, from deep layers of hot magma.

Engineering

Seven Wonders of the World

The Seven Wonders of the World were first designated by Antipater of Sidon in the second century A.D. They are, or were:

Name	Location	Built (circa)
1. Three Pyramids of Gîza (El Gîzeh)* (*Still stand*)	near El Gîzeh, Egypt	from 2,580 B.C.
2. Hanging Gardens of Semiramis, Babylon (*No trace left*)	Babylon, Iraq	600 B.C.
3. Statue of Zeus (Jupiter) by Phidias (*Destroyed by fire*)	Olympia, Greece	*after* 432 B.C.
4. Temple of Artemis (Diana) of the Ephesians (*Destroyed by Goths 262 A.D.*)	Ephesus, Turkey	*before* 350 B.C.
5. Tomb of King Mausolus of Caria (*Fragments survive*)	Halicarnassus (now Bodrum), Turkey	*after* 353 B.C.
6. Statue of Helios (Apollo) by Chares of Lindus, called the Colossus of Rhodes (117 ft. tall) (*Destroyed by earthquakes 224 B.C.*)	Rhodes, Aegean Sea	292–280 B.C.
7. Lighthouse (400 ft.) on island of Pharos (*Destroyed by earthquakes 400 and 1375 A.D.*)	off Alexandria, Egypt	200 B.C.

---

* Built by the Fourth Dynasty Pharaohs, Hwfw (Khufu or Cheops), Kha-f-Ra (Khafre or Khefren) and Menkaure (Mycerinus). The Great pyramid ("Horizon of Khufu") originally had a height of 480 feet 11 inches (now, since the loss of its topmost stone or pyramidion, reduced to 449 feet 6 inches), Khafre's pyramid was 470 feet 9 inches, and Menkaure's was 218 feet tall.

LARGEST INHABITED BUILDINGS: The twin towers of the World Trade Center dwarf all the other high-rises of New York City's waterfront.

TALLEST INHABITED BUILDINGS

Height in feet	No. of Stories	Building and Location
1,454	110	Sears Tower (1974), Chicago, Ill.
1,350	110	World Trade Center (1973), New York City
1,250*	102	Empire State Building (1930), New York City
1,136	80	Standard Oil Building (1973), Chicago, Ill.
1,127	100	John Hancock Center (1968), Chicago, Ill.
1,046	77	Chrysler Building (1930), New York City
950	67	60 Wall Tower, New York City
935	72	First Canadian Place (1977), Toronto, Canada
927	71	40 Wall Tower, New York City
914	46	First National City Corp., New York City
900	71	Bank of Manhattan, New York City
859	74	Water Tower Plaza (1975), Chicago, Ill.
858	62	United California Bank (1974), Los Angeles, Calif.
853	48	Transamerica Pyramid, San Francisco, Calif.
850	60	First National Bank of Chicago (1969), Chicago, Ill.
850	70	R.C.A. Building, New York City
841	64	U.S. Steel Building (1971), Pittsburgh, Pa.
813	60	Chase Manhattan Building, New York City
808	59	Pan American Building (1963), New York City
800	64	MLC Office Tower (1977), Sydney, Australia
792	60	Woolworth Building (1911–13), New York City
790	60	John Hancock Tower, Boston, Mass.
787	28	Mikhail Lomonosov University Building (1953), Moscow, U.S.S.R.
784	57	Commerce Court, Toronto, Ontario
778	52	Bank of America, San Francisco, Calif.
764	57	One Penn Plaza, New York City
756	33	Palace of Culture and Science, Warsaw, Poland
750	52	Prudential Tower, Boston, Mass.
750	54	Exxon Building, New York City

* The Empire State Building was completed in 1930 to a height of 1,250 feet. Between July 27, 1950 and May 1, 1951, a 222-feet TV tower was added.

TALLEST STRUCTURES (excluding Skyscrapers)

Height in   *Structure and Location*
feet

2,120	Warszawa Radio Mast (May 1974,) Konstantynow, nr. Plock, Poland
2,063	KTHI-TV (December 1963), Fargo, N.D.
1,898	KSLA-TV (1966), Shreveport, La.
1,815	CN Tower, Metro Center (April 1975), Toronto, Canada
1,762	Ostankino TV Tower (May 1967) (13 ft added in 1973), (self supporting), Ostankino, Moscow, U.S.S.R.
1,749	WRBL-TV & WTVM (May 1962), Columbus, Ga.
1,749	WBIR-TV (September 1963), Knoxville, Tenn.
1,673	KFVS-TV (June 1960), Cape Girardeau, Mo.
1,638	WPSD-TV, Paducah, Ky.
1,619	WGAN-TV (September 1959), Portland, Me.
1,610*	KSWS-TV (December 1956), Roswell, N.M.
1,600	WKY-TV, Oklahoma City, Okla.
1,572	KWTV (November 1954), Oklahoma City, Okla.
1,521	B.R.E.N. Tower (unshielded atomic reactor) (April 1962), Nevada

Other Tall Structures

1,378	Loran Radio Mast, Snaefellsnes, Iceland
1,345	Danish Govt. Navigation Mast, Greenland
1,312	Peking Radio Mast, Peking, China
1,271	Tower Zero, North West Cape, W. Australia
1,265	IBA TV Mast, Belmont, Lincolnshire, England
1,265	TV Mast, Emley Moor, Yorkshire, England
1,253	Zender Lopik TV Mast, near Lopik, Netherlands
1,251	International Nickel Co. Chimney (1970), Sudbury, Ontario, Canada
1,212	Thule Radio Mast (1953), Thule, Greenland
1,206	American Electric Power Smokestack, Cresap, W. Virginia
1,200	Kennecott Copper Corp. Chimney, Great Salt Lake, Utah
1,185	TV Tower, West Berlin, Germany
1,179	Television Center, Moscow
1,150	TV Tower, Vinnitsa, Ukraine, U.S.S.R.
1,100	Loran Radio Mast, Tomil, Yap Island, Pacific
1,093	CHTV Channel II Mast, Hamilton, Ont., Canada
1,092	Tokyo Television Mast (self supporting), Tokyo, Japan
1,065	Leningrad TV Mast, Leningrad, U.S.S.R.
1,052	La Tour Eiffel (1887–89), Paris, France

* Fell in a gale, 1960; re-erected.

MONT BLANC TUNNEL: Workmen drilling through rock during the construction of the tunnel through the 15,781-foot-high French mountain, completed in 1965.

LONGEST VEHICULAR TUNNELS

Water supply tunnels or aqueducts having only a moderate diameter are lengthier than even the longest vehicular tunnels. The longest example is the 13½-foot diameter West Delaware-New York City aqueduct (1937–45) which runs 85.0 miles from the Rondout Reservoir to Manhattan.

Miles	Name and Location	Built
33.49	Seikan (rail), Tsugaru Channel, Japan	1972–82
17.30	Northern Line (tube), East Finchley-Morden, London	1939
12.31	Simplon II (rail), Brigue, Switzerland-Iselle, Italy	1918–22
12.30	Simplon I (rail), Brigue, Switzerland-Iselle, Italy	1898–1906
11.6	Shin Kanmon (rail), Kanmon Strait, Japan	1975
11.49	Great Appenine (rail), Vernio, Italy	1923–34
10.1	St. Gotthard (road), Göschenen-Airolo, Switzerland	1971–78
10.0	Rokko (rail), Japan	
9.85	Henderson (rail), Rocky Mts., Colorado	1975
9.26	St. Gotthard (rail), Göschenen-Airolo, Switzerland	1872–82
9.03	Lötschberg (rail), Kandersteg-Goppenstein, Switzerland	1906–13
8.61	Hokkuriku (rail), Tsuruga-Imajo, Japan	1957–62
8.5	Mont Cenis (rail extension), Modane, France-Bardonecchia, Italy	1857–81
7.78	Cascade (rail), Berne-Scenic, Wash.	1925–29
7.27	Mont Blanc (road), Pèlerins, France-Entrèves, Italy	1959–65

LONGEST NON-VEHICULAR TUNNELS

Miles

105	Delaware Aqueduct 1937–44	New York State
51.2	Orange-Fish Irrigation 1974	South Africa
44	West Delaware 1960	New York City
31	Central Outfall 1975	Mexico City, Mexico
29.8	Arpa-Sevan hydro-electric u.c.	Armenia, U.S.S.R.
18.8	Thames-Lea Water Supply 1960	Hampton-Walthamstow, London
18.1	Shandfaken Aqueduct 1923	Catskills, New York State
18.0	San Jacinto Aqueduct 1938	California
17.7	Rendalen hydro-electric u.c.	Norway
17.5	Kielder Aqueduct 1980	Tyne-Tees, England
15	Lochaber-hydro-electric 1930	Ben Nevis, Scotland
13.7	Third Water Tunnel 1970–7	New York City
13	Florence Lake Tunnel 1925	California
13	Continental Divide Tunnel 1946	Colorado
12	Ely-Ouse 1969	Cambridgeshire, England

HIGHEST DAMS

Name	River	Country	Completion	Height (ft.)
Nurek	Vakhsh	U.S.S.R.	1979	1017
Grand Dixence	Dixencc-Rhôde	Switzerland	1961	932
Ingurskaya	Inguri	U.S.S.R.	Building	892
Vajont	Piave	Italy	1961	858
Mica	Columbia	Canada	Building	794
Sayany	Yeniseyi	U.S.S.R.	Building	794
Chivor	Bata	Colombia	1975	778
Mauvoisin	Rhône	Switzerland	1957	777
Oroville	Feather-Sacramento	U.S.	1968	770
Chirkyi	Sulak-Caspian Sea	U.S.S.R.	1975	764
Chicoasen	Grijalva	Mexico	1980	761

MOST MASSIVE EARTH AND ROCK DAMS

Name	Volume (millions of cubic yards)
New Cornelia Tailings, Ariz. (1973)	274.0
Tarbela, Indus Pakistan (1975)	186.0
Fort Peck, Mont. (1940)	125.6
Oahe, S.D. (1963)	92.0
Mangla, Jhelum, Pakistan (1967)	85.8
Gardiner, South Saskatchewan, Canada (1968)	85.7
Afsluitdijk, Netherlands	82.9
Oroville, Feather, Calif.	78.0
San Luis, Calif.	77.6
Nurek, Vakhsh, Tadjikistan, U.S.S.R.†	76.0
Garrison, N.D. (1956)	66.5
Cochiti, U.S.A.	64.6
Tabka, Syria	60.1
Kiev, Dnieper, Ukraine, U.S.S.R. (1964)	57.5
W. A. C. Bennett (formerly Portage Mountain), Canada (1968)	57.2
Aswan High Dam (Sadd-el-Aali), Egypt	57.2

† Under construction.

GREATEST MAN-MADE LAKES

Name of Dam	Capacity miles^3
Owen Falls, Uganda (1964)	48.50
Bratsk, Angara River, U.S.S.R. (1964)	40.59
Aswan High Dam, Sadd-el-Aali, Nile, Egypt (1970)	39.36
Kariba, Rhodesia-Zambia (1959)	38.38
Akosombo, Volta, Ghana (1965)‡	35.50
Daniel Johnson, Manicouagan, Quebec, Canada (1968)	34.07
Krasnoyarsk, Yeniseyi, U.S.S.R.	17.58
W. A. C. Bennett (Portage Mountain), Canada (1967)	16.79
Zeya, E. Siberia, U.S.S.R.†	16.41
Wadi Tharthar, Tigris, Iraq (1956)	16.00
Ust-Ilim, Angara, U.S.S.R.†	14.23
V. I. Lenin, Volga, U.S.S.R. (1953)	13.68

† Under construction.
‡ Lake, Volta, Ghana, is the largest artificial lake measured by area (3,275 miles^2).

Note: Owen Falls Dam regulates the natural Victoria Nyanza which is the world's third largest by area.

LONGEST CANALS

Length (Miles)	Name	Year Opened	Min. Depth (Feet)	No. of Locks
141	White Sea (Beloye More)–Baltic (formerly Stalin) Canal	1933	16½	19
	Links the Barents Sea and White Sea to the Baltic with a chain of a lake, canalized river, and 32 miles of canal.			
100.6	Suez Canal	1869	39.3	Nil
	Eliminates the necessity for "rounding the Cape." Deepening in progress.			
62.2	V. I. Lenin Volga–Don Canal	1952	—	13
	Interconnects Black, Azov and Caspian Seas.			
60.9	North Sea (or Kiel) Canal	1895	45	2
	Shortens the North Sea–Baltic passage; south German–Danish border. Major reconstruction 1914.			
56.7	Houston (Texas) Canal	1940	34	Nil
	Makes Houston, although 50 miles from the coast, the United States' eighth busiest port.			
53	Alphonse XIII Canal	1926	25	13
	Makes sea access to Seville safe. True canal only 4 miles in length.			
50.71	Panama Canal	1914	41	6
	Eliminates the necessity for "rounding the Horn." 49 miles of the length was excavated.			
39.7	Manchester Ship Canal	1894	28	4
	Makes Manchester, although 54 miles from the open sea, Britain's third busiest port.			
28.0	Welland Canal	1931	29	7
	Circumvents Niagara Falls and Niagara River rapids.			
19.8	Brussels or Rupel Sea Canal	1922	21	4
	Makes Brussels an inland port.			

Note: 1. The Volga-Baltic canal system runs 1,850 miles from Leningrad *via* Lake Ladoga, Gorky, Kuybyshev and the Volga River to Astrakhan. The Grand Canal of China, completed in the 13th century over a lengh of 1,107 miles from Peking to Hangchou, had silted up to a maximum depth of 6 feet by 1950 but is now being reconstructed.

2. The world's longest inland navigation route is the St. Lawrence Seaway of 2,342 miles from the North Atlantic up the St. Lawrence estuary and across the Great Lakes to Duluth, Minnesota. It was opened on April 26, 1959.

LONGEST BRIDGING

Length (miles)	Name	Date Built	Location
23.87	Lake Pontchartrain Causeway II	1969	Mandeville-Jefferson, La.
23.83	Lake Pontchartrain Causeway I	1956	Mandeville-Jefferson, La.
17.65	Chesapeak Bay Bridge-Tunnel	1964	Delmarva Peninsula–Norfolk, Va.
15.0	Sunshine Skyway	1954	Lower Tampa Bay, Florida
11.85*	Great Salt Lake Viaduct (Lucin cut-off)	1904	Great Salt Lake, Utah
8.7	Ponte Presidente Costa e Silva	1974	Niteroi, Brazil
8.0	Chesapeak Bay I	1952	Virginia
8.0	Chesapeak Bay II	1972	Virginia
7.0	San Mateo-Hayward	1967	San Francisco, Calif.

Other Notable Bridging

Length (miles)	Name	Date Built	Location
4.2	Nanking	1968–9	Yangtze Kiang, China
3.77	Oeland	1972	Sweden
3.75	London Bridge-Deptford Creek (878 brick arches)	1836	London
3.5	North Beveland to Schouwen Duiveland (52 arches)	1966	Netherlands
3.12	Eastern Scheltd	1965	Netherlands
2.28*	Lower Zambezi (46 spans)	1934	Dona Ana-Vila de Sena, Mozambique
2.24*	Lake of Venice (222 arches)	1846	Mestre-Venice, Italy
2.21*	New Tay Bridge (85 spans)	1887	Wormit, Fife-Dundee, Angus, Scotland
1.99	Storstrom (3 arches, 51 piers)	1937	Sjaelland-Falster, Denmark
1.9	Upper Sone	1900	Sone River, India

* Rail viaduct.

LARGEST OIL TANKERS

Name and Flag	Year Completed	High Deadweight (Tons)	Length (ft.)	Breadth (ft.)	High Gross Registered Tons
Pierre Guillaumat (France)	1977	555,031	1,359	206	274,838
Bellamya (France)	1976	553,662	1,359	206	275,276
Batillus (France)	1976	550,000	1,358	206	273,550
Esso Atlantic (Japan)	1977	516,893	1,333	233	234,627
Esso Pacific (Japan)	1977	516,423	1,333	233	234,626
Nissei Maru (Japan)	1975	484,337	1,243	203	238,517
Globtik London (Japan)	1973	483,939	1,243	203	238,207
Globtik Tokyo (Japan)	1973	483,664	1,243	203	238,252
Burmah Endeavour (Taiwan)	1977	447,000	1,241	223	231,629
Esso Mediterranean (Japan)	1976	446,500	1,241	223	170,559
Berge Empress (Japan)	1976	423,700	1,252	223	211,400
Hilda Knudsen (Japan)	1975	423,639	1,240	226	203,996
Esso Deutschland (Japan)	1976	421,678	1,240	226	203,869
Al Rekkah (Japan)	1977	414,366	1,200	229	210,068
Berge Emperor (Japan)	1975	414,000	1,285	223	211,360
Jinko Maru (Japan)	1976	413,549	1,200	229	207,000
Chevron South America (Japan)	1976	413,159	1,200	229	196,334
Aiko Maru (Japan)	1976	413,012	1,200	229	207,000

† Bulk Oil Carrier.

LONGEST BRIDGE: The Verrazano Bridge across the Narrows of New York's inner harbor as seen from 15,000 ft.

LONGEST BRIDGES (Progressive Chart)

Feet	Name and Location	Type	Completion
142	Narni, Nera River, Lucca, Italy.........	Stone Arch	14 A.D.
c. 250	Lan Chin, Yunnan, China	Timber	65 A.D.
251	Trezzo, Italy	Stone Arch	c.1380
1,420	Chak-sam-chö-rilamasery, River Brah-maputra, Tibet	Suspension	1420
580	Menai Straits, Wales.......................	Chain	1826
870	Fribourg, Switzerland	Suspension	1834
1,010	Wheeling-Ohio Bridge	Suspension	1849
1,043	Lewiston Bridge, Niagara River	Suspension	1851
1,057	Covington-Cincinnati Bridge (rebuilt 1898)	Suspension	1867
1,268	Niagara-Clifton, Canada	Suspension	1869
1,596	Brooklyn Bridge, New York City	Suspension	1883
1,710	Forth (rail) Bridge, Scotland	Cantilever	1889
1,800	Quebec Bridge, Canada	Cantilever	1917
1,850	Ambassador Bridge, Detroit	Suspension	1929
3,500	George Washington Bridge, New York City..	Suspension	1931
4,200	San Francisco Golden Gate Bridge......	Suspension	1937
4,260	Verrazano-Narrows Bridge, New York City..	Suspension	1965
4,626	Humber, England	Suspension	1978
5,840	Akashi-Kaikyo, Japan	Suspension	1988

LARGEST PASSENGER LINERS

The largest surviving liner is the *Queen Elizabeth 2* (U.K.) 66,852 gross tons and 963 ft. in length. The largest liner of all-time was the *Queen Elizabeth* (U.K.) of 82,998 gross tons and 1,031 ft. completed in 1940 and destroyed by fire in Hong Kong as *Seawise University* on Jan. 9, 1972. The longest liner is the *France* of 66,348 gross tons and 1,035 ft. in length completed in 1961 and put out of service in 1975. She was bought by a Saudi Arabian interest on Oct. 24, 1977.

SHIPPING TONNAGES

There are four tonnage systems in use, *viz.* Gross tonnage (G.R.T.), net tonnage (N.R.T.), Deadweight Tonnage (D.W.T.) and Displacement Tonnage.

(1) *Gross Registered Tonnage*, used for merchantmen, is the sum in cubic feet of all the enclosed spaces divided by 100, such that 1 g.r.t. = 100 cubic feet of enclosed space.

(2) *Net Registered Tonnage*, also used for merchantmen, is the gross tonnage (above) less deductions for crew spaces, engine rooms and ballast which cannot be utilized for paying passengers or cargo.

(3) *Deadweight Tonnage*, mainly used for tramp ships and oil tankers, is the number of U.K. long tons (of 2,240 lb.) of cargo, stores, bunkers and, where necessary, passengers which is required to bring down a ship from her light line to her load-water line, *i.e.* the carrying capacity of a ship.

(4) *Displacement Tonnage*, used for warships and U.S. merchantmen, is the number of tons (each 35 cubic feet) of sea water displaced by a vessel charged to its load-water line, *i.e.* the weight of the vessel and its contents in tons.

Biology

BIOLOGICAL CLASSIFICATION

The founder of modern taxonomy is usually regarded as Carolus Linnaeus of Sweden. He drew up rules for botanists and zoologists for the assigning of names to both plants and animals. The binomial system was introduced by him in 1758 with the still standard hierarchy of class, order and genus. The full modern hierarchy for an animal can now extend to 20 strata thus:

Kingdom	Order
Subkingdom	Suborder
Phylum or *Division*	Superfamily
Subphylum or Subdivision	*Family*
Superclass	Subfamily
Class	Tribe
Subclass	Genus
Infraclass	Subgenus
Cohort	*Species*
Superorder	Subspecies

KINGDOM PROCARYOTA

The organisms are characterized by an absence of distinct nuclei. Class Microtatobistes comprise viruses and the rickettsiae, which are intermediate between viruses and bacteria in size and biochemistry.

Order Rickettsiales comprises some 60 species, four families, and were named after the virologist Howard T. Ricketts (U.S.) (1871–1910). No general classification of the 1,000 plus viruses identified has yet been adopted. Eventual classification is expected to be based on the capsid (coat protein) symmetry in divisions between DNA— (deoxyribonucleic acid) and RNA—(ribonucleic acid)—containing forms. These infectious agents measured down to a minute 1.4×10^{-6} mm in diameter.

Bacteria, unicellular micro-organisms often spherical or rod-like, generally range from a micron in diameter to filaments several millimeters in length. They belong to the class Schizomycetes (Greek *Schizo* = I split; Mykes = a fungus) in some 1,500 species in ten orders.

Blue-green algae (Cyanophyta; Greek *Kyana* = corn-flower hence dark blue; phyton = a plant) have no motile flagellated cells and no sexual reproduction. Some 1,500 species have been identified.

KINGDOM PROTISTA

This kingdom, first suggested by Ernst Haeckel in 1866, accommodates the mostly microscopic protozoa (Greek *protos* = first; zoon = an animal), of which some 30,000 species have been described embracing flagellates (Latin *Flagellum*, diminutive of *flagrum* = a whip) ciliates (Latin *Ciliatus* = furnished with hairs) and other forms.

Algae possessing the nuclear, mitochondrial and chloroplast membranes are also included in this kingdom.

KINGDOM FUNGI

The fungus group of some 80,000 species, because of dissimilarities to both plants and animals, are now quite usually placed in a separate kingdom.

Sac fungi (order Endomycetales) comprising yeasts (division Mycota); moulds, mildews; truffles (class Ascomycetes) and lichen (order Lecanorales) which have both an algal and a fungal component.

Club fungi include smuts (order Ustilaginales) so called because of black and dusty masses of spores; rusts (order Uredinales) parasitic on vascular plants and hence destructive to agriculture; mushrooms (order Agaricales); puffballs (order Lycoperdales and order Sclerodermatales) and stinkhorns (order Phallales).

KINGDOM PLANTAE

(See Botany)

KINGDOM ANIMALIA

(See Zoology)

Botany

KINGDOM PLANTAE (THE PLANT KINGDOM)

Division *Chlorophyta* (Greek, *chloros*=grass green; *phyton*=a plant). Green algae in which the chromatophores (*i.e.* plastids, or protoplasmic granules in active cells) are green and with the same pigments as vascular plants, *i.e.* those composed of vessels, as opposed to cells, but without their conducting system. About 5,500 species. The plant body never grows by means of an apical cell (*i.e.* the single cell which is the origin of all longitudinal growth) and the reproductive organs are always one-celled and without a sheath of vegetative cells.

Division *Euglenophyta* (Greek, *eu*=true; *glene*=a cavity; *phyton*=a plant). Mostly naked motile (Latin, *motus*=a moving), *i.e.* movable, unicellular organisms, frequently found in stagnant fresh waters. Algae with grass-green chromatophores. The food reserves are either paramylum (an insoluble carbohydrate related to starch) or fats. Flagella (Latin, *flagellum*=a whip), *i.e.* whip-like appendages by which the plants are able to progress through the water, differ from those of other major groups in that they are inserted in a small interior chamber at the anterior end of a cell. Reproduction is by cell division but several genera are known to form thick-walled resting stages. Sexual reproduction is not definitely known for any species.

Division *Charophyta* (Greek, *chairo*=to rejoice). Stoneworts, growing submerged in fresh or brackish waters. The plant body is multicellular, a slender cylindrical axis bearing nodes (Latin, *nodus* = a knot), *i.e.* whorls of short branches ("leaves"), separated by internodes. The growth is initiated by an apical cell. The sex organs (male and female) are surrounded by envelopes of sterile cells.

Division *Phaeophyta* (Greek, *phaios* = brown and swarthy; *phyton* = a plant). Brown algae. About 900 species, all but 3 being strictly marine, growing along rocky ocean shores, predominantly in the algal flora of colder seas, and usually where the water is less than 50 feet deep. These are all multicellular and the primary food reserve is laminarin, a carbohydrate dissolved in the cell sap.

Class *Isogeneratae* (Greek, *isos* = equal to; Latin, *generatio* = a begetting). The life history consists of the alternation of similar generations.

Class *Heterogeneratae* (Greek, *heteros* = other). The life history consists of the alternation of dissimilar generations. The gametophytes (*i.e.* the generations bearing the sexual organs) are always irregularly branched filaments.

Class *Cyclosporeae* (Greek, *kyklos* = a circle). About 350 species, mostly in oceans. In this class there is no gametophytic generation, and the spores function as gametes. The reproductive organs are borne in round cavities (conceptacles) within tips of the sporophytic plant body, and each conceptacle contains many sex organs.

Division *Rhodophyta* (Greek, *rhodon* = a rose [hence a red color]; *phyton* = a plant). Red algae. About 2,500 species, of which about 50 are fresh-water and the rest marine, predominantly in the algal flora of tropical seas. The Rhodophytes have chromatophores in which the photosynthetic pigments are masked by a red pigment (phycoerythrin; from Greek, *erythros* = red); sometimes there is also a blue pigment (phycocyanin). The chief food reserve is an insoluble carbohydrate, floridean starch. Sexual reproduction is unique in that non-flagellate male gametes (spermatia) are passively transported to female sex organs. The plant body is usually a simple blade, a much-divided blade or more complex and differentiated into stem- and blade-like portions.

Division *Chrysophyta* (Greek, *chrysos* = gold; *phyton* = plant). These have golden-brown chromatophores and a storage of reserve foods as leucosin or fats. They form a distinctive type of spore, the endospore, *i.e.* a spore formed within.

Division *Xanthophyceae* (Greek, *xanthos* = yellow) or **Heter okontae** (Greek, *heteros* = other; *kontos* = a pole). Yellowish-green algae, almost exclusively fresh-water. About 200 species. These have yellowish-green chromatophores and store foods as leucosin or as oils, never as starch.

Division *Bacillariophyceae* (Latin, *bacillus* = a staff). Diatoms. Microscopic unicellular or colonial algae. Over 5,500 species. These have cell walls composed of two overlapping halves and a bilateral or radially symmetrical ornamentation of the wall.

Division *Pyrrhophyta* (Greek, *pyrrhos* = flame colored; *phyton* = a plant). The Pyrrophytes are the only algae with yellowish to brownish chromatophores that store reserve foods as starch or starch-like compounds. Motile cells are biflagellate, usually with the flagella unequal in length and movement.

Class Desmophyceae (Greek, *desmos* = a bond). All rare organisms, mostly marine. These have a cell wall vertically divided into two homogeneous, *i.e.* uniform, halves (valves). Motile cells have two apically inserted flattened flagella that differ from each other in type of movement.

Class Dinophyceae (Greek, *dinos* = whirling). About 950 species, almost all marine plankton. Ninety per cent of the genera are unicellular and motile. The cells of most species have numerous golden-brown to chocolate-brown chromatophores, but the cells of certain species lack chromatophores. Motile cells and zoospores are encircled by a transverse groove—the girdle. The two flagella are inserted in or near the girdle; one of them encircles the girdle, the other extends vertically backward.

Division Bryophyta (Greek, *bryon* = a moss) or **Atracheata** (Greek, *a-* = without; Latin, *trachia* = the wind-pipe). The Bryophytes—mosses and liverworts. The sex cells (gametes) are contained in a single-layered jacket of cells, as opposed to a simple cell wall (as in Algae).

Class Hepaticae (from Latin, *hepaticus* = pertaining to the liver). The typical liverworts, sometimes called the hepatics. The spore case (capsule) frequently has sterile slender cells (elaters) among the spores, or in some cases no sterile tissue. The elaters, if present, are unicellular. The cells of the sporophyte have several to many small chloroplasts (*i.e.* green plastids). There are both leafy and thalloid forms. The leafy members of the class often resemble mosses, but usually have two rows of leaves, or two rows of large leaves and a third row of small leaves on the side of the stem towards the substrate. The thalloid forms are flattened ribbons or rosettes without leaflike structures on the stems.

Class Anthocerotae (Greek, *anthos* = a flower; *keras* = a horn). A group of horned liverworts, often called hornworts. Similar to *Hepaticae*, except for the indeterminate basal growth of the needle-shaped sporophyte, so that mature spores may be falling from the top of the apically split sporophyte while new ones are being initiated at the base. The cells of the sporophyte have two large chloroplasts containing starch-producing bodies called pyrenoids. The sporophyte has a sterile central column (columella) and pores (stomata) in the epidermis (the plant-skin or covering). The members of this class usually have irregular multicellular elaters. This class is sometimes included within the Hepaticae. There are about 9,000 liverworts.

Class Musci (Latin, *muscus* = moss). The true mosses. The spore case has a cylinder of sterile tissue (columella) in the center surrounded by many minute spores and usually has a definite lid (operculum) which opens by splitting loose when the spores are ripe. Under the operculum is a single or double row (peristome) of slender, triangular teeth which ring the mouth and are hygroscopic (*i.e.* susceptible to extension or shrinkage on the application or removal of water or vapor) and move in response to changes in moisture. When the teeth are dry they curl back exposing the interior of the capsule; when moist, they curve inward, effectively blocking the mouth of the capsule, thus controlling to some extent the dissemination of spores. The mosses are usually classified into three orders: *Sphagnales* (usually known as bog or peat mosses), *Andreaeales* (slit mosses), and *Bryales*. There are about 14,000 mosses.

Botany (continued)

Division *Tracheophyta* or *Tracheata* (Latin, *trachia*=the wind-pipe). The Tracheophytes—plants possessing tracheae, *i.e.* spiral ducts or water-conducting vessels in the woody tissue of plants, formed from the coalescence of series of cells by the disappearance of the partitions between them. The vascular plants.

Subdivision *Psilopsida* (Greek, *psilos*=naked, smooth). Grasslike plants with a creeping stem, small, scalelike leaves and no true roots. This class contains two orders, *Psilophytales* (comprising only fossil types) and *Psilotales*, which contains the single family *Psilotaceae*. These plants grow epiphytically (*i.e.* on other plants, but not parasitically) or in soil rich in humus.

Subdivision *Lycopsida* (Greek, *lykos*=a wolf). Club-mosses and quillworts. These are in fact vascular plants and quite distinct from the true mosses. The leaves are relatively small and simple in form while the sporangia are seated singly, one in the axil of each leaf of the fertile region, or spreading outwards on its base.

Subdivision *Sphenopsida* (Greek, *sphen*=a wedge; *opsis*=appearance). Horsetails. These are *Pteridophytes* which have their appendages disposed in successive whorls, with long internodes between them. The class contains three orders, *Hyeniales*, *Sphenophyllales* (both extinct now) and *Equisetales* (from Latin, *equus*=a horse; *seta*=a bristle), which has two families—*Calamitaceae* (extinct) and *Equisetaceae*. This latter family contains a single genus, *Equisetum*, comprising the horse-tails—semi-aquatic plants varying in height from a few inches to 30 feet or more, with erect shoots arising from richly branched, subterranean stems, which are themselves rooted in the soil.

Subdivision *Pteropsida* (Greek, *pteris*=a fern).

Class *Filicinidae* (Latin, *filix*=a fern). The ferns— over 9,500 living species. The most distinctive feature of this group is that on the relatively large leaves many sporangia are borne, either singly or in groups (sori). Most ferns flourish under moist conditions with a moderate temperature, and the plant varies in size from a minute herb to a tree-like body, rising to a height of 80 feet. The life cycle is split into two distinct bodily phases, or generations—the leafy spore-bearing fern plant and the prothallus, a small green scale-like body which represents the sexual generation. This subclass contains four orders—the *Coenopteridales* (now extinct), *Marattiales* (from the genus *Marattia*), *Ophioglossales* (adder's tongue ferns), and *Filicales* (the "true" ferns).

Class *Gymnospermidae* or *Gymnospermae* (Greek, *gymnos* =naked; *sperma*=seed or *Pinophyta*). The Gymnosperms form the first of the two groups of living seed plants. The members of this class have naked ovules, exposed to the pollen at the time of pollination, and naked seeds, and the male gametophytes always produce more sterile cells than those of the angiosperms. The female gametophyte is comparatively large and produces large eggs in cellular structures called archegonia. The gymnosperms have several embryos beginning their development, depending upon how many eggs are fertilized, but only one usually survives the intense competition to maturity. The roots are predominantly tap-roots (*i.e.* straight roots tapering to a point growing directly downwards from the stem). The reproductive unit is the strobilus or cone, which consists of a large axis bearing either megasporophylls (the ovule-containing organs), each subtended, in conifers, by a sterile bract (a modified leaf), or microsporophylls (the pollen-containing organs). Living gymnosperms include only woody perennial plants which are usually evergreen trees, seldom shrubs, or lianas. The gymnosperms may be divided into three groups:

Subclass *Cycadopsida*. The cycads and cycad-like plants.

Order *Cycadofilicales* (or *Pteridospermae*)—the so-called seed ferns (now extinct).

Order *Bennettitales* (or *Cycadeioidales*)—cycad-like plants whose relations are uncertain (now extinct).

Order *Cycadales* (Greek, *kykas*, from *kiakos*, plural of *koix*=name of a kind of palm)—the Cycads, of which there are about 100 living species, which all grow very slowly. Those of the columnar type attain their maximum height only after many centuries of growth. They have only a scanty zone of wood surrounding a very large pith and enclosed by a very large cortex (*i.e.* bark or rind), so the stem is relatively weak.

Order *Caytoniales*. A small group, probably of pteridospermous origin with the ovules borne in hollow spherical bodies (cupules). They are sometimes included with Pteridospermales.

Subclass *Coniferopsida*. The conifers and related plants. Order *Cordaitales* (resembling the extinct genus, *Cordaites*). These were mostly trees of considerable size, resembling modern conifers.

Order *Ginkgoales*. This order is almost entirely extinct, being represented by only a single living species, *Ginkgo biloba* (the maidenhair tree), which is native to China. The twigs of this tree are long shoots, bearing many dwarf branches, which continue their growth on the end of long shoots of the previous year, bearing leaves that alternate in a spiral arrangement.

Order *Coniferales* (Latin, *conus*=a cone; *fero*=bear). The conifers, of which there are about 550 living species, such as the pine, spruce, cedar, larch and Douglas fir. The conifers are cone-bearing trees, which are usually evergreen and have profusely branched stems, with needlelike leaves that are usually small and simple and normally persist for about three to ten years. There is a lateral growth zone, or cambium, which gives rise to a large amount of wood surrounded by a thin cortex and enclosing only a small amount of pith. The seed cones may be large and made up of dozens of cone scales, but in some cases the seed-bearing scales are single ovules. All conifers have pollen borne in cones which are usually quite small.

Order *Taxales*. The Taxads (formerly included in *Coniferales*)—yew trees and related plants. The

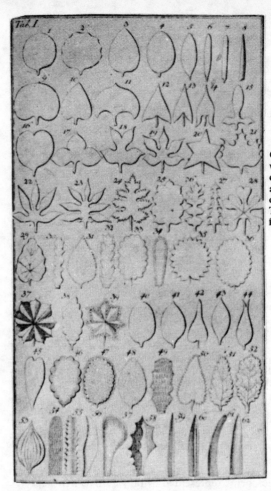

CAROLUS LINNEAUS
was the first to arrange
every known plant and
animal according to their
common characteristics.
This is a page of leaves
from one of his works.

Conifers (continued)

members of this order are, in most respects, similar
to conifers, but it has been discovered that they
have never had ovulate cones, *i.e.* the ovules are
borne terminally and singly on axes of the plant and
are not aggregated into cone-like structures.

Subclass *Gnetopsida*
Order *Gnetales*—contains about 71 species. This
order contains perennial, normally dioecious (*i.e.*
unisexual) plants with opposite simple leaves. The
cones consist of an axis bearing decussate pairs (*i.e.*
alternately at right angles) of bracts or a number of
superposed whorls of bracts, each whorl connate
(united) in a cup-like form. The ovulate or staminate
structures (called "flowers") are axillary to these
bracts (*i.e.* growing in an axil), and consist of one or
two pairs of free or connate scales, the perianth,
enclosing either a single ovule with a long projecting
micropylar tube (*i.e.* from an aperture in the outer
coat of the ovule), or from one to six stamens.

Class *Angiospermae* (from Greek, *angeion*=receptacle; *sperma*=seed) or *Magnoliophyta*. The true flowering plants, of which there are more than 250,000 species. The angiosperms have ovules enclosed within the ovary of a pistil (gynoecium) and the seeds are enclosed within the ripened ovary, which, when matured, becomes a fruit that may be single-seeded or many-seeded. The angiosperms usually have fibrous roots and soft herbaceous stem tissue. The leaves contain extensive mesophytic tissue (*i.e.* requiring only an average amount of moisture). The reproductive unit is the flower, which typically consists of a very short central axis bearing one or more apical megasporophylls, commonly called carpels, subtended by microsporophylls (termed stamens) and by two sets of sterile bract-like appendages collectively termed the perianth (composed of petals and sepals). In the simplest form of the flower, the ovules are borne along the inner margin of the megasporophyll—like peas in the pod. In all modern angiosperms the megasporophyll is closed and fused marginally, with the ovules in the loculus (cavity) thus formed. In this form the carpel is termed the pistil and consists of the ovary (the ovule-containing organ) and its apical stigma (the pollen-receiving part). The microsporophylls are closed until maturity, when they open and their pollen is released. The pollen-producing part is the anther and the supporting stalk the filament. The fertilization (which follows pollination) takes place entirely within the carpel of the flower. After the pollen grain (microgametophyte) reaches the receptive stigmatic surface of the pistil, a pollen tube is developed within, and into it moves the generative nucleus, which divides to form two male nuclei, each of which is a male gamete. Stimulated by the environment created in the stigma, the pollen tube grows through the wall of the pollen grain and into the tissue of the stigma and its style (*i.e.* the usually attenuated part of a pistil between the ovary and the stigma). This growth continues down the style until the tube penetrates the ovary. Growth continues and when the tube reaches the ovule it enters the micropyle (a pore at the tip of the ovule) or elsewhere through the integuments (*i.e.* the two outer layers of the ovule) and finally the female gametophyte (enclosed within the ovule). As pollen-tube growth progresses from stigma to female gametophyte, it carries with it both male nuclei. On approach to the egg nucleus, within the female gametophyte, the two haploid male nuclei are released. One unites with the haploid egg nucleus and forms a diploid sporophyte, called the zygote, and the other unites with the polar nuclei to form a triploid endosperm nucleus. The zygote thus formed is a new generation, and becomes the embryo within the seed. The zygote (enclosed by a membrane) undergoes a series of divisions leading to wall formation (either transverse or longitudinal) separating the terminal cell from the basal cell. The terminal cell continues to divide to produce the axis or hypocotyl of the embryo, from which are later produced the cotyledons (Greek, *kotyledon*=cup-shaped hollow) or seed leaves (either one or two—see below under subclasses). The basal cell divides to form a chain of cells that functions as a suspensor, and the lowest is attached to the embryo and ultimately gives rise to the root and root cap of the embryo. The endosperm nucleus, together with the embryo sac, multiplies to form the endosperm tissue of the seed. This tissue multiplies as the embryo develops, but the bulk of it is digested by the embryo. The angiosperms may be divided into two groups:

Subclass *Dicotyledonae* (Greek, *di*=two) or *Magnoliopsida*. The dicotyledons—over 200,000 species contain angiosperms in which the embryo has two cotyledons (seed leaves). The stems produce a secondary growth by successive cylinders of xylem tissue (Greek, *xyle*= wood), the wood element which, in angiosperms, contains vessels for water conduction and wood fibers for support. The veins of the leaves are typically arranged in a network, *i.e.* reticulate venation. Leaves may be simple, with entire or toothed margins, or compound, with leaflets arranged on either side of, or radiating from a petiole, or footstalk. The petals and sepals of the flowers number mostly four or five, or multiples of four or five, and the pollen grains are mostly tricolpate (with three furrows). This group may be subdivided into 40 or more orders, of which the following are among the larger and more important. They are listed in the general sequence of primitive to advanced:

Order *Ranales* (or *Magnoliales*)—Buttercup, magnolia, tulip tree, marsh marigold, barberry, lotus, custard apple, nutmeg, etc.

Order *Rosales*—Rose, strawberry, blackberry, apple, cherry, legumes, saxifrages, witch hazel, plane tree, etc.

Order *Papaverales* (or *Rhoeadales*)—Poppy, cabbage and relatives, mignonette, bleeding heart, the mustard family (*Cruciferae*), etc.

Order *Geraniales*—Geranium, flax, castor bean, the citrus group, etc.

Order *Umbellales*—The carrot family, English ivy, the dogwoods, etc.

Order *Rubiales*—Madder, honeysuckle, coffee, cinchona, teasel, etc.

Order *Campanulales*—The bellflowers, the aster family (*Compositae*), etc.

Order *Caryophyllales*—The pinks, pigweed, spinach, buckwheat, sea lavender, thrift, etc.

Order *Ericales*—Heath, rhododendron, mountain laurel, blueberry, cranberry, etc.

Order *Gentianales*—Gentian, buddleia, olive, privet, ash, dogbane, milkweed, etc.

Order *Polemoniales*—Polemonium, morning glory, phlox, forget-me-not, potato, tobacco, petunia, etc.

Order *Lamiales*—The mints, salvia, verbena, teak, lantana, etc.

Order *Scrophulariales*—Snapdragon, mimulus, trumpet vine, gloxinia, bladderwort, acanthus, etc.

There are several families of dicotyledons which appear to have no direct relationship with any other group. These include the *Salicaceae* (willows and poplars), *Casuarinaceae* (the Australian pine, not a true pine), *Fagaceae* (beeches and oaks) and the *Proteaceae*.

Subclass *Monocotyledonae* (Greek, *monos*=one) or *Liliatae*. The monocotyledons—about 50,000 species. The embryo has one cotyledon. The members of this subclass have stems without any secondary thickening; the vascular strands are scattered through the stem and no cylinders of secondary xylem tissue are produced. The leaves have entire margins, the blades generally lack a petiole, and the veins are arranged in parallel form. The flower parts are always in multiples of three, and the sepals are often petal-like. The pollen grains are always monocolpate, *i.e.* with one furrow. This subclass contains 15 orders, of which the *Liliales* (Lily order) is considered the most primitive, and the *Orchidales* (Orchid order) the most advanced. This subclass also contains palms, grasses, bamboos, irises, the banana, asparagus, onion, vanilla, pineapple and ginger plants and a great many ornamental herbs, shrubs and vines such as crocus, daffodil, philodendron, dracaena, gladiolus, pothos, amaryllis, and screw pine. This subclass is by far the most important to human subsistence, since it includes such basic food plants as wheat, rice, rye, barley, maize, sugar cane, millet, oats, coconuts and dates.

Fruits

Name	Place of Origin and Date First Known
Apple (*Malus pumila*)	Southwestern Asia; 5th century B.C.
Apricot (*Prunus armeniaca*)	Central and western China; B.C.
Avocado Pear (*Persea americana*)	Mexico and Central America; 1601
Banana (*Musa sapientum*)	Southern Asia; *c.* 1st century A.D.
Cantaloupe (*Cucumis melo*)	Iran and Transcaucasia; *c.* 2400 B.C.
Cherry (*Prunus avium*)	Europe (near Dardanelles); early B.C.
Date (*Phoenix dactylifera*)	unknown; B.C.
Fig (*Ficus carica*)	Syria westward to the Canary Islands; *c.* 4000 B.C.
Grape (*Vitus vinifera*)	around Caspian and Black Seas; *c.* 4000 B.C.
Grapefruit (*Citrus grandis*)	Malay Archipelago and neighboring islands; *c.* 1693
Lemon (*Citrus limon*)	Northern Burma; 11th–13th centuries
Lime (*Citrus aurantifolia*)	Northern Burma; 11th–13th centuries
Mandarin Orange (*Citrus reticulata*)	China; 220 B.C.
Mango (*Mangifera indica*)	Southeastern Asia; *c.* 16th century
Olive (*Olea europaea*)	Syria to Greece; B.C.
Orange (*Citrus sinensis*)	China; 2200 B.C.
Papaya (*Carica papaya*)	West Indian Islands or Mexican mainland; 14th–15th centuries
Peach (*Prunus persica*)	?China; *c.* 2000 B.C.
Pear (*Pyrus communis*)	Western Asia; *c.* 10th century B.C.
Pineapple (*Ananas comosus*)	Guadeloupe; *c.* 1493
Plum (*Prunus domestica*)	Western Asia; *c.* 1500
Persimmon (*Diospyros kaki*)	Southern China; —
Quince (*Cydonia oblonga*)	Northern Iran; B.C.

Fruits (continued)

Rhubarb (*Rheum rhaponticum*) — Eastern Mediterranean lands and Asia Minor; 2700 B.C.

Tomato (*Lycopersicon esculentum*) — Bolivia – Ecuador – Peru; intro. Europe *post* 1523

Watermelon (*Citrullus vulgaris*) — Central Africa; *c.* 2000 B.C.

Vegetables

Vegetables	Place of Origin and Date First Known
Artichoke (*Cynara scolymus*)	Western and central Mediterranean; *c.* 500 B.C.
Asparagus (*Asparagus officinalis*)	Eastern Mediterranean; *c.* 200 B.C.
Beetroot (*Beta vulgaris*)	Mediterranean area; 2nd century B.C.
Broad Bean (*Vicia faba*)	before 4000 B.C.
Broccoli (*Brassica oleracea,* variety *Italica*)	Eastern Mediterranean; 1st century A.D.
Brussels Sprouts (*Brassica oleracea,* variety *Gemmifera*)	Northern Europe; 1587
Cabbage (*Brassica oleracea,* variety *Capitata*)	Eastern Mediterranean lands and Asia Minor; *c.* 600 B.C.
Carrot (*Daucus carota*)	Afghanistan; *c.* 500 B.C.
Cauliflower (*Brassica oleracea,* variety *Botrytis*)	Eastern Mediterranean; 6th century B.C.
Celery (*Apium graveolens*)	Caucasus; *c.* 850 B.C.
Chive (*Allium schoenoprasum*)	Eastern Mediterranean; *c.* 100 B.C.
Corn (*Zea mays,* variety *Saccharata*)	Ancient Andean; intro. Europe *post* 1492
Cucumber (*Cucumis sativus*)	Egypt; 1300 B.C.
Endive (*Cichorium endivia*)	Eastern Mediterranean lands and Asia Minor; B.C.
Garden Pea (*Pisum sativum*)	Central Asia; 3000–2000 B.C.
Garlic (*Allium sativum*)	Middle Asia; *c.* 900 B.C. (Homer)
Gherkin (*Cucumis anguria*)	Northern India; 2nd century B.C.
Kale (*Brassica oleracea,* variety *acephala*)	Eastern Mediterranean lands and Asia Minor; *c.* 500 B.C.
Leek (*Allium porrum*)	Middle Asia; *c.* 1000 B.C.
Lettuce (*Lactuca sativa*)	Iran; 4500 B.C.
Marrow (*Cucurbita pepo*)	Mexican sites; 7000–5500 B.C.
Melon, Musk (*Cucumis melo*)	Africa; 3rd century B.C.
Onion (*Allium cepa*)	Egypt; *c.* 3200 B.C.
Parsnip (*Pastinaca sativa*)	Caucasus; 1st century B.C.
Pepper (*Capsicum frutescens*)	Ancient Peru; intro. Europe 1493
Potato (*Solanum tuberosum*)	Southern Chile; *c.* 1530
Radish (*Raphanus sativus*)	China and central Asia; *c.* 3000 B.C.
Soybean (*Soja max*)	China; *c.* 2850 B.C.
Spinach (*Spinacia oleracea*)	Iran; 647
String Bean (*Phaseolus vulgaris*)	Mexican sites; 7000–5500 B.C.
Swede (*Brassica napobrassica*)	Europe; 1620
Turnip (*Brassica rapa*)	Greece; *c.* 1200 B.C.

Zoology

KINGDOM ANIMALIA or METAZOA (The Animal Kingdom)

A Classification (excluding wholly extinct groups)

The ascending order in animal classifications is subspecies, species, genus, family, superfamily (sometimes), suborder, order, infraclass, class, subphylum, phylum, subkingdom, the animal kingdom.

Animal Kingdom—Dimensions by Species

Scyphozéoa or Scyphomedusae (Jellyfishes). Total number of species in the phylum Cnidaria is 9,600. the jellyfish *Cyanea arctica* with a bell 8 feet in diameter has tentacles extending up to 200 feet in length.

Mollusca—128,000 species: ranging in size between the minute marine gastropods *Homalogyra atomus* and *H. rota* of 0.03 inch, and a known 57 feet 3 inch of the giant squid (*Architeuthis longimanus*), which is the largest of all invertebrates.

Insecta—950,000 (1964) described species of a suspected total of perhaps some 3,000,000: ranging in size from the Battledore wing fairy fly (*Hymenoptera mymaridae*), hairy-winged beetles (family *Trichopterygidae*) 0.008 inch long to the bulky 3.4-ounce, $5\frac{3}{4}$-inch-long African Goliath beetle (*Macrodontia cervicornis*). Insecta embraces the order Lepidoptera of 140,000 species. The wing-span of butterflies range from 12 inches (New Guinea birdwing (*Troides alexandrae*)) to 0.55 inch (South African dwarf blue (*Brephidium barberae*)).

Crustacea—25,000 species: ranging in size from the extremely primitive trilobite-like *Hutchinsonella* and the water flea *Alonella* species at 0.01 inch long to the Giant Japanese Spider Crab (*Macrocheira kaempferi*) with a spread of 12 feet $1\frac{1}{2}$ inches between claws.

Pisces (Fishes), with Selachii and Bradyodontii 23,000 species: ranging from $\frac{3}{8}$-in.-long, 6-milligram Philippine goby (*Pandaka pygmaea*) to the whaleshark (*Rhineodon typus*) weighing up to 40 tons.

Amphibia—2,000 species: ranging in size between the Cuban frog (*Sminthillus limbatus*), less than 0.5 inch long and the $5\frac{3}{4}$-foot-long giant salamander (*Megalobatrachus japonicus*) weighing up to 88 lbs.

Reptilia—5,000 species: ranging in size between the 1.3-inch-long West Indian gecko (*Sphaeodactylus elegans*) and the South American snake anaconda (*Eunectes murinus*), which has been reported to attain $37\frac{1}{2}$ feet in length, and the estuarine crocodile (*Crocodylus porosus*) measuring up to $22\frac{1}{2}$ feet.

Aves—8,600 species: ranging in size from the 0.07-ounce Cuban bee humming bird (*Calypte hellenae*) up to the $12\frac{1}{4}$-foot wingspan Andean condor (*Vultur gryphus*) and the 300-lb., 8-foot-tall ostrich (*Struthio camelus*).

Mammalia—4,500 species: ranging in size, on land, between the 0.1-ounce Savi's white-toothed shrew (*Suncus etruscus*) and the African elephant (*Loxodonta africana*) which may very rarely attain over 11 tons; and, at sea, between the 35-lb. Upper Amazon dolphin Buffeo Negro (*Sotalia fluviotilis*) and the Blue Whale (*Balaenoptera musculus*) which has in an extreme case weighed 195 tons.

Subkingdom *Metazoa* (Greek, *meta*= later in time; *zōon*= an animal). Multicellular animals composed of unlike cells that may lose their boundaries in the adult state, and with at least two cell layers. Contains 21 phyla, as listed below, with about one million described species.

Phylum *Mesozoa* (Greek, *mesos*=middle, the half). Minute parasitic animals, composed of a surface layer of epithelial (*i.e.* nonvascular) cells enclosing reproductive cells. About 50 described species forming two orders, the *Dicyemida* (Greek, *di*=two; *kyēma*=embryo) or *Rhombozoa* (Greek, *rhombos*=turning), which are found only in the kidneys of cephalopods, and the *Orthonectida* (Greek, *orthos*=straight; *nēktos*=swimming), which infest ophiurids, polychaets, nemertines, turbellarians and possibly other groups. Members of this phylum are often considered to be degenerate members of phylum *Platyhelminthes* (see below).

Phylum *Parazoa* (Greek, *para*=near), **also called *Porifera*** (Latin, *porus*=a pore; *fero*=to bear) or ***Spongiida*** (Latin, *spongia*=a sponge).* The sponges. Porous animals whose bodies consist of a rather loose aggregation of several kinds of different cells supported by a framework of spicules or fibers which form intricate skeletal structures. There is an incomplete arrangement into tissues, so there is little co-ordination among the parts of the body. They are fixed objects of indefinite shape, without organ systems or mouth. Reproduction may be either sexual (sponges are often bisexual) or asexual, by means of gemmules. About 4,200 described species, which may be divided into two classes:

> **Class *Nuda*** (Latin, *nudus*=naked) [N.B. Class *Nuda* also occurs in phylum *Ctenophora* (see below)]. Two orders, the *Calcarea* (Latin, *calx*=lime, or chalk) or *Calcispongiae* (Latin, *calcis*, genitive of *calx*), calcareous sponges, whose skeletons have spicules made of calcite ($CaCO_3$); and the *Hexactinellida* (Greek, *hex*=six; *aktis*=a ray; Latin, -*ell*, suffix added to form diminutives), also called *Triaxonida* (Greek, *treis*=three; *axōn*=an axle) or *Hyalospongiae* (Greek, *hyaleos*=glassy, shining), the glass sponges, whose skeletons consist of siliceous spicules, *i.e.* made of opal (SiO_2nH_2O). Includes the Venus's flower basket.

> **Class *Gelatinosa*** (Latin, *gelatina*=a gummy juice) or ***Demospongiae*** (Greek, *dēmos*=multitude). Two orders, the *Tetraxonida* (Greek, *tetra*=four; *axōn*=an axle), including the loggerhead sponge; and the *Keratosa* (Greek, *keratos*, genitive of *keras*=a horn) or horny sponges, including the genus *Spongia* (or *Euspongia*), the bath sponge.

Phylum *Cnidaria* (Greek, *knidē*=nettle) or ***Coelenterata‡*** (Greek, *koilos*=hollow; *enteron*=bowel). The coelenterates, the first group of the *Metazoa* whose cells are completely arranged in tissues, and differentiated into nervous and muscular systems, giving efficient co-ordination of parts and powers of locomotion. The body consists of a small sac, with a single opening at one end (the blastopore). The walls of the sac contain two layers of cells (the inner known as the endoderm, the outer the ectoderm), one passing into the other at the margin of the blastopore. It thus contains only one principal internal cavity, the coelenteron, with one opening to the exterior, the mouth. Coelenterates also bear nematocysts, or stinging cells, and have two types of shape, the polyp (*e.g.* a sea anemone) and the medusa. Coelenterates have a tendency towards asexual reproduction, either by fission or budding. This phylum contains about 9,600 described species, grouped as follows:

---

* The classification used here is by Bidder.

‡ This name is sometimes applied to a group comprising phylum *Cnidaria* and phylum *Ctenophora*.

Class *Hydrozoa* (Greek, *hydōr*=water; *zōon*=an animal) **or *Hydromedusae*** (Latin, *Medusa*, the Gorgon with snaky hair). Six orders, including *Siphonophora* (Greek, *siphon*=a tube; *phoros*=a bearing), which contains the genus *Physalia* (Greek, *physalis*=bubble), or Portuguese man-of-war.

Class *Scyphozoa* or *Scyphomedusae* (Greek, *skyphos*=a cup). The jelly fish. Five orders.

Class *Anthozoa* (Greek, *anthos*=a flower). Three subclasses:

Ceriantipatharia (Greek, *keras*=a horn; *anti*=against; *pathos*=suffering). Two orders, including *Antipatharia* (black corals).

Octocorallia (Latin, *octo*=eight; Greek, *korallion*=coral). The soft corals. Three orders.

Zoantharia (Greek, *zōon*=animal; *anthos*=flower). Five orders, including *Actiniaria* (sea anemones) and *Scleractinia* (true corals, stony corals).

Phylum *Ctenophora* (Greek, *ktenos*, genitive of *kteis*=comb; *phoros*=a bearing). The comb jellies. Marine animals with a body structure similar to coelenterates, *i.e.* a single internal cavity opening by one main aperture, the mouth, but with three layers of tissue, the ectoderm, the endoderm, producing the sex cells, and between these the jellylike mesoderm, containing cells and muscle fibers. The biradially symmetrical body has eight strips of modified ectoderm cells, each bearing a comblike plate whose teeth are made up of large waving cilia (hairs). There are no nematocysts (stinging cells). This phylum contains about 80 described species, grouped as follows:

Class *Tentaculata* (Latin, *tentaculum*=a feeler). Four orders. Includes sea gooseberry and Venus's girdle.

Class *Nuda* (Latin, *nudus*=naked). A single order, *Beroida* (Greek, *Beroë*=one of the nymphs, daughter of Oceanus).

Phylum *Platyhelminthes* (Greek, *platys*=flat; *helminthos*, genitive of *helmins*=a worm) **or *Platodaria*** (Greek, *ploats*=flat; Latin, *-od*=form).† The flatworms. Soft-bodied animals with three layers of cells and bilateral symmetry. Mostly hermaphrodites, *i.e.* each individual is functionally both male and female. Tissues and organs developed from three embryonic layers. Muscles render the body capable of great contraction, elongation and variability in shape. No space between digestive tube and body wall. This phylum contains about 15,000 described species, grouped as follows:

Class *Turbellaria* (Latin, *turbellae*, diminutive of *turba*=a disturbance). The turbellarians. Five orders.

Class *Temnocephaloidea* (Greek, *temnō*=to cut; *kephalē*=a head). One order, *Temnocephalidea*, also called *Dactylifera* (Greek, *daktylos*=a finger, or toe; *fero*=to bear) or *Dactyloda*.

Class *Monogenea* (Greek, *monas*=single; *geneos*, genitive of *genos*=a race, kind) **or *Heterocotylea*** (Greek, *heteros*=other, different; *kotylē*=cup-shaped). Two subclasses:

Monopisthocotylea (Greek, *opisthen*=behind), with five orders.

Polyopisthocotylea, with four orders.

Class *Cestodaria* (Greek, *kestos*=a girdle). Two orders.

Class *Cestoda* (Greek, *kestos*=a girdle). Two subclasses:

---

† The classification given here is by Baer.

Didesmida (Greek, *di-*=two; *desma*=a chain, band). One order, *Pseudophyllidea* (or *Bothriocephaloidea*).

Tetradesmida (Greek, *tetra*=four). Nine orders.

Class *Trematoda* (Greek, *trēmatōdēs*=perforated). The flukes. Two subclasses.

Aspidogastrea (Greek, *aspidos*, genitive of *aspis*=a shield; Greek, *gastēr*=the stomach), also called *Aspidocotylea* (Greek, *kotylē*=cup-shaped) or *Aspidobothria* (Greek, *bothrion*, diminutive of *bothros*=a hole).

Digenea (Greek, *di-*=two; *genos*, genitive of *genos*=a race, kind) or *Malacocotylea* (Greek, *malakos*=soft, gentle; *kotylē*=cup-shaped).

Phylum *Nemertina*, or *Nemertea* (Greek, *Nēmertēs*=the name of a Nereid), **also called *Rhynchocoela*** (Greek, *rhynchos*=a beak, snout; *koilos*=a hollow). The nemertines, or ribbon worms. These have soft, ciliated bodies without external indication of segmentation and without a distinct body cavity, the internal organs being separated by gelatinous parenchyma (soft tissue). The intestine opens at the posterior end. They have a long, muscular proboscis, used to capture food. Most species are free-living and marine, and the sexes are generally separate. This phylum contains about 550 described species, grouped as follows:

Class *Anopla* (Greek, *anoplos*=unarmed). The mouth posterior to the brain. Two orders. Includes the bootlace worm.

Class *Enopla* (Greek, *enoplos*=armed). The mouth anterior to the brain. Two orders, including *Hoplonemertina* (Greek, *hoplon*=a weapon), in which the proboscis is armed with one or more calcareous stylets.

Phylum *Aschelminthes* (Greek, *askos*=a bag or bladder; *helminthos*, genitive of *helmins*=a worm). Small, wormlike animals with a pseudocoelom between the digestive tract and the body wall. They usually have an anus, and almost all have a mouth and digestive tract. This phylum contains about 12,000 described species, grouped as follows:

Class Rotifera (Latin, *rota*=a wheel; *fero*=to bear) or **Rotatoria**. The rotifers, or wheel animalcules. Microscopic aquatic animals. Three orders. About 1,500 described species.

Class *Gastrotricha* (Greek, *gastros* [*gasteros*], genitive of *gastēr*=stomach; *trichos*, genitive of *thrix*=hair). Tiny aquatic animals. Two orders. About 140 described species.

Class *Echinoderida* (Greek, *echinōdēs*=like a hedge-hog) or **Kinorhyncha** (Greek, *kineō*=to move; *rhynchos*=a beak, snout). Minute wormlike animals, living chiefly in the slime of the ocean floor. About 100 described species.

Class *Priapulida* (Greek, *Priapos*=god of gardens and reproduction). Small marine worms. Five described species.

Class *Nematomorpha* (Greek, *nēmatos*, genitive of *nēma*=thread; *morpha*=shape) or **Gordiacea** (Greek, *Gordios*=name of a king of Phrygia; hence the Gordian knot). The horse-hair worms. Two orders. About 250 described species.

Class *Nematoda*, or *Nemata** (Greek, *nēmatos*, genitive of *nēma*=thread). The roundworms. About 10,000 described species. Two subclasses:

Phasmidia. Nematodes with phasmids (lateral caudal pores). Three orders.

Aphasmidia. Nematodes without phasmids. Two orders.

Phylum *Acanthocephala* (Greek, *akantha*=a thorn; *kephalē*=a head). The thorny-headed worms. Parasitic animals with no

---

* The classification given here is by Chitwood and Chitwood (1950) and Thorne (1949).

specialized organs for digestion. They live in the intestines of vertebrates and absorb food through the body wall. The sexes are always separate, and males are usually smaller than females. Their length ranges from less than 1/10th inch to over 20 inches. They have a hook-covered proboscis used as an anchor. Three orders. About 300 described species.

Phylum *Entoprocta*, **or** *Endoprocta* (Greek, *entos* or *endon*=within; *prŏktos*=the anus), **also called** *Calyssozoa* (Greek, *kalos*=beautiful; *yssos*=a javelin; *zōon*=an animal), *Kamptozoa* (Greek, *kamptos*= flexible, bent), *Polyzoa Endoprocta* (Greek, *poly*, singular of *polys*= much, many), **or** *Polyzoa Entoprocta*. These aquatic animals are similar to the *Polyzoa* (see below). In this phylum the anterior end bears the lophophore (the ridge bearing the ciliated tentacles) which is circular, and encloses both mouth and anus. Reproductive organs continuous with ducts. They have definite excretory organs. Three families. About 60 described species.

Phylum *Polyzoa* (Greek, *poly*, singular of *polys*=much, many; *zōon* =an animal), **also called** *Bryozoa* (Greek, *bryon*=a lichen), *Polyzoa Ectoprocta*, **or** *Ectoprocta* (Greek, *ektos*=outside, without; *prŏktos* =the anus). In these tiny aquatic animals, the lophophore (see above) is circular or crescentic, enclosing the mouth but not the anus. Specific excretory organs are absent. Reproductive organs not continuous with ducts. They live in the compartments of tubes which they secrete, and capture their food by sweeping the water with tentacles. The individuals bud and remain attached to each other, to form colonies which are generally about an inch across and sometimes plantlike. The colonies are generally encrusting and resemble the growth of lichens. Mostly marine. About 4,000 described species, grouped as follows:

> **Class** *Phylactolaemata* (Greek, *phylaktos*, genitive of *phylax*=a guard; *laimos*=the throat) **or** *Lophopoda* (Greek, *lophos*=the crest; *podos*, genitive of *pous*=a foot). Lophophore generally horseshoe-shaped, guarded by an epistome, a flap of tissue like a lip.

> **Class** *Gymnolaemata* (Greek, *gymnos*=naked; *laimos*=the throat) **or** *Stelmatopoda* (Greek, *stelma*=a crown). Lophophore circular, without epistome. Five orders, including two exclusively extinct.

Phylum *Phoronida* (Latin, *Phoronis*=surname of Io, daughter of Inachus, who was changed into a white heifer). The phoronids. Small, marine, wormlike hermaphrodite animals which live as adults in self-secreted tubes embedded in the sea bottom or attached to solid surfaces. The body is roughly elongate (from 0.3 inch to 8 inches) and bears at one end a crown of from 50 to over 300 tentacles, each one bearing fine hairs (cilia), and arranged in a double row around the usually crescent-shaped mouth, which is covered by an epistome. The digestive tract is U-shaped, and the anus is immediately outside the tentacles. The larvae are free-swimming. Only two genera and about 16 described species.

Phylum *Brachiopoda* (Greek, *brachiōn*=the upper part of the arm; *podos*, genitive of *pous*=a foot). The brachiopods or lamp shells. Marine animals enclosed in a bivalve shell. Inside the valves two coiled, cirrate appendages (brachia), one on each side of the mouth, serve as food-gathering organs. The sexes are usually separate. The valves are bilaterally symmetrical, and the front (ventral) valve is usually larger than the dorsal (or brachial) valve on the back. About 260 described species, grouped as follows:

> **Class** *Inarticulata* (Latin, *in-*=not; *articulatus*=divided into joints). Two orders.

> **Class** *Articulata* (Latin, *articulatus*=divided into joints). Originally two orders (now discarded) and four suborders.

Phylum *Mollusca* (Latin, *molluscus*=soft). The molluscs. The viscera (entrails) are enclosed in a soft sheath, whose lower part is modified as a muscular organ of locomotion, the foot, while the upper part (the mantle) is extended on each side and hangs down as a free fold around the body, enclosing the mantle-cavity. The mantle usually secretes an external calcareous shell of one or more pieces. The coelom is much reduced by the extensive vascular system. Except in the *Bivalvia* (see below), the anterior tegumentary region is modified as a more or less mobile head, usually provided with sensory appendages and sense organs, and the alimentary system is characterized by a tongue beset with chitinous teeth (radula). This phylum contains about 128,000 described species, grouped as follows:

Class *Polyplacophora** (Greek, *poly*, singular of *polys*=much, many; *plakos*, genitive of *plax*=tablet; *phoros*=a bearing), **or *Loricata*** (Latin, *loricatus*=clad in mail). Marine molluscs, including the chitons, or coat of mail shells, with eight articulated plates. From ½ inch to 8 inches in length. Two orders.

Class *Aplacophora** (Greek, *a-*=without) **or *Solenogastres*** (Greek, *sōlēnos*, genitive of *sōlēn*=a channel; *gastēr*=the stomach). Marine molluscs without shells and with the foot greatly reduced. Two orders.

Class *Monoplacophora* (Greek, *monas*=single). Deep-sea molluscs with a single cap-shaped shell. One order. Two rare and small species.

Class *Gastropoda* (Greek, *gastros* (*gasteros*), genitive of *gastēr* =the stomach; *podos*, genitive of *pous*=a foot). Land, fresh-water and marine molluscs with a flattened foot. The shell is generally a spirally coiled single structure, though may be modified, and sometimes covered by a mantle or entirely absent. From a millimeter to 2 feet in length. Three subclasses:

Prosobranchia (Greek, *pros*=forward, towards, in advance of; *branchia*=fins, or the gills of fishes) or *Streptoneura* (Greek, *streptos*=twisted; *neuron*=tendon). Includes the limpet, periwinkle, cowrie and whelk. Three orders.

Opisthobranchia (Greek, *opisthen*=behind). Includes the sea-hare, sea-butterflies and sea-slugs. Four orders.

Pulmonata (Latin, *pulmonatus*=having lungs). Includes the pond snail, fresh-water limpet, land snail and land-slugs.

Class *Scaphopoda* (Greek, *skaphē*=a bowl; *podos*, genitive of *pous*=a foot). Marine tubular-shelled, burrowing molluscs, commonly called tusk-shells.

Class *Bivalvia* (Latin, *bi*=two; *valva*=a leaf of a folding door), **also called *Lamellibranchia*** (Latin, *lamella*, diminutive of *lamina*=a thin plate; Greek, *branchia*=the gills of fishes) **or *Pelecypoda*** (Greek, *pelekys*=a hatchet; *podos*, genitive of *pous* =a foot). The bivalves. Aquatic headless molluscs, mostly marine, which generally live buried in sand or mud. The shell has two hinged parts. Includes the cockle, mussel, oyster, scallop, gaper and clam. Four orders.

Class *Cephalopoda* (Greek, *kephalē*=a head; *podos*, genitive of *pous*=a foot) **or *Siphonopoda*** (Greek, *siphon*=a tube). Marine molluscs, some without shells. The head and foot are approximate, hence the mouth is situated in the middle of the foot, and the edges of the foot are drawn out into arms and tentacles, equipped with suckers. Includes the cuttle-fish, squid, octopus, pearly-nautilus. Two orders.

Phylum *Sipunculoidea* (Latin, *sipunculus*=a little tube). These animals are marine worms which inhabit burrows, tubes or borrowed

---

* These two classes are sometimes grouped together as *Amphineura* (Greek, *amphi*=double; *neuron*=tendon).

SQUID 250,000,000 YEARS OLD: This fossil of an extinct 10-arm squid was found in northeastern Illinois, an area that was once deep ocean. The center crown is about 30 mm. in diameter, the arms average about 10 mm. in length.

shells. The anus is anterior, situated on the dorsal surface near the base of the proboscis. There is apparently a total lack of segmentation. The body is divided into two regions, a trunk consisting chiefly of the elongated belly of the worm, and a retractile proboscis which bears at its anterior end the mouth, which is partly or completely surrounded by tentacles or tentacle-bearing folds. The proboscis is generally armed with chitinous spines and hooks. About 275 described species.

Phylum *Echiuroidea* (Greek, *echis*=a serpent; *oura*=the tail; *-oideos*=form of). These marine wormlike animals are similar to the *Annelida* (see below), but there is an apparent lack of segmentation. The bodies are generally sac-shaped, and they inhabit U-shaped tubes on sandy-mud bottoms. Attached to the anterior end of the trunk is a preoral lobe (prostomium), about half as long as the trunk and shaped like a hemispherical fan when fully extended. It is ciliated on its ventral surface and forms a funnel around the mouth. Three orders. About 80 described species, including the spoon-worms.

Phylum *Annelida* or *Annulata* (Latin, *annela* or *annulatus*=ringed). The annelids or segmented worms. These animals are generally provided with movable bristles known as setae (or chaetae), each embedded in a setal follicle, the cell which secretes it. The body consists of an outer tube, or body wall, and an inner tube, or alimentary canal, separated by the body cavity (coelom), which is generally divided into compartments by transverse partitions, the septa. This phylum contains about 8,000 described species, grouped as follows:

Class *Polychaeta* (Greek, *poly*, singular of *polys*=much, many; Latin, *chaeta*=a bristle). These are primarily marine and have numerous tufts of setae, borne upon projecting lobes (parapodia) at the sides of the body. Sometimes divided into two subclasses: *Errantia* (Latin, *errantis*, genitive of *errans*=wandering) and *Sedentaria* (Latin, *sedentarius*=sitting), which includes the lugworm.

Class *Myzostomaria* (Greek, *myzō*=to suck in; *stoma*=mouth). Usually external or internal parasites.

Class *Oligochaeta* (Greek, *oligos*=few; Latin, *chaeta*=a bristle). Terrestrial, limicolous or fresh-water worms, sometimes secondarily marine or parasitic. Sometimes divided into two orders. Includes the white worm and earthworms.

Class *Hirudinea* (Latin, *hirudinis*, genitive of *hirudo*=a leech). The leeches. These are annelids with terminal suckers, 34 body segments or somites, no parapodia nor setae. They are hermaphrodites, and the body cavity is largely obliterated. The length is from about $\frac{1}{4}$ inch to 18 inches. Three orders.

Class *Archiannelida* (Greek, *archi*=first). Largely marine or brackish water inhabitants.

Phylum *Arthropoda* (Greek, *arthron*=a joint; *podos*, genitive of *pous*=a foot). The arthropods. Bilaterally symmetrical animals whose bodies are divided into segments, arranged in a chain along a horizontal axis, each segment typically bearing a pair of jointed appendages (legs). The skin is composed of a layer of cells (the hypodermis), a supporting internal basement membrane, and an external layer of chitinous material, which contains hardened or sclerotized areas or plates. This phylum, the largest in the animal kingdom, is grouped as follows:

Class *Onychophora* (Greek, *onychos*, genitive of *onyx*=claw; *phoros*=a bearing). Tropical wormlike arthropods, apparently allied to primitive *Annelida* (see above). 73 described species.

N.B. The next four classes form the old group *Myriapoda* (Greek, *myrias*=the number 10,000, hence many; *podos*, genitive of *pous*=a foot), containing about 11,000 described species.

Class *Pauropoda* (Greek, *pauros*=small; *podos*, genitive of *pous*=a foot). Minute progoneates with nine or ten pairs of legs.

Class *Diplopoda* (Greek, *diploos*=double). The millipedes. Trunk composed of many double segments, each bearing two pairs of legs. Two subclasses:

Pselaphognatha (Greek, *psēlaphaō*=to feel about; *gnathos*=the jaw). Small soft-bodied millipedes bearing bristles (setae) of several kinds arranged in rows and bundles (fascicles). No copulatory organs (gonopods). One order.
Chilognatha (Greek, *cheilos*=a lip). The skin forms a hard shell bearing setae singly. Gonopods well developed. Three superorders, containing ten orders.

Class *Chilopoda* (Greek, *cheilos*=a lip; *podos*, genitive of *pous*=a foot). The centipedes. Wormlike body divided into head and trunk. The many segments of the trunk each bear a single pair of legs. Two subclasses:

A 100,000,000-YEAR-OLD ANT PRESERVED IN AMBER: This member of the
Formicidae (ant) family, sp. *Sphecomyrma fryi*, was discovered in 1966 by two
amateur mineralogists while out collecting rock specimens along the New Jersey shore.
Sphecomyrma fryi has both ant-like and wasp-like characteristics and is presumed to
be a common ancestor of both.

Epimorpha (Greek, *epi*=on, upon; *morphē*=form, shape).
The young hatch with the full number of body segments and
walking legs. Two orders.

Anamorpha (Greek, *ana-*=up, throughout). The young
hatch with usually 7 but sometimes 12 pairs of legs. Additional segments and legs appear later. Two orders.

Class *Symphyla* (Greek, *sym-*=together; *phylē*=a tribe, race).
With long antennae. Trunk with 12 or more single segments
and 12 pairs of legs.

Class *Insecta* (Latin, *in-*=into; *sectus*=cut, cleft) or ***Hexapoda***
(Greek, *hex*=six; *podos*, genitive of *pous*=a foot). The insects.
Body divided into head (with mouth parts and sense organs),
thorax (usually with wings and three pairs of legs) and abdomen (with the digestive, respiratory, reproductive and excretory
organs). About 950,000 described species. Two subclasses:

Apterygota (Greek, *a-*=without; *pterygotōs*=winged), or
Ametabola (Greek, *a-*=without; *metabola*=change). Primitive wingless insects with nine pairs of appendages on the
abdomen and no true metamorphosis, *i.e.* change in form.
Includes spring-tails and bristle-tails. Four orders.

Pterygota (Greek, *pterygotōs*=winged) or *Metabola* (Greek,
metabola=change). Insects which have wings, or vestiges

of wings, and in which metamorphosis takes place. Two divisions:

Palaeoptera (Greek, *palaios*=ancient; *pteron*=wing). May-flies and dragonflies. Two orders.

Neoptera (Greek, *neos*=new, recent; *pteron*=wing). Three sections:

Polyneoptera (Greek, *poly*, singular of *polys*=much, many). Includes cockroaches, termites, grasshoppers, crickets, locusts and earwigs. Nine orders.

Paraneoptera (Greek, *para*=beside, near). Includes lice, thrips and bugs. Four orders.

Oligoneoptera (Greek, *oligos*=few, small), also called *Endopterygota* (Greek, *endon*=within; *pterygotos*= winged) or *Holometabola* (Greek, *holos*=entire; *metabola*=change). Complete metamorphosis. Includes beetles, caddis flies, butterflies, moths, flies, mosquitoes, fleas, ants, wasps and bees. Ten orders.

Class *Crustacea* (Latin, *crustaceus*=having a shell or rind). The crustaceans. Generally aquatic, they have two pairs of antenna-like appendages in front of the mouth. They breathe by gills or by the general surface of the body. Head and thorax usually fused. About 25,000 described species. Seven subclasses:

Branchiopoda (Greek, *branchion*=a fin; *podos*, genitive of *pous*=a foot). The branchiopods. Mostly in fresh water, their limbs are flattened and leaflike. Includes the water fleas. Five orders.

Ostracoda (Greek, *ostrakōdēs*=testaceous, resembling a shell). The ostracods. Minute aquatic clamlike crustaceans, whose body and limbs are completely enclosed in a hinged double shell (bivalve). Four orders.

Copepoda (Greek, *kōpē*=handle, oar; *podos*, genitive of *pous*=a foot). The copepods. Abundant microscopic aquatic crustaceans, an important source of food (as plankton) in the sea. Many are parasitic. Seven orders.

Mystacocarida (Greek, *mystakos*, genitive of *mystax*=upper lip, moustache; Latin, *caridis*, genitive of *caris*=a shrimp). One order.

Branchiura (Greek, *branchia*=the gills of fishes).

Cirripedia (Latin, *cirrus*=a curl; *pedis*, genitive of *pes*=a foot). The cirripedes. Completely sedentary aquatic crustaceans. Many are parasitic. Includes the barnacles and acorn shells. Four orders.

Malacostraca (Greek, *malakos*=soft; *ostrakon*=a shell). Crustaceans whose bodies are composed of nineteen somites, all of which generally have appendages. The thorax has eight parts, and the abdomen six pairs of limbs. Six superorders:

Leptostraca (Greek, *leptos*=thin, small; *ostrakon*=a shell) or *Phyllocarida* (Greek, *phyllon*=a leaf; Latin, *caridis*, genitive of *caris*=a shrimp). Marine and mud-burrowers. The abdomen has seven segments. One order.

Syncarida (Greek, *syn-*=together; Latin, *caridis*, genitive of *caris*=a shrimp). A small fresh-water group. Two orders.

Peracarida (Greek, *pēra*=a pouch). Includes opossum-shrimps, woodlice, the fresh-water shrimp, shore hopper and whale louse.

Hoplocarida (Greek, *hoplon*=a tool, weapon). The mantis shrimps. Exclusively marine. One order.

    Pancarida (Greek, *pan*=all). Minute, blind, creeping crustaceans. One order.

    Eucarida (Greek, *eu-*=true). The eyes are stalked, and the carapace (shell) fused dorsally with all thoracic somites. Includes krill, prawns, shrimps, crayfish, lobsters and crabs. Two orders.

Class *Merostomata* (Greek, *mēros*=the thigh; *stomatos*, genitive of *stoma*=mouth). The king crabs. Large marine arthropods whose bodies are composed of a cephalothorax bearing six pairs of appendages and an abdomen terminated by a long, strong spine. Respiration aquatic. One order. Four described species.

Class *Arachnida* (Greek, *arachnē*=a spider). Arthropods whose bodies are composed of cephalothorax, generally bearing four pairs of legs, and abdomen. There are no antennae. Respiration aerial by means of book-lungs or by tracheae. Includes scorpions, spiders, phalangids, mites and ticks. Ten orders. About 60,000 described species.

Class *Pycnogonida* (Greek, *pyknos*=solid, strong; *gōnia*=a joint), **or** *Pantopoda* (Greek, *pantos*, genitive of *pan*=all; *podos*, genitive of *pous*=a foot). Sea spiders. Marine arthropods whose bodies are composed of a large, five-segmented cephalothorax and a minute abdomen. The genital pores are paired on the second segment of the last two legs of the male and all legs of female. There are no respiratory or excretory organs. Four orders. About 440 described species.

Class *Pentastomida* (Greek, *penta-*=five; *stoma*=mouth) **or** *Linguatulida* (Latin, *linguatus*=with a tongue). The pentastomes. Unsegmented but superficially annulated, wormlike, bloodsucking arthropods which live as internal parasites of vertebrates. Two orders. About 60 described species.

Class *Tardigrada* (Latin, *tardus*=slow; *gradior*=to walk). The tardigrades, or water-bears (bear animalcules). Minute free-living arthropods whose bodies are divided into a well-developed head region and a trunk of four fused segments, each bearing a pair of short unjointed legs, generally with several claws. Found among aquatic vegetation and other damp places. Two orders. About 280 described species.

Phylum *Chaetognatha* (Latin, *chaeta*=a bristle; Greek, *gnathos*=the jaw). The arrow worms. Transparent, mostly pelagic, wormlike animals. The body is usually between 0.4 inch and 1.2 inches, divided into head, trunk and tail, separated from each other by two transverse septa. The head is covered by a retractable hood, and bears upon its side a number of sickle-shaped, chitinous hooks and rows of low spines. They are hermaphrodite and have no gill slits. About 50 described species.

Phylum *Pogonophora* (Greek, *pōgōnos*, genitive of *pōgōn*=beard; *phoros*=a bearing) **or** *Brachiata* (Latin, *brachiatus*=having arms). The beard worms. Wormlike animals which live on the sea-floor. Enclosed in a chitinous tube and may be up to 12 inches long. A "beard" of tentacles at the front end. No mouth or anus. Separate sexes. Two orders, 100 known species.

Phylum *Echinodermata* (Greek, *echinos*=a hedge-hog; *dermatos*, genitive of *derma*=skin). The echinoderms. Marine headless animals in which most of the body structures are divided into five sectors, often giving a radial appearance. The skin contains minute spicules of calcite, which usually grow together into plates, small bones or prickles. There is no definite excretory system. The mouth is originally in a median position but moves to the left as the animal develops. The blood system consists of a number of spaces, and there is no heart or regular circulation. About 5,700 described species, grouped as follows:

Subphylum *Pelmatozoa* (Greek, *pelmatos*, genitive of *pelma*= a stalk; *zōon*=an animal). Mostly deep-water echinoderms. The body is normally borne on a stem, with five arms (brachia) containing the organs and systems. One class:

Class *Crinoidea* (Latin, *crinis*=hair; *oideus*=form of). Includes feather stars and sea lilies. One order.

Subphylum *Eleutherozoa* (Greek, *eleutheros*=free; *zōon*=an animal). Free-moving echinoderms not borne on a stem. Four classes:

Class *Holothuroidea* (Greek, *holos*=whole; *thura* [*thyra*]=a door). The holothurians, or sea cucumbers. The surface turned to the sea-floor is always the same. They normally move only in the direction of the mouth. Five orders.

Class *Echinoidea* (Greek, *echinos*=a hedge-hog). The echinoids. The prickles (radioles) are highly developed, movable and sometimes poisonous. They live with the mouth downwards and can move sideways in any direction. Two subclasses:

Perischoechinoidea (Greek, *peri*=near; *schoinos*=a reed). One order of sea urchins.

Euechinoidea (Greek, *eu-*=true). Four superorders:

Diadematacea (Greek, *dia*=through; *dema*=a bundle). Two orders of sea urchins.

Echinacea (Greek, *echinos*=a hedge-hog). Five orders of sea urchins.

Gnathostomata (Greek, *gnathos*=the jaw; *stoma*=mouth). Includes sand-dollars and cake urchins. Two orders.

Atelostomata (Greek, *atelēs*=imperfect). Includes heart urchins. Four orders.

Class *Asteroidea* (Greek, *asteroeidēs*=like a star). The starfishes. Generally live with the mouth downwards. From it radiate five ciliated grooves. They move by crawling. Three orders.

Class *Ophiuroidea* (Greek, *ophis*=a snake; *oura*=the tail; *ōideos*=form of). The brittle stars. Similar to *Asteroidea* but they move by wriggling. Most have no more than five arms. Includes the serpent stars. Two orders.

Phylum *Chordata* (Latin, *chordata*=having a notochord). The chordates. Sometime during their life these have an elongated skeletal rod, or notochord (Greek, "back-string") which stiffens the body, with a single, hollow nerve chord located on the dorsal side. They possess a pharynx, an enlarged chamber whose sides are perforated by gill slits, just behind the mouth. The blood is contained within vessels and propelled by a heart located on the ventral side, and they generally have a tail extending beyond the anus. About 45,000 described species, grouped as follows:

Subphylum *Hemichordata* (Greek, *hēmi*=half), also called *Stomochordata* (Greek, *stoma*=mouth) or *Branchiotremata* (Greek, *branchion*=a fin; *trēmatos*, genitive of *trēma*=a hole). The hemichordates. Soft-bodied marine wormlike chordates whose notochord is only a tiny tubular rod in the head region. 91 described species, comprising three classes:

Class *Enteropneusta* (Greek, *enteron*=bowel, intestine; *pneustikos*=for breathing). The acorn worms. Burrowing hemichordates whose bodies are composed of a proboscis, a mouth, a ringlike collar and a very long trunk with a terminal anus. The nerve cord is partly tubular and there are numerous gill slits.

Class *Pterobranchia* (Greek, *pteron*=fin; *branchia*=the gills of fishes). The pterobranchs. Small (0.04 inch to 0.3 inch) hemichordates which form colonies of tubes in which they breed by budding as well as by sexual reproduction. The nerve cord is solid and there are few or no gill slits. They have a pair of tentaculated arms. Two orders.

Class *Planctosphaeroidea* (Greek, *plankton*=wandering; *sphaira*=a ball, sphere; *ōideos*=form of). A few larvae of unknown parentage.

Subphylum *Urochordata* (Greek, *oura*=the tail) **or** *Tunicata* (Latin, *tunicatus*=clothed with a tunic). The urochordates or tunicates. Exclusively marine chordates, which are mostly fixed growing organisms, roughly resembling a potato, and without a capacity for locomotion. They produce a free-swimming larva with chordate features, but these, except for the gills, are usually lost in the adult state. A rigid tunic is secreted by the skin and helps to anchor them to some solid structure. About 1,600 described species, grouped as follows:

Class *Ascidiacea* (Greek, *askidion*, diminutive of *askos*=a bag or bladder). The ascidians, or sea squirts. Attached urochordates with a dorsal exhalant siphon. The pharynx has transverse rows of ciliated gill slits. Two orders.

Class *Thaliacea* (Greek, *Thalia*=a muse, patroness of comedy). Pelagic urochordates with inhalant and exhalant siphons at opposite ends of the body. They have long, simple gill slits. Three orders.

Class *Larvacea* (Latin, *larva*=the immature form of a changing animal). Small oceanic urochordates which never bud and have a permanent tail. One order, *Copelata* (Greek, *kōpēlatēs*= a rower).

Subphylum *Cephalochordata* (Greek, *kephalē*=a head), **also called** *Acrania* (Latin, *a-*=without; *cranium*=the skull) **or** *Leptocardii* (Greek, *leptos*=thin, small; *kardia*=heart). The cephalochordates. Small marine fish-like chordates that burrow in sand. Similar to *Urochordata* (see above), but they retain the notochord and powers of locomotion throughout life. 13 described species, including the lancelet.

Subphylum *Vertebrata* (Latin, *vertebratus*=jointed) **or** *Craniata* (Latin, *cranium*=the skull). The vertebrates. Chordates with an internal skeleton, comprising a skull, a vertebral column, or backbone, usually two pairs of limb elements and a central nervous system partly enclosed within the backbone. The muscular system consists primarily of bilaterally paired masses. About 43,000 described species, grouped as follows:

The fishes, 23,000 described species of cold-blooded aquatic vertebrates which swim by fins and breathe by gills, comprising four classes:

Class *Marsipobranchii* (Greek, *marsypos* [*marsipos*]=a bag; *branchion*=a fin) **or** *Agnatha* (Greek, *a-*=without; *gnathos*= the jaw). The marsipobranchs. Mostly marine, eel-like fishes without jaws or paired fins. One existing subclass:

Cyclostomata (Greek, *kyklos*=a circle; *stomatos*, genitive of *stoma*=mouth). The cyclostomes. Blood-sucking fishes, comprising lampreys, hagfishes and slime eels. Two orders.

Class *Selachii* (Greek, *selachos*=shark), **also called** *Chondropterygii* (Greek, *chondros*=a grain; *pterygos*, genitive of *pteryx*=the fin), *Chondrichthyes* (Greek, *ichthys*=a fish) **or** *Elasmobranchii* (Greek, *elasmos*=a thin plate; *branchion*=a fin). The selachians. Fishes with jaws, and branchial arches supporting the gills. They have median and paired fins with horny rays, and the skeleton is a series of cartilaginous rods. The mouth is on the underside of the body. There is no air bladder. Four subclasses, three of them Palaeozoic, one existing:

Euselachii (Greek, *eu-*=true). Includes sharks, dogfishes, angelfishes and rays. Two orders.

Class Bradyodonti (Greek, *bradys*=slow; *odontos*, genitive of *odous*=tooth). Fishes with long tapering tails and large paddle-like pectoral fins. One existing subclass:

Holocephali (Greek, *holos*=whole, entire; *kephalē*=a head). The rabbit fishes.

Class Pisces (Latin, *piscis*=a fish) **or Osteichthyes** (Greek, *osteon*=bone; *ichthys*=a fish). The bony fishes. The skeleton is bony, and the slimy skin is covered with scales or bony plates. The mouth is at the front end. Three subclasses:

Palaeopterygii (Greek, *palaios*=ancient; *pterygos*, genitive of *pteryx*=the fin). Includes the sturgeon, paddle-fish, bichir and reed-fish. Two orders.

Neopterygii (Greek, *neos*=new, recent). The ray-finned fishes. Includes the bow-fins, gar-pikes and all the typical present-day fish, such as the herring, sardine, pilchard, salmon, trout, roach, minnow, carp, cod, whiting, hake, sea-horse, perch, bass, mackerel, tunny, barracuda and eels. 34 orders.

Crossopterygii (Greek, *krossoi*=a fringe, tassels). Includes the coelancanth and lung-fishes. Two orders.

Class Amphibia (Greek, *amphibios*=leading a double life). The amphibians. Cold-blooded vertebrates who breathe air largely through their moist skin. They are mostly four-limbed, live on land, and lay their eggs in water. The larva pass through a fishlike aquatic phase (*e.g.* tadpoles) before metamorphosis. About 3,000 described species, grouped as follows:

Order Caudata (Latin, *caudatus*=having a tail) **or Urodela** (Greek, *oura*=the tail). Amphibians with four legs, a long body and a tail. Some live permanently in water, breathing with gills. Includes the salamanders, axolotl, newts and siren. Five suborders.

Order Salientia (Latin, *salientis*, genitive of *saliens*, present participle of *salio*=to jump) **or Anura** (Greek, *an-*=without; *oura*=the tail). Frogs and toads. Tail-less amphibians with long hind legs adapted for jumping. Five suborders.

Order Gymnophiona (Greek, *gymnos*=naked; *ophioneos*= like a serpent) **or Apoda** (Greek, *a-*=without; *podos*, genitive of *pous*=a foot). The caecilians. Small, primitive, limbless, wormlike, burrowing amphibians with a very short tail. Some have scales. Found in tropical climates.

Class Reptilia (Latin, *reptilis*=creeping). The reptiles. Dry-skinned vertebrates whose body temperature is variable, and who breathe air by lungs. The skin is usually covered with horny scales formed by the epidermis. There is a well-developed tongue. Fertilization is internal. The typical reptile has four five-toed limbs. About 6,000 described species, grouped as follows:

Order Rhynchocephalia (Greek, *rhynchos*=a beak, snout; *kephalē*=a head). Primitive lizardlike reptiles with beaked upper jaws. The only living species is the tuatara of New Zealand.

Order Testudines (Latin, *testudinis*, genitive of *testudo*=a tortoise) **or Chelonia** (Greek, *chelōnē*=a tortoise). Tortoises and turtles. Aquatic and land-dwelling reptiles whose trunk is enclosed in a hard shell built up from a series of dermal bones. They all lay their eggs on land. Two suborders.

Order Crocodilia (Latin, *crocodilus*=a crocodile) **or Loricata** (Latin, *loricatus*=clad in mail). Crocodiles and alligators. Reptiles with short limbs, adapted to aquatic life. They have elongated, heavily-jawed heads and long, flattened tails.

DARWIN'S FAMOUS FINCHES: Charles Darwin noticed that in the Galapagos Islands off Ecuador these birds had developed different species of the same type as on the mainland, and this led to his theory of evolution.

Order *Squamata* (Latin, *squamatus*=scaly). Horny-scaled reptiles. Two suborders:

Sauria (Greek, *sauros*=lizard) or *Lacertilia* (Latin, *lacerta*=a lizard). The lizards.

Serpentes (Latin, *serpentis*, genitive of *serpens*=a serpent) or *Ophidia* (Greek, *ophidion*, diminutive of *ophis*=a snake). The snakes. The jaws are joined by an elastic ligament, and there is no trace of any limbs, except in boas and pythons.

Class *Aves* (Latin, *aves*, plural of *avis*=a bird). The birds. Warm-blooded, egg-laying, feathered vertebrates whose front limbs are modified into wings. Most are thus able to fly. About 8,590 described species, grouped as follows:

Order *Struthioniformes* (Latin, *struthionis*, genitive of *struthio*=an ostrich; *forma*=shape, nature). The ostriches. One family.

Order *Rheiformes* (Greek, *Rhea*=mother of Zeus). The rheas. One family.

Order *Casuariiformes* (Malay, *kasuari*=the cassowary). The emu and cassowary. Two existing families.

Order *Apterygiformes* (Greek, *apterygos*=without wings). The kiwis. One family.

Order *Tinamiformes* (from *tinamou*, the native name) or *Crypturi* (Greek, *kryptos*=hidden; *oura*=the tail). The tinamous. One family.

Order *Gaviiformes** (Latin, *gavia*, the name possibly of the sea-mew). The divers. One family.

Order *Podicipediformes** (Latin, *podicis*, genitive of *podex*=the rump; *pedis*, genitive of *pes*=a foot). The grebes. One family.

Order *Sphenisciformes* (Greek, *sphēniskos*=a small wedge). The penguins. One existing family.

Order *Procellariiformes* (Latin, *procella*=a tempest) or *Turbinares* (Latin, *turbinis*, genitive of *turbo*=something

---

* These two orders are also called *Pygopodes* (Greek, *pyge*=the rump; *podos*, genitive of *pous*=a foot) or *Colymbiformes* (Greek, *kolymbos*=a diving bird).

which spins). Includes the petrels, shearwater, fulmar and albatross. Four families.

Order *Pelecaniformes* (Greek, *pelekan*=a pelican) **or** *Steganopodes* (Greek, *steganos*=covered; *podos*, genitive of *pous*=a foot). Includes the tropic bird, pelican, cormorant, gannet and frigate bird. Six existing families.

Order *Ciconiiformes* (Latin, *ciconia*=a stork) **also called** *Ardeiformes* (Latin, *ardea*=a heron) **or** *Gressores* (Latin, *gressor*=a walker). Includes the herons, the bittern, storks, ibis and spoonbill. Six families.

Order *Phoenicopteriformes* (Greek, *phoinikos*, genitive of *phoinix*=crimson; *pteron*=wing). The flamingos. One existing family.

Order *Anseriformes* (Latin, *anser*=a goose). The screamers, ducks, geese and swans. Two existing families.

Order *Falconiformes* (Latin, *falco*=a falcon) **or** *Accipitres* (Latin, *accipiter*=a bird of prey). Includes the vultures, secretary bird, hawks, kestrel, falcon and osprey. Six existing families.

Order *Galliformes* (Latin, *gallus* [fem. *gallina*]=a fowl). Includes the megapode, curassow, grouse, pheasant, quail, peafowl, turkeys, hoatzin and fowl. Seven existing families.

Order *Gruiformes* (Latin, *gruis*, genitive of *grus*=the crane). Includes the crane, rail, coot and bustard. 12 existing families.

Order *Charadriiformes* (Greek, *charadrios*=a cleft-dwelling bird) **or** *Laro-limicolae* (Greek, *laros*=a ravenous sea-bird [Latin, *larus*=a gull]; Latin, *limus*=mud; *colo*=to inhabit). Includes the plover, gulls, snipe, skua, tern, razorbill, sandpiper, oyster-catcher, puffin, woodcock and avocet. 16 existing families.

Order *Columbiformes* (Latin, *columba*=a dove, pigeon). Includes the sand grouse, pigeon and dove. Three families.

Order *Psittaciformes* (Greek, *psittakē* [*psittakos*]=a parrot). The lories, parrots and macaws. One family.

Order *Cuculiformes* (Latin, *cuculus*=the cuckoo). Includes the plantain-eater and cuckoo. Two families.

Order *Strigiformes* (Greek, *strigos*, genitive of *strix*=an owl). The owls. Two existing families.

Order *Caprimulgiformes* (Latin, *caper* [fem. *capra*]=a goat; *mulgeo*=to milk, to suck). Includes the oil bird, frogmouth and goatsucker, *i.e.* the nightjar. Five families.

Order *Apodiformes* (Greek, *a-*=without; *podos*, genitive of *pous*=a foot), **also called** *Micropodiformes* (Greek, *mikros*=small) **or** *Macrochires* (Greek, *makros*=long, large; *cheir*=hand). The swifts and hummingbirds. Three existing families.

Order *Coliiformes* (Greek, *kolios*=a kind of woodpecker). The colies or mouse birds. One family.

Order *Trogoniformes* (Greek, *trōgōn*=gnawing). The trogons, including the quetzal. One family.

Order *Coraciiformes* (Greek, *korakiao*=a kind of raven). Includes the kingfisher, tody, motmot, bee-eater, roller, hoopoe and hornbill. Nine families.

Order *Piciformes* (Latin, *picus*=a woodpecker). Includes the jacamar, puff-bird, toucan and woodpecker. Six families.

Order *Passeriformes* (Latin, *passer*=a sparrow). The perching birds. Four suborders:

Eurylaimi (Greek, *eurys*=wide, broad; *laimos*=the throat). The broadbills. One family.

Tyranni (Latin, *tyrannus*=a tyrant). Includes the ovenbird and cotinga. 13 families.

Menurae (Greek, *mēnē*=moon; *oura*=the tail). Includes the lyrebird. Two families.

Passeres (Latin, *passer*=a sparrow) or *Oscines* (Latin, *oscines*, plural of *oscen*=a singing bird). The songbirds. Includes the larks, swallow, martins, crows, rook, jackdaw, magpie, jay, bird of paradise, tits, nuthatch, dippers, wren, thrush, blackbird, chats, nightingale, robin, warblers, shrikes, starling, finches and sparrow. 50 existing families.

Class *Mammalia* (Latin, *mammalis*, possessive of *mamma*=breast). The mammals. Warm-blooded, hairy vertebrates whose young are born alive and suckled, *i.e.* nourished with milk from the mother's breasts. About 4,500 described species, grouped as follows:

Subclass *Prototheria* (Greek, *prōtos*=first; *thērion*=a wild animal). The most primitive mammals. One order:

Order *Monotremata* (Greek, *monas*=single; *trematos*, genitive of *trema*=a hole). The monotremes. Egg-laying mammals with a single cloaca, a common outlet for the genital, urinary and digestive organs. They have a beak instead of teeth, no external ears, and milk glands without nipples. Comprises the echidnas, or spiny ant-eaters, and the duck-billed platypus.

Subclass *Theria* (Greek, *thērion*=a wild animal). Mammals with teeth, external ears, separate orifices for the intestine, bladder and reproductive organs and mammary glands with nipples.

Infraclass *Metatheria* (Greek, *meta*=next to). One order:

Order *Marsupialia* (Latin, *marsupium*, from Greek, *marsypion*, diminutive of *marsypos*=a bag). The marsupials. Mammals in which the female has a pouch on the under side, with the nipples of the mammary glands inside the pouch. The young are born in an immature state and finish their development inside the mother's pouch. Includes the opossums, kangaroo, wallaby, wombats, phalanger, bandicoot and koala.

Infraclass *Eutheria* (Greek, *eu-*=true). The eutherians or placental mammals. The developing embryo is fed by the mother's blood indirectly through an organ known as the placenta. 16 orders:

Order *Insectivora* (Latin, *insecta*=insects; *voro*=to devour). The insectivores. Placental mammals with a dentition adapted to an insect diet. The feet generally have five toes, each with a claw. Mostly nocturnal and terrestrial. Includes the tenrec, hedgehog, shrew, mole and desman.

Order *Dermoptera* (Greek, *derma*=skin, leather; *pteron*=wing). Herbivorous, climbing mammals with claws and a gliding membrane. Two species of the colugo or cobego, commonly called flying lemurs.

Order *Chiroptera* (Greek, *cheir*=hand; *pteron*=wing). The bats. The forelimbs are modified to form wings, and these are the only truly flying mammals. Two suborders:

Megachiroptera (Greek, *megas*=great). The fruit bats, including the flying fox.

Microchiroptera (Greek, *mikros*=small). The insectivorous bats.

Order *Primates* (Latin, *primus*=first). The primates. Chiefly tree-dwelling mammals with hands and feet adapted for climbing. The fingers and toes are provided with nails. Three suborders:

Prosimii (Greek, *pro-*=before; Latin, *simia*=ape) or *Lemuroidea* (Latin, *lemures*=shades, ghosts). The lower primates. Includes the tree shrew, loris, bush baby and common lemur.

Tarsii (Greek, *tarsos*=a flat surface). The tarsiers.

Simiae (Latin, *simia*=ape) or *Anthropoidea* (Greek, *anthrōpos*=a man). The brain is highly developed. Includes the marmoset, monkey, baboon, chimpanzee, gorilla and man.

Order *Edentata* (Latin, *e-* [*ex-*]=out, without; *dentatus*=toothed). The edentates. The teeth are either completely absent or undifferentiated, and always absent in the front of the jaws. They have long snouts and long tongues. Includes the sloth, armadillo and anteater.

Order *Pholidota* (Greek, *pholidōtos*=armed with scales). The pangolins, or scaly anteaters. Similar to the edentates, but the body is covered with overlapping horny scales, composed of cemented hairs.

Order *Lagomorpha* (Greek, *lagōs*=a hare; *morphē*=form, shape). Similar to *Rodentia* (see below), but the teeth include two pairs of upper incisors. Includes the pika, hare and rabbit.

Order *Rodentia* (Latin, *rodentis*, genitive of *rodens*=gnawing). The rodents. Gnawing mammals, with one pair of chisel-like incisor teeth, above and below. The feet are generally five-toed. They feed chiefly on plants. Three suborders:

Sciuromorpha (Greek, *skiouros* [Latin, *sciurus*]=a squirrel; *morphē*=form, shape). Includes the squirrel, gopher, beaver, marmot, woodchuck and chipmunk.

Myomorpha (Greek, *myos*, genitive of *mys*=mouse). Includes the mouse, rat, dormouse, vole, hamster, lemming and jerboa.

Hystricomorpha (Greek, *hystrichos*, genitive of *hystrix*=a porcupine). Includes the guinea pig, capybara, chinchilla, coypu and porcupine.

Order *Cetacea* (Greek, *kētos*=a whale). Mammals adapted for aquatic life, mostly marine. The five-fingered skeletal forelimbs are enclosed as paddlelike flippers. The tail has no skeleton, and there is generally a dorsal fin. There is a short neck but no external hind limbs or ears. Hair usually absent. Two existing suborders:

Odontoceti (Greek, *odontos*, genitive of *odous*=tooth). The toothed whales. Includes the sperm whale, porpoise and dolphin.

Mysticeti (Greek, *mystis*=a mystic). The whalebone whales. Includes the rorqual and blue whale.

Order *Carnivora* (Latin, *carnis*, genitive of *caro*=flesh; *voro*=to devour). The carnivores. Mostly flesh-eating mammals, with the teeth adapted for tearing flesh. There are never less than four toes on each foot, each toe with a compressed claw. Two suborders:

Fissipedia (Latin, *fissio*=a cleaving; *pedis*, genitive of *pes*=a foot). Carnivores with paw-like feet divided into toes. The cheek teeth are of several kinds. Includes the dog, wolf, jackal, fox, bear, raccoon, panda, ferret, weasel, mink, ermine, polecat, stoat, marten, sable, badger, skunk, otter, mongoose, hyena, civet, cat, lion, tiger, jaguar, panther, leopard and cheetah.

Pinnipedia (Latin, *pinna*=a wing). Carnivores with limbs adapted to fins. The upper limbs are short and the feet are swimming paddles. The cheek teeth are all alike. Includes the seal, sea lion and walrus.

Order *Tubulidentata* (Latin, *tubulus*, diminutive of *tubus*= a tube; *dentatus*=toothed). The aardvark (Dutch, "earth-pig") or African antbear. A nocturnal burrowing ant-eater, similar to *Edentata* (see above), but with a tubular mouth and long ears.

Order *Proboscidea* (Latin, *proboscidis*, genitive of *proboscis*=a proboscis, from Greek, *proboskis*=an elephant's trunk). The elephants. Large mammals whose heads bear a proboscis (the trunk), a long flexible muscle organ with one or two finger-like processes at its tip.

Order *Hyracoidea* (Greek, *hyrakos*, genitive of *hyrax*=a shrew mouse). Small hoofed mammals, with squat, almost tail-less bodies. Includes the hyrax and coney (or cony).

Order *Sirenia* (Latin, *siren*=a siren, a mermaid). Aquatic mammals with torpedo-shaped bodies. The body has a horizontal tail fluke and very mobile lips. Comprises the dugongs and manatees.

Order *Perissodactyla* (Greek, *perisso*=uneven, odd; *daktylos*=a finger, toe). The perissodactyls, or odd-toed ungulates (hoofed mammals). Herbivorous mammals whose hindfeet each have one or three digits. Two suborders:

Hippomorpha (Greek, *hippos*=a horse; *morphē*=form, shape). Includes the horse, donkey and zebra.

Ceratomorpha (Greek, *keratos*, genitive of *keras*=a horn). Includes the tapir and rhinoceros.

Order *Artiodactyla* (Greek, *artios*=even-numbered; *daktylos*=a finger, toe). The artiodactyls, or even-toed ("cloven-hoofed") ungulates. The hindfeet each have two or four digits. Three suborders:

Suiformes (Latin, *suis*, genitive of *sus*=the pig; *forma*= appearance). Includes the pig, peccary, wart hog and hippopotamus.

Tylopoda (Greek, *tylos*=a knot; *podos*, genitive of *pous*=a foot). Includes the llama, alpaca, vicuna, camel and dromedary.

Ruminantia (Latin, *ruminantis*, genitive of *ruminans*= chewing again). The ruminants. Artiodactyls who "chew the cud." Includes the deer, giraffe, buffalo, cattle, bison, antelope, gazelle, goat and sheep.

The CHEETAH is the fastest land animal. It can run 63 m.p.h. over a short distance.

ANIMAL SPEED

The data on this topic are notoriously unreliable because of the many inherent difficulties of timing the movement of most animals—whether running, flying, or swimming—and because of the absence of any standardization of the method of timing, of the distance over which the performance is measured, or of allowance for wind conditions.

The most that can be said is that a specimen of the species below has been timed to have attained as a maximum the speed given.

m.p.h.

110.07*	Racing Pigeon (*Columba palumbus*)
106.25	Spine-tailed Swift (*Chaetura caudacuta*)
88	Spurwing Goose (*Plectropterus gambensis*)
82*	Peregrine Falcon (*Falco peregrinus*)
80	Red-breasted Merganser (*Mergus serrator*)
68	Sailfish (*Istiophorus americanus*)
65	Mallard (*Anas platyrhynchos*)
63†	Cheetah (*Acinonyx jubatus*)
61	Pronghorn Antelope (*Antilocapra americana*)
57	Quail (*Coturnix coturnix*)
57	Swift (*Apus apus*)
56	Red Grouse (*Lagopus scoticus*)
55	Swan (*Cygnus* sp.)
53	Partridge (*Perdix perdix*)
50	House Martin (*Delichon urbica*)
50	Starling (*Sturnus vulgaris*)
45	Red Kangaroo (*Megaleia rufus*)
45	English Hare (*Lepus timidus*)
43.4	Bluefin Tuna (*Thunnus thynnus*)
43.26	Race Horse (*Equus caballus*) (mounted)
43	Saluki (*Canis familiaris*)
42	Red Deer (*Cervus elephus*)
41.72‡	Greyhound (*Canis familiaris*)
40	Emu (*Dromiceus novae-hollandiae*)
40	Jackdaw (*Corvus monedula*)
40	Flying Fish (*Cypselurius heterurus*) (airborne)
38	Swallow (*Hirundo rustica*)
37	Dolphin (*Delphinus* sp.)

---

* Strong following wind—60 m.p.h. in still air.
† Unable to sustain a speed of over 44 m.p.h. over 350 yards.
‡ Average over 410 yards.

When the DOLPHINS aren't frolicking, they can race through the water at 37 m.p.h.

GIRAFFES have the longest legs but they can run only 37 m.p.h. at their fastest.

Animal Speed (continued)

m.p.h.

36	Dragonfly (*Austrophlebia*)
35	Rhinoceros (*Cerathotherium simus*)
35	Wolf (*Canis lupus*)
33	Hawk Moth (*Sphingidae*)
32	Giraffe (*Giraffa camelopardalis*)
32	Guano Bat (*Tadarida mexicana*)
30	Blackbird (*Turdus merula*)
28	Fox (*Vulpes fulva*)
28	Grey Heron (*Ardea cinerea*)
27	Cuckoo (*Cuculus canorus*)
26.22 §	Man (*Homo sapiens*)
25	California Sealion (*Zalophus californianus*)
24	African Elephant (*Loxodonta africana*)
24	Deer Bot-fly (*Cephenemyia pratti*)
23	Salmon (*Salmo salar*)
22.8	Blue Whale (*Sibbaldus musculus*)
22.3	Gentoo Penguin (*Pygosterlis papua*)
22	Pacific Leatherback Turtle (*Dermochelys coriacea schlegelii*)
22	Wren (*Troglodytes troglodytes*)
20	Monarch Butterfly (*Danaus plexippus*)
18	Race Runner Lizard (*Cnemidophorus sexlineatus*)
16	Flying Frog (*Hyla venulosa*) (gravity glide)
15‖	Black Mamba (*Dendroaspis polylepsis*)
13.3	Hornet (*Vespula maculata*)
12	Wasp (*Vespa vulgaris*)
11	Bee (*Bombus* sp.)
8.5¶	Penguin (Adélie) (*Pygoscelis adeliae*)
4.5**	Flea (Order *Siphonaptera*)
1.2	Spider (*Tegenaria atrica*)
1.1	Centipede (*Scutigera coleoptera*)
0.17	Giant Tortoise (*Testudo gigantea*) (in Mauritius)
0.03	Snail (*Helix aspersa*)

---

§ Over 100 yards (flying start).
‖ Unable to sustain a speed of over 7 m.p.h.
¶ Underwater
** Jumping.

TORTOISES in general have long lives and some exist for 116 to 152 years. They are the longest-living animals.

ANIMAL LONGEVITY

Data are still sparse and in many species unreliable or non-existent. Animals in captivity may not reflect the life span of those in the natural state.

Longest Life Span	Species
152 yrs	Marion's Tortoise (*Testudo sumerii*)
116	Tortoise (*Testudo graeca*)
113	Man (*Homo sapiens*)—highest proven age
c. 100	Deep Sea Clam (*Tindaria callistiformis*)
>90	Killer Whale (*Orcinus orca*)
90	Blue Whale (*Baleanoptera musculus*)
90	Fin Whale (*Baleanoptera physalus*)
82	Sturgeon (*Acipenser transmontanus*)
80	Fresh Water Oyster (*Ostrea edulis*)
73	Cockatoo (*Kukatoe tenuirostris*)
72+	Andean Condor (*Vultur gryphus*)
72	African Gray Parrot (*Psittacus erithacus*)
c. 70	Indian Elephant (*Elephas maximus*)
70	Mute Swan (*Cygnus olor*)
69	Raven (*Corvus corax*)
62	Horse (*Equus caballus*)
62	Ostrich (*Struthio camelus*)
57	Alligator snapping turtle
57	Orang-utan (*Pongo pygmaeus*)
55	Giant Salamander (*Megalobatrachus japonicus*)
54	Hippopotamus (*Hippopotamus amphibius*)
50	Chimpanzee (*Pan troglodytes*)
>50	Koi Fish
>50	Termites (Isoptera sp.)

OLDEST CAT: This tabby, named "Ma," lived in Devon, England, to the age of 34.

50	Lobster (*Homarus americanus*)
c. 49	Carp, Mirror (*Cyprinus carpio* var.)
47	Rhinoceros, Indian (*Rhinoceros unicornis*)
47	Monkey (*Cebus capucinus*)
46	Gray Seal (*Halichoerus grypus*)
43	Ringed Seal (*Pusa hispida*)
40	Common Boa (*Boa constrictor*)
40	Cattle (*Cross-Hereford cow*)
36	Goldfish (*Carassius auratus*)
35	Pigeon (domestic) (*Columba livia domestica*)
34	Cat (domestic) (*Felis catus*)
34	Canary (*Severius Canaria*)
33	Polar Bear (*Thalarctos maritimus*)
30	Giant Clam (*Tridacna gigas*)
29	Dog (Labrador) (*Canis familiaris*)
28	Budgerigar (*Melopsittacus undulatus*)
28	Tarantula (*Mygalomorphae*)
27	Pig (*Sus scofa*)
27	Camel, Bactrian (*Camelas bactriarus*)
26½	Red Deer (*Cervus elephus*)
24	Pike (*Esox lucius*)
>24	Bat (*Myotis lucifugas*)
22	Porcupine (*Atheruras africanus*)
20	Sheep (*Ovis aries*)
19	Wallaroo (*Macropus rubustus*)
18	Goat (*Capra hircus*)
18	Rabbit (*Oryctolagus cuniculus*)
17	Cicada (*Magicicada septendecim*)
13⅓	Guinea Pig (*Cavia porcellus*)
10	Golden Hamster (*Mesocricetus auratus*)

Animal Longevity
(continued)

The POLAR BEAR can exist in extreme cold, but lives for 33 years at most.

$7\frac{1}{3}$	Gerbil (*Gerbillus gerbillus*)
6	House Mouse (*Mus musculus*)
$4\frac{1}{2}$	Snail (freshwater and land species)
4	Rat (house) (*Rattus rattus*)
0.5	Bed Bug (*Cimex lectularius*)
0.2	Fly (house) (*Musca domestica*)

North American Birds

Accentor, Mountain	Prunella montanella
Albatross, Black-browed	Diomedia melanophris
", Black-footed	Diomedia nigripes
", Layson	Diomedia immutabilis
", Short-tailed	Diomedia albatrus
", White-capped	Diomedia cauta
", Yellow-nosed	Diomedia chlororhychos
Ani, Groove-billed	Crotophaga sulcirostris
", Smooth-billed	Crotophaga ani
Auk, Great	Pinguinus impennis
Auklet, Cassin's	Ptychoramphus aleutica
", Crested	Aethia cristatella
", Least	Aethia pusilla
", Parakeet	Cyclorrhynchus psittacula
", Rhinoceros	Cerorhinca monocerata
Avocet, American	Recurvirostra americana
Becard, Rose-throated	Platyptaris aglaiae
Bittern, American	Botaurus lentiginosus
", Least	Ixobrychus exilis
Blackbird	Turdus merula
", Brewer's	Euphagus cyanocephalus
", Red-winged	Agelaius phoeniceus
", Rusty	Euphagus carolinus
", Tawny-shouldered	Agelaius humeralis
", Tricolored	Agelaius tricolor
", Yellow-headed	Xanthocephalus xanthocephalus
Bluebird, Eastern	Sialia sialis
", Mountain	Sialia currucoides
", Western	Sialia mexicana
Bluethroat	Luscinia svecica
Bobolink	Dolichonyx orizovorus
Bobwhite	Colinus virginianus
Booby, Blue-faced	Sula dactylatra
", Blue-footed	Sula nebouxii
", Brown	Sula leucogaster
", Red-footed	Sula sula
Brambling	Fringilla montifringilla
Brant	Branta bernicla
", Black	Branta nigricans
Bufflehead	Becephala albeola
Bullfinch	Pyrrhula pyrrhula
Bunting, Indigo	Passerina cyanea
", Lark	Calamospiza melanocorys
", Lazuli	Passerina amoena
", McKay's	Plectrophenax hyperboreas
", Painted	Passerina ciris
", Rustic	Emberiza rustica
", Snow	Plectrophenax nivalis
", Varied	Passerina versicolor
Bushtit, Black-eared	Psaltriparus melanotis
", Common	Psaltriparus minimus
Canvasback	Aythya valisineria
Caracara	Caracara cheriway
", Guadalupe	Caracara lutosa

DOUBLE-CRESTED CORMORANT, brooding its young, which are covered with short, warm down.

Cardinal	Richmondena cardinalis
Catbird	Dumetella carolinensis
Chachalaca	Ortalis vetula
Chat, Ground	Chamaethlypis poliocephala
" , Yellow-breasted	Icteria virens
Chickadee, Black-capped	Parus atricapillus
" , Boreal	Parus hudsonicus
" , Carolina	Parus carolinensis
" , Chestnut-backed	Parus rufescens
" , Gray-headed	Parus cinctus
" , Mexican	Parus sclateri
" , Mountain	Parus gambeli
Chicken, Greater Prairie	Tympanuchus cupido
" , Lesser Prairie	Tympanuchus pallidicinctus
Chuck-Wills-Widow	Caprimulgus carolinensis
Chukar	Alectoris graeca
Condor, California	Gymnogyps californianus
Coot, American	Fulica americana
" , European	Fulica atra
Cormorant, Brandt's	Phalacrocorax penicillatus
" , Double-crested	Phalacrocorax auritus
" , Great	Phalacrocorax carbo
" , Olivaceous	Phalacrocorax olivaceus
" , Pelagic	Phalacrocorax pelagicus
" , Red-faced	Phalacrocorax urile
Cowbird, Bronzed	Tangavius aenus
" , Brown-headed	Molothrus ater
Crake, Corn	Crex crex
" , Spotted	Porzana porzana
Crane, Sandhill	Grus canadensis
" , Whooping	Grus americana
Creeper, Brown	Certhia familiaris
Crossbill, Red	Loxia curvirostra
" , White-winged	Loxia leucoptera
Crow, Common	Corvus brachyrhynochus
" , Fish	Corvus ossifragus
" , Hooded	Corvus cornix
" , Northwestern	Corvus caurinus

WHITE-WINGED DOVE has become a symbol of peace.

Cuckoo, Black-billed	Coccyzus erythropthalmus
" , Mangrove	Coccyzus minor
" , Oriental	Cuculus saturatus
" , Yellow-billed	Coccyzus americanus
Curlew, Bristle-thighed	Numenius tahitiensis
" , Eskimo	Numenius borealis
" , European	Numenius arquata
" , Long-billed	Numenius americanus
Dickcissel	Spiza americana
Dipper	Cinclus mexicanus
Dotterel	Eudromius morinellus
Dove, Ground	Columbigallina passerina
" , Inca	Scardafella inca
" , Mourning	Zenaidura macroura
" , Ringed Turtle-	Steptopelia risoria
" , Rock	Columba livia
" , Spotted	Streptopelia chinensis
" , White-fronted	Leptotila verreauxi
" , White-winged	Zenaida asiatica
" , Zenaida	Zenaida aurita
Dovekie	Plautus alle
Dowitcher, Long-billed	Limnodromus scolopaceus
" , Short-billed	Limnodromus griseus
Duck, Bahama	Anas bahamensis
" , Black	Anas rubripes
" , Black-bellied Tree	Dendrocygna autumnalis
" , Fulvous Tree	Dendrocygna bicolor
" , Harlequin	Histrionicus histrionicus
" , Labrador	Camptorhynchus labradorium
" , Masked	Oxyura diminica
" , Mexican	Anas diazi
" , Mottled	Anas fulvigula
" , Ring-necked	Aythya collaris
" , Ruddy	Oxyura jamaicensis
" , Ruddy Shield	Casarco ferruginea
" , Sheld-	Tadorna tadorna
" , Tufted	Aythya fuligula

Duck, West Indian Tree	Dendrocygna arborea
” , Wood	Ereunetes alpina
Dunlin	Erolia alpina
Eagle, Bald	Haliaeetus leucocephalus
” , Golden	Aquila chrysaëtos
” , Gray Sea	Haliaeetus albicilla
” , Steller's Sea	Haliaeetus pelagicus
Egret, Cattle	Bubulcus ibis
” , Common	Casmerodius albus
” , Little	Egretta garzetta
” , Reddish	Dichromanassa rufescens
” , Snowy	Leucophoyx thula
Eider, Common	Somateria mollissima
” , King	Somateria spectabilis
” , Spectacled	Lampronetta fischeri
” , Steller's	Polystica stelleri
Falcon, Aplomado	Falcon femoralis
” , Peregrine	Falcon peregrinus
” , Prairie	Falcon mexicanus
Fieldfare	Turdus pilaris
Finch, Black Rosy	Leucosticte atrata
” , Brown-capped Rosy	Leucosticte australis
” , Cassin's	Carpodacus cassinii
” , Gray-crowned Rosy	Leucosticte tephrocotis
” , Guadalupe House	Carpodacus amplus
” , House	Carpodacus mexicanus
” , McGregor's	Carpodacus mcgregori
” , Purple	Carpodacus purpureus
Flamingo, American	Phoenicopterus ruber
Flicker, Gilded	Colaptes chysoides
” , Red-shafted	Colaptes peregrinus
” , Yellow-shafted	Colaptes auratus
Flycatcher, Arcadian	Empidonax virescens
” , Ash-throated	Myiarchus cinerascens
” , Beardless	Camptostoma imberbe
” , Buff-breasted	Empidonax fulvifrons
” , Coves'	Contopus pertinax
” , Dusky	Empidonax oberholseri
” , Fork-tailed	Muscivora tyrannus
” , Gray	Empidonax wrightii
” , Great Crested	Myiarchus crinitus
” , Hammond's	Empidonax hammondii
” , Kiskadee	Pitangus sulphuratus
” , Least	Empidonax minimus
” , Nutting's	Myiarchus nuttingi
” , Olivaceous	Myiarchus tuberculifer
” , Olive-sided	Nuttallornis borealis
” , Scissor-tailed	Muscivora forficata
” , Sulphur-bellied	Myiodynastes luteiventris
” , Traill's	Empidonax traillii
” , Vermillion	Pyrocephalus rubinus
” , Western	Empidonax difficilis
” , Wied's Crested	Myiarchus tyrannulus
” , Yellow-bellied	Empidonax flaviventris
Frigatebird, Magnificent	Fregata magnificens
Fulmer	Fulmarus glacialis
Gadwall	Histrionicus strepera
Gallinule, Common	Gallinula chloropus
” , Purple	Porphyrula martinica
Gannet	Morus bassanus

Gnatcatcher, Black-tailed	Polioptila melanura
” , Blue-gray	Polioptila caerulae
Godwit, Bar-tailed	Limosa lapponica
” , Black-tailed	Limosa limosa
” , Hudsonian	Limosa haemastica
” , Marbled	Limosa fedoa
Goldeneye, Barrows	Becephala islandica
” , Common	Becephala clangula
Goldfinch, American	Spinus tristis
” , European	Carduelis carduelis
” , Lawrence's	Spinus lawrencei
” , Lesser	Spinus psaltria
Goose, Barnacle	Branta leucopsis
” , Bean	Anser fabalis
” , Blue	Chen caerulescens
” , Canada	Branta canadensis
” , Emperor	Philacte canagica
” , Ross'	Chen rossii
” , Snow	Chen hyperborea
” , White-fronted	Anser albifrons
Goshawk	Accipiter gentilis
Grackle, Boat-tailed	Cassidix mexicanus
” , Common	Quiscalus quiscula
Grassquit, Black-faced	Tiaris bicolor
” , Melodius	Tiaris canora
Grebe, Eared	Podiceps caspicus
” , Horned	Podiceps auritus
” , Least	Podiceps dominicus
” , Pied-billed	Podilymbus podiceps
” , Red-necked	Podiceps grisegena
” , Western	Aechmophorus occidentalis
Grosbeak, Black-headed	Pheucticus melanocephalus
” , Blue	Guiraca caerulea
” , Evening	Hesperiphona vespertina
” , Pine	Pinicola enucleator
” , Rose-breasted	Pheucticus ludovicianus

CANADA GEESE migrate in huge V-formations and fly south and north over vast distances.

The HERRING GULL is streamlined so it can fly high and swoop down to pick up fish to eat. Mother is telling chicks what it's all about.

445

North American Birds (continued)

Hawfinch	Coccothraustes coccothaustes
Hawk, Black	Buteogallus anthracinus
" , Broad-winged	Buteo platypterus
" , Cooper's	Accipiter cooperii
" , Ferruginous	Buteo regalis
" , Gray	Buteo nitidus
" , Harlan's	Buteo harlani
" , Harris'	Parabuteo unicinctus
" , Marsh	Cirus cyaneus
" , Pigeon	Falco columbarius
" , Red-shouldered	Buteo lineatus
" , Red-tailed	Buteo jamaicensis
" , Rough-legged	Buteo lagopus
" , Sharp-shinned	Accipiter striatus
" , Short-tailed	Buteo brachyurus
" , Sparrow	Falco sparverius
" , Swainson's	Buteo swainsoni
" , White-tailed	Buteo albicaudatus
" , Zone-tailed	Buteo albonotatus
Heron, Black-crowned Night	Nycticorax nycticorax
" , Gray	Ardea cinerea
" , Great Blue	Ardea herodias
" , Great White	Ardea occidentalis
" , Green	Butorides virescens
" , Little Blue	Florida caerulea
" , Louisiana	Hydranassa tricolor
" , Yellow-crowned Night	Nyctanassa violacea
Honeycreeper, Bahama	Coereba bahamensis
Hummingbird, Allen's	Selasphorus sasin
" , Anna's	Calypte anna
" , Black-chinned	Archilochus alexandri
" , Blue-throated	Lampornis clemenciae
" , Broad-billed	Cyanthus latirostris
" , Broad-tailed	Selasphorus platycercus
" , Buff-bellied	Amazilia yucatanencis
" , Calliope	Stellula calliope
" , Costa's	Calypte costae
" , Heloise's	Atthis heloisa
" , Lucifer	Calothorax lucifer
" , Rieffer's	Amazilia tzacatl
" , Rivoli's	Eugenes fulgens
" , Ruby-throated	Archilochus colubris
" , Rufous	Selasphorus rufus
" , Violet-crowned	Amazilia verticalis
" , White-eared	Hylocharis leucotis
" , Xantus'	Hylocharis xantusii
Ibis, Glossy	Plegadis falcinellus
" , Scarlet	Eudocimus ruber
" , White	Eudocimus albus
" , White-faced	Plegadis chihi
" , Wood	Mycteria americana
Jaçana	Jacana spinosa
Jacksnipe	Lymnocryptes minimus
Jaeger, Long-tailed	Stercorarius longicaudus
" , Parasitic	Stercorarius parasiticus
" , Pomarine	Stercorarius pomarinus
Jay, Blue	Cyanocitta cristata

A brood of young HERONS wait for a signal.

Jay, Gray	Perisoreus canadensis
", Green	Cyanocorax yncas
", Mexican	Aphelocomo ultramarina
", Piñon	Gymnorhinus cyanocephalus
", San Blas	Cissilopha san-blasiana
", Scrub	Aphelocomo coerulescens
", Steller's	Cyanocitta stelleri
Junco, Baird's	Junco bairdi
", Gray-headed	Junco caniceps
", Guadalupe	Junco insularis
", Mexican	Junco phaeonotus
", Oregon	Junco oreganus
", Slate-colored	Junco hyemalis
", White-winged	Junco aikeni
Kestrel	Falco tinnunculus
Killdeer	Charadrius vociferus
Kingbird, Cassin's	Tyrannus vociferans
", Western	Tyrannus verticalis
Kingfisher, Belted	Megaceryle alcyon
", Green	Megaceryle americana
", Ringed	Megaceryle torquata
Kinglet, Golden-crowned	Regulus satrapa
", Ruby-crowned	Regulus calendula
Kite, Everglade	Rostrhamus sociabilis
", Mississippi	Ictinia mississippiensis
", Swallow-tailed	Elanoides forficatus
", White-tailed	Elanus leucurus
Kittiwake, Black-legged	Rissa tridactyla
", Red-legged	Rissa brevirostris
Knot	Calidris canutus
", Great	Calidris tenuirostris
Lapwing	Vanellus vanellus
Lark, Horned	Eremophila alpestris

Limpkin	Aramus guarauna
Longspur, Chestnut-collared	Calcarius ornatus
" , Lapland	Calcarius lapponicus
" , McCown's	Rhynchophes mccownii
" , Smith's	Calcarius pictus
Loon, Arctic	Gavia arctica
" , Common	Gavia immer
" , Red-throated	Gavia stellata
" , Yellow-billed	Gavia adamsii
Magpie, Black-billed	Pica pica
" , Yellow-billed	Pica nuttalli
Mallard	Histrionicus platyrhynchos
Martin, Cuban	Progne cryptoleuca
" , Gray-breasted	Progne chalybea
" , House	Delichon urbica
" , Purple	Progne subis
Meadowlark, Eastern	Sturnella magna
" , Western	Sturnella neglecta
Merganser, Common	Mergus merganser
" , Hooded	Lophodytes cucullatus
" , Red-breasted	Mergus serrator
Mockingbird	Mimus polyglottus
Murre, Common	Uria aalge
" , Thick-billed	Uria lomvia
Murrelet, Ancient	Synthliboramphus antiquum
" , Craveri's	Endomychura craveri
" , Kittlitz's	Brachyramphus brevirostre
" , Marbled	Brachyramphus marmoratum
" , Xantus	Endomychura hypoleuca
Myna, Crested	Acridotheres cristatellus
Nighthawk, Common	Chlordeiles minor
" , Lesser	Chlordeiles acutipennis
Nutcracker, Clark's	Nucifraga columbiana
Nuthatch, Brown-headed	Sitta pusilla
" , Pygmy	Sitta pygmea
" , Red-breasted	Sitta canadensis
" , White-breasted	Sitta carolinensis
Oldsquaw	Clangula hyemalis
Oriole, Baltimore	Icterus galbula
" , Black-headed	Icterus graduacauda
" , Bullock's	Icterus bullockii
" , Hooded	Icterus cucullatus
" , Lichtenstein's	Icterus gularis
" , Orchard	Icterus spurius
" , Scarlet-headed	Icterus postulatus
" , Scott's	Icterus parisorum
" , Spotted-breasted	Icterus pectoralis
Osprey	Pandion haliaetus
Oxenbird	Seiurus aurocapillus
Owl, Barn	Tyto alba
" , Barred	Strix varia
" , Boreal	Aegolius funereus
" , Burrowing	Speotyto cunicularia
" , Elf	Micrathene whitneyi
" , Flammulated	Otus flammeolus
" , Furruginous	Glaucidium brasilianum
" , Great Gray	Strix nebulosa
" , Great Horned	Bubo virginianus
" , Hawk	Surnia ulula

The BALTIMORE ORIOLE here is picking up an ant to put on its wing. This apparently gives the bird pleasure and possibly helps keep it clean.

Owl, Long-eared	Asio otus
", Pygmy	Glaucidium gnoma
", Saw-whet	Aegolius acadicus
", Screech	Otus asio
", Short-eared	Asio flammeus
", Snowy	Nyctea scandiaca
", Spotted	Strix occidentalis
", Whiskered	Otus trichopsis
Oystercatcher, American	Haematopus palliatus
", Black	Haematopus bachmani
", Eastern	Haematopus ostralegus
Parakeet, Carolina	Conuropsis carolinensis
Parrot, Thick-billed	Rhynchopsitta pachyrhyncha
Partridge, Gray	Perdix perdix
Pelican, Brown	Pelecanus occidentalis
", White	Pelecanus erythrorhynchos
Petrel, Ashy	Oceanodroma homochroa
", Bermuda	Pterodroma cahow
", Black	Loomelania melania
", Black-bellied	Fregetta tropica
", Black-capped	Pterodroma hasitata
", Cape	Daption capense
", Cook's	Pterodroma cookii
", Fork-tailed	Oceanodroma furcata
", Galapagos	Oceanodroma tethys
", Guadalupe	Oceanodroma macrodactyla
", Harcourt's	Oceanodroma castro
", Leach's	Oceanodroma leucorhoa
", Least	Halocyptena microsoma
", Scaled	Pterodroma inexpectata
", South Trinidad	Pterodroma arminjoniana
", White-faced	Pelagodroma marina
", Wilson's	Oceanites oceanicus
Pewee, Eastern Wood	Contopus virens
", Western Wood	Contopus sordidulus
Phainopepla	Phainopepla nitens
Phalarope, Northern	Lobipes lobatus
", Red	Phalaropus fulicarius
", Wilson's	Steganopus tricolor
Pheasant, Ring-necked	Phasianus colchicus

Pigeon, Band-tailed	Columba fasciata
" , Passenger	Ectopistes migratorius
" , Red-billed	Columba flavirostris
" , Scaly-naped	Columba squamosa
" , White-crowned	Columba leucocephala
Pintail	Histrionicus acuta
Pipit, Meadow	Anthus pratensis
" , Pechora	Anthus gustavi
" , Red-throated	Anthus cervinus
" , Sprague's	Anthus spragueii
" , Water	Anthus spinoletta
Plover, American	Pluvialis dominica
" , Black-bellied	Squatarola squatarola
" , Eurasian Golden	Pluvialis apricaria
" , Mongolian	Charadrius mongolus
" , Mountain	Eupoda montana
" , Piping	Charadrius melodus
" , Ringed	Charadrius hiaticula
" , Semipalmated	Charadrius semipalmatus
" , Snowy	Charadrius alexandrinus
" , Upland	Bartramia longicauda
" , Wilson's	Charadrius wilsonia
Pochard, Baer's	Aythya baeri
" , Common	Aythya ferina
Poor-Will	Phalaenoptilus nuttalli
Ptarmigan, Rock	Lagopus mutus
" , White-tailed	Lagopus leucurus
" , Willow	Lagopus lagopus
Puffin, Common	Fratercula arctica
" , Horned	Fratercula corniculata
" , Tufted	Lunda cirrhata
Pyrrhuloxia	Pyrrhuloxia sinuata
Quail, California	Lophortyx californicus
" , Gambel's	Lophortyx gambelii
" , Harlequin	Cyrtonyx montezumae
" , Mountain	Oreortyx pictus
" , Scaled	Callipepla squamata
Quail-Dove, Key West	Geotrygon chrysia
" " , Ruddy	Geotrygon montana

HORNED PUFFINS have beaks made for catching and holding small slippery fish.

Rail, Black	Laterallus jamaicencis
” , Clapper	Rallus longirostris
” , King	Rallus elegans
” , Virginia	Rallus limicola
” , Water	Rallus aquaticus
” , Yellow	Coturnicops noveboracencis
Raven, Common	Corvus corax
” , White-necked	Corvus cryptoleucus
Razorbill	Alca torda
Redhead	Aythya americana
Redpoll, Common	Acanthis flammea
” , Hoary	Acanthis hornemanni
Redshank	Totanus totanus
Redstart, American	Setophaga ruticilla
” , Painted	Setophaga picta
Redwing	Turdus musicus
Roadrunner	Geococcyx californianus
Robin	Turdus migratorius
” , San Lucas	Turdus confinis
Rook	Corvus frugilegus
Rubythroat, Siberian	Luscinia calliope
Ruff	Philomachus pugnax
Sanderling	Crocethia alba
Sandpiper, Baird's	Erolia bairdii
” , Buff-breasted	Tryngites subruficollis
” , Curlew	Erolia ferruginea
” , Least	Erolia minutilla
” , Pectoral	Erolia melanotus
” , Purple	Erolia maritima
” , Rock	Erolia ptilocnemis
” , Rufous-necked	Erolia ruficollis
” , Semipalmated	Ereunetes pusillus
” , Sharp-tailed	Erolia acuminata
” , Solitary	Tringa solitaria
” , Spoonbill	Eurynorhynchus pygmeum
” , Spotted	Actitis macularia
” , Stilt	Micropalama himantopus
” , Western	Ereunetes mauri
” , White Rumped	Erolia fuscicollis
” , Wood	Tringa glareola
Sapsucker, Williamson's	Sphyrapicus thyroideus
” , Yellow-bellied	Sphyrapicus varius
Scaup, Greater	Aythya marila
” , Lesser	Aythya affinis
Scoter, Common	Oidemia nigra
” , Surf	Melanitta perspicillata
” , Velvet	Melanitta fusca
” , White-winged	Melanitta deglandi
Seedeater, White-collared	Sporophila torqueola
Shearwater, Audubon's	Puffinus therminieri
” , Black-tailed	Adamastor cinereus
” , Cory's	Puffinus diomedea
” , Greater	Puffinus gravis
” , Little	Puffinus assimilis
” , Manx	Puffinus puffinus
” , New Zealand	Puffinus bulleri
” , Pale-footed	Puffinus carneipes
” , Pink-footed	Puffinus creatopus
” , Slender-billed	Puffinus tenuirostris
” , Sooty	Puffinus griseus
” , Townsend's	Puffinus auricularis
” , Wedge-tailed	Puffinus pacificus
Shoveler	Spatula clypeata

Shrike, Loggerhead	Lanius ludovicianus
" , Northern	Lanius excubitor
Siskin, Pine	Spinus pinus
Skimmer, Black	Rynchops nigra
Skua	Catharacta skua
Skylark	Alauda arvensis
Snipe, Common	Capella gallinago
Solitaire, Townsend's	Myadestes townsendi
Sora	Porzana carolina
Sparrow, Bachman's	Aimophila aestivalis
" , Baird's	Ammodramus bairdii
" , Black-chinned	Spizella atrogularis
" , Black-throated	Amphispiza bilineata
" , Botteri's	Aimophila botterii
" , Cape Sable	Ammospiza mirabilis
" , Cassin's	Aimophila cassinii
" , Chipping	Spizella passerina
" , Clay-colored	Spizella pallida
" , Dusky Seaside	Ammospiza maritima
" , European Tree	Passer montanus
" , Field	Spizella pusilla
" , Fox	Passerella iliaca
" , Golden-crowned	Zonotrichia atricapilla
" , Grasshopper	Ammodramus savannarum
" , Harris'	Zonotrichia querula
" , Henslow's	Passerherbulus henslowii
" , House	Passer domesticus
" , Ipswich	Passerculus princeps
" , Lark	Chondestes grammacus
" , Le Conte's	Passerherbulus caudacutus
" , Lincoln's	Melospiza lincolnii
" , Olive	Arremonops rufivirgata
" , Rufous-crowned	Aimophila ruficeps
" , Rufous-winged	Aimophila carpalis
" , Sage	Amphispiza belli
" , Savannah	Passerculus sandwichensis
" , Seaside	Ammospiza maritima
" , Sharp-tailed	Ammospiza caudacuta
" , Song	Melospiza melodia
" , Swamp	Melospiza georgiana
" , Tree	Spizella arborea
" , Vesper	Pooeretes gramineus
" , White-crowned	Zonotrichia leucophrys
" , White-throated	Zonotrichia albicollis
" , Worthen's	Spizella wortheni
Spoonbill, Roseate	Ajaia ajaja
" , White	Platalea leucorodia
Starling	Sturnus vulgaris
Stilt, Black-necked	Himantopus mexicanus
Stint, Long-toed	Ereunetes subminuta
Surfbird	Aphriza virgata
Swallow, Bahama	Callichelidon cyaneoviridis
" , Bank	Riparia riparia
" , Barn	Hirundo rustica
" , Cave	Petrochelidon fulva
" , Cliff	Petrochelidon pyrrhonota
" , Rough-winged	Stelgidopteryx ruficollis
" , Tree	Iridoprocne bicolor
" , Violet-green	Tachycineta thalassina
Swan, Mute	Cygnus olor
" , Trumpeter	Olor buccinator
" , Whistling	Olor colombianus
" , Whooper	Olor cygnus

WHITE SPOONBILLS between drinks tend their young. With their odd-shaped beaks, they sweep side to side in shallow water and pick up anything edible.

Swift, Black	Cypseloides niger
", Chimney	Chaetura pelagica
", Common	Apus apus
", Vaux's	Chaetura vauxi
", White-rumped	Apus pacificus
", White-throated	Aëronautes saxatalis
Tanager, Hepatic	Piranza flava
", Scarlet	Piranza olivacea
", Summer	Piranza rubra
", Western	Piranza ludoviciana
Tattler, Polynesian	Heteroscelus brevipes
", Wandering	Heteroscelus incanum
Teal, Baikal	Histrionicus formosa
", Blue-winged	Histrionicus discors
", Cinnamon	Histrionus cyanoptera
", Common	Histrionicus crecca
", Falcated	Histrionicus falcata
", Green-winged	Histrionicus cardinensis
Tern, Aleutian	Sterna aleutica
", Arctic	Sterna paradisaea
", Black	Chlidonias niger
", Bridled	Sterna anaethetus
", Caspian	Hydroprogue caspia
", Common	Sterna hirundo
", Elegant	Thalasseus elegans
", Forster's	Sterna forsteri
", Gull-billed	Gelochelidon nilotica
", Least	Sterna albifrons
", Noddy	Anoüs stolidus

453

Tern, Roseate	Sterna dougallii
,, , Royal	Thalasseus maximus
,, , Sandwich	Thalasseus sandvicenis
,, , Sooty	Sterna fuscata
,, , Trudeau's	Sterna trudeaui
,, , White-winged Black	Chlidonias leucopterus
Thrasher, Bendires	Toxostoma bendirei
,, , Brown	Toxostoma rufum
,, , California	Toxostoma redivivum
,, , Crissal	Toxostoma dorsale
,, , Curve-billed	Toxostoma curvivostre
,, , Gray	Toxostoma cinereum
,, , Le Conte's	Toxostoma lecontei
,, , Long-billed	Toxostoma longirostre
,, , Sage	Oreoscoptes montanus
Thrush, Gray-cheeked	Hylocichla minima
,, , Hermit	Hylocichla guttata
,, , Swainson's	Hylocichla ustulata
,, , Varied	Ixoreus naevius
,, , Wood	Hylocichla mustelina
Titmouse, Black-crested	Parus atricristatus
,, , Bridled	Parus wollweberi
,, , Plain	Parus inornatus
,, , Tufted	Parus bicolor
Towhee, Aberti	Pipilo aberti
,, , Brown	Pipilo fuscus
,, , Green-tailed	Chlorura chlorura
,, , Rufous-sided	Pipilo erythrophthalmus
Trogon, Coppery-tailed	Trogon elegans
Tropicbird, Red-billed	Phaëton aethereus
,, , Red-tailed	Phaëton rubricauda
,, , White-tailed	Phaëton lepturus
Turkey	Meleagris gallopavo
Turnstone, Black	Arenaria melanocephala
,, , Ruddy	Arenaria interpres
Veery	Hylocichla fuscescens
Verdin	Auriparus flaviceps
Vireo, Bell's	Vireo bellii
,, , Black-capped	Vireo atricapilla
,, , Black-whiskered	Vireo altiloquus
,, , Gray	Vireo vicinior
,, , Hutton's	Vireo huttoni
,, , Philadelphia	Vireo philadelphicus
,, , Red-eyed	Vireo olivaceus
,, , Solitary	Vireo solitarius
,, , Warbling	Vireo gilvus
,, , White-eyed	Vireo griseus
,, , Yellow-green	Vireo flavoviridis
,, , Yellow-throated	Vireo flavifrons
Vulture, Black	Coragyps atratus
,, , King	Sacoramphus papa
,, , Turkey	Cathartes aura
Wagtail, White	Motacilla alba
,, , Yellow	Motacilla flava
Warbler, Arctic	Phylloscopus borealis
,, , Audubon's	Dendroica auduboni
,, , Bachman's	Vermivora bachmanii
,, , Bay-breasted	Dendroica castanea
,, , Blackburnian	Dendroica fusca

BLUE-WINGED TEALS sport glamorous colors.

Warbler, Blackpoll	Dendroica striata
" , Black and White	Mniotilta varia
" , Black-throated Blue	Dendroica caerulescens
" , Black-throated Gray	Dendroica nigrescens
" , Black-throated Green	Dendroica virens
" , Blue-winged	Vermivora pinus
" , Canada	Wilsonia canadensis
" , Cape May	Dendroica tigrina
" , Cerulean	Dendroica cerulea
" , Chestnut-sided	Dendroica pensylvanica
" , Colima	Vermivora crissalis
" , Connecticut	Oporornis agillis
" , Fan-tailed	Euthlypis lachrymosa
" , Golden-cheeked	Dendroica chrysoparia
" , Golden-winged	Vermivora chrysoptera
" , Grace's	Dendroica graciae
" , Hermit	Dendroica occidentalis
" , Hooded	Wilsonia citrina
" , Kentucky	Oporornis formosus
" , Kirtland	Dendroica kirtlandii
" , Lucy's	Vermivora luciae
" , MacGillivray's	Oporornis tolmiei
" , Magnolia	Dendroica magnolia
" , Middendorf's Grasshopper	Locustella ochotensis
" , Mourning	Oporornis philadelphia
" , Myrtle	Dendroica coronata
" , Nashville	Vermivora ruficapilla
" , Olive	Peucedramus taeniatus
" , Olive-backed	Parula pitiayumi
" , Orange-crowned	Vermivora celata
" , Palm	Dendroica palmarum
" , Parula	Parula americana
" , Pine	Dendroica pinus
" , Prairie	Dendroica discolor
" , Prothonotary	Prothonotaria citrea

Warbler, Red-faced	Cardellina rubrifrons
", Swainson's	Limnothlypis swainsonii
", Tennessee	Vermivora peregrina
", Townsend's	Dendroica townsendi
", Virginia's	Vermivora virginiae
", Willow	Phylloscopus trochilus
", Wilson's	Wilsonia pusilla
", Worm-eating	Helmitheros vermivorus
", Yellow	Dendroica petichia
", Yellow-throated	Dendroica dominica
Waterthrush, Louisiana	Seiurus motacilla
Waxwing, Bohemian	Bombycilla garrulus
", Cedar	Bombycilla cedrorum
Wheatear	Oenanthe oenanthe
Whimbrel	Numenius phaeopus
Whip-poor-will	Caprimulgus vociferens
Willet	Catoptrophus semipalmatus
Widgeon, American	Mareca americana
", European	Mareca penelope
Woodcock, American	Philohela minor
", European	Scolopax rusticola
Woodpecker, Acorn	Melanerpes formicivorus
", Arizona	Dendrocopus arizonae
", Black-backed Three-toed	Picoides articus
", Downy	Dendrocopus plubescens
", Gila	Centurus uropygialis
", Golden-fronted	Centurus aurifrons
", Hairy	Dendrocopus villosus
", Ivory-billed	Campephilus principalis
", Ladder-backed	Dendrocopus scalaris
", Lewis	Asyndesmus lewis
", Northern Three-toed	Picoides tridactylus
", Nuttall's	Dendrocopus nuttallii
", Pileated	Dryocopus pileatus
", Red-bellied	Centurus carolinus
", Red-cockaded	Dendrocopus borealis
", Red-headed	Melanerpes erythrocephalus
", White-headed	Dendrocopus albolarvatus
Wrentit	Chamaea fasciata
Wren, Bewick's	Thrymanes bewickii
", Brown-throated	Troglodytes brunneicollis
", Cactus	Campylorhynchus brunneicapillus
", Cañon	Catherpes mexicanus
", Carolina	Thryothorus ludovicianus
", House	Troglodytes aedon
", Long-billed Marsh	Telmatodytes palustris
", Rock	Salpinctes obsoletus
", Short-billed Marsh	Cistothorus platensis
", Winter	Troglodytes troglodytes
Wryneck	Jynx torquilla
Yellowlegs, Greater	Totanus melanoleucus
", Lesser	Totanus flavipes
Yellowthroat	Geothlypis trichas

Mathematics

Fundamentals

MATH SYMBOLS

.	decimal point (U.S.)	#	numbers to follow
,	decimal comma (Europe)	%	per cent(um) (hundred)
=	equal to	‰	per mille (thousand)
≠	not equal to	∝	varies with
≡	identically equal to	∞	infinity
>	greater than (or remainder)	r! or ⌐r	factorial r
<	less than	√	square root
≯	not greater than	ⁿ√	nth root
≮	not less than	r^n	r to the power n
≥	equal to or greater than	Δ	triangle or increment
≤	equal to or less than	△ or ~	difference,
≏	approximately equal to	Σ	summation
+	plus	∫	integration sign
−	minus	°, ′, ″	degree, minute, second
±	plus or minus		(1° = 60′, 1′ = 60″)
×	multiplication (times)	→	appropriate limit of
÷	divided by	∴	therefore
( ) [ ] { }	brackets, square brackets, enveloping brackets	∵	because
‖	parallel	Ø	diameter
∦	not parallel	3̇	full point over numeral indicates it recurs

MATH CONSTANTS

π	= 3.14159	26535	89793	23846	26433	83280
e	= 2.71828	18284	59045	23536	02874	71353
$\log_{10}e$	= 0.43429	44819	03251	82765	11289	18917
$\log_e 10$	= 2.30258	50929	94045	68401	79914	54684
$\log_{10}\pi$	= 0.49714	98726	94133	85435	12682	88291
$\log_e \pi$	= 1.14472	98858	49400	17414	34273	51353

$180/\pi$ = degrees in 1 rad	= 57.2957795		
$\pi/180$ = rads in 1°	= 0.01745329		
$\pi/10800$ = rads in 1′	= 0.00029	08882	
$\pi/648000$ = rads in 1″	= 0.00000	48481	36811 095
sin 1″	= 0.00000	48481	36811 076
tan 1″	= 0.00000	48481	36811 133

Mathematics (continued)

Number			Log		
π	= 3.14159	65	0.49714	99	
2π	= 6.28318	531	0.79817	99	
4π	= 12.56637	061	1.09920	99	
$1/\pi$	= 0.31830	989	9.50285	01	-10
$1/2\pi$	= 0.15915	494	9.20182	01	-10
$\pi/2$	= 1.57079	633	0.19611	99	
$\pi/3$	= 1.04719	755	0.02002	86	
$\pi/4$	= 0.78539	816	9.89508	99	-10
π^2	= 9.86960	440	0.99429	97	
$1/\pi^2$	= 0.10132	118	9.00570	03	-10
$\sqrt{\pi}$	= 1.77245	385	0.24857	49	
$1/\sqrt{\pi}$	= 0.56418	958	9.75142	51	-10

Formulae

Triangle
(h = vertical height)
Area = $\frac{1}{2}$ base $\times$ h

Square
(x = length of side)
Area = x^2

Circle
(π = 3.14159)
(d = diameter, r = radius)
Diameter d = 2r
Circumference = $2\pi r$ or πd
Area = πr^2 or $\dfrac{\pi d^2}{4}$
quadrant = $90°$, 4 quadrants = 1 circle = $360°$
radian: 2π radians = $360°$

Sphere
Volume = $\dfrac{4}{3}\pi r^3$
Surface area = $4\pi r^2$

Cone
(1 = slant height)
Volume = $\frac{1}{3}\pi r^2 h$
Surface area = $\pi r l$

Cylinder
Volume = $\pi r^2 h$
Curved surface area = $2\pi rh$
Total surface area $2\pi rh + 2\pi r^2 = 2\pi r(h + r)$

Ellipse
(major axis = 2a, minor axis = 2b)
Area = πab

Pyramid
(x = length of side)
(1 = slant height)
Volume = $\frac{1}{3}(x^2 h)$
Surface area = $x^2 + 2lx$

Trapezium
(length of parallel sides m and n)
Area = $h \times \frac{1}{2}(m + n)$

Regular Pentagon, Hexagon, Heptagon and Octagon
(g = length of one side)
Area
Pentagon	$g^2 \times 1.720477$
Hexagon	$g^2 \times 2.598076$
Heptagon	$g^2 \times 3.633912$
Octagon	$g^2 \times 4.828427$
Nonagon	$g^2 \times 6.181824$
Decagon	$g^2 \times 7.694209$

Multiples and Sub-Multiples

Prefix	Symbol	Equivalent	Factor
atto- (Danish *atten*=eighteen)	a	quintillionth part	$\times 10^{-18}$
femto- (Danish *femten*=fifteen)	f	quadrillionth part	$\times 10^{-15}$
pico- (L. *pico*=miniscule)	p	trillionth part	$\times 10^{-12}$
nano- (L. *nanus*=dwarf)	n	billionth part	$\times 10^{-9}$
micro- (Gk. *mikros*=small)	μ	millionth part	$\times 10^{-6}$
milli- (L. *mille*=thousand)	m	thousandth part	$\times 10^{-3}$
centi (L. *centum*=hundred)	c	hundredth part	$\times 10^{-2}$
deci- (L. *decimus*=tenth)	d	tenth part	$\times 10^{-1}$
deca- (Gk. *deka*=ten)	da	tenfold	$\times 10$
hecto- (Gk. *hekaton*=hundred)	h	hundredfold	$\times 10^2$
kilo- (Gk. *chilioi*=thousand)	k	thousandfold	$\times 10^3$
mega- (Gk. *megas*=large)	M	millionfold	$\times 10^6$
giga- (Gk. *gigas*=mighty)	G	billionfold	$\times 10^9$
tera- (Gk. *teras*=monster)	T	trillionfold	$\times 10^{12}$

Odds and Chance

Life is a succession of uncertainties ending only in one absolute certainty—death.

Mathematicians have developed, since about 1650, the art of measuring uncertainties and so became able to compare their degree one with another. This branch of mathematics is known as the mathematics of probability.

Some of the best examples for illustrating probabilities come from gambling games and childbirth.

ODDS ON PERFECT DEALS

The number of possible hands with four players using a full pack of 52 cards is $\dfrac{52!}{(39!)(13!)}$ or 635,013,559,600. Thus the odds against picking up a specific complete suit are 635,013,559,599 to 1 or *any* complete suit 158,753,389,899 to 1.

The number of possible deals is $\dfrac{52!}{(13!)^4 (4!)}$ or 2,235,197,406,895,366,368,301,560,000 or roughly 2.23×10^{27}. A complete suit is thus to be expected once in every 39,688,347,497 deals.

Cases throughout the world of single complete suits are in practice reported about once per year. This being so, cases of two players receiving complete suits could be expected with the present volume of card playing once every 2 billion years and this has only once been recorded. Cases of all four players picking up complete suits might be expected once in 56,000 billion years. This latter occurrence was reported in New Zealand on July 8, 1958, in Illinois, on Feb. 9, 1963, again in Illinois on March 30, 1963, and again 3 days later in Greybull, Wyoming. This is so unlikely, not merely to strain credulity, but to be virtually certain evidence of rigged shuffling or hoaxing.

ODDS IN CONTRACT BRIDGE

The total number of ways that a deck of 52 cards can be dealt is astronomical—more than 1.0×10^{68}.

The odds of pulling a card of a specific suit, say spades, from a pack is 13 to 52, or 1 to 4. The odds of pulling a second spade are not $13/52 \times 13/52$ or 1 to 16 but $13/52 \times 12/51$ or 1 to 17 because for the second pull there are only 12 spades left in the 51 cards. The odds against a third spade would be $13/52 \times 12/51 \times 11/50$ or 1 to 78.

This process can be continued to arrive at odds against being dealt 13 spades of 635,013,559 to 1. The odds against *any* 13-card suit are, of course, 4 times better, or 158,753,389,899 to 1. The odds against each of the four players simultaneously receiving a complete suit, or a "perfect deal," are 2,235,197,406,895,366,301,559,999 to 1.

Such an event having once occurred it should not logically recur, even if the entire world population made up in fours and played 120 hands of bridge a day for another 2,000,000,000,000 years. Nonetheless, "perfect deals" are reported several times in most years.

If further proof were needed that such "perfect deals" are the products of collusion, deceit or pranks it can be provided by the extreme

Mathematics (continued)

rarity of reports of hands in which two players had 13 of a suit. Logically, this should occur 31,201,794 times more frequently than for a "perfect deal" and yet the last report seems to date from Admiral Goodenough in mid-Pacific in 1937.

Descending to less astronomical odds, the chances against

Nine honors	are	104 to 1
Four aces	are	378 to 1
A Yarborough (no honor cards) are		1,827 to 1

In 5-card poker, odds generally become more manageable since "only" 2,598,960 hands are possible. Specific odds are

A pair	137 to 1
A straight	254 to 1
A flush	508 to 1
A full house	693 to 1
A straight flush	72,192 to 1
A royal flush	649,739 to 1

OTHER PROBABILITIES

In roulette, the theory of probability does its deadly work for the house and against the individual player, who is given odds of only 35 to 1 whereas there are 38 options (36 slots plus zero and often a double zero).

Thus the house ensures for itself a built-in long term advantage of 5.26316 per cent on turnover—a veritable license to rob the obstinate.

The basic laws of probability may be expressed as:

1. The chance of two independent events happening is equal to the product of the two separate probabilities, *i.e.*, the odds on tossing tails is 2 to 1, while odds of two tails consecutively is $\frac{2}{1} \times \frac{2}{1}$ or 4 to 1.

2. The chance of two mutually exclusive possibilities turning up equals the sum of the separate chances of each coming true individually, i.e., the odds of throwing a 2 or a 3 with a single 6-faced die would be $\frac{1}{6} + \frac{1}{6}$ or 3 to 1.

An area in which the laws of probability have great scope is in the eternal speculation about "Will it be a boy or a girl?"

Assuming that as with tossing a coin the chances on a boy are one in two and the odds on a girl remain at 50–50 the chance situation is this:

♂ = male   ♀ = female

First birth: ♂ 1 in 2   ♀ 1 in 2

Total family after second birth:

♂ ♂ 1 in 4   ♂ ♀ 2 in 4   ♀ ♀ 1 in 4

Total family after third birth:

♂ ♂ ♂ 1 in 8   ♂ ♂ ♀ 3 in 8   ♂ ♀ ♀ 3 in 8   ♀ ♀ ♀ 1 in 8

Total family after fourth birth:

♂ ♂ ♂ ♂ 1 in 16   ♂ ♀ ♀ ♀ 4 in 16
♂ ♂ ♂ ♀ 4 in 16   ♀ ♀ ♀ ♀ 1 in 16
♂ ♂ ♀ ♀ 6 in 16

Total family after fifth birth:

♂ ♂ ♂ ♂ ♂ 1 in 32   ♂ ♂ ♀ ♀ ♀ 10 in 32
♂ ♂ ♂ ♂ ♀ 5 in 32   ♂ ♀ ♀ ♀ ♀ 5 in 32
♂ ♂ ♂ ♀ ♀ 10 in 32   ♀ ♀ ♀ ♀ ♀ 1 in 32

Total family after sixth birth:

♂ ♂ ♂ ♂ ♂ ♂ 1 in 64   ♂ ♂ ♂ ♀ ♀ ♀ 20 in 64
♂ ♂ ♂ ♂ ♂ ♀ 6 in 64   ♂ ♂ ♀ ♀ ♀ ♀ 15 in 64
♂ ♂ ♂ ♂ ♀ ♀ 15 in 64   ♂ ♀ ♀ ♀ ♀ ♀ 6 in 64
♀ ♀ ♀ ♀ ♀ ♀ 1 in 64

Space prevents listing all recordable permutations in larger families. In 1955, a case was reported from Tennessee of a streak of 13 boys in a family—a phenomenon with a 1 in 8,192 chance.

In practice, chance figures based on 50–50 odds governing the sex of a baby should be refined. Throughout the world the ratio of male births to female births is erratic. In the United States, it runs at about 1,052 boys born for each 1,000 girls. This population disproportion is not in fact maintained because of the physiological inferiority of the male who is more susceptible to mortal disease.

Another factor which slightly distorts the odds is that, for reasons not fully understood, first births tend to include an unusually high preponderance of males.

In the field of multiple births there is a curious correlation in the frequency of twins (1 in 80), triplets (1 in 80^2), quadruplets (1 in 80^3) and quintuplets (1 in 80^4). In the United States, twins occur in about 1 in 83 births. Of twin births, some 718 in 1,000 are dizygotic or fraternal twins of ordinary familial resemblance and 282 are monozygotic or "identical" twins with a very strong resemblance and always of the same sex.

Thus the odds specifically against having "identical" boy twins is not 1 in 80 but worse than 1 in 560.

COINCIDENTAL BIRTH DATES

If one assumes that all years are of equal length (i.e., leap years are disregarded) and birthdays are distributed throughout the year uniformly, then how many people do you need in a room to have a better than even chance of two sharing a birthday? The answer is surprisingly low. If certainty is represented as 1.0 and 0.5 represents an even chance, then with 22 people the probability is 0.493 but with 23 people it is 0.524. It is thus to be expected that 37 U.S. Presidents should provide a coincidental birthday (No. 11 [Polk] and No. 29 [Harding] share November 2nd). Of the 33 deceased Presidents the coincidence is higher than expected chance for three Presidents—John Adams, Jefferson, and Monroe—all died on the Fourth of July and two others—Fillmore and Taft—both died on March 8th.

Logarithms

Logarithms are widely used as a device for substituting the labor of long multiplication and division by the simpler and speedier processes of addition and subtraction.

The multiplication of 17×130 can be done mentally to produce 2210. The multiplication of 17.39×137.4 is more laborious and is more quickly done by logarithms thus:
17.39 is 10 raised to a power between 1 and 2, actually 1.2402
137.4 is 10 raised to a power between 2 and 3, actually 2.1380

The product of the two is 10 raised to the sum of these two powers, namely $10^{3.3782}$ which is 2,389. By long multiplication the answer would be 2389.386. This answer is the product of 4-figure log tables, which suffice for most uses. The bulky 7-figure log tables would, of course, supply an answer the same as the long multiplication sum. Logarithm tables list all numbers in terms of their power to the base 10 while antilogarithm tables enable the product of the additions to be converted back from a power of 10 to the final numerical product.

For fast simple calculations the mantissa or decimal part of the log only is used, i.e. .2402 + .1380 and the index or characteristic 3 supplied

N	0	1	2	3	4	5	6	7	8	9
10	0000	0043	0086	0128	0170	0212	0253	0294	0334	0374
11	0414	0453	0492	0531	0569	0607	0645	0682	0719	0755
12	0792	0828	0864	0899	0934	0969	1004	1038	1072	1106
13	1139	1173	1206	1239	1271	1303	1335	1367	1399	1430
14	1461	1492	1523	1553	1584	1614	1644	1673	1703	1732
15	1761	1790	1818	1847	1875	1903	1931	1959	1987	2014
16	2041	2068	2095	2122	2148	2175	2201	2227	2253	2279
17	2304	2330	2355	2380	2405	2430	2455	2480	2504	2529
18	2553	2577	2601	2625	2648	2672	2695	2718	2742	2765
19	2788	2810	2833	2856	2878	2900	2923	2945	2967	2989
20	3010	3032	3054	3075	3096	3118	3139	3160	3181	3201
21	3222	3243	3263	3284	3304	3324	3345	3365	3385	3404
22	3424	3444	3464	3483	3502	3522	3541	3560	3579	3598
23	3617	3636	3655	3674	3692	3711	3729	3747	3766	3784
24	3802	3820	3838	3856	3874	3892	3909	3927	3945	3962
25	3979	3997	4014	4031	4048	4065	4082	4099	4116	4133
26	4150	4166	4183	4200	4216	4232	4249	4265	4281	4298
27	4314	4330	4346	4362	4378	4393	4409	4425	4440	4456
28	4472	4487	4502	4518	4533	4548	4564	4579	4594	4609
29	4624	4639	4654	4669	4683	4698	4713	4728	4742	4757
30	4771	4786	4800	4814	4829	4843	4857	4871	4886	4900
31	4914	4928	4942	4955	4969	4983	4997	5011	5024	5038
32	5051	5065	5079	5092	5105	5119	5132	5145	5159	5172
33	5185	5198	5211	5224	5237	5250	5263	5276	5289	5302
34	5315	5328	5340	5353	5366	5378	5391	5403	5416	5428
35	5441	5453	5465	5478	5490	5502	5514	5527	5539	5551
36	5563	5575	5587	5599	5611	5623	5635	5647	5658	5670
37	5682	5694	5705	5717	5729	5740	5752	5763	5775	5786
38	5798	5809	5821	5832	5843	5855	5866	5877	5888	5899
39	5911	5922	5933	5944	5955	5966	5977	5988	5999	6010
40	6021	6031	6042	6053	6064	6075	6085	6096	6107	6117
41	6128	6138	6149	6160	6170	6180	6191	6201	6212	6222
42	6232	6243	6253	6263	6274	6284	6294	6304	6314	6325
43	6335	6345	6355	6365	6375	6385	6395	6405	6415	6425
44	6435	6444	6454	6464	6474	6484	6493	6503	6513	6522
45	6532	6542	6551	6561	6571	6580	6590	6599	6609	6618
46	6628	6637	6646	6656	6665	6675	6684	6693	6702	6712
47	6721	6730	6739	6749	6758	6767	6776	6785	6794	6803
48	6812	6821	6830	6839	6848	6857	6866	6875	6884	6893
49	6902	6911	6920	6928	6937	6946	6955	6964	6972	6981
50	6990	6998	7007	7016	7024	7033	7042	7050	7059	7067
51	7076	7084	7093	7101	7110	7118	7126	7135	7143	7152
52	7160	7168	7177	7185	7193	7202	7210	7218	7226	7235
53	7243	7251	7259	7267	7275	7284	7292	7300	7308	7316
54	7324	7332	7340	7348	7356	7364	7372	7380	7388	7396

by common sense. For the multiplication of a lot of numbers or of numbers of widely varying magnitude, *viz.* 0.0001739 × 137,400,000 it is advisable to use the characteristic as an aid.

The characteristic of:

1.739	is 0, hence its log =	0.2402
17.39	is 1, hence its log =	1.2402
173.9	is 2, hence its log =	2.2402
1,739	is 3, hence its log =	3.2402
17,390	is 4, hence its log =	4.2402
173,900	is 5, hence its log =	5.2402
1,739,000	is 6, hence its log =	6.2402
17,390,000	is 7, hence its log =	7.2402

Conversely the characteristic of numbers less than unity are negative. Hence the characteristic of:

0.1739	is $\bar{1}$ hence its log =	1.2402
0.01739	is $\bar{2}$ hence its log =	2.2402
0.001739	is $\bar{3}$ hence its log =	3.2402

These negative characteristics are usually termed bar 1, bar 2, bar 3, etc., and are always greater by one than the number of zeros following the decimal point.

The division process is identical except that instead of adding as with multiplication one subtracts, *e.g.* evaluate:

$$\frac{17.39 \times 137.4}{3.142 \div 0.252}$$

log 17.39 = 1.2402   log 3.142 = 0.4972
log 137.4 = 2.1380   log 0.252 = $\bar{1}$.4014

3.3782   1.0958

Add to get log of the numerator, subtract to get log of the denominator. Now subtract the latter from the former 3.3782 to get the log of the result   1.0958

2.2824

∴ Result = 191.6

A further use of the log tables is in computing squares, cubes, fourth powers, etc., and square roots, cube roots, etc.; *e.g.* the cube of 17.39 is the log × 3 and the cube root the log ÷ 3, thus:

log 17.39 = 1.2402   log 17.39 = $3\overline{)1.2402}$
3   .4134 = 2.590

3.7206 = 5,255

Logarithms other than to the base 10 are of little practical application except hyperbolic logarithms, the base of which is derived from the sum of the series:

$$1 + \frac{1}{1} + \frac{1}{1 \times 2} + \frac{1}{1 \times 2 \times 3} + \textit{et seq.}$$

This base, the value of which approximates to 2.71828, is usually termed e, so that log e N indicates the natural log of N.

Trigonometry

Trigonometry (from the Greek *trigonon*, triangle; *metria*, measurement) as a science may be traced back to work attributed to Hipparchus (*fl.* 150 B.C.), the Greek astronomer. Further contributions were made in India, Iraq, Italy and Persia between 800 and 1400 A.D. The six ratios received their standard names *c.* 1550. The earliest complete trigonometrical tables were published by Rhaeticus in 1596. The word trigonometry in English dates from 1614.

The division of the circle into 360 degrees dates from Ptolemy (85–165 A.D.) but at that time it was the circumference which was divided into 360 equal arcs. The sexagesimal sub-divisions of the degree are named after the Latin *pars minuta prima* for the primary sub-division into 1/60th parts of a degree and *pars minuta secunda* for a second sub-division into 1/3600th parts of a degree, hence the modern terms minute ′ and second ″. The systematic use of decimals *c.* 1580 and of negative numbers *c.* 1610 greatly facilitated the science.

Trigonometry depends upon the fact that the corresponding sides of equiangular triangles are proportional. The three principal ratios are:

$$\text{The tangent of an angle} = \frac{\text{side opposite angle}}{\text{side adjacent to angle}}$$

$$\text{The cotangent of an angle} = \frac{\text{side adjacent to angle}}{\text{side opposite angle}}$$

$$\text{The sine of an angle} = \frac{\text{side opposite angle}}{\text{hypotenuse}}$$

$$\text{The secant of an angle} = \frac{\text{hypotenuse}}{\text{side adjacent to angle}}$$

$$\text{The cosine of an angle} = \frac{\text{side adjacent to angle}}{\text{hypotenuse}}$$

$$\text{The cosecant of an angle} = \frac{\text{hypotenuse}}{\text{side opposite to angle}}$$

TRIGONOMETRICAL IDENTITIES

$\sin (A + B) = \sin A \cos B + \sin B \cos A$

$\sin (A - B) = \sin A \cos B - \sin B \cos A$

$$\tan (A + B) = \frac{\tan A + \tan B}{1 - \tan A \tan B}$$

$$\sin A + \sin B = 2 \sin \frac{A + B}{2} \cos \frac{A - B}{2}$$

$$\sin A - \sin B = 2 \sin \frac{A - B}{2} \cos \frac{A + B}{2}$$

$$\cos A = \frac{1}{\sin A}$$

$$\cot A = \frac{1}{\tan A} = \frac{\cosec A}{\sec A}$$

$$\sec A = \frac{1}{\cos A}$$

$$\cos (A + B) = \cos A \cos B - \sin A \sin B$$
$$\cos (A - B) = \cos A \cos B + \sin A \sin B$$

$$\tan (A - B) = \frac{\tan A - \tan B}{1 + \tan A \tan B}$$

$$\cos A + \cos B = 2 \cos \frac{B - A}{2} \cos \frac{B + A}{2}$$

$$\cos A - \cos B = 2 \sin \frac{B - A}{2} \sin \frac{B + A}{2}$$

$$2 \sin A \sin B = \cos (A - B) - \cos (A + B)$$
$$2 \cos A \cos B = \cos (A - B) + \cos (A + B)$$
$$2 \sin A \cos B = \sin (A + B) + \sin (A - B) \text{ or}$$
$$\sin (A + B) - \sin (B - A)$$

$$\sin 2 A = 2 \sin A \cos A \text{ or } \frac{2 \tan A}{1 + \tan^2 A}$$

$$\cos 2 A = \cos^2 A - \sin^2 A \text{ or } 2 \cos^2 A - 1 \text{ or } 1 - 2 \sin^2 A$$
$$\text{or } \frac{1 - \tan^2 A}{1 + \tan^2 A}$$

$$\tan 2 A = \frac{2 \tan A}{1 - \tan^2 A}$$

$$\sin 3 A = 3 \sin A - 4 \sin^3 A$$
$$\cos 3 A = 4 \cos^3 A - 3 \cos A$$
$$\sin^2 A = \tfrac{1}{2}(1 - \cos 2A)$$
$$\cos^2 A = \tfrac{1}{2}(1 + \cos 2A)$$
$$\sin^2 A + \cos^2 A = 1$$
$$\tan^2 A = \sec^2 A - 1$$
$$\cot^2 A = \cos^2 A - 1$$

$$\tan 3 A = \frac{3 \tan A - \tan^3 A}{1 - 3 \tan^2 A}$$

$$\sin^3 A = \tfrac{1}{4}(3 \sin A - \sin 3A)$$
$$\cos^3 A = \tfrac{1}{4}(\cos 3A + 3 \cos A)$$

$$\sin A = \frac{2t}{1 + t^2}, \cos A = \frac{1 - t^2}{1 + t^2} \text{ and } \tan A = \frac{2t}{1 - t^2}$$

where $t = \tan \tfrac{1}{2}A$

$$\frac{\sin}{\cos} = \tan; \sin (90 - \Theta) = \cos \Theta; \sin \Theta = \sin 180 - \Theta.$$

$$- \cos \Theta = \cos 180 - \Theta; \tan \Theta = \frac{1}{\tan (90 - \Theta)}$$

$$- \tan \Theta = \tan (180 - \Theta)$$

Binary System

The numerical notation in ordinary use is the decimal or denary system with its ten symbols: 0, 1, 2, 3, 4, 5, 6, 7, 8 and 9.

Because electric switches have two essential positions, "on" or "off," the binary system is ideally suited to the programming of computers and is being used increasingly.

To convert the denary number, say 17, to its binary form it is necessary to divide successively through by two, recording the remainders which can only be 1 or 0 thus:

$2/17 = 8 > 1$ which $\div 2 = 4 > 0$ which $\div 2 = 2 > 0$ which $\div 2 = 1 > 0$, thus 17 (decimal) is 10001 binary.

This represents 1×2^4 which is 16, 0×2^3, 0×2^2, 0×2^1 and 1×2^0 which is 1 giving a total of 17.

To convert a binary number to its decimal or denary form, it is simplest to regard the column at the far right as the $2°$ column, thence reading to the left 2^1, 2^2, 2^3, 2^4, etc., columns.

Thus 11101 reads $1 \times 2^4 = 16$, $+ 1 \times 2^3 = 8$, $+ 1 \times 2^2 = 4$, $+ 0 \times 2^1 = 0$, $+ 1 \times 2° = 1$, i.e. 29.

A binary conversion scale thus reads:

Denary	Binary	Denary	Binary	Denary	Binary
1	1	11	1011	32	100000
2	10	12	1100	64	1000000
3	11	13	1101	100	1100100
4	100	14	1110	128	10000000
5	101	15	1111	144	10010000
6	110	16	10000	150	10010110
7	111	17	10001	200	11001000
8	1000	18	10010	250	11111010
9	1001	19	10011	500	111110100
10	1010	20	10100	1000	1111101000

Fractions are also recorded in the binary notation, thus:

Denary		Binary
.5	=	.1
.25	=	.01
.125	=	.001
.0625	=	.0001
.03125	=	.00001
.015625	=	.000001

Thus the binary fraction .10011 is $.5 + 0 + 0 + .0625 + 0.03125 = .59375$.

Computers

Calculation is, except perhaps as a punishment, not an end itself but merely a means to an end. As such much ingenuity has been exercised in order to circumvent its wearisome drudgery.

Both early Chinese (6th century B.C.) and Mediterranean (450 B.C.) civilizations harnessed the *abacus*, which was the pioneer aid to calculating and which even after 25 centuries is still widely employed. The next major step was not taken until 1614 when the Scotsman, John

Neper or Napier (born near Edinburgh in 1550) published his famous *Mirifici Logarithmorum Canonis Descriptio* three years before his death. The advent of logarithms converted at a stroke the tedious processes of long multiplication and division into the less tedious and faster ones of addition and subtraction.

The first actual calculating "machines" were those built by the son of a French tax collector, Blaise Pascal (1623–62) in 1642 for adding, and by Gottfried Wilhelm von Leibniz (1646–1716) (Germany) in 1671 for multiplying by means of repeating additions with a "stepped wheel" device. Charles Xavier Thomas of Alsace invented in 1810 a widely-sold calculating machine, while in 1822 Charles Babbage (1791–1871) (Great Britain) demonstrated the first working model of his "difference engine." Babbage was frustrated in bringing his universal digital calculator to practibility because the production of metal components to such vitally low tolerances necessary was in 1833 nearly a century in advance of metal technology. It is a little known fact that Babbage's ally in his work was the Hon. Augusta Byron, later Lady Lovelace, daughter of the great poet and history's first programmer of computers.

The first really commercial calculating machine was devised in 1885 by William Burroughs of St. Louis, and was manufactured in Chicago in substantial numbers.

For the 1890 decennial census, Herman Hollerith of the U.S. Census Bureau developed the punched card system of recording and analyzing data.

Punched cards had in fact first been used for making weaving patterns on looms in France as early as 1728. They operated simply by permitting (by a hole) or blocking (no hole) a passing needle. Here was the origin of the on-off language of the present-day electronic computer.

Because of their lack of any reasoning mentality, computers are programmed on the binary instead of the customary denary system of counting.

Thus in the binary system, which is counting by the power of 2, 100 becomes 1100100, which indicates from right to left

A block of 64 (or 2^6)?	yes	64
A block of 32 (or 2^5)?	yes	32
A block of 16 (or 2^4)?	no	—
A block of 8 (or 2^3)?	no	—
A block of 4 (or 2^2)?	yes	4
A block of 2	? no	—
A unit	? no	—
		—
		100

or Yes, yes, no, no, yes, no, no rendered 1100100.

The seemingly simple mental process of dividing say 169 by 13 is for the electronic computer an involved laborious process. The secret is that all the plodding steps are taken at such lightning speed that it has the answer in a blink. However, the problem has to be broken down or reasoned by a human programmer, because the computer takes nothing at all for granted.

To illustrate how "simple" a computer is, the first step in programming a division is to establish whether the divisor (or figure to be divided) is made up of zeros. If so, it stands to human reason that no division is possible, but not so to a computer.

The range of jobs that computers can do is phenomenal and often most valuable. These include:—

1. Operational researches such as optimizing the location of manufacturing plants and the movement of ships and aircraft.

Computers (continued)

2. Commercial administration, such as stock control, sales analysis, handling payrolls, distribution of supplies and budgetary control.

3. Engineering design, particularly in transformers and the timing patterns of power-producers, such as 12-cylinder diesels.

4. Linguistic research: in identifying authorship, etc.

5. Economic research: in predicting the effect of monetary and credit factors and constructing models of national economies and trade balances.

6. Pure mathematics: e.g., the discovery of large prime numbers.

7. Astronomical research including the prediction of occultations and extrapolating eclipses.

8. Three-dimensional space calculations without which space flight would be wholly impossible.

Computers have reached the stage where they can perform as many as 16,600,000 additions per second and can multiply 14-digit numbers at the rate of 5,500,000 per second. The cycle time in their central processing units is 16 nanoseconds—a nanosecond being one-thousand-millionth of a second.

Some indication of how brief a time this is can be given by the fact that there are about a thousand million seconds in thirty years. In one nanosecond light, which travels at 670,616,722.8 m.p.h., can move only 11.7 inches.

The ultimate speed at which computers can operate is limited only by the speed of light. All the trends towards microminiaturization, integrated fabrication, tunnelled diodes and the use of super conductivity at a temperature of minus 450°F are being pushed to their physical limits.

The development which gives most concern to the thoughtful and to the individualist is the seemingly inevitable development that every citizen in the more developed countries will be tabbed on every facet of his, or her, being. Social services are growing increasingly complex and the use of computers for the purpose of administrating such services is seemingly only a matter of time.

In their present state of development computers have only about a ten-thousandth part of the performance of a human brain. The gap is closing.

Physics

Laws of Physics

NEWTON'S LAWS OF MOTION

These three self-evident principles were discovered experimentally before Newton's time but were first formulated by him.

Law 1. The law of inertia

A particle will either remain at rest or continue to move with uniform velocity unless acted upon by a force.

Law 2. The law of acceleration

The acceleration of a particle is directly proportional to the force producing it and inversely proportional to the mass of the particle.

Law 3. The law of action and reaction

Forces, the results of interactions of two bodies, always appear in pairs. In each pair the forces are equal in magnitude and opposite in direction.

EQUATIONS OF MOTION

Where
u is the initial velocity of a body;
v is its final velocity after time t;
s is the distance it travels in this time;
a is the uniform acceleration it undergoes.
  Then

$$v = u + at$$
$$s = ut + \tfrac{1}{2}at^2$$
$$v^2 = u^2 + 2as$$

BOYLE'S LAW

$$\frac{p_1}{p_2} = \frac{V_2}{V_1}$$

that is, if the temperature of a gas remains unchanged, its volume varies inversely with its pressure.

Laws of Physics (continued)

CHARLES' LAW

$$\frac{T_1}{T_2} = \frac{V_1}{V_2}$$

that is, if the pressure of a gas remains unchanged, its volume will vary directly with its temperature.

COULOMB'S LAW

$$F = \frac{Q_1 Q_2}{KD^2}$$

where F = force between two bodies
Q_1 = charge on one body
Q_2 = charge on another body
K = a constant
D = distance between the two bodies

KIRCHHOFF'S LAW

1. The algebraic sum of the currents flowing toward any point in an electric circuit is equal to zero.

2. The algebraic sum of the voltages and the drop in current because of resistance in an electric circuit is equal to zero.

OHM'S LAW

$$E = IR$$

where E = electromotive force, in volts
I = current, in amperes
R = resistance, in ohms

LAWS OF THERMODYNAMICS

Thermodynamics (Greek, *thermos*, hot; *dynamis*, power) is the quantitative treatment of the relation of heat to natural and mechanical forms of energy.

There are three Laws of Thermodynamics.

The **First Law,** derived from the principle of Conservation of Energy, may be stated: "Energy can neither be created nor destroyed, so that a given system can gain or lose energy only to the extent that it takes it from or passes it to its environment." This is expressed as:

$$Ef - Ei = \Delta$$

where Ei is the initial energy, Ef the final content of energy and Δ the change of energy. The impossibility of perpetual motion follows directly from this. The law applies only to systems of constant mass.

The **Second Law** concerns the concept of entropy (Greek *en*, into; *tropos*, a changing) which is the relation between the temperature of and the heat content within any system. A large amount of lukewarm water may contain the same amount of heat as a small amount of boiling water. The leveling out of heat within a system, *i.e.* the pouring of a kettle of boiling water into a lukewarm bath, is said to increase the entropy of that system of two vessels. Any system, including the Universe, naturally tends to increase its entropy, *i.e.* to distribute its heat. If the Universe can be regarded as a closed system, it follows from the Law that it will have a finite end, *i.e.* when it has finally dissipated or unwound itself to the point that its entropy attains a maximal level—this is referred to as the "Heat Death" of the Universe. From this it would also follow that the Universe must then have had a finite beginning for if it had had a creation an infinite time ago heat death would by now inevitably have set in. The Second Law, published in Berlin in 1850 by Rudolf Clausius (1822–88), states: "Heat cannot of itself pass from a colder to a warmer body." This is mathematically expressed by the inequality: $$\Delta > O$$

i.e. the change of entropy in any heat exchanging system and its surroundings taken together is always greater than zero.

The **Third Law** is not a general law but applies only to pure crystalline solids and states that at absolute zero the entropies of such substances are zero.

Milestones in Modern Physics

Physics is very much concerned with fundamental particles—the building blocks out of which the Universe is constructed—and the forces which bind and regulate them. Many theories have been proposed from time to time to provide a better understanding of the vast number of facts and observations which have accumulated. The main development of physics is essentially a series of unifications of these theories.

1687 Sir Isaac Newton (1643–1727) produced the great unifying theory of **gravitation** which linked the falling apple with the force which keeps the stars and planets in their courses. This made available for further scientific investigation one of the basic universal forces of nature, the force of gravity. The gravitational force, F, between two bodies of masses, m_1, m_2, distance, r, apart is given by

$$F = G\frac{m_1,\, m_2}{r^2}$$

where G is a Universal constant.

By Newton's time there existed two rival theories to explain the passage of light from source to observer. One was the **particle theory** which maintained that light consists of vast numbers of minute particles ejected by the luminous body in all directions. Newton, who made so many brilliant advances in optics, favored this theory. It accounted in a particularly simple way for the transmission of light through the vacuum of space, for its rectilinear propagation, and for the laws of reflection. The alternative was the **wave theory**, which assumed that light was transmitted by means of a wave motion. This would imply that light would bend round corners, but when it was discovered that the wavelength of the light was very small (about 1/2000th of a millimeter), it was realized that the effect would be small as is in fact observed. Light does not cast a perfectly sharp shadow. Further phenomena were discovered which demonstrated the wave nature of light and added support to that theory, *e.g.* interference and diffraction.

1820 Hans Christian Oersted (1777–1851) of Denmark, discovered that the flow of electric current in a conductor would cause a nearby compass needle to be deflected.

THE FUNDAMENTAL PHYSICAL CONSTANTS

The constants are called "fundamental" since they are used universally throughout all branches of science. Because of the unprecedented amount of new experimental and theoretical work being carried out, thorough revisions are now being published about once every five years, the last being in 1973. Values are reported such that the figure in brackets following the last digit is the estimated uncertainty of that digit, e.g. the speed of light $c = 2.997\ 924\ 58\ (1) \times 10^8$ m s⁻¹ could be written $c = (2.997\ 924\ 58 \pm 0.000\ 000\ 01) \times 10^8$ m s⁻¹. The unit m s⁻¹ represents m/s or meters per second.

	Quantity	Symbol	Value	Units
general constants	Speed of light in vacuo	c	$2.99792458\ (1) \times 10^8$	$m.s^{-1}$
	elementary charge	e	$1.6021892\ (46) \times 10^{-19}$	C
	Planck's constant	h	$6.626176\ (36) \times 10^{-34}$	J.s
		$h = h/2\pi$	$1.0545887\ (57) \times 10^{-34}$	J.s
	gravitional constant	G	$6.6720\ (41) \times 10^{-11}$	$m^3.s^{-2}.kg^{-1}$
matter in bulk	Avogadro constant	N	$6.022045\ (31) \times 10^{23}$	mol^{-1}
	atomic mass unit	$u = 1/N$	$1.6605655\ (86) \times 10^{-27}$	kg
			$9.315016\ (26) \times 10^2$	Mev
	faraday	$F = N\ e$	$9.648456\ (27) \times 10^4$	$C.mol^{-1}$
	normal volume of ideal gas	V	$2.241383\ (70) \times 10^{-2}$	$m^3.mol^{-1}$
	gas constant	R	$8.31441\ (26)$	$J.mol^{-1}.K^{-1}$
			$8.20568\ (26) \times 10^{-5}$	$m^3.atm.mol^{-1}\ K^{-1}$
	Boltzmann constant	$k = R/N$	$1.380662\ (44) \times 10^{-23}$	$J.K^{-1}$
electron	electron rest mass	m	$9.109534\ (47) \times 10^{-31}$	kg
			$0.5110034\ (14)$	Mev
	electron charge to mass ratio	e/m	$1.7588047\ (49) \times 10^{11}$	$C.kg^{-1}$
proton	proton rest mass	m	$1.6726485\ (86) \times 10^{-27}$	kg
			$9.382796\ (27) \times 10^2$	Mev
neutron	neutron rest mass	m	$1.6749543\ (86) \times 10^{-27}$	kg
			$9.395731\ (27) \times 10^2$	Mev
energy conversion	million electron volt unit	Mev	$1.7826758\ (51) \times 10^{-30}$	kg
			$1.6021892\ (46) \times 10^{-13}$	J

Milestones in Modern Physics (continued)

1831 Michael Faraday (1791–1867) the English physicist, uncovered the principle of magnetic induction which led to the invention of the dynamo. He showed that a change in the magnetic field surrounding a conductor could cause a flow of electrical current.

1865 The unification between magnetism and electricity was brought to full flower by the Scottish physicist, James Clerk Maxwell (1831–79), in his great **electromagnetic theory,** which described every known kind of magnetic and electric behavior. The set of equations named after him showed that electromagnetic waves travel at the velocity of light and confirmed that light is, in fact, an electromagnetic radiation. This provided further support for the wave theory of light.

1887 Heinrich Rudolph Hertz (1857–94), the German physicist, performed a classic experiment in which electromagnetic waves were produced and transmitted across the laboratory. This laid the foundation for radio transmission and provided ample vindication for Maxwell's theory.
  As the 19th century drew to a close many of the problems of physics appeared to have been solved and there was a belief that, in principle, if all the observations and calculations could be made, the destiny of the universe could be revealed in full detail. However, following on Hertz's experiment, a quick succession of phenomena presented themselves which threatened to destroy the orderly structure which had been so painstakingly built up over the preceding centuries.

1895 **X-rays** were discovered by Wilhelm Konrad Röntgen (1845–1923) the German physicist. When experimenting with the passage of electrical discharges through gases, he noticed that fluorescent material near his apparatus glowed. He won the first Nobel prize for physics in 1901 for this work.

1896 Antoine Henri Becquerel (1852–1908), the French physicist, discovered that uranium salts, even in the dark, emit a radiation similar to Röntgen's X-rays and would fog a photographic plate. This was **radioactivity.**

1898 Marie Curie (1867–1934), of Poland, working with her French husband, Pierre, (1859–1906) announced the existence of two new chemical elements which powerfully emit radiation. She named the elements radium and polonium. The active phenomenon she gave the name radioactivity. She won the Nobel prize for physics in 1903 with Becquerel and her husband, and in 1911, for chemistry on her own.
  Ernest Rutherford (1871–1937), New Zealand born British physicist and Frederick Soddy (1877–1956), British chemist, formulated a theory of radioactivity which forms the basis of our present understanding of the phenomenon. Three types of radioactivity were identified, α-rays, β-rays, and γ-rays. The γ-rays turned out to be like X-rays, more powerful than those of Röntgen. The β-rays were streams of fast moving electrons. The α-rays were found to consist of electrically charged particles being the nuclei of the element helium. The particles emitted from radioactive materials at such speed provided a means of investigating the structure of the atom itself, and enabled Rutherford to propose in 1911, a model of the atom which is the basis of our modern ideas of atomic structure.

  A further important discovery which contributed to a revision of the ideas of classical physics was the **photoelectric effect.** It was observed that a polished zinc plate, when illuminated with ultra-violet light acquired a positive electric charge. In **1897** Joseph John Thomson (1856–1940), the British physicist, discovered the first of the fundamental particles, the **electron,** which is the basic unit of negative electricity. It became clear that the photoelectric effect was the result of electrons being knocked out of the metal surface by the incident light. It was further discovered that, firstly, the number of electrons emitted was greater for a greater intensity of light and, secondly, that their energy was related only to the wavelength of the light, being greater for shorter wavelengths. The first result was as expected but the second was a mystery.

MODERN PHYSICS

Modern physics could be said to have been born at the beginning of the 20th century, during the course of which a number of radical ideas have been formulated and developed into theories which have completely revolutionized the thinking in physics.

1900 The quantum theory was the first of these, put forward by the German physicist Max Karl Ernst Ludwig Planck (1858–1947). This arose out of yet another problem which had been insoluble up to that time. Calculations showed that the energy emitted from a hot body should be, at very short wavelengths, practically infinite: this was clearly not so. The calculations were satisfactory for radiation of longer wavelengths in that they agreed with experiment. To resolve this difficulty, Planck made the very novel suggestion that energy was radiated from the body, not in a continuous flow of waves as had been supposed up to then, but rather in distinct individual bundles. He called a bundle of energy a **quantum**. The energy of the quantum, E, is given by

$$E = \frac{hc}{\lambda}$$

where λ is the wavelength of the radiation, c is the velocity of light *in vacuo* and h is a fixed, universal constant called Planck's constant. On this theory, energy at the shorter wavelengths would require to be emitted in bigger bundles and thus there would be less of them available for emission in accordance with experimental results. Planck's constant is small and so quantum effects are also small, occurring only in the domain of atomic phenomena.

1905 Albert Einstein (1879–1955), born in Germany, published his theory of the photoelectric effect and for which he was to win the Nobel prize in 1921. Einstein followed Planck's ideas and could see that the incident light must consist of a stream of quanta, that is, bundles of light, which came to be known as **photons**. A photon striking a metal surface is absorbed by an electron in it, the electron having more energy as a result. This causes it to jump from the surface, and since photons have greater energy at shorter wavelengths, so shorter wavelength light causes the emission of higher energy electrons. And, of course, the greater the intensity of the light the more quanta will be striking the surface and so more electrons will be emitted. Thus, the idea of the quantum enabled Einstein to account for the phenomena of the photo electric effect and this was an early triumph for the new quantum theory which was to become a ground force in the subsequent developments in physics.

1905 This year also saw the publication of Einstein's **Special (or Restricted) Theory of Relativity**. It has been said that as a child he had wondered what would happen if it were possible to travel fast enough to catch a ray of light and that this led him some years later to formulate his celebrated theory. This theory arises from an apparent contradiction between two basic postulates:

1. The velocity of light *in vacuo* is a constant for all observers regardless of their state of motion relative to the light source.
2. The special principle of relativity which states that the laws of physics are the same for all observers in uniform motion relative to each other.

Milestones in Modern Physics (continued)

Imagine for a moment a train travelling with a uniform velocity v relative to the railway embankment, and a ray of light transmitted with velocity c along the embankment parallel, and in the direction of the train. For an observer in the train the velocity of the light should appear to be $c-v$: obviously less than c. But this violates the special principle of relativity above: the velocity of light must be the same for an observer on the embankment and an observer on the train. The reconciliation of these two apparently contradictory conclusions is the basis for the special theory and is achieved by surrendering the concepts of absolute time, absolute distance and of the absolute significance of simultaneity. From these ideas, fairly straightforward algebraic manipulation leads to equations which show that when a body is in uniform motion relative to an observer, the length of the body is diminished in the direction of travel and its mass is increased. The equations are:

$$l = l_0 \surd (1 - v^2/c^2) \text{ and } m = \frac{m_0}{\surd (1 - v^2/c^2)}$$

where l and m are the length and mass respectively of a body as seen by an observer, and moving at velocity v in the direction of its length relative to him. l_0 is the velocity of the body at rest and m_0 is its mass at rest.

Thus, if a 20m rocket came past you in space at 149,896 km per sec. (*i.e.* $0.5c$) it would (if you could measure it) be only about 17m long.

If two observers are moving at a constant velocity relative to each other, it appears to each that the other's clocks are slowed down and this is expressed in the equation:

$$t = t_0 \surd (1 - v^2/c^2)$$

where t is one observer's time as read by the other, and t_0 is his own time as read by himself, v being the constant relative velocity of the two observers.

From the theory it can be shown that, at rest, a body possesses energy, E, given by

$$E = m c^2$$

Relativity theory confirms an important unification in physics between two of its very basic concepts; mass and energy.

1911 Ernest Rutherford proposed a model of the atom which is the basis of our ideas of atomic structure to this day. He had from the first recognized the value of the fast moving α-particles emitted naturally from radioactive materials as probes for discovering the nature of the atom. He arranged for α-particles to bombard a thin gold foil and found that while many passed straight through a few were deflected at comparatively large angles, some even "bouncing" back towards the source. He concluded from this that the mass of the atom was concentrated at its center in a minute nucleus consisting of positively charged particles called **protons**. Around the nucleus and at a relatively large distance from it revolved the negatively charged electrons rather like a miniature solar system. The combined negative charges of the electrons exactly balanced the total positive charge of the nucleus. This important model of the atom suffered from a number of defects. One of these was that from Maxwell's electro-magnetic theory the atom should produce light of all wavelengths whereas, in fact, atoms of each element emit light consisting of a number of definite wavelengths—a spectrum—which can be measured with great accuracy. The spectrum for each element is unique.

A further major difficulty was that the electrons, moving round the nucleus, should yield up their energy in the form of radiation and so would spiral into the nucleus bringing about the collapse of the atom. In fact, nothing of the sort occurs: under normal conditions an atom is a stable structure which does not emit radiation.

1913 The difficulties of the Rutherford atom were overcome by the Danish physicist, Neils Henrik David Bohr (1885–1962) who proposed that electrons were permitted only in certain orbits but could jump from one permitted orbit to another. In so jumping the electron would gain or lose energy in the form of photons, whose wavelength followed from Planck's rule:

$$\lambda = \frac{hc}{E}$$

In this way the spectrum of light emitted, or absorbed, by an atom would relate to its individual structure. The theoretical basis to Bohr's work was confirmed by Einstein in 1917 and the Bohr theory went on successfully to explain other atomic phenomena. However, after many outstanding successes over a number of years, an increasing number of small but important discrepancies appeared with which the Bohr theory could not cope.

1919 Rutherford performed the first artificial nuclear disintegration when he bombarded nitrogen atoms with α-particles from radon-C. He demonstrated that protons were emitted as a result of the disintegration and this confirmed that the proton was, indeed, a nuclear particle.

1924 Louis-Victor de Broglie (1892–1976), French physicist, postulated that the dual wave-particle nature of light might be shown by other particles and particularly by electrons. The wavelength, λ, would be given by

$$\lambda = \frac{h}{mv}$$

where m is the mass of the particle, and v is its velocity. Electron waves were demonstrated experimentally in 1927 by C. J. Davisson (1881–1958) and L. H. Germer (b. 1896) of the U.S.A. Subsequently, de Broglie's idea of matter waves was extended to other particles, protons, neutrons, etc. All matter has an associated wave character, but for the larger bodies of classical mechanics, the wavelengths are too small for their effects to be detectable.

1926 Erwin Schrödinger (1887–1961), a physicist from Vienna, took up the ideas of de Broglie waves and applied them to the Bohr atom. The solutions to the resulting wave equation gave the allowed orbits or energy levels more accurately than the quantized orbits in the Bohr atom. Max Born (1882–1970), the German physicist, interpreted these solutions in terms of probability, *i.e.* they gave the probability of finding an electron in a given volume of space within the atom.

1927 The German physicist, Werner Karl Heisenberg (1901–76) formulated his celebrated and profound Uncertainty Principle: this states that there is a definite limit to the accuracy with which certain pairs of measurements can be made. The more accurate one quantity is known, the less accurate is our knowledge of the other. Position and momentum is an example of such a pair of measurements. The more exactly we know the position of, say, an electron, the less will we know about its momentum. This can be expressed:

$$\Delta x. \, \Delta p \sim h$$

where Δx represents the uncertainty in position, Δp the uncertainty in momentum and h is Planck's constant. A further important example relates to time and energy: it is not possible to know how much energy E is possessed by a particle without allowing sufficient time t for the energy to be determined.

$$\Delta E. \, \Delta t \sim h$$

The uncertainty principle provides the main reason why the classical mechanics of Newton do not apply to atomic and sub-atomic phenomena.

1928 Paul Adrien Maurice Dirac (b. 1902), the English mathematician, introduced a theory of the electron which successfully brought together the ideas of quantum mechanics thus far developed with those of relativity. As a result of this, the important concept of electron spin previously advanced by Bohr became theoretically justified.

Dirac's equations revealed a negative quantity which led to the prediction of the existence of the antielectron, a particle identical to the electron, of the same mass but of opposite electric charge. This major idea, that there could exist **antimatter** in the universe composed of antiparticles arises from Dirac's bold prediction.

Heisenberg's uncertainty principle led to the idea of the instantaneous creation and annihilation of short-lived "virtual" particles in the vicinity of stable particles. The basic uncertainty in the energy of a particle enables it to acquire a loan, as it were, of energy for a short time: the length of time, in fact, being inversely related to the amount of energy lent. Provided the loan is repaid in the time available, there is no violation of the law of conservation of energy. The action of forces could now be seen in terms of these "virtual" particles, which behave as force-carriers travelling rapidly from one particle to the other. So, it comes about that particles, not in direct contact, respond each to the presence of the other.

1932 Ernest Orlando Lawrence (1901–58), an American physicist, developed the **cyclotron.** This was one of the first machines constructed for accelerating charged particles artificially to high velocities for research. The particles, which in the first instance were protons, were caused to move with ever increasing velocity in a spiral path by the suitable application of magnetic and electric fields. Lawrence was awarded the Nobel prize in 1939 for this work.

1932 Carl David Anderson (b. 1905), an American physicist of California, announced the discovery of the antielectron predicted a few years previously by Dirac. This was the first particle of antimatter to be discovered and he named it the **positron.**

1932 James Chadwick (b. 1891), the English physicist, discovered the **neutron,** a constituent of the atomic nucleus of zero charge and only slightly heavier than the proton.

1933 Wolfgang Pauli (1900–58) of Austria postulated the existence of the **neutrino,** a neutral particle of negligible mass in order to explain the fact that in β-emission in radioactivity, there was a rather greater loss of energy than could be otherwise explained.

In 1956 Fred Reines and Clyde Cowan in Los Alamos succeeded in detecting neutrinos (electron neutrinos). In 1962 Lederman and Melvin Schwarz of Columbia University demonstrated the existence of the other neutrino, the muon neutrino.

1934 Hideki Yukawa (b. 1907), the Japanese physicist, sought to explain the forces which held the particles in the nucleus together—the **strong force**—and called the force-carrying particles in this case **mesons.** The meson predicted by Yukawa, the **pion,** was discovered by Cecil F. Powell of Bristol University in 1947.

1938 **Nuclear fission** was discovered by Otto Hahn (1879–1968) and Fritz Strassman (b. 1902) by bombarding uranium with neutrons, when trying to produce transuranic elements. They succeeded in producing elements lighter than uranium from the mineral of the periodic table. The incident neutron causes the target nucleus to split into two pieces of almost equal mass. Each of the fragments consists of protons and neutrons and an enormous amount of energy is released in the process. Enrico Fermi (1901–54) suggested that the neutrons released in fission could themselves induce further fission and that it should be possible to sustain a chain reaction.

1942 The first nuclear reactor, set up by Fermi in the University of Chicago became critical.

1945 The first atomic explosion which was experimental took place in July followed by bombs dropped on Hiroshima and Nagasaki in August.

1952 The first hydrogen bomb was exploded in November. This derived its energy from the process of nuclear fusion in which two or more relatively light nuclei combined to form a heavier atomic nucleus releasing thereby a very considerable amount of energy. Considerable effort is being made to develop a fusion reactor and the main difficulty is the problem of containing the enormously high temperatures involved within the reactor for long enough to allow the reaction to proceed. In June 1954 the world's first nuclear powered generator produced electricity at Obnisk near Moscow, and in August 1956 the first large scale nuclear power generating station, Calder Hall, Northumberland, England started up. It was officially opened by Queen Elizabeth II in October when power first flowed into the national grid.

By the 1950's a bewilderingly large number of apparently fundamental particles had been reported and their great number was becoming an embarrassment. Most particles then known fell into two classes: the **leptons** and the **hadrons**.

Hadrons are complex and there was evidence that they themselves possessed an internal structure. Certain of the unstable hadrons were found to take very much longer to decay than expected. These were called **strange** particles.

1953 Murray Gell-Mann (b. 1929) of the U.S.A., introduced a concept he called **strangeness,** a quality akin in some ways to electric charge, which helped to account for the increased life-times of the strange particles. Aided by this idea, it was found that particles could be fitted into patterns according to the amount of strangeness they possessed. This led to the prediction of the existence of a rather unusual particle and it was a great triumph for these theories when in 1964 the omega-minus particle was discovered.

1963 From considerations of these patterns, Gell-Mann was led to the idea that the hadrons were composed of more basic particles called **quarks** (a name he borrowed from the writings of the Irish author, James Joyce). There were three kinds of quark, "up," "down" and "strange" and, for each, a corresponding antiquark. These combined in only one of two ways to form either **baryons** or **mesons** as the table shows. Thus the proton can be pictured as consisting of three quarks —2 up quarks and 1 down quark held together by force-carrying particles called **gluons.**

A free quark has not yet been detected and there is speculation that it never will. But there is experimental evidence suggesting their existence within baryons.

Current theory suggests that the gluons carry an enormously strong force called the **color force.** This is much stronger than the strong nuclear force and permits quarks in the proton, for example, freedom of movement over a very short distance but increases with distance to hold them firmly within the proton.

1974 A particularly heavy particle, a hadron, was discovered and called the J or psi particle. Up to this time, the rules for building hadrons from quarks accounted in a complete and satisfying way for every known hadron and so it was that there appeared to be no room for the new particle. However, it could be explained by assuming it to be composed of a new quark together with its antiquark. This new, fourth quark called the charmed quark had been proposed in 1970 by Sheldon Lee Glashow (b. 1932) for other theoretical reasons. Charm, a property similar to strangeness, was first suggested in 1964 by Glashow on aesthetic grounds: there were two pairs of leptons so the up and down quark also formed a pair leaving the strange quark without a companion. Now, the charmed quark completed the team and also explained this new particle. However, the charm in this psi particle cancelled out because of the charm/anti-charm combination. The search was then for a particle exhibiting "naked" charm, a particle containing a charmed quark in combination with an up, down or strange quark.

1976 In May the D^0 meson was discovered by Gerson Goldhaber, co-discoverer of the psi particle, and Françoise Pièrre at Stanford University. The D^0 particle consisted of a charmed quark and an anti-up quark.

In August, Wonyong Lee of Columbia University announced that a charmed antiproton had been detected, consisting of three antiquarks —up, down and charmed.

Two very heavy Upsilon mesons with masses of 9,400 Mev and 10,000 Mev were announced in Nov. 1977. The tau lepton was announced in Dec. 1978.

Chemistry

THE ELEMENTS

Atomic No.	Name of Element	Date of Discovery	Discoverer
1.	Hydrogen	1766	Henry Cavendish (1731–1810, U.K.)
2.	Helium*	1868*	Pierre Jules Cesar Janssen (1824–1907, France); Sir Joseph Norman Lockyer (1836–1920) and Sir Edward Frankland (1825–99, both U.K.)
3.	Lithium	1817	Johan August Arfwedson (1792–1841, Sweden)
4.	Beryllium	1797	Louis Nicolas Vauquelin (1763–1829, France)
5.	Boron	1808	Joseph Louis Gay-Lussac (1778–1850) and Louis Jacques Thénard (1777–1857, both France); Sir Humphry Davy (1778–1829, U.K.)
6.	Carbon	B.C.	There is no precise knowledge as to the date of discovery
7.	Nitrogen	1772	Karl (or Carl) Wilhelm Scheele (1742–86, Germany–Sweden); Daniel Rutherford (1749–1819) and Joseph Priestley (1733–1804, both U.K.)
8.	Oxygen	1771	Karl Wilhelm Scheele (1742–86, Sweden)
9.	Fluorine	1886	Henri Moissan (1852–1907, France)
10.	Neon	1898	Sir William Ramsay (1852–1916) and Morris William Travers (1872–1961, both U.K.)
11.	Sodium (Natrium)	1807	Sir Humphry Davy (1778–1829, U.K.)
12.	Magnesium	1808	Sir Humphry Davy (1778–1829, U.K.)
13.	Aluminum	1825	Hans Christian Oersted (1777–1851, Denmark)
14.	Silicon	1824	Jöns Jakob Berzelius (1779–1848, Sweden)
15.	Phosphorus	1669	Hennig Brand (17th century, Germany)
16.	Sulphur	B.C.	There is no precise knowledge as to the date of discovery
17.	Chlorine	1774	Karl Wilhelm Scheele (1742–86, Sweden)

* Not discovered on Earth until March, 1895, by Sir William Ramsay (1852–1916, U.K.).

480

Atomic No.	Name of Element	Date of Discovery	Discoverer
18.	Argon	1894	The 3rd Baron Rayleigh (1842–1919) and Sir William Ramsay (1852–1916, both U.K.)
19.	Potassium (Kalium)	1807	Sir Humphry Davy (1778–1829, U.K.)
20.	Calcium	1808	Sir Humphry Davy (1778–1829, U.K.)
21.	Scandium	1879	Lars Fredrik Nilson (1840–1899, Sweden)
22.	Titanium	1791	Rev. William Gregor (1761–1817, U.K.)
23.	Vanadium	1830	Friedrich Wöhler (1800–82, Germany); Nils Gabriel Sefström (1787–1845, Sweden)
24.	Chromium	1798	Louis Nicolas Vauquelin (1763–1829, France)
25.	Manganese	1774	Karl Wilhelm Scheele (1742–86) and Johan Gottlieb Gahn (1745–1818, both Sweden)
26.	Iron (Ferrum)	c. 2000 B.C.	Known to the Sumerian civilization
27.	Cobalt	1742	Georg Brandt (1694–1768, Sweden)
28.	Nickel	1751	Baron Axel Fredrik Cronstedt (1722–65, Sweden)
29.	Copper (Cuprum)	c. 8000 B.C.	Known to Mesolithic man
30.	Zinc	c. 1530	Theophrastus Bombastus von Hohenheim, called Paracelsus (1493–1541, Switzerland)
31.	Gallium	1875	Paul Émile Lecoq de Boisbaudran (1838–1912, France)
32.	Germanium	1886	Clemens Alexander Winkler (1838–1904, Germany)
33.	Arsenic	c. 1250	Albert, Count of Bollstädt, called Albertus Magnus ("Albert the Great") (1206–80, Germany)
34.	Selenium	1818	Jöns Jakob Berzelius (1779–1848, Sweden)
35.	Bromine	1826	Antoine Jérôme Balard (1802–76, France)
36.	Krypton	1898	Sir William Ramsay (1852–1916) and Morris William Travers (1872–1961, both U.K.)
37.	Rubidium	1861	Robert Wilhelm von Bunsen (1811–99) and Gustav Robert Kirchhoff (1824–1887, both Germany)
38.	Strontium	1787	William Cruikshank (U.K.)
39.	Yttrium	1794	Johan Gadolin (1760–1852, Finland)
40.	Zirconium	1789	Martin Heinrich Klaproth (1743–1817, Germany)
41.	Niobium (Columbium [Cb.])	1801	Charles Hatchett (c. 1765–1847, U.K.)
42.	Molybdenum	1782	Peter Jacob Hjelm (1746–1813, Sweden)
43.	Technetium (formerly Masurium)	1937	Emilio Gino Segrè (b. February 1, 1905, Italy—now U.S.) and C. Perrier (France)
44.	Ruthenium	1844	Karl Karlovich Klaus (or Claus) (1796–1864, Estonia, now part of U.S.S.R.)

Atomic No.	Name of Element	Date of Discovery	Discoverer
45.	Rhodium	1803	William Hyde Wollaston (1766–1828, U.K.)
46.	Palladium	1803	William Hyde Wollaston (1766–1828, U.K.)
47.	Silver (Argentum)	c. 4000 B.C.	Known during the period of the Sumerian civilization
48.	Cadmium	1817	Friedrich Strohmeyer (1776–1835, Germany)
49.	Indium	1863	Ferdinand Reich (1799–1882) and Hieronymus Theodore Richter (1824–98, both Germany)
50.	Tin (Stannum)	c. 1500 B.C.	Used during the Egyptiac civilization
51.	Antimony (Stibium)	c. 1450	? Basilius Valentinus (Germany)
52.	Tellurium	1782	Franz Joseph Müller, Baron von Reichenstein (1740–1825, Austria)
53.	Iodine	1811	Bernard Courtois (1777–1838, France)
54.	Xenon	1898	Sir William Ramsay (1852–1916) and Morris William Travers (1872–1961, both U.K.)
55.	Cesium	1860	Robert Wilhelm von Bunsen (1811–99) and Gustav Robert Kirchhoff (1824–87, both Germany)
56.	Barium	1808	Sir Humphry Davy (1778–1829, U.K.)
57.	Lanthanum	1839	Carl Gustav Mosander (1797–1858, Sweden)
58.	Cerium	1803	Martin Heinrich Klaproth (1743–1817, Germany); Jöns Jakob Berzelius (1779–1848) and Wilhelm Hisinger (1766–1852, both Sweden)
59.	Praseodymium	1885	Carl Auer, Baron von Welsbach (1858–1929, Austria)
60.	Neodymium	1885	Carl Auer, Baron von Welsbach (1858–1929, Austria)
61.	Promethium (formerly Illinium)	1947	Dr. Jacob Akiba Marinsky (b. April 11, 1918), Dr. Lawrence Elgin Glendenin (b. November 8, 1918), and Dr. Charles Dubois Coryell (b. February 21, 1912, all U.S.)
62.	Samarium	1879	Paul Émile Lecoq de Boisbaudran (1838–1912, France)
63.	Europium	1901	Eugène Anatole Demarçay (1852–1904, France)
64.	Gadolinium	1880	J. C. Galissard de Marignac (1817–1894, Switzerland)
65.	Terbium	1843	Carl Gustav Mosander (1797–1858, Sweden)
66.	Dysprosium	1886	Paul Émile Lecoq de Boisbaudran (1838–1912, France)
67.	Holmium	1878	J. Louis Soret (France)
68.	Erbium	1843	Carl Gustav Mosander (1797–1858, Sweden)
69.	Thulium	1879	Per Theodor Cleve (1840–1905, Sweden)
70.	Ytterbium (Neoytterbium)	1907	Georges Urbain (1872–1938, France)

Atomic No.	Name of Element	Date of Discovery	Discoverer
71.	Lutetium (Lutecium)	1907	Carl Auer, Baron von Welsbach (1858–1929, Austria); Georges Urbain (1872–1938, France)
72.	Hafnium	1923	George Charles de Hevesy (b. August 1, 1885, Hungary—now Sweden) and Dirk Coster (b. October 5, 1889, Netherlands)
73.	Tantalum	1802	Anders Gustaf Ekeberg (1767–1813, Sweden)
74.	Tungsten (or Wolfram)	1783	Juan José d'Elhuyar and Fausto d'Elhuyar (1755–1833, Spain) (brothers)
75.	Rhenium	1925	Walter Karl Friedrich Noddack (b. 1893), Ida Eva Noddack (née Tacke, b. 1896), and Otto Berg (all Germany)
76.	Osmium	1804	Smithson Tennant (1761–1815, U.K.)
77.	Iridium	1804	Smithson Tennant (1761–1815, U.K.)
78.	Platinum	1748	Antonio de Ulloa (1716–95, Spain)
79.	Gold (Aurum)	c. 3000 B.C.	Known during the Egyptiac civilization
80.	Mercury	c. 1500 B.C.	Known to the Egyptiac, Indic, and Sinic civilizations
81.	Thallium	1861	Professor (later Sir) William Crookes (1832–1919, U.K.)
82.	Lead (Plumbum)	B.C.	Not even an approximate date is known, but this element was used during the Egyptiac civilization
83.	Bismuth	c. 1450	? Basilius Valentinus (Germany)
84.	Polonium	1898	Pierre Curie (1859–1906, France) and Marie Curie (née Marja Sklodowska) (1867–1934, Poland—later France)
85.	Astatine	1940	Dr. Dale Raymond Corson (b. April 5, 1914, U.S.), K. R. Mackenzie (U.S.), and Emilio Gino Segrè (b. February 1, 1905 Italy—now U.S.)
86.	Radon	1900	Friedrich Ernst Dorn (1848–1916, Germany)
87.	Francium	1939	Mlle. Marguerite Perey (b. 1909, France)
88.	Radium	1898	Pierre Curie (1859–1906), Marie Curie (1867–1934) and G. Bémont (all France)
89.	Actinium	1899	André Louis Debierne (France)
90.	Thorium	1828	Jöns Jakob Berzelius (1779–1848, Sweden)
91.	Protactinium	1917	Otto Hahn (b. March 8, 1879, Germany) and Frau Lise Meitner (b. November 8, 1878, Austria)
92.	Uranium	1789	Martin Heinrich Klaproth (1743–1817, Germany)
93.	Neptunium	spring 1940	Drs. Edwin Mattison McMillan (b. September 18, 1907) and Philip Hauge Abelson (b. April 27, 1913, both U.S.)
94.	Plutonium	late 1940	Drs. Glenn Theodore Seaborg (b. April 19, 1912), E. M. McMillan, Arthur C. Wahl, and Joseph W. Kennedy (all U.S.)

Atomic No.	Name of Element	Date of Discovery	Discoverer
95.	Americium	late 1944 and early 1945	Drs. G. T. Seaborg, Ralph Arthur James (b. September 23, 1920), Leon Owen Morgan (b. October 25, 1919), and Albert Ghiorso (b. July 15, 1915, all U.S.)
96.	Curium	summer 1944	Drs. G. T. Seaborg, R. A. James, and A. Ghiorso (all U.S.)
97.	Berkelium	Dec. 1949	Drs. G. T. Seaborg, Stanley Gerald Thompson (b. 1912), and A. Ghiorso (all U.S.)
98.	Californium	Feb. 1950	Drs. G. T. Seaborg, S. G. Thompson, A. Ghiorso, and Kenneth Street, Jr. (b. January 30, 1920— all U.S.)
99.	Einsteinium	Dec. 1952	Dr. A. Ghiorso and his co-workers (U.S.)
100.	Fermium	Jan. 1953	Dr. A. Ghiorso and his co-workers (U.S.)
101.	Mendelevium	Feb. 18, 1955	Drs. G. T. Seaborg, A. Ghiorso, Bernard George Harvey (b. October 5, 1919), Gregory Robert Choppin (b. November 9, 1927), and S. G. Thompson (all U.S.)
102.	Nobelium	Apr. 1958	Drs. G. T. Seaborg, A. Ghiorso, Torbjorn Sikkeland, and John R. Walton (all U.S.)
103.	Lawrencium	Feb. 1961	Drs. A. Ghiorso, T. Sikkeland, Almon E. Larsh, and Robert M. Latimer (all U.S.)
104.	Kurchatovium or Rutherfordium	Aug. 1964 1969	Prof. Georgiy Flerov (U.S.S.R.) Reported
105.	Nielsbohrium or Hahnium	1970 1970	

Note: Elements 106 and 107 reported in 1974 and 1976 remain disputed and hence unnamed by the International Union of Pure and Applied Chemistry. The team claiming the discovery of Element 107 was led by Oyanesyan (U.S.S.R.).

CONFIGURATIONS OF THE ELEMENTS

In the chart on the opposite page the slanted rows numbered from 1 to 7 and running from left to right represent the main orbital shells. The four columns identified by the letters s, p, d, and f represent sub-shells within the main orbitals. Note that each sub-shell is divided by a space into two equal sections. The atomic weight of each element is shown above the symbol for that element; the atomic number is shown below. The atomic number equals, of course, the total number of electrons in an element. Non-metals are indicated by bars above the symbols. Below the chart is shown the group in the periodic table to which the elements in each column belong.

The following examples show how to use the chart.

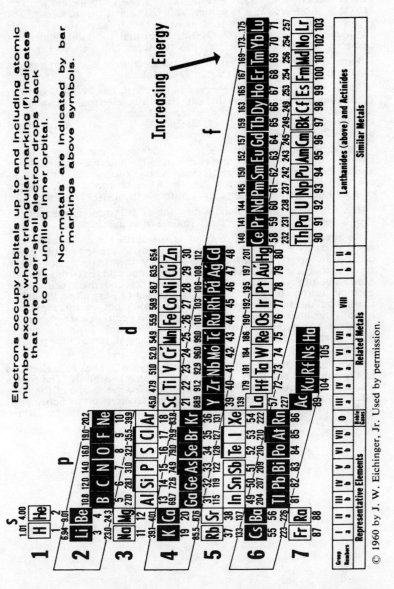

Electrons occupy orbitals up to and including atomic number except where triangular marking (▷) indicates that one outer-shell electron drops back to an unfilled inner orbital.

Non-metals are indicated by bar markings above symbols.

Increasing Energy

© 1960 by J. W. Eichinger, Jr. Used by permission.

ELECTRONIC CONFIGURATIONS OF THE ELEMENTS: Using the chart above, devised by Dr. J. W. Eichinger, Jr., you can readily determine the electronic configuration of each element—the number of electrons in each main orbital shell and the number of electrons in each sub-shell. In particular, you will be able to determine by inspection the number and configuration of electrons in the outer shell of each element. These are the electrons that determine the chemical behavior of the elements.

Configurations of the Elements (continued)

Carbon is No. 6 in the chart; therefore, it has six electrons. How are these electrons arranged? According to the position of the squares numbered from 1 to 6. The two s squares in the 1st orbital are filled. This is written symbolically as follows: $1s^2$. The s sub-shell in the 2nd orbital is also filled. This is written as $2s^2$. The first two squares of the p row are also filled. This is written as $2p^2$. In sum, the electronic configuration of carbon is $1s^22s^22p^2$. Note that the total number of electrons in the element are equal to the superscripts added together.

Vanadium (V) has 23 electrons. By inspection it is evident that its electronic configuration is $1s^22s^22p^63s^23p^64s^23d^3$.

Chromium (Cr), the next element in the chart, has 24 electrons. The small triangle in the square indicates that one electron is transferred from the second-last sub-shell into the last sub-shell. Thus, instead of the electrons being arranged as $1s^22s^22p^23s^23p^64s^24d^4$, they are arranged as $1s^22s^22p^23s^23p^64s^14d^5$.

The ability of atoms to combine with each other chemically depends not only on the total number of electrons in the outermost sub-shell but also on how the electrons are arranged among themselves in the outermost sub-shell. Orbitals within a sub-shell can be unoccupied, they can contain one electron, or they can contain—at most—two electrons.

The following examples show how the arrangement of electrons in the outermost sub-shell can be determined from the chart.

As already noted, the s, p, d, and f sub-shells are divided into two equal parts by a space. Electrons in squares to the left of the space, occupy an orbital within the sub-shell by themselves; electrons in squares to the right of the space double-up with electrons already occupying orbitals. In the p sub-shell of the 2nd main orbital, for example, boron (B), carbon (C), and nitrogen (N) are all to the left of the space. Boron has one electron occupying one of three possible orbitals (the other two orbitals being completely empty), carbon has two electrons occupying two of three possible orbitals (with one empty orbital), and nitrogen has an electron occupying all three of the possible orbitals.

Continuing with the same $2p$ sub-shell, oxygen (O) has four electrons in the sub-shell but there are only three possible orbitals. The fourth electron therefore doubles-up with another electron in one of the three filled orbitals. In the same way, the additional electrons of fluorine (F) and neon (Ne) join orbitals in which there are already two and three electrons present, respectively.

ATOMIC TABLE

Atomic Number	Name of Element	Symbol	Name Derived from	Chemical Atomic Weight	Density (gm/cc) at 20°C. unless otherwise stated
1	Hydrogen	H	Greek, *hydor* = water	1.0079	0.07 at −253° C.
2	Helium	He	Greek, *helios* = sun	4.00260	0.12 at −268.94° C.
3	Lithium	Li	Greek, *lithos* = stone	6.941	0.53
4	Beryllium	Be	Greek, *beryllion* = beryl	9.01218	1.8
5	Boron	B	Persian, *burah* = borax	10.81	2.3
6	Carbon	C	Latin, *carbo* = charcoal	12.011	2.3 (graphite)
7	Nitrogen	N	Greek, *nitron* = saltpeter	14.0067	0.81 at −196° C.
8	Oxygen	O	Greek, *oxys* = acid	15.9994	1.13 at −184° C.
9	Fluorine	F	Latin, *fluo* = flow	18.9984	1.1 at −200° C.
10	Neon	Ne	Greek, *neos* = new	20.179	1.2 at −246° C.
11	Sodium (Natrium)	Na	English, soda	22.98977	0.97
12	Magnesium	Mg	Magnesia, district in Thessaly	24.305	1.7
13	Aluminum	Al	Latin, *alumen* = alum	26.98154	2.7
14	Silicon	Si	Latin, *silex* = flint	28.0855	2.4
15	Phosphorus	P	Latin, from Greek 'light-bringing'	30.97376	1.82 (yellow)
16	Sulfur	S	Latin, *sulfur*	32.0668	2.1 (rhombic)
17	Chlorine	Cl	Greek, *chloros* = green	35.453	1.6 af −34.1° C.
18	Argon	A	Greek, *argos* = inactive	39.948	1.41 at −188°C.
19	Potassium (Kalium)	K	English, potash	39.0983	0.86
20	Calcium	Ca	Latin, *calx* = lime	40.08	1.55
21	Scandium	Sc	Scandinavia	44.9559	3.0
22	Titanium	Ti	Latin, *Titanes* = sons of the earth	47.90	4.5
23	Vanadium	V	Vanadis, a name given to Freyja, the Norse goddess of beauty and youth	50.9414	6.1
24	Chromium	Cr	Greek, *chromos* = color	51.996	7.1
25	Manganese	Mn	Latin, *magnes* = magnet	54.9380	7.4
26	Iron (Ferrum)	Fe	Anglo-Saxon, *iren*	55.847	7.9
27	Cobalt	Co	German, *kobold* = goblin	58.9332	8.9
28	Nickel	Ni	German, abbreviation of *kupfernickel* ('devil's copper'), or niccolite	58.70	8.9

§ The atomic weight of sulfur has a range of ± 0.003.

Atomic Table (continued)

Name of Element	Atomic Number	Symbol	Name Derived from	Chemical Atomic Weight	Density (gm/cc) at 20° C. unless otherwise stated
Copper (Cuprum)	29	Cu	Cyprus	63.546	8.96
Zinc	30	Zn	German, *zink*	65.38	7.1
Gallium	31	Ga	Latin, *Gallia* = France	69.72	5.97
Germanium	32	Ge	Latin, *Germania* = Germany	72.59	5.3
Arsenic	33	As	Latin, *arsenicum*	74.9216	5.7
Selenium	34	Se	Greek, *selene* = moon	78.96	4.8
Bromine	35	Br	Greek, *bromos* = stench	79.904	3.1
Krypton	36	Kr	Greek, *kryptos* = hidden	83.80	2.16 at −146° C.
Rubidium	37	Rb	Latin, *rubidus* = red	85.4678	1.5
Strontium	38	Sr	Strontian, a village in Argyllshire	89.62	2.6
Yttrium	39	Y	Ytterby, in Sweden	88.9059	4.6
Zirconium	40	Zr	Persian, *zargun* = gold-colored	91.22	6.5
Niobium (formerly Columbium [Cb])	41	Nb	Latin, *Niobe,* daughter of Tantalus	95.94	8.6
Molybdenum	42	Mo	Greek, *molybdos* = lead	95.94	10.2
Technetium (formerly Masurium)	43	Tc	Greek, *technetos* = artificial	96.9064	11.49
Ruthenium	44	Ru	Ruthenia (the Ukraine, in the U.S.S.R.)	101.07	12.2
Rhodium	45	Rh	Greek, *rhodon* = rose	102.9055	12.4
Palladium	46	Pd	The asteroid *Pallas*	106.4	12.0
Silver (Argentum)	47	Ag	Anglo-Saxon, *seolfor*	107.868	10.5
Cadmium	48	Cd	Greek, *kadmeia* = calamine	112.41	8.65
Indium	49	In	Its indigo spectrum	118.69	7.3
Tin (Stannum)	50	Sn	Anglo-Saxon, tin	118.70	7.3
Antimony (Stibium)	51	Sb	L. Latin, *antimonium*	121.75	6.7
Tellurium	52	Te	Latin, *tellus* = earth	127.60	6.2
Iodine	53	I	Greek, *iodes* = violet	126.9045	4.9
Xenon	54	Xe	Greek, *xenos* = stranger	131.30	3.5 at −109° C.
Cesium	55	Cs	Latin, *caesius* = bluish-gray	132.9054	1.9

* A star against Chemical Atomic Weight indicates that the figure given is the mass number of the isotope with the longest known half-life (*i.e.* the period taken for its radioactivity to fall to half of its original value).

Element	No.	Symbol	Etymology	Atomic Weight	Density
Barium	56	Ba	Greek, *barys* = heavy	137.33	3.5
Lanthanum	57	La	Greek, *lanthano* = conceal	138.9055	6.2
Cerium	58	Ce	The asteroid *Ceres*	140.12	6.9
Praseodymium	59	Pr	Greek, *prasios* = green, *didymos* = twin	140.9077	6.5
Neodymium	60	Nd	Greek, *neos* = new, *didymos* = twin	144.24	6.9
Promethium (formerly Illinium)	61	Pm	*Prometheus*, the fire-stealer, a Greek demi-god	144.9128	—
Samarium	62	Sm	The mineral Samarskite, named after Col. M. Samarski, a Russian engineer	150.4	7.5
Europium	63	Eu	Europe	151.96	5.1
Gadolinium	64	Gd	Johan Gadolin (1760–1852, Finland)	157.25	8.0
Terbium	65	Tb	Ytterby, in Sweden	158.9254	8.2
Dysprosium	66	Dy	Greek, *dysprositos* = hard to get at	162.50	8.5
Holmium	67	Ho	*Holmia*, a Latinized form of Stockholm	164.9309	8.8
Erbium	68	Er	Ytterby, in Sweden	167.26	9.0
Thulium	69	Tm	Latin and Greek, *Thule* = Northland	168.9342	9.3
Ytterbium	70	Yb	Ytterby, in Sweden	173.04	7.0
Lutetium (formerly Lutecium)	71	Lu	*Lutetia*, Roman name for city of Paris	174.97	9.8
Hafnium	72	Hf	*Hafnia* = Copenhagen	178.49	13.1
Tantalum	73	Ta	*Tantalus*, a mythical Greek king	180.9479	16.6
Tungsten (or Wolfram)	74	W	Swedish, *tung* = heavy; *sten* = stone	183.85	19.3
Rhenium	75	Re	Latin, *Rhenus* = the river Rhine	186.207	21.0
Osmium	76	Os	Greek, *osme* = odor	190.2	22.4
Iridium	77	Ir	Latin, *iris* = a rainbow	192.22	22.65
Platinum	78	Pt	Spanish, *platina* = small silver	195.09	21.45
Gold (Aurum)	79	Au	Anglo-Saxon, gold	196.9665	19.3
Mercury (Hydrargyrum)	80	Hg	*Mercury*, the Roman god of merchandise and merchants	200.59	13.55
Thallium	81	Tl	Greek, *thallos* = a budding twig	204.37	11.85
Lead (Plumbum)	82	Pb	Anglo-Saxon, lead	207.2	11.3
Bismuth	83	Bi	German, *weissmuth* = white matter	208.9804	9.8
Polonium	84	Po	The Polish nationality of the co-discoverer, Mme. Curie	208.9824	—

Atomic Table (continued)

Name of Element	Atomic Number	Symbol	Name Derived from	Chemical Atomic Weight	Density (gm/cc) at 20° C. unless otherwise stated
Astatine	85	At	Greek, *astatos* = unstable	209.987	—
Radon**	86	Rn	Emanation from radium salts	222.0176	4.4 at −62° C.
Francium	87	Fr	The French nationality of Mlle. Perey	223.0197	—
Radium	88	Ra	Latin, *radius* = ray	226.0254	5
Actinium	89	Ac	Greek, *aktinos*, genitive of *aktis* = a ray	227.0278	—
Thorium	90	Th	*Thor*, the Norse god of thunder	232.0381	11.5
Protactinium	91	Pa	Greek, *protos* = first, plus actinium	231.0359	15.4
Uranium	92	U	In honor of the discovery of Uranus	238.029	19.05
Neptunium	93	Np	The planet Neptune	237.482	c. 17.6 to 19.5
Plutonium	94	Pu	The planet Pluto	244.0642	19.737 (αPu)
Americium	95	Am	America	243.0614	11.7 ± 0.3
Curium	96	Cm	The Curies—Pierre (1859–1906) and Marie (1867–1934)	247.0703	—
Berkelium	97	Bk	Berkeley, California	247.0703	—
Californium	98	Cf	California	251.0796	—
Einsteinium	99	Es	Dr. Albert Einstein (1879–1955)	254.0880	—
Fermium	100	Fm	Dr. Enrico Fermi (1901–54), Italian (later U.S.A.) physicist	257.0951	—
Mendelevium	101	Mv	Dmitriy Ivanovich Mendeleyev (1834–1907), Russian chemist	258.099	—
Nobelium	102	No	Alfred Nobel (1833–96), Swedish inventor	259.101	—
Lawrencium	103	Lw	Dr. Ernest Orlando Lawrence (1901–58, U.S.), inventor of the cyclotron	260.105	—
Kurchatovium** (tentative) or Rutherfordium	104	Ku Rf	Dr. Igor V. Kurchatov (1903–60, U.S.S.R.) } Lord (Ernest) Rutherford (1871–1937)	— } 261.109	
Nielsbohrium or Hahnium	105	Ns Ha	Prof. Niels Bohr (1885–1962) } Prof. Otto Hahn (1879–1968)	262.114	
—	106	—	1974	263.120	
—	107	—	1976	261.125	

**Because the discoveries of elements 104, 105, 106 and 107 are disputed, the International Union of Pure and Applied Chemistry has not yet assigned official names to these elements.

Atomic Table (continued)

Name of Element	Atomic Number	Physical Description	Melting Point (for pressure of one standard atmosphere) (°C.)	Boiling Point	Valence (or Valency) Number	No. of Nuclides
Hydrogen	1	Colorless gas	— 259.194	— 252.78	1	3
Helium	2	Colorless gas	— 272.375	— 268.94	0	6
Lithium	3	Silvery-white metal	180.57	1,330	1	5
Beryllium	4	Gray metal	1,289	2,450	2	7
Boron	5	Dark brown powder	2,130	2,550	3	6
Carbon	6	Colorless solid (diamond) or black solid (graphite)	4,550	3,900	2, 3 or 4	9
Nitrogen	7	Colorless gas	— 210.004	— 195.8	3 or 5	7
Oxygen	8	Colorless gas	— 218.789	— 182.970	2	8
Fluorine	9	Pale greenish-yellow gas	— 219.669	— 188.1	1	6
Neon	10	Colorless gas	— 248.589	— 246.1	0	8
Sodium (Natrium)	11	Silvery-white metal	97.86	883	1	7
Magnesium	12	Silvery-white metal	649	1,100	2	9
Aluminum	13	Silvery-white metal	660.46	2,400	3	7
Silicon	14	Dark gray solid	1,414	2,500	4	8
Phosphorus	15	Yellowish or red solid	44.14	280	3 or 5	7
Sulfur	16	Pale yellow solid	115.21 (yellow) (monoclinic)	444.600	2, 4 or 6	10
Chlorine	17	Yellow-green gas	— 100.97	— 34.1	1, 3, 5 or 7	9
Argon	18	Colorless gas	— 189.352	— 185.9	*††	12
Potassium (Kalium)	19	Silvery-white metal	63.50	760	1	12
Calcium	20	Silvery-white metal	840	1,440	2	15
Scandium	21	Metallic	1,541	2,500	3	11
Titanium	22	Silvery metal	1,670	3,300	3 or 4	13
Vanadium	23	Silvery-gray metal	1,920	3,400	2, 3, 4 or 5	9
Chromium	24	Silvery metal	1,860	2,600	2, 3 or 6	10
Manganese	25	Reddish-white metal	1,246	2,100	2, 3, 4, 6 or 7	10
Iron (Ferrum)	26	Silvery-white metal	1,535	2,900	2, 3 or 6	11
Cobalt	27	Reddish-steel metal	1,495	2,900	2 or 3	11

† At 103 atmospheres.

*††Previously regarded as inert and thus of zero valency. Compounds have recently disproved this.

Name of Element	Atomic Number	Physical Description	Melting Point (for pressure of one standard atmosphere) (°C.)	Boiling Point (for pressure of one standard atmosphere) (°C.)	Valence (or Valency) Number	No. of Nuclides
Nickel	28	Silvery-white metal	1,455	2,820	2 or 3	12
Copper (Cuprum)	29	Reddish-bronze metal	1,084.88	2,580	1 or 2	12
Zinc	30	Blue-white metal	419.56	907	2	18
Gallium	31	Gray metal	29.77	2,250	2 or 3	21
Germanium	32	Gray-white metal	938.3	2,880	4	20
Arsenic	33	Steel-gray solid	817||	610¶	3 or 5	19
Selenium	34	Grayish solid	221.18	685	2, 4 or 6	22
Bromine	35	Red-brown liquid	−7.25	58.2	1, 3, 5 or 7	19
Krypton	36	Colorless gas	−157.38	−153.4	*††	23
Rubidium	37	Silvery-white metal	39.30	710	1	25
Strontium	38	Silvery-white metal	768	1,460	2	20
Yttrium	39	Steel-gray metal	1,522	3,000	3	19
Zirconium	40	Steel-white metal	1,855	4,400	4	20
Niobium	41	Gray metal	2,477	5,100	3 or 5	21
Molybdenum	42	Silvery metal	2,623	4,600	2, 3, 4, 5 or 6	20
Technetium	43	Black metal	2,180	—	2, 3, 4 or 6	17
Ruthenium	44	Bluish-white metal	2,330	3,900	3, 4, 6 or 8	18
Rhodium	45	Steel-blue metal	1,963	3,900	3	16
Palladium	46	Silvery-white metal	1,554	3,200	2 or 4	16
Silver (Argentum)	47	Lustrous white metal	961.93	2,180	1	21
Cadmium	48	Blue-white metal	321.108	767	2	23
Indium	49	Bluish-silvery metal	156.634	2,000	1 or 3	28
Tin (Stannum)	50	Silvery-white metal	231.968	2,600	2 or 4	26
Antimony (Stibium)	51	Silvery metal	630.755	1,440	3 or 5	26
Tellurium	52	Silvery-gray solid	449.87	997	2, 4 or 6	31
Iodine	53	Gray-black solid	113.6	183	1, 3, 5 or 7	27
Xenon	54	Colorless gas	111.76	−108.1	*††	30
Cesium	55	Silvery-white metal	28.5	713	1	30
Barium	56	Silvery-white metal	729	1,770	2	25

|| At 35.8 atmospheres.   ¶ Sublimation.   *†† Previously regarded as inert and thus of zero valency. Compounds have recently disproved this.

Atomic Table (continued)

Element	Atomic No.	Appearance			Valence	
Lanthanum	57	Metallic	921	4,200	3 or 4	23
Cerium	58	Steel-gray metal	799	2,900	3 or 4	20
Praseodymium	59	Silvery-white metal	934	3,000	3, 4 or 5	17
Neodymium	60	Yellowish-white metal	1,021	3,170	3	18
Promethium	61	Metallic	1,042	—	3	16
Samarium	62	Light-gray metal	1,077	1,600	2 or 3	18
Europium	63	Steel-gray metal	822	1,400	2 or 3	20
Gadolinium	64	Silver-white metal	1,313	2,700	3	19
Terbium	65	Silvery metal	1,356	2,500	3 or 4	18
Dysprosium	66	Metallic	1,412	2,300	3	19
Holmium	67	Silvery metal	1,474	2,300	3	21
Erbium	68	Grayish-silver metal	1,529	2,600	3	21
Thulium	69	Metallic	1,545	2,100	3	24
Ytterbium	70	Silvery metal	817	1,500	3 or 4	21
Lutetium	71	Metallic	1,665	1,900	3	20
Hafnium	72	Steel-gray metal	2,230	5,100	4	24
Tantalum	73	Silvery metal	3,020	6,000	3 or 5	16
Tungsten (or Wolfram)	74	Gray metal	3,422	5,700	2, 4, 5 or 6	23
Rhenium	75	Whitish-gray metal	3,185	5,900	4	18
Osmium	76	Gray-blue metal	3,100	4,600	2, 3, 4 or 8	30
Iridium	77	Silvery-white metal	2,447	4,350	3 or 4	28
Platinum	78	Bluish-white metal	1,767	3,800	2 or 4	30
Gold (Aurum)	79	Lustrous yellow metal	1,064.43	2,660	1 or 3	29
Mercury	80	Silvery metallic liquid	−38.836	356.58	1 or 2	30
Thallium	81	Blue-gray metal	304	1,460	1 or 3	27
Lead (Plumbum)	82	Steel-blue metal	327.502	1,750	2 or 4	30
Bismuth	83	Reddish-silvery metal	271.442	1,530	2 or 3	27
Polonium	84	Metallic	254	960	2, 3 or 4	26
Astatine	85	Metallic	302	—	1, 3, 5 or 7	24
Radon**	86	Colorless gas	−64.9	−62	0	27
Francium	87	Metallic	23	—	1	26
Radium	88	Silvery metal	707	1,140	2	25

** Also called radium emanation.

493

Atomic Table (continued)

Name of Element	Atomic Number	Physical Description	Melting Point (for pressure of one standard atmosphere) (°C.)	Boiling Point (for pressure of one standard atmosphere) (°C.)	Valence (or Valency) Number	No. of Nuclides
Actinium	89	Metallic	1,050	3,415	3	6
Thorium	90	Gray metal	1,700	4,710	4	10
Protactinium	91	Silvery metal	1,570	4,530	5	9
Uranium	92	Bluish-white metal	1,134	4,270	3, 4, 5 or 6	12
Neptunium	93	Silvery metal	637 ± 1	4,030	3, 4, 5 or 6	10 or 11
Plutonium	94	Metallic	640 ± 2	3,360	3, 4, 5 or 6	15
Americium	95	Metallic	1,176	2,020	3	10
Curium	96	Metallic	1,340	3,110	3	13
Berkelium	97	Metallic	—	—	3 or 4	8
Californium	98	Metallic	986	—	3	11
Einsteinium	99	Metallic	900	—	3	10
Fermium	100	Metallic	—	—	3	7
Mendelevium	101	Metallic	—	—	3	1
Nobelium	102	Metallic	—	—	3	1
Lawrencium	103	Metallic	—	—	3	1
Kurchatovium**	104	Metallic	—	—	?	?
or						
Rutherfordium						
Nielsbohrium	105					
or						
Hahnium						
—	106					
—	107					

**Discoveries of elements 104, 105, 106, 107 are disputed.

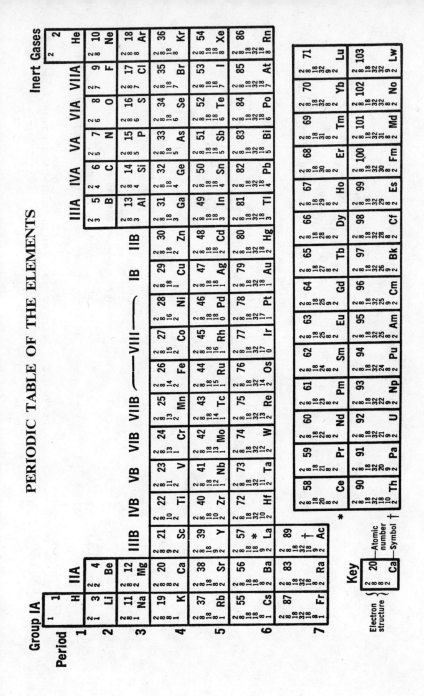

PERIODIC TABLE OF THE ELEMENTS

495

ALLOYS

Mixtures or compounds of a metal with one or more other metals or non-metals.

Name	Composition Expressed as Percentages	Properties and Uses
Alnico	Fe 60, Ni 20, Al 10, Co 10	Permanent magnet
Babbit Metal	Sn (predominates), Sb, Cu, (+Pb)	Used for bearings, anti-friction metal
Brass	Cu with 20–35 Zn	Decorative, condenser tubes
Bronze	Cu with 5–8 Sn	Primitive tools, coinage
Carboloy	W_2C_3, with 10 Co	Very hard alloy, grinding tools
Cast Iron	Impure Fe, C up to $4\frac{1}{2}$ with Mn, P, Si and S traces	Decorative work, weights
Cupronickel	Cu 80, Ni 20 (coinage 75–25)	Marine condenser tubes, Imperial 'silver' coinage
Delta Metal	Cu 55–60, Zn c. 40, Fe 2–4	Bearings, marine propellers
Dow Metal	Al, Mg	Aircraft and car parts
Dental Alloy	Ag_3, Sn ground with Hg	Tooth fillings
Duralumin	Al 93–95$\frac{1}{2}$, Cu 3$\frac{1}{2}$–5$\frac{1}{2}$, Mn $\frac{1}{2}$–$\frac{3}{4}$, Mg $\frac{1}{2}$–$\frac{3}{4}$	Aircraft frames
Dutch Metal	Cu with 30–35 Zn	Bronze in 'gold' leaf form
E-Alloy	Al 78, Zn 20, Cu 2; or Al 96, Zn 2, Cu 2	Castings
Electrum	Au with 15–45 Ag	Coinage (ancient times)
Frary Metal	Pb 97, Ba 2, Ca 1	Bearings
German Metal	Cu 56–65, Zn 24–28, Ni 7–20	Metal fittings, metal ware (often electroplated)
Gun Metal	Cu 88, Sn 8–10, Zn 2–4	Ordnance
Hiduminium	Al with small Cu, Ni, Mg, Si additions	Aircraft parts
Illium	Complex of Co, Cr, Fe, Mn, Mb, Ni and W	Acid resistant
Invar	Fe 64, Ni 35, some C and Mn	Very low expandibility, pendulum rods, steel tape measures
Jae Metal	Ni 70, Cu 30	Shunts on magnetic instruments
Lipowitz's Alloy	Bi 50, Pb 27, Sn 13, Cd 10	Very low melting point (60°C.)
Magnolia Metal	Pb 80, Sb 15, Sn 5	Medium duty bearings
Monel Metal	Ni 68, Cu 29$\frac{1}{4}$, Fe 1$\frac{1}{4}$, Mn 1$\frac{1}{4}$	Resistant to steam corrosion
Muntz Metal	Cu 60, Zn 40	Resistant to sea-water corrosion
Nichrome	Ni 60, Fe 20, Cr 20	Filament wires
Nickel Silver	Cu 55–63, Ni 10–30, Zn 7–35	Electroplated articles, hence E.P.N.S.
Nimonic 80	Ni with Cr 19–22, Fe up to 5, Ti 1$\frac{1}{2}$–3, Al $\frac{1}{2}$–1$\frac{1}{2}$, Mn <1, C < 0.1	Non-creep at high temperatures, gas turbine rotor blades
Pewter	Sn 80, Pb 20, trace of Sb, Tu and Bi (traces)	Modern pewter, Pb replaced by Sb
Permalloy	Ni 77.5, Fe 22.5 (sometimes with traces of Co, Cr, Cu and Mo)	Magnetic properties, transformers, submarine cable parts

Name	Composition	Uses
Phosphorbronze	Cu 90, Sn 9½, P½	Castings, bearings and resilient strip
Pinchbeck	Cu 89–93, Zn 7–11	Imitation gold, jewellery
'Silver' Alloy	Hg-Sn amalgam	'Silver' backing for mirrors, Powdered Al also now used
Solder	Sn 66⅔, Pb 33⅓	Plumbing
Speculum	Cu 60–70, Sn 30–40	High polish surfaces, plating
Stainless Steel	Fe 78–86, Cr 12–20, Ni 2	Corrosion resistant culinary, sterile vessels, decorative
Steel	Essentially Fe with C½–1½ with special purpose additives of Cr, Mn, Mb, Ni, Si, Al, Cu, Co, Ti, W, V	Multifarious
Stellite	Co 43, Cr 43, W 14 et al.	Surgical and other cutting tools
Tombac	Cu 71–90, Zn 10–29	Condenser tubes, cartridge cases
Type Metal	Pb 80–86, Sb 11–20, Sn 3–11	Lino-, Mono- and Stereotype fonts
White Gold	Au with Ni	Platinum substitute
Woods Metal	Bi 50, Pb 25, Sn 12½, Cd 12½	Low melting point, fire sprinklers
X-40	Co 55, Cr 25, Ni 9, W 7, C ½, Fe ½, traces of Mn, Si	Non-creep at high temperatures, gas turbine rotor blades
Y-Alloy	Al 93, Cu 4, Ni 2, Mn 1	

Explosives

Name	Introduced	Description	Inventor
Gunpowder	c. 965	Charcoal 15%, sulfur 10%, potassium nitrate 75%	Sung dynasty of China
Mercuric fulminate	1799	Detonating agent, $Hg(ONC)_2$	(Germany)
Gun cotton	1845	Nitrocellulose	Schonbein
Nitroglycerin	1846	Glyceryl trinitrate	A. Sobrero (Italy)
T.N.T.	1863	Trinitrotoluene, $C_7H_5O_6N_3$	Wilbrand
Dynamite	1866	Nitroglycerin absorbed in kieselguhr or charcoal	A. Nobel (Sweden)
Gelignite	1878	Trinitrocellulose plus nitroglycerin, wood pulp, potassium nitrate	—
Lyddite	1882	Picric acid, trinitrophenol	Woulfe (1771)
Cordite	1888	Gelignite plasticized with acetone solvent	—
Lox (Liquid oxygen)	1895	Porous combustible, e.g. charcoal soaked in liquid oxygen	Linde
RDX	1899	Cyclotrimethylenetrinitramine	Henning
PETN	1901	Pentaergthritol tetranitrate, $C_5H_8N_9O_{12}$	Vignon and Gerin
Amatol	1916	Ammonium nitrate (4 pts.) to 1 pt. T.N.T.	—
Torpex	1939	RDX plus T.N.T. with aluminum powder	Admiralty research
Atomic fission	1945 (July 16)	Fission of uranium isotope 235	E. Fermi (U.S.)
Atomic fusion	1952 (Nov. 1)	Hydrogen-helium fusion triggered by U_{235} or plutonium fission	K. Fuchs and J. von Neumann

ORGANIC CHEMISTRY

Organic chemistry is the chemistry of hydrocarbons and their derivatives. The original division between organic chemical compounds (meaning those occurring in the Animal and Plant Kingdoms) and inorganic chemical compounds (meaning those occurring in the mineral world) was made in 1675 by Léméry. This oversimplified division was upset when in 1828 Wöhler produced urea $[CO(NH_2)_2]$ in an experiment intended to produce ammonium cyanate $(NH_4 \cdot CNO)$ from inorganic sources. Carbon has a valency number (from the Latin *valens*, worth) of 4, *i.e.* a combining-power expressed in terms of the number of hydrogen atoms with which the atom of carbon can combine. In addition, the carbon atom has the unique property of being able to join one to another to form chains, rings, double bonds and triple bonds. Thus, there are almost limitless numbers of organic compounds.

The simplest organic compounds are the straight chain hydrocarbons, in which all the available free positions on the tetravalent carbon are taken up by hydrogen atoms, *viz.*

Methane (CH_4) Ethane (C_2H_6) Propane (C_3H_8)

Members of this series are called the paraffins (from the Latin *parvum affinis*, small affinity), because of their low combining power with other substances.

The higher paraffins are
C_4H_{10} butane
C_5H_{12} pentane
C_6H_{14} hexane
C_7H_{16} heptane
C_8H_{18} octane
C_9H_{20} nonane, *et seq.*

Ring compounds, in which the carbon atoms form a closed ring, are known as the naphthene family and take their names from the corresponding paraffins, *viz.*

Cyclopropane (C_3H_6) Cyclobutane (C_4H_8) Cyclohexane (C_6H_{12})

Cyclohexane is in fact an example of a saturated six atom carbon ring—saturated because each corner represents a CH_2 group.

When carbon atoms are joined to each other by double or triple bonds, *viz.*

there are obviously fewer bonds available for hydrogen atoms and thus their hydrocarbons are said to be unsaturated.

Compounds with one double bond are called olefins or olefines (from the Latin *oleum*, oil; *facio*, to make), *viz.*

$$H—\overset{\overset{\displaystyle H}{|}}{C} = \overset{\overset{\displaystyle H}{|}}{C}—H$$

$$H—\overset{\overset{\displaystyle H}{|}}{\underset{\underset{\displaystyle H}{|}}{C}}—\overset{\overset{\displaystyle H}{|}}{C} = \overset{\overset{\displaystyle H}{|}}{C}—H$$

Ethylene (C_2H_4)   Propylene (C_3H_6)

The higher olefins are
C_4H_8 butylene
C_5H_{10} pentylene
C_6H_{12} hexylene
C_7H_{14} heptylene
C_8H_{16} octylene, *et seq.*

Compounds with one triple bond are called acetylenes (from the Latin *acetum*, vinegar), *viz.*

$$H—C \equiv C—H$$

$$H—\overset{\overset{\displaystyle H}{|}}{\underset{\underset{\displaystyle H}{|}}{C}}—C \equiv C—H$$

$$H—\overset{\overset{\displaystyle H}{|}}{\underset{\underset{\displaystyle H}{|}}{C}}—\overset{\overset{\displaystyle H}{|}}{\underset{\underset{\displaystyle H}{|}}{C}}—C \equiv C—H$$

Acetylene
(C_2H_2)

Methylacetylene
(CH_3C_2H)
Propyne

Ethylacetylene
($C_2H_5C_2H$)
Butyne

The left-hand hydrogen atoms in the first members of these groups are replaced by methyl (CH_3), ethyl (C_2H_5), propyl (C_3H_7) etc. groups. These are known as the alkyl groups. These and other oft-recurring groups are called radicals.

Examples are:

CH_3 methyl, from Gk. *methy*, wine; *hyle*, wood
C_2H_5 ethyl, from Gk. *aither*, clean air (*i.e.* odorless); *-yl*, suffix for substance
C_3H_7 propyl, from Gk. *pro*, before; *peon*, fat, hence radical of fatty acid
C_4H_9 butyl, from Latin *butyrum*, butter, because of rancid smell or amyl
C_5H_{11} pentyl, from Gk. *pente*, five (number of carbon atoms)
C_6H_{13} hexyl, from Gk. *hex*, six (number of carbon atoms)
C_7H_{15} heptyl, from Gk. *hepta*, seven (number of carbon atoms)
C_8H_{17} octyl, from Gk. *okto*, or Latin *octo*, eight (number of carbon atoms)
C_9H_{19} nonyl, from Latin *nonus*, nine (number of carbon atoms)

The parent of the aromatic compounds is the unsaturated six carbon atom ring, benzene

$$\begin{array}{ccc} & \overset{\displaystyle H}{\underset{\displaystyle C}{}} & \\ & \Vert & \\ HC & & CH \\ \Vert & & \vert \\ HC & & CH \\ & \underset{\displaystyle H}{\overset{\displaystyle C}{}} & \end{array}$$

in which alternate carbon atoms are traditionally represented as double-bonded giving in effect a CH group at each corner and a formula of C_6H_6. All bonds are in fact equivalent.

Benzene rings have a facility for forming second rings which may be fused, *e.g.*

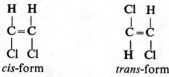

H   H
| |
C = C
| |
Cl Cl

giving naphthalene ($C_{10}H_8$) with two rings condensed, or anthracene ($C_{14}H_{10}$) with a chain of 2 rings joined.

When alternative molecule arrangements can be made with the same complement of atoms, the compounds are termed isomers. For example, though the simple methyl (CH_3) and ethyl (C_2H_5) radicals can have only one form, there are two propyl alcohols (C_3H_7OH), *viz.*

normal or n-propyl alcohol arranged
$$CH_3—CH_2—CH_2—OH$$
and isopropyl alcohol arranged
$$CH_3$$
$$|$$
$$CH_3—CHOH$$

The higher the number of atoms the greater the possibility for permutations. The next higher. alcohol, butyl alcohol (C_4H_9OH), exists in 4 forms—n-Butyl, iso-Butyl, s-Butyl and t-Butyl alcohol where s denotes secondary and t tertiary.

The scope of isomerism when there are more kinds of atoms, *e.g.* carbon, chlorine and hydrogen, is further increased.

H   H
| |
H—C—C—H   is 1:2 dichloroethane or
| | ethylene dichloride
Cl Cl   ($CH_2Cl·CH_2Cl$)

while

H   Cl
| |
H—C—C—H   is 1:1 dichloroethane
| | or ethylidene dichloride
H   Cl   ($CH_2Cl·CH_2Cl$)

This is termed *structural* isomerism.

Where there are carbon atoms linked by a double bond, rotation of this kind is not possible. In these cases isomerism can occur geometrically. For example, dichloroethylene, which has a double carbon bond, may occur in a *cis*-form (from the Latin *cis* = on the near side) or a *trans*-form (from the Latin *trans* = on the far side).

cis-form   *trans*-form

The third class of isomerism is *optical* isomerism. In this class the molecule of one substance is in one form but the molecule of the other substance is laterally inverted as is a mirror image. It was discovered that one isomer has the effect of twisting the plane of polarized light shone through it to the right while its isomer twists it to the left. These are thus known as the d-form (*dextro-*, or right, rotating) and the l-form (*laevo-*, or left, rotating). When the isomers are mixed in equal portions the rotating effect is cancelled out to give an optically inactive or racemic form. The term racemic is derived from the Latin *racemus*, a bunch of grapes, because the mother liquid of fermented grape juice exhibits this characteristic. The practical importance of this phenomenon can be illustrated by the ability of yeast to convert d-grape sugar to alcohol and its powerlessness to effect the l-compound.

Index

Index prepared by Nina Brodsky and Gabriel Weiss.

Picture Credits

The following have been generous in allowing use of photographs on these pages: Alaska Travel Division; American Geographical Society; American Petroleum Institute; American Society of Composers, Authors and Publishers; N. W. Ayer and Son, Inc.; Bell Laboratories; British Airways; British Information Services; British Travel Association; Cambridge Scientific Instruments Ltd.; Frank M. Carpenter, Biological Laboratories; Dominion Observatory, Ottawa, Canada; Egyptian State Tourist Administration; Environmental Science Service Administration; Ford Motor Co. News Bureau; Irish Tourist Board; Italian State Tourist Office; Jordan Tourism Authority; Lawrence Radiation Laboratory, University of California, Berkeley; Mount Wilson and Palomar Observatories; McGraw-Hill, Inc.; National Aeronautics and Space Administration; National Radio Astronomy Observatory; Novosti Press Agency, Moscow; Panama Government Tourist Bureau; Pan American Airways; S. B. Penick and Co., Inc.; Chas. Pfizer & Co., Inc.; Port of New York Authority; United Nations; U.S. Air Force; U.S. Department of the Interior, Geological Survey; U.S. Navy; Carl Zeiss, Inc.

Also: American Museum of Natural History; American Swedish News Exchange; Bahama News Bureau; Canadian Consulate General; Canadian Government Office of Tourism; Victor Chambi; Ecuadorean Government Tourist Commission; K. W. Emmermacher; Robert C. Forsyth; French Embassy Press & Information Division; German Information Center; Greek National Tourist Office; Hsin Hua News Agency; Indonesian Information Office; International Library of Negro Life and History, Library of Congress; Israel Office of Information; E. D. Lacey; Louisiana Tourist Development Commission; National Gallery of Art; Netherlands Information Bureau; Press Information Bureau, New Delhi, India; San Diego Convention & Visitors Bureau; Santa Fe Railway; Sea World, Inc.; The Smithsonian Institution; Tanzania Information Services; Texas Game and Fish Commission; U.S. Department of the Interior, Fish & Wildlife Service; Universal Pictorial Press.